DATA PROTECTION LAW IN THE EU:
ROLES, RESPONSIBILITIES AND LIABILITY

DATA PROTECTION LAW IN THE EU: ROLES, RESPONSIBILITIES AND LIABILITY

Brendan VAN ALSENOY

intersentia
Cambridge – Antwerp – Chicago

KU LEUVEN CiTiP
CENTRE FOR IT & IP LAW

Intersentia Ltd
Sheraton House | Castle Park
Cambridge | CB3 0AX | United Kingdom
Tel.: +44 1223 370 170 | Fax: +44 1223 370 169
Email: mail@intersentia.co.uk
www.intersentia.com | www.intersentia.co.uk

Distribution for the UK and Ireland:
NBN International
Airport Business Centre, 10 Thornbury Road
Plymouth, PL6 7 PP
United Kingdom
Tel.: +44 1752 202 301 | Fax: +44 1752 202 331
Email: orders@nbninternational.com

Distribution for Europe and all other countries:
Intersentia Publishing nv
Groenstraat 31
2640 Mortsel
Belgium
Tel.: +32 3 680 15 50 | Fax: +32 3 658 71 21
Email: mail@intersentia.be

Distribution for the USA and Canada:
Independent Publishers Group
Order Department
814 North Franklin Street
Chicago, IL60610
USA
Tel.: +1 800 888 4741 (toll free) | Fax: +1312 337 5985
Email: orders@ipgbook.com

Data Protection Law in the EU: Roles, Responsibilities and Liability

Cover image: Jorma Puranen, Icy Prospects 29

ISBN 978-1-78068-828-2
ISBN 978-1-78068-845-9 (PDF)
D/2019/7849/47
NUR 822

GPRC
Guaranteed
Peer Reviewed
Content

British Library Cataloguing in Publication Data. A catalogue record for this book is available from the British Library.

FOREWORD

Have you ever considered the discussion on responsibilities and liabilities in the field of the European data protection law as a journey? You should. Brendan Van Alsenoy is inviting you take a trip through the whole history of data protection law in Europe and around the world, as well as through current practice to better understand the roles of different actors in what is a fiendishly complicated environment. You will find him to be a guide who effortlessly offers fresh perspectives on the subject: a relatively young scholar leveraging a surprisingly *ex*tensive and *in*tensive practical experience in a national data protection authority as well as playing a key role in the Working Party Article 29 / European Data Protection Board.

This is a guide to the places that you know and new ones you never thought exist. At times it may explain concepts that you heard about dozens of times before. But Van Alsenoy's explanations are slightly different to the others. He is able to filter his academic knowledge through the lens of the regulatory authorities and their current disputes with other institutional and business players around the world.

One of the first problems the author addresses is the binary concepts of controller and processor. Is this division as clear-cut as when it was first postulated decades ago in European law, or it is rather a case that control is now distributed and should be regulated and applied accordingly? Has the concept of controller evolved to the degree that the explanations proposed in '80s and '90s are no longer useful? How does this model work in practice?

One may say that these are the questions posed over and over again. Be that as it may, this book will nonetheless give you a valuable historical background. It offers use cases illustrating how to understand and interpret the system which the GDPR has inherited from previous European legislation. What will be the effect of different forms of joint controllership on the level of responsibility of each of the players?

It is sometimes surprisingly difficult to distinguish the joint controllership of the GDPR from the exchanges between individual controllers who co-operate with each other using shared resources for different purposes or using different means. I must admit I always thought I was able to discern between the two. But having read this book I can see a fresh methodology may be required. If you think it's enough to read the GDPR and the other legislative reforms in the EU over recent years and compare it with current practices in the market, Brendan

Van Alsenoy invites you to think again. Without the historical background and a rigorous methodology you are likely to repeat the same old mistakes of earlier scholars, regulators and jurisprudence.

Your journey will take in the issues, grammatical, teleological, systemic and historical, along with the same typology of solutions. Then the revised model of liability can be proposed.

My suggestion for the reader of this book is this: before you open it, sit down with a piece of paper and try your best to answer the author's main questions:

1. What is the nature and role of the controller and processor concepts under European data protection law?
2. What is the origin of the controller-processor model and how has it evolved over time?
3. What are the types of issues that arise when applying the controller-processor model in practice?
4. Which solutions have been proposed to address the issues that arise in practice and to what extent are they capable of addressing the issues?

Then – when you finish reading the book – take another piece of paper and try to answer the same questions. Compare your answers. My two sets of answers were quite different.

This journey through almost 700 pages was a unique experience as well as a rewarding academic challenge. I now view certain concepts differently compared to when just a few weeks ago, I had this manuscript in my hands for the first time. There are some ideas which I have to re-think again.

So, now I can invite you to follow the same journey I did. It will be an experience to remember. This book will land on the shelf just next to my desk because I am going to go back to it over and over again in my practical work as a regulator.

Dr. Wojciech Wiewiorowski
European Data Protection Assistant Supervisor

NOTE TO THE READERS

Most of the research for this book was completed on 25 July 2016. Subsequent developments in EU data protection law are only partially addressed. The main updates relate to the judgments of the Court of Justice of the European Union and Advocate General Opinions published until 15 January 2019. Other parts of the text have been revisited or extended in light of the entry into application of the General Data Protection Regulation (GDPR), subsequent regulatory guidance, as well as a selection of academic works.

The contents of this book are based on the contents of my doctoral thesis entitled "*Regulating data protection: the allocation of responsibility and risk among actors involved in personal data processing*", defended at the Law Faculty of KU Leuven on 30 August 2016.

ACKNOWLEDGMENTS

Early in my academic career, a learned professor told me: "the only good PhD is a finished PhD". What he didn't tell me, at the time, was that it takes a village to actually finish it. Completing my thesis would not have been possible without the support of my colleagues, family and friends.

I would like to begin by thanking my supervisor, Prof. Dr. Peggy Valcke, for her guidance, encouragement and trust. She gave me time and space to develop my own research, yet she was there to provide practical direction whenever needed. Warm thanks are also due to my co-supervisor, Dr. Els Kindt, for her insightful comments and continuous support. I am indebted to the members of my advisory committee, Prof. Dr. Geertrui Van Overwalle and Prof. Dr. Serge Gutwirth, for the invaluable feedback and references they provided. I thank Prof. Dr. Giovanni Sartor not only for acting as a member of my examination committee, but also for the fresh and critical perspective one so often encounters in his writing. My gratitude goes out to Em. Prof. Dr. Marc Boes for kindly agreeing to chair the examination committee. Finally, I would like to thank Em. Prof. Dr. Jos Dumortier for his advice and support at the beginning of my PhD project.

Working at the Centre for IT & IP law (CiTiP) has been an honour and a privilege. It is an environment filled with bright minds, dedicated people and a passion for knowledge. I would like to thank every one of my colleagues – past and current – for all the stimulating conversations, comradery and memories. Special thanks go out to Fanny Coudert, Jef Ausloos, Bjorn Coene and Yung Shin Van der Sype for providing me with ideas and feedback throughout the writing process. I would also like to thank Kirsten Van Gossum, Griet Verhenneman, Niels Vandezande, Aleksandra Kuczerawy, Eva Lievens, Eleni Kosta, Valerie Verdoodt, Jessica Schroers, Lina Jasmontaite and Ellen Wauters for the great collaborations in the many projects along the way. Finally, I would like to express my sincere appreciation to Shuki Tang, Carmen Clara, Edith Appelmans and Linda Mees, for their unique combination of professionalism and warmth in supporting our research activities on a daily basis.

The findings in this book have benefited from the input of many people outside my university department. I would especially like to thank Prof. Dr. Spiros Simitis and the Hon. Michael Kirby for sharing valuable insights in relation to the 1970 Hesse Data Protection Act and the 1980 OECD Privacy Guidelines. I am extremely grateful to Michael Donohue for giving me the opportunity to join the OECD Secretariat during the revision of the OECD Privacy Guidelines, as well as for his comments on my research. Dr. Lina Kestemont provided me with invaluable support on how to navigate issues of legal methodology, without which my hermitage perhaps would have been prolonged indefinitely. I thank Joseph Alhadeff for introducing me to the world of multi-stakeholder policy development and for our many lively discussions. I thank Danny De Cock, Günes Açar, Claudia Diaz and Seda Gürses for showing me how cool working with computer scientists can be. Finally, I would like to thank Joelle Jouret for reviewing and commenting on the sections concerning the General Data Protection Regulation.

Last but not least, I would like to thank my family, friends and loved ones. I thank my parents for their unwavering encouragement and support, both in research and in life. I thank my sister for being such an inspiration. I thank Dieter for keeping me grounded and for teaching me that long sentences do not make you seem smarter. I thank Paula for keeping me well-nourished and hydrated during the final stages of the writing process. Finally, I thank Aleksandra for her patience, indulgence and caring, and for giving me the motivation to keep going on.

Brendan Van Alsenoy
July 2016

ABSTRACT

Practically every organisation in the world processes personal data. In fact, it is difficult to imagine a single organisation which does not regularly collect, store or access information about individuals. European data protection law imposes a series of requirements designed to protect individuals against the risks that result from the processing of their data. It also distinguishes among different types of actors involved in the processing and sets out different obligations for each type of actor. The most important distinction in this regard is the distinction between "controllers" and "processors". Together these concepts provide the very basis upon which responsibility for compliance with EU data protection law is allocated. As a result, both concepts play a decisive role in determining the potential liability of an organisation under EU data protection law.

For almost 15 years, Directive 95/46 stood strong as the central instrument of EU data protection law. In 2010, however, the European Commission announced that the time for change had come. The Commission considered that while the objectives and principles of Directive 95/46 remained sound, revisions were necessary in order to meet the challenges of technological developments and globalisation. A public consultation conducted in 2009, had revealed concerns regarding the impact of new technologies, as well as a desire for a more comprehensive and coherent approach to data protection. During the consultation, several stakeholders also raised concerns regarding the concepts of controller and processor. Various solutions were put forward, ranging from minor revision to outright abolition of the concepts. In the end, the EU legislature opted to retain the existing concepts of controller and processor in the General Data Protection Regulation (GDPR). Notable changes were made, however, with regards to the allocation of responsibility and liability among the two types of actors.

Technological and societal developments have rendered it increasingly difficult to apply the concepts of "controller" and "processor" in practice. The complexity of today's processing operations is such that a clear-cut distinction between "controllers" and "processors" is not always possible. Identifying "who's who" can be particularly difficult when the processing involves a large number of actors, who each play their own distinct role in realising the goal(s) of the processing.

Against this background, this book seeks to determine whether EU data protection law should continue to maintain its current distinction between controllers and processors as the basis for allocating responsibility and liability. Specifically, it seeks to determine whether it would be possible to modify the current approach in a manner which would increase legal certainty, without diminishing the legal protections enjoyed by data subjects. To realise these objectives, this book undertakes an analysis consisting of five parts.

After a brief introduction, a detailed analysis of the current state of the art is provided. The state of the art explores the nature and role of the controller and processor concepts, as well as the associated allocation of responsibility and liability. The third part of this book offers a historical-comparative analysis, which traces the origin and development of the controller-processor model over time. Having set out the origins and rationale of the controller-processor model, a number of real-life use cases are examined in part four. The aim of this exercise is to document the issues that arise when applying the controller-processor model in practice. Once the issues have been analysed, an evaluation is made of potential solutions. Finally, the approach adopted by the European legislature in the context of the GDPR is compared with the outcome of the preceding evaluation.

The book concludes that the GDPR has introduced considerable improvements, which are likely to be adequate for the time being. In the long run, however, it may become necessary to introduce further changes. Having this in mind, a number of avenues for possible improvements are presented. First, the possibility of abolishing the distinction between controllers and processors should receive further consideration. It is possible to implement the same policy choices without retaining these problematic concepts. Alternatively, the definitions of each concept could be revised to include less ambiguous or mutually exclusive criteria. Second, the EU legislature should consider the use of standards (as opposed to rules) to mitigate risks of overinclusion in certain situations. Third, the obligation to implement data protection by design should also be made directly applicable to the providers of processing services, given their important role in determining the means of the processing. Fourth, the legal framework should allow for greater contractual flexibility in the relationship between "controllers" and "processors", leaving room for greater specificity in the form of regulatory guidance. Finally, the scope of the personal use exemption should be expanded to apply to all activities which may reasonably be construed as taking place in the course of an individual's private or family life.

For the immediate future, however, practitioners of EU data protection law will have to continue to work with the controller-processor model as it exists today. This book hopes to provide its readers with the right analytical framework to help navigate the intricate relationship among roles, responsibility and liability under EU data protection law.

CONTENTS

PART I

INTRODUCTION

CHAPTER 1
BACKGROUND

1. THE ORIGINS OF DATA PROTECTION LAW – Automated processing of personal information has always been a topic of controversy. As soon as computers became visible to the general public, reflections on how computers might impact the privacy of individuals began to enter the political arena.[1] The first data protection laws emerged during the 1970s, with the aim of protecting individuals against risks resulting from the automated processing of personal data.[2] Regulatory initiatives at the international level soon followed. The first international organisation to formally adopt a normative stance in relation to the processing of personal data was the Council of Europe in 1973.[3] In 1980, the OECD adopted its *Guidelines on the Protection of Privacy and Transborder Flows of Personal Data*.[4] In 1981, the Council of Europe promulgated the *Convention for the protection of individuals with regard to automatic processing of personal data* (Convention 108).[5]

2. INITIATIVES AT EU LEVEL – Even after Convention 108 came into effect, notable differences in national data protection laws remained. As the European Union developed, these differences were perceived as potential obstacles towards the development of the Internal Market.[6] In 1990, the European Commission put forth a draft for a Council Directive on the Protection of Individuals with regard to the processing of personal data and on the free movement of such data. This proposal eventually led to the adoption of *Directive 95/46/EC on the protection*

---

1 See C.J. Bennet, *Regulating privacy. Data Protection and Public Policy in Europe and the United States*, Ithaca, Cornell University Press, 1992, p. 2.

2 P. De Hert and S. Gutwirth, "Privacy, data protection and law enforcement. Opacity of the individual and transparency of power", in E. Claes, A. Duff and S. Gutwirth (eds.), *Privacy and the Criminal Law*, Antwerpen/Oxford, Intersentia, 2006, p. 76. See also R. Gellert, "Understanding data protection as risk regulation", *Journal of Internet Law* 2015, p. 3–16.

3 Committee of Ministers of Council of Europe, Resolution (73)22 on the protection of privacy of individuals vis-à-vis electronic data banks in the private sector, 26 September 1973 (224th meeting of the Ministers' Deputies).

4 Organisation for Economic Co-operation and Development (OECD), *Guidelines on the Protection of Privacy and Transborder Flows of Personal Data*, 23 September 1980.

5 Council of Europe, *Convention for the Protection of Individuals with regard to Automatic Processing of Personal Data*, 28 January 1981.

6 F.H. Cate, "The EU Data Protection Directive, Information Privacy, and the Public Interest", *Iowa Law Review* 1995, Vol. 80, p. 432.

of individuals with regards to the processing of personal data and on the free movement of such data.[7] In 2016, the *Regulation of the European Parliament and of the Council on the protection of natural persons with regard to the processing of personal data and on the free movement of such data* (General Data Protection Regulation) was adopted.[8] This Regulation replaced Directive 95/46 and entered into application on 25 May 2018.

3. THE IMPORTANCE OF ROLES AND RESPONSIBILITIES – As with any legal instrument, it is essential to establish not only the substantive provisions of regulation, but also to identify which actors shall be responsible for ensuring compliance. Data protection law is no different in this regard. Already in 1975, Hondius observed:

> "for an effective system of data protection it is of great importance that the role, rights, and responsibilities of the various persons and parties involved be stated unambiguously".[9]

More than 40 years later, the same premise still holds true. Recital (79) of the GDPR confirms that

> "The protection of the rights and freedoms of data subjects as well as the responsibility and liability of controllers and processors, also in relation to the monitoring by and measures of supervisory authorities, requires a clear allocation of the responsibilities under this Regulation, including where a controller determines the purposes and means of the processing jointly with other controllers or where a processing operation is carried out on behalf of a controller."

4. RELEVANT ACTORS – Under EU data protection law, there are at least two actors implicated by the processing of personal data: a "controller" and a "data subject". A data subject is essentially any individual to whom the data relates, provided that he or she is identified or sufficiently identifiable.[10] The controller is

---

7 Directive 95/46/EC on the protection of individuals with regards to the processing of personal data and on the free movement of such data, OJ 23 November 1995, L 281/31. Hereinafter also referred to as "Directive 95/46/EC" or simply "the Directive".

8 Regulation (EU) 2016/679 of the European Parliament and of the Council of 27 April 2016 on the protection of natural persons with regard to the processing of personal data and on the free movement of such data, and repealing Directive 95/46/EC (General Data Protection Regulation), OJ 4 May 2016, L 119/1. Hereinafter referred to as the "General Data Protection Regulation" or "GDPR".

9 F. W. Hondius, *Emerging data protection in Europe*, Amsterdam, North-Holland Publishing Company, 1975, p. 101.

10 See Article 4(1) GDPR (previously: Article 2(a) Directive 95/46). See also B. Van Alsenoy, J. Ballet, A. Kuczerawy and J. Dumortier, "Social networks and web 2.0: are users also bound by data protection regulations?", *Identity in the information society* 2009, Vol. 2, no.1, p. 68. For a more detailed discussion see Article 29 Data Protection Working Party, "Opinion 4/2007 on the concept of personal data", WP 136, 20 June 2007, 26 p.

defined as the party who alone, or jointly with others, "determines the purposes and means" of the processing.[11] A third important actor identified by EU data protection law is the "processor". A "processor" is defined as a party who processes personal data on behalf of the data controller.[12] Both the controller and the processor concepts are essential to the regulatory scheme of European data protection law. In fact, these concepts provide the very basis upon which responsibility for compliance is allocated. As a result, both concepts play a decisive role in determining the liability exposure of an organisation under EU data protection law.

5. Responsibility and liability – Under Directive 95/46, the allocation of responsibility and liability among controllers and processors resulted from a combination of provisions. As far as the controller's obligations are concerned, the allocation of responsibility was in first instance the result of Article 6(2) of the Directive. This provision stipulated that it shall be the controller who must ensure that the basic principles of data protection are complied with. In addition, the Directive specified a wide range of additional obligations (e.g. accommodation of data subject rights, maintaining an appropriate level of security, etc.) incumbent upon the controller. Finally, Article 23 of the Directive explicitly confirmed that the liability for damages caused by non-compliant behaviour shall be borne by the controller, unless he is able to avail himself of an exemption. As far as the processor's obligations are concerned, the Directive was far more succinct. In fact, it articulated obligations addressed directly towards the processor in only one instance.[13] With the GDPR, a number of new provisions governing the allocation of responsibility and liability among controllers and processors have been introduced. While the controller is still the party who carries primary responsibility for compliance with data protection principles (Article 5(2)), processors have become subject to a host of obligations and may be directly liable towards data subjects in case of an infringement (Article 82).

6. Additional functions – Both the controller and processor concepts are relevant for a range of other legal questions, such as which law applies to the processing.[14] Both concepts are thus pivotal in determining the scope of

11 Article 4(7) GDPR (previously: Article 2(d) Directive 95/46).

12 Article 4(8) GDPR (previously: Article 2(e) Directive 95/46).

13 See Alhadeff, J. and Van Alsenoy, B. (eds.), "Requirements: Privacy, governance and contractual options", *Trusted Architecture for Securely Shared Services* (TAS³), Deliverable 6.1, v2.0, 2009, p. 31 and T. Olsen and T. Mahler, "Identity management and data protection law: Risk, responsibility and compliance in 'Circles of Trust' – Part II", *Computer, Law & Security Review* 2007, Vol. 23, no. 5, p. 418. See in particular Articles 16 and 17 of the Directive.

14 See Article 29 Data Protection Working Party, "Opinion 1/2010 on the concepts of 'controller' and 'processor'", WP169, 16 February 2010, p. 5. Hereinafter simply: "Opinion 1/2010".

European data protection legislation, not only by reason of the type of actor concerned (*ratione personae*), but also as concerns the applicability of national provisions (*ratione loci*). As a result, the interpretation of these concepts shall be determinative for every actor's perception of how the relevant legislation affects him or her, and what measures he or she is expected to put in place.[15]

15 D. Bainbridge, *EC Data Protection Directive*, London, Butterworths, 1996, p. 116.

CHAPTER 2
PROBLEM STATEMENT

7. Outline – Given the fundamental importance of both the controller and processor concepts, it is essential to be able to determine which role an actor has assumed towards a particular processing operation. Unfortunately, it can be quite difficult to apply the distinction between controller and processors in practice.[16] Over time, data protection authorities and courts have provided guidance to inform the practical application of the controller and processor concepts. Notwithstanding the guidance, however, certain scholars have continued to question the utility of the controller-processor model.[17] The following sections outline three perceived vulnerabilities of the current framework.

1. A BROKEN "BINARY"

8. Oversimplification? – Perhaps the most common critique of the controller-processor model is that the "binary" distinction between controllers and processors is too simplistic.[18] While the model may be readily applied in certain situations, the complexity of today's processing operations is such that

---

16 C. Kuner, *European Data Protection Law – Corporate Compliance and Regulation*, second edition, New York, Oxford University Press, 2007, 71–72. For example, portable devices have evolved from single-function apparati to complex and powerful processing systems that have the ability to support a variety of applications (e.g. voice communication, email, social networking, location-based services).

17 See e.g. P. Van Eecke and M. Truyens, "Privacy and social networks", *Computer, Law & Security Review* 2010, Vol. 26, 537–539; W. Kuan Hon, C. Millard and I. Walden, "Who is Responsible for 'Personal Data' in Cloud Computing? The Cloud of Unknowing, Part 2", Queen Mary University of London, School of Law, *Legal Studies Research Paper No. 77/2011*, in particular p. 10–11 and 24; O. Tene, "Privacy: The new generations", *International Data Privacy Law* 2011, Vol. 1, No. 1, p. 26; J.M. Van Gyseghem, "Cloud computing et protection des données à caractère personnel: mise en ménage possible?", *Revue du Droit des Technologies de l'Information* 2011, vol. 42, in particular p. 40 et seq. and P. De Hert and V. Papakonstantinou, "The proposed data protection Regulation replacing Directive 95/46/EC: A sound system for the protection of individuals", *Computer Law & Security Review* 2012, vol. 28, p. 133–134.

18 See in particular P. Van Eecke and M. Truyens, "Privacy and social networks", *l.c.*, p. 537; W. Kuan Hon, C. Millard and I. Walden, "Who is Responsible for 'Personal Data' in Cloud Computing? The Cloud of Unknowing, Part 2", *l.c.*, p. 24.

a clear-cut distinction between controllers and processors is seldom possible.[19] As a result, the binary distinction is considered inadequate to accommodate the increasingly collaborative manner in which businesses operate.[20] Nowadays, control relationships are more complex than the "either/or" approach of the controller-processor model; whereby one party (or group of parties) exercises complete control over the processing, and another party (or group of parties) simply executes the tasks it has been given, without exercising any substantial influence as to either the purposes or means of the processing.

9. Evolving processing practices – At the time Directive 95/46 was adopted, the distinction between parties who control the processing of personal data (data controllers) and those who simply process the data on behalf of someone else (data processors) was considered to be relatively clear.[21] Today we are confronted with a "growing tendency towards organisational differentiation".[22] In both the public and private sector

> "there is a growing emphasis on the development of delivery chains or service delivery across organisations and on the use of subcontracting or outsourcing of services in order to benefit from specialisation and possible economies of scale. As a result, there is a growth in various services, offered by service providers, who do not always consider themselves responsible or accountable […]."[23]

10. Distributed control – To be clear, the diversification and specialization of the market for processing services does not, in and of itself, implicate the providers of those services as controllers or co-controllers. In addition to the expansion of the processing market, however, there is also an increase in collaboration among otherwise autonomous entities whose mutual relationships can no longer be characterized as a simple "principal-delegate" relationship. Similarly, we are also witnessing an increase in services whose use is available to many but the purposes and means of the processing have – at least in the abstract – been determined largely in advance. The assumed power of the controller may

---

19 See in particular C. Kuner, *European Data Protection Law – Corporate Compliance and Regulation*, *o.c.*, p. 72; P. Van Eecke, M. Truyens et al. (eds.), "The future of online privacy and data protection, EU study on the Legal analysis of a Single Market for the Information Society – New rules for a new age?, DLA Piper, November 2009, p. 32; J.M. Van Gyseghem, "Cloud computing et protection des données à caractère personnel: mise en ménage possible?", *l.c.*, p. 40. A prime example in this regard is identity federation. See T. Olsen and T. Mahler, "Identity management and data protection law: Risk, responsibility and compliance in 'Circles of Trust' – Part II", *l.c.*, p. 417–420. See also *infra*, nos. 723 et seq.

20 See e.g. O. Tene, "Privacy: The new generations", *l.c.*, 26; Information Commissioner's Office, "The Information Commissioner's (United Kingdom) response to A comprehensive approach on personal data protection in the European Union", 14 January 2011, p. 9.

21 C. Kuner, *European Data Protection Law – Corporate Compliance and Regulation*, *o.c.*, p. 71–72.

22 Opinion 1/2010, *l.c.*, p. 6.

23 *Id.*

therefore in practice be "carved out", to a greater or lesser extent, by the power of (or choices made by) other parties with whom it interacts, even though the legal obligations for compliance remain with the controller.[24]

2. THE THRESHOLD FOR (JOINT) CONTROL

11. Legal uncertainty – European data protection law advances several criteria to determine whether an entity is acting either as a controller or a processor towards a particular processing operation.[25] While the criteria appear conceptually sound, it often remains debatable whether an entity is either acting as a controller or as a processor towards a particular processing operation. Determining the appropriate qualification of a given actor can be particularly difficult in complex processing environments in which many actors participate. This is, for example, the case for so-called "integrated" services where the final service delivered to the end-user is the result of a complex value chain which may involve any number of intermediary processing operations (e.g. registration, authentication, authorization, discovery, retrieval, enrichment, etc.).[26]

12. Malleability of current criteria – The more actors involved in realizing a particular output or functionality, the more likely one will encounter divergent opinions as to which actor (or actors) "control" the processing from a legal perspective.[27] An additional factor that may complicate the analysis is the fact that existing resources are frequently leveraged to deliver new functionalities, rendering it difficult to assess where the "determinative influence" of each actor (and thus the scope of its respective obligations) begins and ends. While the "purposes and means" of the processing might be determined by more than one actor, it is not always clear which level of influence is required in order to implicate an actor as a (joint) controller.[28]

---

24 P. Van Eecke and M. Truyens, "Privacy and social networks", *l.c.*, p. 538 (in relation to the role of users of social networks as data controllers within social networks). While the cited authors refer to the decision-making power of individual social network users, similar considerations apply to the interactions among organisations.

25 Cf. *infra*, nos. 70 et seq.

26 See also J. Alhadeff and B. Van Alsenoy (eds.), "Legal and Policy handbook for TAS³ implementations", *Trusted Architecture for Securely Shared Services* (TAS³), Deliverable 6.1–6.2, v1.0, 2012, p. 91–92.

27 See, for example, the report issued by the Biometrics & eGovernment Subgroup of the Working Party in relation to the STORK project (acknowledging that the subgroup was not able to come to a concordant conclusion as to whether or not a pan European proxy service ("PEPS") should be considered as a (co-)controller or processor; despite the guidance provided by the Article 29 Working Party in Opinion 1/2010. (Article 29 Data Protection Working Party, Biometrics & eGovernment Subgroup, Written Report concerning the STORK Project, Ref.Ares(2011)424406, 15 April 2011, 6–7). See also *infra*, nos. 819 et seq.

28 See also J. Alhadeff and B. Van Alsenoy (eds.), "Legal and Policy handbook for TAS³ implementations", *l.c.*, p. 91 et seq.; T. Olsen and T. Mahler, "Identity management and data

3. THE IMPLICATIONS OF "GRANULAR" CONTROL

13. More granularity, more problems? – The increased complexity of processing operations has led both doctrine and practitioners to apply a less "monolithic" conception of control (particularly in cases where clearly distinct actors are participating in the processing of personal data).[29] Under this approach, a distinction is first made between the different types of processing operations in order to determine which role each actor plays with regards to each operation. In addition, the controller concept is applied with increased granularity, in particular by recognizing that the "degree" to which a particular actor exercises a determinative influence over the purposes and means of the processing can vary significantly.[30] This more granular and flexible approach seems to create tension with other provisions of EU data protection law, as well as some of its underlying objectives (e.g. the aim to ensure effective and complete protection of data subjects).

14. All or nothing? – The obligations incumbent on a controller in principle befall the controller "as a complete set". A controller shall in principle be accountable for every aspect of the data processing under its control: ranging from its obligation to ensure that the data quality principles are complied with, to the obligation to support the exercise of data subject rights, to notification obligations etc. In practice, the situation often occurs whereby certain obligations may more easily be fulfilled by actors other than the controller(s) himself (themselves). In its 2010 Opinion on the concepts of "controller" and "processor", the Article 29 Working Party emphasized that not being able to directly fulfil all the obligations of a controller does not excuse an actor from its obligations under data protection law. It may engage other actors to achieve compliance with its obligations, but this does not negate the fact that it is the controller that remains ultimately responsible for them.[31] In other opinions, however, the

---

protection law: Risk, responsibility and compliance in 'Circles of Trust' – Part II", *l.c.*, p. 419; C. Kuner, *European data protection law: corporate compliance and regulation*, *o.c.*, p. 70.

[29] See also B. Van Alsenoy, J. Ballet, A. Kuczerawy and J. Dumortier, "Social networks and web 2.0: are users also bound by data protection regulations?", *l.c.*, p. 69. See also J. Alhadeff and B. Van Alsenoy (eds.), "Legal and Policy handbook for TAS³ implementations", *l.c.*, p. 96.

[30] See Opinion 1/2010, *l.c.*, p. 19 and 22 (recognizing that "*in many cases the various controllers maybe be responsible – and thus liable – for the processing of personal data at different stages and to different degrees.*"). See also B. Van Alsenoy, "Allocating responsibility among controllers, processors, and "everything in between": the definition of actors and roles in Directive 95/46/EC, *Computer Law & Security Review* 2012, Vol. 28, p. 36 et seq.

[31] Opinion 1/2010, *l.c.*, 22 (stating "*It may be that in practice those obligations could easily be fulfilled by other parties, which are sometimes closer to the data subject, on the controller's behalf. However, a controller will remain in any case ultimately responsible for its obligations and liable for any breach to them.*").

Working Party has adopted a seemingly contradictory approach, indicating that certain controllers might be dispensed from certain compliance obligations.[32] The absence of a clear framework for assigning responsibilities and delineating potential liability exposure risks creating considerable legal uncertainty.[33]

---

32 See e.g. Article 29 Data Protection Working Party, "Opinion 2/2010 on online behavioural advertising", WP171, 22 June 2010, p. 11–12.

33 See also R. Mahieu, J. van Hoboken, H. Asghari, "Responsibility for Data Protection in a Networked World. On the question of the controller, "effective and complete protection" and its application to data access rights in Europe", *JIPITEC* 2019, vol. 10(1), forthcoming, p. 14.

CHAPTER 3
RESEARCH QUESTIONS

15. MAIN QUESTION – The main research question of this book is the following:

> *Can the allocation of responsibility and liability among actors involved in the processing of personal data, as set forth by EU data protection law, be revised in a manner which increases legal certainty while maintaining at least an equivalent level of data protection?*

16. ALLOCATION OF RESPONSIBILITY AND LIABILITY – "Allocation of responsibility" can be described as the process whereby the legislature, through one or more statutory provisions, imposes legal obligations upon a specific actor. "Allocation of liability", on the other hand, can be described as the process whereby the legislature, through one or more statutory provisions, imputes liability or sanctions to an actor where certain prescriptions or restrictions have not been observed.[34]

17. ACTORS INVOLVED IN THE PROCESSING – The research question is limited to actors *involved* in the processing of personal data. An actor may be "involved" in the processing of personal data either by processing data for themselves, on behalf of others, or by causing others to process personal data on their behalf. The research question does not extend to other stakeholders who might influence the level of data protection, such as system developers, technology designers, standardisation bodies, policymakers, etc.

18. LEGAL CERTAINTY – Legal certainty is a general principle of EU law. It expresses the fundamental premise that those subject to the law must be able to ascertain what the law is so as to be able to plan their actions accordingly.[35] One of the reasons why European data protection law introduced the

---

34 For a comprehensive study of the concept of legal risk see T. Mahler, "Defining legal risk", paper presented at the conference "Commercial Contracting for Strategic Advantage – Potentials and Prospects", Turku University of Applied Sciences, 2007.

35 T. Tridimas, *The General Principles of EU Law*, 2nd edition, Oxford University Press, Oxford, 2006, p. 242 et seq.) See also J. Raitio, "The Expectation of Legal Certainty and Horizontal Effect of EU Law", in U. Bernitz, X. Groussot and F. Schulyok (eds.), *General Principles of EU Law and European Private Law*, 2013, Croyden, Kluwer Law International, p. 199–211.

distinction between controllers and processors was to clarify their respective responsibilities under data protection law, thereby increasing legal certainty.[36] Many stakeholders consider, however, that the distinction reflects an outdated paradigm, which is overly simplistic and has become increasingly difficult to apply.[37] Some even suggested that, because of its decreased relevance and applicability, the distinction actually creates legal uncertainty.[38] The main objective of this book is to explore ways in which legal certainty might be increased, without diminishing the legal protections currently enjoyed by data subjects.

19. At least equivalent – The reference, in the research question above, to "an equivalent level of data protection", refers to the protection offered EU data protection law. Within the context of this book, the substantive requirements and principles of EU data protection law (e.g. finality, proportionality, transparency) are taken as a given. As a result, the research question does not directly concern the substantive principles or requirements of data protection law. Rather, it pertains to the manner in which responsibility and liability for compliance with the requirements and principles are (or should be) allocated. That being said, it remains necessary to include the principles and requirements themselves within the scope of study, if only with a view of ensuring that any proposals to revise the current allocation of responsibility and liability do not result in a lowering of the protection enjoyed by individuals (e.g. by limiting their abilities to obtain redress or by decreasing transparency of processing).

20. Sub-questions – In developing an answer to the main research question, the following sub-questions will help guide the research:

1. What is the *nature* and *role* of the controller and processor concepts under European data protection law?
2. What is the *origin* of the controller-processor model and how has it evolved over time?

---

36 See also Opinion 1/2010, *l.c.*, p. 5.

37 See e.g. Information Commissioner's Office, "The Information Commissioner's (United Kingdom) response to A comprehensive approach on personal data protection in the European Union", *l.c.*, p. 9; P. De Hert and V. Papakonstantinou, "The proposed data protection Regulation replacing Directive 95/46/EC: A sound system for the protection of individuals", *l.c.*, p. 134 and European Privacy Officers Forum (EPOF), "Comments on the Review of European Data Protection Framework", 2009, p. 5.

38 European Privacy Officers Forum (EPOF), "Comments on the Review of European Data Protection Framework", *l.c.*, p. 5; Bird & Bird, "Response to European Commission Consultation on the Legal Framework for the Fundamental Right to Protection of Personal Data", 2009, at paragraph 19. See also International Pharmaceutical Privacy Consortium, "Comments in Response to the Consultation on the Legal Framework for the Fundamental Right to Protection of Personal Data", 2009, p. 7.

3. What are the *types of issues* that arise when applying the controller-processor model in practice?
4. Which *solutions* have been proposed to address the issues that arise in practice and to what extent are they capable of addressing the issues?

CHAPTER 4
STRUCTURE AND METHODOLOGY

21. OUTLINE – This book is divided into five parts, whereby each part aims to answer one or more of the research sub-questions identified in the previous chapter. The following sections will briefly elaborate upon the main topics that are covered by each part, as well as their methodological approach. Further details regarding scope and methodology can be found in the introductory chapter of each part.

1. STATE OF THE ART

22. AIM – Part II of the book will analyse the nature and role of the controller and processor concepts under current EU data protection law. The aim is to obtain a better understanding of the meaning of the concepts, as well as the functions they fulfil within EU protection law. To this end, an analysis shall be made of the regulatory scheme of EU data protection law, with special attention to (a) the definitions of controller and processor; (b) the allocation of responsibility and liability; and (c) the additional functions fulfilled by the controller and processor concepts.

23. SCOPE – Even though the GDPR has repealed Directive 95/46, Part II still contains multiple references to the provisions of Directive 95/46. There are several reasons for doing so. First, the definitions of controller and processor contained in Directive 95/46 were incorporated by the GDPR without substantive modification. Second, most of the literature, guidance and case law interpreting the concepts of controller and processor has been developed in the context of Directive 95/46. Third, Directive 95/46 forms the backdrop against which the GDPR was developed. To properly understand the nature and role of the controller and processor concepts under the GDPR, it is necessary to understand the meaning and role of these concepts under Directive 95/46.[39]

---

39 Moreover, doing so enables a more informed evaluation of the choices made by the EU legislature in the context of the GDPR and to identify areas for further improvement in the future. Cf. *infra*, no. 32.

24. Methodology – Part II of the book will follow an internal approach. The primary sources of analysis shall be the text of the GDPR and of Directive 95/46, their preparatory works, the case law of the CJEU and the guidance issued by the Article 29 Working Party and European Data Protection Board. Where appropriate, reference shall also be made to the preparatory works of national implementations of Directive 95/46 (e.g. the Netherlands, Belgium), as a means to clarify and supplement the insights offered by the primary sources. Finally, regard shall also be had to the Principles of European Tort Law as well as national tort law for issues not addressed explicitly by the GDPR and Directive 95/46.

2. HISTORICAL-COMPARATIVE ANALYSIS

25. Aim – Part III of the book will trace the origin and development of the controller and processor concepts over time. As indicated earlier, European data protection law developed only after several national and international instruments were already in place. By analysing a subset of these instruments, it is possible to further enhance the understanding of the meaning and role of the controller and processor concepts.

26. Scope – The historical-comparative analysis will focus upon the development of the controller and processor concepts at national, international and supra-national level. First, three of the earliest data protection laws (i.e. of Hesse, Sweden and France) are analysed. After that, two international instruments of data protection are discussed, namely the OECD Guidelines on the Protection of Privacy and Transborder Flows of Personal Data ("OECD Guidelines") and Council of Europe Convention for the protection of individuals with regard to automatic processing of personal data ("Convention 108"). Next, two national data protection laws implementing Convention 108 are analysed, namely the UK and Belgian data protection acts, followed by a discussion of the legislative development of Directive 95/46. Finally, the General Data Protection Regulation (GDPR) and its legislative history will be analysed.

27. Methodology – The comparative analysis shall be primarily dogmatic in nature. To the extent possible, reference shall be made to primary sources (i.e. legislation, formal declarations and guidelines issued by the relevant institutions). Where appropriate, however, reference will also be made to preparatory works and explanatory memoranda, jurisprudence, and doctrinal accounts of the meaning and implications of certain concepts.

3. USE CASES

28. AIM – Part IV of the book aims to identify and evaluate the main issues that arise when applying the controller-processor model in practice. To this end, a number of real-life use cases will be examined with the aim of documenting specific issues that arise when applying the concepts of controller and processor. In addition, an assessment shall be made of whether the traditional allocation of responsibility and liability between controller and processor leads to the intended level of protection.

29. SELECTION CRITERIA – Needless to say, it is impossible to document and analyse every possible use case. A selection needs to be made. The primary threshold for eligibility has been the existence of an indication, either in regulatory guidance or doctrine, that the use case in question challenges either the application of the controller and processor concepts or the allocation of responsibility and liability among actors involved in the processing of personal data. Once the initial screening for relevancy was completed, a further selection was made with the aim of ensuring a sufficient degree of variation on the dimensions of theoretical interest and ensuring representativeness.[40]

30. METHODOLOGY – Each of the selected uses cases will be analysed in a structured and focused manner.[41] First, an overview of the main types of actors and interactions will be provided. Next, the legal status and obligations of each actor shall be analysed, taking into account the different interpretations put forward by courts, regulators and scholars. Finally, at the end of each use case, an evaluation will be made of the main issues that have been identified when applying the controller-processor model to the use case in question. The identified issues will serve as the main input for the typology of issues developed in Part V.

4. RECOMMENDATIONS

31. AIM – Part V of the book aims to provide normative recommendations. Specifically, it aims to provide recommendations as to how the current allocation

---

40 See also J. Seawright and J. Gerring, "Case Selection Techniques in Case Study Research – A Menu of Qualitative and Quantitative Options", *Political Research Quarterly* 2008, Vol. 61, No. 2, p. 296.

41 The analysis shall be "structured" in the sense that the analysis of each use case will be composed of the same subsections and answer the same questions in relation to each use case. The analysis shall be "focused" in that the analysis shall extend only to those aspects which are relevant for purposes of the research question which this Part seeks to address. Based on A.L. George and A. Bennet, *Case Studies and Theory Development in the Social Sciences*, *o.c.*, p. 67 et seq.

of responsibility and liability among actors involved in the processing of personal data might be modified in order to increase legal certainty while maintaining at least an equivalent level of data protection.

32. Methodology – The method used to articulate normative recommendations consists of four steps. First, the issues identified in Part IV shall be categorised and presented in a structured manner (typology of issues). Second, an inventory will be made of ways in which these issues might be remedied (typology of solutions). Third, an evaluation will be made of the extent to which the proposed remedies are capable of addressing each of the identified issues. The evaluation of possible solutions shall, for the most part, be based on the typology of issues. Each proposal will be evaluated on the basis of whether, and if so, to what extent, it is capable of addressing each of the identified issues. If multiple solutions have been proposed to remedy a particular issue, an internal comparison will be made. Where appropriate, insights from the field of law and economics will be applied to assist the internal comparison of the proposed solutions.[42] Finally, the approach adopted by the European legislature in the context of the GDPR will be compared with the outcome of the preceding evaluations. Where relevant, recommendations for possible further improvements will be made.

[42] In other words, the typology of issues shall serve as the positive assessment framework to evaluate the proposed solutions. No additional assessment criteria will be used to evaluate the proposed solutions. Only in the context of the internal comparison of possible solutions shall the insights from the field of law and economics be applied in order to enhance the evaluation process.

PART II

STATE OF THE ART

CHAPTER 1
INTRODUCTION

33. OUTLINE – Over the following chapters, the basic regulatory scheme of EU data protection law will be analysed with specific emphasis on the role of the controller and processor concepts. After describing its scope of application and basic protections, a detailed analysis will be made of how EU data protection law allocates responsibility and liability among actors involved in the processing of personal data. First, the key elements of the concepts of controller and processor shall be elaborated. Next, the relationship between controllers, co-controllers and processors will be discussed, followed by an analysis of the liability exposure of each actor. Finally, a number of specific issues relevant to the practical application of the controller and processor concepts shall be discussed.

34. METHODOLOGY – The analysis over the following chapters is based in first instance on the text of both the GDPR and Directive 95/46, their preparatory works, the case law of the CJEU, as well as the guidance issued by the Article 29 Working Party and European Data Protection Board. In certain places, however, the analysis is supplemented by insights offered by the preparatory works which accompanied national implementations of Directive 95/46. This approach is based on the assumption that national deliberations on the topic of how Directive 95/46 should be implemented into national law can yield additional insights as to how policymakers understood the provisions of Directive 95/46 at the time of its enactment.[43] Finally, as regards the liability exposure of controllers and processors, reference shall also be made to the Principles of European Tort Law (PETL) as well as national Belgian tort law. The reason for doing so is that EU data protection law does not exhaustively harmonise the liability exposure of controllers and processors. By incorporating these supplemental sources into the analysis, however, it is possible to complement the analysis of the GDPR and Directive 95/46 with a number of important elements.

---

[43] The preparatory works accompanying the following national laws were consulted: France, Netherlands, Belgium and UK. The reason why the analysis of preparatory works to these national implementations of Directive 95/46 is simply because they are written in languages which I am fluent. After consultation, however, it appeared that mainly the preparatory works of the Dutch and Belgian data protection acts offered additional insights which merited inclusion.

CHAPTER 2
SCOPE OF EU DATA PROTECTION LAW

1. MATERIAL SCOPE

35. Ratione materiae – EU data protection law applies to "*the processing of personal data wholly or partly by automated means and to the processing other than by automated means of personal data which form part of a filing system or are intended to form part of a filing system*".[44]

36. Personal data – The material scope of EU data protection law is in first instance delineated by the concept of "personal data". Personal data is understood as "*any information relating to an identified or identifiable natural person ('data subject')*".[45]

37. "Any information" – The concept of personal data is extremely broad. Any type of information that pertains to an individual is considered personal data. For example, not only text, but also photos qualify as personal data. Even sound can qualify as personal data.[46] The use of the expression "any information" in the definition of personal data reflects the aim of the EU legislature to assign a wide scope to that concept, which is not restricted to information that is sensitive or private, but potentially encompasses all kinds of information, not only objective but also subjective, in the form of opinions and assessments, provided that it 'relates' to the data subject.[47]

38. "Relating to" – Information may be considered as "relating to" the data subject if the information, by reason of its content, purpose or effect, is linked to a particular person.[48] Generally speaking, information can be considered to

---

44 Article 2(1) GDPR (previously: Article 3(1) Directive 95/46).

45 Article 4(1) GDPR (previously: Article 2(a) Directive 95/46).

46 D. De Bot, *Verwerking van persoonsgegevens*, Antwerpen, Kluwer, 2001, 23. See also C. Kuner, *European Data Protection Law – Corporate Compliance and Regulation*, *o.c.*, p. 91–98.

47 Judgment in *Nowak*, C-434/16, ECLI:EU:C:2017:994, paragraph 34.

48 Judgment in *Nowak*, C-434/16, ECLI:EU:C:2017:994, paragraph 35. See also Article 29 Working Party, Opinion 4/2007 on the concept of personal data", WP 136, 20 June 2007, p. 15–17.

"relate" to an individual when it is *about* that individual.[49] In some situations, the information in first instance concerns an object (e.g. a smartphone or other personal device), yet may be considered as indirectly relating to a particular individual.[50] Data also "relates" to an individual if such information is used with the purpose to evaluate an individual (e.g. to determine and establish the performance of a specific person), to treat that person in a certain way or to otherwise influence the status or behaviour of an individual.[51] Finally, information can also be considered to "relate" to an individual because its use is likely to have an effect on the individual's rights and interests, taking into account all the circumstances surrounding a particular case.[52]

39. Identifiability – For EU data protection law to apply, the data must pertain to an identified or identifiable (natural) person. A person is considered "identifiable" if he or she

> "can be identified, directly or indirectly, in particular by reference to an identifier such as a name, an identification number, location data, an online identifier or to one or more factors specific to the physical, physiological, genetic, mental, economic, cultural or social identity of that natural person".[53]

To determine whether or not a person is identifiable, one should take into account all the means which reasonably might be used to identify the data subject, either by the controller or by another person.[54] For information to be treated as "personal data" within the meaning of EU data protection law, there is no requirement that all the information enabling the identification of the data subject must be in the hands of one person.[55] For example, the fact that the additional data necessary to identify the user of a website are held, not by the website operator, but by that user's internet service provider, is insufficient to exclude

---

49 Article 29 Working Party, Opinion 4/2007 on the concept of personal data", WP 136, 20 June 2007, p. 9.

50 *Id.*

51 *Ibid*, p. 10. See also recital (30) GDPR ("*Natural persons may be associated with online identifiers provided by their devices, applications, tools and protocols, such as internet protocol addresses, cookie identifiers or other identifiers such as radio frequency identification tags. This may leave traces which, in particular when combined with unique identifiers and other information received by the servers, may be used to create profiles of the natural persons and identify them.*")

52 Article 29 Working Party, Opinion 4/2007 on the concept of personal data", *l.c.*, p. 11. See also Judgment in *Nowak*, C-434/16, ECLI:EU:C:2017:994, paragraph 39.

53 Article 4(1) GDPR (previously: Article 2(a) Directive 95/46).

54 See recital (26) GDPR (previously: recital (26) Directive 95/46/EC). See also Article 29 Working Party, Opinion 4/2007 on the concept of personal data", *l.c.*, p. 15–17 See also the Opinion of Advocate-General Campos Sánchez-Bordana in *Breyer*, C-582/14, ECLI:EU:C:2016:339, at paragraphs 63–78.

55 Judgment in *Breyer*, C-582/14, EU:C:2016:779, paragraph 43; Judgment in *Nowak*, C-434/16, ECLI:EU:C:2017:994, paragraph 31.

that dynamic IP addresses from being considered as personal data.[56] To ascertain whether means are "reasonably likely to be used" to identify the natural person, account should be taken of all objective factors, such as the costs of and the amount of time required for identification, taking into consideration the available technology at the time of the processing and technological developments.[57]

40. PROCESSING – "Processing of personal data" is understood as

> "any operation or set of operations which is performed on personal data or on sets of personal data, whether or not by automated means, such as collection, recording, organisation, structuring, storage, adaptation or alteration, retrieval, consultation, use, disclosure by transmission, dissemination or otherwise making available, alignment or combination, restriction, erasure or destruction"[58]

Similar to the definition of "personal data", the definition of "processing" is also extremely broad. *Any* operation performed upon personal data by automatic means is covered by the definition of processing.[59] With regards to non-automated processing, EU data protection law only applies to the extent that the personal data is included in a filing system or intended to be part of filing system.[60]

41. EXEMPTIONS – The material scope of the EU data protection law covers all automated processing of personal data, save for the areas excluded by Article 2 of the GDPR, namely the processing of personal data:

> "(a) in the course of an activity which falls outside the scope of Union law;
> (b) by the Member States when carrying out activities which fall within the scope of Chapter 2 of Title V of the TEU;
> (c) by a natural person in the course of a purely personal or household activity;
> (d) by competent authorities for the purposes of the prevention, investigation, detection or prosecution of criminal offences or the execution of criminal penalties, including the safeguarding against and the prevention of threats to public security."[61]

---

56 Judgment in *Breyer*, C-582/14, EU:C:2016:779, paragraph 44.

57 Recital (26) GDPR. In *Breyer*, the CJEU considered that having at one's disposal legal means which enable it to identify the data subject with the help of additional data which is held by third parties (e.g. an internet service provider) about that person may be considered as means which may likely reasonably be used in order to identify the data subject. Judgment in *Breyer*, C-582/14, EU:C:2016:779, paragraph 48.

58 Article 4(2) GDPR (previously: Article 2(b) Directive 95/46).

59 See also C. Kuner, *European Data Protection Law – Corporate Compliance and Regulation*, *o.c.*, p. 98–99; Judgment in *Google Spain*, C-131/12, ECLI:EU:C:2014:317, paragraphs 25–31.

60 Article 2(1) GDPR (previously: Article 3(1) Directive 95/46). See also the Judgment in *Jehovah's Witnesses*, C-25/17, ECLI:EU:C:2018:551, at paragraphs 52–62.

61 Article 2(2) GDPR (previously: Article 3(2) Directive 95/46). For the processing of personal data by the Union institutions, bodies, offices and agencies, Regulation (EU) 2018/1725 applies (previously Regulation (EC) No 45/2001). See Articles 100–101 of Regulation

2. TERRITORIAL SCOPE

42. Ratione loci – The territorial scope of the GDPR is determined by Article 3. For the purposes of this book, the two most important triggers are (1) the presence of a relevant establishment of a controller or processor on EU territory and (2) the monitoring or targeting of EU data subjects.[62] While the first ground governs the situation in which the controller or processor has an establishment on EU territory, the second ground governs the situation where there is no such establishment.

43. Establishment criterion – Article 3(1) provides that the GDPR shall apply

> "to the processing of personal data in the context of the activities of an establishment of a controller or a processor in the Union, regardless of whether the processing takes place in the Union or not."

Determining the territorial scope of the GDPR pursuant to Article 3(1) implies prior identification of the entity which is acting as a "*controller*" or "*processor*" of the processing, as well as the location of its "*establishment(s)*". Equally important, however, is the reference to the "*context of activities*": this criterion implies that the establishment must be involved in activities implying the processing of personal data in question.[63] Or rather, the establishment must be involved in a "*real and effective exercise of activities in the context of which the personal data are being processed*".[64] The notion of "in the context of the activities" does not, however, require that the establishment in question itself is actively engaged in the processing.[65]

(EU) 2018/1725 of the European Parliament and of the Council of 23 October 2018 on the protection of natural persons with regard to the processing of personal data by the Union institutions, bodies, offices and agencies and on the free movement of such data, and repealing Regulation (EC) No 45/2001 and Decision No 1247/2002/EC, OJ, 21.11.2018, L 295/39.

62 In addition to these "main criteria", the GDPR also specifies in Article 3(3) that the GDPR applies to the processing of personal data by a controller not established in the Union, but in a place where Member State law applies by virtue of public international law. Recital (25) indicates that this might be the case, for example, as regards the processing of personal data carried out in a Member State's diplomatic mission or consular post.

63 Article 29 Data Protection Working Party, "Opinion 8/2010 on applicable law", WP 179, 16 December 2010, p. 2.

64 *Ibid*, p.11.

65 Judgment in *Google Spain*, C-131/12, ECLI:EU:C:2014:317, paragraph 52. For a detailed discussion of the concepts of "establishment" an "in the context of" in light of existing CJEU case law, see B. Van Alsenoy, "Reconciling the (extra)territorial reach of the GDPR with public international law", in G. Vermeulen and E. Lievens (eds.), *Data Protection and Privacy under Pressure Transatlantic tensions, EU surveillance, and big data*, Antwerp, Maklu, 2017,

44. Changes to directive 95/46 – Article 3(1) GDPR is the successor of Article 4(1)a of Directive 95/46, with two notable changes. First, Article 3(1) GDPR makes reference not only to an establishment of a controller, but also to an establishment of a processor. As a result, the processing of personal data might also be subject to EU data protection law by virtue of a *processor* having an establishment located within the EU.[66] Second, Article 3(1) explicitly indicates that it is not necessary for the processing of personal data to take place within the EU in order for the GDPR to apply. In other words, Article 3(1) GDPR still has the potential for extra-territorial reach: EU data protection law shall apply to processing taking place outside EU territory as long as it is being carried out "in the context of the activities of an establishment of the controller or processor" located within the EU.[67]

45. Targeting or monitoring – Article 3(2) GDPR explicitly addresses the territorial scope of the GDPR in case of processing of personal data by a controller or processor not established in the Union. It provides that the GDPR shall be applicable to

> "the processing of personal data of data subjects who are in the Union by a controller or processor not established in the Union, where the processing activities are related to:
>
> (a) the offering of goods or services, irrespective of whether a payment of the data subject is required, to such data subjects in the Union; or
> (b) the monitoring of their behaviour as far as their behaviour takes place within the Union."

While Article 3(2) only applies in case the controller or processor is not established in the Union, the processing of personal data must concern data subjects located in the Union. The first activity triggering the application of Article 3(2) is the "offering of goods or services". Recital (23) clarifies that Article 3(2)a requires conduct on the part of the controller or processor which demonstrates its *intention* to offer goods or services to data subjects located in the Union:

---

p. 80–85 and European Data Protection Board, "Guidelines 3/2018 on the territorial scope of the GDPR (Article 3) – Version for public consultation", 16 November 2018, p. 4–12.

66 For a discussion of implications of this addition see E.J. Kindt, "Why research may no longer be the same: About the territorial scope of the New Data Protection Regulation", *Computer Law & Security Review* 2016, vol. 32, p. 741 and L. Moerel, "The data transfer regime for processors does not make sense and requires clarification", GDPR Conundrums: Data Transfer, 9 June 2016, https://iapp.org/news/a/gdpr-conundrums-data-transfer.

67 See also B. Van Alsenoy and M. Koekkoek, "Internet and jurisdiction after Google Spain: the extraterritorial reach of the 'right to be delisted'", *International Data Privacy Law* 2015, Vol. 5, No. 2, p. 107.

> "In order to determine whether such a controller or processor is offering goods or services to data subjects who are in the Union, it should be ascertained whether it is apparent that the controller or processor envisages offering services to data subjects in one or more Member States in the Union."[68]

The second activity triggering the application of Article 3(2) is "monitoring of behaviour". Recital (24) indicates that Article 3(2)b is first and foremost concerned with online tracking and profiling activities:

> "In order to determine whether a processing activity can be considered to monitor the behaviour of data subjects, it should be ascertained whether natural persons are tracked on the internet including potential subsequent use of personal data processing techniques which consist of profiling a natural person, particularly in order to take decisions concerning her or him or for analysing or predicting her or his personal preferences, behaviours and attitudes."[69]

46. Changes to directive 95/46 – Article 3(2)b GDPR can be considered as the successor of Article 4(1)c of Directive 95/46, which provides that Member States must apply their national data protection laws if a controller who is not established in the EU "*makes use of equipment*" situated on its territory. While the term "equipment" in first instance referred to physical objects[70], the Article 29 Working Party had given the term a broad interpretation, which comprises both human and technical resources.[71] More specifically, the Working Party understood the term "equipment" to have the same meaning as the term "means" used in Article 2(d) of the Directive (i.e. the definition of controller).[72]

---

68 As a result, mere accessibility of a website is considered insufficient to ascertain such an intention. Conversely, use of a currency or language generally used in one or more EU Member States, in particular where that language is not generally used in the third country where the controller or processor is established, or the mentioning of customers or users who are in the Union, may make it apparent that the controller envisages offering goods or services to data subjects in the Union. (Recital (23) GDPR). For more information see also B. Van Alsenoy, "Reconciling the (extra)territorial reach of the GDPR with public international law", *l.c.*, p. 85–87 and European Data Protection Board, "Guidelines 3/2018 on the territorial scope of the GDPR (Article 3) – Version for public consultation", p. 14–17.

69 Recital (24) explicitly refers to internet tracking and profiling techniques, suggesting either that an element of intentional or active tracking is required, or that the monitoring must reach a certain level or intrusiveness. See also European Data Protection Board, "Guidelines 3/2018 on the territorial scope of the GDPR (Article 3) – Version for public consultation", p. 17–18.

70 M. Czerniawski, "Do We Need the 'Use of Equipment' as a factor for the territorial applicability of the EU Data Protection Regime?", *l.c.*, p. 227. The legislative history of Directive 95/46 suggests that its drafters only had physical objects in mind when using the word 'equipment'. See also L. Moerel, 'The long arm of EU data protection law: Does the Data Protection Directive apply to processing of personal data of EU citizens by websites worldwide?', *l.c.*, p. 33 and 36.

71 Article 29 Data Protection Working Party, 'Opinion 8/2010 on applicable law', *l.c.*, p. 20.

72 *Id.*

On the basis of this broad interpretation, the Working Party considered that the use of JavaScript banners or cookies might also be considered as "means" within the meaning of Article 4(1)c.[73] As a result, the use of cookies by non-EU controllers to track data subjects located in the EU was considered to fall within the territorial scope of Directive 95/46. While this interpretation has been the subject of considerable criticism, the EU legislature has apparently chosen to embrace it by providing it with a more explicit legal footing.

73 *Ibid*, p. 21–22.

CHAPTER 3
BASIC PROTECTIONS

47. Outline – EU data protection law seeks to protect individuals with regard to the processing of their personal data by (1) requiring compliance with a number of key principles; (2) providing individuals with a right to information as well as other data subject rights; (3) imposing an obligation to ensure the confidentiality and security of processing; (4) requiring the establishment, at national level, of supervisory authorities dedicated to monitoring compliance with the substantive provisions of EU data protection law; and (5) requiring controllers to able to demonstrate compliance with these principles.

1. KEY PRINCIPLES

48. Lawfulness, fairness & transparency – Article 5(1)a of the GDPR provides that personal data must be processed "*lawfully, fairly and in a transparent manner*".[74] Fairness of processing is considered an overarching principle of data protection law.[75] It is a generic principle which has provided the foundation for other data protection requirements. As such, the fairness principle provides a "lens" through which the other provisions in the Directive should be interpreted.[76] The principle of lawfulness of processing reaffirms that data controllers must stay in line with other legal obligations, even outside of the

[74] Article 5(1)a GDPR (previously: Article 6(1)a Directive 95/46).

[75] L.A. Bygrave, *Data Protection Law. Approaching its Rationale, Logic and Limits*, Kluwer International 2002, Den Haag, p. 58. See also B. Van Alsenoy, A. Kuczerawy and J. Ausloos, "Search Engines after *Google Spain*: Internet@Liberty or Privacy@Peril?", *ICRI Working Paper Series*, Working paper 15/2013, September 2013, p. 31.

[76] B. Van Alsenoy, A. Kuczerawy and J. Ausloos, "Search Engines after *Google Spain*: Internet@ Liberty or Privacy@Peril?", *l.c.*, p. 31. See also A. Kuczerawy and F. Coudert, "Privacy Settings in Social Networking Sites: Is It Fair?," in *Privacy and Identity Management for Life*, 2011, p. 237–238 ("*The collection and processing of personal data must be performed in a way that does not intrude unreasonably upon the data subjects' privacy nor interfere unreasonably with their autonomy and integrity*") with reference to L.A. Bygrave, *Data Protection Law, Approaching its rationale, logic and limits, o.c.*, p. 58. The open-ended nature of the fairness principle seems to place a general obligation on controllers to act in a responsible way. This requirement becomes particularly relevant in situations where the extent to which data subjects can exercise control over the processing is limited (e.g. because of a significant power imbalance between controllers and subjects, because of the complexity of processing, etc.) (B.

GDPR, regardless of whether these obligations are general, specific, statutory or contractual.[77] The principle of transparency is in many ways a logical extension of the requirement that personal data shall be processed "fairly and lawfully".[78] It is based on the idea that even if one doesn't have a say in the matter, an individual should generally[79] at least be informed when his personal data are being processed and/or be in a position to acquire additional information. The transparency principle is given further substance within the context of the data subject's right to information and right of access.[80]

49. Finality – Article 5(1)b of the GDPR dictates that personal data must be "*collected for specified, explicit and legitimate purposes and not further processed in a manner that is incompatible with those purposes.*"[81] This provision embodies the so-called "*principle of finality*", which comprises two basic rules. First, it requires controllers to clearly articulate the purposes for which personal data are being collected (purpose specification).[82] Second, it requires controllers to limit their subsequent use of this information to practices compatible with the purposes defined at the moment of collection (use limitation).[83] By defining

Van Alsenoy, A. Kuczerawy and J. Ausloos, "Search Engines after *Google Spain*: Internet@ Liberty or Privacy@Peril?", *l.c.*, p. 31).

77 B. Van Alsenoy, A. Kuczerawy and J. Ausloos, "Search Engines after Google Spain: Internet@ Liberty or Privacy@Peril?", *l.c.*, p. 31; C. De Terwangne, "Les principes relatifs au traitement des données à caractère personnel et sa licéité", in C. De Terwangne and K. Rosier (eds.), *Le Règlement Général sur la Protection des Données (RGPD/GDPR) – Analyse approfondie*, CRIDS, Brussels, Larcier, 2018, p. 89–90. Alternatively, the argument can also be made that the requirement to respect legal requirements outside of the GDPR might stem from the requirement of legitimacy of purpose. See also Opinion of Advocate-General Bobek in *Fashion ID*, C-40/17, ECLI:EU:C:2018:1039, paragraph 122 ("*There is no type of interest that is excluded per se, as long of course as they are themselves legal.*")

78 See e.g. L.A. Bygrave, *Data Protection Law. Approaching its Rationale, Logic and Limits*, Kluwer International 2002, Den Haag, 59; M.-H. Boulanger, C. De Terwangne, Th. Léonard, S. Louveaux, D. Moreau and Y. Poullet, 'La protection des données à caractère personnel en droit communautaire, *Journal des Tribunaux* 1997, 127; T. Léonard and Y. Poullet, 'La protection des données à caractère personnel en pleine (r)évolution – La loi du 11 décembre 1998 transposant la directive 95/46/C.E. du 24 octobre 1995, *Journal des Tribunaux* 1999, 385; D. De Bot, *Verwerking van Persoonsgegevens*, Antwerpen, Kluwer, 2001, 115.

79 Obviously exceptions derogations may be necessary (e.g. in the course of undercover operation). However, such derogations must be established pursuant to the provisions of the GDPR (unless of course, the processing operation falls outside of its scope altogether).

80 See *infra*, nos. 54 et seq. For a further discussion of the rationale underlying the transparency principle see B. Van Alsenoy, E. Kosta and J. Dumortier, "Privacy notices versus informational self-determination: Minding the gap", *International Review of Law, Computers & Technology* 2013, p. 185–203.

81 Article 5(1)b GDPR (previously: Article 6(1)b Directive 95/46).

82 B. Van Alsenoy, A. Kuczerawy and J. Ausloos, "Search Engines after Google Spain: Internet@ Liberty or Privacy@Peril?", *l.c.*, p. 32.

83 *Ibid*, p. 32. See e.g. Article 29 Data Protection Working Party, "Opinion 03/2013 on purpose limitation", WP 203, 2 April 2013, 70 p.; L.A. Bygrave, "Core principles of data protection", *Privacy Law and Policy Reporter*, vol. 7, issue 9, 2001; E. Kosta and J. Dumortier, "The Data Retention Directive and the principles of European Data protection legislation", *Medien*

the purpose at the outset, the data controller establishes the benchmark against which the other data quality principles will be measured.[84] This makes it possible to assess the fairness, lawfulness and proportionality of processing, as well as to evaluate the data controller's compliance with the use limitation principle.[85]

50. LEGITIMACY – The purposes of the processing must not only be specified, they must also be legitimate and lawful. EU data protection law restricts the instances in which the processing of personal data may take place. In particular, Article 6(1) of the GDPR enumerates several legal grounds, of which at least one must be present in order for the processing of personal data to be considered "lawful" for purposes of EU data protection law (e.g. data subject consent, necessity for the performance of a contract, etc.).[86] It is worth observing that Article 6(1) of the GDPR refers to "lawfulness", whereas previous Article 7 of Directive 95/46 spoke of "criteria for making data processing legitimate". It has been pointed out that the GDPR generally uses the concept of "lawfulness" in a more narrow and precise way in comparison to Directive 95/46.[87] The basic requirement has however remained the same: the processing of personal data shall only be permitted to the extent that at least one of the recognized grounds for processing applies.

---

und Recht International, issue 3, 2007, p. 133; C. Kuner, *European Data Protection Law – Corporate Compliance and Regulation*, *o.c.*, p. 99–100 and D. Elsegem, "The structure of rights in Directive 95/46/EC on the protection of individuals with regard to the processing of personal data and the free movement of such data", *Ethics and Information Technology* 1999, vol. 1, p. 287–288.

84 B. Van Alsenoy, A. Kuczerawy and J. Ausloos, "Search Engines after *Google Spain*: Internet@Liberty or Privacy@Peril?", *l.c.*, p. 32.

85 *Id.* and S. Gutwirth, *Privacy and the information age*, *o.c.*, p. 97–102. See also B. Van Alsenoy, A. Kuczerawy and J. Ausloos, "Search Engines after *Google Spain*: Internet@Liberty or Privacy@Peril?", *l.c.*, p. 33, with reference to M.-H. Boulanger, C. De Terwangne, T. Léonard, S. Louveaux, D. Moreau and Y. Poullet, "La Protection des Données à caractère personnel en droit communautaire", *Journal de Tribunaux Droit Européen* 1997, p. 127 and 145–147; D. De Bot, *Verwerking van persoonsgegevens*, *o.c.*, p. 118–121 and T. Léonard, "La protection des données à caractère personnel et l'entreprise", Brussels, Kluwer, 2004, livre 112.1, p. 29.

86 Article 6(1) GDPR (previously: Article 7 Directive 95/46). See also B. Van Alsenoy, A. Kuczerawy and J. Ausloos, "Search Engines after *Google Spain*: Internet@Liberty or Privacy@Peril?", *l.c.*, p. 33, with reference to M.-H. Boulanger, C. De Terwangne, T. Léonard, S. Louveaux, D. Moreau and Y. Poullet, "La Protection des Données à caractère personnel en droit communautaire", *l.c.*, p. 147–148. See also L.A. Bygrave, *Data Protection Law, Approaching its rationale, logic and limits*, *o.c.*, p. 61–62 and C. Kuner, *European Data Protection Law – Corporate Compliance and Regulation*, second edition, New York, Oxford University Press, 2007, p. 74–46 and p. 90; Article 29 Data Protection Working Party, Opinion 06/2014 on the notion of legitimate interests of the data controller under Article 7 of Directive 95/46/EC, 9 April 2014, WP 217, p. 13–33 and J. Ausloos, *The Right to Erasure: Safeguard for informational self-determination in a digital society?*, Dissertation presented in partial fulfilment of the requirements for the degree of Doctor in Laws, KU Leuven, 2018, p. 189–197.

87 J. Ausloos, *o.c.*, p. 187.

51. Data minimisation & storage limitation – Article 5(1)c GDPR specifies that the processing of personal data should be limited to data that are "*adequate, relevant and limited to what is necessary in relation to the purposes for which they are processed ('data minimisation')*".[88] EU data protection law requires that there exists a sufficiently narrow correlation, both in terms of adequacy and relevancy, between the legitimate purpose articulated by the controller and the data being collected. Moreover, only data which are *necessary* to achieve the legitimate aims of the controller may be processed.[89] Article 5(1)e further provides that personal data may not be kept in a form which permits identification of data subjects for longer than necessary to realise for the purposes for which the data were collected (or for which they are further processed) ('*storage limitation*').[90]

52. Accuracy – Every controller is under the obligation to ensure the accuracy of the personal data it processes.[91] This provision in first instance requires controllers to put in place mechanisms and procedures which enable them to establish the accuracy of data with a level of assurance proportionate to the interests at stake. Article 5(1)d of the GDPR also stipulates that data must be kept up-to-date where necessary. This implies that controllers are in principle obliged to meet the requirement of accuracy not only at the moment of collection, but as long as the data is being processed under their control.[92]

53. Special categories of personal data – Finally, it is worth noting that EU data protection law imposes additional restrictions regarding the processing of so-called special (or "sensitive") categories of data, which include personal data revealing racial or ethnic origin, political opinions, religious or philosophical beliefs, or trade union membership, and the processing of genetic data, biometric

---

88 Article 5(1)c GDPR (previously: Article 6(1)c Directive 95/46). This provision is generally considered a manifestation of a more general data protection principle, namely the principle of proportionality. (B. Van Alsenoy, A. Kuczerawy and J. Ausloos, "Search Engines after *Google Spain*: Internet@Liberty or Privacy@Peril?", *l.c.*, p. 33). For a more comprehensive overview of the role of the proportionality principle in the Data Protection Directive and EU law in generals see C. Kuner, "Proportionality in European Data Protection Law And Its Importance for Data Processing by Companies", *Privacy & Security Law Report* 2008, vol. 07, no. 44, p. 1615 and European Data Protection Supervisor, Assessing the necessity of measures that limit the fundamental right to the protection of personal data: A Toolkit, 11 April 2017, p. 4–5.

89 B. Van Alsenoy, A. Kuczerawy and J. Ausloos, "Search Engines after *Google Spain*: Internet@ Liberty or Privacy@Peril?", *l.c.*, p. 33, with reference to M.-H. Boulanger, C. De Terwangne, T. Léonard, S. Louveaux, D. Moreau and Y. Poullet, "La Protection des Données à caractère personnel en droit communautaire", *l.c.*, p. 147. See also D. De Bot, *Verwerking van persoonsgegevens, o.c.*, p. 124–125.

90 Article 5(1)e GDPR (previously: Article 6(1)e Directive 95/46).

91 Article 5(1)d GDPR (previously: Article 6(1)d Directive 95/46).

92 B. Van Alsenoy, N. Vandezande, K. Janssen, a.o., "Legal Provisions for Deploying INDI services", *l.c.*, p. 22.

data for the purpose of uniquely identifying a natural person, data concerning health or data concerning a natural person's sex life or sexual orientation.[93] The processing of such data is in principle prohibited, subject to certain exceptions.[94] It is important to note that the restrictions for special categories of personal data apply in addition to the general requirement of lawfulness (or "legitimacy") of processing.[95]

2. TRANSPARENCY AND DATA SUBJECT RIGHTS

54. Outline – Articles 12 and following of the GDPR set forth the transparency obligations of controllers and list the rights data subjects can exercise towards controllers when their personal data is being processed. Underlying these provisions is the idea that the data subject should in principle:

(a) be notified of the processing of her personal data (right to information);
(b) have means to obtain further information (right of access); and
(c) have immediate means of recourse towards the controller in case she feels her data are being processed improperly (right to rectification, erasure or restriction).[96]

55. Duty to inform – Articles 13 and 14 of the GDPR specify which types of information controllers must provide to data subjects with regards to the processing of their personal data.[97] As a rule, each data subject must be informed of at least the identity and contact details of the controller (and, if applicable,

---

93 Article 9 GDPR (previously: Article 8 Directive 95/46). In comparison to Directive 95/46, the GDPR has added the processing of genetic data, biometric data for the purpose of uniquely identifying a natural person and the processing of data concerning a natural person's sexual orientation to the list of processing of special categories of data.

94 Article 29 Data Protection Working Party, Opinion 06/2014 on the notion of legitimate interests of the data controller under Article 7 of Directive 95/46/EC, *l.c.*, p. 14.

95 *Ibid*, p. 14–15.

96 B. Van Alsenoy, N. Vandezande, K. Janssen, a.o., "Legal Provisions for Deploying INDI services", *l.c.*, p. 28. See also B. Van Alsenoy, E. Kosta and J. Dumortier, "Privacy notices versus informational self-determination: Minding the gap", *International Review of Law, Computers & Technology* 2013 and Bygrave, *Data Protection Law, Approaching its rationale, logic and limits, o.c.*, p. 63–66.

97 Articles 13 and 14 GDPR (previously: Articles 10–11 Directive 95/46) address two different scenarios, respectively: one in which the information is obtained directly from the data subject (Article 13), and one in which the information is collected indirectly (i.e. from an entity other than the data subject) (Article 14). The duty to inform is similar in both scenarios; the main relevance of the distinction concerns (a) the moment by which notice must be provided and (b) the exemptions to the notice provision. For a detailed comparison and discussion of the difference between Article 13 and Article 14 see Article 29 Data Protection Working Party, Guidelines on transparency under Regulation 2016/679, WP260 rev.01, 11 April 2018, p. 35–40.

of his representative and/or data protection officer) and the purposes and legal basis of the processing.[98] Other relevant information concerns the recipients or categories of recipients of the personal data, the period for which the personal data will be stored, data subject rights, etc.[99] It is worth noting that the GDPR explicitly requires controllers to provide such information in a concise, transparent, intelligible and easily accessible form.[100]

56. Right of access – Article 15(1) of the GDPR stipulates that every data subject shall have the right to obtain from the controller confirmation as to whether or not personal data concerning him or her are being processed, and, where that is the case, access to the personal data and the following information:

(a) the purposes of the processing;
(b) the categories of personal data concerned;
(c) the recipients or categories of recipient to whom the personal data have been or will be disclosed, in particular recipients in third countries or international organisations;
(d) where possible, the envisaged period for which the personal data will be stored, or, if not possible, the criteria used to determine that period;
(e) the existence of the right to request from the controller rectification or erasure of personal data or restriction of processing of personal data concerning the data subject or to object to such processing;
(f) the right to lodge a complaint with a supervisory authority;

---

98 The use of plural "purposes", in Articles 13–14, implies that the data subject has to be informed not only about the main purpose to be accomplished, but also about any secondary purposes for which the data will be used. (B. Van Alsenoy, E. Kosta and J. Dumortier, "Privacy notices versus informational self-determination: Minding the gap", *l.c.*, at note 7).

99 Previously, Directive 95/46 stipulated that Member States must require controllers to provide the data subject with supplemental information "*in so far as such further information is necessary, having regard to the specific circumstances in which the data are collected, to guarantee fair processing in respect of the data subject*". Subsequent Member State laws varied considerably with regard to the kinds of information that must actually be provided in order to ensure fairness of processing. Sometimes the examples given in the Directive were repeated, other times somewhat different examples are included, and sometimes there are no examples at all. See Article 29 Data Protection Working Party, "Opinion on More Harmonised Information Provisions", WP100, 25 November 2004, p. 3. As far as the duty to inform under the GDPR is concerned, the Article 29 Working Party has taken the position that by default all of the information identified in Articles 13 and 14 (as set out in both their first and second paragraphs) should be provided to the data subject unless one or more categories of the information does not exist or is not applicable. Article 29 Data Protection Working Party, Guidelines on transparency under Regulation 2016/679, *l.c.*, p. 24. These Guidelines were subsequently endorsed by the EDPB.

100 See Article 12(1) GDPR, which sets out the general rules which apply to the provision of information to data subjects (under Articles 13–14); communications with data subjects concerning the exercise of their rights (under Articles 15–22); and communications in relation to data breaches (under Article 34). Article 29 Data Protection Working Party, Guidelines on transparency under Regulation 2016/679, *l.c.*, p. 6.

(g) where the personal data are not collected from the data subject, any available information as to their source;
(h) the existence of automated decision-making, including profiling, referred to in Article 22(1) and (4) and, at least in those cases, meaningful information about the logic involved, as well as the significance and the envisaged consequences of such processing for the data subject.[101]

The controller is obliged to provide a copy of the personal data undergoing processing, free of charge.[102] For any further copies requested by the data subject, the controller may charge a reasonable fee based on administrative costs. Where the data subject makes the request by electronic means, and unless otherwise requested by the data subject, the information shall be provided in a commonly used electronic form.[103]

57. Rectification, erasure and restriction – EU data protection law provides that the data subject shall have the right to obtain from the controller without undue delay the rectification of inaccurate personal data concerning him or her.[104] Data subjects also have the right to obtain the erasure of personal data in a number of circumstances, for example where it appears the data have been unlawfully processed or when the personal data are no longer necessary in relation to the purposes for which they were collected or otherwise processed.[105] The right to restriction of processing applies for example when the accuracy of the personal data is contested by the data subject (for the period enabling the controller to verify the accuracy of the personal data) or the controller no longer needs the personal data for the purposes of the processing, but they are required by the data subject for the establishment, exercise or defence of legal claims.[106] In instances where the data subject's request for rectification, erasure or restriction is granted, she may also request that controller provides notification thereof to any third parties to whom the data have been disclosed. The only grounds for the controller to refuse such a request would be to assert that such notification is impossible or involves a disproportionate effort.[107]

---

101 Where personal data are transferred to a third country or to an international organisation, the data subject shall additionally have the right to be informed of the appropriate safeguards pursuant to Article 46 relating to the transfer (Article 15(2) GDPR).

102 Articles 15(3) and 12(5) GDPR.

103 Article 15(3) GDPR.

104 Article 16 GDPR (previously: Article 12(b) Directive 95/46). Taking into account the purposes of the processing, the data subject shall have the right to have incomplete personal data completed, including by means of providing a supplementary statement (Article 16 GDPR, second sentence).

105 Article 17 GDPR (previously: Article 12(b) Directive 95/46). For a detailed analysis of all the circumstances in which the right to erasure can be invoked see J. Ausloos, *The Right to Erasure: Safeguard for informational self-determination in a digital society?*, *o.c.*, p. 161–195.

106 Article 18 GDPR (previously: Article 12(b) Directive 95/46).

107 Article 19 GDPR (previously: Article 12(c) Directive 95/46).

58. Data portability – For the most part, the GDPR has limited itself to further developing rights of data subjects which were already recognized under Directive 95/46. A notable exception to this statement is the so-called right to "data portability" enshrined in Article 20 of the GDPR. The right to data portability is closely related to the right of access, but also differs from it in many ways.[108] It allows for data subjects to receive, under certain conditions, the personal data that they have provided to a controller, in a structured, commonly used and machine-readable format, and to transmit those data to another data controller.[109]

3. CONFIDENTIALITY AND SECURITY

59. Basic principle – EU data protection law requires organisations that handle personal data to implement appropriate technical and organisational measures to ensure the confidentiality and security of processing.[110] In particular, appropriate measures must be implemented to protect personal data against accidental or unlawful destruction, loss, alteration, and unauthorised disclosure or access. The security obligation is defined as an obligation of means. There are various criteria for determining the extent of this obligation, namely state-of-the-art, the costs of implementation and the nature, scope, context and purposes of processing as well as the risk of varying likelihood and severity for the rights and freedoms of natural persons.[111] The general security obligation can be broken down into a number of components, each of which corresponds with one or more security objectives.[112]

60. Confidentiality – A first security objective is to maintain the confidentiality of information. Confidentiality as a security objective can be described as keeping the content of information secret from all parties except those that are authorized to access it.[113] There are numerous approaches to

108 Article 29 Data Protection Working Party, Guidelines on the right to data portability, WP 242 rev. 01, 5 April 2017, p. 3. These guidelines have in the meantime been endorsed by the European Data Protection Board (EDPB).

109 *Id.*

110 Article 5(1)f and 32 GDPR (previously: Articles 16 and 17 Directive 95/46).

111 Article 32(1) GDPR (previously: Article 17(1) Directive 95/46). B. Van Alsenoy, E. Kindt and J. Dumortier, "Privacy and data protection aspects of e-government identity management", in S. Van der Hof, M.M. Groothuis (eds.), *Innovating Government – Normative, Policy and Technological Dimensions of Modern Government*, Information Technology and Law Series (IT & Law), Vol. 20, T.M.C. Asser Press – Springer, 2011, p. 257. See also Article 29 Data Protection Working Party, "Guidelines on Personal data breach notification under Regulation 2016/679", WP250 rev.01, 6 February 2018, p. 6 et seq.

112 B. Van Alsenoy, N. Vandezande, K. Janssen, a.o., "Legal Provisions for Deploying INDI services", *l.c.*, p. 30.

113 X. Huysmans and B. Van Alsenoy (eds.), "Conceptual Framework – Annex I. Glossary of Terms", *IDEM*, Deliverable D1.3, v1.07, 2007, p. 12.

providing confidentiality, ranging from physical protection to the use of access control and cryptographic algorithms.[114] In addition to safeguarding the confidentiality of information, the processing capabilities (read, write, modify ...) of each party should be limited to that which is necessary to realize the goals of the processing. These requirements apply not only at the level of each organisation, but also at the level of each individual user.[115]

61. Integrity and authenticity – In addition to protecting the confidentiality of personal data, appropriate measures are also necessary to ensure the integrity and authenticity of the data. Integrity as a security objective is understood as ensuring data has not been altered by unauthorized or unknown means.[116] Authenticity as a security objective is generally understood as verifiable assurance that data has emanated from the appropriate entity and has not been altered by unauthorized or unknown means (and thus the "authenticity" of data also implies data integrity).[117]

62. Availability – Another component of the security obligation is to protect personal data against accidental destruction or loss. This requirement can be approximated to the security objective of availability, which can be described as the property of being accessible and useable upon demand by an authorized entity.[118]

63. Breach notification – The GDPR has introduced the requirement to notify personal data breaches[119] to supervisory authorities, unless the personal data breach is unlikely to result in a risk to the rights and freedoms of natural persons.[120] When the personal data breach is likely to result in a high risk to the rights and freedoms of natural persons, the personal data breach must also be communicated to the data subject without undue delay.[121]

---

114 J.C. Buitelaar, M. Meints and E. Kindt, "Towards requirements for privacy-friendly identity management in eGovernment", *FIDIS*, Deliverable D16.3, 2009, p. 19.

115 *Ibid*, p. 20. See also B. Van Alsenoy, E. Kindt and J. Dumortier, Privacy and data protection aspects of e-government identity management", *l.c.*, p. 258.

116 Menezes, A.J., Van Oorschot, P.C. and Vanstone, S.A., *Handbook of Applied Cryptography*, Boca Raton, CRC Press, 1997, p. 3.

117 *Ibid*, p. 25.

118 ITU-T SG 17, "Security Compendium. Part 2 – Approved ITU-T Security Definitions", 13 May 2005, available at http://www.itu.int/ITU-T/studygroups/com17/def005.doc (last accessed 20 January 2019).

119 Article 4(12) defines a "personal data breach" as "*a breach of security leading to the accidental or unlawful destruction, loss, alteration, unauthorised disclosure of, or access to, personal data transmitted, stored or otherwise processed*".

120 Article 33(1) GDPR.

121 For more information see Article 29 Data Protection Working Party, "Guidelines on Personal data breach notification under Regulation 2016/679", WP250 rev.01, 6 February 2018.

4. SUPERVISORY AUTHORITIES

64. Basic princple – EU data protection law requires Member States to have in place an independent supervisory authority which is dedicated to monitoring compliance.[122] Each supervisory authority must be endowed with a number of powers, including (a) investigative powers; (b) corrective powers[123]; and (c) the power to engage in legal proceedings and to bring infringements to the attention of the judicial authorities.[124] Every individual who feels his or her rights and freedoms are being harmed by the processing of personal data has the right to file a complaint with a supervisory authority.[125]

65. Article 29 Working Party – Article 29 of Directive 95/46 called for the creation of a "Working Party", composed of a representative of the supervisory authority or authorities designated by each Member State. The mission of the Working Party was to

(a) examine any question covering the application of the national measures adopted under Directive 95/46 in order to contribute to the uniform application of such measures;
(b) give the Commission an opinion on the level of protection in the Community and in third countries;
(c) advise the Commission on any proposed amendment of this Directive, on any additional or specific measures to safeguard the rights and freedoms of natural persons with regard to the processing of personal data and on any other proposed Community measures affecting such rights and freedoms;
(d) give an opinion on codes of conduct drawn up at Community level.[126]

66. European Data Protection Board – With the entry into application of the GDPR, the Article 29 Working Party has been replaced by the European Data Protection Board (EDPB). Like the Working Party before it, the EDPB is composed of a representative of the supervisory authority of each Member

122 Article 51 GDPR (previously: Article 28 Directive 95/46).

123 See Article 58(2) GDPR, which includes the power to issue warnings, the power to order that the processing be brought into compliance with the GDPR, in a specified manner and within a specified period, the power to impose a temporary or definitive limitation including a ban on processing, and the power to impose administrative fines. Under Directive 95/46, examples of "effective powers of intervention" included the delivering opinions before processing operations are carried out, ordering the blocking, erasure or destruction of data, of imposing a temporary or definitive ban on processing, warning or admonishing the controller, or that of referring the matter to national parliaments or other political institutions (Article 28(3) Directive 95/46).

124 Article 51(5) GDPR (previously: Article 28(3) Directive 95/46).

125 Article 77(1) GDPR (previously Article 28(4) Directive 95/46).

126 Article 30(1) of Directive 95/46.

State.[127] The EDPB, however, also has legal personality[128] and its own secretariat, which is provided by the European Data Protection Supervisor yet performs its tasks exclusively under the instructions of the Chair of the EDPB.[129] The mission of the EDBP is to ensure the consistent application of the GDPR, inter alia by

(a) examining, on its own initiative, on request of one of its members or on request of the Commission, any question covering the application of the GDPR and issue guidelines, recommendations and best practices in order to encourage consistent application of the GDPR;
(b) advising the Commission on any issue related to the protection of personal data in the Union, including on any proposed amendment of the GDPR;
(c) encouraging the drawing-up of codes of conduct and the establishment of data protection certification mechanisms and data protection seals and marks;
(d) issuing opinions on draft decisions of supervisory authorities pursuant to the consistency mechanism referred to in Article 64(1), on matters submitted pursuant to Article 64(2) and to issue binding decisions pursuant to Article 65 (dispute resolution), including in cases referred to in Article 66.[130]

5. ACCOUNTABILITY

67. Basic principle – Accountability is a concept with many dimensions.[131] It has been characterized by scholars as being an "elusive" and even "chameleon-like" concept, because it can mean very different things to different people.[132] In its core meaning, accountability refers to the existence of a relationship whereby one entity has the ability to call upon another entity and demand an explanation and/or justification for its conduct.[133] Over time, different data protection instruments have advanced different types of accountability mechanisms.[134]

[127] Article 68(3) GDPR (previously: Article 29(2) Directive 95/46).

[128] Article 68(1) GDPR.

[129] Article 75(1)-(2) GDPR.

[130] See Article 70 GDPR.

[131] See e.g. J. Koppell, "Pathologies of Accountability: ICANN and the Challenge of "Multiple accountabilities Disorder"", *Public Administration Review* 2005, vol. 65, p. 94–99 and R. Mulgan, ""Accountability": an ever-expanding concept?", *Public Administration* 2000, vol. 78, p. 555–556.

[132] A. Sinclair, "The Chameleon of Accountability: Forms and Discourses", *Accounting, Organisations and Society* 1995, Vol. 20, p. 219 and M. Bovens, "Analysing and Assessing Accountability: A conceptual Framework", *European Law Journal* 2007, vol. 13, p. 448.

[133] J. Alhadeff, B. Van Alsenoy and J. Dumortier, "The accountability principle in data protection regulation: origin, development and future directions", *l.c.*, p. 71.

[134] *Id.* The principle of accountability made its formal debut in the field of international data protection in the 1980 OECD Privacy Guidelines. For a discussion of the role of the accountability principle in different data protection instruments see J. Alhadeff, B. Van

In the GDPR, the principle of accountability is mainly used to signal that controllers are not only *responsible* for implementing appropriate measures to comply with the GDPR, but must also be able to *demonstrate* compliance at the request of supervisory authorities.[135]

68. Implementing accountability – Article 24(1) of the GDPR confirms that the controller is obliged to implement appropriate technical and organisational measures to ensure compliance. Generally speaking, this will require controllers to put in place internal policies and procedures dedicated to ensure organisational compliance (Article 24(2)). The actual measures adopted by controllers must be tailored to the nature, scope, context and purposes of the processing, as well as the risks presented by the processing.[136] Beyond these general statements of principle, the GDPR also specifies a number of specific obligations which aim to give further substance to the accountability principle, such as obligations concerning:

(a) data protection by design and by default (Article 25)[137]
(b) the legal binding of processors (Article 28(3))[138];

Alsenoy and J. Dumortier, "The accountability principle in data protection regulation: origin, development and future directions", *l.c.*, p. 52–64. When reviewing these instruments, it is apparent where these instruments purport to rely on the same principle of accountability, notable differences exist in terms of the definition of norms, the designation of accountors and accountees, oversight mechanisms and sanctions. (*Id.*).

135 Article 5(2) of the GDPR specifies that the controller shall be responsible for, and be able to demonstrate compliance with the principles relating to the processing of personal data. In the same vein Article 24(1) provides that the controller shall *implement* appropriate technical and organisational measures to ensure and to be able to *demonstrate* that processing is performed in accordance with this Regulation. See also Article 29 Data Protection Working Party, "Opinion 3/2010 on the principle of accountability", 13 July 2010, WP 173, paragraph 34. In the same vein, paragraph 15 of the Revised OECD Privacy Guidelines provides that a controller should put in place a privacy management programme which "gives effect" to the Guidelines for all personal data under its control, and should be prepared to demonstrate its privacy management programme as appropriate, in particular at the request of a competent privacy enforcement authority.

136 Article 24(1) GDPR; Recital (74) GDPR. See also Paragraph 15(a)ii of the Revised OECD Privacy Guidelines (which provides that every controller should have in place a privacy management programme that is tailored "to the structure, scale, volume and sensitivity of its operations" and "provides for appropriate safeguards based on privacy risk assessment".

137 See also recital (78) ("*In order to be able to demonstrate compliance with this Regulation, the controller should adopt internal policies and implement measures which meet in particular the principles of data protection by design and data protection by default*").

138 The legal binding of processors is related to the principle of accountability in the sense that it reinforces the notion of controller accountability for all personal data under its control, regardless of whether it is processed by the controller itself or by an agent on its behalf. See also OECD, *Supplementary explanatory memorandum to the revised recommendation of the council concerning guidelines governing the protection of privacy and transborder flows of personal data*, 2013, p. 23.

(c) the keeping of appropriate records of the processing (Article 30)[139];
(d) co-operation with supervisory authorities (Article 31);
(e) personal data breach notification (Article 33–34);
(f) data protection impact assessments and prior consultation (Article 35–36);
(g) designation of data protection officer (Article 37–39); and
(h) codes of conduct and certification (Article 40–43).

[139] See in particular also Article 30(4), which provides that the controller or the processor shall make the record available to the supervisory authority on request.

CHAPTER 4
ALLOCATION OF RESPONSIBILITY

69. Outline – EU data protection law assigns primary responsibility for compliance with its provisions to the controller(s) of the processing. It also assigns responsibility to the processor(s), as a means to address the situation where a controller enlists another actor to process personal data on its behalf. Given the central importance of these concepts to the research question of this book, it is necessary to analyse the meaning of these concepts in some detail. The following subsections will analyse

(1) the key elements of the controller and processor concepts;
(2) the legal relationship between controllers and processors; and
(3) the legal relationship between joint controllers.

1. KEY ELEMENTS OF THE "CONTROLLER" AND "PROCESSOR" CONCEPTS

70. Preliminary remarks – With the adoption of Directive 95/46, the key principles for allocating responsibility and liability among controllers and processors were established. How these principles were to be applied in practice would be determined by a steadily growing body of materials (opinions, recommendations, enforcement actions) developed by national data protection authorities. For quite some time, only limited EU-wide guidance existed on how to apply the concepts of "controller" and "processor" practice. While the Article 29 Working Party was called upon to interpret these concepts in relation to specific cases, the resulting guidance was generally closely tied to the specific issue at hand.[140]

140 See e.g. "Working Document on online authentication services", WP68, 29 January 2003; "Opinion 10/2006 on the processing of personal data by the Society for Worldwide Interbank Financial Telecommunication (SWIFT)", WP128, 22 November 2006; "Opinion 7/2007 on data protection issues related to the Internal Market Information System (IMI)", WP140, 20 September 2007; "Opinion 5/2009 on online social networking", WP163, 12 June 2009.

71. Opinion 1/2010 – In 2010, the Article 29 Working Party published an Opinion on the concepts of "controller" and "processor".[141] The main motivation for the Opinion was a desire to promote a consistent and harmonized approach in the interpretation of these concepts among the Member States.[142] Opinion 1/2010 of the Article 29 Working Party represents the most comprehensive attempt to clarify the meaning of the "controller" and "processor" concepts to date. Given the authority enjoyed by WP29 opinions, as well as their strategic importance, Opinion 1/2010 will serve as the main source of reference when analysing the key elements of the controller and processor concepts over the following sections.

72. CJEU case law – Since the adoption Opinion 1/2010, the CJEU has been called upon to clarify to interpret the concepts of controller, joint controller and processor in a number of cases. The most important of those cases are *Google Spain*[143], *Wirtschaftsakademie* (or "*Fan pages*")[144], *Jehovah's witnesses*[145] and *Fashion ID*.[146] Where relevant, reference shall also be made to those judgments of the CJEU and the accompanying AG Opinions.

73. GDPR changes – The GDPR, in turn, has also introduced a number of important clarifications. To be clear, the definitions of the concepts of controller and processor as such have essentially remained unchanged. As a result, most of the WP29 guidance and CJEU case law clarifying the interpretation of these concepts remains valid. Nevertheless, the GDPR also contains a number of new provisions, which further clarify the allocation of responsibility and liability among the actors involved in the processing of personal data. Where appropriate, the changes made by GDPR in comparison to Directive 95/46 will be highlighted.

1.1. CONTROLLER

74. Controller – A controller is defined by Article 4(7) GDPR as

> "the natural or legal person, public authority, agency or other body which, alone or jointly with others, determines the purposes and means of the processing of personal data; where the purposes and means of such processing are determined by Union or Member State law, the controller or the specific criteria for its nomination may be provided for by Union or Member State law".[147]

---

[141] Article 29 Data Protection Working Party, "Opinion 1/2010 on the concepts of "controller" and "processor"", WP 169, 16 February 2010, 31 p.

[142] *Ibid*, p. 3.

[143] Judgment in *Google Spain*, C-131/12, EU:C:2014:317.

[144] Judgment in *Wirtschaftsakademie*, C-210/16, ECLI:EU:C:2018:388.

[145] Judgment in *Jehovah's witnesses*, C-25/17, ECLI:EU:C:2018:551.

[146] Opinion of Advocate-General Bobek in *Fashion ID*, C-40/17, ECLI:EU:C:2018:1039.

[147] Previously: Article 2(d) of Directive 95/46.

75. "ANY BODY" – Under EU data protection law, a controller can be "a natural or legal person, public authority, agency or other body".[148] This means that there is in principle no limitation as to which type of actor might assume the role of a controller. It might be an organisation, but it might also be an individual or group of individuals.[149] For example, in *Jehovah's witnesses*, the CJEU considered that a religious community of Jehovah's witnesses acted as a controller, jointly with its members, of the processing of personal data carried out by the latter in the context of door-to-door preaching organised, coordinated and encouraged by that community.[150]

76. "DETERMINES" – A second key element of the controller concept refers to the controller's *factual influence* over the processing, by virtue of an *exercise of decision-making power*.[151] In order to assess which actor(s) wield(s) relevant influence over the processing, one should look at the entirety of factual elements surrounding the processing. Useful questions to ask at this stage include: "*Why is this processing taking place?*" and "*Who initiated it?*"[152] The exercise of factual influence or decision-making power can also take place by contributing to the processing of personal data in a certain way (e.g. through the setting of parameters).[153] It may therefore be sufficient that the entity in question somehow impacts the manner in which (or whether or not) personal data are being processed for a particular purpose.[154] What matters is whether

---

148 This portion of the controller definition is quasi identical to that the definition of a data controller in both the OECD Guidelines and Convention 108. Cf. *infra*, no. 433 and no. 462. See also Opinion 1/2010, *l.c.*, p. 15. According to the Working Party, this portion of the definition was simply assimilated from Article 2 of Convention 108 and was not the object of any specific discussion during the preparation of Directive 95/46/EC (*Id.*). In Article 4(7) GDPR, the word "any" has been removed just before the word "other" in comparison to Article 2(d) of Directive 95/46.

149 According to the Article 29 Working Party, it is generally better to consider a company or organisation as a controller rather than a specific person within a company or organisation. See Opinion 1/2010, *l.c.*, p. 15. The extent to which individuals within organisations might be considered as controllers will be discussed *infra*, nos. 217 et seq.

150 Judgment in *Jehovah's witnesses*, C-25/17, ECLI:EU:C:2018:551, paragraph 75. See also *infra*, no. 230.

151 Opinion 1/2010, *l.c.*, p. 8–9.

152 *Ibid*, p. 8.

153 Judgment in *Wirtschaftsakademie*, C-210/16, ECLI:EU:C:2018:388, at paragraphs 31, 36 and 39. See also the Opinion of Advocate-General Bobek in *Fashion ID*, C-40/17, ECLI:EU:C:2018:1039, paragraphs 63–64. In Wirtschaftsakademie, for example, the CJEU considered that the operator of a Facebook "Fan page", by its definition of parameters (depending in particular on its target audience and the objectives of managing and promoting its activities), takes part in the determination of the purposes and means of processing the personal data of the visitors to its fan page. Judgment in *Wirtschaftsakademie*, C-210/16, ECLI:EU:C:2018:388, at paragraph 39. For detailed discussion see *infra*, nos. 887.

154 It is therefore possible that the personal data at issue are already being processed for a certain purpose and that the entity in question only later joins in the determination of the purposes and means of the processing.

the entity has any influence, in law or in fact, over the purposes and means of the processing.[155]

77. "Purposes and means" – The third key element of the controller concept refers to the object of the controller's influence, namely the "purposes and means" of the processing. The Article 29 Working Party has paraphrased this portion of the definition by saying that the controller is the actor deciding about *the "why" and the "how"* of the processing[156]: given a particular processing operation, the controller is the actor who has determined *why* the processing is taking place (i.e. "to what end"; or "what for"[157]) and *how* this objective shall be reached (i.e. which means shall be employed to attain the objective[158]).[159] A natural or legal person who exerts influence over the processing of personal data for his own purposes, and who participates, as a result, in the determination of the purposes and means of that processing, may be regarded as a controller within the meaning of Article 4(7) GDPR.[160]

78. "Alone or jointly with others" – Article 4(7) recognizes that the "purposes and means" of the processing might be determined by more than one actor. It alludes to this possibility by stating that the controller is the actor who "alone or jointly with others" determines the purposes and means of the processing.[161] This implies that the controller concept does not necessarily refer to a single entity and may concern several actors taking part in that processing, with each of them then being subject to the applicable data protection provisions.[162] The extent to which two or more actors jointly exercise control may take on different forms, as will be clarified later on.[163]

---

155 Opinion of Advocate General Bot in *Wirtschaftsakademie*, C-210/16, ECLI:EU:C:2017:796, paragraph 54. According to the Advocate General, it is also this element of the definition ("determines") that indicates that the controller is not the person that carries out the personal data processing, but the person that determines the means and purposes of that data processing. (*Id.*).

156 Opinion 1/2010, *l.c.*, p. 13. See also the Opinion of Advocate General Bot in *Wirtschaftsakademie*, C-210/16, ECLI:EU:C:2017:796, paragraph 46.

157 See also Opinion 1/2010, *l.c.*, p. 13 (citing a dictionary definition of "purpose" as "*an expected result that is intended or guides planned actions*").

158 See also Opinion 1/2010, *l.c.*, p. 13 (citing a dictionary definition of "*how a result is obtained or an end is achieved*").

159 Of the two objects of the controller's influence, regulators appear to place greater weight on the controller's determination of finality ("purpose") than upon his determination of "means". This aspect will be discussed in greater detail *infra*, nos. 109et seq.

160 Judgment in *Jehovah's witnesses*, C-25/17, ECLI:EU:C:2018:551, paragraph 68.

161 See also T. Olsen and T. Mahler, "Identity management and data protection law: Risk, responsibility and compliance in 'Circles of Trust' – Part II", *l.c.*, p. 419.

162 Judgment in *Wirtschaftsakademie*, C-210/16, ECLI:EU:C:2018:388, paragraph 29.

163 Cf. *infra*, nos. 122 et seq.

79. "Of the processing of personal data" – The purposes and means determined by the controller must relate to the "processing of personal data". Article 4(2) GDPR defines the processing of personal data as "*any operation or set of operations which is performed on personal data or on sets of personal data*". As result, the concept of a controller can be linked either to a single processing operation or to a set of operations. According to the Article 29 Working Party, the question of which party is acting as a controller should be looked at "*both in detail and in its entirety*".[164] In practice, this may mean that the control exercised by a particular entity may extend to the entirety of processing at issue but may also be limited to particular stage in the processing.[165]

80. "Provided for by national or community law" – Finally, it is worth observing that Article 4(7) explicitly foresees that a "controller" might also be provided for by Union or Members law, particularly in situations "*where the purposes and means of processing are determined by Union or Member State law*".[166]

81. Effective & complete protection – The case law of the CJEU indicates that the concept of a controller has been defined broadly in order to ensure *effective and complete protection* of data subjects.[167] The CJEU has interpreted the concept of controller expansively, applying it to actors who do not necessarily have the ability to exercise full control over every aspect of the processing.[168] For example, the CJEU does not consider it necessary that every entity involved in the processing to have access the personal data concerned in order to be considered a (joint) controller.[169] The CJEU's approach to interpreting the controller concept is not purely mechanical but also teleological, based on the

164 Opinion 1/2010, *l.c.*, p. 3 and 20–21. See also *infra*, no. 116 and 530.

165 See also the Opinion of Advocate-General Bobek in *Fashion ID*, C-40/17, ECLI:EU:C:2018:1039, paragraph 99, who appears to favour an analysis at the level of discrete processing operations ("*Even if the notion of processing is, similar to the notion of controller, rather broad, it clearly underlines and aims at a stage in the processing: it refers to an operation or a set of operations, with an illustrative list of what such individual operations might be. But then logically, the issue of control should rather be assessed with regard to the discrete operation in question, not with regard to an undetermined bundle of everything and anything called processing.*") The definition of a controller itself appears to be flexible enough allow for both approaches. This is even more so now that the definition of "processing" in Article 4(2) GDPR additionally clarifies that it refers to "*any operation or set of operations which is performed on personal data or on sets of personal data*". See also *infra*, nos. 116–117.

166 See also *infra*, no. 235. Article 2(d) of Directive 95/46 previously referred to "national or Community laws or regulations".

167 Judgment in *Google Spain*, C-131/12, EU:C:2014:317, paragraph 34; Judgment in *Wirtschaftsakademie*, C-210/16, ECLI:EU:C:2018:388, paragraphs 27–28; Judgment in *Jehovah's witnesses*, C-25/17, ECLI:EU:C:2018:551, paragraph 66.

168 Judgment in *Google Spain*, C-131/12, EU:C:2014:317, paragraph 34; Opinion of Advocate General Bot in Wirtschaftsakademie, C-210/16, ECLI:EU:C:2017:796, paragraph 62.

169 Judgment in *Wirtschaftsakademie*, C-210/16, ECLI:EU:C:2018:388, paragraph 38; Judgment in *Jehovah's witnesses*, C-25/17, ECLI:EU:C:2018:551, paragraph 69.

assessment of whether or not the involvement of the actor concerned plays a decisive role in whether or how the processing interferes with an individual's right to data protection.[170] The broad interpretation of the controller concept is clearly motivated by a desire to ensure full effect of EU data protection law, to avoid lacunae and to and to prevent possible circumvention of the rules.[171]

1.2. PROCESSOR

82. Definition – A processor is defined by Article 4(8) GDPR as "a natural or legal person, public authority, agency or other body which processes personal data on behalf of the controller".[172]

83. "Any body"– Similar to the definition of a controller, the definition of a processor envisages a broad range of actors: any natural or legal person, public authority, agency "or other body" can assume the role processor.[173] The only requirement in this respect is that the actor in question is an entity separate from the controller.[174]

84. "On behalf of" – The main substantive component of the processor concept is that a processor acts "on behalf" of a controller. The Article 29 Working Party has approximated this wording with the legal concept of *delegation*, whereby one party requests another party to undertake certain actions on its behalf.[175] The term "delegation" is often used in reference to figures of legal representation.[176] The term can also be used, however, to refer to

170 Judgment in *Google Spain*, C-131/12, EU:C:2014:317, paragraph 36; Opinion of Advocate General Bot in *Wirtschaftsakademie*, C-210/16, ECLI:EU:C:2017:796, paragraphs 64–65.

171 *Id.* See also the Opinion of Advocate General Bot in *Wirtschaftsakademie*, C-210/16, ECLI:EU:C:2017:796, paragraph 65 and the Opinion of Advocate General Mengozzi, in *Jehovah's witnesses*, C-25/17, ECLI:EU:C:2018:57, paragraphs 63 and 68.

172 The definition of processor contained in Article 4(8) GDPR is unchanged in comparison to the definition of Article 2(e) Directive 95/46, with the exception of the removal of the word "any" just before the word "other".

173 See also Opinion 1/2010, *l.c.*, p. 24.

174 *Ibid*, p. 25.

175 *Id.*

176 In the case of legal representation, one party (the principal) bestows upon another party (the agent), the authority to undertake one or more legal actions on the principal's behalf. (See O. Lando and H. Beale (eds.), *Principles of European Contract Law – Parts I and II*, prepared by the Commission on European Contract Law, The Hague, Kluwer Law International, 2000, 197 et seq.) The legal effects of these actions shall, as a rule, be attributed directly to the principal (provided the agent acts with in the scope of his authority). Even where the agent exceeds his authority, his actions might still be attributed to the principal under the theory of apparent authority. For more information see also B. Van Alsenoy, D. De Cock, K. Simoens, J. Dumortier and B. Preneel, "Delegation and digital mandates: Legal requirements and security objectives", *Computer, Law and Security Review* 2009, Vol. 25, no 5, p. 415–420.

the process whereby one party requests another party to perform one or more actions of a non-legal nature. The Working Party appears to have used the term "delegation" in the latter sense, as the type of services typically associated with processors consist mainly in the performance of technical operations.[177]

85. In accordance with instructions – In order for an actor to be qualified as a "processor" rather than a "controller", it is required that the actor is processing personal data pursuant to someone else's instructions (i.e. the instructions issued by the controller).[178] Although this is not explicitly mentioned in the definition of a "processor", it follows from a combined reading of Article 4(8) and Articles 28–29 GDPR.[179] The latter set of provisions regulates the legal relationship between controller and processors, which shall be further elaborated in the course of the following subsection.

2. THE RELATIONSHIP BETWEEN CONTROLLERS AND PROCESSORS

86. Outline – Article 28 and 29 of the GDPR[180] set out the level of control that a controller must exercise over the processor which it appoints. These provisions also specify that a processor must act only on the controller's instructions and that a contract or other legal act binding the processor to the controller must be in place.[181] The objective of these provisions is to ensure that the externalisation of processing (from controller to processor) does not affect the level of protection of personal data enjoyed by data subjects.[182]

2.1. DUE DILIGENCE

87. Choice of processor – Article 28(1) GDPR stipulates that

> "Where processing is to be carried out on behalf of a controller, the controller shall use only processors providing sufficient guarantees to implement appropriate

177 Of course, a processor might also perform legal acts on behalf of a controller, e.g. in case of further subcontracting pursuant to the instructions of the controller; or where the processor also operates the front-office for consent registration and acceptance of the terms of use of a particular service.

178 Judgment in *Probst*, C-119/12, ECLI:EU:C:2012:748, paragraph 25.

179 Previously: Article 2(e) and Articles 16–17 of Directive 95/46/EC. In the same vein: Commissie voor de Persoonlijke Levenssfeer, Decision of 9 December 2008 regarding the Control and recommendation procedure initiated with respect to the company SWIFT, at paragraph 120.

180 Previously: Articles 16–17 Directive 95/46.

181 See also Judgment in *Probst*, C-119/12, ECLI:EU:C:2012:748, paragraph 25.

182 *Ibid*, paragraphs 26–27. See also *infra*, nos. 551.

technical and organisational measures in such a manner that processing will meet the requirements of this Regulation and ensure the protection of the rights of the data subject."

88. Vetting – Article 28(1) GDPR essentially requires controllers to exercise appropriate care when selecting a processor.[183] Specifically, it requires controllers to ascertain whether a processor provides *sufficient guarantees* in respect of the technical and organisational measures that will govern the processing to be carried out. Recital (81) clarifies that "sufficient guarantees" provided by the processor shall in particular concern guarantees in terms of expert knowledge, reliability and resources, to implement technical and organisational measures which will meet the requirements of this Regulation, including for the security of processing.[184]

89. Standards, codes or certificates – The selection of an appropriate processor shall generally be easier if the processor documents its practices with reference to one or more external standards.[185] Absent such an indication, the controller must himself assess whether the processor provides sufficient guarantees in respect of the processing to be carried out (although he may of course engage an external expert to make the assessment for him).[186] Article 28(5) GDPR explicitly confirms that adherence of a processor to an approved code of conduct[187] or an approved certification mechanism[188] may be used as an element by which to demonstrate the presence of sufficient guarantees.

90. Oversight – Previously, Article 17(2) Directive 95/46 provided that the controller must not only choose a processor providing sufficient guarantees in respect of technical and organisational measures, but it also that it "*must ensure compliance with those measures*". In other words, Directive 95/46 explicitly stipulated that controllers needed to ensure that processors in fact lived up to their commitments. For example, simply obtaining copies of the processor's

---

183 While the GDPR does not explicitly impose a similar obligation of "due dilligence" when a controller makes use of the services provided by another – separate or joint – controller, the argument can be made that every controller should also conduct reasonable due diligence in such circumstances. See M. Hintze, "Data Controllers, Data Processors, and the Growing Use of Connected Products in the Enterprise: Managing Risks, Understanding Benefits, and Complying with the GDPR", *Journal of Internet Law* August 2018, p. 6.

184 See also A. Delforge, "Les obligations générales du responsable du traitement et la place du sous-traitant", in C. De Terwangne and K. Rosier (eds.), *Le Règlement Général sur la Protection des Données (RGPD/GDPR) – Analyse approfondie*, CRIDS, Brussels, Larcier, 2018, p. 397.

185 U. Dammann and S. Simitis, *EG-Datenschutzrichtlinie*, *o.c.*, p. 230.

186 *Id.*

187 As referred to in Article 40 GDPR.

188 As referred to in Article 42 GDPR.

security policies was not considered sufficient.[189] The controller also had to verify that the relevant measures were in fact implemented in practice.[190] It was not considered necessary, however, that the controller conducted such a verification in person. The controller could also rely upon the assessment of an external expert or upon information provided by a supervisory authority.[191]

While Article 28(1) GDPR does not explicitly stipulate that the controller "must ensure compliance with those measures", the same principle still applies. Indeed, the obligation to use only processors "providing sufficient guarantees" should be seen as an ongoing obligation. The controller should therefore verify the presence of appropriate guarantees not only when it first enlists the processor, but throughout the entire duration of the processing.[192] As a result, the controller should ensure periodic validation in case of processing contracts which span a longer a period of time.[193] This explains why Article 28(3)h GDPR now provides that the contract or other legal act that governs the processing must also stipulate that the processor:

> "makes available to the controller all information necessary to demonstrate compliance with the obligations laid down in this Article and allow for and contribute to audits, including inspections, conducted by the controller or another auditor mandated by the controller."

2.2. BOUND BY INSTRUCTIONS

91. Basic principle – Article 29 GDPR provides that

> "The processor and any person acting under the authority of the controller or of the processor, [...] shall not process those data except on instructions from the controller, unless required to do so by Union or Member State law"[194]

Article 29 GDPR can be explained by the fact that the GDPR bestows upon the controller the primary duty to ensure compliance. Because the processor is seen as a mere "delegate" of the controller, it would arguably undermine the effectiveness of the regulatory framework if a processor were free to process data

---

189 U. Dammann and S. Simitis, *EG-Datenschutzrichtlinie*, *o.c.*, p. 230.

190 *Id.*

191 *Id.*

192 *Id.* If there is reason to suspect that the security measures are no longer adequate (e.g. in case of a security breach), the controller must undertake the necessary steps to ensure that an appropriate level of security is reinstated. If he is not able to remove all doubts, he must end his contract with the processor and demand that the data be provided back to him (*Id.*).

193 See also U. Dammann and S. Simitis, *EG-Datenschutzrichtlinie*, *o.c.*, p. 230.

194 Previously Article 16 Directive 95/46.

beyond the instructions received from the controller.[195] Indeed, within the logic of the GDPR, the legality of an entity's processing activities as "processor" is determined by the mandate given by a controller (who is considered ultimately responsible for ensuring the lawfulness of processing). If a processor goes beyond the scope of its instructions, it would lose its legal status of "processor" because it would then no longer be processing data "on behalf of" the controller. Its legal status would in principle then change from that of a "processor" to that of a controller.[196] This is further confirmed by Article 28(10) GDPR, which provides that:

> "Without prejudice to Articles 82, 83 and 84, if a processor infringes this Regulation by determining the purposes and means of processing, the processor shall be considered to be a controller in respect of that processing."

92. Not a "subordinate" of the controller – While the processor is legally prohibited from processing the data "except on the instructions of the controller", he is not necessarily a "subordinate" of the controller.[197] A processor is typically an independent contractor, who is not in a hierarchical relationship with the controller.[198]

93. Degree of autonomy – In practice, processors enjoy considerable discretion in deciding how to organize their services.[199] This gives rise to the following question: to what extent may an actor influence the processing before it can no longer be considered a mere "processor"? According to the Article 29 Working Party, processors can enjoy a certain degree of autonomy when processing personal data on behalf of others. Specifically, the Working Party accepts that a processor has a certain "margin of manoeuvre" in deciding *how* the processing shall be organized.[200]

---

195 See also U. Dammann and S. Simitis, *EG-Datenschutzrichtlinie*, *o.c.*, p. 224.

196 See also Opinion 1/2010, *l.c.*, p. 25. The reader should note, however, the distinction between the situation where a processor acting *beyond* the instructions of the controller and the situation where a processor merely fails to implement the controller's instructions. See also *infra*, nos. 165–167.

197 Tweede Kamer der Staten-Generaal, Regels inzake de bescherming van persoonsgegevens (Wet bescherming persoonsgegevens) – Memorie van Toelichting, Vergaderjaar 1997–1998, 25 892, no. 3, p. 61.

198 *Id.* The specific issue of the role of individuals within organisations as well as the possible impact of corporate structures shall be discussed *infra*, nos. 217–224 (individuals within organisations) and nos. 231–234 (corporate concerns).

199 One of the main reasons why organisations outsource certain processing activities is precisely because they do not have the requisite expertise in-house. By definition such outsourcing arrangements imply that the service provider will enjoy certain discretion in deciding how the processing will be organised.

200 Opinion 1/2010, *l.c.*, p. 13–14. See also *infra*, nos. 110 et seq.

94. SUB-PROCESSING – The degree of autonomy enjoyed by the processor is by no means unlimited. By way of example, Article 28(2) GDPR stipulates that the processor shall not engage another processor without prior specific or general written authorisation of the controller. In the case of general written authorisation, the processor must inform the controller of any intended changes concerning the addition or replacement of other processors, thereby giving the controller the opportunity to object to such changes.

95. DOCUMENTATION – The GDPR further envisages that the instructions issued by the controller shall be documented. Article 28(3)a provides that the contract or other legal act that governs the processing (see below) must also stipulate that the processor shall only process the personal data on *documented* instructions from the controller, including with regard to transfers of personal data to a third country or an international organisation. The processor may only process the personal data beyond the documented instructions of the controller if it is required to do so by Union or Member State law to which the processor is subject. In such a case, the processor must inform the controller of that legal requirement before processing, unless that law prohibits the processor from providing such information on important grounds of public interest.

2.3. LEGAL BINDING

96. "CONTRACT OR OTHER LEGAL ACT" – A controller that decides to enlist a processor must ensure that the processing shall be governed by a contract or other legal act under Union or Member State law, that is binding on the processor with regard to the controller.[201] The aim of the "contract or other legal act" is to bind the processor to the controller and to put in place legally enforceable rules that will help ensure that the level of protection for data subjects is not undermined. In practice, the legal act binding the processor to the controller shall most often take the form of a contract. The reference to "other" legal acts in Article 28(3) GDPR mainly concerns the public sector, where a processor might be appointed either directly by way of legislation or by way of a unilateral decision of a public body.[202]

97. IN WRITING – Article 28(9) GDPR specifies that

> "The contract or the other legal act referred to in paragraphs 3 and 4 shall be <u>in writing, including in electronic form</u>".[203]

---

201 Article 28(3) GDPR (previously: Article 17(3) Directive 95/46).

202 U. Dammann and S. Simitis, *EG-Datenschutzrichtlinie*, *o.c.*, p. 231.

203 Previously Article 17(4) Directive 95/46 ("*For the purposes of keeping proof, the parts of the contract or the legal act relating to data protection and the requirements relating to the [security measures] shall be in writing or in another equivalent form*").

The requirement that the contract or other legal act be laid down in writing makes it easier for parties to demonstrate that the necessary arrangement has been put in place.[204] The presence (or absence) of a written arrangement, however, is not decisive for the existence of a controller-processor relationship.[205] As Advocate General Bot observed:

> "Indeed, the division of tasks indicated in the contract can only suggest the actual roles of the parties to the contract in the processing of personal data. If it were otherwise, the parties would be able artificially to assign responsibility for the data processing to one or other of themselves. That is especially true when the general terms and conditions are drawn up in advance […] and are not negotiable."[206]

Where there is reason to believe that the contract does not correspond with reality in terms of actual control, the agreement may be set aside by the adjudicating body.[207] Conversely, a controller-processor relationship might still be held to exist in absence of a written processing agreement.[208] This absence would, however, imply a violation of Article 28(3) GDPR and provide a first indication that the relationship between the parties is not a controller-processor relationship.

98. Minimum content under Directive 95/46 – Directive 95/46 provided very few details regarding content of the arrangement that was to be concluded between controllers and processors. Specifically, Article 17(3) of Directive 95/46 provided that

> "The carrying out of processing by way of a processor must be governed by a contract or legal act binding the processor to the controller and stipulating in particular that:
>
> - the processor shall act only on instructions from the controller,
> - the obligations set out in paragraph 1, as defined by the law of the Member State in which the processor is established, shall also be incumbent on the processor."

---

204 *Ibid.* p. 232. Indeed, Article 17(4) of Directive 95/46 explicitly stated that the obligation to lay down the contract or legal act in writing or equivalent from is imposed "for the purposes of keeping proof". Putting down the arrangement in writing also has the benefit of formalising parties' mutual understanding as to what they may expect from one and other when it comes to the fulfillment of the obligations imposed by the GDPR.

205 Opinion 1/2010, *l.c.*, p. 26–27.

206 Opinion of Advocate General Bot in *Wirtschaftsakademie*, C-210/16, ECLI:EU:C:2017:796, paragraph 60.

207 Opinion 1/2010, *l.c.*, p. 27.

208 See also the Opinion of Advocate General Mengozzi, in *Jehovah's witnesses*, C-25/17, ECLI:EU:C:2018:57, paragraph 68 ("*For the purposes of determining the 'controller' within the meaning of Directive 95/46, I am inclined to consider […] that excessive formalism would make it easy to circumvent the provisions of Directive 95/46 and that, consequently, it is necessary to rely upon a more factual than formal analysis […].*")

In other words, only two elements were explicitly identified as being mandatory, namely (1) the stipulation that the processor is obliged to follow the controller's instructions at all times and (2) the stipulation that the processor is obliged to implement appropriate technical and organisational measures to ensure the security of processing.[209] The Article 29 Working Party emphasized, however, that Article 17(3) only mentioned the *minimum* content that should be included in an arrangement between controllers and processors. According to the Working Party, the contract or other legal act should additionally include "*a detailed enough description of the mandate of the processor*".[210]

99. Minimum content under GPDR – The GDPR has increased considerably the number of elements to be included in the arrangement between controllers and processors. Under Article 28(3), the arrangement must at a minimum stipulate that the processor:

(a) only processes the personal data only on *documented instructions* from the controller[211];
(b) ensures that persons authorised to process the personal data are bound to *confidentiality*[212];
(c) takes all appropriate measures to ensure *security of processing*[213];
(d) respects the *conditions for engaging another processor* ("sub-processing");
(e) assists the controller, insofar as this is possible and taking into account the nature of the processing, for the fulfilment of the controller's obligation to accommodate *data subject rights*;
(f) assists the controller in ensuring compliance with the obligations regarding *security* of processing (Article 32), *data breach* notification and communication (Articles 33–34) and *data protection impact assessment* and prior consultation (Articles 35–36), taking into account the nature of processing and the information available to the processor;
(g) at the choice of the controller, *deletes or returns* all the personal data to the controller after the end of the provision of services relating to processing, and deletes existing copies unless Union or Member State law requires storage of the personal data;

---

209 Opinion 1/2010, *l.c.*, p. 26.

210 *Id.* See also U. Dammann and S. Simitis, *EG-Datenschutzrichtlinie*, *o.c.*, p. 232 (noting that the contract or legal act should generally address all data protection issues including, for example, how to deal with access requests by governments or other interested third parties).

211 Cf. *supra*, no. 95.

212 The duty of confidentiality may result either from the fact the persons in question have committed themselves to confidentiality or are under an appropriate statutory obligation of confidentiality (Article 28(3)b GDPR).

213 In contrast to Directive 95/46, the GDPR also imposes the security obligation directly upon processors (Article 32). For comparison between the obligations directly incumbent upon processors under Directive 95/46 and the GDPR respectively, see *infra*, no. 671.

(h) makes available to the controller all information necessary to *demonstrate compliance* with the obligations laid down in Article 28 GDPR and allow for and *contribute to audits, including inspections*, conducted by the controller or another auditor mandated by the controller.[214]

Article 28(3) GDPR confirms the minimum elements already required by Directive 95/46, but foresees a considerable number of additional elements. The additional elements in first instance appear to be motivated by the aim of ensuring that the controller in fact *remains in control* over the processing. In addition, the GDPR foresees that the processor shall be bound by a *duty to assist* the controller with respect to certain obligations. Finally, Article 28(3) also contains provisions designed to promote the *accountability* of both controllers and processors.

100. Staying in control – Article 28(3) GDPR seeks to ensure that the controller remains capable of exercising "control" over the processing notwithstanding the fact that it has decided to outsource the processing. By providing that the processor may only process the personal data on *documented* instructions of the controller, the processor to will effectively share in the burden of proof of demonstrating that the processing is in fact being undertaken with the knowledge, awareness and approval of the controller.[215] Article 28(3) also reinforces the conditions for sub-processing, as set forth by Article 28(2) and 28(4) GDPR. Article 28(2) GDPR provides that a processor may not engage another processor without prior specific or general written authorisation of the

---

214 Article 28(3) GDPR in fine adds that with regard to point (h) of the first subparagraph, the processor shall immediately inform the controller if, in its opinion, an instruction infringes this Regulation or other Union or Member State data protection provisions. For a more detailed discussion see A. Delforge, "Les obligations générales du responsable du traitement et la place du sous-traitant", *l.c.*, p. 403 and A. Cruquenaire and J.F. Henrotte, "Le devoir de Conseil dans le Règlement géneral sur la protection des données: bis repetita placent?", in C. De Terwangne a.o. (eds.), *Law, Norms and Freedoms in cyberworld / Droit, Normes et Libertés dans le cybermonde – Liber amicorum Yves Poullet*, p. 612–613.

215 To be clear, the existence of '"documented instructions" is not a prerequisite for an entity to be considered as a controller. See also Judgment in *Jehovah's witnesses*, C-25/17, ECLI:EU:C:2018:551, at paragraph 75 ("*Having regard to the foregoing considerations, the answer to Questions 3 and 4 is that Article 2(d) of Directive 95/46, read in the light of Article 10(1) of the Charter, must be interpreted as meaning that it supports the finding that a religious community is a controller, jointly with its members who engage in preaching, of the processing of personal data carried out by the latter in the context of door-to-door preaching organised, coordinated and encouraged by that community, without it being necessary that the community has access to those data, or to establish that that community has given its members written guidelines or instructions in relation to the data processing.*"). As a result, a controller-processor relationship might still be held to exist in absence of documented instructions. This would, however, imply a violation of Article 28(3)a GDPR and provide a first indication that the relationship between the parties is not a controller-processor relationship. See also A. Delforge, "Les obligations générales du responsable du traitement et la place du sous-traitant", *l.c.*, p. 401. Compare also *supra*, no. 97.

controller.[216] Article 28(4) adds that in case of sub-processing, the same data protection obligations as set out in the contract or other legal act between the controller and the processor must be imposed on that other (sub-)processor, in particular providing sufficient guarantees to implement appropriate technical and organisational measures in such a manner that the processing will meet the requirements of the GDPR. Finally, the obligation for the processor to delete or return all the personal data to the controller after the end of the provision of its services, is also a clear of example of an obligation which seeks to ensure that the controller remains "in control" over the processing.

101. Duty to assist – Article 28(3) GDPR foresees that the processor shall be bound by a duty to assist the controller in ensuring compliance with several of its obligations under the GDPR. The (contractual) duty to assist the controller in ensuring compliance goes beyond the security of processing, extending to the controller's obligations regarding data breach notifications, data protection impact assessments and data subject rights. As regards data subject rights, it is worth noting that Article 28(1) GDPR also explicitly calls out the need for appropriate measures to ensure the protection of data subject rights when assessing whether or not a processor provides sufficient guarantees.[217] These provisions clearly indicate that the EU legislature envisages a particular role for processors in relation to the accommodation of data subject rights.[218] The various duties to assist can be explained by the fact that the controller shall de facto be dependent on the assistance of the processor, either by lending material support and/or by providing information, to be able to comply with its own obligations under the GDPR.[219]

102. Accountability – Article 28 GDPR also contains a number of provisions seeking to promote the accountability of both controllers and processors. In addition to the obligation for processors to process data only on *documented*

216 In the case of general written authorisation, the processor shall inform the controller of any intended changes concerning the addition or replacement of other processors, thereby giving the controller the opportunity to object to such changes.

217 Cf. *supra*, no. 88–90.

218 In contrast, Article 17(2) of Directive 95/46 referred only to "technical security measures and organizational measures governing the processing to be carried out".

219 The obligations to assist the controller are not expressed in absolute terms. Indeed, the extent of the processors' (contractual) obligations shall be determined by reference to "the nature of the processing", "what is possible" (Article 28(3)e) and/or "the information available to the processor (Article 28(3)f). This makes it all the more important for controllers to only use processors offering sufficient guarantees, and to establish *ex ante* how compliance the obligations concerning security, data breach, DPIA and data subject rights shall be ensured prior to proceeding with the choice to outsource the processing to a particular processor. For a detailed discussion of the processor's "duty to assist" the controller see A. Cruquenaire and J.F. Henrotte, "Le devoir de Conseil dans le Règlement géneral sur la protection des données: bis repetita placent?", *l.c.*, p. 599–617.

instructions from the controller[220], Article 28(3)h envisages an obligation for processors to make available to the controller

> "all information necessary to demonstrate compliance with the obligations laid down in this Article and allow for and contribute to audits, including inspections, conducted by the controller or another auditor mandated by the controller."

In the same vein, Article 28(4) *in fine* provides that in case a sub-processor fails to fulfil its data protection obligations as set out in the contract or other legal act between the controller and the processor, the initial processor shall remain fully liable to the controller for the performance of that other processor's obligations.

103. Standard clauses – Finally, it is worth noting that Article 28 contemplates the possibility to use standard contractual clauses as a means of binding the processor to the controller (or the sub-processor to the processor).[221] Such contractual clause can be established either the by the European Commission[222] or by a supervisory authority in accordance with the consistency mechanism (i.e. after submitting its draft decision to an opinion of the European Data Protection Board).[223]

2.4. DISTINGUISHING BETWEEN CONTROLLERS AND PROCESSORS

104. Outline – In Opinion 1/2010, the Article 29 Working Party recognized that it may be difficult to distinguish between controllers and processors in practice.[224] To help guide the application of these concepts, the Working Party developed additional criteria to make it easier for practitioners to determine whether someone is acting as "controller" or "processor". The following paragraphs summarize the main points of guidance provided by the Working Party.

---

220 Cf. *supra*, no. 95.

221 Article 28(6) GDPR provides that "*[w]ithout prejudice to an individual contract between the controller and the processor, the contract or the other legal act referred to in paragraphs 3 and 4 of this Article may be based, in whole or in part, on standard contractual clauses referred to in paragraphs 7 and 8 of this Article, including when they are part of a certification granted to the controller or processor pursuant to Articles 42 and 43.*"

222 Article 28(7) provides that the Commission "*may lay down standard contractual clauses for the matters referred to in paragraph 3 and 4 of this Article and in accordance with the examination procedure referred to in Article 93(2)*".

223 Article 28(8) provides that a supervisory authority "*may adopt standard contractual clauses for the matters referred to in paragraph 3 and 4 of this Article and in accordance with the consistency mechanism referred to in Article 63.*"

224 Opinion 1/2010, *l.c.*, p. 6.

A. *Circumstances giving rise to "control"*

105. Functional concept – The concept of a controller is a functional concept: rather than allocating responsibility on the basis of formal criteria, it aims to allocate responsibilities where the factual influence is.[225] This implies that the legal status of an actor as either a "controller" or a "processor" must in principle be determined by its actual activities (influence) in a specific context, rather than upon the formal designation of an actor as being either a "controller" or "processor" (e.g. in a contract or in a notification to a supervisory authority).[226]

106. Need for predictability – Because the question of "who controls the processing?" is a question of fact, determining who actually controls a particular processing activity may sometimes require an in-depth and lengthy analysis.[227] According to the Article 29 Working Party, however, regulatory effectiveness also requires predictability.[228] Specifically,

> "[...] the need to ensure effectiveness requires that a pragmatic approach is taken with a view to ensure predictability with regard to control. In this perspective, rules of thumb and practical presumptions are needed to guide and simplify the application of data protection law. This calls for an interpretation of the Directive ensuring that the "determining body" can be easily and clearly identified in most situations, by reference to those – legal and/or factual – circumstances from which factual influence normally can be inferred, unless other elements indicate the contrary."[229]

107. Categories of circumstances – According to the Article 29 Working Party, the circumstances which typically give rise to "control" can be classified into three main categories, namely[230]:

---

225 *Ibid*, p. 9.

226 *Ibid*, p. 25–27. See also the Opinion of Advocate General Mengozzi, in *Jehovah's witnesses*, C-25/17, ECLI:EU:C:2018:57, paragraph 68 ("*For the purposes of determining the 'controller' within the meaning of Directive 95/46, I am inclined to consider [...] that excessive formalism would make it easy to circumvent the provisions of Directive 95/46 and that, consequently, it is necessary to rely upon a more factual than formal analysis [...].*") See also Opinion 1/2010, *l.c.*, p. 12: "*the definition of data controller should be considered as a mandatory legal provision, from which parties cannot simply derogate or deviate*". Of course, a formal designation or declaration remains an important factual element which can be taken into account when assessing the legal status of a particular entity, but it is not decisive. (*Id.*) See also *infra*, no. 231 et seq.

227 Opinion 1/2010, *l.c.*, p. 9.

228 *Id.*

229 *Id.*

230 Opinion 1/2010, *l.c.*, p. 10–12.

a) Control stemming from *explicit legal competence* (e.g. when the controller or the specific criteria for its nomination are designated by national or Community law);
b) Control stemming from *implicit competence*, whereby an analysis of the traditional roles associated with a certain actor will assist in identifying the controller (e.g. an employer in relation to data on his employees, the publisher in relation to data on subscribers); or
c) Control stemming from *factual influence*, whereby the qualification of controller is attributed on the basis of an assessment of factual circumstances which warrant the conclusion that this party exercises a "dominant role" with respect to the processing.

108. Assessment – The need to ensure predictability of "control" was discussed at length in the context of the preparation of the revisions to the Dutch Data Protection Act of 1989.[231] The Dutch government argued that "control" should in principle be linked to formal competences and criteria (e.g. formal designation, legal authority) as much as possible.[232] Only in cases where multiple actors influence the processing without a clear indication of who the controller is, should the determination of "control" be based on a functional approach. In such instances, responsibility for the processing should above all be determined "*on the basis of generally accepted standards of societal interaction*" (in Dutch: "*algemeen in het maatschappelijk verkeer geldende maatstaven*").[233] The Working Party's guidance bears some resemblance to this approach: while recognizing

---

231 See Tweede Kamer der Staten-Generaal, Regels inzake de bescherming van persoonsgegevens (Wet bescherming persoonsgegevens) – Memorie van Toelichting, *l.c.*, in particular p. 55–57.

232 The main argument in favour of this approach is that the relationships and power structures between different organisations involved in the processing will generally be opaque towards the data subject. (*Ibid*, p. 15) ("*De formele bevoegdheden zijn duidelijker en dienen daarom het aanknopingspunt te zijn in plaats van de feitelijke machtsverhoudingen met betrekking tot de te verwerken persoonsgegevens. Deze laatste zijn voor de betrokkene minder transparant.*") In response, the Dutch Raad van State pointed out that if the intention of the legislature was to link control to formal competences as much as possible, the definition should also refer to the term "competence" ("*De Raad stelt in de eerste plaats vast dat in dit artikelonderdeel, anders dan de toelichting doet voorkomen, het element bevoegdheid ontbreekt*") (Tweede Kamer der Staten-Generaal, Regels inzake de bescherming van persoonsgegevens (Wet bescherming persoonsgegevens) – Advies Raad van State en Nader rapport", Vergaderjaar 1997–1998, no. 25 892, p. 4). The Dutch government dismissed the suggestion, however, both to stick as closely as possible to the wording of Directive 95/46 (*ibid*, p. 5) and in order to ensure that entities who undertake to process personal without proper legal authority were brought within the scope of the act (Tweede Kamer der Staten-Generaal, Regels inzake de bescherming van persoonsgegevens (Wet bescherming persoonsgegevens) – Memorie van Toelichting, *l.c.*, p. 55) ("*Overeenkomstig artikel 2, onderdeel d, van de richtlijn wordt in de begripsomschrijving niet meer gesproken van de natuurlijke persoon enz. die bevoegd is doel van en middelen voor de verwerking vast te stellen. Indien onbevoegd gegevens worden verwerkt dient immers eveneens een verantwoordelijke te kunnen worden aangewezen en op zijn handelen te kunnen worden aangesproken.*").

233 *Ibid*, p. 55.

the functional nature of the controller concept, it also tries to link the question of "control" to both formal criteria (e.g. explicit competences) and traditional roles (implicit competences) as much as possible.[234]

B. "Purpose" over "means"

109. The primacy of purpose – Article 4(7) GDPR defines the controller as the entity which determines both "purposes" and "means" of the processing. Of the two objects of the controller's influence, it would appear that greater weight is placed on the controller's determination of finality ("purpose") than upon his determination of "means".[235] For example, the Article 29 Working Party considered that the determination of purpose(s) is something that is reserved to the controller: whoever decides the purpose acts as a controller.[236] The determination of the "means" of the processing, however, might be (partially) delegated to the processor.[237]

110. Subordination of the "means" criterion – As far as the determination of the "means" of the processing is concerned, the Working Party felt that Directive 95/46 supports a certain degree of flexibility. Specifically, it accepted that when a controller relies upon a processor to realize the purpose(s) of the processing, it may leave its processor(s) a certain "margin of manoeuvre" in specifying how the processing shall be organised.[238] In other words, while the determination of purpose "automatically" triggers the qualification of controller, this would not necessarily be the case where an entity only influences the means of the processing.[239]

111. "Essential" vs. "non-essential" means – The margin for manoeuvre accorded to processors is not unlimited. According to the Article 29 Working Party, the influence of the processor may not extend to either the "purpose" or the "essential" means of the processing:

---

[234] See also M. Overkleeft-Verburg, *De Wet persoonsregistraties – norm, toepassing en evaluatie*, Proefschrift ter verkrijging van de graad van doctor aan de Katholieke Universiteit Brabant, Hilvarenbeek, 1995, p. 400 et seq. (noting that Dutch scholars generally advocate linking control to prevailing norms of social interaction). Interestingly, the cited scholars also conceive of this approach as being a "functional" approach, as it links responsibility for data processing to the function fulfilled by the processing in the relationships between the controller and the data subject (*Ibid*, footnote 1416: "*Het begrip "functioneel" ziet derhalve primair op de functionaliteit van de gegevensverwerking in samenhang met de op overeenkomst en/of de WPR gebaseerde rechts-/informatiebetrekkingen tussen de registratiehouder en de geregistreerde*").

[235] See also P. Van Eecke and M. Truyens, "Privacy and social networks", *l.c.*, p. 539.

[236] Opinion 1/2010, *l.c.*, p. 15.

[237] *Id.*

[238] *Ibid*, p. 13–14.

[239] *Ibid*, p. 14.

> "while determining the purpose of the processing would in any case trigger the qualification as controller, determining the means would imply control only when the determination concerns the essential elements of the means."[240]

"Essential means", according to the Working Party, are those elements which are traditionally and inherently reserved to the determination of the controller, such as "*which data shall be processed?*", "*for how long shall they be processed?*", and "*who shall have access to them?*".[241] "Non-essential means" concern more practical aspects of implementation, such as the choice for a particular type of hard- or software.[242] Under this approach, the Working Party considers it possible that the technical and organisational means of the processing are determined exclusively by the data processor.[243] A provider of processing services shall only be considered a joint controller if it determines either the purpose or the "essential elements" of the means which characterize a controller.[244]

112. Assessment – The tendency to emphasize the purpose over the means of the processing as being determinative for control can also be found in earlier

---

240 *Id.*

241 The Article 29 Working Party derived these criteria from the legislative development of the controller and processor concepts. Previous iterations of the controller concept referred to four elements ("*purpose and objective*", "*which personal data are to be processed*", "*which operations are to be performed upon them*" and "*which third parties are to have access to them*"). Cf. *infra*, no. 548. According to the Working Party, the word "means" should be understood as comprising these elements. ("*[T]he final definition must rather be understood as being only a shortened version comprising nevertheless the sense of the older version.*") (*Ibid*, p. 14). See also Tweede Kamer der Staten-Generaal, Regels inzake de bescherming van persoonsgegevens (Wet bescherming persoonsgegevens) – Memorie van Toelichting, *l.c.*, p. 57 ("*Iemand die voor zichzelf verwerkt of doet verwerken, is verantwoordelijke. Hieraan doet niet af dat hij daarmee derden van dienst wil zijn. Van belang is dat hij zelf bepaalt welke soort gegevens hij verwerkt, hoe lang en met welke middelen. Degene daarentegen die krachtens een contract dat blijkens zijn aard betrekking heeft op de gegevensverwerking ten behoeve van een derde, waarbij de wederpartij bepaalt welke gegevens, waartoe, hoelang enz. worden verwerkt, moet worden aangemerkt als bewerker.*").

242 Opinion 1/2010, *l.c.*, p. 14. The Article 29 Working Party draws a parallel to the figure of delegation, which allows imply a certain degree of discretion about how to best serve the controller's interests, allowing the processor to choose the most suitable technical and organisational means. (*Ibid*, p. 25).

243 *Id.* See also Tweede Kamer der Staten-Generaal, Regels inzake de bescherming van persoonsgegevens (Wet bescherming persoonsgegevens) – Memorie van Toelichting, *l.c.*, p. 61–62.

244 *Ibid*, p. 19. Van Eecke and Truyens point out that the Working Party's distinction between "essential" and "non-essential" means is at odds with the literal wording of Article 2(d). (P. Van Eecke and M. Truyens, "Privacy and social networks", *l.c.*, p. 539). Specifically, they argue that it reduces a dual legal requirement ("and") to a single requirement ("or"), by stating that it is sufficient for a party to determine either the purpose or the essential aspects of the means in order to qualify as a data controller (*Id.*). This criticism is further analysed *infra*, no. 1190.

doctrine[245] and regulatory guidance.[246] The weight given to the "purpose" element undoubtedly stems from the fact that "purpose" also fulfils such a central role in determining the scope of a controller's obligations (see in particular Article 5(1)b-e; Article 6(1)b-f; Articles 13–14; Articles 24–25; Article 32, Article 35, Article 37 and Article 39).[247]

C. *Additional criteria*

113. Stronger "bargaining position"? – Article 28(3) GDPR obliges the controller to ensure that processing by a processor is governed by a contract or other legal act, which must stipulate that the processor is to follow the controller's instructions at all times. The phrasing of this provision might suggest that the controller should enjoy a stronger "bargaining position" than its processor. The Working Party has, however, clearly stated that this is not a prerequisite. According to the Working Party, service providers specialized in certain processing of data

> "will set up standard services and contracts to be signed by data controllers, de facto setting a certain standard manner of processing personal data".[248]

The mere fact that an entity does not have any other choice than to simply "take it or leave it" does not prevent its qualification as a controller.[249] Along the same line, the Article 29 Working Party has emphasized that the fact that there exists an imbalance in the contractual power of a "small" data controller with respect to "big" service providers does not excuse these "smaller" entities from compliance with data protection law.[250] Advocate General Bot defended the same position as follows:

> "The view cannot, therefore, be taken that a person who may do no more than accept or refuse the contract cannot be a controller. Once such a party has concluded the contract of his own volition he may always be regarded as a controller, given his actual influence over the means and purposes of the data processing."[251]

114. Additional criteria – When it comes to distinguishing between controllers and processors, the Working Party considered that the following

---

245 See e.g. D. De Bot, *Verwerking van persoonsgegevens*, *o.c.*, p. 46.
246 See e.g. Office of the Information Commissioner, "Data Protection Act, 1998 – Legal Guidance", Version 1, not dated, p. 16.
247 See also S. Gutwirth, *Privacy and the information age*, *o.c.*, p. 97. See also *infra*, no. 117.
248 Opinion 1/2010, *l.c*, p. 26.
249 *Id.*
250 *Id.*
251 Opinion of Advocate General Bot in *Wirtschaftsakademie*, C-210/16, ECLI:EU:C:2017:796, paragraph 61.

criteria may be helpful in determining the qualification of the various subjects involved[252]:

(1) *Level of prior instructions given* (the greater the level of instruction, the more limited the margin of manoeuvre of the processor);
(2) *Monitoring of the execution of the service* (a constant and careful supervision of compliance provides an indication of being in control of the processing operations);
(3) *Image given to the data subject*[253]; and
(4) *Expertise of the parties* (if the expertise of the service provider plays a predominant role in the processing, it may entail its qualification as data controller).[254]

D. Dynamic perspective

115. Variability of control – The functional nature of the controller concept implies that the legal status of an actor may vary (1) over time and (2) across activities. The same actor may act as a "controller" for certain activities and as a "processor" for others. Likewise, the legal status of an actor might change from that of a "processor" to that of a "controller" (et vice versa) if there is a substantial change in its influence over the processing.[255] In each case, the qualification of an actor as either controller or processor has to be assessed with regard to specific sets of data or operations.[256]

116. Operation or set of operations – According to Article 4(7) GDPR, the influence of a controller extends to the "processing of personal data". Article 4(2) GDPR defines the processing of personal data as "*any operation or set of operations which is performed on personal data or on sets of personal data*". As result, the concept of a controller can be linked either to a single processing operation or to a set of operations. According to Advocate General

252 Opinion 1/2010, *l.c.*, p. 28.

253 See Opinion 1/2010, *l.c.*, p. 28 (example of a call centre using the identity of the controller when communicating with data subjects).

254 According to the Working Party, the traditional role and professional expertise of the service provider play a predominant role and may entail its qualification as data controller. See Opinion 1/2010, *l.c.*, p. 28–29 (describing the situation of barristers and accountants). See also Tweede Kamer der Staten-Generaal, Regels inzake de bescherming van persoonsgegevens (Wet bescherming persoonsgegevens) – Memorie van Toelichting, *l.c.*, p. 62 (noting that if the processing of personal data is a correlary of another service being provided, than the service provider is a controller rather than a processor).

255 For example, if a processor suggests to the controller to use personal data for a new purpose and both parties determine how this processing shall be organized, the processor will likely be considered a (joint) controller with respect to these further processing activities.

256 Opinion 1/2010, *l.c.*, p. 25.

Bobek, one should analyse the issue of control at the level of discrete processing operations:

> "Even if the notion of processing is, similar to the notion of controller, rather broad, it clearly underlines and aims at a stage in the processing: it refers to an operation or a set of operations, with an illustrative list of what such individual operations might be. But then logically, the issue of control should rather be assessed with regard to the discrete operation in question, not with regard to an undetermined bundle of everything and anything called processing."[257]

According to the Article 29 Working Party, the question of which entity is acting as a controller should be looked at "*both in detail and in its entirety*".[258] Specifically:

> "In some cases, various actors process the same personal data in a sequence. In these cases, it is likely that at micro-level the different processing operations of the chain appear as disconnected, as each of them may have a different purpose. However, it is necessary to double check whether at macro-level these processing operations should not be considered as a "set of operations" pursuing a joint purpose or using jointly defined means."[259]

117. Assessment – The definition of a controller itself appears to be flexible enough allow for an approach at both micro- and macro-level. This is even more so now that the definition of "processing" in Article 4(2) GDPR additionally clarifies that it refers operations or sets of operations performed on *sets of* personal data. The Working Party did not explicitly state when control should be assessed either at the level of a specific operation or set of operations. The examples provided suggest that the pursuit of a jointly defined purpose should be determinative.[260] An alternative approach, advanced by the Dutch legislature, would be to again simply look at general perception. If the "prevailing norms of societal interaction" treat a series of processing operations as a "cohesive whole", control should be assessed in relation to the set of operations rather than at the level of each individual operation.[261] Given the central importance of the purpose specification principle to the regulatory scheme of EU data protection law, however, the delineation of "the processing" should be made in light of the purposes pursued.[262] As Gutwirth argues:

---

257 Opinion of Advocate-General Bobek in *Fashion ID*, C-40/17, ECLI:EU:C:2018:1039, paragraph 99.

258 Opinion 1/2010, *l.c.*, p. 3 and 20–21.

259 *Ibid*, p. 20.

260 See also *infra*, no. 530.

261 See also Tweede Kamer der Staten-Generaal, Regels inzake de bescherming van persoonsgegevens (Wet bescherming persoonsgegevens) – Memorie van Toelichting, *l.c.*, p. 51.

262 Gutwirth, S., *Privacy and the information age*, *o.c.*, p. 97.

"[T]he delineation and separation of purposes is decisive in the establishment of the number of processing operations. Finality is the key to pinpoint what the processing operation is. And since the whole protection system is engrafted onto the processing operation, it will succeed or fail based on the way in which processing is delineated. Personal data processing is each processing operation or series of operations with personal data which aims to realize one purpose, one finality."[263]

2.5. IMPORTANCE OF THE DISTINCTION

118. Outline – The distinction between controllers and processors forms the basis upon which compliance with the requirements of the GDPR is allocated. Determining the role of each actor involved in the processing is therefore essential to properly understand its responsibilities are under the GDPR. Certain obligations are only applicable to controllers and not to processors. Other obligations are only indirectly applicable to processors. Finally, the extent of certain obligations also varies depending controller or processor status.

119. Subject to different obligations – Under the GDPR, the controller carries "primary" or "overarching" responsibility for ensuring compliance. Any infringement of the GDPR is, as a matter of principle, attributable to the controller, regardless of whether it carries out the processing or relies on a processor. The GDPR also recognizes, however, that processors have an important role to play in ensuring compliance. The GDPR therefore also imposes a number of obligations directly upon processors. In contrast to the controller, however, the processor is in principle only responsible for compliance with those requirements which specifically directed towards processors. The following table provides a comparative overview of the obligations incumbent upon controllers and processors respectively:

Table 1. Comparison obligations controller – processor under the GDPR

Relevant provisions	**Controller**	**Processor**
Principles	✓	✗
Lawfulness of processing	✓	✗
Special categories of data	✓	✗
Transparency and modalities	✓	✗
Data subject rights	✓	Duty to assist

263 *Id.*

Relevant provisions	Controller	Processor
Data protection by design and by default	✓	✗
Documentation	✓	✓
Co-operation with supervisory authority	✓	✓
Security	✓	✓
Data breach notification[264]	✓	✓
DPIA, prior authorization	✗	Duty to assist
Data protection officers	✓	✓
Codes of conduct, certification	✓	✓
International transfers	✓	✓

120. Indirect obligations – Several of the obligations mentioned in the above table are directly applicable to processors. For example, with or without a contract, processors are obliged to maintain documentation, ensure an appropriate level of security and co-operate with supervisory authorities. Other obligations, such as the duty to assist the controller (insofar as this is possible and taking into account the nature of the processing) in relation to data subject rights, are imposed indirectly: those obligations are to be included in the contract or other legal act governing the processing.[265]

121. Modulations – Certain obligations also apply differently to controllers and processors. The duty to maintain a record of (categories) of processing activities, for example, is slightly different for controllers and processors respectively.[266] The duty to notify a personal data breach is another example. The controller is obliged to notify a relevant personal data breach "*without undue delay and, where feasible, not later than 72 hours after having become aware*

[264] As regards the obligation to notify data breaches, a distinction must be made between the obligation to inform breaches to the controller and the obligation to notify breaches to supervisory authorities and data subjects. Only the controller is obliged to notify the data subject and supervisory authorities. The processor is only obliged to notify the controller.

[265] Article 28(3) does not specify whether the obligation to have in place a "contract or other legal" is incumbent upon the controller or processor or both. As Article 28(3) uses a passive formulation, the argument could be made that the obligation applies to both actors. If that is indeed the case, it would appear to be less significant whether an obligation is seen to apply directly by virtue of the GDPR or by virtue of the "contract or other legal act" that binds the processor to the controller. Indeed, the enforceability of those obligations should then not be contingent upon the existence of a "contract or other legal act" (as to hold otherwise would allow a processor to limit its obligations by not complying with another obligation to which it is subject).

[266] Compare Article 30(1) and 30(2) GDPR.

of it" to the competent supervisory authority.[267] A processor, on the other, is not obliged to notify the breach to the supervisory authority but rather to the controller and must do so "*without undue delay*".

3. THE RELATIONSHIP BETWEEN (JOINT) CONTROLLERS

122. Outline – Article 4(7) GDPR recognises the possibility that more than one actor exercises control over the processing ("alone or jointly with others"). The relationship among two actors that determine the purposes and means of the processing *together* is referred to as a relationship of "joint control" or "co-control". Joint control should be clearly distinguished, however, from situations where multiple actors each determine their own purposes and means *independently* of one and other ("separate control").

3.1. "JOINT CONTROL" VS. "SEPARATE CONTROL"

A. *Joint control*

123. Concept – Article 26(1) GDPR specifies that where two or more controllers jointly determine the purposes and means of processing, they shall be "joint controllers". The concept of joint control was already recognized under Directive 95/46, as it was already included in the definition of controller itself. Indeed, as the CJEU stated in *Wirtschaftsakademie*:

> "[S]ince, as Article 2(d) of Directive 95/46 expressly provides, the concept of 'controller' relates to the entity which 'alone or jointly with others' determines the purposes and means of the processing of personal data, that concept does not necessarily refer to a single entity and may concern several actors taking part in that processing, with each of them then being subject to the applicable data protection provisions."[268]

124. Different forms of joint control – During the preparatory works of Directive 95/46, the European Commission noted that

> "for a single processing operation a number of parties may jointly determine the purpose and means of the processing to be carried out. It follows from this that, in such a case, each of the co-controllers must be considered as being constrained by the

[267] Article 33(1) GDPR.

[268] Judgment in *Wirtschaftsakademie*, C-210/16, ECLI:EU:C:2018:388, paragraph 29.

obligations imposed by the directive so as to protect the natural persons about whom the data are processed."[269]

According to the Article 29 Working Party, the Commission's opinion offered only a partial view of the different forms of joint control that may be possible:

> "The Commission opinion did not completely reflect the complexities in the current reality of data processing, since it focused only on the case where all the controllers equally determine and are equally responsible for a single processing operation. Instead, the reality shows that this is only one of the different kinds of 'pluralistic control' which may exist. In this perspective, "jointly" must be interpreted as meaning "together with" or "not alone" in different forms and combinations."[270]

In other words, the decision-making power of each co-controller may vary. For example, the co-controllers may be "on an equal footing" in terms of decision-making, or there might be a dominant party among them. In fact, an indeterminable number of variations are possible.[271] The Working Party put it as follows:

> "in the context of joint control the participation of the parties to the joint determination may take different forms and does not need to be equally shared. [...] A broad variety of typologies for joint control should be considered [...] in order to cater for the increasing complexity of current data processing reality."[272]

125. Different levels of responsibility – The existence of shared responsibility does not imply equal responsibility.[273] As various controllers may be involved in the processing of personal data "at different stages and to differing degrees", their responsibilities should be assessed accordingly. The CJEU confirmed this viewpoint in its *Wirtschaftsakademie* judgment

> "[I]t should be pointed out [...] that the existence of joint responsibility does not necessarily imply equal responsibility of the various operators involved in the processing of personal data. On the contrary, those operators may be involved at different stages of that processing of personal data and to different degrees, so that

269 Commission of the European Communities, Opinion of the Commission pursuant to Article 189 b (2) (d) of the EC Treaty, on the European Parliament's amendments to the Council's common position regarding the proposal for a European Parliament and Council directive on the protection of individuals with regard to the processing of personal data and on the free movement of such data, COM(95) 375 final- COD287, 18 July 1995, p. 3.

270 Opinion 1/2010, *l.c.*, p. 18.

271 *Ibid*, p. 18–19.

272 *Ibid*, p. 19.

273 Opinion of Advocate General Bot in in *Wirtschaftsakademie*, C-210/16, ECLI:EU:C:2017:796, paragraph 75.

the level of responsibility of each of them must be assessed with regard to all the relevant circumstances of the particular case."[274]

What this means practically, in terms of the allocation of responsibility and liability, may not always be immediately apparent. As the CJEU itself indicates, a case-by-case approach is necessary to properly assess the extent of the obligations incumbent upon each joint controller. As far as liability is concerned, consideration must also be given to the additional provisions introduced by the GDPR, which specifically govern the situation where more than one controller may be involved in the processing.[275]

B. Separate control

126. Concept – Multiple controllers can interact in the processing of personal data without being considered as "joint" or "co-controllers". If an exchange of data takes place between two parties without shared purposes and means, the exchange should be viewed only as a transfer between separate controllers.[276] For instance, if each controller processes personal data for its own distinct purposes, each is likely to be considered as a controller independently of the other.

127. Recital (47) Directive 95/46– Neither Article 2(d) of Directive 95/46 nor Article 4(7) GDPR explicitly recognise the possibility of "separate control". Under Directive 95/46, clear support could be found in recital (47), which concerned the provisioning of electronic transmission services:

> "Whereas where a message containing personal data is transmitted by means of a telecommunications or electronic mail service, the sole purpose of which is the transmission of such messages, the controller in respect of the personal data contained in the message will normally be considered to be the person from whom the message originates, rather than the person offering the transmission services; whereas, nevertheless, those offering such services will normally be considered controllers in respect of the processing of the additional personal data necessary for the operation of the service".

Recital (47) is important for two reasons. First, it signals that when the processing involves multiple operations and multiple actors, there can be more than one controller, for each of the different actions that occur. Secondly, it suggests that if one actor decides to entrust personal data to another actor, the former is

274 Judgment in *Wirtschaftsakademie*, C-210/16, ECLI:EU:C:2018:388, paragraph 43; Judgment in *Jehovah's witnesses*, C-25/17, ECLI:EU:C:2018:551, paragraph 66.
275 See in particular Article 82(2) GDPR, which will be discussed *infra*, at nos. 205–207.
276 Opinion 1/2010, *l.c.*, p. 19.

probably acting as a controller with regards to the transmitted content.[277] The actor receiving the data might be acting as a processor, but it might also be acting as a controller. Recital (47) indicates that the latter is likely to be the case with respect to the processing of "additional personal data necessary for the operation of the service".[278] While recital (47) of Directive 95/46 was not incorporated in the GDPR, the same considerations still apply.

C. *Decisive factor*

128. Principle – The distinction between "joint" and "separate" control may be difficult to draw in practice. The decisive factor is whether or not the different parties jointly determine the purposes and means of the processing at issue.[279] If the parties do not pursue the *same objectives* ("purpose"), or do not rely upon the *same means* for achieving their respective objectives, their relationship is likely to be one of "separate controllers" rather than "joint controllers". Conversely, if the actors in question do determine the purposes and means of a set of processing operations together, they will be considered to act as "joint controllers" or "co-controllers".[280]

129. 1984 UK Data Protection Act – The distinction between joint and separate control was rendered more explicit in the 1984 UK Data Protection Act, which defined a data user as the person that "either alone or jointly or in common with other persons" controls the contents and use of the data.[281] As clarified by the Data Protection Registrar at the time:

> "Control may be shared with others. It may be shared jointly or in common. 'Jointly' covers the situation where control is exercised by acting together. Control 'in common" is where each shares a pool of information, changing, adding to or using the information for his own purposes independently of the other".[282]

277 See also B. Van Alsenoy, J. Ballet, A. Kuczerawy and J. Dumortier, "Social networks and web 2.0: are users also bound by data protection regulations?", *l.c.*, p. 69

278 See also Tweede Kamer der Staten-Generaal, Regels inzake de bescherming van persoonsgegevens (Wet bescherming persoonsgegevens) – Memorie van Toelichting, *l.c.*, p. 59–60 for a discussion of the respective obligations of the provider of an electronic communication service and the sender of the message, e.g. regarding data accuracy ("*Wat betreft de juistheid van de gegevens beperkt zich deze verantwoordelijkheid tot de zorg te waarborgen dat de gegevens in overeenstemming zijn met de gegevens zoals deze zijn aangeleverd door degene die van deze dienst gebruik maakt*"). See also Opinion 1/2010, *l.c.*, p. 29 (example of a lost & found website).

279 Opinion 1/2010, *l.c.*, p. 19 ("*joint control will arise when different parties determine with regard to specific processing operations either the purpose or those essential elements of the means which characterize a controller*").

280 See also Opinion 1/2010, *l.c.*, p. 25.

281 Section 1(5) of the 1984 Data Protection Act.

282 The Data Protection Registrar, "The Data Protection Act 1984: The Definitions", Great Britain. Office of the Data Protection Registrar, Wilmslow, 1989, p. 10–11). See also the Data

130. AG Fashion ID – In his Opinion for Fashion ID, Advocate General Bobek takes the position that in order to be able to establish "joint control", there must be an *identity of the purposes and means* between the different actors involved:

> "[T]he notion of joint control is not specifically defined by Directive 95/46. But logically, that notion builds on the notion of controller in Article 2(d): the situation of joint control appears when two or more persons determine the means and the purposes of processing of personal data together. In other words, for two (or more) persons to qualify as joint controllers, there must be identity of the purposes and means of the personal data processing between them."[283]

While Advocate General Bobek initially refers to an "identity" of purposes and means, his subsequent analysis clearly suggests that it is not necessary that the purposes be completely identical. Instead, it may be sufficient that there exists a "*unity*" or "*mutual complementarity*" between the purposes pursued and the means used:

> "[I]n general both [parties] seem to pursue commercial purposes in a way that appears to be mutually complementary. In this way, although not identical, there is unity of purpose: there is a commercial and advertising purpose.
>
> On the facts in the present case, it thus appears that the [parties] co-decide on the means and purposes of the data processing at the stage of the collection and transmission of the personal data at issue."[284]

3.2. THE TYPOLOGY OF OLSEN AND MAHLER

131. Outline – In 2005, Olsen and Mahler developed a very interesting visualization and typology of the different types of relationships among (co-) controllers and processors.[285] The typology encompasses, for the most part, the different forms of collaboration subsequently outlined by the Article 29 Working Party in Opinion 1/2010. In the interest of brevity, the following sections will

---

Protection Registrar, "The Data Protection Act 1984: An introduction to the act and guide for data users and computer bureaux", Data Protection Registrar, Wilmslow, 1985, p. 12. Cf. *infra*, no. 497.

283 Opinion of Advocate-General Bobek in *Fashion ID*, C-40/17, ECLI:EU:C:2018:1039, paragraph 100.

284 Opinion of Advocate-General Bobek in *Fashion ID*, C-40/17, ECLI:EU:C:2018:1039, paragraphs 105–106.

285 T. Olsen and T. Mahler, "Privacy – Identity Management Data Protection Issues in Relation to Networked Organisations Utilizing Identity Management Systems", *Legal IST project*, Deliverable D11, 4 November 2005, p. 40–47. The relevant parts of the Legal IST report were later published as T. Olsen and T. Mahler, "Identity management and data protection law: Risk, responsibility and compliance in 'Circles of Trust' – Part II", *l.c.*, p. 419–420.

combine the typology developed by Olsen and Mahler with examples given by the Article 29 Working Party in Opinion 1/2010.[286]

Figure 1. Modes of collaboration among (co-)controller(s) and processor(s)

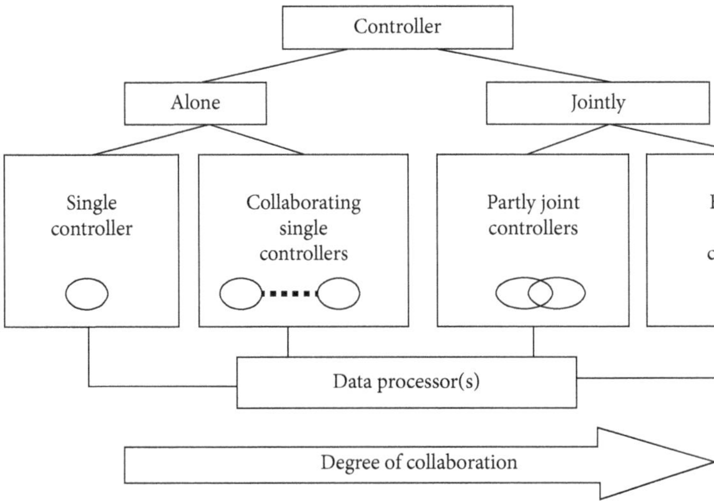

© T. Olsen and T. Mahler.

A. *Single controller*

132. Basic characteristics – The most straightforward scenario is that in which there is only one entity acting as a controller, without having any relationship whatsoever with other data controllers.[287] This controller might be carrying out the processing by itself, or rely on the services of a processor. Insofar as the latter only acts pursuant to instructions provided by the former, there shall be little doubt as to which actor is legally responsible for ensuring compliance under EU data protection law.

B. *Collaborating single controllers*

133. Basic characteristics – In this scenario, there is an interaction between data controllers, but they do not make any joint decisions about the

286 Due to the wide range of possible ways in which joint control might be exercised, the Article 29 Working Party decided not to develop a former typology of co-control. (See Opinion 1/2010, *l.c.*, p. 18). The examples it provided can, however, for the most part, be categorized within the Olsen-Mahler typology.

287 *Ibid*, p. 419.

purposes and means of any specific processing operation.[288] The "collaborating single controllers" do exchange personal data with one and other, but each party has its own (distinct) reasons to process the data.[289] The relationship among collaborating single controllers has also been referred to by the Article 29 Working Party as a relationship among "separate controllers".[290]

134. Example – A travel agency sends personal data of a customer to an airline and a chain of hotels in order to make reservations. Once the airline and hotel have confirmed the availability of the rooms requested, the travel agency issues the relevant tickets and vouchers. In such a scenario, the travel agency, the airline and the hotel are to be considered as three separate data controllers, each subject to the data protection obligations relating to its own processing of personal data.[291]

C. *Partly joint controllers*

135. Basic characteristics – The third type of collaboration envisaged by Olsen and Mahler is the situation where the purposes and means of certain processing operations are determined jointly by more than one controller, while other processing operations are performed separately under the sole control of one controller.[292]

136. Example – A typical scenario in which partial joint control arises is when several (otherwise autonomous) business entities decide to create a common web portal. Imagine, for example, that the travel agency, hotel chain and airline from the previous example decide to create a common web portal to manage their respective reservations. They all agree on the means to be used (e.g. which data will be stored, who can have access, etc.) and the overall purpose for each actor is the same. Furthermore, they pool their customer information to carry out integrated marketing actions. In this scenario the travel agency, hotel and airline are to be considered joint controllers for the processing operations which are accomplished on the jointly controlled portal, but as single controllers with regard to further processing carried outside of the portal.[293]

---

288 *Id.*

289 T. Olsen and T. Mahler, "Privacy – Identity Management Data Protection Issues in Relation to Networked Organisations Utilizing Identity Management Systems", *l.c.*, p. 44.

290 Opinion 1/2010, *l.c.*, p. 19.

291 *Id.* Recital (47) offers another example of "collaborating single controllers". Cf. *supra*, no. 127.

292 T. Olsen and T. Mahler, "Identity management and data protection law: Risk, responsibility and compliance in 'Circles of Trust' – Part II", *l.c.*, p. 420.

293 Opinion 1/2010, *l.c.*, p. 20.

137. Variations – "Partial joint control" can be seen as a combination of "collaborating single control" (type *B*) and "full scope joint control" (type *D*). It should be reiterated, however, that the decision-making power of each joint controller may vary, whereby the actors involved determine the purposes and means to a different extent. In other words, the exercise of control may be "symmetric" or "asymmetric": (co)controllers may be "on an equal footing" in terms of decision-making, or there might be a dominant party among them.[294]

D. Full scope joint controllers

138. Basic characteristics – Collaborating entities shall be considered to be acting as "full scope" (or "full-fledged"[295]) joint controllers when they jointly determine *all* the purposes and means of the data processing operations involved in a particular application or in the provisioning of a particular service.[296] In this scenario the collaborating entities shall in principle be jointly responsible for compliance with all applicable data protection requirements.[297]

139. Example – An example of full scope joint control might occur when two or more research institutions jointly process personal data as part of a common research project.[298]

3.3. THE ARRANGEMENT BETWEEN JOINT CONTROLLERS

140. Directive 95/46 – Directive 95/46/EC did not contain any requirements regulating the relationship among controllers as such.[299] While the Directive did not explicitly require controllers to conclude a contract with each other, the Article 29 Working Party stated that an agreement should be in place as to how compliance with data protection rules shall be ensured. Collaborating controllers were said to enjoy a degree of flexibility when allocating responsibility amongst

294 See also Opinion 1/2010, *l.c.*, p. 22.
295 *Ibid*, p. 21.
296 T. Olsen and T. Mahler, "Identity management and data protection law: Risk, responsibility and compliance in 'Circles of Trust' – Part II", *l.c.*, p. 420.
297 *Id.*
298 *Id.*
299 One notable exception has resulted from the administrative practice surrounding international transfers. Article 26 (2) has provided the basis for the use of contractual clauses as a means to enable transfers to jurisdictions not providing an "adequate" level of protection. Pursuant to the powers conferred by Article 26(4), the Commission has developed standard contractual clauses for transfers to both data controllers and data processors established outside the EU/EEA. For more information on the regulation of transborder data flows see C. Kuner, "Regulation of Transborder Data Flows under Data Protection and Privacy Law: Past, Present, and Future", *TILT Law & Technology Working Paper Series*, 2010, 90 p.

each other, "as long as they ensure full compliance".[300] More specifically, the bottom line should be that:

> "[...] even in complex data processing environments, where different controllers play a role in processing personal data, compliance with data protection rules and responsibilities for possible breach of these rules are clearly allocated, in order to avoid that the protection of personal data is reduced or that a "negative conflict of competence" and loopholes arise whereby some obligations or rights stemming from the Directive are not ensured by any of the parties."[301]

141. Article 26 GDPR – Article 26 GDPR appears to have codified, to a large extent, the Working Party's guidance. It requires joint controllers to determine, in a transparent manner, their respective responsibilities for compliance with the obligations under GDPR.[302] The arrangement that is to be concluded between joint controllers should particularly address how the exercise of data subject rights shall be accommodated and how their respective duties to provide information shall be organized. While it is not a mandatory requirement in every circumstance, the arrangement may designate a contact point for data subjects.[303]

142. Unless provided by law – Joint controllers are not required to conclude an arrangement between them in so far as the respective responsibilities of the controllers are determined by Union or Member State law to which the controllers are subject.

143. Duly reflect – Article 26(2) GDPR provides that the arrangement between joint controllers must "duly reflect" the respective roles and relationships of the joint controllers vis-à-vis the data subjects. This provision also appears to have been inspired by the guidance of the Article 29 Working Party, which stated that

> "Rules on how to exercise joint responsibilities should be determined in principle by controllers. However, factual circumstances should be considered also in this case, with a view to assessing whether the arrangements reflect the reality of the underlying data processing."[304]

In other words, the ability for joint controllers to freely allocate responsibilities among each other is not unlimited: the arrangement must also duly reflect the actual roles and relationship of the joint controllers vis-à-vis the data subjects.

---

300 Opinion 1/2010, *l.c.*, p. 24.
301 *Ibid*, p. 22.
302 Article 26(1) GDPR.
303 Article 26(1) in fine GDPR.
304 Opinion 1/2010, *l.c.*, p. 24.

144. No limitation of data subject rights – Joint controllers are required to make the essence of their mutual arrangement available to data subjects.[305] Irrespective of the terms of the arrangement, however, the data subject may exercise his or her rights under the GDPR in respect of and against each of the controllers.[306] In other words, the terms of the arrangement cannot in any limit the data subjects' ability to seek recourse or to exercise its rights under the GDPR. This also has important implications for the liability exposure of joint controllers, which will be analysed further in the following chapter.

305 Article 26(2) *in fine* GDPR.
306 Article 26(3) GDPR.

CHAPTER 5
LIABILITY EXPOSURE OF CONTROLLERS AND PROCESSORS

145. Outline – The GDPR has introduced a number of important clarifications and changes when it comes to liability under EU data protection law. The main principles underlying the liability model have, however, essentially remained the same. To provide a comprehensive account of the liability exposure of controllers and processors, both the liability regime of Directive 95/46 and the liability regime GDPR shall be analysed.

146. Relevant sources – The main sources used for the analysis are the texts of Directive 95/46 and the GDPR, their preparatory works and the guidance issued by the Article 29 Working Party. Where appropriate, however, reference shall also be made to the preparatory works of national implementations of Directive 95/46 (e.g. the Netherlands, Belgium), as a means to supplement the insights offered by the primary sources. Last but not least, the Principles of European Tort Law (PETL), as well as national tort law, are also considered for issues not addressed explicitly by Directive 95/46 or the GDPR.

1. DIRECTIVE 95/46: "STRICT" LIABILITY FOR CONTROLLERS

147. Basic principle – Under Directive 95/46, a controller was, as a matter of principle, liable for any damages caused by the unlawful processing of personal data. Article 23(1) of Directive 95/46 stipulates that Member States must provide that the controller shall be liable towards data subjects for any damages suffered as a result of an unlawful processing operation. A controller could be exempted from liability, however, in whole or in part, if he proved that he was "*not responsible for the event giving rise to the damage*" (Article 23(2)). Directive 95/46 does not contain any provisions regarding the liability exposure of processors. While Article 16 stipulates that processors may only process the data in accordance with the instructions of the controller, the Directive does not explicitly allocate liability in case of a disregard for instructions.

1.1. CONTROLLER LIABILITY

A. The nature of controller obligations

148. "Means" or "result" – To properly understand the liability exposure of controllers, it is necessary to first understand the nature of controller obligations. Directive 95/46 imposes a variety of obligations upon controllers. In certain instances, the obligations specify a *result* to be achieved (e.g. "personal data must be collected for legitimate purposes and not further processed in a way incompatible with those purposes").[307] In other instances, the obligations are specified as an obligation to make *reasonable efforts* to do something ("obligation of means"). For example, Article 6(1)d of Directive 95/46 provides that the controller must take "every reasonable step" to ensure that data which are inaccurate or incomplete shall be erased or rectified. Similarly, Article 17(1) of Directive 95/46 requires the controller to implement "appropriate" measures to ensure the confidentiality and security of processing.[308] Finally, it should be noted that certain requirements necessitate a further assessment in light of the specific circumstances of the processing (e.g. whether or not personal data are "excessive" will depend inter alia on the purposes of the processing). The precise nature of the controller's obligations must therefore always be determined in light to the specific wording of each provision.

149. A form of strict liability? – Article 23(1) of Directive 95/46 provides that the controller shall be liable towards data subjects for any damages suffered "*as a result of an unlawful processing operation or of any act incompatible with the national provisions adopted pursuant to this Directive*". The liability rule of Article 23 has been characterised as a form of "strict" (i.e. "no fault") liability.[309]

---

[307] Article 6(1)b Directive 95/46.

[308] See in the same vein also High Court of Justice, *Various Claimants v Wm Morrisons Supermarket PLC* [2017] EWHC 3113 at paragraphs 57–58, 62 and 67–68 ("*The mere fact of disclosure or loss of data is not sufficient for there to be a breach. Rather, "appropriate" sets a minimum standard as to the security which is to be achieved. This is expressly subject to both the state of technological development and the cost of measures. Thus, the fact that a degree of security may technologically be achievable, which has not been implemented, does not of itself amount to failure to reach an appropriate standard: an example might be if particular security measures might be introduced which are very costly at the present stage of development, whereas after a few more years the cost might reduce significantly, as is the case with many new technologies.*") and Court of Appeal, *Various Claimants v Wm Morrisons Supermarket PLC*, [2018] EWCA Civ 2339, paragraphs 40–41.

[309] Memorie van Toelichting, Wetsontwerp ter bescherming van de persoonlijke levenssfeer ten opzichte van de verwerking van persoonsgegevens, *Parl. St.* Kamer, 1990–1991, 6 May 1991, no. 1610–1, p. 54 and D. De Bot, *Verwerking van persoonsgegevens*, *o.c.*, p. 241. See also T. Léonard and Y. Poullet, "La protection des données à caractère personnel en pleine (r)évolution", *Journal des Tribunaux* 1999, p. 394 at no. 65. Certain authors also refer to the "objective liability" of the controller. Although the terms "strict" and "objective" appear to be used interchangeably at times, some authors associate different legal consequences to the

The reason for this characterisation is the finding that the controller cannot escape liability simply by demonstrating the absence of a "personal fault". Likewise, it is not necessary for data subjects to demonstrate that the unlawful act was personally committed by the controller.[310] One should be careful however, to not overstate the "strict" nature of controller liability.[311] Even though the data subject is not required to demonstrate a "personal fault" on the part of the controller, he or she must in principle still succeed in proving the performance of an "unlawful act".[312] Demonstration of an "unlawful act" generally amounts to a demonstration of "fault" for tort law purposes.[313] Conversely, if the controller can establish that the processing complies with the requirements of the Directive, he will effectively exempt himself from liability on data protection grounds.[314] The characterisation of controller liability as "strict" liability (i.e. the notion that a controller may be still be held liable in absence of a personal fault) is therefore mainly relevant in relation to (1) controller obligations which impose an obligation of result; and (2) the liability of a controller for acts committed by his processor.

B. *A non-delegable duty of care*

150. Basic principle – Under Directive 95/46, the controller has a general duty to ensure compliance. Because the processor is seen as a "mere executor", who simply acts in accordance with the instructions issued by the controller,

---

respective terms. For purposes of conceptual clarity, only the term "strict liability" shall be used here.

310 Memorie van Toelichting, Wetsontwerp ter bescherming van de persoonlijke levenssfeer ten opzichte van de verwerking van persoonsgegevens, *Parl. St.* Kamer, 1990–1991, 6 May 1991, no. 1610–1, p. 54 and D. De Bot, *Verwerking van persoonsgegevens, o.c.*, p. 241.

311 See also E. Reid, "Liability for Dangerous Activities: A Comparative Analysis", *The International and Comparative Law Quarterly* 1999, p. 736–737 (noting that strict liability is not always "stricter "than fault-based liability, particularly in cases where the circumstances giving rise to liability coincide in large measures with those used in negligence analysis) and E. Karner, "The Function of the Burden of Proof in Tort Law", in Koziol and Steininger (eds.), *European Tort Law 2008*, Springer, 2009, p. 76–77 (arguing that in practice "fault-based" liability and "strict" liability are not two clearly distinct categories of liability, but rather two extremes in a continuum, with many variations between them as regards the possibility of exculpation).

312 See also *infra*, no. 155. See also Tweede Kamer der Staten-Generaal, Regels inzake de bescherming van persoonsgegevens (Wet bescherming persoonsgegevens) – Memorie van Toelichting, *l.c.*, p. 176.

313 See Article 4:101 and 4:102(3) of the Principles of European Tort law (PETL): "*A person is liable on the basis of fault for intentional or negligent violation of the required standard of conduct*" and "*Rules which prescribe or forbid certain conduct have to be considered when establishing the required standard of conduct.*") See however also V. Ulfbeck and M.-L. Holle, "Tort Law and Burden of Proof – Comparative Aspects. A Special Case for Enterprise Liability?", in H. Koziol and B.C. Steininger (eds.), *European Tort Law 2008* (Springer, 2009), p. 35–36.

314 See also Judgment of 19 June 2003, Kh. Kortrijk, 1st Ch., *Tijdschrift voor Gentse Rechtspraak* 2007, p. 96.

the Directive maintains that the responsibility for ensuring compliance remains with the controller. The mere fact that the unlawful action was performed by the processor rather than the controller does not diminish the controller's liability exposure.[315] The controller shall in principle be liable for any violation of the Directive resulting from the operations carried out by a processor acting on its behalf ("*as if they were performed by the controller*"). In other words, Directive 95/46 imposes upon controllers a "non-delegable duty of care": the duty of care that a controller owes data subjects cannot be transferred to an independent contractor.[316]

151. No due diligence defence – A controller cannot escape liability for actions undertaken by its processors by demonstrating an absence of fault in either his choice or supervision of the processor.[317] This is a consequence of the strict liability imposed upon controllers: a controller can only escape liability by demonstrating that the processing complies with the requirements of the Directive or by proving an "event beyond his control" (Article 23[2]).[318] The EU legislature chose to attach liability to the quality of a person as data controller (*qualitate qua*), without making any reference to possible exemptions other than the one mentioned in Article 23(2).[319]

---

315 See also Tweede Kamer der Staten-Generaal, Regels inzake de bescherming van persoonsgegevens (Wet bescherming persoonsgegevens) – Memorie van Toelichting, *l.c.*, p. 176 and C. De Terwangne and J.-M. Van Gyseghem, "Analyse détaillée de la loi de protection des données et de son arrêté royal d'exécution", in C. De Terwangne (ed.), *Vie privée et données à caractère personnel*, Bruxelles, Politeia, 2013, p. 125.

316 Compare E. Reid, "Liability for Dangerous Activities: A Comparative Analysis", *l.c*, p. 752–753 (explaining that a principal may be liable for the negligence of its contractors in cases where the law imposes a non-delegable duty of care). Liability for breach of non-delegable duty of care is not the same as vicarious liability, although the two can easily be confused. In case of vicarious liability, liability is "substitutional", whereas in case of a non-delegable duty of care, liability is personal (i.e. originates from a duty which is personal to the defendant). For a more detailed discussion see C. Witting, "Breach of the non-delegable duty: defending limited strict liability in tort", 2006 *University of New South Wales Law Journal*, p. 33–60.

317 Contra: U. Dammann and S. Simitis, *EG-Datenschutzrichtlinie*, *o.c.*, p. 264 (arguing that the intent of the European legislature was to exempt the controller not only in case of force majeure but also in cases where the controller had taken all the appropriate measures required by Article 17).

318 Cf. *infra*, nos. 158–161.

319 The legislative history of Article 23(2) makes clear that the EU legislature intended to render the controller strictly liable for the actions committed by his processor by removing the reference to "suitable measures" (which had been present in both the initial and amended European Commission proposal) and by limiting the possible defense of the controller to "events beyond his control", such as force majeure. It stands to reason that the EU legislature thus deliberately chose to derogate from the general principle that a person shall not be liable for the actions performed by independent contractors. Compare also with Article 7:102 of the Principles of European Tort Law (PETL) ("Strict liability can be excluded or reduced if the injury was caused by an unforeseeable and irresistible (a) force of nature (force majeure), or (b) conduct of a third party.").

152. Similar to liability for auxiliaries – The liability of the controller for the actions performed by its processor is similar to the vicarious liability of a principal for the actions undertaken by its auxiliaries, whereby "a person is liable for damage caused by his auxiliaries acting within the scope of their functions provided that they violated the required standard of conduct".[320] In case of processors, however, the relationship with the controller in principle is not hierarchical in nature. While the processor is legally prohibited from processing the data "except on the instructions of the controller", he is not necessarily a "subordinate" of the controller.[321] As a result, the processor will in principle not be formally considered as an "auxiliary" of the controller for tort law purposes, although the outcome may be similar in practice.[322]

153. *Ratio legis* – The preparatory works make clear that the liability of a controller for the activities of its processor stems from the fact that the controller is the person or body who "ultimately" decides about the design and operation of the processing carried out. A processor, on the other hand, is seen as someone who merely carries out the controller's instructions.[323] The preparatory works are silent as to why the decision was made to impose *strict* liability upon the controller. It stands to reason that the decision was the result of a compromise between the position of the European Commission (which favoured a more lenient approach) and that of the European Parliament (who favoured an even stricter approach).[324] Possible motivations for the imposition of a strict liability regime include: (1) the risks presented by the processing of personal data; (2) the wish to stimulate highly diligent behaviour on the part of the controller; or (3) the wish to ensure the compensation of data subjects that suffer harm as result of the unlawful processing activities.[325]

---

320 Article 6:102 of the Principles of European Tort Law (PETL). See also C. von Bar a.o. (eds.) "Principles, Definitions and Model Rules of European Private Law – Draft Common Frame of Reference (DCFR)", Study Group on a European Civil Code and the Research Group on EC Private Law, 2009, p. 3318 et seq. See also *infra*, no. 219 et seq.

321 Tweede Kamer der Staten-Generaal, Regels inzake de bescherming van persoonsgegevens (Wet bescherming persoonsgegevens) – Memorie van Toelichting, *l.c.*, p. 61.

322 Needless to say, in cases where the processor is a natural person, it may not be excluded that he or she might *de facto* operate in a hierarchical relationship with the controller, despite being labelled as an "independent contractor" in his or her contract with the employer. In cases where the person carrying out the services should legally be qualified as an "employee" rather than an "independent contractor", he or she will of course be treated as an "auxiliary" for tort law purposes.

323 Commission of the European Communities, Amended proposal for a council directive on the protection of individuals with regard to the processing of personal data and on the free movement of such data, COM(92) 422 final – SYN 287, 15 October 1992, p. 10.

324 Cf. *infra*, no. 552 et seq.

325 Based on H. Cousy and D. Droshout, "Belgium", *l.c.*, p. 62, who further note that strict liability regimes are typically justified by an amalgam of motives.

154. Contractual vs. non-contractual liability – The liability of the controller is in principle non-contractual in nature. The "fault" giving rise to liability is a breach of the law rather than the breach of a contractual agreement. As a result, it is by no means required that there exists a contractual relationship between the data subject and the controller. In cases where a contractual agreement exists, however, the unlawful processing operation may additionally constitute a violation of a contractual agreement. The rules governing a plaintiff's ability to combine contractual and non-contractual liability claims (concurrence of claims) may vary from Member State to Member State.[326]

C. *Burden of proof*

155. Basic principle – To hold a controller liable, the data subject must succeed in demonstrating three elements: namely (1) the performance of an "unlawful act" (i.e. an unlawful processing operation or other act incompatible with the national provisions adopted pursuant to the Directive); (2) the existence of damages; and (3) a causal relationship between the unlawful act and the damages incurred.[327] In addition, the data subject must also establish, as a

[326] See e.g. Study Group on a European Civil Code and the Research Group on EC Private Law, "DCFR", *l.c.*, p. 3023–3028. In Belgium, there are certain limits as to the extent a plaintiff can invoke extra-contractual liability against a contracting party (in Dutch this is referred to as: "*samenloop*"). See e.g. S. Stijns, *Verbintenissenrecht*, *o.c.*, p. 128–142 and H. Bocken, "Samenloop contractuele en buitencontractuele aansprakelijkheid", *NjW* 2007, no. 169, p. 722–731. In cases where the tort ("fault") giving rise to liability also amounts to a crime (which may often be the case where unlawful data processing is involved), the plaintiff in principle is not restricted from invoking extra-contractual liability (see S. Stijns, *o.c.*, p 125–128). The distinction between contractual and extra-contractual liability is relevant inter alia for the determination of eligible damages (see H. Cousy and D. Droshout, "Belgium", *l.c.*, p. 61).

[327] D. De Bot, "Art. 15*bis* Wet Persoonsgegevens", in X., *Personen- en familierecht. Artikelsgewijze commentaar met overzicht van rechtspraak en rechtsleer*, Kluwer, 2001, looseleaf. See also Raad van State, Advies van de Raad van State bij het voorontwerp van wet tot omzetting van de Richtlijn 95/46/EG van 24 oktober 1995 van het Europees Parlement en de Raad betreffende de bescherming van natuurlijke personen in verband met de verwerking van persoonsgegevens en betreffende het vrij Verkeer van die gegevens, 2 February 1998, *Parl. St.* Kamer 1997–1998, no. 1566/1, p. 145. See also U. Dammann and S. Simitis, *o.c.*, p. 264. It should be noted that certain authors consider that it may be sufficient for the data subject demonstrate the performance of an "unlawful act" and the existence of damages in order to hold the controller liable, without additionally requiring a demonstration of a causal relationship between the unlawful act and the damages suffered. See e.g. C. De Terwangne and J.-M. Van Gyseghem, "Analyse détaillée de la loi de protection des données et de son arrêté royal d'exécution", in C. De Terwangne (ed.), *Vie privée et données à caractère personnel*, Bruxelles, Politeia, 2013, p. 125. In my view, this interpretation runs counter to the literal wording of Article 23(1) of the Directive, which stipulates that the controller is obliged to indemnify the data subject for damages suffered "*as a result of*" an unlawful processing operation. As will be discussed later however, there exist certain judicial constructs through which the evidentiary burden of the data subject in this respect may be alleviated.

preliminary matter, that the defendant is (or was) acting as the "controller" of the processing.[328]

156. Practical difficulties – The burden of proof incumbent upon data subjects can be quite onerous. First, identifying the controller of the processing at issue may be a complicated exercise, especially where more than one party is involved in the processing. Second, demonstrating the performance of an "unlawful act" may also be a challenge, particularly in cases where the Directive specifies an obligation of means (rather than an obligation of result), or requires further interpretation (e.g. an assessment of proportionality).[329] Demonstrating causality can also be difficult especially in cases where a particular outcome may be caused by different factors. For example, it may be difficult to prove that the unlawful collection of information (e.g. information regarding the ethnicity of a loan applicant) actually caused the damages to occur (e.g. the denial of a loan may be attributed to many different factors).[330] Finally, demonstrating recoverable damages (e.g. loss of reputation, emotional distress) can also be a challenge.[331]

157. Judicial constructs – A major difficulty for data subjects is that the evidence relevant to their case is often only accessible to the controller or its processor. Because personal data processing is generally conducted "behind closed doors", it can be difficult for data subjects to obtain solid evidence substantiating their claims.[332] Depending on the facts at hand however, the data subject may be able to invoke a *presumption* or other *judicial construct* with similar effect to help substantiate its claim. For example, in a case involving the

---

328 See also C. von Bar a.o. (eds.) "Principles, Definitions and Model Rules of European Private Law – Draft Common Frame of Reference (DCFR)", *l.c.*, p. 2994, at paragraph 31 ("*The axiom [...], as far as tort law is concerned, is as far as tort law is concerned, is that the plaintiff must plead/establish and prove all of the requirements pertaining to his claim, in particular damage, grounds of liability and causation save where express regulations permit departures from this rule, whereas it is incumbent upon the defendant to show and prove certain requirements which give rise to a ground of defence, thereby displacing the claimant's assertions*"). See also the Judgment in *Fotios Nanopoulos*, F-30/08, EU:F:2010:43, paragraph 161 and the Judgment in *Kalliopi Nikolaou*, T-259/03, EU:T:2007:254, paragraph 141.

329 T. Léonard and Y. Poullet, "La protection des données à caractère personnel en pleine (r) évolution", *l.c.*, p. 394 at no. 65 and D. De Bot, "Art. 15*bis* Wet Persoonsgegevens", *l.c.*, looseleaf.

330 *Id.* De Bot indicates the doctrine of "loss of a chance" might be useful in this respect: see D. De Bot, "Art. 15*bis* Wet Persoonsgegevens", *l.c.*, looseleaf. For a comparative discussion of the "loss of a chance" doctrine see V. Ulfbeck and M.-L. Holle, "Tort Law and Burden of Proof – Comparative Aspects. A Special Case for Enterprise Liability?", *l.c.*, p. 40–43.

331 See also P. Larouche, M. Peitz and N. Purtova, "Consumer privacy in network industries – A CERRE Policy Report, Centre on Regulation in Europe, 25 January 2016, p. 58.

332 P. De Hert, V. Papakonstantinou, D. Wright and S. Gutwirth, "The proposed Regulation and the construction of a principles-driven system for individual data protection", *The European Journal of Social Science Research* 2013, p. 141.

unauthorised disclosure of personal data, the European Union Civil Service Tribunal has considered that the burden of proof incumbent upon the applicant may be relaxed:

> "in cases where a harmful event may have been the result of a number of different causes and where the [defendant] has adduced no evidence enabling it to be established to which of those causes the event was imputable, although it was best placed to provide evidence in that respect, so that the uncertainty which remains must be construed against it".[333]

The reasoning of the Civil Service Tribunal can be seen as an application of the so-called "proof-proximity principle", which allocates the evidential burden of proof on the party to whom the evidence is available, or whomever is better situated to furnish it easily and promptly.[334] Another judicial construct which may benefit certain data subjects is the adage of "*res ipsa loquitur*" ("*the thing speaks for itself*"), pursuant to which negligence may be inferred in cases where the harm would not ordinarily have occurred in the absence of negligence.[335] It should be noted however, that the ability for the data subject to avail him- or herself of a particular presumption or construct, may vary according to the domestic legal system of each Member State.

D. *Defences*

158. Escape clause – Article 23(2) stipulates that "the controller may be exempted from this liability, in whole or in part, if he proves that he is not responsible for the event giving rise to the damage". The question inevitably arises as to the nature of the evidentiary burden of proof incumbent upon controllers. Which evidence must controllers offer to successfully exempt themselves from liability, either for their own actions or for the actions performed by their processors or auxiliaries?

---

333 Judgment in *Fotios Nanopoulos*, F-30/08, EU:F:2010:43, paragraph 161. See also the Judgment in *Kalliopi Nikolaou*, T-259/03, EU:T:2007:254, paragraphs 141–142.

334 C. Volpin, "The ball is in your court: Evidential burden of proof and the proof-proximity principle in EU competition law", *Common Market Law Review* 2014, p. 1173–1177. See also E. Karner, "The Function of the Burden of Proof in Tort Law", *l.c.*, p. 72–73.

335 See V. Ulfbeck and M.-L. Holle, "Tort Law and Burden of Proof – Comparative Aspects. A Special Case for Enterprise Liability?", *l.c.*, p. 32–35; F.E. Heckel and F.V. Harper, "Effect of the doctrine of res ipsa loquitur", 22 *Illinois Law Review*, p. 724–725 and F. Dewallens and T. Vansweevelt, *Handboek gezondheidsrecht Volume I*, 2014, Intersentia, p. 1329. While the doctrine of *res ipsa loquitur* appears similar to reasoning of Civil Service Tribunal, there is a difference: the presumption of the Civil Service Tribunal pertained to the *attribution* of an act of negligence, whereas *res ipsa loquitur* concerns the *existence* of negligence. In case of *res ipsa loquitur* however, the requirement of attribution shall also be satisfied as one of the conditions for application of the doctrine is that the object which caused harm was under the exclusive control of the defendant (*Id.*).

159. Legislative history – During the legislative history of Directive 95/46, the escape clause of Article 23(2) underwent several revisions. In the initial Commission proposal, the escape clause provided that the controller of the file would not be liable for damages resulting from the *loss or destruction of data* or from *unauthorized access* if he could prove that he had taken "*appropriate measures*" to comply with requirements of Articles 18 and 22 (security and due diligence).[336] The European Parliament amended the text to state that the controller must compensate the data subject for *any* damage "*resulting from storage of his personal data that is incompatible with this directive.*"[337] The Parliament's change had the effect of removing the escape clause contained in the initial Commission proposal.[338] The European Commission felt strongly, however, that the Member States should be able to exempt controllers from liability, if only in part, for damage resulting from the loss or destruction of data or from unauthorized access "*if he proves that he has taken suitable steps to satisfy the requirements of Articles 17 and 24.*"[339] In the end, the issue was settled by the Council, which drafted the final version of 23(2), which provides that:

> "The controller may be exempted from this liability, in whole or in part, if he proves that he is not responsible for the event giving rise to the damage."

The Council clarified the meaning of Article 23(2) by way of a recital which stipulated that

---

336 Commission of the European Communities, Commission Communication on the Protection of individuals in relation to the processing of personal data in the Community and information security, COM(90) 314 final, SYN 287 and 288, 13 September 1990, p. 40.

337 European Parliament, Position of the European Parliament on Proposal for a directive I COM(90) 0314 – C3-0323/90 – SYN 287 / Proposal for a Council directive concerning the protection of individuals in relation to the processing of personal data T3-0140/1992, 11 March 1992 (First Reading) OJ 13 April 1992, C 94/192.

338 The change proposed by the Parliament should be neither overstated nor understated. In both versions, the controller only risks liability in case of failure to comply with the obligations imposed by the Directive. A key difference however, concerns the lack of reference to the "due diligence requirement" of (former) Article 22. By explicitly referring to (former) Article 22, the initial Commission proposal implied that a controller might escape liability for a security breach if he could demonstrate having exercised appropriate care in choosing his processor. In the European Parliament version, however, it is clear that the controller would remain liable for ensuring compliance with the security obligation, even if the controller had exercised appropriate care in choosing his processor.

339 Commission of the European Communities, Amended proposal for a council directive on the protection of individuals with regard to the processing of personal data and on the free movement of such data, COM(92) 422 final – SYN 287, 15 October 1992, OJ 27 November 1992, C 311/54. See also Commission of the European Communities, Amended proposal for a council directive on the protection of individuals with regard to the processing of personal data and on the free movement of such data, COM(92) 422 final – SYN 287, 15 October 1992, p. 33.

"[...] whereas any damage which a person may suffer as a result of unlawful processing must be compensated for by the controller, who may be exempted from liability if he proves that he is not responsible for the damage, in particular in cases where he reports an error on the part of the data subject or in a case of force majeure".

160. Defence – In order to prove that he is "not responsible for the event giving rise to the damage", the controller must demonstrate three things: (1) the occurrence of an event; (2) which caused the damage; and (3) which cannot be attributed to the controller.[340] In principle, mere demonstration of an absence of fault on the part of the controller is not sufficient.[341] Once it is established that the damage was caused by an unlawful processing operation, the controller can only escape liability by demonstrating that the damages occurred only as the result of an event that cannot be attributed to him.[342]

161. An event beyond control – The wording "not responsible for the event giving rise to the damage" recalls the concept of an "external cause" or "event beyond control", which in many jurisdictions is accepted either (1) as a justification ground excluding fault, or (2) as a means to demonstrate the absence of a causal relationship.[343] According to the Draft Common Frame of Reference, an event beyond control is "an abnormal occurrence which cannot be averted by any reasonable measure" and which does not constitute the realisation of a risk for which the person is strictly liable.[344] The aim of the liability exemption is therefore not to reduce the "strict" liability of the controller. Rather, its aim is to keep the strict liability within the borders of the risk for which it exists.[345] Recital (55) provides two examples of events for which the controller cannot be

340 This point was emphasized by the Belgian Council of State during its evaluation of the bill implementing Directive 95/46. See Raad van State, Advies van de Raad van State bij het voorontwerp van wet tot omzetting van de Richtlijn 95/46/EG van 24 oktober 1995 van het Europees Parlement en de Raad betreffende de bescherming van natuurlijke personen in verband met de verwerking van persoonsgegevens en betreffende het vrij Verkeer van die gegevens, 2 February 1998, *Parl. St.* Kamer 1997–1998, no. 1566/1, p. 145.

341 *Ibid*, p. 146.

342 See in the same vein also M. Thompson, "Beyond Gatekeeping: The Normative Responsibility of Internet Intermediaries", (2015) *University of Hong Kong Faculty of Law Research Paper*, No. 2015/45, p. 23–24 (noting that the language of Article 23(2) does not concern itself with the imputation of fault or culpability to the controller, but with the imputation of the facts themselves).

343 See C. von Bar a.o. (eds.) "Principles, Definitions and Model Rules of European Private Law – Draft Common Frame of Reference (DCFR)", *l.c.*, p. 3538 et seq. and Article 7:102 of the Principles of European Tort Law (PETL) (defences against strict liability).

344 *Id.*

345 C. von Bar a.o. (eds.) "Principles, Definitions and Model Rules of European Private Law – Draft Common Frame of Reference (DCFR)", *l.c.*, p. 3539.

held responsible: namely, (1) an error on the part of the data subject[346]; and (2) a case of force majeure.[347, 348]

162. Other defences – Article 23(2) of Directive 95/46 provides the only valid defence for controllers once the data subject has satisfied its burden of proof. In practice, controllers will not wait until the burden of proof shifts to them. Most controllers will try to ward off liability by arguing that the conditions of liability are simply not met, e.g. by demonstrating the absence of illegality in the processing. Again, the nature of the controller obligation at issue will be determinative here. Where an obligation of means is concerned, controllers can effectively avoid liability by demonstrating that they implemented every reasonable measure that might be expected of them. Even where an obligation of result is involved, controllers may seek to avoid liability by reference to the *Google Spain* ruling, where the Court of Justice indicated that there may also be practical considerations which limit the responsibilities of controllers.[349] In particular, when qualifying search engine providers as

---

346 The reference to "an error on the part of the data subject" recalls the concept of "contributory negligence" or "contributory fault", whereby a victim whose own faulty behaviour has contributed to the occurrence of his own damage, is not entitled to compensation to the extent that his behaviour contributed to the damage. See C. von Bar a.o. (eds.) "Principles, Definitions and Model Rules of European Private Law – Draft Common Frame of Reference (DCFR)", *l.c.*, p. 3475–3500 and p. 3539. See also H. Cousy and D. Droshout, "Fault under Belgian Law", in P. Widmer (ed.), *Unification of Tort Law: Fault*, Kluwer Law International, 2005, p. 36.

347 "*Force majeure*" or "*Act of God*" can be described as an unforeseeable and unavoidable event which occurs independent of a person's will. For a discussion of the specific requirements for *force majeure* in different Member States see C. von Bar a.o. (eds.) "Principles, Definitions and Model Rules of European Private Law – Draft Common Frame of Reference (DCFR)", *l.c.*, p. 3540 et seq.

348 According to the parliamentary works relating to the implementation of Directive 95/46 into Belgian law, other events which cannot be attributed to the controller can also be considered as a possible defence (e.g. the act of a third party for which the controller is not accountable). See Memorie van Toelichting, Wetsontwerp ter bescherming van de persoonlijke levenssfeer ten opzichte van de verwerking van persoonsgegevens, *Parl. St.* Kamer, 1990–1991, 6 May 1991, no. 1610–1, p. p. 54 and D. De Bot, *Verwerking van persoonsgegevens*, *o.c.*, p. 241. Of course, the presence of a justification ground does not suspend the general duties of care of a controller. If the controller could have foreseen the damages and prevent them by taking anticipatory measures, normal rules of negligence apply. See also C. von Bar a.o. (eds.) "Principles, Definitions and Model Rules of European Private Law – Draft Common Frame of Reference (DCFR)", *l.c.*, p. 3538.

349 See also H. Hijmans, "Right to Have Links Removed – Evidence of Effective Data Protection", *Maastricht Journal of European and Comparative Law* 2014, p. 55 and Article 29 Working Party, "Guidelines on the Implementation of the Court of Justice of the European Union Judgment on "Google Spain and Inc. v Agencia Española de Protección de Datos (AEPD) and Mario Costeja González" C-131/12" (2014), WP 225, p. 6) ("The ruling does not oblige search engines to permanently carry out that assessment in relation to all the information they process, but only when they have to respond to data subjects' requests for

"controllers", the Court of Justice indicated that there may be practical limits to the scope their obligations:

> "[...] the operator of the search engine as the person determining the purposes and means of that activity must ensure, within the framework of its responsibilities, powers and capabilities, that the activity meets the requirements of Directive 95/46 [...]".[350]

By explicitly referring to the "powers and capabilities" of the search engine operator, the Court of Justice implicitly acknowledged that there may be practical limits to the ability of a search engine operator to meet all the obligations resulting from Directive 95/46.[351] In particular, it can be argued that *Google Spain* does not oblige search engine providers to exercise preventative control over the information it refers to.[352] In fact, the reasoning of the Court of Justice suggests that the obligations of search engine providers concerning third-party data is essentially only "reactive"; only after the provider has been made aware of the fact that the display of specific search results following a name search adversely impacts the data subject, must the provider assess whether or not delisting is necessary.[353]

E. *Eligible damages*

163. Material and non-material – In principle, there is no restriction as to the type or amount of damages that data subjects may claim. Data subjects can claim both material (e.g. loss of a chance) and non-material damages (e.g. loss of

---

the exercise of their rights."). These considerations are particularly relevant as regards the general prohibition to process certain "sensitive" categories of data, which is in principle formulated as an obligation of result. Cf. *infra* , no. 1167.

350 Judgment in *Google Spain*, C-131/12, EU:C:2014:317, paragraph 38, emphasis added.

351 For a more narrow reading see M. Thompson, "Beyond Gatekeeping: The Normative Responsibility of Internet Intermediaries", *l.c.*, p. 26.

352 See also H. Hijmans, "Right to Have Links Removed – Evidence of Effective Data Protection", *Maastricht Journal of European and Comparative Law* 2014, p. 559 ("*For me, it is obvious that this judgment does not mean that a search engine provider should exercise preventive control over the information it disseminates, nor that it is in any other manner limited in its essential role of ensuring a free internet. In essence, the Court confirms that a search engine – which has as its core activity the processing of large amounts of data with potentially important consequences for the private life of individuals – cannot escape from responsibility for its activities.*"). See also *infra*, no. 1162 et seq.

353 See also Article 29 Working Party, "Guidelines on the Implementation of the Court of Justice of the European Union Judgment on "Google Spain and Inc. v Agencia Española de Protección de Datos (AEPD) and Mario Costeja González" C-131/12" (2014), WP 225, p. 6).

reputation, distress).[354] Of course, the general rules on damages shall also apply here (e.g. personal interest, actual loss, etc.).[355]

1.2. PROCESSOR LIABILITY

164. Outline – Directive 95/46 does not contain any provision regulating the liability of processors. It also does not impose any obligations directly upon processors, with one exception: Article 16 of Directive 95/46 requires the processor not to process personal data "*except on the instructions from the controller*". While Directive 95/46 does foresee additional obligations for processors, it envisages them as being of a contractual nature. In particular, Article 17(3) of Directive 95/46 provides that when a controller engages a processor to carry out certain processing operations on his behalf, their relationship must be governed by a contract or other legal act "binding the processor to the controller", which must specify that the processor is obliged (1) to follow the controller's instructions at all times, and (2) to implement appropriate technical and organisational measures to ensure the security of processing.[356] Article 17(3) mentioned only the minimum content that should be included in an arrangement between controllers and processors. According to the Working Party, the contract or other legal act should additionally include "a detailed enough description of the mandate of the processor".[357]

165. Two scenarios – The absence of a clear liability model for processors under Directive 95/46 begs the question of whether processors could be held liable by data subjects. In answering this question, a distinction should be made between two scenarios. In the first scenario (scenario A), the processor merely fails to give effect to the instructions issued by the controller (e.g. fails to implement the security measures instructed by the controller or fails to update information as instructed by the controller). In the second scenario (scenario B), the processor decides to process personal data for his own purpose(s), beyond the instructions received by the controller (in other words, to act outside the scope of his "processing mandate").

354 U. Dammann and S. Simitis, *o.c.*, p. 263 and D. De Bot, "Art. 15*bis* Wet Persoonsgegevens", *l.c.*, looseleaf. See also Court of Appeal (Civil Division), *Google Inc v Vidal-Hall & Ors* [2015] EWCA Civ 311 (27 March 2015), at paragraphs 70–79.

355 For a discussion of the general rules of damages under Belgian law see e.g. S. Stijns, *Verbintenissenrecht*, Boek 1*bis*, die Keure, 2013, p. 101–104.

356 Opinion 1/2010, *l.c.*, p. 26.

357 Cf. *supra*, no. 98.

A. *Failure to implement controller instructions*

166. Scenario A – In scenario A, the data subject shall in principle only be able to hold the processor liable on the basis of data protection law if this is provided by the national legislation implementing Directive 95/46.[358] Article 49(3) of the Dutch Data Protection Act, for example, provides that the processor can be held liable by data subjects insofar as the damages resulted from his activities.[359] In contrast, the Belgian Data Protection Act does not recognise a right for data subjects to hold processors liable as such. A data subject might nevertheless be able to hold a processor liable if he can demonstrate that the actions of the processor constituted "negligence" or violated another legal provision.[360] The standard of care incumbent upon the processor may, however, be informed by the contract between controller and processor.[361] In any event, the controller who has been held liable by the data subject, should be able to claim back the damages from the processor on the basis of the contract between them.[362]

---

358 See also Opinion 1/2010, *l.c.*, p. 28 ("*[W]hile the Directive imposes liability on the controller, it does not prevent national data protection laws from providing that, in addition, also the processor should be considered liable in certain cases.*").

359 Wet van 6 juli 2000, houdende regels inzake de bescherming van persoonsgegevens (Wet bescherming persoonsgegevens), *Staatsblad* 302 (Netherlands). See also Tweede Kamer der Staten-Generaal, Regels inzake de bescherming van persoonsgegevens (Wet bescherming persoonsgegevens) – Memorie van Toelichting, *l.c.*, p. 62 and p. 176. Another example of a national law which imposes liability directly upon processors is the Czech Data Protection Act (see Article 8 of Act No. 101/2000 Coll., on the Protection of Personal Data, 4 April 2000).

360 D. De Bot, "Art. 15*bis* Wet Persoonsgegevens", *l.c.*, looseleaf. Generally speaking, it will be more appealing for the data subject to seek damages from the controller, because (a) the identity of the processor may not be known to the data subject (b) it will generally be more difficult for the data subject to establish a violation of general duty of care by processor.

361 See e.g. A. De Boeck, "Aansprakelijkheid voor gebrekkige dienstverlening", in X., *Bestendig Handboek Vennootschap & Aansprakelijkheid* (Kluwer, 2008), II.3-84o-p. See also S. Demeyere, I. Samoy and S. Stijns, *Aansprakelijkheid van een contractant jegens derden – De rechtspositie van de nauw betrokken derde*, die Keure, 2015, p. 37 et seq. The standard of care incumbent upon processor may in principle also be assessed in light of the professional occupation and knowledge of the processor: see e.g. H. Cousy and D. Droshout, "Fault under Belgian Law", *l.c.*, p. 32 and p. 39. In Belgium, plaintiffs may also need to consider the so-called "*rule of the (quasi-)immunity of the contractor's agent*" in cases where there is a contractual relationship between the controller and the data subject. This rule may further limit the data subject's ability to seek redress directly from the processor. If the action by the processor amounts to a crime however, such limitations will not apply. For more information see H. Cousy and D. Droshout, "Liability for Damage Caused by Others under Belgian Law", in J. Spier (ed.), *Unification of Tort Law: Liability for Damage Caused by Others*, Kluwer law International, 2003, p. 50; S. Stijns, *Verbintenissenrecht*, p. 143 et seq.

362 See also Tweede Kamer der Staten-Generaal, Regels inzake de bescherming van persoonsgegevens (Wet bescherming persoonsgegevens) – Memorie van Toelichting, *l.c.*, p. 176.

B. *Acting outside of processing mandate*

167. SCENARIO B – In scenario B, the processor does not merely fail to observe the instructions issued by the controller, but also decides to process the personal data for his own purposes. In such instances, the processor shall be considered to be acting as a controller in his own right, by virtue of determining his own "purposes and means" of the processing.[363] As a result, the (former) processor could be held liable in any event on the basis of national legislation implementing Article 23 of Directive 95/46.[364] In principle, data subjects might also turn to the initial controller (who had entrusted the data to the (former) processor) for compensation. This is a result of the strict liability regime of Article 23. The initial controller cannot escape liability by demonstrating an absence of fault in either his choice or supervision of the processor.[365] In practice, this means that the data subject will typically have the choice whether or not to sue both parties and whether or not to do so simultaneously or consecutively (although national tort law may specify otherwise).[366] Again, the initial controller should be able to claim back the awarded damages from the processor for disregarding his instructions on the basis of the contract between them.[367]

1.3. MULTIPLE CONTROLLERS

168. SEPARATE VS. JOINT CONTROL – As indicated earlier, not every collaboration among actors involving the processing of personal data implies the

---

363 See also Opinion 1/2010, *l.c.*, p. 25. A (former) processor shall be (re)qualified as a (co-) controller where he acquires a relevant role in determining either the purpose(s) and/or the essential means of the processing (*Id.*). See also Tweede Kamer der Staten-Generaal, Regels inzake de bescherming van persoonsgegevens (Wet bescherming persoonsgegevens) – Memorie van Toelichting, *l.c.*, p. 62.

364 In principle, the processor could also be held liable on the basis of the national provision implementing Article 16 of Directive 95/46, which specifies that the processor may not process personal data "*except on the instructions of the controller*", which is a requirement directly applicable to processors. Depending on the jurisdiction, a breach of confidentiality by processors could also amount to a crime: see e.g. Article 38 of the Belgian Data Protection Act.

365 This outcome is similar to the liability of principals for torts committed by their auxiliaries "*in the course of the service*" for which they have been enlisted (although results may vary depending on national tort law). See e.g. T. Vansweevelt and B. Weyts, *Handboek Buitencontractueel Aansprakelijkheidsrecht*, 2009, Antwerp, Intersentia, p. 416–421 and H. Vandenberghe, "Aansprakelijkheid van de aansteller", *Tijdschrift voor Privaatrecht* (TPR) 2011, p. 604–606.

366 In Belgium, victims of concurrent faults may hold both the tortfeasor and the vicariously liable party liable *in solidum*. See H. Cousy and D. Droshout, "Multiple Tortfeasors under Belgian Law", *l.c.*, p. 33–35. See also Article 9:101 PETL.

367 See also Tweede Kamer der Staten-Generaal, Regels inzake de bescherming van persoonsgegevens (Wet bescherming persoonsgegevens) – Memorie van Toelichting, *l.c.*, p. 176.

existence of a controller-processor relationship. It is equally possible that each actor processes personal data for its own distinct purposes, in which case each entity is likely to be considered a controller independently of the other ("separate controllers"). It is also possible that the actors jointly exercise decision-making power concerning the purposes and means of the processing, in which case they are considered to act as "joint controllers" or "co-controllers".[368]

A. *Separate controllers*

169. Basic principle – Separate controllers exchange personal data with one another, but do so without making any joint decisions about the purposes and means of any specific processing operation.[369] In such cases, each party is independently (yet fully) responsible for ensuring compliance of its own processing activities. In principle, the liability exposure of each party is also strictly limited to the processing activities under its own control. In exceptional cases however, liability may nevertheless be shared, particularly where failure to ensure compliance by one controller contributes to the same damages caused by the fault by another controller.

170. Separate control, separate responsibilities – In the case of separate controllers, the starting point is that each controller is only responsible for ensuring compliance with its own activities ("*separate control, separate responsibilities*"). As Olsen and Mahler put it:

> "In this type of multiple data controller relationship, the data controllers separately process personal data, but there is a data flow from one controller to the other. Each controller is responsible for his own processing, and the communication of personal data to the other data controllers is one example of such processing. One controller is not responsible for acts or omissions of the other data controller."[370]

Because each controller is separately responsible for his own processing activities, only one controller shall in principle be liable in case of an unlawful processing operation (scenario A).[371] Liability may nevertheless be shared, however, if the fault of one controller brings about the *same damage* as the fault of another controller (scenario B).

---

368 Cf. *supra*, nos. 123 et seq.

369 Opinion 1/2010, *l.c.*, p. 19 and T. Olsen and T. Mahler, "Identity management and data protection law: Risk, responsibility and compliance in 'Circles of Trust' –Part II", *l.c.*, p. 419.

370 T. Olsen and T. Mahler, "Privacy – Identity Management Data Protection Issues in Relation to Networked Organisations Utilizing Identity Management Systems", Legal IST project, 2005, p. 41.

371 Tweede Kamer der Staten-Generaal, Regels inzake de bescherming van persoonsgegevens (Wet bescherming persoonsgegevens) – Memorie van Toelichting, *l.c.*, p. 58.

171. Example of scenario A – A hospital routinely shares information about a patient's treatments with an insurance company in order to obtain payment for the expenses relating to the patient's care. The sharing of personal information takes place with the explicit consent of the data subject and/or pursuant to national legislation. One day, the insurance company suffers a data breach as a result of insufficient security measures. Information about the patient's medical treatment is exposed, leading to considerable emotional harm. In principle, the patient will only be able to obtain compensation from the insurance company for the damages suffered because the hospital is not the controller of the processing operations undertaken by the insurance company.[372]

172. Example of scenario B – One day a hospital mistakenly transmits information about a patient's treatment to the wrong insurance company. The next day, the insurance company suffers a data breach as a result of inadequate security measures. In such cases, the patient may be able to obtain compensation from both the hospital and the insurance company for the damages suffered as they each committed a fault contributing to the same damage.

173. Concurring faults – Scenario B offers an example of *concurring faults*, whereby several distinct faults may be considered to have caused the same legally relevant damage.[373] What precisely constitutes "*the same damage*" is open to interpretation.[374] In certain jurisdictions, concurring faults lead either to solidary liability or liability *in solidum*.[375] If that is the case, each "concurrent tortfeasor" shall be obliged to indemnify the victim for the entire damage, irrespective of the severity of the fault leading to its liability.[376]

---

372 See in the same vein also High Court of Justice, *Various Claimants v Wm Morrisons Supermarket PLC* [2017] EWHC 3113, at paragraph 46 ("*In closing, Mr Barnes thus accepted that if Company A copied da ta which it held as data controller, and transmitted that copy to Company B, then if Company B did not handle that data in accordance with any one of the data protection principles, Company B would be liable. It would be liable alone, unless it were to process the data for Company A, for it would now be the data controller in respect of the data copied to it: Company A would not. The fact that Company A would remain data controller of the data from which the copy was made would be beside the point.*").

373 See H. Cousy and D. Droshout, "Multiple Tortfeasors under Belgian Law", *l.c.*, p. 29–35; S. Stijns, *Verbintenissenrecht*, p. 110–111 and T. Vansweevelt and B. Weyts, *Handboek Buitencontractueel Aansprakelijkheidsrecht*, *o.c.*, p. 835–839.

374 *Ibid*, p. 44–45 and S. Guiliams, "Eenzelfde schade of andere schade bij pluraliteit van aansprakelijken", *Nieuw Juridisch Weekblad* (NJW) 2010, afl. 230, p. 699–700 (arguing that different faults will be considered to have contributed to "the same damage" *if it is practically impossible to distinguish* to what extent the damage is attributable to each of the concurring faults).

375 See C. von Bar a.o. (eds.) "Principles, Definitions and Model Rules of European Private Law – Draft Common Frame of Reference (DCFR)", *l.c.*, p. 3599 et seq. See also Article 9:101 of the Principles of European Tort Law (PETL).

376 *Id.* The difference between solidary liability and *in solidum* liability is minimal: in both cases, the injured party is able to sue each of the debtors for relief of the whole amount. For more

The internal allocation of liability between the concurrent tortfeasors may nevertheless take into account the extent or severity of the fault.[377] In the case of scenario B, it would mean that the hospital would be obliged to indemnify the patient for the whole of the damages suffered, even though the hospital was not responsible as a controller for the poor security measures employed by the insurance company.

B. *Joint controllers*

174. Basic principle – In the case of joint control, several parties jointly determine the purposes and means of one or more processing activities. The distinction between "joint" and "separate" control may be difficult to draw in practice. The decisive factor is whether or not the different parties *jointly* determine the purposes and means of the processing at issue.[378] If the parties do not pursue the *same objectives* ("purpose"), or do not rely upon the *same means* for achieving their respective objectives, their relationship is likely to be one of "separate controllers" rather than "joint controllers". Conversely, if the actors in question do determine the purposes and means of a set of processing operations together, they will be considered to act as "joint controllers" or "co-controllers".[379]

175. Joint control, joint responsibilities – Directive 95/46 EC is essentially silent on how responsibility and liability should be allocated in case of joint control. The only guidance that can be found in the legislative history of Directive 95/46 is the following statement made by the European Commission:

> "each of the co-controllers must be considered as being constrained by the obligations imposed by the Directive so as to protect the natural persons about whom the data are processed".[380]

---

information see H. Cousy and D. Droshout, "Multiple Tortfeasors under Belgian Law", *l.c.*, p. 29–36.

377 *Id.* In Belgium, the apportionment of liability among the concurrent tortfeasors must in principle be based on the extent to which each concurring fault may be said to have caused the damage, rather than the severity of the fault. (S. Stijns, *Verbintenissenrecht*, p. 111 and S. Guiliams, "De verdeling van de schadelast bij samenloop van een opzettelijke en een onopzettelijke fout", *Rechtskundig Weekblad* (R.W.) 2010, p. 475.

378 Opinion 1/2010, *l.c.*, p. 19 ("*joint control will arise when different parties determine with regard to specific processing operations* *either the purpose* *or those* *essential elements* *of the means which characterize a controller*").

379 *Ibid*, p. 25. Cf. *supra*, nos. 123 et seq.

380 Commission of the European Communities, Opinion of the Commission pursuant to Article 189 b (2) (d) of the EC Treaty, on the European Parliament's amendments to the Council's common position regarding the proposal for a European Parliament and Council directive on the protection of individuals with regard to the processing of personal data and on the free movement of such data, COM(95) 375 final- COD287, 18 July 1995, p. 3. See also Opinion 1/2010, *l.c.*, p. 17–18.

The cited passage suggests that each co-controller is individually responsible for ensuring compliance of the processing as a whole and should therefore in principle be liable for any damages resulting from non-compliance ("*joint control, joint responsibilities*"). The liability among joint controllers shall in principle be solidary in nature (i.e. the harmed data subject may bring a claim against any of them for the entire amount of the damage).[381] Of course, the solidary liability of joint controllers only extends to those processing activities for which they in fact exercise joint control. In case of "partial joint control" (whereby certain processing operations are performed under the sole control of one controller)[382], responsibility and liability will only be shared with regard to the common (i.e. jointly controlled) processing activities.[383]

176. Common faults – The solidary liability of joint controllers can be justified on the basis of the "common fault" committed by each controller. A "common fault" arises when multiple parties knowingly and willingly contribute to the same circumstance or event giving rise to the damage.[384] Common faults typically induce solidary liability.[385]

177. Benefits – Solidary liability provides victims with a number of advantages. First, the risk of insolvency of one of the tortfeasors is shifted from the victim to the other tortfeasors.[386] In addition, the victim escapes the burden of specifying to which extent each tortfeasor has contributed to the damage.[387] As noted by the DCFR,

> "[t]he victim should not be expected to establish the respective shares of liability; this issue must be ironed out by the liable persons between themselves. It would be unfair to require the injured person always to sue each and every liable person and dispute with them all and it would be especially unfair to require the injured person to bear the risk of personal insolvency of one of the liable persons. The injured person should

---

381 T. Olsen and T. Mahler, "Privacy – Identity Management Data Protection Issues in Relation to Networked Organisations Utilizing Identity Management Systems", *l.c.*, p. 46–48. See also Tweede Kamer der Staten-Generaal, Regels inzake de bescherming van persoonsgegevens (Wet bescherming persoonsgegevens) – Memorie van Toelichting, *l.c.*, p. 58.

382 T. Olsen and T. Mahler, "Identity management and data protection law: Risk, responsibility and compliance in 'Circles of Trust' –Part II", *l.c.*, p. 420.

383 T. Olsen and T. Mahler, "Privacy – Identity Management Data Protection Issues in Relation to Networked Organisations Utilizing Identity Management Systems", *l.c.*, p. 46–48.

384 See H. Cousy and D. Droshout, "Multiple Tortfeasors under Belgian Law", *l.c.*, p. 30; T. Vansweevelt and B. Weyts, *Handboek Buitencontractueel Aansprakelijkheidsrecht*, *o.c.*, p. 839.

385 See Article 9:101 of the Principles of European Tort Law (PETL). See also C. von Bar a.o. (eds.) "Principles, Definitions and Model Rules of European Private Law – Draft Common Frame of Reference (DCFR)", *l.c.*, p. 3599 et seq. and E. Karner, "The Function of the Burden of Proof in Tort Law", *l.c.*, p. 74.

386 H. Cousy and D. Droshout, "Multiple Tortfeasors under Belgian Law", *l.c.*, p. 32.

387 *Id.* See also Study Group on a European Civil Code and the Research Group on EC Private Law, "DCFR", *l.c.*, p. 3599.

> in fact have the option of pursuing the person from whom reparation can probably be obtained most quickly and most easily."[388]

178. Recourse – If the data subject decides to address only one of the joint controllers for the damages, that controller should be able to obtain redress from his fellow joint controllers for their contribution to the damages.[389] In principle, nothing prevents joint controllers from deciding how to allocate responsibility and liability among each other (e.g. by way of a joint controller contract).[390] The terms of such arrangements shall generally not however be opposable to data subjects, based on the principle of solidary liability for common faults.[391]

179. The approach of WP29 – It should be noted that the Article 29 Working Party has defended an alternative point of view. Specifically, it has argued that joint control should not necessarily entail solidary ("joint and several") liability.[392] Instead, joint and several liability:

> "should only be considered as a means of eliminating uncertainties, and therefore assumed only insofar as an alternative, clear and equally effective allocation of obligations and responsibilities has not been established by the parties involved or does not clearly stem from factual circumstances".[393]

180. Assessment – The approach of the Article 29 Working Party seems fair when it comes to the internal allocation of liability among joint controllers, but may potentially be unjust towards the harmed data subject. The approach suggests that a contract between joint controllers may be opposable to data subjects, and that a harmed data subject may carry the burden of deciding which of the joint controllers is "ultimately" responsible for the damages suffered. In my opinion, the viewpoint of the Article 29 Working Party does not find sufficient support in either the text or legislative history of Directive 95/46. In cases where joint control exists, each joint controller should in principle incur solidary liability for damages resulting from the "common" processing. Any arrangements between joint controllers, including those regarding liability,

---

388 *Id.*

389 See also Tweede Kamer der Staten-Generaal, Regels inzake de bescherming van persoonsgegevens (Wet bescherming persoonsgegevens) – Memorie van Toelichting, *l.c.*, p. 58.

390 T. Olsen and T. Mahler, "Privacy – Identity Management Data Protection Issues in Relation to Networked Organisations Utilizing Identity Management Systems", *l.c.*, p. 48.

391 See also Tweede Kamer der Staten-Generaal, Regels inzake de bescherming van persoonsgegevens (Wet bescherming persoonsgegevens) – Memorie van Toelichting, *l.c.*, p. 58.

392 Opinion 1/2010, *l.c.*, p. 22. In this context, the term "solidary liability" is synonymous with the term "joint and several liability".

393 *Ibid*, p. 24.

should not be opposable to data subjects, based on the principle of solidary liability for common faults.[394]

2. THE GDPR: "CUMULATIVE" LIABILITY FOR CONTROLLERS AND PROCESSORS

181. Outline – The GDPR has introduced several changes to the allocation of responsibility and liability among controllers and processors. While the controller is still the party who carries primary responsibility for compliance, processors have become subject to a host of obligations and are directly liable towards data subjects in case of non-compliance (Article 82(2)). In situations involving more than one controller or processor, every controller or processor involved in the processing may in principle be held liable for the entire damage, provided the damage results from its failure to comply with an obligation to which it is subject (Article 82(4)). The result is a "cumulative" liability regime, whereby each actor can be held liable in light of its role in the processing.

2.1. CONTROLLER LIABILITY

182. Basic principle – The liability model for controllers under the GDPR is essentially the same as under Directive 95/46. Article 82(2) of the GDPR provides that "*[a]ny controller involved in processing shall be liable for the damage caused by processing which infringes this Regulation.*" In other words, the controller remains generally liable for any damages arising from the unlawful processing of personal data. The controller may be exempted from liability, in whole or in part, "*if it proves that it is not in any way responsible for the event giving rise to the damage*" (Article 82(3)).

A. The nature of controller obligations

183. "Means" or "result" – As under Directive 95/46, the actual liability exposure of controllers depends on the nature of the obligation in question. Many controller obligations under the GDPR are formulated as an obligation of means. For example, Article 17(2) of the GDPR requires controllers who are obliged to erase data pursuant to the right to erasure, to take "reasonable steps" to inform other controllers that the data subject has requested the erasure. Moreover, it is worth noting that many controller obligations make reference to the notion of "risk" (e.g. data protection by design (Article 25(1) GDPR),

394 Again: in cases of partial joint control, responsibility and liability will only be shared with regard to the common (i.e. jointly controlled) processing activities.

implying that the evaluation of risk may be a determinative factor in liability disputes. Only few controller obligations contained in the GDPR can be qualified as obligations of result. An interesting example is provided by Article 13(3) of the GDPR, which concerns the duty to provide information to the data subject in case a controller who collected information from the data subject intends to further process data for a purpose other than that for which the data were collected.[395]

B. *Non-delegable duty of care*

184. Basic principle – The liability regime for controllers has remained "strict" under the GDPR: once an infringement has been established, the controller cannot escape liability simply by demonstrating the absence of personal fault.[396] The controller shall therefore remain liable for unlawful processing activities undertaken by the processor on its behalf, even if the controller were to demonstrate an absence of fault in either his choice or supervision of the processor. Under the GDPR, a controller may in principle be exempted from liability (in whole or in part) in only two situations: (1) if the controller can prove it is not in any way responsible for the event giving rise to the damage (Article 82(3)); and (2) if the controller satisfies the conditions for liability exemption for intermediary service providers contained in Directive 2000/31 (Article 2(4)).[397]

C. *Burden of proof*

185. The principle of accountability – According to Article 5(2) of the GDPR, controllers are under a general obligation to be able to demonstrate their compliance with the basic principles of data protection ("accountability"). Moreover, a number of other provisions additionally stipulate that the controller must be able to demonstrate compliance, such as the provisions regarding the conditions for consent (Article 7), processing which does not allow identification (Articles 11 and 12(2)), and the general obligation to adopt appropriate technical and organisational measures to ensure compliance (Article 24).

186. Shifting the burden of proof? – Strictly speaking, the requirement that the controller should "be able" to demonstrate compliance does not alter the burden of proof incumbent upon data subjects. After all, requiring the

[395] Interestingly, only in the situation where the personal data have been collected from the data subject is the duty to inform defined as an obligation of result. If the data have been obtained elsewhere, Article 14(5)a GDPR provides an exemption in case of disproportionate effort.
[396] Compare *supra*, nos. 150–154.
[397] See also *infra*, nos. 187–188.

ability to demonstrate is not the same as requiring *actual* demonstration.[398] Such a formalistic reading would, however, run contrary to the principle of accountability which the GDPR seeks to promote.[399] The EU legislature did not introduce these provisions merely to promote better organisational practices, but also to require controllers to stand ready to demonstrate compliance when called upon to do so. As a result, one can argue that the data subject no longer carries the burden of proof of demonstrating exactly where the processing went wrong.[400] At the very least, the argument can be made that the provisions of the GDPR regarding accountability (which require controllers to "be able to demonstrate compliance") reinforce the notion that the controller is in fact "best placed" to proffer evidence of the measures it has taken to ensure compliance. Even if the legal burden of proof is still borne by the data subject, the evidential burden of proof should *de facto* shift to the controller as soon as the data subject has offered *prima facie* evidence of an unlawful processing activity.[401]

D. *Defences*

187. Escape clause – Article 82(3) GDPR provides that a controller or processor shall be exempt from liability if it proves that it is "not in any way" responsible for the event giving rise to the damage. Article 82(3) GDPR clearly echoes the escape clause of Article 23(2) of Directive 95/46.[402] Interestingly, the GDPR does not contain a recital similar to recital (55) of Directive 95/46, which provides two examples of how a controller might prove that it is "not responsible for the event giving rise to the damage" (i.e. force majeure or error on the part of the data subject). Nevertheless, it is reasonable to assume that the words "not responsible for the event giving rise to the damage" should in principle still be interpreted in the same way. As a result, the escape clause of Article 82(3) still refers to "events beyond control", i.e. an abnormal occurrence which cannot be averted by any reasonable measures and which does not constitute the realisation

398 Only in Article 21 (right to object) does the GDPR specify that it is up to the controller to actually demonstrate the legality of his processing activities towards the data subject.

399 For a detailed discussion regarding the origin and development of the principle of accountability see J. Alhadeff, B. Van Alsenoy and J. Dumortier, "The accountability principle in data protection regulation: origin, development and future directions", *l.c.*, p. 49–82.

400 See also P. De Hert, V. Papakonstantinou, D. Wright and S. Gutwirth, "The proposed Regulation and the construction of a principles-driven system for individual data protection", *l.c.*, p. 141 and K. Rosier and A. Delforge, "Le régime de responsabilité civile du responsable du traitement et du sous-traitant dans le RGPD", *l.c.*, p. 682–683.

401 Regarding the distinction between *legal* burden of proof and the *evidential* burden of proof see C. Volpin, "The ball is in your court: Evidential burden of proof and the proof-proximity principle in EU competition law", *Common Market Law Review* 2014, p. 1177–1179. Regarding the requirement of causality when bringing an action on the basis of Article 82 GDPR see K. Rosier and A. Delforge, "Le régime de responsabilité civile du responsable du traitement et du sous-traitant dans le RGPD", *l.c.*, p. 688–689.

402 Cf. *supra*, no. 158.

of the risk for which the person is strictly liable.[403] If anything, the addition of the words "in any way" (in comparison to Article 23(2) of Directive 95/46), suggests a desire to tighten the scope of the escape clause even further.[404]

188. Additional escape clause – A more significant development has been the formal recognition of the liability exemptions for internet intermediaries contained in the E-Commerce Directive. Article 2(4) GDPR specifies that the Regulation "shall be without prejudice to the application of Directive 2000/31/EC, in particular of the liability rules of intermediary service providers in Articles 12 to 15 of that Directive". The clarification provided by Article 2(4) GDPR is most welcome, given the uncertain status of these liability exemptions under Directive 95/46. Article 1(5)b of the E-Commerce Directive provides that it does not apply to "*questions relating to information society services covered by Directive 95/46 […]*". A literal reading would suggest that the liability exemptions provided in the E-Commerce Directive should not be applied in cases concerning the liability of "controllers", as this is a matter regulated by Directive 95/46.[405]

189. Assessment – The practical importance of Article 2(4) of the GDPR should not be overstated. A reasonable interpretation of controller obligations shall generally not result in the imposition of liability in absence of both knowledge and control. The decision of the Court of Justice in *Google Spain*[406], as well as the decision of the Italian Supreme Court in *Google Video*[407], clearly support this proposition. Nevertheless, the incorporation of the liability exemptions for internet intermediaries is likely to yield certain benefits.

403 Cf. *supra*, no. 161.

404 See also P. Larouche, M. Peitz and N. Purtova, "Consumer privacy in network industries – A CERRE Policy Report", 2016, Centre on Regulation in Europe, p. 58.

405 It should be noted, however, that even in relation to Directive 95/46 certain scholars have argued that controllers should in principle be able to benefit from the liability exemptions contained in the E-Commerce Directive, including in situations where the dispute concerns the unlawful processing of personal data. See e.g. G. Sartor, "Providers' liabilities in the new EU Data Protection Regulation: A threat to Internet freedoms?", *International Data Privacy Law* 2013, p. 5 et seq.; G. Sartor, "Search Engines as Controllers – Inconvenient implications of a Questionable Classification", *Maastricht Journal of European and Comparative Law* 2014, p. 573 et seq. and M. de Azevedo Cunha, L. Marin and G. Sartor, " Peer-to-peer privacy violations and ISP liability: data protection in the user-generated web", *International Data Privacy Law* 2012, p. 57–58.

406 Cf. *supra*, no. 162.

407 Corte di Cassazione, sez. III Penale, Sentenza 17 dicembre 2013 – deposit ail 3 febbraio 2014, n. 5107/14, at paragraph 7.2 ("*[…] as long as the offense is unknown to the service provider, it cannot be regarded as the controller of the processing, because it lacks any decision-making power on the data itself, and when, instead, the provider is aware of the illegal data and is not active for its immediate removal or makes it inaccessible, however, it takes a full qualification of the data controller*".) A special word of thanks is owed to Professor Giovanni Sartor for assisting me with this translation.

First, it should further the development of a more horizontal and uniform approach to the issue of intermediary liability.[408] In addition, Article 15 of the E-Commerce Directive clearly provides that Member States may not impose general monitoring obligations upon internet intermediaries. While most would agree that internet intermediaries should not be expected to proactively monitor whether the personal data disseminated through their platform is being processed lawfully, the formal applicability of Article 15 of Directive 2000/31 would offer certain providers greater legal certainty. But Article 2(4) of the GDPR is by no means a panacea: the concepts of "hosting, "mere conduit", and "caching" contained in Directive 2000/31 are subjects of continuous debate and have themselves given rise to a fair degree of legal uncertainty.[409] Moreover, the liability exemptions of Directive 2000/31 would only affect the liability exposure of controllers in relation to mere distribution or storage activities. An absence of liability for mere distribution or storage does not however, imply an absence of responsibility with regard to other operations performed on that content. Many service providers perform additional operations which go beyond a purely "intermediary", "passive", or "neutral" capacity.[410] As a result, it may still be necessary to interpret the obligations of internet intermediaries as controllers in light of their "responsibilities, powers and capabilities", as suggested by the CJEU in *Google Spain*.[411]

E. *Eligible damages*

190. Material and non-material – Article 82(1) GDPR explicitly recognises that data subjects may seek compensation for both material and non-material damages. The EU legislature has thereby clarified that the right to compensation extends to "non-pecuniary damages". While this was arguably already the case under Directive 95/46, the clarification is nevertheless welcome with a view of removing doubt and ensuring a harmonised approach among EU Member States. Recital (146) further clarifies that

> "The concept of damage should be broadly interpreted in the light of the case-law of the Court of Justice in a manner which fully reflects the objectives of this Regulation."

---

408 M. de Azevedo Cunha, L. Marin and G. Sartor, "Peer-to-peer privacy violations and ISP liability: data protection in the user-generated web", *l.c.*, p. 57–58.

409 See e.g. P. Van Eecke, "Online service providers and liability: a plea for a balanced approach", *Common Market Law Review* 2011, 1481 et seq.; E. Montéro, "Les responsabilités liées au web 2.0", *Revue du Droit des Technologies de l'Information* 2008, p. 364 et seq. and B. Van der Sloot, "Welcome to the Jungle: the Liability of Internet Intermediaries for Privacy Violations in Europe", *JIPITEC* 2015, p. 214–216.

410 B. Van Alsenoy, J. Ballet, A. Kuczerawy and J. Dumortier, "Social networks and web 2.0: are users also bound by data protection regulations?", 2009 *Identity in the information society*, p. 62.

411 Cf. *supra*, no. 162.

As a result, the concept of damages, like the concepts of controller and processor, is to be seen as an autonomous concept of EU law which must be interpreted in light of the jurisprudence of the CJEU.[412]

2.2. PROCESSOR LIABILITY

191. Direct responsibility and liability – In contrast to Directive 95/46, the GDPR imposes a range of obligations directly upon processors and renders them liable towards data subjects in the case of non-compliance (Article 82(2)).

A. The nature of processor obligations

192. "Means" or "result" – As is the case for controller liability, the liability exposure of processors depends on the nature of the obligation concerned. Many obligations incumbent upon processors are formulated as obligations of means rather than as obligations of result. For example, the obligation to secure the processing of personal data (Article 32) is clearly an obligation of means. On the other hand, the obligation not to process personal data except on the instructions of the controller (Article 29), has been formulated as an obligation of result. The precise nature of a processor's liability exposure must therefore also be determined in light of the specific wording of each obligation.

193. It should be noted that the GDPR has added considerable detail as regards to the legal binding of processors towards controllers (Article 28(3)). Processors must comply not only with requirements that are directly applicable, but also with requirements imposed by way of contract. For example, Article 28(3) foresees that the contract or other legal act between the controller and processor shall stipulate that the processor shall assist the controller in the fulfilment of its obligation to respond to requests for exercising the data subject's rights – insofar as this is possible and taking into account the nature of the processing.[413]

---

[412] K. Rosier and A. Delforge, "Le régime de responsabilité civile du responsable du traitement et du sous-traitant dans le RGPD", in C. De Terwangne and K. Rosier (eds.), *Le Règlement Général sur la Protection des Données (RGPD/GDPR) – Analyse approfondie*, CRIDS, Brussels, Larcier, 2018, p. 687.

[413] Regarding the data subject's ability to rely on the terms of the contract between the controller and processor when initiating a legal action on the basis of Article 82, see also K. Rosier and A. Delforge, "Le régime de responsabilité civile du responsable du traitement et du sous-traitant dans le RGPD", *l.c.*, p. 674.

194. Other obligations that are directly relevant to processors are the obligation to maintain a record of processing activities (Article 30(2)), the obligation to notify data breaches to the controller (Article 33(2)), the obligation to appoint a data protection officer (Article 37), the adherence to codes of conduct and requirements of certification (Articles 41 and 42), and restrictions regarding international transfers (Article 44 et seq.).

B. Proportional liability

195. Basic principle – Despite the increased number of obligations incumbent upon processors, the relationship between controllers and processors has remained largely the same. Like before, the processor is essentially conceived of as an "agent" or "delegate" of the controller, who may only process personal data in accordance with the instructions of the controller (Articles 29 and 28(10)). As a result, the liability exposure of processors remains more limited in scope than the liability exposure of controllers. Whereas controllers can in principle be held liable for damages arising from *any* infringement of the GDPR, processors can in principle only be held liable in case of failure to comply with obligations of the GDPR specifically directed to processors or where it has acted outside or contrary to lawful instructions of the controller (Article 82(2)). This is essentially a "proportional" liability model, as the processor can in theory only be held liable in relation "for his segment" in the processing.[414] The processor will be liable for the entire damage, however, insofar as it is – at least partially – responsible for the harm suffered (Article 82(4)). To properly understand the meaning of Article 82(4), it is worth elaborating upon its legislative history.

196. Legislative history – In the initial proposal for the GDPR, the Commission provided that processors would be jointly and severally liable, together with any controller involved in the processing, for the entire amount

---

414 See Council of the European Union, Note from CZ, DE, IE, ES, FR, HR, NL, AT, PL, PT, FI and UK delegations to the Working Group on Information Exchange and Data Protection (DAPIX), 2012/0011 (COD), 7586/1/15 REV 1, 10 April 2015, in particular at p. 11 (Germany); 23–24 (France); p. 27 (Croatia) and 63 (Portugal). The concept of "proportional liability" is not always neatly defined and can be used to mean different things. See I. Gilead, M.D. Green and B.A. Koch, "General Report – Causal uncertainty and Proportional Liability: Analytical and Comparative Report", in I. Gilead, M.D. Green and B.A. Koch (eds.), *Proportional Liability: Analytical and Comparative Perspectives, Tort and Insurance Law* 2013, Vol 33, p. 1 et seq. Here the term is used to signal that each party's liability exposure is limited to their proportional share in causing the damages. If one party proves insolvent, the loss shall in principle be borne by the data subject. By contrast, in case of joint and several liability, each party can be held liable by data subjects for the full amount. See also J. Boyd and D.E. Ingberman, "The 'Polluter pays principle': Should Liability be Extended When the Polluter Cannot Pay?", *The Geneva Papers on Risk and Insurance* 1996, Vol. 21, No. 79, p. 184.

of the damage.[415] Mere "involvement" in the processing would be sufficient to render the processor liable, unless the processor could prove it was not responsible for the event giving rise to the damage. The Council revised the text to differentiate between the liability exposure of controllers and processors more clearly.[416] The changes introduced by the Council, which were retained in the final version of the GDPR, made clear that a processor would only be liable in case of failure to comply with those obligations of the Regulation which are specifically directed to processors, or if it acted contrary to or outside of the lawful instructions of the controller. As a result, mere "involvement" in the processing is not sufficient to give rise to liability: the liability of the processor is conditional upon a prior finding of responsibility in causing the damage. Only in cases where the processor can be deemed responsible in accordance with paragraphs 2 and 3 of Article 82 GDPR can it be held liable for the entire damage. It is important to note however, that there is no threshold regarding the *degree* of responsibility of the processor in contributing to the damage. Even if the processor is only partially responsible, the processor can be held liable for the entire amount of the damage.[417]

197. Cumulative liability – From the perspective of the data subject, Article 82(4) of the GDPR results in a "cumulative" liability regime.[418] The controller carries a general responsibility for the processing and can be held liable for damages in the event of an unlawful processing activity. The data subject additionally has the possibility to sue the processor directly in case he or she has reasons to believe that the processor and not (only) the controller is in fact responsible for the damage.[419] In such cases, the data subject will effectively have a choice whether to sue the controller, the processor, or both.[420] In cases where a controller and processor have been joined to the same judicial proceedings,

415 European Commission, Proposal for a Regulation of the European Parliament and of the Council on the protection of individuals with regard to the processing of personal data and on the free movement of such data (General Data Protection Regulation), COM(2012) 11 final, 2012/0011 (COD), 25 January 2012, p. 91.

416 Council for the European Union, Proposal for a Regulation of the European Parliament and of the Council on the protection of individuals with regard to the processing of personal data and on the free movement of such data (General Data Protection Regulation) – Preparation of a general approach", 11 June 2015, 2012/0011 (COD), 9565/15, p.185.

417 See also Council of the European Union, Note from Presidency to JHA Counsellors on the proposed General Data Protection Regulation – Chapter VIII, 9083/15, 27 May 2015, p. 3 ("*[E]ach non-compliant controller and/or processor involved in the processing are held liable for the entire amount of the damage. However a controller or processor is exempted from this liability if it demonstrates that it is not responsible for the damage (0% responsibility). Thus only controllers or processors that are at least partially responsible for non-compliance (however minor, e.g. 5%) with the Regulation, and/or in case of a processor, with the lawful instructions from the controller, can be held liable for the full amount of the damage.*")

418 *Id.*

419 *Ibid*, p. 2.

420 *Id.*

compensation may be apportioned according to the responsibility of each controller or processor for the damage caused by the processing, provided that full and effective compensation of the data subject who suffered the damage is ensured.[421] In cases where the processor is not joined to the same proceeding, the controller is entitled to claim back any compensation from the processor that was paid for in damages for which the processor was responsible (Article 82[5] GDPR).

198. Similar to PETL – The cumulative liability regime of Article 82(4) of the GDPR reflects the Principles of European Tort Law (PETL) regarding multiple tortfeasors. According to Article 9:101 of the PETL, liability is solidary "where the whole or a distinct part of the damage suffered by the victim is attributable to two or more persons".[422] The same provision also stipulates that where persons are subject to solidary liability, the victim may claim full compensation from any one or more of them, provided that the victim may not recover more than the full amount of the damage suffered by him.[423] The main innovation of the GDPR in comparison to Directive 95/46 therefore does not relate to the imposition of cumulative or solidary liability as such (as the GDPR merely codifies general tort law principles), but rather to the fact that the GDPR also imposes an increasing number of obligations directly upon processors.

199. From processor to controller – Finally, it is worth noting that Article 28(10) explicitly states that if a processor infringes the GDPR by determining the purposes and means of processing, it shall be considered to be a controller in respect of that processing. The rule of Article 28(10) applies "without prejudice to Articles 82, 83 and 84", meaning that a failure to abide by the controller's instructions could still give rise to liability, even if the processing might theoretically have been legitimate if the processor had obtained the data through other means. It also implies that the initial controller remains liable towards the data subject even in cases where the processor re-purposes the data.[424]

C. *Burden of proof*

200. Basic principle – To hold a processor liable, the data subject must succeed in demonstrating three elements: namely, (1) the performance of an "unlawful act" (i.e. failure to comply with those obligations of the GDPR which are specifically directly to processors or an act contrary to or outside of the

---

421 Recital (146) GDPR.
422 Article 9:101(1) PETL.
423 Article 9:101(2) PETL.
424 See also *supra* no. 167.

lawful instructions of the controller); (2) the existence of damages; and (3) a causal relationship between the unlawful act and the damages incurred.

201. Shifting the burden of proof? – As indicated earlier, the data subject may be able to invoke one or more presumptions in order to help substantiate its claims.[425] While the GDPR does not impose upon processors a general obligation to "be able to demonstrate" compliance, processors will often still be "best placed" to provide evidence of their efforts to comply with the obligations applicable to processors. As a result, the evidential burden of proof may also shift to the processor as soon as the data subject offers *prima facie* evidence of a failure to comply with those obligations of the GDPR, which are incumbent upon processors.[426] Again, it should be noted that the ability for the data subject to avail him- or herself of such a presumption may vary according to the domestic legal system of each Member State.

D. Defences

202. Escape clause – Processors can in principle benefit from the same liability exemptions as controllers. A processor who is considered (at least partly) responsible for the damage may be exempted from liability – in whole or in part – if it proves that it is not in any way responsible for the event giving rise to the damage (Article 82(3)).[427] In addition, processors acting as internet intermediaries within the meaning of Articles 12 to 15 of the E-Commerce Directive, may also be exempted from liability provided the conditions listed in these articles are met.

E. Sub-processing

203. Non-delegable duty of care – An interesting issue to consider is the liability of processors in the case of sub-processing. Article 28(4) of the GDPR provides that in the case of sub-processing, the initial processor remains fully liable towards the controller for the performance of the relevant obligations by the sub-processor. The GDPR does not, however, explicitly state that the initial processor also remains liable towards the data subject. Nevertheless, the argument can easily be made that this should be the case. After all, the GDPR imposes obligations directly upon processors. Every processor involved in the processing must therefore accept personal responsibility for those requirements directed towards processors, even in the case of outsourcing. The formulation of the escape clause of Article 82(3) makes clear that the GDPR also imposes a non-delegable duty of care upon processors.

---

425 Compare *supra*, no. 157.
426 Compare *supra*, no. 186.
427 See also *supra*, no. 187.

F. Eligible damages

204. Material and non-material – Under the GDPR, data subjects can claim both material and non-material damages from processors (Article 82(1)).

2.3. MULTIPLE CONTROLLERS

A. Separate controllers

205. Basic principle – Pursuant to Article 82(2) GDPR, any controller involved in the processing can in principle be held liable for the damages suffered. Read in isolation, one might assume that both joint and separate controllers face equal liability exposure. This is not the case. While joint controllers can theoretically always be held liable for damages caused by processing activities under their joint control, separate controllers can only be held liable if the damage was caused by a processing activity which was under the control of that particular controller (or may otherwise be attributed to him). After all, Article 82(4) provides that every controller involved in the processing may only be held liable "for the entire damage" insofar that they can be held responsible in accordance with paragraphs 2 and 3. As a result, separate controllers shall in principle only be liable for the entire damage if they acted as a controller towards the processing activity which gave rise to the damage or in case of "concurring faults".[428]

B. Joint controllers

206. Basic principle – The GDPR introduced a new provision dedicated specifically to situations of joint control. Article 26(1) provides that joint controllers must determine their respective responsibilities for compliance with the GDPR, in particular as regards to the exercise of data subject rights and their respective duties to provide information by means of an "arrangement" between them.[429] The arrangement must duly reflect the respective roles and relationships of the joint controllers vis-à-vis the data subjects (Article 26(2)).[430]

---

428 Compare *supra*, no. 173. See also K. Rosier and A. Delforge, "Le régime de responsabilité civile du responsable du traitement et du sous-traitant dans le RGPD", *l.c.*, p. 680.

429 Joint controllers are not obliged to put in place such an arrangement in so far as the respective responsibilities of the controllers are determined by Union or Member State law to which the controllers are subject.

430 Cf. *supra*, nos. 141–144.

207. Liability exposure remains – For the most part, Article 26 of the GDPR can be seen as a codification of the earlier guidance provided by the Article 29 Working Party regarding the legal implications of joint control.[431] A notable difference, however, is that every joint controller in principle remains liable towards data subjects for the entire damage even if there exists an appropriate arrangement between them (Article 82(4)).[432] A joint controller can only escape liability if it succeeds in demonstrating that it is not in any way responsible for the event giving rise to the damage (Article 82(3)), or that it satisfies the conditions for liability exemption for intermediary service providers contained in Directive 2000/31 (Article 2(4)).

C. *Apportioning liability*

208. Joined proceedings – In case where more than one controller has been joined to the same judicial proceedings, compensation may be apportioned according to the responsibility of each controller for the damage caused by the processing, provided that full and effective compensation of the data subject who suffered the damage is ensured.[433]

209. Recourse – In cases where one of the controllers responsible for the damage was not joined to the same proceeding, the controller that indemnified the data subject is entitled to claim back any compensation that was paid for in damages for which the other controller was responsible, in accordance with its part of responsibility for the damage (Article 82(5) GDPR).

3. CONCLUSION

210. GDPR novelties – The GDPR has not fundamentally altered the basis for apportioning liability among organisations involved in the processing of

---

431 Opinion 1/2010, *l.c*, p. 22. See also *supra*, no. 174–180.

432 In its First Reading, the European Parliament had proposed to add to limit the joint and several liability between controllers and processors in cases where there existed an appropriate written agreement determining their respective responsibilities (European Parliament legislative resolution of 12 March 2014 on the proposal for a regulation of the European Parliament and of the Council on the protection of individuals with regard to the processing of personal data and on the free movement of such data (General Data Protection Regulation), (COM(2012)0011 – C7-0025/2012 – 2012/0011(COD)), P7_TA(2014)0212, p. 291. This approach was undesirable, however, as it implied that the data subjects would carry the burden of determining which of the joint controllers was ultimately responsible for the damage. The revisions introduced by the Council brought the final text of the GDPR in line with the general principles of European tort law, according to which liability is solidary "*where the whole or a distinct part of the damage suffered by the victim is attributable to two or more persons*". See Article 9:101 of the Principles of European Tort Law (PETL).

433 Recital (146) GDPR.

personal data. The distinction between "controllers" and "processors" is still a decisive factor. Nevertheless, a number of important changes and clarifications have been made. From a liability perspective, the main novelties of the GDPR are:

(1) the increased number of obligations directly applicable to processors and the recognition of their liability towards data subjects;
(2) the formal recognition of a cumulative liability regime where more than one controller or processor are involved in the processing;
(3) the incorporation of the liability exemptions contained in Articles 12–15 of Directive 2000/31;
(4) explicit recognition of the eligibility of non-material damages.

211. Liability for controllers and processors – The liability model for controllers has essentially remained the same as under Directive 95/46: a controller shall in principle be liable for any damages arising from the unlawful processing personal data. The liability of the controller is also still "strict" in the sense that, once an infringement has been established, the controller cannot escape liability simply by demonstrating the absence of personal fault. Contrary to Directive 95/46, the GDPR also explicitly recognises processor liability. The liability exposure of processors, however, remains much more limited in scope than the liability exposure of controllers. Whereas controllers can in principle be held liable for damages arising from *any* infringement of the GDPR, a processor can in principle only be held liable in case of failure to comply with obligations of the GDPR specifically directed to processors, or where it has acted outside or contrary to lawful instructions of the controller.

212. Cumulative liability – The GDPR has retained the general principle that the controller carries "general" (or "primary") liability exposure for any processing activity under its control. It also recognises, in contrast to Directive 95/46, that processors should be directly liable towards data subjects. In addition, by rendering more obligations directly applicable to processors, the enforceability of certain obligations is no longer contingent upon the existence of a "contract or other legal act" between the controller and processor. The result is a cumulative liability regime, in which the data subject has a choice whether to sue the controller, the processor, or both – at least in cases where both controller and processor are at least partially responsible for the damage.[434] In cases where the processor is not in any way responsible for the damage however, the only avenue for remedy shall be against the controller(s) involved in the processing.

434 The cumulative liability regime of Article 82(4) of the GDPR reflects the general principles of tort law regarding multiple tortfeasors.

213. Consistent with PETL – The liability model of the GDPR is consistent with the Principles of European Tort Law (PETL), provided one takes into account the "general" liability of controllers and the "proportional" liability of processors. In many ways, the changes introduced by the GDPR merely constitute a (further) codification of general tort law principles. The main innovation of the GDPR in comparison to Directive 95/46 therefore does not relate to the imposition of cumulative or solidary liability as such, but rather to the fact that the GDPR also imposes an increasing number of obligations directly upon processors.

214. Directive 2000/31/EC – The incorporation of the liability exemptions contained in Directive 2000/31 is likely to provide greater legal certainty to the providers of certain processing services, but there will still be many grey areas. In those cases, a balanced approach is necessary, which takes into account the "*responsibilities, powers and capabilities*" of the actor(s) in question.

215. Eligible damages – Finally, it is also worth noting the GDPR also explicitly recognises the eligibility of non-material damages. While this was arguably already the case under Directive 95/46, the clarification is nevertheless welcome with a view of removing doubt and ensuring a harmonised approach among EU Member States.

216. Burden of proof – While the GDPR has provided for greater clarity regarding the liability exposure of actors involved in the processing of personal data, it has not given special consideration to the difficult position that data subjects may find themselves in when trying to substantiate their claims. While certain data subjects may be able to avail themselves of one or more presumptions, the ability to effectively do so will depend on their domestic legal system. Absent the possibility to invoke such presumptions, the burden of proof incumbent upon data subjects remains quite onerous. The question may be asked therefore, whether it would not be desirable to formally recognise a shift in the burden of proof towards controllers and processors as soon as the data subject has offered *prima facie* evidence of an unlawful processing operation. Doing so would likely enhance the accountability of both actors towards data subjects.

CHAPTER 6
SPECIFIC ISSUES

1. INDIVIDUALS WITHIN ORGANISATIONS

217. Problem statement – Article 4(7) GDPR defines a controller as being a "*natural person, legal person, public authority, agency or other body*". The definition thus refers to a broad range of subjects, ranging from natural to legal persons and including any "other body".[435] In practice, the question may arise whether an individual within an organisation should be considered as the "controller", or whether instead this role should be attributed to the organisation of which he or she is a part. According to the Article 29 Working Party,

> "preference should be given to consider as controller the company or body as such rather than a specific person within the company or the body. It is the company or the body which shall be considered ultimately responsible for data processing and the obligations stemming from data protection legislation, unless there are clear elements indicating that a natural person shall be responsible. In general, it should be assumed that a company or public body is responsible as such for the processing activities taking place within its realm of activities and risks."[436]

218. Relationship with other areas of law – In Opinion 1/2010, the Working Party emphasizes that it is important to stick as closely as possible to the rules established by other areas of law, such as civil, administrative and criminal law.[437] These rules indicate to what extent individuals, organisations or other bodies may be held responsible and will in principle help to determine which actor should be labelled as the "controller".[438] The following paragraphs will briefly look at the civil and criminal liability of organisations – and the individuals working on their behalf – from the perspective of Belgian law.

---

435 Opinion 1/2010, *l.c.*, p. 15.

436 *Id.* See also A. Delforge, "Les obligations générales du responsable du traitement et la place du sous-traitant", *l.c.*, p. 374.

437 *Id.* ("*The identification of 'the controller' in a data protection perspective will be interconnected in practice with the civil, administrative or criminal law rules providing for the allocation of responsibilities or sanctions to which a legal or a natural person can be subject.*") (*Ibid*, p. 16).

438 *Ibid*, p. 15. See also M. Overkleeft-Verburg, *De Wet persoonsregistraties – norm, toepassing en evaluatie*, *o.c.*, p. 387.

219. Liability for auxiliaries and agents – Article 1384, subsection 3 of the Belgian Civil Code (C.C.) provides that masters and principals are liable for damage caused by their servants and appointees ("auxiliaries"). For Article 1384, subs. 3 to apply, the following three conditions must be met:

a) there must be a relationship of *subordination* between the principal and the auxiliary;
b) the auxiliary must have committed a *fault* (i.e. negligence or unlawful act); and
c) the fault must have been committed *in the course of the service* for which the auxiliary has been enlisted.[439]

Article 1384, subs. 3 C.C. is generally applied to hold employers (and legal persons more generally) vicariously liable for actions of their employees and other subordinates.[440] Public servants and directors of private corporations, on the other hand, are generally viewed as "organs", whose tortious behaviour can be imputed directly to the State or legal person on the basis of the theory of organic representation.[441]

220. Employee liability – In principle, any processing of personal data by employees which takes place within the "realm of activities" of an organisation may be presumed to take place under that organisation's control.[442] Employees are generally not considered as "controllers", but rather as "persons acting under the authority of the controller" within the meaning of Article 29 GDPR.[443] Nevertheless, employees may be subject to liability on the basis of national legislation adopted in accordance with the GDPR. Recital (149) provides that "*Member States should be able to lay down the rules on criminal penalties for infringements of this Regulation, including for infringements of national rules*

439 See H. Cousy and D. Droshout, "Liability for Damage Caused by Others under Belgian Law", *l.c.*, p. 46; H. Vandenberghe, "Aansprakelijkheid van de aansteller", *Tijdschrift voor Privaatrecht* (TPR) 2011, afl. 2, p. 596 et seq. and T. Vansweevelt and B. Weyts, *Handboek Buitencontractueel Aansprakelijkheidsrecht*, *o.c.*, p. 399 et seq. See also Study Group on a European Civil Code and the Research Group on EC Private Law, "DCFR", *l.c.*, p. 3318 et seq. and Article 6:102 of the Principles of European Tort Law (PETL).

440 Under Belgian law, the requirements concerning the vicarious liability of employers are interpreted quite broadly. For example, an act shall be considered to have been committed "*in the course of the service*" as soon as there exists some (even indirect) connection between the tort and the service for which the person has been enlisted. For more information see T. Vansweevelt and B. Weyts, *Handboek Buitencontractueel Aansprakelijkheidsrecht*, *o.c.*, p. 418 et seq.

441 H. Cousy and D. Droshout, "Liability for Damage Caused by Others under Belgian Law", *l.c.*, p. 42 and B. Samyn, "Raad van Bestuur", in X., *Bestendig Handboek Vennootschap & Aansprakelijkheid*, II.1-26a et seq.

442 Opinion 1/2010, *l.c.*, p. 15. See also M.B.J. Thijssen, *De Wbp en de vennootschap*, Deventer, Kluwer, 2009, p. 106–107.

443 Previously: Article 16 Directive 95/46.

adopted pursuant to and within the limits of this Regulation."[444] It should be noted, however, that national laws may also limit the extent to which employees can be held liable for wrongful acts committed in the course of their duties. For example, Article 18 of the Belgian Employment Contracts Act provides that employees shall remain exempt from *civil* liability except in case of "fraud, gross negligence or habitual light negligence".[445]

221. Disregard for instructions – The question may arise whether an employee might be considered a controller if he or she decides to use personal data for his or her own purposes. According to the Article 29 Working Party,

> "[s]pecial analysis is needed in cases where a natural person acting within a legal person uses data for his or her own purposes outside the scope and the possible control of the legal person's activities. In this case the natural person involved would be controller of the processing decided on, and would bear responsibility for this use of personal data. The original controller could nevertheless retain some responsibility in case the new processing occurred because of a lack of adequate security measures."[446]

222. Assessment – Article 29 GDPR prohibits any person "acting under the authority of the controller" from processing personal data "except on instructions from the controller, unless he is required to do so by law". The employee who decides to use personal data for his or her own purposes may indeed be considered as a controller in his own right, by virtue of determining his own "purposes and means" of the processing. In my opinion, data subjects may in principle also seek compensation from the organisation under whose authority the personal data was being processed – even if the employee processes the data for purposes "outside the scope of the organisation's activities", provided that an infringement of the GDPR can be established that is somehow attributable to the controller (e.g. a failure to implement appropriate security measures). This is a result of the "strict" liability regime of Article 82 and the general rules of liability for actions undertaken by agents and auxiliaries.[447] In practice, this means that the data subject may have the choice whether or not to sue both parties and whether or not to do so simultaneously or consecutively

---

444 Previously, recital (55) of Directive 95/46 provided that "*[...] sanctions must be imposed on any person, whether governed by private of public law, who fails to comply with the national measures taken under this Directive*". See e.g. Articles 38–39 of the Belgian Data Protection Act of 1992. Recital (149) GDPR goes on to state that "*[t]hose criminal penalties may also allow for the deprivation of the profits obtained through infringements of this Regulation. However, the imposition of criminal penalties for infringements of such national rules and of administrative penalties should not lead to a breach of the principle of ne bis in idem, as interpreted by the Court of Justice.*"

445 See also H. Cousy and D. Droshout, "Fault under Belgian Law", *l.c.*, p. 30.

446 Opinion 1/2010, *l.c.*, p. 16.

447 See also *supra*, no. 184.

(although national tort law may specify otherwise).[448] Under Belgian law, the organisation shall be able to obtain redress from his employee where his actions constituted fraud, gross negligence or habitual light negligence.[449]

223. Interplay vicarious liability – It is also possible that a data subject may not be able to claim compensation on the basis of an infringement of the GDPR, but still be able to do on the basis of the vicarious liability of the employer. In *Morrisons*, for example, it was held that Morrisons was not directly liable for the breach under data protection law, but was still vicariously liable for a rogue employee's actions.[450] The case involved a personal data breach which had been deliberately caused by a disgruntled employee. The employee had exploited his access privileges to steal and post online the personal details of almost 100,000 employees.[451] In first instance, the High Court of Justice held that Morrisons was not directly liable under the UK data protection act[452], but was nevertheless vicariously liable.[453] The Court of Appeal confirmed the High Court's reasoning:

> "[T]he DPA says nothing at all about the liability of an employer, who is not a data controller, for breaches of the DPA by an employee who is a data controller. [...] It is common ground on this appeal that he, and not Morrisons, was the data controller under the DPA in respect of that data. [I]n terms of processing duties and liability,

448 In Belgium, victims of concurrent faults may hold both the tortfeasor and the vicariously liable party liable *in solidum*. See H. Cousy and D. Droshout, "Multiple Tortfeasors under Belgian Law", *l.c.*, p. 33–35 and H. Cousy and D. Droshout, "Belgium", *l.c.*, p. 68–69.

449 See also E. Dirix, "Aansprakelijkheid van en voor hulppersonen", *l.c.*, p. 346; L. Wynant, "Aansprakelijkheid voor en van derden die voor de vennootschap werken: Personeel ter beschikking stellen van werknemers, onderaannemers", in X., *Bestendig Handboek Vennootschap & Aansprakelijkheid*, 2000, p. II.3–41 and M. Lauvaux, "De burgerlijke aansprakelijkheid van werknemers", *Oriëntatie (Or.)* 2005, afl. 3, p. 69–71.

450 R. Hopkins, "Vicarious liability for data breaches: Court of Appeal dismisses Morrisons' challenge", *Panopticon blog*, 22 October 2018, https://panopticonblog.com/2018/10/22/vicarious-liability-for-data-breaches-court-of-appeal-dismisses-morrisons-challenge/ (last accessed 31 December 2018).

451 *Id.*

452 Specifically, the High Court considered that Morrison's had in fact, for the most part, implemented "appropriate" security measures, as required by the UK Data Protection Act. Only one shortcoming was identified, but it did not stand in causal relationship to the damage suffered. High Court of Justice, *Various Claimants v Wm Morrisons Supermarket PLC*, [2017] EWHC 3113 at paragraphs 79, 94–95, 109–110, 122 and 196 ("*In conclusion, I hold that the DPA does not impose primary liability upon Morrisons; that Morrisons have not been proved to be at fault by breaking any of the data protection principles, save in one respect which was not causative of any loss; and that neither primary liability for misuse of private information nor breach of confidentiality can be established*".)

453 *Ibid*, at paragraphs 123–125, 154–161 and 196–198 ("*I reject, however, the arguments that the DPA upon a proper interpretation is such that no vicarious liability can be established, and that its terms are such as to exclude vicarious liability even in respect of actions for misuse of private information or breach of confidentiality. Having rejected them, I hold that, applying Mohamud principles, secondary (vicarious) liability is established*").

> the DPA is only concerned with the primary liability and obligations of the data controller. It has nothing at all to say about the liability of someone else for wrongful processing by the data controller. [...]
>
> [T]he concession that the causes of action for misuse of private information and breach of confidentiality are not excluded by the DPA in respect of the wrongful processing of data within the ambit of the DPA, and the complete absence of any provision of the DPA addressing the situation of an employer where an employee data controller breaches the requirements of the DPA, lead inevitably to the conclusion that the Judge was correct to hold that the common law remedy of vicarious liability of the employer in such circumstances (if the common law requirements are otherwise satisfied) was not expressly or impliedly excluded by the DPA."[454]

224. Director liability – The directors of a company may also face civil or criminal liability for data protection violations. For example, section 198 of the UK Data Protection Act 2018 provides that:

> "Where an offence under this Act has been committed by a body corporate, and it is proved to have been committed with the consent or connivance of or to be attributable to neglect on the part of a director, manager, secretary or similar officer of the body corporate, or a person who was purporting to act in such a capacity, [t]he director, manager, secretary, officer or person, as well as the body corporate, is guilty of the offence and liable to be proceeded against and punished accordingly."[455]

Under certain conditions, crimes committed by directors may also be attributable to the legal person, depending on national legislation.[456]

2. BRANCHES, DEPARTMENTS AND SUBSIDIARIES

225. Outline – Large corporations and public bodies typically consist of multiple departments. In addition, large corporations may have multiple physical locations ("branches") in several different countries. A corporation may also be part of a larger concern, whereby its primary shareholder may be a parent

---

454 Court of Appeal, *Various Claimants v Wm Morrisons Supermarket PLC*, [2018] EWCA Civ 2339, paragraphs 57 and 60. In paragraph 59, the Court of Appeal notes that "*the contrast between the fault based primary liability on an employer data controller under the DPA and the imposition of a strict vicarious liability on an employer for the defaults of an employee data controller is in truth no more of an anomaly than the position at common law. The common law imposes the same strict liability on an employer who is guilty of no fault. The legal policy which limits the imposition of that strict liability is the requirement of a sufficient connection between the default of the employee and the running of the employer's enterprise.*"

455 A similar provision could already be found in section 61(1) of the 1998 UK Data Protection Act.

456 Opinion 1/2010, *l.c.*, p. 16–17. For the situation under Belgian law see H. Cousy and D. Droshout, "Liability for Damage Caused by Others under Belgian Law", *l.c.*, p. 41–42.

or holding company. In practice, such configurations may make it difficult to determine which actor should be labelled as the "controller".[457] To what extent can the branch of a company, which does not enjoy separate legal personality, be considered a controller? Can a subsidiary, despite the existence of a hierarchical relationship with a parent company, be considered as a controller? Likewise, can an administrative department of a public body be its own controller, despite its formal dependence on a ministry or other administrative body?

A. *An (over)emphasis on legal personality?*

226. Emphasis on legal personality – Despite the open-ended language of Article 4(7) GDPR, certain commentators argue that legal personality should be decisive when determining whether or not an entity can act as a "controller".[458] Under this approach, branches or organisational departments without separate legal personality in principle cannot be considered as controllers. The argument in favour of this approach is essentially two-fold. First, it is argued that only natural or legal persons can be holders of rights and obligations. Second, the actions of branches and organisational departments are ultimately attributed to the legal person under which they reside in accordance with rules of civil and corporate law. As noted by Moerel

> "Only formal (legal) persons can have rights and obligations. In the case of a branch this would be the parent entity (to avoid one natural person within the branch being personally accountable for the processing of its employer). Any claim could only result in legal liability if it were brought against the legal entity controlling (under corporate law) the controller (under data protection law). Thus legal certainty would be best served if only the formal (legal) person being responsible for the processing at hand could qualify as a controller."[459]

227. Pragmatic approaches – Other commentators have argued that it would not be appropriate to hinge the question of "who is the controller?" entirely on the question of legal personality. For example, Bainbridge has argued that

---

457 See e.g. M. Overkleeft-Verburg, *De Wet persoonsregistraties – norm, toepassing en evaluatie*, *o.c.*, p. 387 et seq.; M.B.J. Thijssen, "Data Protection and group companies", 17th BILETA Annual Conference April 5th–6th, 2002, 12 p.; C. Kuner, *European Data Protection Law – Corporate Compliance and Regulation*, *o.c.*, p. 70–71; G.-J. Zwenne, A.-W. Duthler, M. Groothuis a.o., "Eerste fase evaluatie Wet bescherming persoonsgegevens Literatuuronderzoek en knelpuntenanalyse", Ministerie van Justitie (NL), 2007, p. 100 and L. Moerel, "Back to basics: when does EU data protection law apply?", *International Data Privacy Law* 2011, Vol. 1, No. 2, p. 99–100.

458 L. Moerel, "Back to basics: when does EU data protection law apply?", *l.c.*, p. 99. In the same vein: Tweede Kamer der Staten-Generaal, Regels inzake de bescherming van persoonsgegevens (Wet bescherming persoonsgegevens) – Memorie van Toelichting, *l.c.*, p. 56.

459 L. Moerel, "Back to basics: when does EU data protection law apply?", *l.c.*, p. 99.

> "It would be sensible if the acid test of who should be a controller was based on legal personality. However, this may not always be appropriate. A local authority has but one legal personality, as a corporation. This is unlike the group of companies where each has its distinct and separate legal personality. On the other hand, a partnership does not have its own legal personality distinct from its partners and it would be ridiculous if each partner had to register separate as a controller. In practice there may be some leeway and it may be up to organisations with complex structures to decide how to approach this issue."[460]

Bainbridge goes on to argue that large organisations which are a single legal entity but have several branches or departments may choose whether to operate the whole organisation as a single controller or to set up each branch office or department as a controller in its own right.[461]

228. Public vs. private sector – In her 1995 Ph.D. thesis, Overkleeft-Verburg argues that the concept of a "controller" should be interpreted in accordance with the basic principles of private and public law.[462] Under private law, only natural or legal persons are recognized as legal subjects (i.e. can be holders of rights and obligations). As a result, she argues, only natural or legal persons can be "controllers" in the private law context.[463] Under public law, however, the main legal subject of regulation is not the legal person but rather the "competent body" (in Dutch: "*bevoegd orgaan*") as defined by administrative and public law.[464] This could be a Minister, but it might also for example be a City Council of Aldermen.[465] It stands to reason, therefore, that when the EU legislature adopted the terms "*public authority, agency or other body*", it did so to accommodate the myriad of subjects recognized by Member States' public and administrative law, rather than to invent a new category of legal subjects.[466]

229. Assessment – The issue of whether or not an entity without legal personality may be considered a "controller" is not merely academic. It may have practical implications in terms of applicable law, transparency of processing and data subject rights. The wording of Article 4(7) suggests that the EU legislature intended to bring entities without legal personality within the scope of this article. On the other hand, it is clear that branches and departments in principle

---

460 D. Bainbridge, *EC Data Protection Directive*, *o.c.*, p. 118.

461 *Ibid*, p. 118–119.

462 M. Overkleeft-Verburg, *De Wet persoonsregistraties – norm, toepassing en evaluatie*, *o.c.*, p. 378–381.

463 *Ibid*, p. 387.

464 *Ibid*, p. 379. See also U. Dammann and S. Simitis, *EG-Datenschutzrichtlinie*, *o.c.*, p. 112.

465 *Ibid*, p. 387.

466 In this regard, it is also worth noting that the initial proposal of the European Commission for Directive 95/46 had assimilated the wording of Convention 108, which defined the controller of the file as "*the natural or legal person, public authority, agency or any other body who is competent according to the national law to decide* […]".

act under the authority of the company or public body that created them. In addition, it seems reasonable to argue that EU legislature would have sought to align the concept of the controller with existing concepts of private and public law as much as possible. For the public sector, this means that the controller shall in principle be the "competent body", i.e. the entity which (according to public law and administrative law) is in charge of the natural person(s) or department(s) engaged in the processing of personal data.[467] In the private sector, the controller shall in principle be the entity (natural or legal person) under whose authority the processing of personal data is taking place, rather than the natural person(s) or branch(es) tasked with implementing the processing.[468]

230. Religious communities – In *Jehovah's witnesses*, the CJEU considered that a religious community of Jehovah's witnesses acted as a controller, jointly with its members, of the processing of personal data carried out by the latter in the context of door-to-door preaching.[469] Not all religious communities have separate legal personality. The Jehovah's Witnesses enjoy recognition as a religious organisation in many EU countries.[470] In Finland, for example, Jehovah's Witnesses was registered as a religious association under the Act on Freedom of Religion.[471] In accordance with this act, a registered religious community "*may acquire rights and make commitments and appear as a party in a court of law and before other authorities*".[472] The consideration of the religious community of Jehovah's witnesses as a controller, therefore did not create a "new category of legal subjects". Implicitly, it was aligned with the fact that a registered religious community constitutes a recognized legal subject under Finnish law. It must be noted, however, that the CJEU considered that the Jehovah's witnesses acted as a controller *jointly with its members*. As a result, there may be still be a situation in which not only the entity that "organises, coordinates and encourages" a particular processing, but also the members of that entity, shall be considered as (joint) controllers.

In my opinion, one should be careful not to interpret this portion of the CJEU's ruling too broadly. There are certain factual elements underlying the

467 *Ibid*, p. 387.

468 *Ibid*, p. 387–388. See also Commission of the European Communities, Amended proposal for a council directive on the protection of individuals with regard to the processing of personal data and on the free movement of such data, COM(92) 422 final – SYN 287, 15 October 1992, p. 10 and D. De Bot, *Verwerking van persoonsgegevens*, *o.c.*, p. 46. See also *supra*, no. 217.

469 Judgment in *Jehovah's witnesses*, C-25/17, ECLI:EU:C:2018:551, paragraph 75.

470 Jehovah's Witnesses, "Recognition in the European Union", not dated, available at https://www.jw.org/en/news/legal/legal-resources/information/packet-recognition-in-european-union.

471 *Id.*

472 English translation of Section 17 of the Freedom of Religion Act No. 453 of 6 June 2003, available at https://www.prh.fi/en/yhdistysrekisteri/uskonnolliset_yhdyskunnat/lyhennysote_uskonnonvapauslaista.html (last accessed 2 January 2019).

judgment in Jehovah's witnesses which are worth recalling in this context. The CJEU was called upon to specifically address the question of whether or not a religious community could be considered as a "controller" in the absence of written guidelines or instructions from the community and without the community having access to the personal data. In this context, it was clear that the individual members still have the ability to exercise considerable influence over the processing. As noted by Advocate General Mengozzi:

> "[A]ny finding of control by the religious community in no way excludes a parallel finding of shared control by the members of that community [...]. [I]t seems apparent from the facts as presented to the Court by the referring court that members of the religious community can have a practical effect on the means of processing (in targeting the persons who will be visited, deciding whether to take notes, choosing the medium for those notes, determining the extent of the data collected, etc.)."[473]

The CJEU likewise emphasized the significant role played by the members themselves:

> "70. In the present case, as is clear from the order for reference, it is true that members of the Jehovah's Witnesses Community who engage in preaching determine in which specific circumstances they collect personal data relating to persons visited, which specific data are collected and how those data are subsequently processed. However, as set out in paragraphs 43 and 44 of the present judgment, the collection of personal data is carried out in the course of door-to-door preaching, by which members of the Jehovah's Witnesses Community who engage in preaching spread the faith of their community. That preaching activity is, as is apparent from the order for reference, organised, coordinated and encouraged by that community. In that context, the data are collected as a memory aid for later use and for a possible subsequent visit. Finally, the congregations of the Jehovah's Witnesses Community keep lists of persons who no longer wish to receive a visit, from those data which are transmitted to them by members who engage in preaching.

The qualification of the Jehovah's Witness community as joint controller for the processing stemmed from the fact that it organised, coordinated and encouraged the preaching activities of its members:

> 71 Thus, it appears that the collection of personal data relating to persons contacted and their subsequent processing help to achieve the objective of the Jehovah's Witnesses Community, which is to spread its faith and are, therefore, carried out by members who engage in preaching for the purposes of that community. Furthermore, not only does the Jehovah's Witnesses Community have knowledge on a general level of the fact that such processing is carried out in order to spread its faith, but that

473 Opinion of Advocate General Mengozzi in *Jehovah's witnesses*, C-25/17, ECLI:EU:C:2018:57, paragraph 72.

> community organises and coordinates the preaching activities of its members, in particular, by allocating areas of activity between the various members who engage in preaching.
>
> 72 Such circumstances lead to the conclusion that the Jehovah's Witnesses Community encourages its members who engage in preaching to carry out data processing in the context of their preaching activity.
>
> 73 In the light of the file submitted to the Court, it appears that the Jehovah's Witnesses Community, by organising, coordinating and encouraging the preaching activities of its members intended to spread its faith, participates, jointly with its members who engage in preaching, in determining the purposes and means of processing of personal data of the persons contacted, which is, however, for the referring court to verify with regard to all of the circumstances of the case."[474]

As a result, it can be argued that in the case of *Jehovah's witnesses*, the control over the processing as distributed in such a manner between the community and its members that both exercise sufficient influence over the processing to be labelled as (joint) controllers.

B. *Corporate concerns*

231. Problem statement – Multinational corporate concerns typically comprise a number of distinct legal persons, which may include one or more parent companies, holding companies and subsidiaries. In practice, the decision is sometimes made to endow one of these legal persons (e.g. the parent company or a subsidiary) with decision-making power regarding the processing of personal data on behalf of the corporate concern.[475] The legal person in question might even be formally designated as the "controller" of the corporate group. Such configurations give rise to several questions: to what extent are corporate actors able to freely designate the controller of the processing? Second, should a parent company not always be viewed as the controller in relation to processing undertaken by a subsidiary?

232. General criteria apply – First off, it should be recalled that the general criteria of Article 4(7) apply irrespective of whether the entities involved in the processing of personal data belong to the same corporate group. Any entity that determines the purposes and means of the processing of personal data shall be considered a controller, regardless of its corporate ties. In principle, the controller of a particular processing operation shall be the legal person under

---

474 Judgment in *Jehovah's witnesses*, C-25/17, ECLI:EU:C:2018:551, paragraphs 70–73.

475 A "corporate concern" does not have separate legal personality.

whose authority the processing is taking place.[476] Legal persons belonging to the same corporate group may, however, decide to pool certain resources or functions. In such cases, the legal persons involved will typically be considered as either "joint controllers" or "collaborating single controllers", depending on the circumstances.[477]

233. Formal designation – EU data protection law does not explicitly prohibit arrangements (e.g. contracts or articles of incorporation) which designate one (or more) legal person(s) as "controller(s)" on behalf a corporate concern.[478] As is the case for controller-processor arrangements, however, the existence of a formal designation is not decisive. Such arrangements will only be recognized insofar as they are not contradicted by the facts.[479] Where there is reason to believe that the formal designation does not correspond with the reality in terms of actual control, the arrangement may be set aside by the adjudicating body.[480] Only if the legal person in question actually determines the purposes and means of the processing, shall the arrangement enjoy full legal effect.

234. Corporate control – The concept of "control" under data protection law is a very different concept than "control" under corporate law.[481] The existence of a hierarchical relationship between corporate entities (control in the corporate sense) is not determinative for "control" in the data protection sense.[482] Parent companies are therefore not automatically considered

---

476 M. Overkleeft-Verburg, *De Wet persoonsregistraties – norm, toepassing en evaluatie*, *o.c.*, p. 387–388; Tweede Kamer der Staten-Generaal, Regels inzake de bescherming van persoonsgegevens (Wet bescherming persoonsgegevens) – Memorie van Toelichting, *l.c.*, p. 56 and D. De Bot, *Verwerking van persoonsgegevens*, *o.c.*, p. 48–49.

477 Tweede Kamer der Staten-Generaal, Regels inzake de bescherming van persoonsgegevens (Wet bescherming persoonsgegevens) – Memorie van Toelichting, *l.c.*, p. 58 and D. De Bot, *Verwerking van persoonsgegevens*, *o.c.*, p. 48–49.

478 See also Tweede Kamer der Staten-Generaal, Regels inzake de bescherming van persoonsgegevens (Wet bescherming persoonsgegevens) – Memorie van Toelichting, *l.c.*, p. 56.

479 In the same vein: D. De Bot, *Verwerking van persoonsgegevens*, *o.c.*, p. 49 with reference to J. Dumortier, "De toepassing van de Privacywet bij het personeelsbeheer: een stand van zaken", *Oriëntatie* (Or.) 1994, No. 11, p. 222.

480 Cf. *supra*, no. 96. See also M. Overkleeft-Verburg, *De Wet persoonsregistraties – norm, toepassing en evaluatie*, *o.c.*, p. 384. This viewpoint has recently also been confirmed by the case law of the CJEU in a case involving Facebook. According to Facebook's policies and terms, it is Facebook Ireland (and not Facebook Inc.) that acts as the (sole) controller for the processing in relation to the processing of personal data. Both the Advocate General and the CJEU took the position, however, that Facebook Ireland and Facebook Inc must be regarded as jointly responsible for processing of personal data at issue (See Opinion of Advocate General Bot in in *Wirtschaftsakademie*, C-210/16, ECLI:EU:C:2017:796, paragraphs 47–51 and Judgment in *Wirtschaftsakademie*, C-210/16, ECLI:EU:C:2018:388, paragraphs 55 and 59–60).

481 C. Kuner, *European Data Protection Law – Corporate Compliance and Regulation*, *o.c.*, p. 71.

482 See also Tweede Kamer der Staten-Generaal, Regels inzake de bescherming van persoonsgegevens (Wet bescherming persoonsgegevens) – Memorie van Toelichting, *l.c.*,

"controllers" of the processing activities undertaken by their subsidiaries. At the same time, a parent company cannot exempt itself from its own data protection responsibilities simply by designating one of its subsidiaries as controller for the whole corporate concern. Again, the factual influence over the processing remains determinative.[483]

C. Governmental bodies

235. Designation by national or community law – Article 4(7) provides that

> "where the purposes and means of such processing are determined by Union or Member State law, the controller or the specific criteria for its nomination may be provided for by Union or Member State law".

Processing of personal data by public bodies requires a legal basis. Ideally, when the legislature passes a law which requires the processing of personal data, it would indicate which entity shall act as a controller. In practice, however, this is seldom the case. As observed by the Article 29 Working Party:

> "The explicit appointment of the controller by law is not frequent and usually does not pose big problems. In some countries, the national law has provided that public authorities are responsible for processing of personal data within the context of their duties. However, more frequent is the case where the law, rather than directly appointing the controller or setting out the criteria for his appointment, establishes a task or imposes a duty on someone to collect and process certain data."[484]

236. "Competent body" – In cases where the national or EU legislature has not explicitly designated the controller(s), but merely entrusted the processing of personal data to a particular governmental body, it may generally be assumed that the body in question is to be considered as "controller".[485] This viewpoint has been confirmed by the Article 29 Working Party as follows

p. 56–57 and M. Overkleeft-Verburg, *De Wet persoonsregistraties – norm, toepassing en evaluatie*, *o.c.*, p. 388.

483 See also M. Overkleeft-Verburg, *De Wet persoonsregistraties – norm, toepassing en evaluatie*, *o.c.*, p. 384 and p. 397–398.

484 Opinion 1/2010, *l.c.*, p. 10.

485 D. De Bot, *Verwerking van persoonsgegevens*, *o.c.*, p. 51; D. De Bot, *Privacybescherming bij e-government in België. Een kritische analyse van het Rijksregister, de Kruispuntbank van Ondernemingen en de elektronische identiteitskaart*, Brugge, Vandenbroele, 2005, p. 35. See also M. Overkleeft-Verburg, *De Wet persoonsregistraties – norm, toepassing en evaluatie*, *o.c.*, p. 385–386 and Tweede Kamer der Staten-Generaal, Regels inzake de bescherming van persoonsgegevens (Wet bescherming persoonsgegevens) – Memorie van Toelichting, *l.c.*, p. 57.

> "For example, this would be the case of an entity which is entrusted with certain public tasks (e.g., social security) which cannot be fulfilled without collecting at least some personal data, and sets up a register with a view to fulfil them. In that case, it follows from the law who is the controller. More generally, the law may impose an obligation on either public or private entities to retain or provide certain data. These entities would then normally be considered as the controller for any processing of personal data in that context."[486]

In practice there may still be instances in which it is difficult to determine which governmental body (or bodies) is acting as the controller of the processing. For instance, several governmental entities might be charged with complementary tasks of public interest. This, in turn, might require multiple governmental entities, each within their respective domain, to carry out certain processing operations. If there is no clear specification in the law as to which entity shall act as a controller, their respective roles are determined by the general criteria of the controller concept (purposes, means).[487]

3. THE ROLE OF "THIRD PARTIES" AND "RECIPIENTS"

237. Outline – In addition to the three main actors (i.e. controller, processor and data subject), EU data protection law also recognizes two other actors, namely "third parties" and "recipients". Both concepts have received relatively limited attention in the literature.[488] The following sections will briefly elaborate upon the meaning of these concepts, their role within the regulatory framework of EU data protection law, as well as the importance of distinguishing between them.

A. *Third party*

238. Definition of a "third party" – Article 4(10) defines a third party as

486 Opinion 1/2010, *l.c.*, p. 10.

487 B. Van Alsenoy, E. Kindt and J. Dumortier, "Privacy and data protection aspects of e-government identity management", in S. Van der Hof, M.M. Groothuis (eds.), *Innovating Government – Normative, Policy and Technological Dimensions of Modern Government*, Information Technology and Law Series (IT & Law), Vol. 20, T.M.C. Asser Press, Springer, 2011, p. 263–264. See also Tweede Kamer der Staten-Generaal, Regels inzake de bescherming van persoonsgegevens (Wet bescherming persoonsgegevens) – Memorie van Toelichting, *l.c.*, p. 57.

488 A notable exception is the contribution by J.A. Salom, "'A third party to whom data are disclosed': A third group among those processing data", *International Data Privacy Law*, 2014, Vol. 4, No. 3, p. 177–188.

> "a natural or legal person, public authority, agency or body <u>other than</u> the data subject, controller, processor and persons who, under the direct authority of the controller or processor, are authorised to process personal data".[489]

According to the Article 29 Working Party, the concept of a "third party" should be understood similarly to how this concept is normally used in civil law, where a "third party" refers to a subject which is not part of an entity or of an agreement.[490] In the data protection context, a "third party" refers to any party which is not part of the "inner circle" of a particular data processing, which includes only the data subject, the controller and possibly a processor, as well as their respective employees.[491]

239. External to data controller and processor – Article 4(10) defines "third party" in a negative fashion: it refers to entities *other than* the data subject, controller, processor or their employees.[492] It is in fact a "residual" category.[493] Because a third party is not part of the "inner circle" of a particular data processing, it does not *a priori* enjoy any legitimacy or authorization for processing personal data.[494] Instead, a third party receiving personal data should in principle be viewed as a controller in his own right, which is separately responsible for ensuring compliance with the provisions of EU data protection law.[495]

240. Emphasis on legal personality – In a private law context, legal personality shall in principle be determinative to decide whether or not an entity should be considered as a "third party" or not.[496] As a result, persons working for a separate organisation, even if they belong to the same group or holding companies would be considered "third parties". On the other hand, branches processing customer information under the direct authority of their headquarters would not be considered third parties.[497] For the same

---

489 Previously: Article 2(f) Directive 95/46.
490 Opinion 1/2010, *l.c.*, p. 31.
491 *Ibid*, p. 8.
492 D. De Bot, *Verwerking van persoonsgegevens*, *o.c.*, p. 55.
493 Opinion 1/2010, *l.c.*, p. 35.
494 *Id.*
495 *Ibid*, p. 31.
496 See also Tweede Kamer der Staten-Generaal, Regels inzake de bescherming van persoonsgegevens (Wet bescherming persoonsgegevens) – Memorie van Toelichting, *l.c.*, p. 64. Regarding the distinction between public and private sector see also *supra*, nos. 228 et seq.
497 Commission of the European Communities, Amended proposal for a council directive on the protection of individuals with regard to the processing of personal data and on the free movement of such data, COM(92) 422 final – SYN 287, 15 October 1992, p. 11. See also Opinion 1/2010, *l.c.*, p. 31 and European Union Agency for Fundamental Rights (FRA) and Council of Europe, *Handbook on European Data Protection Law*, 2014, p. 54.

reason, employees of either the controller or processor shall in principle not be considered as "third parties".[498]

241. Role of the concept – Directive 95/46 uses the concept of a "third party" in several provisions. It is mainly used with a view *to establish prohibitions, limitations or obligations* in cases where personal data might be processed by parties not envisaged at the moment of initial collection.[499] For example, recital (39) provides that

> "Whereas certain processing operations involve data which the controller has not collected directly from the data subject; whereas, furthermore, data can be legitimately disclosed to a third party, even if the disclosure was not anticipated at the time the data were collected from the data subject; whereas, in all these cases, the data subject should be informed when the data are recorded or at the latest when the data are first disclosed to a third party".[500]

The third party concept plays a similar role in relation to the right to correction[501] and the right to object.[502] Article 7 (legitimacy) explicitly recognizes the interests of third parties to whom the data might be disclosed.[503] Article 8 (sensitive data), on the other hand, prohibits disclosure of sensitive data by certain bodies without the consent of the data subject.[504] Finally, the

498 Tweede Kamer der Staten-Generaal, Regels inzake de bescherming van persoonsgegevens (Wet bescherming persoonsgegevens) – Memorie van Toelichting, *l.c.*, p. 64.

499 Opinion 1/2010, *l.c.*, p. 31.

500 See also Article 11(1) of Directive 95/46.

501 Article 12(c) provides that Member States must guarantee that every data subject shall have the right to obtain from the controller "*notification to third parties to whom the data have been disclosed of any rectification, erasure or blocking carried out in compliance with (b), unless this proves impossible or involves a disproportionate effort*".

502 Article 14(b) provides that Member States shall grant the data subject the right "*to object, on request and free of charge, to the processing of personal data relating to him which the controller anticipates being processed for the purposes of direct marketing, or to be informed before personal data are disclosed for the first time to third parties or used on their behalf for the purposes of direct marketing, and to be expressly offered the right to object free of charge to such disclosures or uses.*"

503 Article 7(e) of Directive 95/46 provides that personal data may be processed if the "*processing is necessary for the performance of a task carried out in the public interest or in the exercise of official authority vested in the controller or in a third party to whom the data are disclosed*". Article 7(f) of Directive 95/46 allows the processing of personal data if the "*processing is necessary for the purposes of the legitimate interests pursued by the controller or by the third party or parties to whom the data are disclosed, except where such interests are overridden by the interests for fundamental rights and freedoms of the data subject which require protection under Article 1 (1).*" Article 6(1)f GDPR now refers to processing which is "*necessary for the purposes of the legitimate interests pursued by the controller or by a third party, except where such interests are overridden by the interests or fundamental rights and freedoms of the data subject which require protection of personal data, in particular where the data subject is a child.*"

504 Article 8(2)d provides that the general prohibition regarding the processing of "*special categories of data*" shall not apply where the "*processing is carried out in the course of its*

concept of a third party also plays a small role in relation to international data transfers.[505] While the GDPR has retained the concept of a third party, it clearly makes less use of the concept. Reference to the concept of a "third party" is still made in the context of lawfulness of processing (Article 6(1)f, recital (47), recital (69)) and in the context of the duty to inform (Article 13(1)d–14(2)b). Very often, the GDPR simply uses different language to convey a similar meaning (e.g. by referring to "another natural or legal person").

B. *Recipient*

242. Definition of recipient – According to Article 4(10) GDPR, a "recipient" shall mean

> "a natural or legal person, public authority, agency or another body, to which the personal data are disclosed, whether a third party or not. However, public authorities which may receive personal data in the framework of a particular inquiry in accordance with Union or Member State law shall not be regarded as recipients; the processing of those data by those public authorities shall be in compliance with the applicable data protection rules according to the purposes of the processing"[506]

The term "recipient" should in principle be understood in its natural language meaning. It refers to *any* entity to whom data are disclosed. "Disclosure" should also be interpreted broadly in this context, referring to any type of divulgation of data regardless of the medium or modalities. For example, granting online remote access to data should in principle also be considered as form of disclosure.[507]

---

legitimate activities with appropriate guarantees by a foundation, association or any other non-profit-seeking body with a political, philosophical, religious or trade-union aim and on condition that the processing relates solely to the members of the body or to persons who have regular contact with it in connection with its purposes and that the data are not disclosed to a third party without the consent of the data subjects." Article 9(2)d GDPR now makes reference to "*processing is carried out in the course of its legitimate activities with appropriate safeguards by a foundation, association or any other not-for-profit body with a political, philosophical, religious or trade union aim and on condition that the processing relates solely to the members or to former members of the body or to persons who have regular contact with it in connection with its purposes and that the personal data are not disclosed outside that body without the consent of the data subjects*".

505 Article 26(1)(c) of Directive 95/46 provides that that a transfer or a set of transfers of personal data to a third country which does not ensure an adequate level of protection may nevertheless take place on the condition that the "*transfer is necessary for the conclusion or performance of a contract concluded in the interest of the data subject between the controller and a third party.*" Article 49(1)c GDPR now refers to a transfer which is "*necessary for the conclusion or performance of a contract concluded in the interest of the data subject between the controller and another natural or legal person*".

506 Previously: Article 2(g) of Directive 95/46.

507 D. De Bot, *Verwerking van persoonsgegevens*, *o.c.*, p. 56.

243. Internal or external to controller or processor – The concept of a "recipient" is much broader than the concept of a third party.[508] It may be an entity outside the organisation of the controller or processor (in which case the recipient is also a "third party"), but it may also be an entity who is part of the controller or processor, such as an employee or another division within the same company or department.[509]

244. Role of the concept – The term "recipient" was introduced primarily to help ensure *transparency* of processing towards data subjects.[510] For example, Articles 13 and 14 GDPR stipulate that the data subject must in principle be informed of the "recipients or categories of recipients" of the data, if any. Data subjects who exercise their right of access must be provided with information at least as to "*the recipients or categories of recipients to whom the data have been or will be disclosed, in particular recipients in third countries or international organisations*".[511] Article 19 GDPR also provides that in case of rectification, erasure or restriction of processing following the exercise of rights by the data subject, each recipient to whom the personal data have been disclosed must be informed thereof, unless this proves impossible or involves disproportionate effort. The controller shall inform the data subject about those recipients if the data subject requests it.[512]

245. Exclusion of "authorities" – Article 4(10) *in fine* provides that "public authorities" which may receive data "in the framework of a particular inquiry" shall not be regarded as recipients. The "public authorities" envisaged here are essentially judicial or administrative authorities.[513] The reference to "a particular inquiry" further suggests that the exclusion only concerns disclosures

---

508 European Union Agency for Fundamental Rights (FRA) and Council of Europe, *Handbook on European Data Protection Law*, *o.c.*, p. 54.

509 *Id.* See also Tweede Kamer der Staten-Generaal, Regels inzake de bescherming van persoonsgegevens (Wet bescherming persoonsgegevens) – Memorie van Toelichting, *l.c.*, p. 64.

510 Council of the European Union, Common position (EC) No 1/95 adopted by the Council on 20 February 1995 with a view to adopting Directive 95/…/EC of the European Parliament and of the Council of … on the protection of individuals with regard to the processing of personal data and on the free movement of such data, OJ 13 April 1995, C 93, p. 22. Articles 10 and 11, for instance, may require controllers to inform data subjects of the "recipients or categories of recipients" of their personal data.

511 Article 15(1)c GDPR. Previously: Article 12(a) of Directive 95/46.

512 Interestingly, the corresponding article in Directive 95/46 (Article 12(c)) refers to "third parties" rather than to "recipients". As a result, it would appear that Article 19 GDPR may have a broader scope of application (by virtue of the fact that it envisages all recipients, not just third parties).

513 See also recital (31) GDPR ("*Public authorities to which personal data are disclosed in accordance with a legal obligation for the exercise of their official mission, such as tax and customs authorities, financial investigation units, independent administrative authorities, or financial market authorities responsible for the regulation and supervision of securities markets should not be regarded as recipients if they receive personal data which are necessary to carry*

which are of a limited and specific (as opposed to systemic) nature. Examples might include a targeted fiscal inspection or a judicial inquiry.[514] According to De Bot, the rationale for the exclusion is that such disclosures by definition cannot be anticipated at the moment of collection. As a result, it would not make sense to require controllers to mention such recipients (either towards data subjects at the moment of collection or towards supervisory authorities as part of a notification).[515] Bulk disclosures of personal data between public administrations, outside the context of a specific inquiry, shall in principle not be covered by the exclusion.[516]

C. *Importance of the distinction*

246. Legitimacy of disclosure – The main difference between "third parties" and "recipients" concerns their relationship to the controller and their authorization to access personal data held by the controller.[517] A recipient may belong to the "inner circle" of a particular data processing, by being part of the organisation of either controller or processor. A disclosure to recipients therefore does not *ipso facto* require an additional lawful basis.[518] A third party, on the other hand, is by definition external to the organisation of a controller. The receipt of personal data by the third party will therefore always require an additional lawful basis.[519]

247. Applicable requirements – "Third parties" to whom personal data are disclosed are by definition "recipients", but not all "recipients" are by definition third parties.[520] Every disclosure to a "third party" must therefore comply with provisions regarding third parties and recipients (but not *vice versa*). A processor is always deemed a recipient, but never a third party.[521]

---

out a particular inquiry in the general interest, in accordance with Union or Member State law.")

514 D. De Bot, *Verwerking van persoonsgegevens*, *o.c.*, p. 57.

515 *Ibid*, p. 57–58.

516 See also the Judgment in *Smaranda Bara and Others*, C-201/14, EU:C:2015:638. Interestingly, the issue of whether the CNAS might be considered an "authority" within the meaning of Article 2(g) of Directive 95/46 was not even considered by either the Advocate General or the Court of Justice.

517 European Union Agency for Fundamental Rights (FRA) and Council of Europe, *Handbook on European Data Protection Law*, *o.c.*, p. 54.

518 *Id.*

519 *Id.* ("*The employees of a controller or processor may without further legal requirement be recipients of personal data if they are involved in the processing operations of the controller or processor. On the other hand, a third party, being legally separate from the controller or processor, is not authorised to use personal data processed by the controller, unless on specific legal grounds in a specific case. 'Third-party recipients' of data will, therefore, always need a legal basis for lawfully receiving personal data.*")

520 D. De Bot, *Verwerking van persoonsgegevens*, *o.c.*, p. 57.

521 *Ibid*, p. 55.

D. *A "third group" among those processing personal data?*

248. A "THIRD GROUP"? – Under Directive 95/46, certain commentators argued that the concept of a "*third party to whom personal data are disclosed*", which is mentioned in Article 7(f) of Directive 95/46, should be considered as a separate category of actor which is distinct from controller and processor.[522] According to Salom, Article 7(f) allowed

> "third parties to whom the data are disclosed [...] to process personal data to satisfy a legitimate, unique, and personal interest, however, they must adapt data processing to the purposes and means determined by another entity that controls that process."[523]

Salom categorically rejected the notion that a third party should be in principle be viewed as a controller in his own right:

> "Interpreting that the role of the third party is an interim situation, at the end of which this party will become data controller or data processor depending on the circumstances, is not admissible because the contrast arising between the terms 'data controller' and 'third party' makes this impossible and, moreover, the definition itself of data controller given in Article 2 (d) also prevents undefined situations from arising temporarily."[524]

Examples of such "third parties to whom data are disclosed" are providers of telecommunications or electronic mail service, credit bureaus, list brokers and internet search engines.[525]

249. RATIONALE – At least part of Salom's rationale for carving out a "third group" stems from the difficulties that arise when trying to subject anyone who processes personal data to the legal regime applicable to controllers or processors.[526] Recognition of the "third group" would allow certain data disclosures to take place without bringing its recipients within the direct purview of Directive 95/46. Salom's main argument appears to have been that the interests of data subjects are sufficiently protected by the obligations incumbent upon the controller in case of disclosure to a third party, i.e. prior information, rights of rectification, cancellation and opposition.[527] In addition, recognition of the "third group" would resolve the legal questions and problems that arise when

---

522 J.A. Salom, "'A third party to whom data are disclosed': A third group among those processing data", *l.c.*, p. 177–188.
523 *Ibid*, p. 179–180.
524 *Ibid*, p. 179. Contra: Opinion 1/2010, *l.c.*, p. 31.
525 *Ibid*, p. 183–187.
526 *Ibid*, p. 177.
527 *Ibid*, p. 181–183.

treating all "third parties to whom data are disclosed" as either controllers or processors.[528]

250. Assessment – While both intriguing and innovative, there are reasons to question Salom's argumentation. First, the provisions of Directive 95/46 are written mainly from the perspective of a particular processing operation, as undertaken by a particular controller at a particular moment in time. The textual arguments provided by Salom therefore do not preclude that a "third party to whom data are disclosed" might also, upon receipt, be considered a controller in his own right. Second, the provisions of the Directive which concern disclosures to third parties were not introduced with a view of limiting the obligations of certain entities. Rather, they were introduced because disclosures to third parties were viewed as presenting greater risks to data subjects, requiring additional (rather than less) safeguards.[529] Third, Salom did not offer clear criteria to distinguish between, on the one hand, a third party who merely has a "legitimate interest" and, on the other hand, a third party who determines his own purposes and means.[530] Fourth, the approach advanced by Salom would prevent data subjects from exercising their rights directly against the third party in question, even though data subjects might benefit from the ability to do so.

251. GDPR changes – Article 6(1)f GDPR, which has now replaced Article 7(1)f Directive 95/46, no longer refers to the legitimate interests pursued by the "*third party to whom personal data are disclosed*". Instead, it simply refers to the legitimate interests of "a third party". The textual basis for asserting that the EU legislature would envisage a separate type ("third group") of actor among those processing personal data, is therefore no longer present.

4. SUB-PROCESSING

A. *Directive 95/46*

252. A plurality of processors – Directive 95/46 did not explicitly address the issue of sub-processing. In Opinion 1/2010, the Article 29 Working Party noted, however, that controllers increasingly outsource the processing of personal data to a plurality of processors.[531] The processors in question may

528 *Ibid*, p. 188.
529 See e.g. Commission of the European Communities, Commission Communication on the Protection of individuals in relation to the processing of personal data in the Community and information security, *l.c.*, p. 23.
530 See J.A. Salom, "'A third party to whom data are disclosed': A third group among those processing data", *l.c.*, p. 181.
531 Opinion 1/2010, *l.c.*, p. 27.

each have direct relationship with the controller, or be sub-contractors to which a processor has delegated part of the processing activities entrusted to it ("sub-processors").[532] The possibility of sub-processing was also explicitly recognized in the context of the 2010 standard contractual clauses for international data transfers.[533]

253. Authorisation by the controller – According to the Article 29 Working Party, a processor could only enlist a sub-processor with the prior written consent of the controller.[534] The ability to subcontract a whole or part of the processing could be specified in the initial processing agreement (between controller and processor), or could be agreed upon at a later stage. As to the level of detail, the Working Party considered that

> "while it is not necessary that the controller defines and agrees on all the details of the means used to pursue the envisaged purposes – it would still be necessary that he is at least informed of the main elements of the processing structure (for example, subjects involved, security measures, guarantees for processing in third countries, etc), so that he is still in a position to be in control of the data processed on his behalf."[535]

The Working Party also considered it necessary that there be a clear duty for the processor to name all subcontractors involved and to inform the controller of any intended changes.[536] In addition, the controller should at all times retain the possibility to object to such changes or to terminate the contract.[537] Finally, the Working Party also recommended that the controller should enjoy contractual recourse possibilities in case of breaches of contracts caused by the sub-processors.[538]

---

532 *Id.*

533 Commission Decision of 5 February 2010 on standard contractual clauses for the transfer of personal data to processors established in third countries under Directive 95/46/EC of the European Parliament and of the Council (notified under document C(2010) 593), 2010/87/EU, OJ 12 February 2010, L 39/5–18. Since then, the Article 29 Working Party has developed draft ad hoc contractual clauses for subprocessing from EU based-processor to non-EU based sub-processors: see Article 29 Data Protection Working Party, "Working document 01/2014 on Draft Ad hoc contractual clauses "EU data processor to non-EU sub-processor", WP 214, 21 March 2014.

534 See also Article 29 Data Protection Working Party, "Opinion 05/2012 on Cloud Computing", WP 196, 1 July 2012 p. 10 and Information Commissioner's Office (ICO), "Outsourcing – A guide for small and medium-sized businesses", 28 February 2012, v1.0, p. 6.

535 Opinion 1/2010, *l.c.*, p. 27–28.

536 Article 29 Data Protection Working Party, "Opinion 05/2012 on Cloud Computing", *l.c.*, p. 10.

537 *Id.*

538 *Id.* See also Clause 11 of the Standard Contractual Clauses for (Processors) of 5 February 2010. For more information regarding the contractual elements to be included see also M. Schmidl, "The Challenges of Subprocessing and Suggested Solutions under German and EU Privacy Law", *Bloomberg BNA World Data Protection Report* 2013, Vol. 13, No. 2, p. 1–5.

254. General consent possible – While sub-processing in principle could not take place without the agreement of the controller, the Working Party appeared to accept that a controller might provide a "general prior consent" to allow sub-processing.[539] According to the Article 29 Working Party,

> "it is up to the controller to decide if general prior consent would be sufficient or if specific consent is required for each new sub processing. This decision will probably vary depend on the context of the processing, the type of data (sensitive or not), and the level of involvement of the controller for this type of choice. Some controllers may decide that a full prior check of the identity of each sub processor is necessary while others may consider that prior information [...], the duty to communicate the clause [...] and the guarantee to have the same level of protection [...] are enough."[540]

255. Legal binding – The Article 29 Working Party considered that sub-processors are in essence subject to the same rules as processors. To retain their status as "processor", they must abide by the controller's instructions at all times.[541] The sub-processing contract between processor and sub-processor should also formally bind the sub-processor to adhere to the controller's instructions, as well as to implement the appropriate technical and organisational security measures.[542]

256. Liabilty of initial processor – The initial processor remains liable towards the controller for failure to fulfil his own data processing obligations under the contract.[543]

B. GDPR

257. Codification WP29 guidance – The GDPR has essentially codified much the guidance of Article 29 Working Party regarding sub-processors, at least insofar as it concerns (1) the requirement of prior authorisation; (2) legal

539 Article 29 Data Protection Working Party, "FAQs in order to address some issues raised by the entry into force of the EU Commission Decision 2010/87/EU of 5 February 2010 on standard contractual clauses for the transfer of personal data to processors established in third countries under Directive 95/46/EC", WP176, 12 July 2010, p. 5. See also B. Wojtan, "The new EU Model Clauses: One step forward, two steps back?", *International Data Privacy Law* 2011, Vol. 1, No. 1, p. 77.

540 *Id.*

541 Opinion 1/2010, *l.c.*, p. 27.

542 Tweede Kamer der Staten-Generaal, Regels inzake de bescherming van persoonsgegevens (Wet bescherming persoonsgegevens) – Memorie van Toelichting, *l.c.*, p. 63. See also Clause 11 of the Standard Contractual Clauses (for processors) of 5 February 2010.

543 Tweede Kamer der Staten-Generaal, Regels inzake de bescherming van persoonsgegevens (Wet bescherming persoonsgegevens) – Memorie van Toelichting, *l.c.*, p. 63. See also recital (18) of the Standard Contractual Clauses for (Processors) of 5 February 2010.

binding; and (3) the liability of the initial processor for the sub-processor's failure to fulfil its data protection obligations.

258. Specific or general authorisation – Article 28(2) GDPR stipulates that the processor shall not engage another processor without prior specific or general written authorisation of the controller. In the case of general written authorisation, the processor must inform the controller of any intended changes concerning the addition or replacement of other processors, thereby giving the controller the opportunity to object to such changes.

259. Legal binding – Article 28(4) GDPR provides that:

> "Where a processor engages another processor for carrying out specific processing activities on behalf of the controller, the <u>same data protection obligations</u> as set out in the contract or other legal act between the controller and the processor as referred to in paragraph 3 <u>shall be imposed on that other processor</u> by way of a contract or other legal act under Union or Member State law, in particular providing sufficient guarantees to implement appropriate technical and organisational measures in such a manner that the processing will meet the requirements of this Regulation."

260. Liability of initial processor – Finally, Article 28(4) *in fine* confirms that in case a sub-processor fails to fulfil its data protection obligations as set out in the contract or other legal act between the controller and the processor, the initial processor shall remain fully liable to the controller for the performance of that other processor's obligations.

CHAPTER 7

ADDITIONAL FUNCTIONS OF THE CONTROLLER AND PROCESSOR CONCEPTS

261. Outline – The qualification of an actor as either a controller or processor has implications beyond the allocation of responsibility and liability. To begin with, the qualification is important to determine whether EU data protection law applies to the processing, and if so, to what extent.[544] In addition, determining the appropriate qualification of the actors involved may also be necessary to comply with a number of substantive provisions, in particular provisions regarding (a) transparency of processing; (b) data subject rights; (c) balance of interests and (d) legal binding between controllers and processors.[545] The aim of this section is to briefly elaborate upon the additional functions which the controller and processor concepts fulfil within the regulatory scheme of EU data protection law.

1. TERRITORIAL SCOPE

262. Establishment of controller or processor – Article 3 sets forth when processing of personal data falls within the territorial scope of the GDPR.[546] One of the main factors in each of these instances is the territory in which the controller or processor is established. For example, Article 3(1) stipulates that the GDPR shall apply to the processing of personal data in the context of the activities of an establishment of a controller or a processor in the Union. Determining the territorial scope of the GDPR pursuant to Article 3(1) therefore implies prior identification of the entity which is acting as a "*controller*" or "*processor*" of the processing, as well as the location of its "*establishment(s)*".

---

544 See Opinion 1/2010, *l.c.*, p. 5.

545 See also M. Overkleeft-Verburg, *De Wet persoonsregistraties – norm, toepassing en evaluatie*, *o.c.*, p. 381.

546 Cf. *supra*, nos. 42 et seq.

263. SEPARATE APPLICATION – The EDPB has taken the view that when it comes to the identification of the different obligations triggered by the applicability of the GDPR, the processing by each entity (controller or processor) must be considered separately. The GDPR envisages different and dedicated provisions or obligations applying to data controllers and processors respectively, and as such, should a data controller or processor be subject to the GDPR, the related obligations would apply to them respectively and separately.[547] As a result, the EDPB also considers it important to consider the establishment of the controller and processor separately for purposes of Article 3.[548]

264. TARGETING OR MONITORING – Similar considerations also apply in the context of Article 3(2) GDPR. Article 3(2) determines the territorial scope of the GDPR in case of processing of personal data by a controller or processor not established in the Union. Again, the determination of whether or not the GDPR applies is linked to the identification of which entity is acting as a "controller" or "processor". Article 3(2) only applies when the controller or processor does not have a relevant establishment on EU/EEA territory.[549]

265. DIMINISHED RELEVANCE – The territorial scope of the GDPR is triggered by the establishment (or not) of both controllers and processors. Under Directive 95/46, only the establishment (or not) of the controller was a relevant consideration. Under the GDPR, the distinction between controllers and processors is longer decisive. While Article 3 still includes a reference to both the concept of "controller" or "processor", the importance of the right qualification shall mainly be relevant in determining the extent of obligations applicable to the entity in question (as it also in case of intra-EU processing).

---

547 European Data Protection Board, "Guidelines 3/2018 on the territorial scope of the GDPR (Article 3) – Version for public consultation", 16 November 2018, p. 9.

548 *Ibid*, p. 10. In this context, the EDPB has also stated that the existence of a processor in the EU should not be considered to be an "establishment" of a data controller within the meaning of Article 3(1) merely by virtue of its status as processor. The existence of a relationship between a controller and a processor does not necessarily trigger the application of the GDPR to both, should one of these two entities not be established in the Union. (*Ibid*, p. 9).

549 See also Article 29 Data Protection Working Party, "Opinion 8/2010 on applicable law", *l.c.*, p. 19. Arguably, the application of Article 3(2) is not prevented if the controller only has an "irrelevant" establishment on EU territory. (*Id.*) The Article 29 Working Party has thus chosen to give this phrase a functional rather than literal interpretation of the phrase "*the controller is not established on EU territory*".

2. COMPLIANCE WITH SUBSTANTIVE PROVISIONS

2.1. TRANSPARENCY OF PROCESSING

266. Identity disclosure – Articles 13 and 14 of the GDPR, which set forth the information to be given by the controller to the data subject, specify that the data subject must in principle be informed of the identity of the controller and/or his representative.[550] When the processing involves multiple actors, compliance with this obligation will require them to formally establish the role of each actor in order to determine whether or not the data subject must be informed of their identity as such.[551] As a rule, the identity of any controller(s) involved in the processing must always be disclosed. In contrast, the identity of the processor must not necessarily be communicated to the data subject. Indeed, in accordance with Article 13(1)e and 14(1)e, it may be sufficient to inform the data subject of the categories of recipients rather than providing the name of the recipients as such.

2.2. DATA SUBJECT RIGHTS

267. Accommodation – Every controller is obliged to accommodate data subject rights.[552] Even if he appoints another entity to act as a point of contact, he cannot escape the fact that he remains ultimately responsible for ensuring an appropriate accommodation data subject rights. The data subject may always approach a (joint) controller directly to request access, erasure or restriction.[553] Determining the appropriate qualification of the actors involved is therefore necessary to properly organize the accommodation of data subject rights.

268. Authority to decide – The controller is in principle also the entity who has the authority to decide whether to grant or refuse a request made by a data subject.[554] Pursuant to Article 29 GDPR, the processor may only process the data on instructions from the controller, unless he is required to do so by

---

550 Cf. *supra*, no. 54 et seq.

551 This shall particularly be the case where the notice that is provided to the data subject seeks to address the notice obligations of multiple controllers. This may be done for a variety of purposes, e.g. to address the fact that not every controller has the ability to communicate directly with the data subject at the moment of data collection.

552 See Articles 12–22 GDPR. See also *supra*, no. 56 et seq.

553 In case of joint control, Article 26(3) GDPR stipulates that irrespective of the terms of any arrangement among the joint controllers, the data subject may exercise his or her rights in respect of and against each of the controllers. See also *supra*, nos. 141–144.

554 See also M. Overkleeft-Verburg, *De Wet persoonsregistraties – norm, toepassing en evaluatie*, *o.c.*, p. 381.

law.[555] As a result, a processor may not accommodate data subject rights on his own initiative, without prior authorisation by the controller.

2.3. BALANCE OF INTERESTS

269. Interested parties – EU data protection law restricts the instances in which the processing of personal data may take place. In particular, Article 6(1) of the GDPR enumerates several legal grounds, of which at least one must be present in order for the processing of personal data to be considered "lawful" for purposes of EU data protection law.[556] Article 6(1)f makes reference to the legitimate interests pursued "*by the controller or by a third party*". The potential interests of the processor are not mentioned. As a result, only the legitimate interests of the controller or of "third parties" may be taken into account when determining the legitimacy of processing pursuant to Article 6(1)(f). Articles 6(1) e, 9(2)b and 10 GDPR similarly only make reference to the rights, obligations or authority of the controller, not of the processor.

2.4. LEGAL BINDING

270. Contract or other act – Article 28(3) of the GDPR stipulates that when a controller engages a processor to carry out certain processing operations on his behalf, their relationship must be governed by a contract or other legal act which contains certain mandatory provisions.[557] Article 26(1) GDPR, in turn, stipulates that joint controllers shall in principle determine their respective responsibilities for compliance, in particular as regards the exercise of data subject rights and their respective duties to provide the information, by means of an arrangement between them. The arrangement may designate a contact point for data subjects.[558] The qualification of an actor as either a controller, joint controller, or processor therefore has immediate implications for the contractual arrangements that should be in place between the entities involved in the processing. The same also applies in the context of an international data transfer, where an appropriate qualification of each actor is necessary for determining what type of EU model contract should be used.[559]

555 Previously: Article 16 Directive 95/46.
556 Cf. *supra*, no. 50.
557 Cf. *supra*, no. 96. Previously: Article 17(3) of Directive 95/46.
558 Cf. *supra*, no. 141.
559 See also P. Van Eecke, M. Truyens et al. (eds.), "The future of online privacy and data protection", *l.c.*, p. 32 at note 162.

CHAPTER 8
CONCLUSION

271. Allocation of responsibility and liability – Within the regulatory scheme of EU data protection law, the controller carries the primary responsibility for ensuring compliance. At the moment of its enactment, the EU legislature was mindful of the practice whereby one organisation requests another organisation to perform certain processing operations on its behalf. By introducing the concept of a "processor", the EU legislature hoped to be able address this situation and to ensure a continuous level of protection.[560]

272. Relationship controller-processor – The Article 29 Working Party has approximated the relationship between controllers and processors with the figure of delegation. The analogy appears to be founded on a number of considerations. In first instance, a processor acts "on behalf" of a controller and is called upon to abide by the instructions given by the controller.[561] Secondly, the consequences of the processor's actions are in principle attributed to the controller, provided that the processor merely follows the latter's instructions. Finally, the delegation figure also permits the delegate (processor) to exercise a certain amount of discretion on how to best serve the principal's (controller's) interests.[562]

273. Mulitplicity of control – Not every collaboration involving the processing of personal data among two separate actors implies the existence of a controller-processor relationship. It is equally possible that each actor processes personal data for their own distinct purposes, in which case each actor is likely to be considered a controller independently of the other. It is also possible that collaborating actors jointly exercise decision-making power concerning the purposes and means of the processing, in which case they are considered to act as joint or (co) controllers.

---

560 The provisions which regulate the relationship between controllers and processors were in fact intended to ensure that such outsourcing arrangements did not result in a lowering of protection enjoyed by data subjects. Cf. *supra*, nos. 86 et seq. See also *infra*, no. 551.

561 Opinion 1/2010, *l.c.*, p. 25.

562 See Opinion 1/2010, *l.c.*, p. 25.

274. Varying degrees of contractual flexibility – The GDPR has devoted several provisions to the relationship between controllers and processors. Article 28(3) specifies that the relationship between controller and processor shall be governed by a contract or other legal act, which must contain, at a minimum, all the elements mentioned in this provision. As far as joint controllers are concerned, Article 26(1) GDPR stipulates that they shall in principle determine their respective responsibilities for compliance, in particular as regards the exercise of data subject rights and their respective duties to provide the information, by means of an arrangement between them. The contrast, in terms of detail, between Article 28(3) and Article 26(1) of the GDPR is striking. Already under Directive 95/46, the Article 29 Working noted that controllers and joint controllers enjoy considerable freedom when determining how to best allocate responsibility amongst each other, "as long as they ensure full compliance".[563] The result is that collaborating (co-)controllers are in principle free to assign responsibilities, whereas controller-processor relationships must be modelled according to a pre-defined format.

275. Various degrees of responsibility – The distinction between controllers and processors forms the basis upon which compliance with the requirements of the GDPR is allocated. Determining the role of each actor involved in the processing is therefore essential to properly understand its responsibilities under the GDPR. Certain obligations are only applicable to controllers and not to processors. Other obligations are only indirectly applicable to processors. Finally, the extent of certain obligations also varies depending controller or processor status.[564]

276. Varying liability exposure – Whether an actor is considered a controller, co-controller or processor has important implications in terms of liability exposure. Controllers can face liability not only for their own activities, but also for the activities of their processors. Processors, on the other hand, shall in principle only be liable if they have not complied with obligations of the Regulation specifically directed to processors or where they have acted outside or contrary to lawful instructions of the controller. Moreover, the liability exposure of different controllers working together may vary depending on whether or not they are seen to act as "separate" controllers or "joint" controllers.

277. Additional functions – The legal status of an actor as either a controller or processor is not only important for issues of liability, but also has important implications. First, the qualification of an actor as either a controller or processor

563 Opinion 1/2010, *l.c.*, p. 24.
564 Cf. *supra*, no. 118 et seq.

is an important element in determining whether EU data protection law applies to the processing, and if so, to what extent. Second, several other provisions of the Directive make explicit reference to either the "controller" or a "processor". This is quite natural, as these concepts serve primarily as vehicles to convey the respective obligations of these actors. However, for certain provisions of the GDPR it is also necessary to know which role a particular actor has assumed towards the processing in order to be able to comply with them.[565]

565 Cf. *supra*, nos. 266-270.

PART III

HISTORICAL-COMPARATIVE ANALYSIS

CHAPTER 1
INTRODUCTION

"You have to know the past to understand the present".
Dr. Carl Sagan, 1980[566]

278. Preface – The concepts of controller and processor were not created out of thin air. Prior to Directive 95/46 and the GDPR, many other data protection instruments incorporated concepts with similar meaning and scope. The objective of this Part of the book is to enhance the understanding of the meaning and role of the controller and concepts by tracing the origin and development of these concepts over time.

279. Relevant periods – When one looks at EU data protection law from a historical perspective, four main periods can be distinguished, namely:

(1) the emergence of national data protection laws (1970–1980);
(2) internationalisation (1980–1981);
(3) national implementation (1982–1994);
(4) European harmonisation (1995–2016).

280. Selection criteria – In principle, every data protection instrument adopted during each of the aforementioned periods is worthy of analysis. A selection must be made, however, if only for practical reasons. Two criteria have guided the selection made here, namely (1) the desire to be comprehensive (i.e. to avoid large gaps in terms of chronology); and (2) ease of access and language considerations.[567]

281. Application – For the first period, three data protection laws were chosen, namely the data protection laws of Hesse, Sweden and France. The Hessian and Swedish acts were chosen simply because they represent the very

566 Carl Sagan, "One Voice in the Cosmic Fugue", *Cosmos*: Episode 2, available at https://www.youtube.com/watch?v=7-I7jP5fNcE (55:35) (last accessed 20 January 2019).
567 For a discussion of potential selection criteria for comparative law purposes see A.E. Oderkerk, *De preliminaire fase van het rechtsvergelijkend onderzoek*, Ph. D. Thesis, 1999, Amsterdam Center for International Law (ACIL), p. 47–60 and p. 221–239.

first national data protection laws. The French data protection act was selected to bridge the gap between the first data protection laws the first international instruments of data protection and on the basis of language considerations. For the second period, Convention 108 and the OECD Guidelines on the Protection of Privacy and Transborder Flows of Personal Data ("OECD Guidelines") and Council of Europe Convention for the protection of individuals with regard to automatic processing of personal data ("Convention 108") were selected. An analysis of Convention 108 was deemed indispensable, as it provided the normative framework of the national implementations in the period that followed. The analysis of the OECD guidelines was deemed beneficial as the Guidelines were developed in parallel with Convention 108, and therefore offer additional insights into the meaning of the concepts employed by Convention 108. For the third period, two data protection laws were selected, namely the 1984 UK Data Protection Act and the 1992 Belgian data protection act. Again, this selection was driven by the desire to be comprehensive from a chronological perspective as well as by language considerations. Finally, Directive 95/46 and the GDPR were selected as the two instruments of European harmonisation simply because they are the focal point of this book.

282. Sources – The historical-comparative analysis conducted in this Part shall be primarily dogmatic in nature. To the extent possible, the analysis shall be based on primary sources (i.e. legislation, formal declarations and guidelines issued by the relevant institutions). Where appropriate, however, reference may also be made to preparatory works and explanatory memoranda, jurisprudence, and doctrinal accounts.

283. Analysis – Each of the selected instruments of data protection regulation will be analysed in a structured and focused manner.[568] Specifically, each instrument will include an analysis of:

(1) the origin and development of the instrument in question;
(2) its scope *ratione materiae*;
(3) its basic protections; and
(4) the manner in which responsibility and liability are allocated (scope *ratione personae*).

With respect to the fourth element, the following questions will guide the analysis:

568 The analysis is "structured" in the sense that the analysis of each law is composed of the same subsection and seeks to answer the same questions in relation to each use case. The analysis is "focused" in that the analysis extends only to those aspects which are relevant for purposes of the research question which this Part seeks to address. Based on A.L. George and A. Bennet, *Case Studies and Theory Development in the Social Sciences*, *o.c.*, p. 67 et seq.

(1) how are actors and roles defined?
(2) how is responsibility and liability allocated among the identified actors?
(3) what is the threshold for responsibility and liability?
(4) how prescriptive is the regulation of the relationship among actors involved in the processing?

284. Outline – Before delving into the analysis of specific national data protection laws, a brief overview shall be given of how European data protection laws came into existence. Next, three of the earliest data protection laws (i.e. of Hesse, Sweden and France) are analysed. After that, two international instruments of data protection are discussed, namely the OECD Guidelines on the Protection of Privacy and Transborder Flows of Personal Data ("OECD Guidelines") and Council of Europe Convention for the protection of individuals with regard to automatic processing of personal data ("Convention 108"). Next, two national data protection laws implementing Convention 108 are analysed, namely the UK and Belgian data protection acts, followed by a discussion of the legislative development of Directive 95/46. Finally, the General Data Protection Regulation (GDPR) and its legislative development will be analysed. By way of conclusion, a summary overview will be provided of how the controller and processor concepts evolved over time.

CHAPTER 2

THE EMERGENCE OF DATA PROTECTION LAW

1. HISTORICAL CONTEXT

285. Introduction – Data protection emerged as a policy issue in a time of profound social and economic change.[569] In the 1960s, as society continued its transition from an industrial to a post-industrial economy, many European nations introduced comprehensive social reforms.[570] Administering these reforms would oblige governments to collect and process significant amounts of data about their citizens.[571] Thanks to the advances in computing technology, governments would be able to process these data in an automated fashion. Initially, the use of computer applications had been confined to tasks related to research and planning.[572] Towards the middle of the 1960s, however, computers started to make their appearance in daily administration, thereby increasing public awareness.[573] This awareness in turn led to the realization that the application of information technology might alter the nature of the relationship between the individual and the state.[574]

286. Catalysts – The public debate regarding the use of automated data processing techniques was fuelled by a number of catalysts. First, several governments were developing plans for centralized and computerized *population data banks*.[575] These plans triggered public concerns regarding the ability of the state to infringe upon the privacy of its citizens, for example by creating "crib-to-grave dossiers", or by developing "comprehensive systems of

569 C.J. Bennet, *Regulating privacy. Data Protection and Public Policy in Europe and the United States*, *o.c.*, p. 14.

570 V. Mayer-Schönberger, "Generational Development of Data Protection in Europe", in P.E. Agre and M. Rotenberg (eds.), *Technology and Privacy: The New Landscape*, 1998, London, MIT Press, p. 222.

571 *Id.*

572 F.W. Hondius, *Emerging data protection in Europe*, *o.c.*, p. 3–4.

573 *Id.*

574 C.J. Bennet, *Regulating privacy. Data Protection and Public Policy in Europe and the United States*, *o.c.*, p. ix.

575 *Ibid*, p. 46–49. See also V. Mayer-Schönberger, "Generational Development of Data Protection in Europe", *l.c.*, p. 222–223.

data surveillance".[576] Closely related to this issue were the proposals to introduce (or extend the use of) *personal identification numbers* for citizens.[577] As these numbers facilitate the linkage of information across record-keeping systems, these proposals augmented the concern that governments might at some point start to use citizens' information against them. A third cause for public alarm were the scheduled *population censuses*.[578] Several censuses scheduled around 1970 helped bring privacy questions to the public attention, both because of the seemingly intrusive nature of the questions asked, as well as the use of automation in the census processes.[579] Finally, an array of "*alarmist" publications* which emerged in the late 1960s and 1970s also served to draw public attention to the dangers computers might pose to the rights and freedoms of individuals.[580]

287. Little brother – Of course, the use of information technology was not limited to the public sector alone. Private sector entities were likewise exploring the use of automated data processing to improve the efficiency of their daily operations.[581] Many felt that individuals should also be protected from intrusive data processing carried out by private sector entities. However, the establishment of data protection rules for the public sector was generally regarded as the most urgent matter.[582] As a result, the earliest instruments of data protection regulation focused on the use of automated data processing by the public sector. Quite soon, however, legislative initiatives which encompassed private sector processing activities were being considered as well.[583]

2. RATIONALE

288. Why data protection? – The growing use of computing applications was perceived as posing a threat to individuals' rights and freedoms, in particular

576 R. Turn and W.H. Ware, "Privacy and Security Issues in Information Systems", *IEEE Transactions on Computers* 1976, Vol. C-25, No. 12, p. 153.

577 C.J. Bennet, *Regulating privacy. Data Protection and Public Policy in Europe and the United States, o.c.*, p. 49. See also G. Stadler and T. Herzog, "Data Protection: International Trends and the Austrian Example", Guest Seminar at the International Institute for Applied Systems analysis, Laxenburg, Austria, 1981, p. 5 and L.A. Bygrave, *Data Protection Law. Approaching its Rationale, Logic and Limits, o.c.*, p. 94.

578 C.J. Bennet, *Regulating privacy. Data Protection and Public Policy in Europe and the United States, o.c.*, p. 51.

579 *Id.*

580 *Ibid*, p. 53.

581 See e.g. A.R. Miller, "Personal Privacy in the Computer Age: The Challenge of a New Technology in an Information-Oriented Society", *Michigan Law Review* 1969, vol. 67, p. 1105; F.W. Hondius, *Emerging data protection in Europe, o.c.*, p. 7–8; L.A. Bygrave, *Data Protection Law. Approaching its Rationale, Logic and Limits, o.c.*, p. 97–98.

582 F.W. Hondius, *Emerging data protection in Europe, o.c.*, p. 22–23.

583 F.W. Hondius, *Emerging data protection in Europe, o.c.*, p. 20 (Table 6).

their right to privacy.[584] This perception of risk was closely related to the new capabilities offered by emerging computing technologies.[585] First, computers were making it increasingly easy to aggregate large amounts of information.[586] Until then, records containing personal information generally remained scattered across different filing systems in different departments and organisations.[587] Simply finding a particular piece of information could be a challenge.[588] With the help of computers, however, the information retrieval process would be greatly facilitated and accelerated. Computers also made it easier and cheaper to store information. As a result, one could expect that, over time, more and more data would be recorded and that these records would be kept for increasingly long periods of time.[589] This information could in turn be made readily available to an increasing number of parties, who could use it for a variety of purposes.[590] The combination of these elements gave rise to a vision of a future in which the individual would become completely transparent; whereby personal freedom would be dependent on the outcome of obscure data processing practices.[591]

3. GOALS OF DATA PROTECTION REGULATION

289. Overview – The primary goal of data protection legislation is to protect individuals (and by extension, society) against harms resulting from the misuse of their personal data.[592] To this end, these laws have instituted a variety of

584 *Ibid*, p. 7 (noting that "The demand for appropriate measures was motivated not so much by indications that abuse had actually occurred but rather by the fear and risk of abuses".) See also the discussion of future risks in Commission Informatique et Libertés, *Rapport de la Commission Informatique et libertés*, 1975, La Documentation Française, Paris, p. 14–17.

585 L.A. Bygrave, *Data Protection Law. Approaching its Rationale, Logic and Limits*, *o.c.*, p. 93. See also e.g. Home Office (Great Britain), *Computers and Privacy*, Cmnd. 653, Her Majesty's Stationary Office (HMSO), London, 1975; reproduced by Home Office (Great Britain), *Report of the Committee on Data Protection*, Cmnd. 7341, London, HMSO, 1978, p. 451.

586 G. Stadler and T. Herzog, "Data Protection: International Trends and the Austrian Example", *l.c.*, p. 4–5.

587 J. A. Cannataci, *Privacy and Data Protection Law: International Development and Maltese Perspectives*, Norwegian University Press, Oslo, 1986, p. 65.

588 *Id.*

589 See C.J. Bennet, *Regulating privacy. Data Protection and Public Policy in Europe and the United States*, *o.c.*, p. 17 (citing P. Sieghart, *Privacy and Computers*, London, Latimer, 1976, p. 75–76).

590 *Id.*

591 See also L.A. Bygrave, *Data Protection Law. Approaching its Rationale, Logic and Limits*, *o.c.*, p. 94–95. In 1968, one member of the UK Parliament *"could picture the stage being reached when a button was pressed and if the computer gave the "thumbs down" sign, he would never get a license"*. (C.J. Bennet, *Regulating privacy. Data Protection and Public Policy in Europe and the United States*, *o.c.*, p. 45; citing M. Warner and M. Stone, *The Data Bank Society: Organisations, Computers and Social Freedom*, London, Allen & Unwin, 1970, p. 105).

592 P. De Hert and S. Gutwirth, "Privacy, data protection and law enforcement. Opacity of the individual and transparency of power", *l.c.*, p. 76.

procedural safeguards to protect individuals, in particular their right to privacy, in relation to such processing.[593] Generally speaking, one can discern three sets of interrelated goals underlying the provisions of data protection legislation, namely a desire to[594]:

1. Protect individuals' privacy and related societal values;
2. Enhance the accountability of record-keepers and users of personal information; and
3. Improve the integrity and efficiency of decision-making processes.

290. Privacy and related values – Most data protection instruments identify privacy protection as one of the primary justifications for their enactment.[595] A shaky foundation, one might say, as the right to privacy is generally considered "notoriously difficult to define".[596] Over time, privacy has been construed in a variety of ways, most notably as (a) a right "to be let alone"; (b) limited access to the "self"; (c) confidentiality; (d) control over one's personal information; and (e) the ability to make personal choices and develop relationships without undue interference.[597] Privacy is also generally considered instrumental for the protection of a range of related societal values, such as individuality, autonomy and dignity.[598] While there is no consensus regarding a definition of the right to privacy, the various conceptualizations have – to a lesser or greater extent – found their application in provisions of data protection regulation.[599] For example, the data subject rights of erasure or restriction of

---

593 *Ibid*, p. 77; P. De Hert and S. Gutwirth, "Data Protection and the Case Law of Strasbourg and Luxemburg: Constitutionalism in Action", in S. Gutwirth, Y. Poullet, P. De Hert, J. Nouwt and C. De Terwangne (eds.), *Reinventing data protection?*, Springer Science, Dordrecht, 2009, p. 9.

594 Based on C.J. Bennet, *Regulating privacy. Data Protection and Public Policy in Europe and the United States*, *o.c.*, p. 44; P. De Hert and S. Gutwirth, "Privacy, data protection and law enforcement. Opacity of the individual and transparency of power", *l.c.*, p. 77; L.A. Bygrave, *Data Protection Law. Approaching its Rationale, Logic and Limits*, *o.c.*, p. 107–112. See also J. Bing, "A Comparative Outline of Privacy Legislation", *Comparative Law Yearbook* 1978, Vol. 2, p. 170 et seq., who differentiates between "the interest in adequate information", "the interest in discretion" and "the interest in being informed".

595 See also J. Bing, "A Comparative Outline of Privacy Legislation", *l.c.*, p. 170.

596 See e.g. P.E. Agre, "Introduction", in P.E. Agre and M. Rotenberg (eds.), *Technology and Privacy: The New Landscape*, 1998, London, MIT Press, p. 6; L.A. Bygrave, *Data Protection Law. Approaching its Rationale, Logic and Limits*, *o.c.*, p. 126.

597 For a comprehensive overview of the various meanings attributed to the concept of privacy see D. Solove, "Conceptualising Privacy", *California Law Review* 2002, Vol. 90, p. 1087–1155. See also L.A. Bygrave, *Data Protection Law. Approaching its Rationale, Logic and Limits*, *o.c.*, p. 125 et seq; P.E. Agre, "Introduction", *l.c.*, p. 6–7.

598 L.A. Bygrave, *Data Protection Law. Approaching its Rationale, Logic and Limits*, *o.c.*, p. 133–136. Privacy is at times also seen as a necessary condition for the effective enjoyment of other fundamental rights, such as the freedom of expression.

599 See also J. Bing, "A Comparative Outline of Privacy Legislation", *l.c.*, p. 174–175.

processing[600] can be seen as (partial) manifestations of a right to control the circulation of one's personal information. Similarly, the special treatment of certain types of "sensitive" data (e.g. data relating to health or sex life)[601], can be seen as an effort to limit access to individuals' more intimate personal details.[602] None of the aforementioned conceptualizations of privacy can, however, provide a comprehensive (let alone exhaustive) account of all the rights and obligations found in data protection law.

291. Knowledge is power – A second set of concerns surrounding the increase in computer usage revolved around the issue of information asymmetry. While individuals were becoming increasingly transparent, the organisational practices involving their personal data were becoming increasingly opaque. This was perceived as a threat to the balance of power that existed between individuals, organisations and governments.[603] The use of computing technology would make it much easier to collect and analyse personal data, thereby increasing record-keepers' abilities to surreptitiously manipulate individuals' behaviour or to exercise other forms of social control.[604] Many data protection laws have sought to mitigate these risks by introducing specific duties to inform and dedicated oversight mechanisms.[605] These measures can be seen both as efforts to reduce the information asymmetries among the various stakeholders (by imposing transparency) and/or as "checks" against abusive record-keeping practices (by enhancing the accountability of public and private record-keepers).[606]

---

600 See e.g. Articles 17–18 GDPR (previously: Article 12(c) Directive 95/46/EC).

601 See e.g. Article 9 GDPR (previously: Article 8 Directive 95/46/EC).

602 For a more comprehensive account of the legal manifestations of the various conceptualizations of privacy and related societal values see L.A. Bygrave, *Data Protection Law. Approaching its Rationale, Logic and Limits*, *o.c.*, p. 153–156.

603 G. Stadler and T. Herzog, *l.c.*, p. 4; R. Turn and W.H. Ware, *l.c.*, p. 1354; L.A. Bygrave, *Data Protection Law. Approaching its Rationale, Logic and Limits*, *o.c.*, p. 107. For a more detailed treatise of "information as power" see also P. Seipel, "The Right to Know – Computers and Information Power", in P. Blume (ed.), *Nordic Studies in Information Technology and Law*, Computer/Law series no. 7, Deventer, Kluwer, 1991, p. 7–43. Some were also fearful that computers might unduly strengthen the power of the executive vis-à-vis the legislative branch of government, as evidenced by the Hessian Data Protection Act. See F.W. Hondius, *Emerging data protection in Europe*, *o.c.*, p. 5–6 and H. Burkert, "Privacy – Data Protection A German/European Perspective", in C. Engel K.H. Keller (eds.), *Governance of Global Networks in the Light of Differing Local Values*, 2000, Baden-Baden, Nomos, p. 45.

604 L.A. Bygrave, *Data Protection Law. Approaching its Rationale, Logic and Limits*, *o.c.*, p. 103 and 107; C.J. Bennet, *Regulating privacy. Data Protection and Public Policy in Europe and the United States*, *o.c.*, p. 19 and 29; J. A. Cannataci, *Privacy and Data Protection Law: International Development and Maltese Perspectives*, *o.c.*, p. 60 and 64.

605 See also J. Bing, "A Comparative Outline of Privacy Legislation", *l.c.*, p. 176–178 (relating such provisions to a general "interest in being informed").

606 See also S. Rodotà, "Data Protection – Some problems for Newcomers", in Council of Europe, *Legislation and Data Protection. Proceedings of the Rome Conference on problems relating to the development and application of legislation on data protection*, 1983, Rome, Camera dei

292. Data quality – A third objective common to most data protection laws is improving the integrity and efficiency of decision-making processes.[607] The use of inaccurate, incomplete or irrelevant information in a decision-making process can be more detrimental to the individual concerned than a breach of confidentiality.[608] As computers made it easier to store information for prolonged periods of time, and to make the same information available to a wide variety of users, the risk of harms resulting from the reliance upon erroneous data was expected to increase.[609] Several data protection requirements can be seen as efforts to "sanitize the informational environment"[610]; in particular those provisions which seek to impose limits upon the collection[611] and storage[612] of information, or provisions which require that recorded information be kept up-to-date[613] or limit the use of such data to a particular context.[614]

4. NATIONAL AND INTERNATIONAL DEVELOPMENT

293. National data protection laws before 1980 – The first data protection law was adopted at regional rather than national level, namely by the German Land of Hesse. The Hessian Act of 7 October 1970 was the first

Deputati, p. 188. Of course, transparency and accountability are closely related to one and other: "what is in the dark cannot be scrutinized" (M. Hildebrandt and B.J. Koops, "The Challenges of Ambient Law and Legal Protection in the Profiling Era", *The Modern Law Review* 2010, p. 449. On the role of accountability as a data protection principle over time see also J. Alhadeff, B. Van Alsenoy and J. Dumortier, "The accountability principle in data protection regulation: origin, development and future directions", in D. Guagnin, L. Hempel, C. Ilten a.o. (eds.), *Managing Privacy through Accountability*, Houndmills (UK), Palgrave Macmillan, 2012, p. 49–82.

607 C.J. Bennet, *Regulating privacy. Data Protection and Public Policy in Europe and the United States*, *o.c.*, p. 44; L.A. Bygrave, *Data Protection Law. Approaching its Rationale, Logic and Limits*, *o.c.*, p. 105 et seq.

608 See also J. Bing, "A Comparative Outline of Privacy Legislation", *l.c.*, p. 170–171 ("*One prime form of misuse is the use of non-relevant information in a decision process; or the negligence to take into consideration information which the person in question himself holds as relevant.*").

609 C.J. Bennet, *Regulating privacy. Data Protection and Public Policy in Europe and the United States*, *o.c.*, p. 35. See e.g. A.R. Miller, "Personal Privacy in the Computer Age: The Challenge of a New Technology in an Information-Oriented Society", *l.c.*, p. 1114.

610 L.A. Bygrave, *Data Protection Law. Approaching its Rationale, Logic and Limits*, *o.c.*, p. 137.

611 See e.g. Article 5(1)c GDPR (previously: Article 6(1)c Directive 95/46/EC).

612 See e.g. Article 5(1)e GDPR (previously: Article 6(1)e Directive 95/46/EC).

613 See e.g. Article 6(1)d GDPR (previously: Article 6(1)d Directive 95/46/EC).

614 See e.g. Article 5(1)a GDPR (previously: Article 6(1)a Directive 95/46/EC). Of course, limitations upon the collection, storage and use of information can also be seen as an attempt to help secure privacy and related societal values (by imposing limits on the collection of privacy-sensitive information and reducing the risk that information be used out of context). However, it is clear that the drafters of data protection laws were concerned with information quality in addition to privacy and integrity (see L.A. Bygrave, *Data Protection Law. Approaching its Rationale, Logic and Limits*, *o.c.*, p. 137).

legislative act to establish data protection rules of general application.[615] The first national data protection law was adopted by Sweden in 1973, followed in 1978 by Germany, France, Denmark, Norway and Austria. By the end of 1970s a total of seven European countries had enacted general data protection laws.[616] In the following chapter, the data protection laws of Hesse, Sweden and France will be investigated as exemplifications of the regulatory approach embodied by the earliest data protection laws.

294. International instruments – Although individual accounts vary, the first discussions among international policymakers on the need for data protection may be situated towards the end of the 1960s.[617] By the beginning of the 1970s, both the Council of Europe and the OECD were engaged in dedicated efforts to evaluate the privacy issues related to data banks.[618] Eventually, those efforts resulted in the Guidelines on the Protection of Privacy and Transborder Flows of Personal Data (OECD) and the Convention for the protection of individuals with regard to automatic processing of personal data (Council of Europe), which were finalized in 1980 and 1981 respectively.

295. National data protection laws after 1981 – Following the adoption of Convention 108, several Member States of the Council of Europe enacted their first national data protection laws.[619] Despite the growing convergence among national data protection laws, notable differences remained, reflecting the different national traditions in policymaking, constitutional norms and socio-economic environments.[620]

296. European harmonisation – By the mid-1980s it was becoming clear that further harmonization would be necessary in order to secure the proper functioning of the EU internal market.[621] In 1990, the European Commission

615 M. D. Kirby, "Transborder Data Flows and the "Basic Rules" of Data Privacy, *Stanford Journal of International Law* 1980, vol. 16, p. 39.

616 N. Platten, "Chapter 2: Background to and History of the Directive", in D. Bainbridge, *EC Data Protection Directive*, London, Butterworths, 1996, p. 14.

617 Compare e.g. F.H. Cate, "The EU Data Protection Directive, Information Privacy, and the Public Interest", *l.c.*, 431 with D. Campbell and J. Fisher (eds.), *Data transmission and privacy*, Center for International Legal Studies, Martinus Nijhoff Publishers, Dordrecht, 1994, vii.

618 H. Burkert, "Privacy – Data Protection A German/European Perspective", *l.c.*, p. 51.

619 For a chronological overview see C.J. Bennet, *Regulating privacy. Data Protection and Public Policy in Europe and the United States*, p. 57.

620 For a detailed discussion of the different factors contributing to divergence see C.J. Bennet, *Regulating privacy. Data Protection and Public Policy in Europe and the United States*, p. 194 et seq. who describes five possible explanations for policy divergence: (1) formal constitutional norms; (2) preferences and influence of dominant social groups; (3) electoral politics and partisan ideology; (4) the position and power of national bureaucracies; and (5) economic constraints.

621 N. Platten, "Chapter 2: Background to and History of the Directive", *l.c.*, 23–24.

put forth its first draft for a "Council Directive on the Protection of Individuals with regard to the processing of personal data and on the free movement of such data", which eventually led to the adoption of Directive 95/46/EC. Fifteen years later, many stakeholders felt that even greater harmonisation was necessary. In 2012, the Commission released its initial proposal for a General Data Protection Regulation, which in turn eventually led to the adoption of the GDPR in 2016.

CHAPTER 3

NATIONAL DATA PROTECTION LAWS BEFORE 1980

297. OUTLINE – This chapter will analyse three of the earliest data protection laws, namely the Hessian Data Protection Act of 7 October 1970[622], the Swedish Data Act of 11 May 1973[623] and the French Law on Informatics, Files and Liberties of 6 January 1978.[624] The objective of this analysis is to ascertain how the early data protection laws allocated responsibility for complying with the norms they contained. For each instrument, the analysis will commence with a discussion of the origin and development of the instrument in question. Next, the scope *ratione materiae* of each instrument shall be discussed, followed by an overview of the basic protections it contains. Finally, a separate section shall be dedicated to an analysis of how each instrument allocates responsibility and liability.

1. THE HESSE DATA PROTECTION ACT (1970)

1.1. ORIGIN AND DEVELOPMENT

298. A TALE OF HOPE AND DISENCHANTMENT – Following the "Great Hessen plan" of 1965, the German Federal State ("*Land*") of Hesse embarked upon a large-scale data collection exercise. The goal of this exercise was to assist the government in its development of long-term policies in economic and social matters, such as finance and social security.[625] In 1969, the government enacted

---

[622] Hesse Data Protection Act of 7 October 1970 ["*Hessen Datenschutzgesetz vom 7. Oktober 1970*"], *Gesetz- und Verordnungsblatt für das Land Hessen* (HE GVBl), 12 October 1970, no. 41, Part I, p. 625–627.

[623] Swedish Data Act of 11 May 1973 ["*Datalagen*"], SFS 1973: 289.

[624] Law no. 78-17 of 6 January 1978 concerning informatics, files and liberties ["*Loi n° 78-17 du 6 janvier 1978 relative à l'informatique, au fichiers et aux libertés*"], Official Journal of the French Republic 7 January 1978, p. 227–231 (corr. 25 January 1978).

[625] S. Simitis, "Privacy – An Endless Debate?", *California Law Review* 2010, Vol. 98, p. 1995. See also S. Simitis, "Zwanzig Jahre Datenschutz in Hessen – eine kritische Bilanz", in Hessischer Landtag, *Neunzehnter Tätighkeitsbericht des hessischen Datenshutzbeauftragten*, 1990, Drucksache 12/7651, p. 68–75.

legislation which authorized the creation of an integrated data processing system for state and communal data.[626] By using automated data processing techniques, policy makers would be able to "*replace the most intuitive political decisions by rational conclusions based on knowledge of all the relevant data*".[627] Towards the end of the '60s, however, euphoria regarding the benefits of automation started to dwindle, as critical reflections regarding the consequences of such automation began to increase.[628] Two concerns in particular permeated the debate: destabilization of the balance of powers ("*Gewaltenteilung*") and the loss of privacy ("*Verlust jeglicher Privatheit*").[629]

299. Upsetting the balance – A first area of concern related to the balance of power between the legislature and the executive. Some worried that the use of automated data processing techniques would unduly strengthen the power of the executive vis-à-vis the legislative branch (by providing the former with an "informational advantage" over the latter).[630] A second set of concerns revolved around the relationship between the State and its citizens. The involvement of nearly all Hesse citizens, combined with the sensitive nature of the data being stored, as well as the databank's capacity to exploit information for different purposes, increased the demands for a public investigation.[631]

300. History in the making – After drawing inspiration from a series of (mainly U.S.) congressional reports and the then burgeoning privacy literature, a draft bill was prepared.[632] On 30 September 1970, the Hessian parliament

---

626 A. Newman, *Protectors of Privacy: Regulating personal data in a global economy*, 2008, Cornell University, New York, p. 46. See also Hessischer Landtag, *Vorlage des Datenshutzbeauftragten betreffend den Ersten Tätighkeitsbericht*, 1972, Drucksache 7/1495, p. 8. The law in question was the Law of 16 December 1969 establishing the data processing centre of the State of Hesse and regarding the data processing centres of local communities ["*Gesetz über die Errichtung der Hessischen Zentrale für Datenverarbeitung (HZD) und Kommunaler Gebietsrechenzentren (KGRZ)*"], *HE GVBI*, 22 December 1969, No. 32, Part I, p. 304–307. See also H. Burkert, "Privacy – Data Protection A German/European Perspective", *l.c.*, p. 45. As the title suggests, the law also provided a legal basis for the creation of data processing centres at the level of the local communities, which would be under an obligation to co-operate with the State data processing centre (see section 18).

627 S. Simitis, "Zwanzig Jahre Datenschutz in Hessen – eine kritische Bilanz", *l.c.*, p. 69, citing Minister-President Oswald's preface to the Great Hessen plan (own translation).

628 *Id.* See also S. Simitis, "Datenschutz", in H. Meyer and M. Stolleis (eds.), *Staats- und Verwaltungsrecht für Hessen*, 1996, fourth edition, Baden-Baden, Nomos Verlagsgesellschaft, p. 110–111.

629 *Ibid*, p. 69–70. See also Hessischer Landtag, *Plenarprotokolle der 77. Sitzung*, 8 July 1970, 6. Wahlperiode (1966–1970), p. 4057–4063.

630 S. Simitis, "Zwanzig Jahre Datenschutz in Hessen – eine kritische Bilanz", *l.c.*, p. 70 and F.W. Hondius, Emerging data protection in Europe, *o.c.*, p. 5.

631 S. Simitis, "Privacy – An Endless Debate?", *l.c.*, p. 1995.

632 *Id.*

adopted[633] the world's first data protection act.[634] This Act was the first separate law laying down rules of general application for data protection (i.e. not merely a part of a law by which a data centre was established).[635] As will become apparent over the following sections and paragraphs, the basic tenets of this law would influence the future development of data protection legislation in Europe for decades to come.[636]

1.2. SCOPE

301. PUBLIC SECTOR – The scope of the law was limited to data which was being handled by (or on behalf of[637]) public sector bodies of the State of Hesse. More specifically, the Hessian Act applied to

> "all records prepared for the purposes of automatic data processing, all stored data and the results of processing such records and data within the purview of the State authorities and the public corporations institutions and establishments under the jurisdiction of the State".[638]

302. AUTOMATIC PROCESSING – The Hessian Act applied to all forms of automatic processing.[639] The Act also applied to the "input" and "output" of automated processing activities, insofar as the records or data concerned had

---

633 Hessischer Landtag, *Plenarprotokolle der 80. Sitzung*, 30 September 1970, 6. Wahlperiode (1966–1970), p. 4271–4272.

634 S. Simitis, "Privacy – An Endless Debate?", *l.c.*, p. 1995. (noting 10 October 1970 as the date of parliamentary adoption; this appears to be a typographical error).

635 F.W. Hondius, *Emerging data protection in Europe*, *o.c.*, p. 35; M. D. Kirby, "Transborder Data Flows and the "Basic Rules" of Data Privacy, *l.c.*, p. 39. Clauses to protect the confidentiality of personal information had already been introduced in the form of administrative regulations to one of the organisational laws seeking to implement data processing public administration, namely the law of 2 April 1968 of Schleswig Hollstein. (H. Burkert, "Privacy – Data Protection A German/European Perspective", *l.c.*, p. 45).

636 Section 1 of the Hessian Data Protection Act. See also H. Burkert, "Privacy – Data Protection: A German/European Perspective", *l.c.*, p. 46.

637 See Hessischer Landtag, *Vorlage des Datenshutzbeauftragten betreffend den Ersten Tätighkeitsbericht*, *l.c.*, p. 11 (stating that the requirements contained in the Act would also apply in cases where a public entity commissioned a private entrepreneur to process data on its behalf). See also *infra*, no. 160. It is worth noting that the regulation of private enterprises was only debated after the adoption of the Hesse law, seeing as the competence towards private sector activities was (and is) reserved to the Federal Government.

638 The citations of the Hessian Data Protection Act included in this chapter have been taken from the translation found in U. Dammann, O. Mallmann and S. Simitis (eds.), *Data Protection Legislation. An International Documentation. English – German*, 1977, Frankfurt am Main, Alfred Metzner Verlag GmbH, p. 113–119.

639 Limiting the scope to electronic data processing would have allegedly constituted a discrimination towards computers. (H. Burkert, "Privacy – Data Protection A German/European Perspective", *l.c.*, p. 47).

either been prepared for the purposes of automatic processing or had undergone such processing.[640]

303. (Non-)personal data – From a contemporary perspective, it is interesting to note that the Hesse Data Protection Act did not limit its scope to personal data.[641] As a result, the requirements of the Act in principle applied to all types of data, regardless of whether such data related to a natural person or not.[642] Section 5 of the Act did, however, authorize the communication and publication of data *"containing no individual details concerning natural or legal persons and permitting no such details to be inferred"* (provided there was no legal prohibition or important public interest preventing it).

1.3. BASIC PROTECTIONS

304. Overview – The Hesse Data Protection Act had essentially three objectives: (1) to prevent unauthorized access to government data files; (2) to protect individuals against the potential dangers of automated data processing and (3) to secure the legislature's access to information.[643] The Act also provided for institutional control by creating a Data Protection Commissioner's office which would be tasked with oversight.[644]

A. Protection of data

305. Security and confidentiality – Section 2 of the Hessian Data Protection Act provided that all records, data and results covered by its scope

> "shall be obtained, transmitted and stored in such a way that they cannot be consulted, altered, extracted or destroyed by unauthorized persons".[645]

This provision essentially obliged the relevant public authorities to ensure the security of the data being processed through appropriate technical and

640 See also Hessischer Landtag, *Vorlage des Datenshutzbeauftragten betreffend den Ersten Tätighkeitsbericht*, *l.c.*, p. 22.

641 The Hesse Data Protection Act sought to prevent unauthorized access to government data files in general. See Hessischer Landtag, *Plenarprotokolle der 77. Sitzung*, *l.c.*, p. 4057.

642 See also *ibid*, p. 27.

643 Hessischer Landtag, *Plenarprotokolle der 77. Sitzung*, *l.c.*, p. 4057; Council of Europe, *Legislation and Data Protection. Proceedings of the Rome Conference on problems relating to the development and application of legislation on data protection*, 1983, Rome, Camera dei Deputati, p. 18 (intervention by S. Simitis).

644 See also F.W. Hondius, *Emerging data protection in Europe*, *o.c.*, p. 35.

645 See also section 5(2), which imposed access control restriction in the case of data banks and information systems.

organisational measures. Section 3(1) goes on to state that the persons charged with the handling of data "shall be prohibited from communicating or making available to other persons the records, data and results gained during the course of their duties and from enabling other persons to obtain such information", except where this is authorized by law or by the consent of "*those entitled to exercise control*"[646] over the records, data and results.

B. *Rights for individuals*

306. Claim to data protection – Section 4 of the Hessian Data Protection Act introduced two rights, namely (1) a right to rectification and (2) a right of "blocking". The former enabled any aggrieved party to demand the rectification of incorrect data (section 4(1)). The latter enabled any person whose rights were infringed by unlawful access, alteration, destruction or extraction, to demand that such action be discontinued if there was a danger of further infringement (section 4(2)). In addition to these two specific rights, section 11 also introduced a general right of complaint to the Data Protection Commissioner for anyone who considered that his or her rights had been infringed by automated data processing.

C. *Access to information by legislature*

307. Right to information – One of the main objectives of the Hessian Act was to secure the legislature's access to information. To this end, section 6 of the Act obliged the administrative bodies who operated data processing centres[647] to provide the State legislature and its parliamentary parties any information they requested from the stored data.[648] The same right was also provided to the district and local councils, their political groups, as well as other public bodies, each within their sphere of responsibility (section 6(2)).[649] If a request for information was not met or not fully satisfied, each beneficiary could require the Data Protection Commissioner to investigate the matter (section 12).

---

646 Cf. *infra*, no. 316.

647 More specifically, this provision of the Act refers to the Hesse data processing centre, the local district computer centres and the State authorities operating data processing installations.

648 This general right to information was subject to 4 conditions: (1) the request was within the jurisdiction of that entity ["*im Rahmen ihrer Zuständigkeiten*"]; (2) the information in question did not contain details concerning natural or legal persons and permitted no such details to be inferred; (3) there was no legal prohibition against it and (4) no important public interest to prevent it.

649 The scope of this right was slightly different than that of the State parliament, in that it referred to "relevant" local district computer centres and other data processing operated by the municipalities and counties (compare *supra*, footnote 648).

D. *Data Protection Commissioner*

308. Mission – In order to promote the effective implementation of its rules, the Hessian Data Protection Act created a Data Protection Commissioner's office. This entity had the responsibility of ensuring that all public sector entities which fell within the scope of the act acted in compliance with its provisions. Its mission also extended to other regulations governing the confidential handling of information provided by citizens and of records relating to individual citizens (section 10(1)). In addition, the Data Protection Commissioner was charged with monitoring the effects of automatic data processing on the operation and powers of the public sector entities that fell within the scope of the Act and to note whenever there was (risk of) displacement in the distribution of powers (section 10(2)).

309. Powers – In case of infringement, the Data Protection Commissioner was required to inform the responsible supervisory authorities ("*Aufsichtsbehörde*") and to suggest appropriate measures to improve data protection (section 10(1) and 10(2)). All public sector bodies falling within the scope of the Act were required to provide the Data Protection Commissioner with the information he needed in the performance of his duties (section 13). Each year, the Data Protection Commissioner would be required to submit an annual report documenting the results of his activity to the State Parliament and the Prime Minister (section 14).

1.4. ALLOCATION OF RESPONSIBILITY AND LIABILITY

310. Absence of general criteria – The Hesse Data Protection Act did not explicitly define which actors (or types of actors) would be responsible for ensuring compliance with its provisions, at least not within the scope section of the law. Section 1 did include a reference to "*Land authorities and public corporations, institutions and establishments*" in defining the scope *ratione materiae* (cf. *supra*, no. 301); but provided no general criteria[650] to determine which of these entities would be deemed responsible for the actual implementation of data protection measures in a specific instance.

311. Conferred authority – One possible explanation for the absence of general criteria relates to the context in which this Act would be applied. Seeing as the scope of the Act was limited to data processing carried out by (or on behalf of) public sector bodies, the activities would be governed by the general

650 By "general criteria" I mean to refer to criteria of general application, i.e. a standard, rule or test on which a decision can be based and which can be applied in a wide variety of instances.

principles of public law. As a rule, the activities of public sector bodies require a basis in law in order for them to be legitimate. Data processing may therefore in principle only be undertaken if there is a legal basis authorizing it.[651] If one expects that to be the case, one might have also considered it unnecessary at that time to include further criteria, as the roles and responsibilities of each actor would be ascertainable from the relevant legislation.[652]

312. Specific responsibilities – While the Hesse Data Protection Act did not use any general criteria to allocate responsibility, several of its provisions were targeted at specific entities. In particular, references can be found to "responsible persons" ("*betrauten Personen*")[653], the "supervisory authority" ("*die Aufsichtsbehörde*")[654] and "those entitled to exercise control" ("*derjenigen die verfügungsberechtigt sind*").[655]

313. Responsible persons – It is reasonable to infer that the term "responsible persons" ("*betrauten Personen*"), as it is used in section 3 of the Act, was intended to refer to the administrative staff who were engaged in the actual handling of data. This inference is supported both by the language of this provision as well as the fact that the duty contained in this provision was considered to be complementary to the general duty of confidentiality incumbent upon public servants.[656]

314. Operators of data processing centres – The Hesse Data Protection Act also addressed the administrative bodies who were in charge of operating

---

651 This principle was later explicitly codified in the Hessian Data Protection Act of 31 January 1978 (*HE GVBl.* 7 February 1978, no. 4, I, p. 96), specifically in section 7. See also S. Simitis, "Datenschutz", *l.c.*, p. 125 ("*Ohne gesetzliche Grundlage dürfen die öffentlichen Stellen keine personenbezogene Daten verwenden.*")

652 This explanation was proffered to me by Spiros Simitis in the course of an email exchange which took place in March 2013. Specifically, Prof. Simitis explained to me that: "*It is correct [...] that the Hesse law did not explicitly indicate criteria. But there was a clear reason. Each entity has specific tasks. And it is precisely these tasks that not only legitimate the existence of a particular entity, but also define the legally acceptable choice of the data to be processed. The Hesse Act was nonetheless linked to the expectation that a growing consciousness of the importance of data protection would also support the efforts to precisely name the purposes of the various entities and thus avoid the risks of an enlarging expansion of their activities.*"

653 See section 3(1).

654 See section 6(1). From a contemporary perspective, it is also interesting to note that this term has also been translated in the past as "the *controlling* authority", e.g. in the translation found in U. Dammann, O. Mallmann and S. Simitis (eds.), *Data Protection Legislation. An International Documentation. English - German*, 1977, Frankfurt am Main, Alfred Metzner Verlag GmbH, p. 113–119 (which was an unofficial translation made by the OECD, Informatics Studies No. 2, 1971, p. 47).

655 See section 3(1) ("*derjenigen die verfügungsberechtigt sind*" can also be translated as: "*those authorized to dispose of*").

656 See Hessischer Landtag, *Plenarprotokolle der 77. Sitzung*, 8 Juli 1970, 6. Wahlperiode (1966–1970), p. 4057.

the data processing centres.[657] In particular, section 6 of the Act obliged these entities to provide the legislative (and associated) bodies with any information they requested from the stored data, provided this request resided within their sphere of responsibility.[658] In addition, even though this was not spelt out explicitly in the Act, compliance with data protection was also deemed to be an essential component of their administrative task.[659]

315. SUPERVISORY AUTHORITY – The term "supervisory authority" ("*Aufsichtsbehörde*") appeared twice in the Hessian Data Protection Act, namely in section 6(3) and section 10(1).[660] While the term "supervisory authority" was not defined within this Act, it previously appeared in the Law of 16 December 1969 establishing the data processing centre of the State of Hesse and regarding the data processing centres of local communities.[661] As the Hessian Data Protection Act was regarded as a follow-up to the aforementioned law[662], it is reasonable to assume that this term was intended to have a similar meaning within both laws.[663] The term "*Aufsichtsbehörde*" should not, however, be confined to any particular supervisory authority. This term is used as a general reference for any government office exercising supervisory authority and especially control functions. Any reference to the "responsible" supervisory authority must be therefore understood in the context of the activities at issue.[664]

657 More specifically, section 6(1) of the Act refers to the Hesse data processing centre, the local district computer centres and the State authorities operating data processing installations.

658 Cf. *supra*, no. 155.

659 See Hessischer Landtag, *Vorlage des Datenshutzbeauftragten betreffend den Ersten Tätighkeitsbericht*, *l.c.*, p. 24: "*The Hessian Data Processing Centre and the Data Processing Centres of the local communities process data as a service; it is the purpose of their establishment, not a tool supporting their activities. Hence data protection is an essential component of their administrative task, both in terms of the protection of personality ["persönlichkeitsschutzes"] as well as in terms of data security*".

660 Section 6(3), which deals with the Legislature's right of access, specifies that "*in case of doubt the decision of the supervisory authority shall be final*" (referring to instances in which there may be a disagreement as to whether or not a particular legislative body should in fact be provided with access). Section 10(1) deals with the duties and powers of the Data Protection Authority. It provides that the Data Protection Commissioner "*shall inform the responsible supervisory authorities of any infringements committed and shall suggest appropriate measures to improve data protection*".

661 Cf. *supra*, footnote 627.

662 See Hessischer Landtag, *Plenarprotokolle der 77. Sitzung*, 8 Juli 1970, 6. Wahlperiode (1966–1970), p. 4057. See also H. Burkert, "Privacy – Data Protection A German/European Perspective", *l.c.*, p. 45.

663 Section 14 of the Law of 16 December 1969 identified the Hessian Prime Minister as the "supervisory authority" of the data processing centre of the State of Hesse. Section 21 of the same law assigned the Hessian Minister of Interior the task of supervising the data processing centres of the local communities.

664 This explanation was proffered to me by Spiros Simitis in the course of an email exchange which took place in April 2013. Specifically, Prof. Simitis explained to me that: ""*Aufsichtsbehörde" is a term generally used for Government offices exercising supervisory and especially control functions. Their specific tasks and duties can consequently only be indicated as long as the*

316. Those entitled to exercise control – Section 3(1) provides that persons charged with the handling of data may only share such data with others when this is authorized either by law or by the consent of "those entitled to exercise control" ("*derjenigen die verfügungsberechtigt sind*").[665] In his first annual report, the Data Protection Commissioner highlighted some of the difficulties arising from the fact that the Hesse Data Protection Act did not specify who would be authorized to decide over the disclosure of data (or under which conditions).[666] The Data Protection Commissioner did not, however, advocate for a statutory definition of these actors. Instead, he recommended that, in particular where intimate data were concerned, administrative arrangements be put in place to ensure that the decision is made by either the head of the "issuing authority" ("*abgebenden Behörde*") or an especially designated civil servant ("*besonderes verpflichteter Bediensteter*").[667]

317. Issuing authority – It stands to reason that the terms "issuing authority" ("*abgebenden Behörde*") (which can also be translated as: "leaving" or "submitting" authority) in first instance referred to the public bodies who had requested the processing of certain data to support the exercise of their official duties. Section 5 of the Law of 16 December 1969 provided that every member or customer of the State data processing centre had a right to access its own data file. This language, together with language used by the Data Protection Commissioner in his first annual report, suggests that the term "issuing authority" referred to those entities who had entrusted the processing of data to either a State or local processing centre (thereby effectively "leaving" or "submitting" the data with (to) the processing centre).

318. A shared responsibility – Based on the foregoing considerations, one can conclude that the responsibility for ensuring compliance with the Hesse Data Protection Act was shared, at least in part, by all entities involved in the preparation and execution of automatic data processing. Four sets of actors in particular are targeted by the law: (1) the administrative staff engaged in the actual handling of data; (2) the operators of the data processing centres[668];

---

particular context of their activities is considered. The references to the "Aufsichtsbehörden" in sections 6(3) and 10(1) must be read and understood in precisely this sense."

665 Cf. *supra*, no. 305.

666 See Hessischer Landtag, *Vorlage des Datenshutzbeauftragten betreffend den Ersten Tätighkeitsbericht*, *l.c.*, p. 25–26.

667 *Ibid*, p. 33. In subsequent annual reports, however, the Data Protection Commissioner did call for a statutory definition of criteria to determine when the disclosure of data should be deemed permissible. See e.g. Hessischer Landtag, *Vorlage des Datenshutzbeauftragten betreffend den Vierten Tätighkeitsbericht*, 1975, Drucksache 8/438, p. 8.

668 See also F.W. Hondius, *Emerging data protection in Europe*, *o.c.*, at p. 35: "[The Hessian Data Protection Act] lays down norms on data confidentiality *which should observed by the authorities in charge of data processing and computer personnel*".

(3) the public authorities who requested data processing to take place; and (4) the relevant supervisory authorities. The fact that data protection was considered part of the statutory duty of the operators of the data centres is an indication that that those engaged in the actual processing operations were considered responsible for implementing appropriate data protection measures.[669] At the same time, the reference to "those entitled to exercise control" in section 3 suggests that the decision-making power over the disclosure of data (and the responsibility to exercise this power appropriately) may lie elsewhere than with the actual holders of the data.

319. OUTSOURCING – The Hesse Data Protection Act also applied in situations where a public authority commissioned a private entrepreneur to process data on its behalf.[670] The Data Protection Commissioner emphasized that in such cases the public authorities concerned with the automatic data processing remain responsible and accountable for the implementation of appropriate data protection measures.[671] He also indicated that, in case of co-operation with private entities, additional security measures might be necessary. Specifically, the public sector entities concerned were responsible for ensuring that an equivalent level of protection is maintained at all times.[672]

320. LIABILITY – Section 16 of the Hesse Data Protection Act provided that it shall be an offence of any person to, either intentionally or through negligent participation, provide an unauthorized person with access to information protected by the Act in violation of Section 3.[673] The Hesse Data Protection Act does not make reference to any other liabilities or sanctions in case of non-compliance. While Section 3 mainly targets the administrative staff who were

---

669 See also Hessischer Landtag, *Vorlage des Datenshutzbeauftragten betreffend den Ersten Tätighkeitsbericht, l.c.*, p. 24 ("*The Hessian Data Processing Centre and the Data Processing Centres of the local communities process data as a service; it is the purpose of their establishment, not a tool supporting their activities. Hence data protection is an essential component of their administrative task, both in terms of the protection of personality ["persönlichkeitsschutzes"] as well as in terms of data security*").

670 Hessischer Landtag, *Vorlage des Datenshutzbeauftragten betreffend den Ersten Tätighkeitsbericht, l.c.*, p. 11.

671 *Ibid*, at p. 33 ("*Verantwortlichkeit der Verwaltungen – Entgegen manchen Äusserungen und Erwartungen ist daran zu erinnern, dass die volle verantwortung für die Durchführen des Datenschutzes den Behörden und Stellen obliegt, die mit der maschinellen Datenverarbeitung befasst sind*")

672 *Id.*

673 This provision was modified by the Law of 4 September 1974 (*HE GVBl.* 9 sept. 1974, no. 27, I, p. 365) to stipulate that such offences may be punished by imprisonment up to one year or by a fine. The same penalty would apply if this person collaborated with another person who improperly obtained access to information or if the responsible person made improper use of the information. If the offender were acting for consideration or with the intention of obtaining financial benefit for himself or for another, or of harming another person, the penalty could be increased to two years (section 16(2)).

tasked with handling the data ("*betrauten personen*"), one can nevertheless assume that the authorities in charge of the data processing centres and/or the public authorities who were requesting data processing to take place might be held accountable (or even liable) in case of failure to implement appropriate data protection measures, particularly where this failure falls short of a reasonable standard of care.

1.5. CONCLUSION

321. Experimental nature – The Hesse Data Protection Act has been characterized as "trial and error" legislation: a considerable portion of the law focused on the establishment of a Data Protection Commissioner, who would watch over the application of the law and gather experience.[674] By defining the Commissioner's role in broad terms, the Act allowed for continuous adjustment to the progressively increasing automation of public administration.[675]

322. A source of inspiration – While the level of detail may have been limited, the Hessian Act contained several elements which would influence data protection legislation for decades to come.[676] First, the Act put in place a default confidentiality rule for data processing: in principle, all data undergoing automated processing should be kept confidential, unless there was an explicit authorization to disclose.[677] The Act also attributed rights to individuals who might be affected by the processing, in particular the right to rectification and the right of "blocking".[678] A third element of influence was the establishment of institutional oversight.[679] While the powers of supervisory bodies would vary from country to country, the basic notion of charging a governmental entity with oversight of data protection rules was echoed in data protection laws throughout Europe.

323. Responsibility and liability – The 1970 Hesse Data Protection Act did not formally define how responsible entities should be identified. However, a number of its terms, such as "those entitled to exercise control" and "data

---

674 H. Burkert, "Privacy – Data Protection A German/European Perspective", *l.c.*, p. 46.

675 See Hessischer Landtag, *Vorlage des Datenshutzbeauftragten betreffend den Ersten Tätighkeitsbericht, l.c.*, p. 12 ("*[...] the Data Protection Act defines the scope of the mission of Data Protection Commissioner in broad terms and allows for the adjustment to the progressively increasing automation of public administration and the development of the techniques of data processing*") (own translation).

676 H. Burkert, "Privacy – Data Protection A German/European Perspective", *l.c.*, p. 46.

677 *Ibid*, p. 45.

678 Cf. *supra*, no. 306.

679 F.W. Hondius, *Emerging data protection in Europe*, *o.c.*, p. 35; H. Burkert, "Privacy – Data Protection A German/European Perspective", *l.c.*, p. 46.

processing centres", display both a conceptual and linguistic similarity with the terms "controller" and "processor" later adopted by Directive 95/46/EC and the GDPR. In addition, the first annual reports of the Hessian Data Protection Commissioner identified a number of issues which would become recurring themes in subsequent discourse, such as the need for additional measures when entrusting data processing to other entities who are not directly subject to the act.

2. THE SWEDISH DATA ACT (1973)

2.1. ORIGIN AND DEVELOPMENT

324. Early adopters – In comparison to other countries, Sweden was relatively early in achieving widespread adoption of computers.[680] In the beginning of 1960s, the Swedish government began to significantly expand its use of automated data processing ("ADP") within the public sector.[681] It developed a comprehensive system of centralized data banks, which progressively became operational starting in 1963.[682] At first, this "computerization" of public administration was largely perceived as a rational and positive development.[683] Towards the end of the 60s, however, general perception had become less equivocal.[684] The ensuing political debate centred around two core issues: transparency and privacy.

325. A tradition of open government – Many commentators attribute Sweden's early adoption of data protection legislation – at least partially – to its unique tradition of openness and transparency.[685] For more than two centuries, Sweden has recognized a general principle of free access to all public

680 C.J. Bennet, *Regulating privacy. Data Protection and Public Policy in Europe and the United States*, *o.c.*, p. 62. See also D.H. Flaherty, *Protecting Privacy in Surveillance Societies. The Federal Republic of Germany, Sweden, France, Canada, & the United* States, 1989, Chapel Hill, The University of North Carolina Press, p. 96.

681 See L. Ilshammar, "When Computers Became Dangerous: The Swedish Computer Discourse of the 1960s", *HUMAN IT* 2007, Vol. 9, No. 1, p. 9.

682 F.W. Hondius, *Emerging data protection in Europe*, *o.c.*, p. 44. Prominent examples included the population registry, motor vehicle registration, register of business firms, land records, police files, social service and employment offices. (*Id.*) See also D.H. Flaherty, *Protecting Privacy in Surveillance Societies*, *o.c.*, p. 96 (characterizing Sweden as "a paradise for registers").

683 L. Ilshammar, "When Computers Became Dangerous: The Swedish Computer Discourse of the 1960s", *l.c.*, p. 9.

684 *Ibid*, p. 9–10.

685 C.J. Bennet, *Regulating privacy. Data Protection and Public Policy in Europe and the United States*, *o.c.*, p. 62. See also R. Pagano, "Panorama of Personal Data Protection Laws", in Council of Europe, *Legislation and Data Protection. Proceedings of the Rome Conference on problems relating to the development and application of legislation on data protection*, 1983,

documents.[686] Pursuant to this principle, everyone has a right to view all official documents and request a copy.[687] Any exception to this principle must be established by law and is construed narrowly.[688] As the use of computers became more widespread, fears arose that this might threaten the public's ability to exercise their rights of access.[689] Specifically, there was a concern that members of the public, who could find their own way through a manual file, would experience difficulties in the face of an electronic register.[690]

326. Too much of a good thing ... – A second set of concerns, somewhat contradictory to the former, related to the privacy of individuals.[691] The computerization of public records, in combination with the principle of publicity, was making it possible for private actors to obtain massive amounts of information on individuals.[692] Among these private actors were also commercial enterprises, such as credit agencies and advertising agencies.[693] Moreover, the ability to link information about specific individuals was facilitated considerably

---

Rome, Camera dei Deputati, p. 305 and D.H. Flaherty, *Protecting Privacy in Surveillance Societies*, *o.c.*, p. 94.

686 R. Pagano, "Panorama of Personal Data Protection Laws", *l.c.*, p. 305 ("public documents" in this context comprise all documents transmitted to public bodies or drawn up by them). (*Id.*) This "publicity principle" was first codified in 1766 by way of an Ordinance Relating to the Freedom of Writing and the Press (see J. Mustonen (ed.), *The World's First Freedom of Information Act. Anders Chydenius' Legacy Today*, Anders Chydenius Foundation's Publications 2, 2006. This publicity principle was later reaffirmed in the Freedom of the Press Act of 1949, which is one of the four basic laws of the Swedish constitution. For purposes of completeness, we must note that the principle of publicity was suspended several times during this time period.

687 R. Pagano, "Panorama of Personal Data Protection Laws", *l.c.*, p. 305. This principle can only be limited by specific legislation. (*Id.*) See also C.G. Källner, "Personal Data: The Open Access Approach", in OECD, *Policy issues in data protection and privacy. Concepts and perspectives*, Proceedings of the OECD Seminar 24th–26th June 1974, OECD Informatics Studies, no. 10, 1976, Paris, p. 59–60 and J. Freese, "The Swedish Data Act", *Current Sweden* 1977, No. 178, p. 1 (noting that it was "*[...] very easy to take advantage of this right. Anyone can visit the offices of government agencies and ask to look at their documents*") (*Id.*).

688 J. Freese, "The Swedish Data Act", *l.c.*, p. 1. The so-called "Secrecy Act" ("Sekreteslag") of 28 May 1937 provided the legislative basis for exceptions to the general principle of publicity (*Id.*).

689 C.J. Bennet, *Regulating privacy. Data Protection and Public Policy in Europe and the United States*, *o.c.*, p. 63.

690 F.W. Hondius, *Emerging data protection in Europe*, *o.c.*, p. 46. Even though the public's right of access extended to computerized records, there was still the concern that members of the public might require special computer facilities or aid of specialized personnel to enable them to exercise their right of access (*Id.*).

691 *Id.*

692 F.W. Hondius, *Emerging data protection in Europe*, *o.c.*, p. 46; C.J. Bennet, *Regulating privacy. Data Protection and Public Policy in Europe and the United States*, *o.c.*, p. 63. See also C.G. Källner, "Personal Data: The Open Access Approach", *l.c.*, p. 59–60.

693 *Id.* See also L. Ilshammar, "When Computers Became Dangerous: The Swedish Computer Discourse of the 1960s", *l.c.*, p. 22 (describing a case involving the commercial use of local housing authorities records which triggered the discussion of the privacy problem at the level of the Riksdag in December 1967).

by the fact that the Swedish government employed a highly developed system of personal identification numbers.[694] Given the comprehensive nature of Sweden's public sector data banks, fears grew that these developments would upset the existing social equilibrium and result in invasion of individuals' privacy.[695]

327. Committee on publicity and secrecy – As time passed, the call for a governmental investigation into the balance between openness and privacy grew.[696] In April 1969, the Swedish government set up the Committee on Publicity and Secrecy Legislation (*"Offentlighets och Sekretesslagstifningskommiten"* – OSK).[697] This multi-stakeholder expert group was asked to prepare legislation on the publicity and secrecy of public documents in light of electronic processing techniques.[698] While the Committee initially focused on the publicity issue (i.e. how could the principle of public access be extended to computer media), privacy issues came to the fore during the latter part of 1970.[699] In 1972, after having carried out a number of inquiries, consultations and hearings, the OSK presented its report, entitled *"Data and Integrity"* (*"Data och integritet"*), which proposed a number of legislative amendments.[700]

---

694 C.J. Bennet, *Regulating privacy. Data Protection and Public Policy in Europe and the United States*, *o.c.*, p. 62 and D.H. Flaherty, *Protecting Privacy in Surveillance Societies*, *o.c.*, p. 94 and 98 (noting that the use of national identification numbers as the standard identifier for individuals in a public and private information systems facilitates the linkage of information, which can lead to surveillance and/or abusive personality profiling).

695 F.W. Hondius, *Emerging data protection in Europe*, *o.c.*, p. 46. The population and housing and housing census of 1970 is said to have been the "spark" that set off the privacy debate in earnest: see L. Ilshammar, "When Computers Became Dangerous: The Swedish Computer Discourse of the 1960s", *l.c.*, p. 13–16. See also P.G. Vinge, *Swedish Data Act*, Federation of Swedish Industries, No. 43, Svanbäck & Nymans Boktr., Stockholm, 1974 (original release: 1973), p. 6 (signalling an exceptional high number of complaints occasioned by the 1970 Census).

696 C.J. Bennet, *Regulating privacy. Data Protection and Public Policy in Europe and the United States*, *o.c.*, p. 63.

697 R. Pagano, "Panorama of Personal Data Protection Laws", *l.c.*, p. 306; C.J. Bennet, *Regulating privacy. Data Protection and Public Policy in Europe and the United States*, *o.c.*, p. 63 and L. Ilshammar, "When Computers Became Dangerous: The Swedish Computer Discourse of the 1960s", *l.c.*, p. 23. The so-called "Secrecy Act" ("Sekreteslag") of 28 May 1937 provided exceptions to the general principle of publicity (F.W. Hondius, *Emerging data protection in Europe*, *o.c.*, p. 45). This Act had for long time governed access to sensitive data, including the results of population and housing censuses. However, many felt that these regulations were insufficient in an increasingly computerized society. (L. Ilshammar, "When Computers Became Dangerous: The Swedish Computer Discourse of the 1960s", *l.c.*, p. 14)

698 R. Pagano, "Panorama of Personal Data Protection Laws", *l.c.*, p. 306.

699 L. Ilshammar, "When Computers Became Dangerous: The Swedish Computer Discourse of the 1960s", *l.c.*, p. 24. As indicated earlier, the population and housing and housing census of 1970 is said to have been the "spark" that set off the privacy debate in earnest (cf. *supra*, footnote 696). See also C.J. Bennet, *Regulating privacy. Data Protection and Public Policy in Europe and the United States*, *o.c.*, p. 63.

700 R. Pagano, "Panorama of Personal Data Protection Laws", *l.c.*, p. 306–307.

328. Legislative proposals – With regard to the publicity issue, the OSK proposed an amendment to the Freedom of the Press Act.[701] This amendment would ensure that the rules applicable to paper documents would also apply to computer media and other technical recordings; with specific rules on the handing out of such recordings.[702] With regard to the issue of privacy protection, the OSK proposed an all-new "Data Act" ("*Datalag*"), which would essentially subject the creation of computerized records containing personal information to prior approval.[703]

329. The First National Data Protection Act – The proposed Data Act was formally adopted on 11 May 1973.[704] The Swedish Data Act[705] represented the first piece of data protection legislation adopted at national level.[706] It came into (partial) force on 1 July 1973.[707]

2.2. SCOPE

330. Public and private sector – Because of the principle of free access to public records, the Swedish government felt the need to address the private and public sector in conjunction with one and other.[708] The Swedish Data Act was therefore equally applicable to both public and private sector data processing.[709]

---

701 F.W. Hondius, *Emerging data protection in Europe*, *o.c.*, p. 46.

702 L. Ilshammar, "When Computers Became Dangerous: The Swedish Computer Discourse of the 1960s", *l.c.*, p. 25. See also P.G. Vinge, *Swedish Data Act*, *o.c.*, p. 7.

703 *Id.*

704 F.W. Hondius, *Emerging data protection in Europe*, *o.c.*, p. 46.

705 Data Act (Datalagen), SFS 1973: 289. An English translation can be found in U. Dammann, O. Mallmann and S. Simitis (eds.), *Data Protection Legislation. An International Documentation. English – German*, *o.c.*, p. 129–145 and in OECD, *Policy issues in data protection* and privacy, *o.c.*, p. 298–305.

706 F.W. Hondius, *Emerging data protection in Europe*, *o.c.*, p. 44; R. Pagano, "Panorama of Personal Data Protection Laws", *l.c.*, p. 305; M. D. Kirby, "Transborder Data Flows and the "Basic Rules" of Data Privacy, *l.c.*, p. 39; C.J. Bennet, *Regulating privacy. Data Protection and Public Policy in Europe and the United States*, *o.c.*, p. 60; H. Burkert, "Privacy – Data Protection: A German/European Perspective", *l.c.*, p. 48 and L. Ilshammar, "When Computers Became Dangerous: The Swedish Computer Discourse of the 1960s", *l.c.*, p. 26.

707 R. Pagano, "Panorama of Personal Data Protection Laws", *l.c.*, p. 307. The entirety of its provision came into force on 1 July 1974, after the amendment of the Freedom of the Press Act was completed. See also J. Freese, "The Swedish Data Act", *l.c.*, p. 1; P.G. Vinge, *Swedish Data Act*, *o.c.*, p. 18–19.

708 F.W. Hondius, *Emerging data protection in Europe*, *o.c.*, p. 46 and C.J. Bennet, *Regulating privacy. Data Protection and Public Policy in Europe and the United States*, *o.c.*, p. 161.

709 J. Bing, "A Comparative Outline of Privacy Legislation", *l.c.*, p. 161; M. D. Kirby, "Transborder Data Flows and the "Basic Rules" of Data Privacy, *l.c.*, p. 39 and C.J. Bennet, *Regulating privacy. Data Protection and Public Policy in Europe and the United States*, *o.c.*, p. 161.

331. Personal registers – The Act applied to "personal registers", which were defined in Section 1 as *"any register or other notes made by automatic data processing and containing personal information that can be assigned to the individual concerned"*.[710] The Swedish Data Act thus only applied to *automatic* data processing which involved personal information (not to manual records).[711]

332. Personal information – "Personal information" was defined in the Act as "information concerning an individual" (section 1). Hence property registers or motor vehicle registers were also covered if they contained information by which the owners could be identified.[712] A "registered individual" was in turn defined as *"an individual in respect of whom personal information occurs in a register"* (section 1).

2.3. BASIC PROTECTIONS

333. Outline – The Swedish Data Act sought to protect individuals' privacy by subjecting the creation of personal registers to prior approval and regulation and by imposing a number of duties upon the "responsible keeper" of a register. It also established a Data Inspection Board (DIB) endowed with broad supervisory powers.

A. *Prior authorization*

334. Controlling the computer – Section 2 of the Swedish Data Act provided that *"no personal register may be started or kept without permission by the Data Inspection Board"*. The rationale behind this provision was to prevent the creation of new registers which unduly interfered in individuals' privacy.[713] By doing so, the Act sought to protect privacy without detracting from the open access principle: all publicly held information would remain accessible as it was before, whereas the automated processing of this information could be regulated to protect privacy.[714]

---

710 The citations of the Swedish Data Act included in this chapter have been taken from the translation found in U. Dammann, O. Mallmann and S. Simitis (eds.), *Data Protection Legislation. An International Documentation. English – German*, *o.c.*, p. 129–145.

711 P.G. Vinge, *Swedish Data Act*, *o.c.*, p. 9; C.J. Bennet, *Regulating privacy. Data Protection and Public Policy in Europe and the United States*, *o.c.*, p. 161. See also D.H. Flaherty, *Protecting Privacy in Surveillance Societies*, *o.c.*, p. 104.

712 C.J. Bennet, *Regulating privacy. Data Protection and Public Policy in Europe and the United States*, *o.c.*, p. 161. See also P.G. Vinge, *Swedish Data Act*, *o.c.*, p. 9 and J. Bing, "A Comparative Outline of Privacy Legislation", *l.c.*, p. 159.

713 C.G. Källner, "Personal Data: The Open Access Approach", *l.c.*, p. 61–62.

714 *Id.*

335. A COMPREHENSIVE LICENSING SCHEME – In principle, all automatic processing of personal information was subject to prior approval by the Data Inspection Board (DIB). A basic premise underlying the Data Act had been that "*all information about the conditions of individuals may concern privacy*".[715] As a result, any computerization of personal information in principle required a license from the DIB. The only exception to this rule were the personal registers established by the King or Parliament (section 2). However, even in those instances the DIB still needed to be heard and had the authority to suggest regulations (see section 7).[716]

336. INTERNATIONAL TRANSFERS – Under section 11 off the Data Act, special permission by the DIB was also required "*if there is reason to believe that personal information will be used for ADP abroad*". This effectively meant that computerized personal information could not be transferred to another country without a specific license issued by the DIB.[717] This restriction applied also in case of transfer to other EU countries.

337. ASSESSMENT CRITERIA – The DIB was to grant permission if there was no reason to assume that it would lead to "*undue encroachment on the privacy of individuals*" (section 3, first indent). This assessment was to take into account in particular (1) the kind and quantity of personal information meant to be included in the register and (2) the attitude towards the register shown or expected from the individuals meant to be registered (section 3, second indent).[718]

338. REGISTERS CONTAINING SENSITIVE INFORMATION – For certain types of personal registers, a particularly compelling justification was required if the requestor was someone other than a government agency which had been mandated by law or statute to keep such records.[719] This was, for example, the case for personal registers containing information about criminal convictions

---

715 C.J. Bennet, *Regulating privacy. Data Protection and Public Policy in Europe and the United States*, *o.c.*, p. 64, citing Sweden, Commission on Publicity and Secrecy of Official Documents, *Computers and Privacy* (English translation of the report *Data och Integritet*), Stockholm, Ministry of Justice, 1972, p. 5. See also P.G. Vinge, *Swedish Data Act*, *o.c.*, p. 11, seemingly citing the same report ("*Even if each item of information may be considered harmless in isolation, the totality of accumulated information may still constitute a serious threat to privacy*")

716 See also C.G. Källner, "Personal Data: The Open Access Approach", *l.c.*, p. 61. See also P.G. Vinge, *Swedish Data Act*, *o.c.*, p. 10.

717 See also M. D. Kirby, "Transborder Data Flows and the "Basic Rules" of Data Privacy", *l.c.*, p. 28.

718 See also P.G. Vinge, *Swedish Data Act*, *o.c.*, p. 10 and D.H. Flaherty, *Protecting Privacy in Surveillance Societies*, *o.c.*, p. 104–106 (highlighting the vagueness of the criteria "privacy" and "undue encroachment").

719 J. Freese, "The Swedish Data Act", *l.c.*, p. 3. Section 4, first indent speaks of "extraordinary reasons", whereas section 4 second indent speaks of "special reason". See also P.G. Vinge, *Swedish Data Act*, *o.c.*, p. 11.

or coercive actions under the Child Welfare Act. Similarly, permission to start and keep a personal register containing information about anybody's political or religious views could only be granted where there were special reasons for this (section 4, first indent).[720]

339. Modalities of license – When granting a permission, the DIB was to issue specific "regulations" or "directives" which would constrain the license that was given. Certain directives were mandatory, namely directives as to the *purpose of the register* and the personal *information that could be included* (section 4).[721] In addition, the DIB could also, if it considered it necessary to prevent undue encroachment on privacy, issue *additional regulations* (e.g. concerning the technical equipment used, information to be provided to the registered persons, security measures, deletion of personal information etc.) (See section 6, first indent).[722] These regulations were not, however, allowed to restrict the duties of public authorities under the Freedom of the Press Act (section 6, second indent).

340. Practical difficulties – Needless to say, the act of licensing every personal register in Sweden entailed a considerable administrative burden. Quite soon after the Data Act entered into force, the DIB introduced a "simplified procedure" which was used for applications involving "routine" data processing.[723] The simplified procedure, which bore greater resemblance to a registration procedure than to a licensing procedure, allowed the DIB to dispose of the majority of applications in summary fashion.[724] This standard operating procedure was later sanctioned by amendments introduced in 1979.[725]

B. Duties of a "responsible keeper"

341. Overview – Processing of personal information was in first instance regulated by the directives issued by the DIB. As indicated earlier, these directives would at a minimum concern the purpose of the register and the

720 This restriction did not apply to personal registers that an association wanted to keep of its own members (section 4, third indent *in fine*).

721 J. Freese, "The Swedish Data Act", *l.c.*, p. 3.

722 See also P.G. Vinge, *Swedish Data Act, o.c.*, p. 12–13.

723 C.G. Källner, "Personal Data: The Open Access Approach", *l.c.*, p. 63; J. Freese, "The Swedish Data Act", *l.c.*, p. 6 and C.J. Bennet, *Regulating privacy. Data Protection and Public Policy in Europe and the United States, o.c.*, p. 164–165. This procedure was applied in cases where a personal data register would not include more information than stipulated on the standardized form and was not going to be used otherwise than granted by the form (*Id.*).

724 *Id.*

725 R. Pagano, "Panorama of Personal Data Protection Laws", *l.c.*, p. 307. A further step was taken with the amendments of 1982, which introduced a formal distinction between "licenses" and "permissions". (*Ibid*, p. 307–308). See also D.H. Flaherty, *Protecting Privacy in Surveillance Societies, o.c.*, p. 95 and C.J. Bennet, *Regulating privacy. Data Protection and Public Policy in Europe and the United States, o.c.*, p. 165.

information that could be included.[726] In addition to abiding by these directives, the entity responsible for a personal register (i.e. its "responsible keeper"[727]) needed to observe a number of duties, which were specified in sections 8–14 of the Data Act. These duties concerned *inter alia* (1) the accuracy and completeness of personal information; (2) the right to information of a registered individual; (3) restrictions upon dissemination of personal information and (4) secrecy requirements.[728]

342. Correction – Section 8, first indent of the Data Act provided that

> "if there is reason to suspect that personal information in a personal register is incorrect, the responsible keeper of the register shall, without delay, take the necessary steps to ascertain the correctness of the information and, if needed, to correct it or exclude it from the register".

This provision essentially entailed a duty to ensure accuracy of registered information.[729] If a piece of information was corrected or excluded due to its inaccurate nature, the registered individual had the right to demand that the responsible keeper notify any person who had been handed the information in question of its correction or exclusion (section 8, second indent).[730]

343. Supplementation – If a personal register did not include an item of information that ought to have been included, the responsible keeper was obliged to supplement the register with that which is needed to render it complete (section 9). Whether or not a register needed to be supplemented was determined by taking into account, on the one hand, the purpose of the register and, on the other hand, the risk of "undue encroachment" on individuals' privacy or loss of rights (section 9 *in fine*).[731]

344. Right to information – If a registered person so requested, the responsible keeper was obliged to inform him of the personal information

---

726 Cf. *supra*, no. 339.

727 Cf. *infra*, no. 349

728 The Swedish Data Act also included specific provisions on the duties of a responsible keeper in case of discontinuance of a register (section 12) and the use of information from an ADP recording for the purpose of judicial or administrative proceedings (section 14).

729 The extent of this duty, of course, needed be interpreted within reason. An acceptable level of accuracy should be reached, taking into account the uses of the data. (D.H. Flaherty, *Protecting Privacy in Surveillance Societies*, *o.c.*, p. 107). For example, the DIB accepted a lower level of reliability for information used for statistical as opposed to administrative purposes (*Id.*).

730 If there were special circumstances, the DIB could exempt the responsible keeper from this duty to notify (section 8, second indent *in fine*).

731 See also J. Freese, "The Swedish Data Act", *l.c.*, p. 4. See also P.G. Vinge, *Swedish Data Act*, *o.c.*, p. 14.

concerning him contained in the register (section 10, first indent).[732] Such information was to be provided free of charge, unless the DIB had permitted otherwise (section 10, second indent). The duty to inform a registered persons did not apply in cases where a law, statute or decision by an authority prohibited the disclosure of this information to the individual concerned (section 10, third indent).

345. Restrictions upon dissemination – Section 11, first indent, provided that personal information contained in a personal register "may not be issued if there is reason to assume that the information will be used for ADP contrary to this act." This meant that personal information should not be disclosed if there was reason to believe that this information might be used to further undue encroachment on personal privacy.[733]

346. Secrecy – A further restriction upon dissemination was stipulated in section 13 of the Swedish Data Act, which provided that "the responsible keeper of a personal register and any other person who has concerned himself with it may not without authorization reveal what he has learnt from it about the personal circumstances of an individual". This provision essentially obliged responsible keepers to observe professional secrecy with respect to what they have found out about private persons in the course of their data processing.[734]

C. Data Inspection Board

347. Mission – The mission of the Data Inspection Board was to "ensure that ADP does not cause undue encroachment on privacy" (section 15). In addition to its extensive licensing authority (cf. *supra*), the DIB was also charged with monitoring compliance with the Act. Finally, the DIB also served as a department for complaints from the general public.[735]

348. Powers – Section 16 of the Data Act provided the DIB with the power to inspect any premise where ADP was being carried out or where computers

---

732 The DIB could also issue a directive which required the responsible keeper to actively notify registered persons of the existence of the register. However, the general rule included in the Data Act itself only provided for a passive information obligation (i.e. upon request). See J. Freese, "The Swedish Data Act", *l.c.*, p. 4.

733 D.H. Flaherty, *Protecting Privacy in Surveillance Societies*, *o.c.*, p. 108. In case of publicly held documents, restrictions were contained in the Act on Restrictions of the Right to obtain public documents (a.k.a. the "Official Secrets Act") (section 11 *in fine*). See also P.G. Vinge, *Swedish Data Act*, *o.c.*, p. 14–15. As already indicated earlier, section 11 also contained a restriction upon the disclosure of personal information if there was reason to believe that it would be used for purposes of ADP abroad. Cf. *supra*, no. 336.

734 J. Freese, "The Swedish Data Act", *l.c.*, p. 4.

735 C.G. Källner, "Personal Data: The Open Access Approach", *l.c.*, p. 63.

or other equipment was being kept. The same provision also entitled the DIB to access any documents relating to ADP.[736] The DIB was free to perform such inspections either at its own initiative or pursuant to a complaint.[737] The DIB also had the authority, if it considered it necessary, to alter the regulations it had previously issued, issue new regulations, or revoke a license altogether (section 18). Finally, the DIB also had the authority to issue fines for certain violations of the Data Act (section 24).[738]

2.4. ALLOCATION OF RESPONSIBILITY AND LIABILITY

349. "Responsible keeper" – The Swedish Data Act allocated the responsibility for compliance with its provisions to the "responsible keeper of a register" ("*registeransvarig*").[739] As the meaning of this term is of central importance to the research objectives of this book, several different translations will be considered over the following paragraphs.

350. Translation by Council of Europe – The translation made by the Council of Europe in 1973, reproduced by U. Dammann, O. Mallmann and S. Simitis in 1977, defines the "responsible keeper of a register" as

> "anyone for whose activity ADP is being carried out, if the register is at his disposal".[740]

351. Translation by OECD – In 1974, the OECD organized a seminar on the topic of data protection and privacy, the proceedings of which were published in 1976. These proceedings include a translation of the Swedish Data Act in its annexes, where the term "person responsible for a register" is defined as

> "any person on whose behalf a personal register is kept, if the register is at his entire disposal".[741]

---

736 See also C.J. Bennet, *Regulating privacy. Data Protection and Public Policy in Europe and the United States*, *o.c.*, p. 166. Section 17 of the Data Act obliged the responsible keeper of a register to deliver to the DIB any "*information and particulars concerning the ADP which the Board requires for its supervision*". This disclosure obligation also applied to anyone who handled a personal register on behalf of the responsible keeper of the register (section 17 *in fine*). See also *infra*, no. 357.

737 See also R. Pagano, "Panorama of Personal Data Protection Laws", *l.c.*, p. 309.

738 See also *infra*, no. 360.

739 See also C.J. Bennet, *Regulating privacy. Data Protection and Public Policy in Europe and the United States*, *o.c.*, p. 167.

740 U. Dammann, O. Mallmann and S. Simitis (eds.), *Data Protection Legislation. An International Documentation. English – German*, *o.c.*, p. 130.

741 OECD, *Policy issues in data protection and privacy*, *o.c.*, p. 298.

352. Translation by P.G. Vinge – In 1973, P.G. Vinge published one of the earliest commentaries on the Swedish Data Act.[742] In this booklet, the term "responsible keeper" is defined as

> "the party for whose purposes a personal file is maintained, and who controls the file".[743]

353. General criteria – Although there exist notable differences among the translations reproduced here, it seems reasonable to conclude that the concept of a "responsible keeper" consisted of two main components. The first component signals that the responsible keeper was in a sense the "*main beneficiary*" of the personal register: the data processing was carried out "for its activity", "on its behalf" or "for its purposes". The second part of the definition suggests that *mastery* over the register was also an important element: the responsible keeper was an entity who had the register "at his disposal", "at his entire disposal" or under his "control".

354. From "file keeper" to "responsible keeper" – In the early stages of the preparation of the Swedish Act, the term "file keeper" had been used in lieu of the term "responsible keeper".[744] The replacement was reportedly made because the term "responsible keeper" made it clearer that the term referred to the party that actually controlled the file and made decisions on its contents.[745] The concept therefore excluded service bureaus and other parties that might have been involved in the processing of a personal register without actually "controlling" it.[746]

355. "Control" vs. "ownership" – As regards the relationship between control and ownership, Hondius made a distinction between two scenarios.[747] In the first scenario, the person, enterprise or agency who controls the register is also the owner of the data bank that is used to keep the register. This entity is then considered both the owner and responsible keeper of the register contained in the data bank. In the second scenario, the data bank used for keeping the register is owned by a party who processes this information for another party (i.e. on its behalf). According to Hondius, it was the decision of the OSK "*to concentrate responsibility with the party that controls the file and orders the data*

742 P.G. Vinge, *Swedish Data Act*, *o.c.*, 22 p.

743 P.G. Vinge, *Swedish Data Act*, *o.c.*, p. 9. The term "file" refers to the term "personal file", which is Vinge's translation of what we have previously referred to as a "personal register".

744 P.G. Vinge, *Swedish Data Act*, *o.c.*, p. 9. As highlighted in the previous footnote, the term "file" refers to the term "personal file", which is Vinge's translation of what we have previously referred to as a "personal register".

745 P.G. Vinge, *Swedish Data Act*, *o.c.*, p. 9.

746 *Id.*

747 F.W. Hondius, *Emerging data protection in Europe*, *o.c.*, p. 101–102.

processing operations concerned, and not the party that actually carries out the instructions, such as a service bureau".[748] This decision was purportedly based on pragmatic considerations, given the widespread practice whereby one data bank would house several different registers.[749] At the time, only very large organisations owned their own data banks, *"and even there a clear distinction [was] drawn between the party that controls the system and the party that operate[d] it under the controller's instructions".*[750]

356. Natural or legal persons – According to P.G. Vinge, both individuals and organisations could be identified as responsible keepers.[751] It seems reasonable to infer that the notion of a "responsible keeper" thus comprised both natural and legal persons, provided the criteria contained in section 1, fourth indent were met.

357. Entities acting "on behalf of" a responsible keeper – The Swedish Data Act contained two provisions which explicitly mentioned persons or organisations acting "on behalf of" a responsible keeper. Specifically, section 17 *in fine*, stipulated that the duty to provide the DIB with information was also incumbent upon anyone who handled a personal register on behalf of the responsible keeper.[752] Failure to do so could result in a fine (section 24). In addition, section 13, first indent, included a reference to "any other person who has concerned himself with [a personal register]". This provision, which provided for a general duty of confidentiality (cf. *supra*), also concerned the employees of the responsible keeper as well as service bureaus who acted on its behalf.[753]

358. Civil liability – If a registered individual suffered damage because a personal register contained incorrect information about him, he or she could demand compensation from the responsible keeper of the register (section 23). This provision encompassed a strict tort liability (i.e. no demonstration of fault required), which extended to both economic and non-economic loss.[754]

---

748 *Ibid*, p. 102.
749 *Id.*
750 *Id.*
751 P.G. Vinge, *Swedish Data Act, o.c.*, p. 9.
752 See also P.G. Vinge, *Swedish Data Act, o.c.*, p. 16. Although not spelt out specifically as such in section 16, the DIB's right of access also extended to the premises of third parties such as service bureaus (see section 24). See also J. Freese, "The Swedish Data Act", *l.c.*, p. 5 (*"If the responsible keeper does not have the hardware at its own disposal but resorts to someone else, e.g. a service bureau, the obligations to assist the Board for control purposes will rest on the latter correspondingly"*).
753 P.G. Vinge, *Swedish Data Act, o.c.*, p. 15.
754 J. Freese, "The Swedish Data Act", *l.c.*, p. 5. The Data Act did not explicitly provide for civil liability for reasons other than harm suffered from incorrect data processing. However, it seems reasonable to assume that any harm resulting from a failure to observe any of the other

359. Punitive provisions – Section 20 of the Data Act made it a criminal offence for any person to, either wilfully or by negligence, (1) start or keep a personal register without the necessary permission; (2) disregard one of the regulations issued by the DIB; (3) engage in the unauthorized dissemination of personal information; or to (4) provide incorrect information regarding the register to either the DIB or a registered person. The Data Act also created a new category of criminal offence, known as "data trespass", which was defined as unauthorized access or alteration of "recordings for ADP" (section 21).[755]

360. Forfeiture and fines – Section 21 provided that personal registers created or maintained without the necessary permission would be forfeit (unless this would be manifestly unreasonable).[756] Section 24 stipulated that the responsible keeper of a registers, or a person who administers a personal register on his behalf, could be fined if they failed to provide access to the premises or to provide relevant documentation when so requested by the DIB. A responsible keeper could also receive a fine from the DIB for failure to observe the duties of a responsible keeper specified in sections 8, 9 or 10 (section 24 *in fine*).

2.5. CONCLUSION

361. Experimental nature – Several commentators have described the Swedish Data Act as an "experiment" or as "a strategy for gaining experience".[757] At the time, the Data Act was seen as part of a gradual development towards regulation of all privacy problems.[758] Like the Hessian Act before it, the Swedish Data Act placed considerable emphasis on the institutional body that would be charged with ensuring compliance.[759] By doing so, the Swedish government hoped to maintain flexibility whilst gaining experience for later policy decisions in this area.[760]

---

duties of a responsible keeper would still give rise to remedy under general tort law (albeit that a demonstration of fault would most likely still have been necessary).

755 See also J. Freese, "The Swedish Data Act", *l.c.*, p. 5.

756 *Id.*

757 J. Bing, "A Comparative Outline of Privacy Legislation", *l.c.*, p. 150. See also C.J. Bennet, *Regulating privacy. Data Protection and Public Policy in Europe and the United States, o.c.*, p. 61.

758 P.G. Vinge, *Swedish Data Act, o.c.*, p. 19.

759 Compare *supra*, no. 321.

760 C.J. Bennet, *Regulating privacy. Data Protection and Public Policy in Europe and the United States, o.c.*, p. 169. See also J. Bing, "A Comparative Outline of Privacy Legislation", *l.c.*, p. 151.

362. A SOURCE OF INSPIRATION – The Swedish Data Act would (also) serve as a source of inspiration for decades to come.[761] In many of its provisions, one can detect precursors to several modern day data protection principles and obligations. Examples include: restrictions regarding sensitive data and international transfers, the use of prior authorization schemes as a regulatory tool, the duty to ensure accuracy and completeness of information and the granting of rights to data subjects.

363. ALLOCATION OF RESPONSIBILITY – The Swedish Data Act imposed its obligations almost exclusively upon the "responsible keeper of a register". Contrary to the Hessian Act, the Swedish Data Act did provide general criteria to determine which actor was responsible for compliance. These criteria were designed to allocate responsibility with the party that actually "controlled" the register, as opposed to those who were merely passively following instructions. In doing so, the Data Act implicitly exempted, for the most part, service bureaus and other parties that might have been involved in the processing of a personal register but did not actually "control" it.[762] This situation did not, however, detract from the DIB's supervisory authority: even in case of outsourcing, the DIB would be able to effectuate on-site inspection at the premises of a service bureau and it would be obliged to co-operate.[763] None of the provisions of the Swedish Data Act, however, explicitly regulated the relationship between responsible keepers and service bureaux.

364. ALLOCATION OF LIABILITY – The Swedish Data Act allocated the risk of non-compliance primarily with the responsible keeper of the register. Its liability exposure explicitly included (1) liability for damages resulting from the use of inaccurate information (section 23), as well (2) fines levied for failure to abide by the duties of a responsible keeper (section 24). In addition, the Data Act also contained punitive provisions of a more general nature, whose scope was not limited to any specific type of actor (but rather extended to all persons who might interact with the personal information contained in a register).

---

761 See also C.J. Bennet, *Regulating privacy. Data Protection and Public Policy in Europe and the United States*, *o.c.*, p. 61.

762 As indicated earlier, the 1973 Data Act only explicitly addressed persons who handled a personal register "on behalf of" its responsible keeper in two instances, namely in section 17 and section 24 (cf. *supra*, no. 357).

763 Cf. *supra*, no. 348 and 357.

3. THE FRENCH LAW ON INFORMATICS, FILES AND LIBERTIES (1978)

3.1. ORIGIN AND DEVELOPMENT

365. Computers in the public sector – Similarly to the debates that took place in Hesse and Sweden, the French debate on the use of automated data processing was occasioned by plans to expand computer usage within the public sector.[764] In 1970, the French government proposed two bills which implied increased data sharing among public administrations.[765] The parliamentary debate surrounding these proposals evidenced a need for the elaboration of data protection principles.[766] Although a provision recognizing a general right to privacy was introduced in the Civil Code during that same year[767], the precise meaning of this provision was left largely undefined.[768]

366. La chasse aux français – The public debate regarding computers culminated in 1974 as a result of the "Safari" plan, in which it was proposed that all automated files in the public sector should be made accessible by means of one unique identifier.[769] The French newspaper *Le Monde* reported on this plan with an article entitled '*"Safari" ou la chasse aux Français*' ('*"Safari", or the hunt on the French*').[770] This article evoked visions of powerful computers capable of integrating citizen data from all areas of government.[771] The push towards

---

764 F.W. Hondius, *Emerging Data Protection in Europe*, *o.c.*, p. 32.

765 *Ibid*, 32. The first bill aimed to reinforce traffic safety by integrating information held by the Ministry of the Interior on driver's licenses and that of the Ministry of Justice on convictions for traffic offences (Law no. 70-539 of 24 June 1970 on the centralization of the documentation relative to road traffic), whereas the second bill (i.e. Law of 31 December 1970 on hospital reform) contained a provision aiming to establish a centralized system for electronic health records. (*Id.*) See also R. Pagano, "Panorama of Personal Data Protection Laws", *l.c.*, p. 256.

766 F.W. Hondius, *Emerging Data Protection in Europe*, *o.c.*, p. 33–34.

767 See Article 22 of the Law no. 70-643 of 17 July 1970 aimed at strengthening the protection of the rights of individuals and citizens ["*Loi n° 70-643 du 17 juillet 1970 tendent à renforcer la garantie des droits individuels et citoyens*"], Official Journal of the French Republic 19 July 1970, p. 6755.

768 F.W. Hondius, *Emerging Data Protection in Europe*, *o.c.*, p. 34.

769 A.C.M. Nugter, *Transborder Flow of Personal Data within the EC. A comparative analysis of the privacy statutes of the Federal Republic of Germany, France, the United Kingdom and The Netherlands and their impact on the private sector*, Deventer, Kluwer, Computer/Law Series no. 6, 1990, p. 77. ("SAFARI" stood for "Système Automatisé pour les Fichiers Administratifs et le Répertoire des Individus") See also R. Pagano, "Panorama of Personal Data Protection Laws", *l.c.*, p. 256 and D.H. Flaherty, *Protecting Privacy in Surveillance Societies*, *o.c.*, p. 166. The report made by the Commission on Informatics and Liberties points out that it was not only the Safari plan, but also the creation of vast data banks and computer networks more generally which gave rise to public concerns. See Commission Informatique et Libertés, *Rapport de la Commission Informatique et libertés*, La Documentation Française, Paris, 1975, p. 7. See also H. Burkert, "Privacy – Data Protection A German/European Perspective", *l.c.*, p. 49–50.

770 Ph. Boucher, ""Safari" ou la chasse aux Français", Le Monde, 21 March 1974, p. 9. See also A.C.M. Nugter, *Transborder Flow of Personal Data within the EC*, *o.c.*, p. 77.

771 Ph. Boucher, ""Safari" ou la chasse aux Français", *l.c.*, p. 9.

centralization of governmental files was characterized as a serious threat to individual freedom and the balance of powers.[772]

367. COMMISSION INFORMATIQUE ET LIBERTÉS – The public unrest over the Safari plan further fuelled the call for action, which eventually led to the appointment of a Commission on Informatics and Liberties ("*Commission Informatique et Libertés*" – "CIL").[773] The mandate of this Commission was to propose "measures to ensure that the development of data processing in the public, semi-public and private sectors will take place in the context of respect for private life, individual liberties and public liberties".[774] The CIL concluded that, although the use of informatics had not yet resulted in many infringements of individual liberties, significant risks existed for the future.[775] An increase of social control, together with an aggravation of already unequal relationships within society, were perceived as key areas of concern.[776]

368. LEGISLATIVE DEVELOPMENT – The CIL report, which was published in 1975, was accompanied by a preliminary draft bill aimed at regulating the processing of personal information.[777] This draft bill served as the basis for the subsequent proposal put forth by the French government in 1976.[778] After substantial modifications by the Senate, the bill was accepted by both houses of Parliament in December of 1977.[779] It was enacted on 6 January of 1978 as Law no. 78–17 concerning Informatics, Files and Liberties (LIFL).[780]

772 *Id.*

773 Decree no. 74-938 of 8 November 1974 establishing the Committee on Informatics and Liberties ["*Décret n° 74-938 du 8 novembre 1974 portant création de la Commission Informatique et Libertés*"], Official Journal of the French Republic 13 November 1974, p. 11403. See also Commission Nationale de l'Informatique et des libertés, *Premier rapport au Président de la République et au Parlement 1978-1980*, La Documentation Française, Paris, 1980, p. 8.

774 Article 1 of Decree no. 74-938. See also D.H. Flaherty, *Protecting Privacy in Surveillance Societies, o.c.*, p. 166. The CIL did not need to start its work from scratch. In addition to the studies carried out in other countries, the CIL could also benefit from studies carried out by the French Conseil d'Etat et Chancellerie carried out in in 1971 and 1972 respectively. (Commission Informatique et Libertés, *Rapport de la Commission Informatique et libertés, o.c.*, p. 7).

775 Commission Informatique et Libertés, *Rapport de la Commission Informatique et libertés, o.c.*, p. 11–17.

776 *Ibid*, p. 17. See also D.H. Flaherty, *Protecting Privacy in Surveillance Societies, o.c.*, p. 166.

777 While the report of the CIL was made public, the draft bill itself was not. (A.C.M. Nugter, *Transborder Flow of Personal Data within the EC, o.c.*, p. 78).

778 Assemblé Nationale, *Projet de loi relatif à l'informatique et aux libertés*, Enregistré à la Présidence de l'Assemblée national le 9 aout 1976, Annexe au procès-verbal de la séance du 2 octobre 1976, Document Parl. no. 2516, p. 1–18. See also A.C.M. Nugter, *Transborder Flow of Personal Data within the EC, o.c.*, p. 78).

779 See Commission nationale de l'Informatique et des libertés, *Premier rapport au Président de la République et au Parlement 1978-1980, o.c.*, p. 9; R. Pagano, "Panorama of Personal Data Protection Laws", *l.c.*, p. 257 and A.C.M. Nugter, *Transborder Flow of Personal Data within the EC, o.c.*, p. 78.

780 Law no. 78–17 of 6 January 1978 concerning informatics, files and liberties ["*Loi n° 78-17 du 6 janvier 1978 relative à l'informatique, aux fichiers et aux libertés*"], Official Journal of the French Republic 7 January 1978, p. 227–231. (corr. 25 January 1978).

3.2. SCOPE

369. PUBLIC AND PRIVATE SECTOR – The LIFL applied to both public and private sector data processing (Article 14).[781] However, as will be made clear over the following paragraphs, a different regime applied to public and private data processing respectively.

370. AUTOMATED, NON-AUTOMATED AND MECHANIZED PROCESSING – The LIFL governed automated, non-automated and mechanized processing of personal data.[782] Article 5 defines automated processing as

> "any set of operations, performed by automatic means, relating to the collection, recording, development, modification, storage and deletion of personal data as well as any set of operations of a similar nature relating to the use of files or data bases, in particular the interconnection or linkage, consultation or communication of personal data".[783]

The notions of "non-automated" and "mechanized" (or "machine") processing of personal data were not further defined in the law.[784] Although most of the law affected only the automated processing of personal data, several of its provisions also applied to non-automated or mechanized files.[785]

---

781 See also J. Bing, "A Comparative Outline of Privacy Legislation", *l.c.*, p. 157 (noting that while Article 14 essentially served to articulate the duties of the CNIL, it also identifies the scope of the LIFL.

782 A.C.M. Nugter, *Transborder Flow of Personal Data within the EC*, *o.c.*, p. 81.

783 The translations of the provisions of the LIFL in this section are based on the original version of the LIFL, together with the translation provided by A.C.M. Nugter, *Transborder Flow of Personal Data within the EC*, *o.c.*, p. 81 et seq. Generally speaking, the concept of "processing" was intended to refer to processing *systems* (i.e. sets of processing operations) rather than individual data processing operations (see Commission Nationale de l'Informatique et des libertés, *Premier rapport au Président de la République et au Parlement 1978-1980*, *o.c.*, p. 25). However, certain provisions did also refer to specific data processing operations such as the collection, storage or access to data.

784 A.C.M. Nugter, *Transborder Flow of Personal Data within the EC*, *o.c.*, p. 81–82.

785 D.H. Flaherty, *Protecting Privacy in Surveillance Societies*, *o.c.*, p. 175. See Article 45 LIFL (specifying that Articles 25, 27, 29–33 also applied to the non-automated and/or mechanized processing of personal data unless such processing was intended exclusively for personal use ("*dont l'usage relève strict exercice du droit à la vie privée*") (A.C.M. Nugter, *Transborder Flow of Personal Data within the EC*, *o.c.*, p. 82). The argument for including non-automated and mechanized processing within the scope of the LIFL was to avoid 'privileging' non-automated techniques over automated ones, as well as to avoid circumvention of the law (Commission Informatique et Libertés, *Rapport de la Commission Informatique et libertés*, *o.c.*, p. 21). See also N. Lenoir, "La loi 78-17 du 6 janvier 1978 et la Commission national de l'informatique et des libertés: Éléments pour un premier bilan de cinq années d'activité", *La Revue adminstrative* 1983, Vol. 36, no. 215, p. 453 and P. Kayser, *La protection de la vie privée. Protection du secret de la vie privée*, Economica, Paris, 1984, p. 289–290 (highlighting that the inclusion of non-automated files in the scope of the LIFL was also driven by the risks they presented).

371. PERSONAL DATA – The LIFL applied to the processing of personal data ("*informations nominatives*"), which are defined by Article 4 as "*data which permit, in any form, directly or indirectly, the identification of natural persons to whom they relate*".[786]

372. EXEMPTIONS AND DEROGATIONS – The LIFL provided for certain exemptions to its scope, as well as derogations to a number of its provisions. For example, non-automated or mechanized of personal data was exempted entirely from the law if such processing was intended purely for personal use (e.g. addresses entered into a personal diary).[787] A partial derogation was also provided for processing of personal data by entities of the press.[788] In addition, Article 17 also created the opportunity for the issuance of "simplified rules" for processing that did not present a danger to individual privacy or basic freedoms (cf. *infra*; no. 377).[789]

3.3. BASIC PROTECTIONS

373. OVERVIEW – The LIFL sought to protect privacy and individual liberties by (1) putting in place procedures for prior consultation or declaration; (2) imposing a number of restrictions and obligations in relation to the processing of personal data; (3) providing individuals whose data were being processed with certain rights and (4) establishing a National Committee on Informatics and Liberties (CNIL) endowed with broad supervisory powers.

---

786 A.C.M. Nugter, *Transborder Flow of Personal Data within the EC*, *o.c.*, p. 82. The LIFL thus did not apply to the processing of data concerning legal persons, although this had been the intention of the initial government draft bill. See A. Holleaux, "La loi du 6 Janvier 1978 sur l'informatique et les libertés (I)", *La Revue Administrative* 1978, Vol. 31, no. 181, p. 32 and P. Kayser, *La protection de la vie privée. Protection du secret de la vie privée*, *o.c.*, p. 290–291.

787 A.C.M. Nugter, *Transborder Flow of Personal Data within the EC*, *o.c.*, p. 82 (based on Article 45 LIFL). This exemption was said to encompass "non-professional" files, which are "not related to any activity which places those that hold them in an "organisational" relationship [*rapport organique*] with third parties" (A. Holleaux, "La loi du 6 janvier 1978 sur l'informatique et les libertés (II)", *l.c.*, p. 165). *Automated* processing of personal data by individuals would, strictly speaking, fall within the remit of the LIFL, even if it were carried out for a purely private purpose. See N. Lenoir, "La loi 78-17 du 6 janvier 1978 et la Commission national de l'informatique et des libertés: Éléments pour un premier bilan de cinq années d'activité", *La Revue adminstrative* 1983, Vol. 36, no. 215, p. 465.

788 See Article 33 LIFL.

789 A.C.M. Nugter, *Transborder Flow of Personal Data within the EC*, *o.c.*, p. 82. It is interesting to note that the LIFL did apply, as a matter of principle, to matters concerning national security, defense and public safety. Several provisions of the LIFL did, however, contain specific derogations for such instances. See e.g. Article 19 (contents of request for an opinion); Article 39 (right of access).

A. *Prior consultation or declaration*

374. PUBLIC SECTOR – Pursuant to Article 15, automated processing of personal data on behalf of a public or semi-public[790] entity required a legal or regulatory basis.[791] This law or regulation could only be adopted after obtaining a motivated opinion from the CNIL.[792] In case of an unfavourable opinion, the processing could only take place on the basis of a decree which was adopted in accordance with an opinion issued by the Council of State (Article 15, second indent).[793]

375. PRIVATE SECTOR – Processing of personal data on behalf of private sector entities[794] was not subject to a requirement of prior consultation, but rather to a declaration procedure (Article 16). Any private sector entity seeking to initiate personal data processing first needed to submit a declaration to the CNIL. Upon submission, the CNIL would verify whether all the requisite information was included in the declaration. If so, it would issue a receipt. Only upon obtaining this receipt would the applicant be allowed to initiate the processing (Article 16, second indent).[795]

---

790 In addition to "the State", Article 15 also mentions "public institutions" ("*établissement public*"), institutions of a collective territory ("*établissement d'une collectivité territoriale*") and private legal persons operating a public service ("*personne moral de droit privé gérant un service public*").

791 Whether or not a formal law was required (or another form of regulation might suffice) was determined by Article 34 of the French Constitution. See A. Holleaux, "La loi du 6 Janvier 1978 sur l'informatique et les libertés (I)", *l.c.*, p. 35–36 and P. Kayser, *La protection de la vie privée. Protection du secret de la vie privée*, *o.c.*, p. 295–298.

792 Commission Nationale de l'Informatique et des libertés, *Premier rapport au Président de la République et au Parlement 1978-1980*, *o.c.*, p. 24. In situations where the processing of personal data required a basis in law, the government was required to attach the opinion of the CNIL to the draft bill when submitting it to Parliament (Article 20 of the Decree of 17 July 1978). (N. Lenoir, "La loi 78-17 du 6 janvier 1978 et la Commission national de l'informatique et des libertés: Éléments pour un premier bilan de cinq années d'activité", *l.c.*, p. 453)

793 Due to the requirement of a favourable opinion by CNIL or Council of State, one might argue that the requirement of prior consultation was in fact a system of prior authorization or licensing (similar to the procedure that existed in Sweden). While the withholding of a favourable opinion could have similar effects in practice, it would be more correct to view the French system of prior consultation as a procedure to ensure that privacy considerations are taken into account, rather than as a formal licensing procedure. (See J. Bing, "A Comparative Outline of Privacy Legislation", *l.c.*, p. 165).

794 Article 16 mentioned "entities other than those subject article 15".

795 A.C.M. Nugter, *Transborder Flow of Personal Data within the EC*, *o.c.*, p. 92. The primary objective of the declaration procedure was to ensure that the CNIL remained abreast of technological developments within society, rather than to create a procedure of prior approval (see Commission Informatique et Libertés, *Rapport de la Commission Informatique et libertés*, *o.c.*, p. 34). However, the CNIL did have the authority, if it deemed it appropriate, to issue recommendations regarding the declared processing (N. Lenoir, "La loi 78-17 du 6 janvier 1978 et la Commission national de l'informatique et des libertés: Éléments pour un premier bilan de cinq années d'activité", *l.c.*, p. 454). If necessary the CNIL also had the ability to bring matters to the attention of the Prosecutor's office (Article 21, 4° LIFL).

376. CONTENT OF A REQUEST OR DECLARATION – Article 19 enumerated the different elements that needed to be included in a request for an opinion or declaration.[796] Both types of documents were required to specify[797]:

- the identity of the person presenting the request [or declaration], as well as the identity of the person who has the power to decide whether personal data shall be processed ("celle qui a pouvoir de décider la création du traitement")[798];
- the *characteristics*, *purposes*, and, if applicable, the *name* of the processing;
- the department or the departments responsible for implementing the processing;
- the department where the *right of access* provided by chapter 5 can be exercised as well as the measures taken to facilitate the exercise of these rights;
- the *categories of persons who*, by reason of their duties or for the needs of the department, *have direct access to the registered data*;
- the *personal data processed*, their source, the *duration* for which they shall be stored, as well as the *recipients or categories of recipients* authorized to receive these data;
- the *links, interconnections or any other form of linkage* of these data as well as their transfer to third parties;
- the steps taken to ensure the *security of processing and data* and to guarantee secrets protected by law;
- whether the processing is intended for *dispatch of personal data between the French territory and a foreign country*, in any form, including the case where it involves operations carried out partly in France on the basis of operations previously carried out outside of France.

Any modification relating to the information listed above, or any cancellation of processing, was to be notified to the CNIL (Article 19). In case of data processing based on a regulatory act, the act in question was required to specify several of the elements listed above (Article 20).[799]

(see also Commission Informatique et Libertés, *Rapport de la Commission Informatique et libertés*, *o.c.*, p. 34).

796 Commission Nationale de l'Informatique et des libertés, *Premier rapport au Président de la République et au Parlement 1978-1980*, *o.c.*, p. 24.

797 Translation based on the original version of the LIFL and A.C.M. Nugter, *Transborder Flow of Personal Data within the EC*, *o.c.*, p. 80 and p. 93.

798 In case this person resided outside of France, the name of his or her representative in France was to be provided (Article 19, first indent).

799 The regulation in question would have to specify in particular (1) the name and purpose of the processing; (2) the department where the right of access provided by chapter 5 can be exercised, as well as (3) the categories of registered information as well as the recipients or categories of recipients authorized to receive these data.

377. "SIMPLIFIED RULES" – Article 17 LIFL allowed the CNIL to adopt so-called "simplified rules" ("*normes simplifiées*") for very common types of processing, provided they "*clearly do not pose any risk to privacy or freedom*" ("*qui ne comportent manifestement pas d'atteinte à la vie privée ou aux libertés*"). Such simplified rules could be adopted vis-à-vis both private and public sector data processing. In situations where "simplified rules" applied, the actor responsible for such processing needed only to declare that the processing conformed to their provisions (rather than submitting a request or declaration of its own) (Article 17, second indent).[800]

B. Data processing requirements

378. OVERVIEW – In addition to the procedures of prior consultation and declaration, the LIFL also articulated a number of restrictions and obligations. In particular, the LIFL contained (1) general principles concerning the use of information technology; (2) rules concerning the collection and storage of personal data; (3) a requirement of security of processing; and (4) restrictions upon the use of sensitive data and national identification numbers.

379. GENERAL PRINCIPLES – Article 1 provided that

> "Informatics must be at the service of every citizen. [...]
> It shall infringe neither human identity nor the rights of man, nor private life, nor individual or public liberties."

The broad language of this provision reaffirmed that the concerns regarding the use of informatics were not limited to the issue of privacy. One of the basic premises of the drafters of the LIFL was that information technology had the ability to affect all areas of community and social life, not merely the private life of individuals.[801]

800 See also Commission Nationale de l'Informatique et des libertés, *Premier rapport au Président de la République et au Parlement 1978-1980, o.c.*, p. 31 et seq. and N. Lenoir, "La loi 78-17 du 6 janvier 1978 et la Commission national de l'informatique et des libertés: Éléments pour un premier bilan de cinq années d'activité", *l.c.*, p. 454. Early examples of such simplified rules concerned processing in the areas of human resource management, utility consumption, loaning of books, tax collection, etc. (Commission Nationale de l'Informatique et des libertés, *Premier rapport au Président de la République et au Parlement 1978-1980, o.c.*, p. 33–34).

801 See A.C.M. Nugter, *Transborder Flow of Personal Data within the EC, o.c.*, p. 79. In its report, the CIL had underlined that informatics had the ability to affect more than just the private life of individuals (even though the latter had admittedly been the focus of its attention). See Commission Informatique et Libertés, *Rapport de la Commission Informatique et libertés, o.c.*, p. 29 et seq. Even though the bulk of the provisions of the LIFL focus on regulating the automated processing of personal data, the broad language of Article 1 led the CNIL to construe its mission in an equally broad fashion. See D.H. Flaherty, *Protecting Privacy in Surveillance Societies, o.c.*, p. 176–177.

380. PROFILING – Article 2 provided that *"no judicial decision involving an assessment of human behaviour may be based on an automated processing of data which describes the profile or personality or the individual concerned"*. A similar restriction was articulated in relation to administrative and private decisions. However, the impact of this latter provision was limited significantly due to the additional qualification that automated processing may not be "sole" basis of the decision (Article 2, second indent).[802]

381. DATA COLLECTION – The drafters of the LIFL sought to "discipline" the collection and recording of personal data in several ways.[803] As indicated earlier, any automated processing of personal data first needed to be included in a request for an opinion or a declaration (cf. *supra*). As part of its supervisory activities, the CNIL would also check whether these data were in fact necessary to realize the stated purpose of the processing.[804] If not, the CNIL would seek to limit any collection it deemed excessive.[805] Finally, Article 25 provided that the collection of personal data by fraudulent, dishonest or illegal means was prohibited. For example, it would be unlawful to collect personal data from files which were not intended for third-party disclosure.[806]

382. FINALITY – The principle of finality was a fundamental principle of the LIFL.[807] Each request for an opinion or declaration needed to state the purpose(s) of the processing (cf. *supra*).[808] This stated purpose would then in principle determine the authorized usage of the collected data.[809] Any use of

---

802 For more information regarding the rationale underlying this provision see A. Holleaux, "La loi du 6 Janvier 1978 sur l'informatique et les libertés (I)", *l.c.*, p. 32.

803 See Commission Informatique et Libertés, *Rapport de la Commission Informatique et libertés*, *o.c.*, p. 45–49.

804 N. Lenoir, "La loi 78-17 du 6 janvier 1978 et la Commission national de l'informatique et des libertés: Éléments pour un premier bilan de cinq années d'activité", *l.c.*, p. 460. Although this requirement of "collection limitation" cannot be found explicitly in the original version of the LIFL, it appears to have been a matter of administrative practice, inspired by the laws of other countries. See Commission Nationale de l'Informatique et des libertés, *Premier rapport au Président de la République et au Parlement 1978-1980*, *o.c.*, p. 27. The CIL had previously also noted the importance of the rule according to which "only data corresponding to a legitimate purpose should be taken into account". See Commission Informatique et Libertés, *Rapport de la Commission Informatique et libertés*, *o.c.*, p. 48–49.

805 N. Lenoir, "La loi 78-17 du 6 janvier 1978 et la Commission national de l'informatique et des libertés: Éléments pour un premier bilan de cinq années d'activité", *l.c.*, p. 460.

806 A.C.M. Nugter, *Transborder Flow of Personal Data within the EC*, *o.c.*, p. 89.

807 N. Lenoir, "La loi 78-17 du 6 janvier 1978 et la Commission national de l'informatique et des libertés: Éléments pour un premier bilan de cinq années d'activité", *l.c.*, p. 459. See also Commission Informatique et Libertés, *Rapport de la Commission Informatique et libertés*, *o.c.*, p. 53–54.

808 For each declaration or request for an opinion, the CNIL would verify (1) whether the stated purpose was compatible with the duties (*"missions"*) of the declaring entity and (2) whether the recorded data corresponded to the stated purpose. (N. Lenoir, *l.c.*, p. 459).

809 The same processing operations could in principle serve multiple purposes. The CNIL also allowed certain "extensions" to the purposes of the processing, in particular for statistical or

personal data for purposes other than those mentioned in the request for an opinion or declaration was illegal (Article 44).

383. Accuracy and completeness – If the entity holding a file containing personal data obtained knowledge of its inaccuracy or incompleteness, these data were to be corrected or completed (Article 37). Should these data have previously been disclosed to a third party, the entity was in principle also obliged to notify them of the correction (Article 38).[810]

384. Storage limitation – Article 28 provided that "*unless otherwise provided for by law, personal data may not be stored in personal form beyond the period stated in the request for an opinion or declaration, unless such storage is authorized by the commission*". The provision was based on the recommendation made by the CIL that data should not be stored indefinitely, but rather be preserved only as long as they are useful for the purposes of the processing.[811]

385. Security – Article 29 stipulated that

> "any person ordering or performing a processing of personal data shall commit himself, towards the individuals concerned, to see that all necessary precautions are taken to protect the data and in particular to prevent these from being distorted, damaged or disclosed to unauthorized third parties".[812]

This obligation to ensure security of processing was also reflected in the punitive provisions of the act (cf. *infra*; 405).[813]

386. Sensitive data – The LIFL imposed additional restrictions on the processing of certain types of "sensitive" data. These data were regarded as sensitive either because of their intimate nature or because they could readily serve as a basis for unfair discrimination.[814] The restrictions concerned data regarding criminal offences, convictions or security measures (Article 30), as well as data revealing racial origin, political, philosophical or religious opinions, or union

research purposes. N. Lenoir, "La loi 78-17 du 6 janvier 1978 et la Commission national de l'informatique et des libertés: Éléments pour un premier bilan de cinq années d'activité", *l.c.*, p. 459.

810 This obligation existed unless the CNIL exempted them from it (Article 38 *in fine*).

811 Commission Informatique et Libertés, *Rapport de la Commission Informatique et libertés*, *o.c.*, p. 50. See also D.H. Flaherty, *Protecting Privacy in Surveillance Societies*, *o.c.*, p. 180. See also A. Holleaux, "La loi du 6 Janvier 1978 sur l'informatique et les libertés (I)", *l.c.*, p. 38–39.

812 See Commission Informatique et Libertés, *Rapport de la Commission Informatique et libertés*, *o.c.*, p. 63 et seq. for a discussion of security measures envisaged by the CIL.

813 A.C.M. Nugter, *Transborder Flow of Personal Data within the EC*, *o.c.*, p. 95. See also A. Holleaux, "La loi du 6 Janvier 1978 sur l'informatique et les libertés (I)", *l.c.*, p. 38.

814 Commission Informatique et Libertés, *Rapport de la Commission Informatique et libertés*, *o.c.*, p. 47.

membership (Article 31). Processing of these data was generally prohibited. Data regarding criminal offences, convictions or security measures could in principle only be processed by "*the jurisdictions and public authorities acting within the scope of their legal powers and, on the favourable opinion of the national commission, companies managing public services*".[815] Data revealing racial origin, political, philosophical or religious opinions, or union membership could in principle only be processed with the express consent of the individual concerned.[816]

387. NATIONAL IDENTIFICATION REGISTER – Article 18 stipulated that the use of the national identification register of national persons ("*répertoire national d'identification des personnes physiques*") was to be authorized by a decree from the Council of State, adopted after receiving an opinion from the CNIL. The terms "use of the national register" was interpreted broadly. It referred not only to the consultation of this register, but also to any use of the national register number (e.g. for purposes of identification or interconnection).[817]

388. INTERNATIONAL TRANSFERS – Article 24 provided that

> "the transfer, between the French territory and a foreign country, in any form, of personal data whose automated processing is governed by article 16 […], can be made subject to a requirement of prior authorization or regulation in accordance with terms established by a decree issued by the Council of State […]".

The reason why this article only expressly targeted private sector data processing was because public sector data transfers could protected by means of the legal or regulatory act providing a basis for the processing.[818]

---

815 Translation by D.H. Flaherty, *Protecting Privacy in Surveillance Societies*, *o.c.*, p. 180.

816 Exceptions to this rule of express consent were provided for religious, philosophical, political or organisations who kept an automated record of data regarding their members or correspondents (Article 31, second indent). In addition, other exceptions to this rule could be adopted for reasons of public interest, on the Commission's proposal or favourable opinion by a decree made by the Council of State (Article 31, second indent). See also N. Lenoir, "La loi 78-17 du 6 janvier 1978 et la Commission national de l'informatique et des libertés: Éléments pour un premier bilan de cinq années d'activité", *l.c.*, p. 455; D.H. Flaherty, *Protecting Privacy in Surveillance Societies*, *o.c.*, p. 180; P. Kayser, *La protection de la vie privée. Protection du secret de la vie privée*, *o.c.*, p. 306–310 and A.C.M. Nugter, *Transborder Flow of Personal Data within the EC*, *o.c.*, p. 90.

817 See Commission Informatique et Libertés, *Rapport de la Commission Informatique et libertés*, *o.c.*, p. 55 et seq.; Commission Nationale de l'Informatique et des libertés, *Premier rapport au Président de la République et au Parlement 1978-1980*, *o.c.*, p. 29–30 and N. Lenoir, "La loi 78-17 du 6 janvier 1978 et la Commission national de l'informatique et des libertés: Éléments pour un premier bilan de cinq années d'activité", *l.c.*, p. 455. Because of the close relationship between the national register number ("*Numéro d'Inscription au Repertoire*" – NIR) and the identification number used by the social security administration (the latter being identical to the former with the addition of a three-digit number), both numbers were regulated in the same fashion (*Id.*).

818 A. Holleaux, "La loi du 6 Janvier 1978 sur l'informatique et les libertés (I)", *l.c.*, p. 36. See also P. Kayser, *La protection de la vie privée. Protection du secret de la vie privée*, *o.c.*, p. 348–350.

C. *Data subject rights*

389. Overview – The LIFL accorded individuals whose personal data was being processed ("*personnes concernées*") a number of rights, including (1) a right to be informed; (2) a right to object; (3) a right to access; (4) a right to know and to contest; and (5) a right to correction.

390. Right to information – Article 27 provided that individuals, from whom personal data are collected, shall be informed of:

- whether providing the solicited information is mandatory or optional;
- what consequences they might face in case of a failure to respond;
- the natural or legal persons that will be recipients of the information;
- the existence of a right of access and rectification.[819]

391. Right to object – Article 26 provided that individuals shall have the right to object to the processing of their personal data. Such an objection would have to be founded on a legitimate reason. Whether or not a legitimate reason existed was not further defined by the LIFL and therefore needed to be decided on a case-by-case basis.[820]

392. Right to access – Every individual had a right to obtain, from any actor or service engaged in the processing of personal data, (1) confirmation as to whether or not data about them was being processed and, if so, (2) to have these data communicated to him (Article 34).[821] No motivation was necessary to justify an access request.[822] The individual concerned needed only to prove his or her identity and submit the request in accordance with the modalities stipulated by the CNIL.[823] Obtaining a copy of one's personal data

---

819 For more information see A.C.M. Nugter, *Transborder Flow of Personal Data within the EC*, *o.c.*, p. 85

820 A.C.M. Nugter, *Transborder Flow of Personal Data within the EC*, *o.c.*, p. 85–86. See also A. Holleaux, "La loi du 6 Janvier 1978 sur l'informatique et les libertés", *l.c.*, p. 37–38.

821 A discussion of the rationale behind this provision can be found in Commission Informatique et Libertés, *Rapport de la Commission Informatique et libertés*, *o.c.*, p. 37–43. It is worth noting that the right of access was perceived as complementary to the public's ability to access the list of processing operations maintained by the CNIL (Article 22 LIFL; cf. *infra*). By consulting this list, it was reasoned, individuals would be capable of determining in which files personal data about them might be included (if they did not know already) and learn where they might obtain more information. See also N. Lenoir, "La loi 78-17 du 6 janvier 1978 et la Commission national de l'informatique et des libertés: Éléments pour un premier bilan de cinq années d'activité", *l.c.*, p. 463.

822 N. Lenoir, "La loi 78-17 du 6 janvier 1978 et la Commission national de l'informatique et des libertés: Éléments pour un premier bilan de cinq années d'activité", *l.c.*, p. 463.

823 *Id.* Where medical data were concerned, however, the right of access was to be exercised via a doctor (Article 40 LIFL). Where the processing activity affects national security, defense, or

could be subjected to a flat fee established by the CNIL (Article 35, second indent).[824]

393. Right to know and to contest – In addition to the right to object and the right of access, the LIFL also provided individuals with a right to contest the processing of their personal data. Specifically, Article 3 provided that every person had the right "*to know and contest the information and reasoning used in automated processing of which the results are used against him*". This provision implied that an individual had a right to learn, not only what data about him were being processed, but also what the logic was of the processing itself (at least in situations where the results of this processing were used against him).[825]

394. Right to correction, completion or clarification – Finally, Articles 36 also provided individuals with a right to correction. Specifically, Article 36 stipulated that "*the holder of a right of access may demand that any data regarding him which are incorrect, incomplete, ambiguous or outdated be corrected, completed, clarified or deleted*". The same right existed in relation to data of which the collection, use or communication was prohibited.[826] If the individual so requested, the department or entity concerned had to send him a copy of the modified data free of charge (Article 36, second indent).[827]

D. National Committee on Informatics and Liberties (CNIL)

395. Mission – The National Committee on Informatics and Liberties ("*Commission Nationale Informatique et Liberté*" – "CNIL") was established to

> "ensure compliance with the provisions of [the LIFL], in particular by informing all individuals concerned of their rights and obligations, by consulting with them and by supervising the use of informatics for the processing of personal data".[828]

The mission of the CNIL was thus to inform, advise and supervise individuals engaged in (or affected by) the processing of personal data.[829] In addition, the

---

public safety, the right of access was to be exercised via the CNIL (Article 39). See also A.C.M. Nugter, *Transborder Flow of Personal Data within the EC*, *o.c.*, p. 85–86.

824 For more information regarding the right of access see A. Holleaux, "La loi du 6 Janvier 1978 sur l'informatique et les libertés (II)", *l.c.*, p. 160–163.

825 See also A.C.M. Nugter, *Transborder Flow of Personal Data within the EC*, *o.c.*, p. 84–85.

826 In cases of data processing concerning national security, defense and public safety, the right to correction was to be exercised via the CNIL (Article 39).

827 In case of a modification, the individual concerned was also to be reimbursed for any charges levied pursuant to the exercise of the right of access (Article 36, third indent). As indicated earlier, the entity holding the file was in principle also obliged to notify any third parties to whom this information had previously been disclosed (Article 38) (cf. *supra*).

828 Article 6 LIFL.

829 The exercise of these tasks could take on a variety of forms. See Commission Informatique et Libertés, *Rapport de la Commission Informatique et libertés*, *o.c.*, p. 71; Commission

CNIL was also responsible for maintaining a publicly available list of all public and private data processing (Article 22 LIFL). This list was to specify, for each processing system:

- the law or regulatory act which decided about the creation of the processing or the date of its declaration;
- its name and its purpose;
- the service with which one can exercise one's right of access;
- the types of personal data registered as well as the recipients or categories of authorized recipients.

396. Powers – The LIFL endowed the CNIL with broad supervisory powers. In addition to its authority to review declarations or requests for private and public sector data processing, as well as to issue simplified norms (cf. *supra*), the CNIL also had the authority to (Article 21):

- conduct investigations and on-site inspections;
- develop recommendations and model regulations regarding the security of processing;
- receive and mediate complaints;
- render certain decisions in specific cases (e.g. to allow an exception to the granting of a right of access[830]);
- issue warnings and inform the public prosecutor of any infractions that come to its knowledge; and
- propose any legislative or regulatory measure it deemed appropriate to protect individual freedoms in light of technological developments.[831]

The entities in charge of (public or private) organisations, as well as the entities that hold or use files containing personal data were obliged to co-operate with the CNIL in the exercise of its tasks (Article 21 *in fine*).

3.4. ALLOCATION OF RESPONSIBILITY AND LIABILITY

397. Absence of a formal definition – The 1978 LIFL did not formally define which actor (or type of actor) would be responsible for compliance with its

Nationale de l'Informatique et des libertés, *Premier rapport au Président de la République et au Parlement 1978-1980*, *o.c.*, p. 16–17 and A.C.M., *Transborder Flow of Personal Data within the EC*, *o.c.*, p. 96–97.

830 See Article 35, second indent LIFL.

831 See also Commission Nationale de l'Informatique et des libertés, *Premier rapport au Président de la République et au Parlement 1978-1980*, *o.c.*, p. 16–17; D.H. Flaherty, *Protecting Privacy in Surveillance Societies*, *o.c.*, p. 186–188 and A.C.M. Nugter, *Transborder Flow of Personal Data within the EC*, *o.c.*, p. 97–101.

provisions. Instead, the LIFL articulated its commands either in general terms (as generally applicable requirements or prohibitions) or by imposing certain responsibilities on specific entities (using varying terminology).

398. CIL REPORT: PUBLIC SECTOR – The CIL report, which had preceded the drafting of the LIFL, stated that the responsibilities of each actor involved in the processing of personal data should be clearly specified.[832] In case of public sector data processing, the CIL expected that the law or regulation, which was to provide the legal basis for the processing, would also specify the responsibilities of the different entities involved.[833] In this regard, it considered it insufficient that the act in question

> "would limit itself to the declaration that a minister or manager was the 'master' of a particular file. While it is good to affirm the responsibility for the whole (with regard to its finality, its general organisation and its supervision), one must also decompose the processing in its successive operation, without ignoring that which precedes it, accompanies it, or follows it, and decide who must do what".[834]

As far as the local communities and public institutions were concerned, the CIL considered it equally necessary for them to define and distribute responsibilities amongst each other.[835] In regard to the allocation of liability, the CIL noted that

> "[i]f the processing of personal data were to cause harm to a third party, the community would be liable. However, it is not sufficient for the mayor or secretary general to push himself forward to cover their subordinates. The mission and duties of each must be specified and it must be possible to identify the people who were really responsible."[836]

399. CIL REPORT: PRIVATE SECTOR – The CIL report was extremely succinct with regards to the allocation of responsibility for private sector data processing. It merely stated: "*similar considerations seem to be valid*".[837] As regards allocation of liability, the CIL noted that

---

832 Commission Informatique et Libertés, *Rapport de la Commission Informatique et libertés*, *o.c.*, p. 69.

833 *Id.* See also p. 31–32 of the same report.

834 *Id.* For example, the head of one particular administrative agency might be responsible for certain operations and for part of the security of the processing, but not be responsible for the collection of the data or what happens to the data once it's been transmitted to its intended recipients. Also, in the event a security officer is appointed, this person would have certain responsibilities without "absorbing" the responsibilities of others (*Id.*).

835 *Id.*

836 *Id.*

837 *Ibid*, p. 70.

"it hopes that the use of informatics will not present an occasion to excessively multiply [the number of] criminal offences, nor to create instances of vicarious criminal responsibility. [The Commission] also considered that the general principles of civil liability should be sufficient, at least for a while, to ensure compensation for damages suffered".[838]

400. Inconsistent terminology – Both the CIL report and the LIFL used various terms to identify the actor (or actors) responsible for ensuring compliance. For example, the CIL report at times spoke of "the entity responsible for the file" ("*l'organisme responsable du fichier*") and the holder of the file ("*détenteur du fichier*").[839] The LIFL itself employed an even wider variety of terms, which included:

- entities "on whose behalf" ("*pour le compte de*") data processing is taking place (Articles 15–16)[840];
- the "person who has the power to decide whether personal data shall be processed" ("*celle qui a pouvoir de décider la création du traitement*") (Article 19)[841];
- the department or departments charged with implementing the processing ("*le service ou les services chargés de mettre en œuvre le traitement*") (Article 19)[842];
- the "holders" or "users" ("*les détenteurs ou utilisateurs*") of the files (Article 21)[843];
- a "person ordering or performing" ("*toute personne ordonnant ou effectuant*") the processing of personal data (Article 29)[844];
- "entities charged with performing the processing" ("*organismes chargées de mettre en œuvre le traitement*") (Article 34)[845];
- the entity responsible for the file ("*le responsable du fichier*") (Article 35)[846]
- the entity holding the file ("*l'organisme qui le tient*") (Article 37).[847]

838 *Id.*

839 See e.g. Commission Informatique et Libertés, *Rapport de la Commission Informatique et libertés*, *o.c.*, p. 42–44. In relation to private sector data processing, the CIL also referred to "private actors that manage personal files or have them managed by third parties" (as responsible entities who must submit a declaration). (*Ibid*, p. 34).

840 Articles 15 and 16 concerned the obligation to submit a request for an opinion or declaration. Cf. *supra*, nos. 374 et seq.

841 Article 19 concerned the contents of a request or declaration. Cf. *supra*, no. 376.

842 *Id.*

843 Article 21 concerned the obligation to co-operate with members to the CNIL in the exercise of their tasks. Cf. *supra*, no. 396.

844 Article 29 concerned the obligation to ensure the security of processing. Cf. *supra*, no. 385.

845 Article 34 concerned the right of access of individuals. Cf. *supra*, no. 392.

846 Article 35 also concerned the right of access of individuals. Cf. *supra*, no. 392.

847 Article 37 concerned the right of correction. Cf. *supra*, no. 394.

401. General criteria – Although the LIFL did not formally define its scope *ratione personae*, it did contain criteria that could be used to identify "the responsible entity". Basing itself on Article 19, the CNIL concluded that the entity that should submit a declaration ("*organisme déclarant*") was "the physical or legal person who has *the power to decide* about whether personal data shall be processed".[848] The language of Articles 15–16 suggested that this "*organisme déclarant*" was also the entity "*on whose behalf*" ("*pour le compte de*") personal data processing would be taking place.[849] As a result, it seems reasonable to conclude that the (implicit) concept of a "responsible entity" under the LIFL was akin to that of a "responsible keeper" under the Swedish Data Act: both the element of *mastery* (decision-making power) and of *benefit* ("on its behalf" were incorporated in the law's provisions.[850]

402. Entities acting "on behalf of" – The LIFL also contained several provisions referring to persons or organisations that might be processing personal data on behalf of others. For example, Articles 19, 29 and 34 referred to entities "performing the processing".[851] Articles 21 and 37 likewise referred to the "holders" of the file. These provisions made clear that entities performing data processing on behalf of others also faced certain responsibilities and restrictions.[852] For example, any "holder" of a file containing personal data was obliged to co-operate with the members to the CNIL in the exercise of their tasks (Article 21). He or she was seemingly also obliged to rectify or complete inaccurate or incomplete information upon obtaining knowledge of its

848 Commission Nationale de l'Informatique et des libertés, *Premier rapport au Président de la République et au Parlement 1978-1980*, *o.c.*, p. 26. By way of example, the CNIL noted that an entity who both initiates and performs the processing of personal data would meet this concept. The same qualification would apply, however, to an entity that initiates the processing but outsources its operations to a third party. In situations whereby one entity initiates the processing of personal data, then transfers some of these data to a third party, who then processes them further for his own account, both these entities would be considered responsible for submitting a declaration (*Id.*).

849 This interpretation is also implicitly confirmed by the examples provided in the first activity report of the CNIL (Commission Nationale de l'Informatique et des libertés, *Premier rapport au Président de la République et au Parlement 1978-1980*, *o.c.*, p. 26).

850 Compare *supra*, no. 400. The decision-making power of "responsible entities" under the LIFL in principle concerned every aspect of the processing (its organisation, collection methods used, etc.). First and foremost, however, it concerned the decision to *initiate* the processing of personal data ("*décider la création*"). See also Commission Informatique et Libertés, *Rapport de la Commission Informatique et libertés*, *o.c.*, p. 29–31 (which referred to "*la décision de recourir à l'informatique*" and "*la décision d'entreprendre traitements*").

851 According to the CNIL, the reference in Article 19 to "the department or departments charged with implementing the processing" ("*le service ou les services chargés de mettre en œuvre le traitement*") referred to the entity or entities who were appointed by the "*organisme déclarant*" to act as its "technical contact point(s)" ("*interlocuteur technique*"). See Commission Nationale de l'Informatique et des libertés, *Premier rapport au Président de la République et au Parlement 1978-1980*, *o.c.*, p. 26.

852 *Contra*: A.C.M. Nugter, *Transborder Flow of Personal Data within the EC*, *o.c.*, p. 96.

incompleteness or inaccuracy (Article 37).[853] Data subjects also had the ability to exercise their right of access vis-à-vis the entities charged with performing the processing (Article 34). Finally, the obligation to ensure security of processing was also incumbent on those who performed the processing of personal data (Article 29).

403. A SHARED RESPONSIBILITY – Based on the foregoing considerations, one can conclude that the responsibility for ensuring compliance with the LIFL was shared, at least in part, among (1) those who had made the decision that personal data processing should take place (*la personne "ordannant" ou "décidant la création"*) and (2) those engaged the actual performance of the processing (*ceux qui "mettent en oeuvre" ou "performent"*). In certain provisions, the allocation of responsibility upon either (or both) types of actors was explicit. In other provisions such explicit allocation was absent, meaning that the precise nature and scope of each actor's obligations would have to be analysed on a case-by-case basis.

404. DEGREE OF FLEXIBILITY – While certain provisions of the LIFL specified which actor (or actors) should comply with its prescriptions, there were many requirements for which the "responsible entity" was free to determine how compliance would be ensured – and by whom.[854] As indicated earlier, the CIL report had called for a clear specification of the responsibilities among actors involved in the processing of personal data.[855] Particularly in the case of outsourcing, the CIL wished to draw attention to the

> "risk that, if strict precautions are not taken with regard to the mission delegated in a service contract, and then in an outsourcing contract, it would become difficult to know what the responsibilities of each entity are".[856]

---

853 Article 37 makes a reference to "l'organisme qui le tient". Given the earlier reference to "*détenteurs ou utilisateurs*" (Article 21), it seems reasonable to infer that Article 37, by using the verb "to hold" ("*tenir*") in first instance referred to the entity who actually "held" the file (which would not necessarily be the same as the entity who "ordered" the processing to take place). However, given the absence of a formal terminology, one must be cautious in concluding that this provision applied only to a certain type of entity (the holder or "*détenteur*") and not the other (the "responsible entity" or "*organisme declarant*"). In any event, it seems reasonable conclude that the individual concerned had the ability to request the correction or completion of information directly from the entity holding his or her data, without having to first contact the "*organisme déclarant*" (in situations where the "holder" and "declarer" or the processing were not the same entity).

854 Undertaking this exercise was (at least in part) necessitated by Article 19, which mandated the inclusion of certain elements in any request for an opinion or declaration (e.g. a designation the department or departments "implementing" the processing; a designation of the department or departments where the right of access can be exercised; indication of steps undertaken to ensure the security of processing). Cf. *supra*, no. 376.

855 Commission Informatique et Libertés, *Rapport de la Commission Informatique et libertés*, *o.c.*, p. 69. Cf. *supra*, no. 398.

856 *Ibid*, p. 70.

In order to address this risk, the CIL suggested that the supervisory authority charged with overseeing the law (i.e. the CNIL) would develop or approve standardised agreements for these situations.[857]

405. Punitive provisions – The LIFL provided for a number of new criminal offences in Articles 41–44 of the law. Article 41 made it a crime for anyone "to carry out or have others carry out" ("*aura procédé ou fait procéder*") automated processing of personal data before (a) publication of regulatory act authorizing the processing or (b) having submitted the requisite declaration.[858] Article 42 criminalized the registration or storage of data in violation of Articles 25 (collection of personal data by fraudulent, dishonest or illegal means), 26 (legitimate objection by data subject), 28 (limitation of storage duration), 29 (security of processing), 30 and 31 (sensitive data).[859] Article 43 made it a crime for anyone to engage in an unauthorized disclosure of personal data that would damage the reputation of the person concerned, as well as the intimacy of his or her private life.[860] Finally, Article 44 penalized any entity that used personal data for a purpose other than the one defined in the declaration or regulatory act authorizing the processing.[861]

406. Civil remedy – The LIFL did not contain any specific provisions concerning damages resulting from a violation of the law.[862] Normal rules regarding civil liability would apply in those cases.[863]

---

857 *Id.* Strictly speaking this remark only concerned processing operations undertaken on behalf of public sector entities. However, the following sentence in the CIL's report is that "*similar considerations seem to apply for the private sector*". The CIL also noted that "*the contracts usually offered to users by manufacturers or service providers are quite inconspicuous about the obligations of service providers and it would opportune to seek out more balanced formulations*" (*Id.*).

858 Violation of this provision was punishable by a fine and/or imprisonment of not less than 6 months with a maximum of 3 years. In addition, a convicted person could also be ordered by the courts to publish the sentence (in part or in full) at his own expense (Article 41, second indent). (A.C.M. Nugter, *Transborder Flow of Personal Data within the EC*, *o.c.*, p. 102). See also P. Kayser, *La protection de la vie privée. Protection du secret de la vie privée*, *o.c.*, p. 292.

859 Violation of this provision was punishable by a fine and/or imprisonment of not less than 1 year with a maximum of 5 years. Again, the convicted person could also be ordered by the courts to publish the sentence (in part or in full) at his own expense (Article 42, second indent). (A.C.M. Nugter, *Transborder Flow of Personal Data within the EC*, *o.c.*, p. 102–103).

860 Violation of this provision was punishable by a fine and/or imprisonment of not less than 2 months with a maximum of 6 months. (A.C.M. Nugter, *Transborder Flow of Personal Data within the EC*, *o.c.*, p. 103).

861 Violation of this provision was punishable by a fine and/or imprisonment of not less than 1 year with a maximum of 5 years. (A.C.M. Nugter, *Transborder Flow of Personal Data within the EC*, *o.c.*, p. 103).

862 A.C.M. Nugter, *Transborder Flow of Personal Data within the EC*, *o.c.*, p. 105.

863 *Id.* See also *supra*, no. 399 (noting that the CIL had considered that the general principles of civil liability should be sufficient, at least for a while, to ensure compensation for damages

3.5. CONCLUSION

407. Staying the course – The French Law on Liberties, Informatics, Files and Liberties followed the footsteps of its German and Swedish predecessors. In some respects it bore resemblance to the data protection laws of Hesse[864] and the Federal Republic of Germany[865], in others it more closely resembled the Swedish Data Act.[866] Many of its key provisions, such as the right of access, the limitation of storage duration and the right to know still echo in contemporary data protection legislation.

408. Responsibility and liability – The LIFL did not formally define which actor (or type of actors) would be responsible for compliance with its provisions. Instead, it employed a range of different terms to refer, on the one hand, to the actor that carried primary responsibility for the processing (i.e. the entity that "*decided about the creation of data processing*", "*ordered*" the processing or "*carried out or had others carry out*" personal data processing) and, on the other hand, to actors who might be engaged in the processing of personal data on behalf of others (i.e. the entities "*performing the processing*", the "*holders*" of the files). The latter group of actors were not exempted from compliance however: several provisions of the LIFL were directly applicable to actors that performed data processing on behalf of others.[867]

---

suffered). (Commission Informatique et Libertés, *Rapport de la Commission Informatique et libertés*, *o.c.*, p. 70).

864 E.g. as regards the consultative role of the entity charged with supervising compliance with the act (as opposed to a default licensing scheme). Compare *supra*, nos. 308 et seq.

865 Gesetz zum Schutz vor Mißbrauch personenbezogener Daten bei der Datenverarbeitung of 27 January 1977, *Bundesgesetblatt* 1 February 1977, I, No. 7, p. 201.

866 E.g. as regards its applicability to public and private sector data processing and the duties of the "responsible keeper". Compare *supra*, no. 330 and no. 341 et seq.

867 The punitive provisions of the LIFL also did not distinguish between those processing on their own account and those processing on behalf of others. The CIL report had, however, indicated a desire not to introduce instances of vicarious criminal liability (cf. *supra*, no. 399). As a result, one might argue that those acting "on behalf" of others might not be criminally responsible as long as they acted in accordance with the instructions issued to them.

CHAPTER 4
INTERNATIONAL INSTRUMENTS

1. INTRODUCTION

409. Data crosses borders – During the 1970s, policy makers became increasingly concerned with the international dimension of data protection.[868] Transborder flows of personal data were gradually becoming a reality to be reckoned with. Certain policymakers feared that protections offered by national laws might be circumvented by "offshoring" data processing activities.[869] Any restrictions on the international transfer of personal data, however, would disrupt free information flow and trade.[870] To address this issue, international organisations started to form working groups of experts to explore the necessities and implications of data protection at the international level.[871]

410. International initiatives – Although individual accounts vary, the first international discussions on the need for data protection may be situated towards the end of the 1960s.[872] The increasingly international dimension of data flows made it imperative that certain "basic rules" be established and agreed upon at international level.[873] Data protection was discussed at various intergovernmental and non-governmental fora.[874] In the end, however, there were

---

868 A.C.M. Nugter, *Transborder Flow of Personal Data within the EC*, *o.c.*, p. 20, C.J. Bennet, *Regulating privacy. Data Protection and Public Policy in Europe and the United States*, *o.c.*, p. 130.

869 C.J. Bennet, *Regulating privacy. Data Protection and Public Policy in Europe and the United States*, *o.c.*, p. 130

870 *Id.* Additional concerns related to jurisdictional conflicts resulting from discrepancies among national laws, as well issues regarding remedies and enforcement (*Ibid*, p. 130–131). See also M.D. Kirby, "Transborder Data Flows and the 'Basic Rules' of Data Privacy", *l.c.*, p. 27–28.

871 G. Stadler and T. Herzog, "Data Protection: International Trends and the Austrian Example", *l.c.*, p. 6.

872 Compare e.g. F.H. Cate, "The EU Data Protection Directive, Information Privacy, and the Public Interest", *l.c.*, 431 with D. Campbell and J. Fisher (eds.), *Data transmission and privacy*, Center for International Legal Studies, Martinus Nijhoff Publishers, Dordrecht, 1994, vii and C.J. Bennet, *Regulating privacy. Data Protection and Public Policy in Europe and the United States*, *o.c.*, p. 131–132.

873 M.D. Kirby, "Transborder Data Flows and the 'Basic Rules' of Data Privacy", *l.c.*, p. 29

874 See C.J. Bennet, *Regulating privacy. Data Protection and Public Policy in Europe and the United States*, *o.c.*, p. 132–133.

two international organisations which would contribute most to the development of harmonised data protection standards, namely the Organisation for Economic Cooperation and Development (OECD) and the Council of Europe.[875]

2. THE OECD GUIDELINES (1980)

2.1. ORIGIN AND DEVELOPMENT

411. Economic relevance – The Organisation for Economic Co-Operation and Development (OECD) took an early interest in information processing and computerization.[876] From the 1960s onward, the OECD considered information to be an increasingly important economic asset.[877] When the first data protection laws emerged, concerns arose as to how such legislation might affect the free flow of data across borders.[878] Transborder data flows ("TBDF") were generally perceived as being beneficial to economic and social development. Any restrictions upon TBDF could impede those benefits from accruing and therefore required careful consideration.[879]

412. Preparation – Between 1968 and 1974, the OECD undertook a range of studies and organised multiple seminars regarding the technological, economic and legal implications of computing.[880] In 1977, an intergovernmental

875 *Id.*

876 C.J. Bennet, *Regulating privacy. Data Protection and Public Policy in Europe and the United States*, *o.c.*, p. 136.

877 *Id.* See also B. Godin, "The information economy: the history of a concept through its measurement, 1949–2005", *History and Technology: An International Journal* 2008, Vol. 24, n. 3, p. 256 et seq.

878 M.D. Kirby, "Transborder Data Flows and the "Basic Rules" of Data Privacy", *l.c.*, p. 42.

879 See also M. Kirby, "The history, achievement and future of the 1980 OECD guidelines on privacy", *International Data Privacy Law* 2011, Vol. 1, No. 1, p. 8 ("*It was the potential of TBDF to occasion restrictions, regulations and even treaties within the global community of free markets and for these to impose 'barriers' on the free flow of data that attracted the interest of the OECD. Specifically, they enlivened its mission to contribute to (and defend) free flows deemed suitable to market information economies. Put bluntly, the OECD concern was that the response of European nations (and European regional institutions) to the challenges of TBDF for privacy might potentially erect legal and economic barriers against which it was essential to provide effective exceptions.*") See also OECD, "The Evolving Privacy Landscape: 30 Years After the OECD Privacy Guidelines", *OECD Digital Economy Papers* 2011, No. 176, OECD Publishing, Paris, p. 7 and 11.

880 In 1968, the OECD's Committee on Science and Policy decided that the topic of "computer utilization" should be examined, leading to the subsequent establishment of a "Computer Utilization Group". (C.J. Bennet, *Regulating privacy. Data Protection and Public Policy in Europe and the United States*, *o.c.*, p. 136). The group produced a number of studies under the series "OECD Informatics studies". See also P. Svenonius, "Address", OECD, "Policy issues in data protection and privacy. Concepts and perspectives", *OECD Informatics Studies*, no. 10, 1976, OECD, Paris, p. 48; F. W. Hondius, *Emerging data protection in Europe*, *o.c.*, p. 58; H.P. Gassman, "30 Years After: The Impact of the OECD Privacy Guidelines", Speech delivered

Expert Group on "Transborder Data Barriers and Privacy Protection" was established.[881] The mission of this Expert Group was to (1) develop guidelines on basic rules governing transborder flow and the protection of personal data and privacy with a view of facilitating harmonization and (2) investigate the legal and economic problems relating to the transborder flow of nonpersonal data.[882] The Expert Group was to carry out its activities "in close co-operation and consultation" with the Council of Europe and the European Community.[883]

413. Adoption – In 1979, the Expert Group presented its draft Guidelines, together with an Explanatory Memorandum, to the Committee for Scientific and Technological Policy.[884] On 23 September 1980, the OECD Council formally adopted the *Guidelines on the Protection of Privacy and Transborder Flows of Personal Data*.[885]

2.2. SCOPE

414. Public and private sector – The OECD Guidelines were to govern both public and private sector data processing (paragraph 2). In principle, no distinction was made with regards their application to either sector.[886] However, the Guidelines did recognize that exceptions could be made in the name of national sovereignty, national security and public policy.[887]

---

at the Joint Roundtable of the Committee for Information, Computer and Communications Policy (ICCP), and its Working Party on Information Security and Privacy (WPISP), 10 March 2010, Parisand OECD, "The Evolving Privacy Landscape: 30 Years After the OECD Privacy Guidelines", *l.c.*, p. 9.

881 M.D. Kirby, "Transborder Data Flows and the 'Basic Rules' of Data Privacy", *l.c.*, p. 43. See also the Explanatory Memorandum to the OECD Guidelines on the Protection of Privacy and Transborder Flows of Personal Data, paragraph 18 (hereinafter: "Explanatory Memorandum"). The Expert Group was established under the OECD's Directorate for Science, Technology and Industry's Committee for Information, Computer and Communications Policy (DSTI/ICCP) (M. Kirby, "The history, achievement and future of the 1980 OECD guidelines on privacy", *l.c.*, p. 7). It was chaired by Honourable Justice Michael Kirby of Australia. (Explanatory Memorandum, paragraph 19).

882 M.D. Kirby, "Transborder Data Flows and the 'Basic Rules' of Data Privacy", *l.c.*, p. 43.

883 *Id.* See also Explanatory Memorandum, paragraph 19.

884 M.D. Kirby, "Transborder Data Flows and the 'Basic Rules' of Data Privacy", *l.c.*, p. 43.

885 Organisation for Economic Co-operation and Development (OECD), "Recommendation of the Council concerning Guidelines governing the protection of privacy and transborder flows of personal data", 23 September 1980 (hereinafter: "OECD Guidelines"). This was the same month that the Council of Europe's Convention for the Protection of Individuals with regard to Automatic Processing of Personal Data (Convention 108) was adopted. However, the Convention was not opened for ratification until 1981. (OECD, "The Evolving Privacy Landscape: 30 Years After the OECD Privacy Guidelines", *l.c.*, p. 12) See also *infra*, no. 447.

886 See also A.C.M. Nugter, *o.c.*, p. 22.

887 Even though the OECD Guidelines were expressed as a non-binding Recommendation, its drafters nevertheless considered it important to incorporate guidance with regard to potential exemptions or derogations. (Explanatory Memorandum, paragraph, 46).

415. Personal data – The OECD Guidelines applied only to the processing of personal data, which were defined as "*any information relating to an identified or identifiable individual*" (paragraph 1(b)).

416. Automated and non-automated – The Guidelines in principle applied both to automated and non-automated data processing.[888] Neither term was explicitly defined.[889]

2.3. BASIC PROTECTIONS

417. Overview – The OECD Guidelines were divided into four substantive parts, namely (1) basic principles of national application, (2) basic principles of international application; (3) national implementation; and (4) international co-operation.

A. *Basic principles of national application*

418. Minimum standards – The first substantive part of the OECD Guidelines set forth a number of "basic rules" for the processing of personal data. These rules, which were articulated in the form of "principles", were intended as benchmarks for national policies aiming to protect privacy.[890] It is important to note, however, that the OECD Guidelines were promulgated as minimum standards, "*capable of being supplemented by additional measures for the protection of privacy and individual liberties*" (paragraph 6). This meant that national policies (or other international instruments) could introduce additional (and perhaps more restrictive) measures to protect privacy and individual liberties.[891]

419. Degree of abstraction – The basic principles of national application were articulated with varying levels of detail. These differences were attributable to (a) the degree of consensus, within the Expert Group, as to how these principles should be given effect, and (b) existing knowledge and experience

888 *Ibid*, paragraphs 34–38. Paragraph 3(c) of the Guidelines did however grant that "*[t]hese Guidelines should not be interpreted as preventing the application of the Guidelines only to automatic processing of personal data*".

889 According the Explanatory Memorandum, guidance for the interpretation of the concept of "automatic data processing" could be obtained from sources such as standard technical vocabularies. (*Ibid*, paragraph 36).

890 M.D. Kirby, "Transborder Data Flows and the 'Basic Rules' of Data Privacy", *l.c.*, p. 27–29.

891 In other words, the principles contained in the OECD Guidelines provided "a floor, not a ceiling" for the protection of privacy and individual liberties. This qualification, because it was specified in the scope section of the Guidelines, applied to the Guidelines as a whole – not only to the principles of national application.

relating to such measures.[892] Because the Guidelines were intended as a frame of reference for many different countries (who each had varying legal systems and traditions), a certain degree of abstraction was unavoidable.[893]

420. Collection limitation – The first principle of national application was the collection limitation principle. According to paragraph 7,

> "[t]here should be limits to the collection of personal data and any such data should be obtained by lawful and fair means and, where appropriate, with the knowledge or consent of the data subject."

421. Data quality – According to the data quality principle,

> "[p]ersonal data should be relevant to the purposes for which they are to be used, and, to the extent necessary for those purposes, should be accurate, complete and kept up-to-date."[894]

The requirement of "relevancy" implied that the collected data should not be "more far-reaching" than was necessary to achieve the purposes of the processing.[895] The duty to maintain data accuracy, supplement data, or to ensure it remained up-to-date was likewise to be assessed in light of the purposes pursued.[896]

422. Purpose specification – The purpose specification principle (paragraph 9) was closely associated with its two surrounding principles, namely the data quality principle and the use limitation principle.[897] Paragraph 9 provided that "*the purposes for which personal data are collected should be specified not later than at the time of data collection*". Any subsequent use of these data was to be limited to the fulfilment of those purposes – or at least be "compatible" with them.[898]

---

892 Explanatory Memorandum, paragraph 27.

893 By the time the Guidelines were adopted, one third of the OECD Member countries had already undertaken to regulate the processing of personal data, among which notable differences existed (for an overview see OECD, "The Evolving Privacy Landscape: 30 Years After the OECD Privacy Guidelines", *l.c.*, p. 8 and C.J. Bennet, *Regulating privacy. Data Protection and Public Policy in Europe and the United States*, *o.c.*, p. 57). Any attempt to consolidate and/or harmonize basic principles from these different instruments would necessarily involve a certain degree of abstraction. See also Explanatory Memorandum, paragraph 6.

894 Paragraph 8 of the Guidelines.

895 Explanatory Memorandum, paragraph 53.

896 According to the Explanatory Memorandum, this "*'purpose test' will often involve the problem of whether or not harm can be caused to data subjects because of lack of accuracy, completeness and up-dating*" (*Id.*).

897 Explanatory Memorandum, paragraph 54.

898 Explanatory Memorandum, paragraph 54. It is interesting to note that the Explanatory Memorandum also infers from this principle that "*when data no longer serve a purpose, and*

423. Use limitation – Paragraph 10 stated that

> "Personal data should not be disclosed, made available or otherwise used for purposes other than those specified in accordance with Paragraph 9 except:
>
> a) with the consent of the data subject; or
> b) by the authority of law".

The use limitation principle built further upon the purpose specification principle: the purposes specified prior to collection of personal data in principle determined how those data could be used. However, paragraph 10 also indicated that a deviation of purpose might be permissible in two instances, namely (a) where the individual concerned provided his or her consent or, (b) where the new use was authorized by law.[899]

424. Security safeguards – The security safeguards principle stipulated that personal data should be protected, by reasonable security measures, against "*loss or unauthorised access, destruction, use, modification or disclosure of data*" (paragraph 11).

425. Openness – The openness principle (paragraph 12) was formulated in relatively abstract terms. According to this principle,

> "[t]here should be a general policy of openness about developments, practices and policies with respect to personal data. Means should be readily available of establishing the existence and nature of personal data, and the main purposes of their use, as well as the identity and usual residence of the data controller."

426. Individual participation – The principle of individual participation was generally considered as one of the most important privacy safeguards.[900] As a result, it was articulated in rather direct and specific terms. Paragraph 13 of the Guidelines provided that data subjects should have a right (1) to access their data (i.e. to receive communication of data relating to him in a reasonable manner) and (2) to challenge data relating to him and, if the challenge is successful to have the data erased, rectified, completed or amended.

427. Accountability – The principle of accountability was of central importance to the OECD Guidelines. Paragraph 14 provided that:

---

if it is practicable, it may be necessary to have them destroyed (erased) or given an anonymous form. The reason is that control over data may be lost when data are no longer of interest; this may lead to risks of theft, unauthorised copying or the like.") (*Id.*).

899 See also Explanatory Memorandum, paragraph 55.

900 *Ibid*, paragraph 58.

> "A data controller should be accountable for complying with measures which give effect to the principles stated above".

The objective of this principle was two-fold. First, it served to assign (primary) responsibility for compliance to the "data controller".[901] Secondly, this principle encouraged Member countries to institute mechanisms which ensure that data controllers are held answerable in case this responsibility is not met.[902] The Explanatory Memorandum to the Guidelines elaborated upon the rationale and implications of this principle as follows:

> "The data controller decides about data and data processing activities. It is for his benefit that the processing of data is carried out. Accordingly, it is essential that under domestic law accountability for complying with privacy protection rules and decisions should be placed on the data controller who should not be relieved of this obligation merely because the processing of data is carried out on his behalf by another party, such as a service bureau."[903]

The Guidelines themselves did not prescribe to whom the controller should be accountable, nor did it prescribe any specific accountability mechanisms. The Memorandum merely indicated that "*accountability under Paragraph 14 refers to accountability supported by legal sanctions, as well as to accountability established by codes of conduct, for instance.*"[904]

B. *Basic principles of international application*

428. Purpose – The main driver behind the development of the OECD Guidelines was, as mentioned earlier, the concern that privacy laws might create artificial barriers to the free flow of data.[905] In an attempt to mitigate this risk, paragraphs 15–18 of the Guidelines called upon Member countries to (a) remain mindful of each other's interests in relation to the processing of personal data; (b) ensure the security and continuity of transborder data flows; and (c) avoid unnecessary restrictions upon transborder data flows.

C. *National implementation*

429. A general framework – Paragraph 19 provided a general outline of how the Guidelines might be implemented at national level. Recognizing that

901 See also M.D. Kirby, "Transborder Data Flows and the 'Basic Rules' of Data Privacy", *l.c.*, p. 60. The "data controller" was defined by paragraph 1(a) as "*a party who, according to domestic law, is competent to decide about the contents and use of personal data regardless of whether or not such data are collected, stored, processed or disseminated by that party or by an agent on its behalf*". See also *infra*, no. 432.

902 J. Alhadeff, B. Van Alsenoy and J. Dumortier, "The accountability principle in data protection regulation: origin, development and future directions", *l.c.*, p. 53.

903 Explanatory Memorandum, paragraph 62.

904 *Id.*

905 Cf. *supra*, no. 411.

this implementation was bound to vary according to different legal systems and traditions, this paragraph merely attempted to signal, in broad terms, what kind of "national machinery" was envisaged for putting the Guidelines into effect.[906]

430. Elements – According to paragraph 19, the following elements merited consideration when implementing the Guidelines: (a) the adoption of appropriate legislation; (b) the promotion of self-regulation; as well as (c) the administration of sanctions and remedies in cases of failure to comply with measures implementing the Guidelines. In addition, paragraph 19 also envisaged "reasonable means for individuals to exercise their rights" and measures to prevent "unfair discrimination against data subjects".[907]

D. International co-operation

431. Elements – The final section of the OECD Guidelines specified a number of areas in which Member countries were encouraged to co-operate further, namely:

a) exchange of information regarding the implementation of the Guidelines[908];
b) the development of compatible procedures for TBDF[909];
c) procedural and investigative matters, particularly among data protection authorities and entities dealing with information policy issues[910]; and
d) the development of conflict of laws rules.[911]

2.4. ALLOCATION OF RESPONSIBILITY AND LIABILITY

432. Formal definition – The OECD Guidelines formally defined the actor which should be responsible for ensuring compliance with its provisions. The responsible actor was the "data controller", which was defined by paragraph 1(a) as

> "a party who, according to domestic law, is competent to decide about the contents and use of personal data regardless of whether or not such data are collected, stored, processed or disseminated by that party or by an agent on its behalf."[912]

---

906 Explanatory Memorandum, paragraph 69. This aspect of "flexible implementation" is considered to have been key to the success of the OECD Guidelines. See M. Kirby, "The history, achievement and future of the 1980 OECD guidelines on privacy", *l.c.*, p. 11.
907 See Explanatory Memorandum, paragraph 70.
908 Paragraph 20 of the Guidelines. See also Explanatory Memorandum, paragraphs 71–72.
909 *Id.*
910 Paragraph 21 of the Guidelines. See also Explanatory Memorandum, paragraph 73.
911 Paragraph 22 of the Guidelines. See also Explanatory Memorandum, paragraphs 74–76.
912 Paragraph 1(a) of the OECD Guidelines (emphasis added).

A number of general criteria can be extrapolated from this definition, each of which shall be elaborated over the following paragraphs.

433. A PARTY – Under the OECD Guidelines, a data controller could be a natural or legal person, public authority, agency or any other body.[913]

434. DECISION-MAKING POWER – The data controller was the actor who, according to domestic law, was "*competent to decide*" about the collection and use of personal data. A first constitutive element of the data controller concept was thus a competency to exercise decision-making power. The reference to "according to domestic law" underlined that Member countries retained discretion in developing additional criteria for determining such competency.[914]

435. CONTENTS AND USE – The second constitutive element of the data controller concept concerned the object of its decision-making power, namely the "contents and use" of personal data. According to the Explanatory Memorandum, the data controller was the actor who "*decide[d] about data and data processing activities*".[915] Arguably, this encompassed various aspects of the processing, such as the types of data to be collected, the purposes of the processing, which entities would have access to the data, the logic of the processing, etc.[916] In other words: the data controller was the actor that decided about the "input" of the processing as well as how this input was to be applied.

436. CUI BONO – According to the Explanatory Memorandum, the data controller was the party *for whose benefit* the processing of personal data is being carried out.[917] This aspect was also reflected implicitly in paragraph 1(a), which stated that a party might be considered a data controller "*regardless of whether or not such data are collected, stored, processed or disseminated by that party* ***or by an agent on its behalf***" (emphasis added). The reference to "on his behalf" suggested that the processing was undertaken to serve the controller's interests.

437. EXCLUDED ENTITIES – The Explanatory Memorandum stated that certain types of actors, although they might be involved in the processing of data, should

---

913 Explanatory Memorandum, paragraph 40.

914 P.H. Patrick, "Privacy Restrictions on Transnational Data Flows: A Comparison of the Council of Europe Draft Convention and OECD Guidelines", *Jurimetrics Journal* 1980–1981, Vol. 21, p. 410.

915 Explanatory Memorandum, paragraph 62.

916 This interpretation is corroborated by the latter portion of paragraph 40 of the Explanatory Memorandum, which indirectly paraphrases the controller's decision-making power as being entitled to decide "*what activities should be carried out and for what purposes*" and "*what data should be stored, who should be able to use them, etc*".

917 Explanatory Memorandum, paragraph 62.

not be considered data controllers.[918] Specifically, the data controller concept reportedly excluded

> "(a) licensing authorities and similar bodies which exist in some Member countries and which authorise the processing of data but are not entitled to decide (in the proper sense of the word) what activities should be carried out and for what purposes; (b) data processing service bureaux which carry out data processing on behalf of others; (c) telecommunications authorities and similar bodies which act as mere conduits; and (d) "dependent users" who may have access to data but who are not authorised to decide what data should be stored, who should be able to use them, etc."[919]

This portion of the Explanatory Memorandum made clear that not every actor with the ability to influence the processing should necessarily be considered a data controller. It also made clear that an actor might be engaged in the processing of personal data without acting as a data controller.[920]

438. Genesis of the "data controller" concept – The term "data controller" had not figured in any of the national laws adopted prior to the Guidelines. While several of those laws formally defined a "responsible actor", none of them used a term which was etymologically related to the word "controller". How this term came to be introduced is therefore somewhat uncertain. However, the limited documentation that exists regarding the introduction of this concept provides some indication. Speaking at an OECD symposium in 1977, F.W. Hondius, a representative of the Directorate of Legal Affairs of the Council of Europe, commented on the difficulties in developing a common understanding of key concepts as follows:

---

918 *Ibid*, paragraph 40.

919 *Id.*

920 The exclusion of "service bureaux" from the data controller concept echoes one of the recommendations submitted to the 1977 OECD symposium on Transborder Data Flows and the Protection of Privacy. Specifically, it was recommended that a distinction be maintained between, on the one hand, the "*use* of data" and the "*processing* of data" and, on the other hand, between the organisation or individual "on whose behalf and under whose direction" data processing work is done (the "*beneficial user*") and the individual or organisation on whose computing systems processing is carried out (the "*agency*"). The former should be subject to applicable data protection laws, whereas the latter should be capable of providing a level of security appropriate to the level of sensitivity of the data. See A.A. Benjamin, "Privacy and Computers", in OECD, *Transborder Data Flows and the Protection of Privacy*, *o.c.*, p. 175–176. It is worth noting the affiliation of the author, i.e. the UK Computing Services Association. The contribution by P.C. Onstad, Chairman of the Association of Data Processing Services, followed a similar vein: see P.C. Onstad, "Data Processing Services and Transborder Data Flows", in in OECD, *Transborder Data Flows and the Protection of Privacy*, *o.c.*, p. 180 (comparing data processing services to a "safety box" leased by a bank to the customer; whereby the customer is totally responsible and "in complete control" of all input and output to the box; whereas the bank can at most assume responsibility for the physical security of the box).

> "The main difficulty we encountered in preparing this draft was, to use a computer term, to create interfaces between widely different concepts of the various national legal systems. [...] But we found it worth the effort, after having made an analytical survey of the key concepts of national legislation, to try our hand at international standards. Mr. Benjamin will be pleased to recognize, for example, his 'beneficial user' concept, which is disguised in our text as 'controller of the record', a clumsy English rendering of the marvellous French expression 'maître du fichier'."[921]

It seems reasonable to conclude, on the basis of this text, that the term "controller of the file" emerged in the course of the discussions surrounding the preparation of Convention 108 and the OECD Guidelines.[922] This term was not, however, created *de novo*. Its inspiration seems to have stemmed from computer science literature, in particular the writings of Rein Turn.[923]

439. Entities "acting on behalf of" – The OECD Guidelines allocated "ultimate" responsibility for compliance with the data controller.[924] They did not assign any responsibility to entities acting on behalf of a data controller. The Explanatory Memorandum noted, however, that Member countries remained free to develop "*more complex schemes of levels and types of responsibilities*" when implementing the Guidelines.[925] For example,

> "[...] nothing in the Guidelines prevents service bureaux personnel, "dependent users" [...] and others from also being held accountable. For instance, sanctions against breaches of confidentiality obligations may be directed against all parties

---

921 F.W. Hondius, "The Action of the Council of Europe with regard to International Data Protection", in OECD, "Transborder Data Flows and the Protection of Privacy", *o.c.*, p. 260 (emphasis added). See also *supra*, footnote 921.

922 The Committee of Experts tasked with preparing Convention 108 also comprised participants from countries outside of Europe, as well as members of the OECD Expert Group on Transborder Data Barriers and Privacy Protection. The suggestion to use the term "controller" may therefore have originated from either forum.

923 In his 1975 book, Hondius noted that Rein Turn used the term "controller" to refer to what he would refer to as the "user" of a data bank (see F.W. Hondius, *Emerging data protection in Europe*, *o.c.*, p. 101–103). Turn had also used the term "controller" in his contribution to the 1974 OECD seminar on Policy issues in data protection and privacy (see R. Turn, "Data security: costs and constraints" in OECD, *Policy issues in data protection and privacy. Concepts and perspectives*, *o.c.*, p. 244 et seq.), as well as in anterior publications (dating back at least to 1967). See e.g. H.E. Peterson and R. Turn, "System implications of information privacy", in *Proceeding AFIPS '67*, (Spring) Proceedings of the April 18–20, 1967, spring joint computer conference, ACM, New York, p. 293. Turn's use of the term "controller" displayed strong conceptual similarity with the terms "data controller" and "controller of the file". In his contribution to 1974 OECD seminar, for example, he defined the "controller" as "*(an agency) with authority over the data-base system, which specifies the population of subjects, type of data collected, and the protection policies*". (R. Turn, "Data security: costs and constraints", *l.c.*, p. 244).

924 Explanatory Memorandum, paragraph 40.

925 Explanatory Memorandum, paragraph 40.

> entrusted with the handling of personal information (cf. Paragraph 19 of the Guidelines)."[926]

As we have seen earlier, the privacy laws of Hesse, Sweden and France all allocated certain responsibilities upon entities acting "on behalf of" the "responsible" entity, whether they were acting in the capacity of a service provider or as an employee.[927] For the most part, their responsibilities were limited to (a) duties of confidentiality; (b) an obligation to ensure security of processing; as well as (c) a general duty to co-operate with supervisory authorities.[928]

440. Role of the accountability principle – Within the OECD Guidelines, the principle of accountability served as a vehicle to assign responsibility for compliance "*with measures which give effect to the principles*".[929] Rather than limiting the scope of the Guidelines *ratione personae*, the drafters chose to introduce an additional principle as a means of assigning responsibility. This choice was reflective of the fact that the OECD Guidelines were directed towards Member countries, rather than being directly applicable to data controllers. As noted by Kirby, the principle of accountability

> "sought to identify a duty-bearer so that there would be no doubt as to who had the obligation to comply with the Guidelines in particular cases. The passive voice and subjunctive mood of hortatory language, common in international instruments, can sometimes weaken the power of their instruction. The value of the 'accountability

926 *Ibid*, paragraph 62. For a detailed discussion of the "processing services" and "data services" offered by "(computer) service bureaux" at the time see J. Bing, P. Forsberg and E. Nygaard, "Legal problems related to transborder data flows", in OECD, *An Exploration of Legal Issues in Information and Communication Technologies*, Information Computer Communication Policy no. 8, Paris, OECD, 1983, p. 129–131.

927 Cf. *supra*, no. 319 (Hesse); no. 357 (Sweden) and no. 402 (France).

928 *Id.* It is worth noting that the federal data protection act of (West) Germany (1977) imposed a more comprehensive set of obligations upon the "data protection representative" ("*Datenschutzbeauftragten*"), who acted as a "responsible person" within an organisation that had decided to process personal data. See paragraph 29 of the Act on the Protection against the Misuse of Personal Data in Data Processing ("*Gesetz zum Schutz vor Missbrach Peronenbezogener Daten bei der Datenverarbeitung – Bundesdatenshutzgesetz*") of 27 January 1977 (*Bundesgesetzblatt* No. 7 of 1 February 1977, Part I (Teil I), p. 201). See also M.D. Kirby, "Transborder Data Flows and the 'Basic Rules' of Data Privacy", *l.c.*, p. 61. For a critical evaluation see S. Simitis, "Establishing Institutional Structures to Monitor and Enforce Data Protection", in OECD, "Policy issues in data protection and privacy. Concepts and perspectives", *OECD Informatics Studies*, *o.c.*, p. 85–86.

929 Cf. *supra*, no. 427. Kirby has noted that the accountability principle was to some extent an OECD novelty: see M. Kirby, "The history, achievement and future of the 1980 OECD guidelines on privacy", *l.c.*, p. 10 ("*The OECD Guidelines added the 'accountability principle' (para.14). That principle had not been included, as such, in the earlier European work.*") As noted by the same author, the principle of accountability had already figured in the 1974 US Privacy Act: see M.D. Kirby, "Transborder Data Flows and the 'Basic Rules' of Data Privacy", *l.c.*, p. 38.

> principle' is that it permits elaboration and identification of the duty-bearer. This is important for the effective implementation of the Guidelines."[930]

As indicated earlier, the principle of accountability also served a second purpose, namely as the articulation of a governance principle.[931] It postulated that accountability mechanisms should be in place to ensure that data controllers would be answerable in case of failure to comply with measures giving effect to the Guidelines. While the Guidelines did not specify precisely which accountability mechanisms should be in place, it signalled the importance of such mechanisms for the practical effectiveness of the Guidelines.

441. Allocation of liability – The Guidelines did not specify which mechanisms of civil or criminal liability Member countries should introduce. Paragraph 19(d) merely encouraged Member countries to

> "provide for adequate sanctions and remedies in case of failures to comply with measures which implement the principles set forth in Parts Two and Three."

As indicated earlier, the OECD Guidelines recognized that Member countries had varying regulatory cultures and traditions; and thus might employ different means to pursue effective enforcement. In relation to the accountability principle, the Explanatory Memorandum noted this principle "*refers to accountability supported by legal sanctions, as well as to accountability established by codes of conduct, for instance*".[932]

2.5. CONCLUSION

442. Building on predecessors – The OECD Guidelines represented the first internationally agreed statement of core privacy protection principles.[933] The Guidelines were not, however, developed from scratch. The drafters of the Guidelines "*did not set out to reinvent the wheel or needlessly to alter sensible approaches that had been adopted by [their] predecessors*".[934] The chairman of the Expert Group, Michael Kirby, has noted the input received from academic writing, as well as from governmental reports available at the time, such as those

---

930 M. Kirby, "The history, achievement and future of the 1980 OECD guidelines on privacy", *l.c.*, p. 10.

931 Cf. *supra*, no. 440.

932 Explanatory Memorandum, paragraph 70.

933 OECD, "The Evolving Privacy Landscape: 30 Years After the OECD Privacy Guidelines", *l.c.*, p. 2.

934 M. Kirby, "The history, achievement and future of the 1980 OECD guidelines on privacy", *l.c.*, p. 10.

developed in the United States, the United Kingdom and France.[935] In addition, Mr. Kirby also noted the input provided by Frits Hondius, representative of the Council of Europe, who assisted them in drawing on the Council's work as they "translated that work into an inter-continental context".[936]

443. Responsibility and liability – The OECD Guidelines, together with its accompanying Memorandum, foreshadowed a number of developments in data protection regulation. First, the Guidelines placed the primary responsibility for compliance on the "data controller". This term, or minor variations thereof, would be echoed in subsequent national and international instruments. Second, the Guidelines indicated that the data controller's responsibilities should not necessarily end once data is transferred to another party. Specifically, the Guidelines suggested that a data controller should remain accountable in relation to processing carried out by a third party on its behalf. At the same time, they also recognized that there may be instances in which it is appropriate for a service bureau, that processes data on behalf of a data controller, to also be held accountable for certain aspects related to the processing. Finally, the accountability mechanisms suggested by the Guidelines, namely legal sanctions and codes of conduct, still remain relevant today.[937]

3. CONVENTION 108 (1981)

3.1. ORIGIN AND DEVELOPMENT

444. Human rights relevance – The efforts of the Council of Europe (CoE) in the field of data protection were born of the recognition that certain technological developments posed a threat to the rights and freedoms of individuals, in particular their right to privacy.[938] Of particular concern were "*newly developed techniques such as phone-tapping, eavesdropping, surreptitious observation, the illegitimate use of official statistical and similar surveys to obtain private information, and subliminal advertising and propaganda*".[939]

445. Early initiatives – In 1968, the Parliamentary Assembly of the CoE adopted a Recommendation concerning human rights and modern scientific

935 *Id.*

936 *Id.*

937 J. Alhadeff, B. Van Alsenoy and J. Dumortier, "The accountability principle in data protection regulation: origin, development and future directions", *l.c.*, p. 54–55.

938 See Parliamentary Assembly of the Council of Europe, "Recommendation 509 (1968) concerning Human rights and modern scientific and technological developments", 31 January 1968 (16th Sitting), at paragraph 3.

939 *Id.*

and technological developments.[940] This Recommendation called for a study to examine whether member States' laws and the European Convention of Human Rights (ECHR) sufficiently protected the right to privacy "*against violations which could be committed by the use of modern scientific and technical methods*".[941] In 1970, a preliminary report was produced which answered this question in the negative.[942] Seeing as the increased usage of computers was at the focus of concern, the decision was made to concentrate further study efforts on electronic data banks.[943] In order to facilitate the development of common European norms, a Committee of experts developed two resolutions containing basic principles with regard to the gathering, storing, processing and dissemination of personal data by means of computers.[944] The first resolution, adopted by the Committee of Ministers in 1973, concerned the protection of individuals' privacy vis-à-vis electronic data banks in the private sector.[945] The second resolution, adopted in 1974, called for the application of similar principles to the public sector.[946]

446. PREPARATION – In 1976, the Committee of Ministers tasked a Committee of Experts on Data Processing "*to prepare a convention for the protection of privacy in relation to data processing abroad and transfrontier data processing*".[947] This decision was motivated by the recognition that data flows were becoming increasingly transnational in nature. Concerned that national legislature might otherwise erect barriers to the free flow of information, the development of an

---

940 *Id.* For a more detailed account of the discussions that took place see P. Vegleris, "Preadvies", in X., *Privacy en de rechten van de mens. Handelingen van het Derde Internationaal Colloquium over het Europees Verdrag tot Bescherming van de Rechten van de Mens*, Leuven, Acco, 1974, p. 337–342 and A.C. Evans, "Data Protection Law", *The American Journal of Comparative Law* 1981, Vol. 29, No. 4, p. 572.

941 Recommendation 509 (1968), at paragraph 8.1. See also F.W. Hondius, *Emerging data protection in Europe*, *o.c.*, p. 65.

942 F.W. Hondius, *Emerging data protection in Europe*, *o.c.*, p. 65; A.C. Evans, "Data Protection Law", *l.c.*, p. 573; C.J. Bennet, *Regulating privacy. Data Protection and Public Policy in Europe and the United States*, *o.c.*, p. 133. One of the main reasons for this conclusion was the finding that the European Convention of Human Rights did not offer sufficient protection to individuals in relation to other private parties. (F.W. Hondius, *Emerging data protection in Europe*, *o.c.*, p. 65).

943 F.W. Hondius, *Emerging data protection in Europe*, *o.c.*, p. 66 and C.J. Bennet, *Regulating privacy. Data Protection and Public Policy in Europe and the United States*, *o.c.*, p. 133–134.

944 F.W. Hondius, *Emerging data protection in Europe*, *o.c.*, p. 68.

945 Committee of Ministers of the Council of Europe, "Resolution (73) 22 on the protection of the privacy of individuals vis-à-vis electronic data banks in the private sector", 26 September 1973 (224th meeting of the Ministers' Deputies).

946 Committee of Ministers of the Council of Europe, "Resolution (74)29 on the protection of the privacy of individuals vis-à-vis electronic data banks in the public sector", 20 September 1974 (236th meeting of the Ministers' Deputies).

947 Explanatory Report accompanying the Convention for the Protection of Individuals with regard to Automatic Processing of Personal Data, ETS. 108, paragraph 13, (hereinafter: "Explanatory Report").

internationally binding instrument was deemed necessary.[948] It is worth noting that experts from the Asia-Pacific region (Australia, Canada, Japan), the United States, the European Communities and the OECD participated in the work of the Expert Committee.[949]

447. Adoption – The draft text of the Convention was finalized in April of 1980.[950] It was subsequently adopted by the Committee of Ministers on 17 September 1980.[951] The *Convention for the Protection of Individuals with regard to Automatic Processing of Personal Data* ("Convention 108") was opened for signature on 28 January 1981.[952] The five ratifications, which were necessary before the Convention could enter into force, were received on 1 October 1985.[953]

3.2. SCOPE

448. Public and private sector – Pursuant to Article 3(1), Parties to Convention 108 were obliged to apply its provisions to "*automated personal data files and automatic processing of personal data in the public and private sectors*". The provisions of the Convention thus in principle applied equally to public and private sector activities. However, the Convention also recognized that exceptions could be made in the name of State security, public safety, monetary interests, or the suppression of criminal offences.[954]

449. Personal data – Convention 108 only applied to the automated files or automatic processing involving personal data, which were defined by Article

948 G. Buquicchio, "The work of the Council of Europe in the field of data protection", in Council of Europe, *Legislation and Data Protection. Proceedings of the Rome Conference on problems relating to the development and application of legislation on data protection*, 1983, Rome, Camera dei Deputati, p. 230.

949 *Id.* See also Explanatory Report, paragraph 15.

950 Explanatory Report, paragraph 17.

951 C.J. Bennet, *Regulating privacy. Data Protection and Public Policy in Europe and the United States*, *o.c.*, p. 135; R. Pagano, "Panorama of Personal Data Protection Laws", *l.c.*, p. 321.

952 Council of Europe, "Convention for the Protection of Individuals with regard to Automatic Processing of Personal Data", ETS. 108, Strasbourg, 28 January 1981.

953 C.J. Bennet, *Regulating privacy. Data Protection and Public Policy in Europe and the United States*, *o.c.*, p. 135. See also Article 22 Convention 108.

954 Article 9 enabled the Parties to Convention 108 to limit the effect of several of its provisions. Specifically, the Convention allowed exceptions to the provisions of Article 5 (data quality), 6 (special categories of data) and 8 (data subject rights); provided such derogations were provided for by law and constituted a necessary measure in a democratic society. Moreover, such restrictions needed to serve the interests of (a) protecting State security, public safety, the monetary interests of the State or the suppression of criminal offences or (b) protecting the data subject or the rights and freedoms of others. Restrictions on the exercise of certain data subject rights could also be provided with respect to automated personal data files used for statistics or for scientific research purposes if there was obviously no risk of an infringement of the privacy of the data subjects (Article 9(3)).

2(a) as *"any information relating to an identified or identifiable individual ('data subject')"*.[955]

450. Automated data files & automatic processing – The term "automated data file" was defined as *"any set of data undergoing automatic processing"* (Article 2(b)). It was intended to cover

> "not only data files consisting of compact sets of data, but also sets of data which are geographically distributed and are brought together via computer links for purposes of processing".[956]

The term "automatic processing" included operations such as *"the storage of data, the carrying out of logical and/or arithmetical operations on those data, their alteration, erasure, retrieval or dissemination"*; provided such operations were carried out in whole or in part by automated means (Article 2(c)).[957] Non-automated processing of personal data thus in principle fell outside the scope of Convention 108. However, Article 3(2)c recognized Parties' ability to extend similar protections to personal data files which were not processed automatically.

3.3. BASIC PROTECTIONS

451. Overview – Convention 108 was comprised of three main parts: (1) substantive law provisions in the form of basic principles; (2) special rules on transborder data flows; and (3) mechanisms for mutual assistance and consultation between the Parties.[958]

A. *Basic principles for data protection*

452. Minimum standards – Chapter II of Convention 108 set forth a number of "basic principles for data protection". These principles were designed

---

955 According to the Explanatory Report, the term "identifiable" referred only to situations in which the individual could be identified with relative ease (excluding situations where individuals could only be identified by means of very sophisticated methods). (Explanatory Report, paragraph 28). Processing of data relating to legal persons thus in principle fell outside the scope of Convention 108. However, Article 3(2)b recognized Parties' ability to extend similar protections to *"groups of persons, associations, foundations, companies, corporations and any other bodies consisting directly or indirectly of individuals, whether or not such bodies possess legal personality"*, subject to the submission of a declaration to the Secretary General of the Council of Europe.

956 Explanatory Report, paragraph 30.

957 See also Explanatory Report, paragraph 31.

958 Explanatory Report, paragraph 18.

to protect individuals' rights and fundamental freedoms with regard to the automatic processing of their personal data (Article 1).[959]

453. NATURE – While Convention 108 was a legally binding instrument, it was not designed to be self-executing. This meant that it did not intend to procure rights to individuals directly.[960] Instead, the Convention obliged each Party to take the necessary measures in its domestic law to give effect to the Convention's basic principles (Article 4).[961]

454. DATA QUALITY – According to Article 5, personal data undergoing automatic processing needed to be

> "a) obtained and processed fairly and lawfully;
> b) stored for specified and legitimate purposes and not used in a way incompatible with those purposes;
> c) adequate, relevant and not excessive in relation to the purposes for which they are stored;
> d) accurate and, where necessary, kept up to date;
> e) preserved in a form which permits identification of the data subjects for no longer than is required for the purpose for which those data are stored."

This provision consolidated the basic principles of data protection as introduced in earlier CoE resolutions and national data protection laws.[962]

455. SPECIAL CATEGORIES OF DATA – Contrary to the OECD Guidelines, Convention 108 did identify several types of data for which additional protection was required. The Explanatory Report reasoned that

---

959 It is important to note, however, that these "basic principles" of Convention 108 were promulgated as minimum standards. Every Party remained free to grant data subjects a wider measure of protection than was stipulated in the Convention (Article 11). See also Explanatory Report, paragraph 61.

960 Explanatory Report, paragraph 38.

961 Such measures could take different forms, depending on the depending on the legal and constitutional system of the State concerned (e.g. laws, regulations, administrative guidelines). However, legally binding measures were considered necessary to ensure full compliance with the Convention. (Explanatory Report, paragraph 39).

962 Explanatory Report, paragraph 40. Seeing as these principles, save for certain nuances, bear a close resemblance to those contained in the OECD Guidelines, the reader may wish to consult the earlier discussion of the OECD privacy principles: cf. *supra*, nos. 418 et seq. For a more detailed comparison between the provisions of Convention 108 and the OECD Guidelines see P.H. Patrick, "Privacy Restrictions on Transnational Data Flows: A Comparison of the Council of Europe Draft Convention and OECD Guidelines", *l.c.*, p. 405–420; J. Bing, "The Council of Europe Convention and the OECD Guidelines on Data Protection", *Michigan Yearbook of International Legal Studies* 1984, Vol. 5, p. 271–303 and P. Kayser, *La protection de la vie privée. Protection du secret de la vie privée*, *o.c.*, p. 362–364.

> "[w]hile the risk that data processing is harmful to persons generally depends not on the contents of the data but on the context in which they are used, there are exceptional cases where the processing of certain categories of data is as such likely to lead to encroachments on individual rights and interests."[963]

The sensitive categories of data included personal data revealing racial origin, political opinions or religious or other beliefs, as well as personal data concerning health or sexual life and personal data relating to criminal convictions.[964] Such data could not be processed automatically unless domestic law provided for appropriate safeguards (Article 6).

456. Data security – Article 7 provided that

> "appropriate security measures shall be taken for the protection of personal data stored in automated data files against accidental or unauthorised destruction or accidental loss as well as against unauthorised access, alteration or dissemination."

Which security measures were "appropriate" would depend *inter alia* on the risks presented, the specific function of the file, as well as the existing state of the art of data security methods and techniques.[965]

457. Safeguards for data subjects – Article 8 provided for a number of "safeguards for data subjects", designed to encourage the creation of subjective rights for data subjects.[966] These rights would enable individuals to obtain:

- knowledge about the existence of an automated data file;
- knowledge about the contents of the information, if any, stored about data subjects in a file;
- rectification of erroneous or inappropriate information;
- a remedy if any of the previous elements are not respected.[967]

B. Transborder data flows

458. Purpose – A main driver behind Convention 108, in addition to privacy concerns, was the fear that national privacy laws might erect barriers to the free flow of information among contracting parties. Article 12 attempted to mitigate

963 Explanatory Report, paragraph 43.

964 For more information regarding these data types see Explanatory Report, paragraphs 44–48.

965 Explanatory Report, paragraph 49.

966 Explanatory Report, paragraph 50. Article 8 expressed them in the form of "safeguards" which Contracting States were to offer in view of the non-self-executing character of the convention (*id.*).

967 Explanatory Report, paragraph 50. Similar to the OECD Guidelines, the Convention recognized that Member States might implement these safeguards in various ways. For more information see paragraphs 50–54 of the Explanatory Report.

this risk by limiting the instances in which Parties to Convention 108 might prohibit or otherwise restrict transborder flows of personal data.

459. Free flow and legitimate restrictions – In principle, Parties to Convention were prohibited from restricting, for the sole purpose of protecting privacy, transborder flows of personal data going to the territory of another Party (Article 12(2)). Nevertheless, each Party remained entitled to derogate from this rule (Article 12(3)):

> "a) insofar as its legislation includes specific regulations for certain categories of personal data or of automated personal data files, because of the nature of those data or those files, except where the regulations of the other Party provide an equivalent protection;
> b) when the transfer is made from its territory to the territory of a non-Contracting State through the intermediary of the territory of another Party, in order to avoid such transfers resulting in circumvention of the legislation of the Party referred to at the beginning of this paragraph."[968]

C. Mutual assistance

460. Elements – Chapter IV of Convention 108 specified a number of areas in which Parties were to render each other mutual assistance, namely:

a) exchange of information regarding the implementation of the Convention as well as any factual information to specific automatic processing carried out in its territory[969]; and
b) assistance to data subjects resident abroad.[970]

3.4. ALLOCATION OF RESPONSIBILITY AND LIABILITY

461. Formal definition – Convention 108 contained a formal definition of the entity that would be responsible for ensuring compliance with its provisions. The responsible entity was the "controller of the file", which was defined by Article 2(d) as:

> "the natural or legal person, public authority, agency or any other body who is competent according to the national law to decide what should be the purpose of the automated data file, which categories of personal data should be stored and which operations should be applied to them."[971]

968 See also Explanatory Report, paragraphs 62–70.
969 Article 13 Convention 108. See also Explanatory Report, paragraphs 71–76.
970 Article 14 Convention 108. See also Explanatory Report, paragraphs 77–78. Articles 15–17 further regulated the modalities of requests for assistance.
971 Article 2(d) of Convention 108 (emphases added).

462. Any body – Under Convention 108, a controller could be a natural or legal person, public authority, agency or any other body.

463. Decision-making power – The controller of the file was the party who, according to national law, was "*competent to decide*" about the automated data file. A first constitutive element of the data controller concept was thus the authority to exercise decision-making power. The reference to "according to national law" indicated that national laws might contain additional criteria for determining such competency.[972]

464. Purpose, categories of data & operations – The second constitutive element of the "controller of the file" concept concerned the object of its decision-making power. The controller of the file was understood to have decision-making power over the following three elements:

- the purpose of the automated data file;
- the categories of personal data that will be stored;
- the nature of the operations applied to those data.

465. Excluded entities – The Explanatory Report indicated that the concept of the "controller of the file" only referred to the person or body "ultimately responsible" for the file and not to "*persons who carry out the operations according to the instructions given by the controller of the file*".[973]

466. Comparison with the "data controller" – While the respective definitions of the terms "controller of the file" and "data controller" bear a close resemblance, they are not identical. In particular, the terms used to describe the object of a controller's decision-making power are slightly different. Under the OECD Guidelines, the data controller decides about the "*contents and use*" of personal data.[974] Under Convention 108, the controller of the file decides about the "*purposes*" of the file, the "*categories of personal data*" that will be stored, and which "*operations*" should be applied to the data. A second difference concerns the absence of language suggesting that the controller is also the "beneficiary" of the file. Neither the text of Convention 108 nor its Explanatory Report contained any language to suggest that the controller of the file was also the party "for

---

972 See Explanatory Report, paragraph 32 ("*The reference to the "national law" takes into account the fact that the various national data protection laws contain precise criteria for determining who is the competent person.*") See also P.H. Patrick, "Privacy Restrictions on Transnational Data Flows: A Comparison of the Council of Europe Draft Convention and OECD Guidelines", *l.c.*, p. 410.

973 Explanatory Report, paragraph 32.

974 Cf. *supra*, no. 435.

whose benefit" the processing of personal data was being carried out.[975] Nevertheless, it seems reasonable to argue that the terms "controller of the file" and "data controller" (as contained the OECD Guidelines) essentially intended to refer to the same type of entity.[976] Moreover, as noted by Bing, even though Convention 108 did not contain an explicit provision regarding "accountability", it similarly (albeit less explicitly) rendered the controller of the file ultimately responsible for compliance with its provisions.[977]

467. FROM "USERS" TO "CONTROLLERS" – Convention 108 represented the first instance in which the term "controller of the file" appeared in an official Council of Europe instrument. Its earlier resolution regarding private sector data banks (Resolution (73)22) had not formally specified to whom its principles applied.[978] However, the Explanatory Report suggested that the "*users*" of such data banks were responsible for them.[979] The Explanatory Report went on to note that the "user" or "owner" of a data bank was not necessary the same entity:

> "Data banks [...] may be organised in different ways. The data processing equipment (hardware) and techniques (software) are usually sold or leased by the manufacturers to data processing centres, which contain the data banks. Sometimes the user of the data banks is also the owner and operator of the centre. In most cases, however, the centre is managed by a separate organisation, which has its own operating staff and provides computer facilities to several organisations with data banks."[980]

468. GENESIS OF THE "DATA CONTROLLER" CONCEPT – The term "controller" had not figured in any of the national laws adopted prior to Convention 108. As explained earlier, it appears as if the term "controller of the file" emerged in the course of the discussions surrounding the preparation of Convention 108 and the OECD Guidelines.[981]

---

975 Compare *supra*, no. 436.

976 See also J. Bing, "The Council of Europe Convention and the OECD Guidelines on Data Protection", *l.c.*, p. 282. It is also worth noting that F.W. Hondius, who acted as Head of Division II for the Directorate of Legal Affairs of the Council of Europe, approximated the concept of "controller of the record" (which had figured in an earlier draft of Convention 108), with that of a "beneficial user". See F.W. Hondius, "The Action of the Council of Europe with regard to International Data Protection", in OECD, "Transborder Data Flows and the Protection of Privacy", *o.c.*, p. 260. See also *infra*, no. 468.

977 J. Bing, "The Council of Europe Convention and the OECD Guidelines on Data Protection", *l.c.*, p. 282. See also O. Estadella Yuste, "The relevance of the data protection principles set out in Convention 108 and its additional Protocol", report for the *European Conference on Data Protection on "Council of Europe Convention 108 for the Protection of Individuals with regard to Automatic Processing of Personal Data: Present and Future" (Warsaw, Poland, 19–20 November 2001)*, p. 57.

978 See also F.W. Hondius, *Emerging data protection in Europe*, *o.c.*, p. 101.

979 Explanatory Report accompanying Resolution (73)22, paragraph 15.

980 *Id.*

981 Cf. *supra*, no. 438.

469. Allocation of liability – Convention 108 did not prescribe specific mechanisms of civil or criminal liability. Article 10 merely obliged Parties to establish *"appropriate sanctions and remedies for violations of provisions of domestic law giving effect to the basic principles for data protection set out in this chapter"*. This formulation essentially left each State free to determine the nature of these sanctions (civil, administrative and/or criminal).[982]

3.5. CONCLUSION

470. Strong similarity – The provisions of Convention 108 are in many respects similar to those contained in the OECD Privacy Guidelines. Their mutual resemblance comes as no surprise, seeing as many of the delegations to the OECD and Council of Europe meetings were composed of the same experts.[983] Perhaps the most important differences concern the nature of each instrument (a legally binding convention vs. a non-binding recommendation) as well as the geographic constituency of the forum which adopted it (the membership of the OECD notably including countries such as the United States, Canada and Japan).

471. Responsibility and liability – As we have seen, a strong similarity also exists with regards to how both instruments allocate responsibility and liability. Both instruments designated the "controller" as the actor that should be "ultimately responsible". Convention 108 referred to the "controller of the file" whereas the OECD Guidelines referred to the "data controller". Notwithstanding subtle differences in their respective definitions, both terms seemingly intended to refer to the same type of actor. Conspicuously absent from Convention 108 and its Explanatory Report, however, is a reference to any obligations of entities which might be acting "on behalf" of the controller. Contrary to the OECD Guidelines, there is no mention in Convention 108 of the Parties' ability to introduce "more complex schemes of levels and types of responsibilities" (e.g. by imposing certain obligations on so-called "service bureaux" or "data processing centres").[984] However, given the close relationship between the two texts, one must remain cautious not to overstate the significance of this omission.

---

982 Explanatory Report, paragraph 60.

983 J. Bing, "The Council of Europe Convention and the OECD Guidelines on Data Protection", *l.c.*, p. 285; C.J. Bennet, *Regulating privacy. Data Protection and Public Policy in Europe and the United States*, *o.c.*, p. 130–140; H. Burkert, "Privacy – Data Protection A German/European Perspective", *l.c.*, p. 52.

984 Compare *supra*, no. 439.

CHAPTER 5

NATIONAL DATA PROTECTION LAWS AFTER 1981

472. Outline – This chapter will analyse two data protection laws enacted after 1981, namely the UK Data Protection Act of 1984 and the Belgian Data Protection Act of 1992. The objective of this analysis is to track the further development of EU data protection laws leading up to Directive 95/46. In the interest of brevity, the discussion of each act shall be reduced in scope. The discussion will be limited to (1) the origin and development of the act (in order to place it in context) and (2) the allocation of responsibility and liability. Substantive rights and obligations are not discussed separately, as these provisions correspond, by and large, to the provisions of Convention 108 and the OECD Privacy Guidelines.

1. UNITED KINGDOM (1984)

1.1. ORIGIN AND DEVELOPMENT

473. Early initiatives – The UK Data Protection Act of 1984 had been a long time coming. The first legislative proposals concerning privacy emerged in the early 1960s, under the form of private member bills. These bills mainly sought to introduce a general right to privacy.[985] None of these proposals made much of an impact, however, until the *Right to Privacy* bill of 1969.[986] This bill was closely connected to a controversial Justice report entitled "*Privacy and the Law*" (1970).[987] While the Right to Privacy bill was not adopted, the ensuing debate

---

985 See Home Office (Great Britain), *Report of the Committee on Data Protection*, Cmnd. 7341, HMSO, London, 1978, p. 3; F.W. Hondius, *Emerging data protection in Europe*, *o.c.*, p. 49 and J. A. Cannataci, *Privacy and Data Protection Law: International Development and Maltese Perspectives*, *o.c.*, p. 40–41.

986 Right to Privacy Bill, *HC Deb* 26 November 1969, vol. 792, c. 430. Appendix F of the report of the Younger Committee contains a copy of this bill as well other privacy-related bills. (See Home Office (Great Britain), *Report of the Committee on Privacy*, Cmnd. 5012, HMSO, London, 1972, p. 273 et seq.) A summary of the discussions surrounding the proposals can be found at p. 185–202.

987 Home Office (Great Britain), *Report of the Committee on Privacy*, *o.c.*, p. 1; F.W. Hondius, *Emerging data protection in Europe*, *o.c.*, p. 49 and A.C.M. Nugter, *Transborder Flow of*

did induce the Government to appoint a Committee on Privacy, better known as the "Younger Committee".[988]

474. Younger committee – The Younger Committee was tasked to investigate whether legislation was necessary *"to give further protection [...] against intrusions into privacy by private persons and organisations, or by companies"*.[989] Its mandate of inquiry was thus confined to the private sector.[990] In 1972, the Committee found that it would be unwise to create a general right to privacy.[991] It also felt that the introduction of data protection legislation would be premature as the use of computers did not yet form a threat to privacy.[992] It did, however, recommend that computer users voluntarily adopt certain principles for handling personal information on computers.[993] It also recommended that the Government *"provide itself with machinery, such as a standing commission, for keeping under review the growth and techniques of gathering personal information on computers"*.[994]

475. Government white paper – After some years of delay, the UK Government issued a White Paper entitled "*Computers and Privacy*" (1975).[995]

Personal Data within the EC, o.c., p. 107. The Justice report was met with hostility from the UK press, who felt that a general right to privacy might restrict their freedom of speech. See G. Dworkin, "The Younger Committee Report on Privacy", *The Modern Law Review* 1973, Vol. 36, No. 4, p. 399 and C.J. Bennet, *Regulating privacy. Data Protection and Public Policy in Europe and the United States, o.c.*, p. 84–85.

988 Home Office (Great Britain), *Report of the Committee on Privacy, o.c.*, p. 1. See also A.C.M. Nugter, *Transborder Flow of Personal Data within the EC, o.c.*, p. 107 and C.J. Bennet, *Regulating privacy. Data Protection and Public Policy in Europe and the United States, o.c.*, p. 85.

989 Home Office (Great Britain), *Report of the Committee on Privacy, o.c.*, p. 1.

990 Home Office (Great Britain), *Report of the Committee on Privacy, o.c.*, p. 2. See also G. Dworkin, "The Younger Committee Report on Privacy", *l.c.*, p. 399. The Younger Committee analysed many different aspects of the "privacy problem" (the concept, areas of concern, practices in specific sectors) as well as technological developments relating to surveillance devices and computers.

991 Home Office (Great Britain), *Report of the Committee on Privacy, o.c.*, p. 202 et seq. See also G. Dworkin, "The Younger Committee Report on Privacy", *l.c.*, p. 401 and F.W. Hondius, *Emerging data protection in Europe, o.c.*, p. 50.

992 Home Office (Great Britain), *Report of the Committee on Privacy, o.c.*, p. 191.

993 Id. See also p. 183–185. These principles, which had been developed by the British Computer Society, proved quite influential and informed not only the later development of the UK Data Protection Act, but also the development of data protection laws around Europe. (F.W. Hondius, *Emerging data protection in Europe, o.c.*, p. 52 and A.C.M. Nugter, *Transborder Flow of Personal Data within the EC, o.c.*, p. 107).

994 Home Office (Great Britain), *Report of the Committee on Privacy, o.c.*, p. 191. For a general evaluation of all the recommendations proposed by the Younger Committee see G. Dworkin, "The Younger Committee Report on Privacy", *l.c.*, p. 401 and F.W. Hondius, *Emerging data protection in Europe, o.c.*, p. 400–406.

995 Home Office (Great Britain), *Computers and Privacy*, Cmnd. 653, Her Majesty's Stationary Office (HMSO), London, 1975; reproduced by Home Office (Great Britain), *Report on the Committee on Data Protection, o.c.*, p. 449–460.

The White Paper outlined the position of the Government following the Younger Report as well as the Government's inquiry into its own use of computer systems. Somewhat surprisingly, the White Paper announced that there was a need for data protection legislation after all.[996] While maintaining that fears about improper use of computers were still unjustified, the Government considered that legislation for both the public and private sector was necessary in order to prevent misuse in the future.[997] The White Paper went on to describe what this legislation should look like, leaving further details to be defined by yet another committee.[998]

476. The Lindop committee – The Committee on Data Protection, chaired by Sir Norman Lindop, presented its findings in December 1978. The Committee recommended the establishment of an independent body (the "Data Protection Authority" or "DPA"), whose duty it would be to supervise compliance with a set of statutory principles defined in the future data protection act.[999] These data protection principles would not be directly enforceable in courts.[1000] Rather, the principles would serve as the basis for future *Codes of Practice* which would govern different types of personal data handling activities.[1001] One of the main tasks of the Data Protection Authority was to draw up such Codes of Practice in consultation with the affected users.[1002]

477. Legislative development – It was not until 1982 that the UK Government published a new White Paper confirming its intent to legislate.[1003] On 21 December 1982, the Government presented a draft data protection bill in Parliament.[1004] This bill differed from the recommendations offered by

---

996 Commentators have ascribed this change of heart to the fact that UK data processing companies were losing business because of restrictions imposed by data protection legislation in other countries. See e.g. J. A. Cannataci, *Privacy and Data Protection Law: International Development and Maltese Perspectives*, *o.c.*, p. 41.

997 Home Office (Great Britain), *Report of the Committee on Data Protection*, *o.c.*, p. 6.

998 *Id.*

999 Home Office (Great Britain), *Report of the Committee on Data Protection*, *o.c.*, p. 163; A.C.M. Nugter, *Transborder Flow of Personal Data within the EC*, *o.c.*, p. 108.

1000 Home Office (Great Britain), *Report of the Committee on Data Protection*, *o.c.*, p. 163.

1001 *Ibid*, p. 164. The main objective of this approach was to ensure sufficient flexibility, given wide range of contexts in which personal data are used. See also A.C.M. Nugter, *Transborder Flow of Personal Data within the EC*, *o.c.*, p. 108 and A. Crook, "Data Protection in the United Kingdom, Part 2", *Journal of Information Science* 1983, Vol. 7, p. 48.

1002 Home Office (Great Britain), *Report of the Committee on Data Protection*, *o.c.*, p. 164.

1003 Home Office (Great Britain), *Data Protection: the Government's proposal for Legislation*, Cmnd. 8539, HMSO, London, 1982, 23 p. The second push towards the enactment of legislation has likewise been attributed to the UK computer industry: see e.g. J. McBride, "Citizen's Privacy and Data Banks: Enforcement of the Standards in the Data Protection Act 1984 (U.K.)", *Les Cahiers de Droit* 1984, vol. 25, no. 3, p. 535; A.C.M. Nugter, *Transborder Flow of Personal Data within the EC*, *o.c.*, p. 108 and C.J. Bennet, *Regulating privacy. Data Protection and Public Policy in Europe and the United States*, *o.c.*, p. 90–91.

1004 House of Lords (HL) Debates (Deb), 21 December 1982, vol. 437 c. 926.

the Lindop Committee in several respects.[1005] Most notably, the previously recommended "Data Protection Authority" had been reduced to a mere "Data Protection *Registrar*", whose powers were more limited in scope.[1006] According to commentators, the main objective of the 1982 bill was simply to enable the UK to ratify Convention 108, which the UK had already signed in 1981.[1007] The bill was reintroduced on 23 June of 1983.[1008] After a series of legislative amendments, the UK Data Protection Act was finally signed into law on 12 July 1984.[1009]

1.2. ALLOCATION OF RESPONSIBILITY AND LIABILITY

478. Outline – The long legislative history of the UK Data Protection Act left behind a rich body of literature. The following sections will analyse how the views of UK policymakers evolved over time with regard to the allocation of responsibility and liability. Specifically, an analysis shall be made of the views of (A) the Younger Committee (1972); (B) the Lindop Committee (1978); and (C) the drafters of the UK Data Protection act (1984).

A. *The Younger Committee*

479. Professional discipline – As mentioned earlier, the Younger Committee had decided that the time for data protection legislation was not yet ripe.[1010] However, the Committee did propose a set of principles for the handling of personal information by computers.[1011] These principles were to be observed, on a voluntary basis, by "*computer manufacturers, operators and users*".[1012] The Younger Committee further envisaged a system of control through professional discipline, whereby one or more professional associations would impose a set of ethical standards upon those "*responsible for programming and operating computers*".[1013]

1005 A.C.M. Nugter, *Transborder Flow of Personal Data within the EC, o.c.*, p. 109.

1006 *Id.*

1007 One member of the House of Lords commentator later characterized the bill as trying to do nothing more than achieve "bare compliance with the terms of the European Convention" See HL Deb 20 January 1983 vol. 437 cc 1551. See also C.J. Bennet, *Regulating privacy. Data Protection and Public Policy in Europe and the United States, o.c.*, p. 93.

1008 J. McBride, "Citizen's Privacy and Data Banks: Enforcement of the Standards in the Data Protection Act 1984 (U.K.)", *l.c.*, p. 533. The bill needed to be introduced a second time due to the dissolution of Parliament for the general election (*Id.*).

1009 Data Protection Act, 1984 c. 35. For a summary overview of the Parliamentary debates see A. Crook, "Data Protection in the United Kingdom, Part 2", *Journal of Information Science* 1983, Vol. 7, p. 47–57.

1010 Cf. *supra*, no. 474.

1011 See Home Office (Great Britain), *Report of the Committee on Privacy, o.c.*, p. 182 et seq.

1012 *Ibid*, p. 184.

1013 *Ibid*, p. 185. However, the Committee concluded that it was "*premature to expect the successful establishment in the near future of an effective voluntary professional discipline which could properly be endorsed by legislation*" (*Id.*).

480. Concept of a "responsible person" – The Younger Committee also recommended to consider whether it might be useful if each organisation handling computerized personal information were to appoint a "responsible person" within its organisation.[1014] Such a responsible person would be

> "the person to whom the owner or user of a computerized personal information store has delegated the responsibility for ensuring that whatever principles the legislation requires him to enforce are complied with [...]".[1015]

While the final responsibility for compliance would remain with the "owner" or "user" of the data processing system, the responsibility for the enforcement within the organisation would be delegated to this responsible person.[1016]

481. Users vs. computer bureaux – The Younger Committee recognized that not every user of a computer system owned the underlying equipment. Specifically, it recognized the existence of so-called "computer bureaux", who provided computing services on an agency basis.[1017] The Younger Committee considered that

> "[i]n the case of a commercial computing bureau, only some of the requirements contained in the principles would fall within the competence of the bureau operator/owner, the remainder being the responsibility of the user. Nevertheless it would probably be necessary that bureaux also should appoint "responsible persons", as to secure to the maximum degree the enforcement of those requirements which are within their competence."[1018]

482. Distribution of responsibility – When discussing the division of responsibility between the users and providers of computing services, the Younger Committee made a distinction between three areas, namely:

> "i. The computer services area, which includes the translation of the designed system into programs of instruction to the machine installation, the operation of the installation together with its input and output facilities and the monitoring of the installation's performance and of the required security provisions.
> ii. An area where there is joint involvement between the user and the person or persons who provide the computer services. This area will include, inter alia,

---

1014 *Ibid*, p. 16 and p. 191.

1015 *Ibid*, p. 336. The Younger Committee compared the function of the "responsible person" to that of a "Security Administration Officer" who is tasked with ensuring the efficient operation and audit of measures prescribed for data security (*Id.*).

1016 *Id.* Again, the Younger Committee felt that further study was necessary before introducing a legal requirement mandating the appointment of a "responsible person" (*Ibid*, p. 192).

1017 *Ibid*, p. 192. The role of computer bureaux was studied at length by the Lindop Committee. Cf. *infra*, nos. 485 et seq.

1018 *Ibid*, p. 336.

the design of systems to meet the user's requirements, the checking of such systems to ensure that the requirements have been met, the nature and extent of security provisions to be incorporated into the systems and the safeguarding of information in transit between the user and the computer service whether by document, telephone, teleprinter or terminal.

iii. The area where responsibility must lie with the ultimate user of the service who will initiate and specify the requirements to be met, will probably be responsible for routine assembly of the information for input to the computer and who will use the processed information when it is supplied to him from the computer. [...]"[1019]

The Younger Committee thus clearly foresaw responsibilities for both users and bureaux, each within their own sphere of competence.

B. The Lindop Committee

483. Terminology – The Lindop Committee had been tasked to provide recommendations for the enactment of data protection legislation.[1020] With this task in mind, the Committee set out to find appropriate terminology to identify the subjects of the future data protection act.[1021] After discarding several alternatives (such as "operator" and "owner"), the Committee eventually settled on the term "user" to denote the main subject of regulation.[1022] The Committee selected this term because it was generally used in computing circles to refer to "*those who use computers for their own purposes – as opposed to those who provide others with a computer service for a fee*".[1023] The latter were referred to as "data handling bureaux" or "computer bureaux". While bureaux would not be subject to the same obligations as users, they would nevertheless become subjects of the Lindop Committee's recommendations.

484. Definition of a "user" – In its "principal legislative recommendations", the Lindop Committee defined a "user" as:

> "any person who, alone or with others, carries on or causes to be carried on any automatic handling of personal data in any part of the UK wholly or partly for his own interest, and determines what data are handled."[1024]

The Committee likened the concept of a user to that of the "beneficial user", which had previously been defined by the Computing Services Association (CSA) as

1019 *Ibid*, p. 337 (emphasis added).
1020 Cf. *supra*, no. 476.
1021 Home Office (Great Britain), *Report of the Committee on Data Protection*, *o.c.*, p. 149–150.
1022 *Ibid*, p. 150.
1023 *Id.*
1024 *Ibid*, p. 289.

> "the organisation or individual who uses personal data in his business or other activities and who is entitled to give instructions for a personal record data system to be designed and programmed (including subsequent amendments), processed or operated".[1025]

485. Definition of a "bureau" – Although the Lindop Committee did not propose a definition for the term "bureau", it had studied the phenomenon of bureaux in detail.[1026] The Committee described a data handling bureau as an organisation which made its (computing) facilities available to others for the purpose of executing their data handling applications.[1027] The services offered by a bureau could vary widely, ranging

> "from just the hire of computer time for use by the user's own staff to the full range of ad hoc systems design, programming, data preparation, computer output handling to meet individual user needs, and the provision of standardised and packaged comprehensive information services which are sold in identical form to many clients. [...] Statistical aggregations or customer billing or payroll are the sorts of tasks which are commonly taken on from day to day."[1028]

486. Distinguishing "users" from "bureaux" – According to the Lindop Committee, there were two attributes distinguishing users from bureaux. First, a user handles data (or has them handled) for his own interest, and not as an agent for someone else.[1029] Second, a user also determines what data are to be handled.[1030] These two characteristics set users and bureaux apart from one another.

487. Relationship between users and bureaux – The bureau was seen by the Lindop Committee as an agent of the user, who acted under the latter's instructions.[1031] Usually, the specific responsibilities of the bureaux would be set out in a contract between the user and the bureau.[1032] While the bureau's services might be constrained by its resources (e.g. available equipment), it would in principle not be selective in what it did.[1033] It was the user (and not

---

1025 *Ibid*, p. 150.
1026 *Ibid*, p. 252–259.
1027 *Ibid*, p. 252.
1028 *Ibid*, p. 255. It is worth noting that a bureau was not necessarily aware of the fact that it was handling personal data (or why). In some cases a bureau might have had knowledge and understanding of the data it handles (and of the meaning of the products which result from that handling), in other cases it might not. For example, if the bureau's facilities were operated by the user's own staff (something which was frequently done by terminal access), the bureau staff might not have been aware of what programs were used or of the processes that were undertaken (*Id.*).
1029 *Ibid*, p. 150.
1030 *Id.*
1031 *Ibid*, p. 255–256.
1032 *Id.*
1033 *Id.*

the bureau) who decided what services would be provided and how the data would be used.[1034] However, in many cases the customer would also rely heavily on the bureau for technical advice on how the work should be handled.[1035] Furthermore, it was not uncommon for all stages of a job, from data collection to dissemination, to be handled on an agency basis.[1036]

488. Bureaux as subjects of regulation – For the Lindop Committee, it was clear that the decision-making power of bureaux was much more limited in comparison to that of users.[1037] At the same time, it also recognized that certain aspects of data protection did reside within the competence of a bureau. For example,

> "[t]he maintenance of the accuracy of the data during handling [...] and the maintenance of an adequate standard of security, are matters which depend on the efficiency and reliability of staff and equipment, the design of software and the physical safeguards at the location of data handling".[1038]

The Lindop Committee felt that bureaux should be made directly responsible "*for complying with data protection rules in those matters over which they had control*".[1039] It explicitly rejected the approach advocated by the CSA, according to which only users would be directly responsible for compliance.[1040] It motivated this conclusion by reasoning that

> "Users are generally not in a position to assess the reliability or competence of bureau, no matter how strong the incentive on them to do so may be. Consequently, compliance with data protection rules where applications are handled by bureaux would not be effectively supervised."[1041]

1034 *Id.*

1035 *Id.*

1036 *Ibid*, p. 256. Despite the potential latitude of a bureau's role, the Lindop Committee considered that "*it is the final user of the information who decides what will be done once the bureau has produced what is wanted.*" (*Ibid*, p. 255).

1037 *Ibid*, p. 256.

1038 *Id.* The Committee considered moreover that "*the user-bureau relationship brings with it certain additional potential hazards to data protection, which are not present where the data are handled by the user's own staff and on his own facilities. One such risk arises from the fact that the user's application may run side by side with the applications of other users employing the same bureau: in some circumstances this could give rise to possibilities for accidently allowing one user access to another's data [...].*" (*Id.*).

1039 *Ibid*, p. 257 and 295.

1040 *Ibid*, p. 256–257. Under this approach, users might be required to exercise reasonable care when entrusting their data handling to a third party. In their contracts with bureau, users could require indemnities in case of any breach of a Code of Practice caused by the bureau. In this way, "*[l]iability for matters within its competence would pass to the bureau indirectly through the civil law, since it would be required to compensate the user for any penalties or civil damages incurred by him [...].*" (*Ibid*, p. 257).

1041 *Ibid*, p. 257.

Moreover, the Committee reasoned, some users might be deterred from taking full advantage of the benefits of automation if they risked being penalized for breaches caused by a bureau without being able to recover damages.[1042]

489. ALLOCATION OF RESPONSIBILITY – According to the Lindop Committee, each party subject to the act should be responsible for those aspects over which they have control. The exact distribution of responsibility would not, however, be specified in the act itself. Instead, the Data Protection Authority would have the task of defining the appropriate division of responsibilities in *Codes of practice.*[1043] It was already clear from the beginning, however, that users would be subject to the bulk of the act's obligations:

> "In the relationship between user and bureau, it is the user who retains control over the nature of the data being handled, the methods by which it is collected, the degree of access which he accords to his data subjects, and the purposes to which the data are put. [...] [T]he bureau often has no effective means of controlling these aspects [...] We agree therefore with the CSA that there can be no question of placing legal responsibility for complying with these matters on any person other than the user."[1044]

The obligations incumbent upon bureaux would mainly concern security measures for safeguarding the confidentiality and integrity of data.[1045] Nevertheless, each Code of Practice would specify in it "*those provisions which become binding on any bureau which handle applications in the relevant category*".[1046] Breach of those provisions would be an offence, and

> "it would therefore be incumbent on a bureau to avoid taking on an application if it was unable to meet the safeguards and standards required for that application under the relevant code".[1047]

The Lindop Committee also considered that the Data Protection Authority may wish to draft one or more Codes of Practice which would be applicable to bureaux "as a class".[1048] Finally, it is worth noting that the Committee even

1042 *Id.*

1043 *Ibid*, p. 258. As mentioned earlier, the Lindop Committee recommended that future data protection act should contain "a set of statutory principles" (e.g. data accuracy, purpose specification). These data protection principles would not be directly enforceable in courts. Rather, the principles would serve as the basis for future Codes of Practice, which would govern different types of personal data handling activities. It was expected that the Data Protection Authority would define, for each class of personal data handling applications, which measures users should be taken. Cf. *supra*, no. 476.

1044 *Ibid*, p. 256 (emphasis added).

1045 *Ibid*, p. 258.

1046 *Id.*

1047 *Id.*

1048 *Id.* Such codes might deal with "*such matters as the need to avoid any linking of the different applications of different users, and the need to avoid any accidental or deliberate retention of*

foresaw an advisory role for bureaux, especially towards small users who may not be aware of the contents of the relevant Codes of Practice.[1049]

490. ALLOCATION OF LIABILITY – Both users and bureau would be liable in case of a violation of a relevant Code of Practice. However, each party would only be liable for its own offences and for matters within its control.[1050] As a result, the overall liability exposure of bureaux was considered to be more limited as their sphere of competence primarily concerned security measures.[1051] Nevertheless, it would be an independent offence for a bureau to fail to comply with provisions of codes of practice which reside with the bureau's competence.[1052] Finally, it is also worth observing that the Data Protection Authority would have similar powers of supervision over bureaux as it would over users, meaning that bureaux could be held accountable in a manner similar to users.[1053]

C. *The 1984 Data Protection Act*

491. TERMINOLOGY – The 1984 Data Protection Act retained, by and large, the terminology developed by the Lindop Committee. The Act employed the term "data user" to denote the main subject of regulation. It also followed the Committee's recommendation to bring "computer bureaux" within the scope of the act. The definition of each term, however, was extended in order to align it with the other terms defined in the act.

i. Data user

492. DATA USER – Section 1(5) of the 1984 Data Protection Act defined a data user as

> "a person who holds data, and a person 'holds' data if –
>
> (a) the data form part of a collection of data processed or intended to be processed by or on behalf of that person [...]; and
> (b) that person (either alone or jointly or in common with other persons) controls the contents and use of the data comprised in the collection; and

data when the bureau ceased to carry out work for a user." (*Id.*).

1049 *Ibid*, p. 259.

1050 The Lindop Committee explicitly rejected the notion of vicarious liability, at least insofar as criminal liability was concerned. It considered that it would be "*distasteful to impose on users absolute criminal liability of the transgression of others who were beyond their control*". (*Ibid*, p. 257).

1051 *Ibid*, p. 258.

1052 *Id.*

1053 *Id.*

(c) the data are in the form in which they have been or are intended to be processed [...]."[1054]

493. "A PERSON" – In principle, every natural or legal person could be characterized as a data user.[1055] The term encompassed both individuals as well as bodies of persons, such as corporate bodies, unincorporated bodies, trade unions, governmental departments[1056], trade associations, etc.[1057] The concept was not confined to commercially operating entities.[1058] However, individuals holding personal data "*which concerned only the management of his personal, family or household affairs or held by him for recreational purposes*" were exempted from compliance with the DPA (section 33(1)).[1059]

494. "CONTROLS THE CONTENT AND USE" – Not every person processing personal data was considered a data user.[1060] A person was only considered a data user if this person actually "held" the data within the meaning of Section 1(5).[1061] "Holding" in this context did not mean "possession".[1062] A person was considered

1054 Emphasis added. The term "data" was defined by Section 1(2) as "*information recorded in a form in which it can be processed by equipment operating automatically in response to instructions given for that purpose*".

1055 A.C.M. Nugter, *Transborder Flow of Personal Data within the EC*, *o.c.*, p. 111.

1056 See HL Deb, 24 March 1983, vol. 440, at cc 1275–1276 for a discussion of the possibility that government departments be qualified as data users.

1057 C. Edwards and N. Savage, "Data Privacy: the UK Experience", *o.c.*, p. 81. Employees or individuals acting on behalf of an organisation were generally considered as data users themselves (in such case the data user was the employer or organisation for whom they worked). See The Data Protection Registrar, "The Data Protection Act of 1984: Questions and Answers on the Act (1–20)", Office of The Data Protection Registrar, Cheshire, 1985, p. 2 (Question 3); The Data Protection Registrar, "The Data Protection Act 1984: The Definitions", Guideline: number 2, Office of the Data Protection Registrar, Cheshire, 1989, p. 26–27.

1058 A.C.M. Nugter, *Transborder Flow of Personal Data within the EC*, *o.c.*, p. 111.

1059 See also HL Deb 10 March 1983 vol. 440, at cc373, for a discussion of the rationale behind the "personal use" exemption. Strictly speaking, data held for private purposes was only partially exempted from the 1984 Data protection act (see section 33(1)). In principle, the users of these data still needed to comply with the general principles of data protection contained in Section 1 of the act. However, in practice there was a total exemption as the principles were only enforceable against registered data users. A.C.M. Nugter, *Transborder Flow of Personal Data within the EC*, *o.c.*, p. 118 footnote 21. The 1984 Data Protection Act provided similar blanket exemptions for personal data (1) which the law requires to be made public; (2) which safeguard national security; (3) held for payroll, pensions and accounts purposes; (4) from unincorporated member clubs and (5) in mailinglists. In addition, the DPA also contained exemptions from certain obligations in certain situations (e.g. exemption to non-disclosure obligation in case the disclosure is required by law). See A.C.M. Nugter, *Transborder Flow of Personal Data within the EC*, *o.c.*, p. 118–119.

1060 The Data Protection Registrar, "The Data Protection Act 1984: An introduction to the act and guide for data users and computer bureaux", Guideline: number 1, Office of the Data Protection Registrar, Cheshire, 1984, p. 12; A.C.M. Nugter, *Transborder Flow of Personal Data within the EC*, *o.c.*, p. 111.

1061 The Data Protection Registrar, "The Data Protection Act 1984: An introduction to the act and guide for data users and computer bureaux", *l.c.*, p. 12.

1062 The Data Protection Registrar, "The Data Protection Act 1984: The Definitions", Guideline: number 2, Office of the Data Protection Registrar, Cheshire, 1989, p. 9.

to "hold" data only if that person *controlled its contents and use*.[1063] The term "control" was thus at the heart of the definition of a data user.[1064] In 1985, the term was further clarified by Data Protection Registrar as follows:

> "Controls – this is a vital element of the definition. You are not a "Data User" and do not "hold" data unless you are entitled to take the final decision as to the information which is to be recorded and as to the purposes for which the data are to be used."[1065]

A person was said to control the "contents" of a data collection if he is "*in a position to decide which item and type of information are to be recorded as data*".[1066] A person controls the "use" of the collection if he is "*able to determine the purpose for which the data are to be processed*".[1067]

In 1989, the Data Protection Registrar further expanded on the notion of "control" as follows:

> "Control means having the power to decide what information about an individual is to be recorded, whether the information should be added to, amended or deleted and to what use the recorded information may be put either by the data user or by others. This is not the same as physically controlling either the processing operations or the disk or tapes on which the data are recorded."[1068]

495. "DATA PROCESSED OR INTENDED TO BE PROCESSED" – Mere collection or storage of data without any intention to see these data processed automatically fell outside the scope of the DPA.[1069]

496. "BY OR ON BEHALF OF" – It was not necessary to possess a computerized system in order to be considered a data user.[1070] A company which made use of

---

1063 As noted by Lord Elton: "*The key concept here is the control of the contents and use of data. That is the crucial element in the definition of data user because it is only the person who controls contents and use who can sensibly be expected to fulfil the responsibilities and obligations that the Bill places on data users.*" HL Deb, 19 July 1983, vol. 443, cc1068. Effective control over how the data was to be used was considered to be especially important. See also HL Deb 10 March 1983 vol. 440, at cc. 408–409 (stating that "the person to be held responsible under the Bill is the person who actually controls what is to be done with the data").

1064 See HL Deb 19 July 1983 vol. 443, at cc 1069.

1065 The Data Protection Registrar, "The Data Protection Act 1984: An introduction to the act and guide for data users and computer bureaux", *l.c.*, p. 12 (emphasis added).

1066 The Data Protection Registrar, "The Data Protection Act of 1984: Questions and Answers on the Act (1–20)", *l.c.*, p. 1.

1067 *Id.*

1068 The Data Protection Registrar, "The Data Protection Act 1984: The Definitions", *l.c.*, p. 10.

1069 *Id.* and A.C.M. Nugter, *Transborder Flow of Personal Data within the EC*, *o.c.*, p. 111. See also HL Deb, 19 July 1983, vol. 443, at cc 1054–1055 (discussing a proposed amendment to add the word "collecting" to the definition of data user) and cc 1067–1068 (discussing the relevance of the intention to process). Processing" was defined by Section 1(7) as "*amending, augmenting, deleting or re-arranging the data or extracting the information constituting the data and, in the case of personal data, means performing any of those operation by reference to the data subject*".

1070 A.C.M. Nugter, *Transborder Flow of Personal Data within the EC*, *o.c.*, p. 112.

the services of a computer bureau would also be considered as a data user within the meaning of the DPA, provided that it exercised control over the contents and use of automated personal data.[1071]

497. "Alone or jointly or in common" – The drafters of the 1984 Data Protection Act recognized that control could be exercised by more than one entity.[1072] As stated by the Data Protection Registrar:

> "The control does not need to be exclusive to one data user. Control may be shared with others. It may be shared jointly or in common. 'Jointly' covers the situation where control is exercised by acting together. Control 'in common" is where each shares a pool of information, changing, adding to or using the information for his own purposes independently of the other".[1073]

ii. Computer bureau

498. Computer bureau – According to Section 1(6) of the 1984 Data Protection Act, a person carries on a computer bureau if

> "he provides other persons with services in respect of data, and a person provides such services –
>
> (a) as agent for other persons he causes data held by them to be processed [...]; or
> (b) he allows other persons the use of equipment in his possession for the processing [...] of data held by them."[1074]

499. "A person" – In principle, both natural and legal persons could act as a computer bureau.[1075] A person did not have to be in business as a bureau in order to meet the definition of a computer bureau.[1076] Nor was it necessary that

---

1071 *Id.*

1072 See HL Deb 19 July 1983 vol. 443, at cc 1069 (discussing a scenario of "joint control").

1073 The Data Protection Registrar, "The Data Protection Act 1984: The Definitions", l.c., p. 10–11. See also the Data Protection Registrar, "The Data Protection Act 1984: An introduction to the act and guide for data users and computer bureaux", *l.c.*, p. 12 (*""jointly or in common" – covers the situation where control is exercised by a number of persons acting together or by each of a group of persons."*). It is interesting to note that while the definition of a data user provided by the Lindop committee recognized that control might be exercised together with others (i.e. "jointly"), it did not explicitly recognize that multiple entities might be controlling data at the same time, but each for their own purposes (compare *supra,* no. 485).

1074 Emphasis added.

1075 A.C.M. Nugter, *Transborder Flow of Personal Data within the EC, o.c.*, p. 112 and C. Edwards and N. Savage, "Data Privacy: the UK Experience", in C. Edwards and N. Savage (eds), *Information Technology & The* Law, 1986, MacMillan Publishers, p. 81.

1076 The Data Protection Registrar, "The Data Protection Act 1984: An introduction to the act and guide for data users and computer bureaux", *l.c.*, p. 12.

the person takes part in the actual processing of the data. It was sufficient that he made equipment in his possession available for use by a data user.[1077]

500. "SERVICES IN RESPECT OF DATA" – The 1984 Data Protection Act distinguished between two types of services offered by a computer bureau, namely (a) the processing of personal data held by others and (b) the making available of equipment to process data held by others. This definition reportedly covered a variety of arrangements

> "from the traditional batch bureau offering [...], such as batch accounting or payroll functions, to those where the user, inputting his own materials, has direct access to mainframe processing capabilities [...]".[1078]

501. "AS AGENT" – The definition of a computer bureau implied that any processing of personal data by the bureau occurred on an agency basis. According to the Data Protection Registrar, however, "agency" in this context merely meant "*a person acting for others*" rather than as an agent in a contractual sense.[1079] Because a computer bureau acted "on behalf" of a data user, it was in principle not allowed to disclose personal data without prior authorization by the data user who controls that data (section 15(1)).[1080]

502. "ALLOWING THE USE OF EQUIPMENT" – Paragraph (b) of the definition covered the situation where a person allowed others to make use of computer equipment in his possession, without taking active part in the processing.[1081] The term "possession" did not refer to ownership but merely implied physical control of the equipment.[1082]

iii. Distinguishing "users" from "bureaux"

503. KEY CHARACTERISTICS – Similar to the definitions provided by to the Lindop Committee, there appear to be two key characteristics distinguishing

---

1077 *Id.*

1078 T. Cook, "The law relating to computer bureaux", in C. Edwards and N. Savage (eds), *Information Technology & The* Law, 1986, MacMillan Publishers, p. 159. The author further notes that for many computer bureau their computer activities might be but a small part of the overall service which they offer. For example, a traditional batch bureau payroll service could be combined with the secure delivery of wages, or a remote access bureau could be combined with the writing of customized programs to the requirements of the user. (*Ibid*, p. 160).

1079 The Data Protection Registrar, "The Data Protection Act 1984: The Definitions", *l.c.*, p. 12.

1080 See also HL Deb, 21 July 1983, vol. 443, at cc 1299–1300 (discussing the exemption to the non-disclosure requirement for access requests by law enforcement and its relationship to computer bureaux).

1081 The Data Protection Registrar, "The Data Protection Act 1984: The Definitions", *l.c.*, p. 12.

1082 *Id.*

data users from computer bureaux. First, a data user processes data (or has them processed) for his own purpose(s), and not as an agent for someone else. Second, the data user also decides what data (contents) are to be handled.[1083]

504. Scenarios – Already in 1985, the Data Protection Registrar observed there might be scenarios in which it could be difficult to distinguish between "data users" and "computer bureaux":

> "Difficulties in identifying the Data User may arise where one organisation (A) has services provided to it by another organisation (B) and, in order to provide those services, B automatically processes personal information supplied by A."[1084]

By way of illustration, the Registrar described 3 scenarios to clarify the distinction between data users and computer bureaux in such cases:

ii) "Where A instructs or requests B to process the information on A's behalf, the nature of the output and the purposes of which it is to be used is being determined by A, then B is merely carrying out the processing on behalf of A. If this is done automatically than A is a Data User and B is a Computer Bureau. [...][1085]"
iii) "Where the automatic processing of the information is merely incidental to some other service which B provides to A, the decisions as to the information to be processed and the purpose of processing being made by B on his own account, the B is the data user. [...][1086]"
iv) "If B is both processing on behalf of A and providing some other service then both A and B may be Data Users [...] In respect of this information A and B control the contents and use of the data in common and both are Data Users. [...]"[1087]

The Registrar also described the scenario in which the service provider does not receive the data from the client, but rather is in a situation where he collects information and maintains records which he decides are necessary to provide the service. The example provided is that of an estate agent, who manages residential properties on behalf of its owner. Because the estate agent had been given a "wide discretion" by the property owner as to the actual contents and use

1083 Compare *supra*, no. 486.
1084 The Data Protection Registrar, "The Data Protection Act of 1984: Questions and Answers on the Act (1–20)", *l.c.*, p. 2 (Question 2).
1085 The example provided by the Registrar is that of an accounting firm, whereby B both keeps the accounts of A's business and calculates the salaries of its employees.
1086 The example provided by the Registrar is that of a tax consultancy firm, whereby B processes the information provided by A in order to provide advice on the A's tax affairs.
1087 In the example provided by the Registrar B both keeps the accounts A and provides tax advice to A. (The Data Protection Registrar, "The Data Protection Act of 1984: Questions and Answers on the Act (1–20)", *l.c.*, p. 2 (Question 2)).

of the records, the estate agent was considered to be the data user rather than the owner (because the owner's interest was essentially only in the income received rather than in the contents of the individual records).[1088]

505. Role of contracts – The UK Data Protection Act did not formally require the creation of contracts among data users and computer bureaux. Where such contracts existed, however, its terms could be relied on by the Registrar to determine whether a party was acting either as data user or as a computer bureaux.[1089] The Registrar immediately added, however, that a contract to decide which of the parties is the data user "*must not be a sham*".[1090] According to the Registrar, the contract should leave the data user free to make at least some of the following decisions:

- "to what extent records containing information about individuals should be kept;
- what sort of information about individuals they should contain;
- from where that information should be obtained;
- when and how the information should be processed;
- whether or not the information is accurate or should be updated;
- whether and when the information should be added to, amended or deleted;
- whether and when the information should be available to the other party;
- whether the information may be disclosed to and used by third parties;
- what information should be made available to an individual who makes a subject access request under the Act and whether information should be withheld in reliance on one of the exemptions from the subject access provisions; and
- whether the data user may keep the information after the contract has ended."[1091]

1088 The Data Protection Registrar, "The Data Protection Act of 1984: Questions and Answers on the Act (21–34)", Office of The Data Protection Registrar, Cheshire, 1986, p. 3–4 (Question 22). See also The Data Protection Registrar, "The Data Protection Act 1984: The Definitions", *l.c.*, p. 29–31 (providing further examples to determine whether the customer or the service provider should be considered the data user).

1089 The Data Protection Registrar, "The Data Protection Act 1984: The Definitions", *l.c.*, p. 27. ("*If it is clear from the contract that one of the parties accepts all of the responsibilities under the Act and that he is genuinely in a position to fulfil those responsibilities, then there should be no difficulty in concluding that that person is the data user and that the other party is not. It will, therefore, be sensible for those who are in this situation to review their contracts and to consider whether their positions are already clear or whether some more terms should be added to the contract to clarify the situation.*")

1090 *Id.*

1091 *Ibid*, p. 28. Interestingly, the Data Protection Registrar also linked the concept of the data user to the *business interests* of the parties involved. The customer of the service will need to retain its role of data user if he is not able to surrender control over the contents and use of the information without losing control over the running of its own business. (*Ibid*, p. 29) In an earlier text, the Registrar also linked the concept of a data user to the concept of *ownership*,

iv. Allocation of responsibility and liability

506. Outline – The 1984 Data Protection Act was underpinned by eight data protection principles based on the Younger Committee's Report and Council of Europe Convention 108.[1092] Because of their general nature, the principles were not directly enforceable through the courts, but only indirectly through the Registrar.[1093] The first seven principles applied only to data users, i.e. those who controlled the content and use of the data held.[1094] The eighth principle (security) applied both the data users and computer bureaux (Section 2(2)).[1095] Both data users and computer bureaux were under an obligation to register themselves with the Data Protection Registrar (Section 5(2) and 5(4)).[1096]

507. Data protection principles – Data users were bound to comply with eight data protection principles enumerated in Schedule 1 of the Act, i.e. the principles of

(1) Fairness and lawfulness;
(2) Purpose specification;
(3) Disclosure and use limitation;
(4) Proportionality;
(5) Accuracy;
(6) Limitation of storage duration;
(7) Data subject rights; and
(8) Security.[1097]

---

by asking to whom the data resulting from the processing "belong". See The Data Protection Registrar, "The Data Protection Act of 1984: Questions and Answers on the Act (21–34)", *l.c.*, p. 3 (Question 22).

1092 C. Edwards and N. Savage, "Data Privacy: the UK Experience", *o.c.*, p. 78. See also HL Deb, 5 July 1983, vol. 443, at cc 509.

1093 C. Edwards and N. Savage, "Data Privacy: the UK Experience", *o.c.*, p. 78. See also HL Deb, 5 July 1983, vol. 443, at cc 509–510. In case of non-compliance, the Registrar had the power to issue an enforcement notice (section 10). In principle, such notices could be directed to either data users or computer bureau. For more information on the types of notices which the Registrar might issue see C. Edwards and N. Savage, "Data Privacy: the UK Experience", *o.c.*, p. 119 et seq.; A.C.M. Nugter, *Transborder Flow of Personal Data within the EC*, *o.c.*, p. 136 et seq.

1094 C. Edwards and N. Savage, "Data Privacy: the UK Experience", *o.c.*, p. 78.

1095 *Id.*

1096 K. Wong, "Data Protection Law", *Data Processing* 1984, Vol. 26, no. 1, p. 13.

1097 Part II of Schedule 1 of the Act contained interpretative provisions with regard to the data protection principles. For a discussion of the 1984 data protection principles see also C. Edwards and N. Savage, "Data Privacy: the UK Experience", in C. Edwards and N. Savage (eds), *Information Technology & The Law*, Basingstoke, MacMillan Publishers, 1986, p. 126. It is also worth noting section 2(3) enabled the Secretary of State to impose additional requirements or restrictions in relation to sensitive data.

As indicated above, only the eighth principle (security) was directly applicable to computer bureaux. The eighth principle read as follows:

> "Appropriate security measures shall be taken against unauthorized access to, or alteration, disclosure or destruction of, personal data and against accidental loss or destruction of personal data."

508. Registration – In its application for registration, a data user was obliged to provide the following pieces of information (section 4(3)):

(1) name and address;
(2) *description of the personal data* to be held by him and of the *purpose(s)* for which the data are to be held or used;
(3) a *description of the source(s)* from which he intends or may wish to obtain the data or the information to be contained in the data;
(4) a description of any *person(s) to whom he intends* or may wish *to disclose* the data;
(5) the names or a description of any *countries* or territories outside the United Kingdom to which he intends or may wish directly or indirectly to transfer the data; and
(6) one or more addresses for the receipt of *requests from data subjects* for access to the data.

Persons carrying on a computer bureaux were also under an obligation to register their activities with the Data Protection Registrar. However, bureaux were only obliged to specify their name and address in their application for registration (section 4(4)).

509. Role of registration – Registration under the 1984 Data Protection Act served several important functions. First, registration was designed to enable the Registrar to assess compliance.[1098] Second, because the register itself was to be open to the public, it was expected to provide a starting point for data subjects who wished to investigate who held which data on them and why.[1099] Finally, section 5 of the DPA obliged data users and their agents to abide by the terms of the registration. Section 5(3) explicitly stated that users and agents alike were bound to comply with any restrictions regarding use, disclosure or transfer of the data resulting from the terms of the registration.[1100] For this reason, it was recommended that the contract between users and bureau specify that the user shall be bound to supply the bureau with a copy of the user's register entry in

1098 See section 7 of the DPA.
1099 A.C.M. Nugter, *Transborder Flow of Personal Data within the EC*, *o.c.*, p. 126.
1100 The term "agent" encompasses computer bureaux (see section 1(6).

respect of data processed by the bureau, and to keep the bureau informed of any alterations.[1101]

510. Data subject rights – The 1984 Data Protection Act provided data subjects with a right of access, correction and erasure (see section 21 and 24). These rights could only be exercised towards the data user. Computer bureaux were under no obligation to comply with such requests.[1102]

511. Criminal liability – The 1984 DPA exposed both data users and computer bureau to the risk of criminal liability. Certain offences could, by definition, only be committed by data users (e.g. "holding" personal data not described in the registry). Other offences could only be committed by a computer bureau (e.g. operating as a computer bureau without being registered). However, many of the offences created by the DPA could be committed by both users and bureaux (e.g. disclosing data other than as described in the register). The 1984 Data Protection Act created the following offences[1103]:

(1) holding personal data *without being registered* (or without having applied for registration) (section 5 (5));
(2) knowingly or recklessly *holding personal data not described* in the register entry (section 5(5));
(3) knowingly or recklessly *using, obtaining, disclosing or transferring* personal data *other than as described* in the register entry (section 5(3) and 5(5));
(4) knowingly or recklessly operating as a computer bureau in respect of personal data without being registered as such (section 5(5));
(5) knowingly or recklessly *disclosing personal data without the authority* of the person to whom computer bureau service are provided (section 15(3));
(6) failure to comply with an *enforcement notice* (section 10(9));
(7) failure to comply with a *transfer prohibition notice* (section 12(10));

1101 T. Cook, "The law relating to computer bureaux", *l.c.*, p. 164. According to the Data Protection Registrar, not all computer bureaux needed to know what was contained in the register entry of the data user to whom it was providing services. A computer bureau which only performed the limited service of "causing data to be processed automatically" would not do anything which constituted an offence under section 5(3). If the computer bureaux provided a wider service, however, which involved collecting information on behalf of the data user or disclosing it in accordance with its instructions, it would run the risk of committing an offence if departed from the particulars contained in the user's register entry. See The Data Protection Registrar, "The Data Protection Act of 1984: Questions and Answers on the Act (1–20)", *l.c.*, p. 6 (Question 9).

1102 T. Cook, "The law relating to computer bureaux", *l.c.*, p. 165 and A.C.M. Nugter, *Transborder Flow of Personal Data within the EC*, *o.c.*, p. 122. In fact, computer bureaux were generally prohibited from making any disclosure other than those authorized by the data user.

1103 A.C.M. Nugter, *Transborder Flow of Personal Data within the EC*, *o.c.*, p. 139.

(8) knowingly or recklessly supplying the Registrar with *false or misleading information* on an application for registration (or for alteration of a register entry) (section (6));
(9) failure to keep the *registered address* up to date (section 6(5));
(10) intentional *obstruction* of a person executing a search warrant or failure, without a reasonable excuse, to give help reasonably required by a person executing a search warrant (schedule 4 section (12)).

The DPA further provided that, in cases where an offence is committed by a corporate body, any director, manager, secretary or similar officer could be found personally guilty of an offence if it was proved that the offence was committed with the "consent or connivance" of the person concerned, or to be attributable to neglect on that person's part (section 20(1)). In such a scenario, both the person concerned as well as the corporate body would be punishable for the offence.[1104]

512. Civil liability – The 1984 Data Protection Act provided data subjects with a claim for compensation of damages in two situations, namely (1) in case of damages suffered by reason of inaccuracy of data (section 22); or (2) in case of damages suffered by reason of loss, unauthorized disclosure, or access to data (section 23). While compensation for inaccuracy could only be obtained from the data user, an award for damages in case of a security breach could in principle also be obtained from a computer bureau.[1105] According to the Data Protection Registrar, the computer bureau would only be liable in so far as the destruction, disclosure or access occurs without the authority of the computer bureau (sic).[1106]

1104 Section 20(2) continued by stating that "Where the affairs of a body corporate are managed by its members subsection (1) above shall apply in relation to the acts and defaults of a member in connection with his functions of management as if he were a director of the body corporate." See also A.C.M. Nugter, *Transborder Flow of Personal Data within the EC*, *o.c.*, p. 139–140.

1105 It is interesting to note that the civil remedies provided by the 1984 Data Protection Act did not cover all data protection principles (effectively only the fifth and eighth principle were covered). For example, there is no provision for compensation in case of unlawfully obtained data or unauthorized use of data. This was reportedly a deliberate choice, as policymakers felt that existing civil law remedies (such as torts for breach of confidence, breach of contract or negligence) would be sufficient. Nevertheless, the limited scope of the claims recognized by the DPA was criticized at length by several scholars. See J. McBride, "Citizen's Privacy and Data Banks: Enforcement of the Standards in the Data Protection Act 1984 (U.K.)", *l.c.*, p. 544–545 and C. Edwards and N. Savage, "Data Privacy: the UK Experience", *o.c.*, p. 130–131.

1106 The Data Protection Registrar, "The Data Protection Act 1984: An introduction to the act and guide for data users and computer bureaux", *l.c.*, p. 22 and (note: while the text in both instances states "without the Computer Bureau's authority", one may venture to suggest this was an error and should have read "without the Data User's authority").

1.3. CONCLUSION

513. CONSISTENCY – Despite its long legislative history, the basic concepts underlying the 1984 Data Protection Act remained largely unchanged. From the outset, both the Younger and Lindop Committee recognized the difference between the "users", "operators", and "owners" of computer services. In the end, two distinct roles were recognized: that of the "computer bureau" and that of the "data user". The former was viewed primarily as a facility provider, whereas the latter was considered to be the product beneficiary.[1107]

514. FORMAL RECOGNITION OF COMPUTER BUREAUX – The 1984 Data Protection Act was not the first act to recognize the existence of computer bureaux.[1108] Nevertheless, the appearance of the term "computer bureau" is noteworthy.[1109] The reports of the Younger and Lindop Committees suggest that the recognition of bureaux was mainly a result of lobbying on the part of the UK computer industry. In their contributions, representatives of computer industry eagerly differentiated the providers of computing services from their customers. The main objective was seemingly to ward off any direct responsibility or accountability for their service offerings.

515. RESPONSIBILITY AND LIABILITY – Like the Lindop Committee before it, the House of Lords wound up rejecting the notion that computer bureaux should be left outside the scope of the Data Protection Act. Bureaux would be subject to the Act, but would have far fewer responsibilities bestowed upon them. Computer bureaux were mainly obliged to (1) register their activities; (2) act in conformity with instructions of the data user as well as the terms of the relevant register entries; and (3) ensure the security of processing. The remainder of the obligations provided under the Act were directed almost exclusively to data users. Nevertheless, bureaux were subject to the supervision of the Registrar and

---

1107 See also Home Office (Great Britain), *Report of the Committee on Data Protection*, *o.c.*, p. 255.

1108 The first data protection act to regulate computer bureaux as distinct entities was the Danish Private Register Act of 1978 which similarly required "computer service bureaux" to register their activities with the data protection registrar (See paragraph 20 of the Private Register Act (*lov om private register*) of 8 June 1978 (no. 293). The reader may note that the three data protection acts adopted before 1981 which were analysed in this book (i.e. Hesse, Sweden and France) also contained provisions which were directly applicable to entities processing data "on behalf of" other persons. However, the Danish act of 1978 appears to the first occasion whereby the term "computer service bureau" was explicitly mentioned in a piece of legislation and used to vest such entities with particular responsibilities.

1109 While Convention 108 recognized the existence of computer bureaux in its Explanatory Memorandum, it refrained from formally recognizing them as a separate entity within the body of the Convention. The UK was thus not under any international obligation to provide explicit recognition to this category of entities.

were exposed to the risk of both civil and criminal liability for activities residing within their sphere of control.[1110]

516–517. Recognition of pluralistic control – Another notable feature of the 1984 data protection act was its recognition of pluralistic control. Not only did it recognize that control might be exercised by more than one party, it also recognized two different ways in which control might be shared ("jointly or in common").

2. BELGIUM (1992)

2.1. ORIGIN AND DEVELOPMENT

518. Early initiatives – The first Parliamentary proposal to introduce data protection legislation in Belgium was submitted in 1971.[1111] Many other like-minded proposals would follow, none of which would become law.[1112] Throughout the 1970s, the Belgian government showed remarkably little appetite for data protection legislation.[1113] Instead, it contented itself with the view that existing laws offered adequate protections and that it should await the outcome of ongoing international initiatives, in particular by the Council of Europe.[1114]

519. A piecemeal approach – Beginning in the early 1980s, Belgium began to adopt laws regulating the use of certain categories of data. The scope of application of these laws was, however, strictly limited to a specific sector or database.[1115] Most notable were the Law on the National Register[1116] (1983) and

---

1110 The analysis of the activities of computer bureaux by the Lindop Committee reports suggest that that UK policymakers had a particular relationship and business model in mind when deciding that bureau should be brought within the scope of the act (see Home Office (Great Britain), *Report of the Committee on Data Protection*, *o.c.*, p. 252–259).

1111 Voorstel van wet betreffende de bescherming van het privé-leven en de persoonlijkheid, *Parl. St.*, Senaat, 1970–1971, 19 juli 1971, no. 706. The legislative proposal was based on an academic publication by C. Aronstein, "Défense de la vie privée. Essai pour contribuer à la survie de notre civilisation", *Journal des Tribunaux* 1971, p. 453–463. See also P. De Hert, S. Gutwirth and W. Debeuckelaere, *Anthologie privacy: referentietekst*, published by Commissie voor de Bescherming van de Persoonlijke Levenssfeer, 2013, p. 47.

1112 R. Pagano, "Panorama of Personal Data Protection Laws", *l.c.*, p. 243 (noting that between July 1971 and May 1981 a total nine parliamentary bills and a government bills were brought before the Belgian parliament, none of which were enacted into law).

1113 R. Pagano, "Panorama of Personal Data Protection Laws", *l.c.*, p. 244.

1114 F.W. Hondius, *Emerging Data Protection in Europe*, *o.c.*, p. 27.

1115 P. De Hert, S. Gutwirth and W. Debeuckelaere, *Anthologie privacy: referentietekst*, *o.c.*, p. 25–26.

1116 Wet van 8 augustus 1983 tot regeling van een Rijksregister van de natuurlijke personen, *B.S.* 21 april 1984.

the Law establishing the Crossroadsbank of Social Security[1117] (1990). Both laws imposed substantial restrictions on the extent to which certain information could be used or made available. At the same time, both laws were equally (if not more so) concerned with a desire to legitimate and further facilitate the automated exchange of personal information.[1118]

520. Mounting international pressure – Belgium had signed Convention 108 of the Council of Europe as early as 1982. Ratification, however, did not take place until 1991.[1119] In the end, the final push for ratification came from growing pressure within the international community.[1120] The Schengen Implementation Agreement[1121] explicitly required Contracting Parties to provide for a level of protection at least equal to that resulting from the principles laid down in Convention 108.[1122] The Schengen obligation, combined with an increasingly negative reputation of Belgium as a "data processing haven", eventually led the Belgian government to ratify Convention 108 and propose comprehensive data protection legislation.[1123]

521. Legislative development – A first draft of the Belgian Data Protection Act was submitted by the government on 16 May 1991.[1124] Despite repeated calls of urgency, the draft bill still underwent several substantive revisions.[1125] Throughout the legislative debate, a recurring point of criticism was that the bill would require many implementing acts before it could take full effect. The final text of the act was signed into law on 8 December 1992.[1126]

1117 Wet van 15 januari 1990 houdende oprichting en organisatie van een Kruispuntbank van de sociale zekerheid, *B.S.* 22 februari 1990.

1118 See P. De Hert, S. Gutwirth and W. Debeuckelaere, *Anthologie privacy: referentietekst, o.c.*, p. 34–46 and 54–55.

1119 Wet van 17 juni 1991 houdende goedkeuring van het Verdrag tot bescherming van personen ten opzichte van de geautomatiseerde verwerking van persoonsgegevens, opgemaakt te Straatsburg op 28 januari 1981, *B.S.* 30 december 1993.

1120 P. De Hert, S. Gutwirth and W. Debeuckelaere, *Anthologie privacy: referentietekst, o.c.*, p. 57.

1121 Convention implementing Schengen agreement of 14 June 1985 between the Governments of the States of the Benelux Economic Union, the Federal Republic of Germany and the French Republic on the gradual abolition of checks at their common borders, 19 June 1990.

1122 Article 117 of the Schengen Implementation Agreement.

1123 P. De Hert, S. Gutwirth and W. Debeuckelaere, *Anthologie privacy: referentietekst, o.c.*, p. 57. See also Centrum voor Internationaal Strafrecht, "De Belgische privacy-wetgeving, een eerste analyse", *Rechtskundig Weekblad* 1992–1993, no. 34, p. 1145.

1124 Wetsontwerp tot bescherming van de persoonlijke levenssfeer ten opzichte van de verwerking van persoonsgegevens, *Parl. St.* Kamer, 1990–1991, 6 May 1991, no. 1610–1.

1125 P. De Hert, S. Gutwirth and W. Debeuckelaere, *Anthologie privacy: referentietekst, o.c.*, p. 49 and 56–57.

1126 Wet van 8 december 1992 tot bescherming van de persoonlijke levenssfeer ten opzichte van de verwerking van persoonsgegevens, *B.S.* 18 maart 1993.

2.2. ALLOCATION OF RESPONSIBILITY AND LIABILITY

522. Terminology – Not surprisingly, the terminology of the 1992 Data Protection Act was quite similar to that of Convention 108. The definitions were not, however, identical. For instance, the Belgian definition of the "controller of the file" was notably shorter than its counterpart in Convention 108. The Belgian data protection act also formally recognized the concept of a "processor", which was similar to the concept of the "computer bureau" recognized by the 1984 UK Data Protection Act.[1127]

A. *"Controller of the file"*

523. Formal definition – Article 1, §6 defined the "controller of the file" (in Dutch: "*houder van het bestand*"[1128]) as

> "the natural or legal person or association which is competent to decide about the purpose of the processing or about the types of data that shall be included in the processing.
>
> In case the purpose of the processing or the types of data to be included are specified by law, the controller of the file shall be the natural or legal person that is appointed by law to process the data."

524. "Natural or legal person or association" – The controller of the file could be either a natural or legal person, or an association (in Dutch: "*feitelijke vereniging*"). The Act in principle applied to both the public and private sector, but it contained exemptions and derogations for certain public sector entities.[1129] The Act also contained an exemption for "*data kept by natural persons, which are intended for private, family or household use and which keep this purpose*" (Article 3, §2, 1°).[1130]

1127 Cf. *supra*, no. 498.

1128 The Dutch term "houder van het bestand" would translated more accurately into English as "the keeper of the file". However, as the term "houder van het bestand" was the official translation of the term "controller of the file" as it appeared in Convention 108, the same English term is used here.

1129 F. Robben, "Toepassingsgebied en begripsdefinities", in J. Dumortier en F. Robben, *Persoonsgegevens en privacybescherming. Commentaar op de wet tot bescherming van de persoonlijke levenssfeer*, Brugge, die Keure, 1995, p. 41 (referring to Article 3§3 and Article 4§1).

1130 For a discussion see Memorie van Toelichting, Wetsontwerp ter bescherming van de persoonlijke levenssfeer ten opzichte van de verwerking van persoonsgegevens, *Parl. St.* Kamer, 1990–1991, 6 May 1991, no. 1610–1, p. 7; Verslag namens de Minister van Justitie uitgebracht door Mevr. Merckx-Van Goey, Wetsontwerp ter bescherming van de persoonlijke levenssfeer ten opzichte van de verwerking van persoonsgegevens, *Parl. St.* Kamer, 1991–1992 (B.Z.), 2 juli 1992, no. 413–12, p. 23; F. Robben, "Toepassingsgebied en begripsdefinities", *o.c.*, p. 35–36 and Centrum voor Internationaal Strafrecht, "De Belgische privacy-wetgeving, een eerste analyse", *l.c.*, p. 1147.

525. "Competent to decide" – The controller of the file was the party "competent to decide" about the processing. The definition thus adopted a *functional approach* by allocating responsibility for compliance with the party that could exercise final decision-making power with regards to the processing.[1131]

526. "Purpose or types of data" – The second element of the definition concerned the object of the controller's decision-making power. The controller of the file was understood to have decision-making power "about the *purpose* of the processing *or* about the *types of data* that shall be included in the processing".

527. Primacy of purpose – In cases where the actor deciding about the processing was not the same as the actor deciding about the types of data to be processed, it appeared that preference should be given to the actor deciding about the purpose of the processing.[1132] According to the preparatory works, the controller is the *actor who decides to process personal data for a particular purpose*, rather than the technicians who decide which data are necessary to achieve the chosen purpose.[1133]

528. CBPL proposal – It is worth noting that the Belgian Privacy Commission (CBPL)[1134] had proposed to extend the definition of "controller of the file", to state the controller must also hold decision-making power regarding

(a) the types of processing activities to be performed;
(b) third parties to whom the data might be disclosed; and
(c) the processor to whom the processing of personal data might be entrusted.[1135]

The CBPL justified the proposal by saying that these elements are important aspects of the processing and therefore the controller of the file should also have

1131 Centrum voor Internationaal Strafrecht, "De Belgische privacy-wetgeving, een eerste analyse", *l.c.*, p. 1147 and S. Gutwirth, "De toepassing van het finaliteitsbeginsel van de Privacywet van 8 december 1992 tot bescherming van de persoonlijke levenssfeer ten opzichte van de verwerking van persoonsgegevens", *Tijdschrift voor Privaatrecht* 1993, Vol. 4, 14, p. 1443.

1132 F. Robben, "Toepassingsgebied en begripsdefinities", *o.c.*, p. 43–44.

1133 Centrum voor Internationaal Strafrecht, "De Belgische privacy-wetgeving, een eerste analyse", *l.c.*, p. 1147, with reference to Verslag namens de commissie voor de Justitie uitgebracht door de heer Vandenberghe, *Gedr. St., Senaat*, 1991–1992 (B.Z.), 27 October 1992, no. 445-2, p. 52–53.

1134 The Belgian Privacy Commission (in Dutch: "*Commissie voor de Bescherming van de Persoonlijke Levenssfeer*" – CBPL) had previously been established by the Law on the National Register and reformed by the Law on the Crossroadsbank for Social Security. See P. De Hert, S. Gutwirth and W. Debeuckelaere, *Anthologie privacy: referentietekst, o.c.*, 45.

1135 Commissie voor de Bescherming van de Persoonlijke Levenssfeer, Advies nr 7/92 betreffende het wetsontwerp tot bescherming van de persoonlijke levenssfeer ten opzichte van de verwerking van persoonsgegevens, 12 May 1992, p. 9.

the power to decide about them.[1136] The government, however, declined to take up the proposal.[1137] It reasoned that in practice the decisions about these aspects might be taken by several different actors. If the proposal of the CBPL were to be adopted, it would lead to situations in which there is no actor that satisfied the definition.[1138]

529. Continued reference to "the file" – The decision to keep the term "controller of the file" was heavily criticized.[1139] After all, the Act also covered completely automated processing, which meant that one could be labelled "controller of the file" without an actual "file" being present.[1140] The decision to keep the term "controller of the file" was justified mainly by a desire for consistency with the terminology of Convention 108.[1141]

530. "Processing" as a set of operations – The decision-making power of the controller extended to the "processing" of personal data. The term "processing" was defined in the Act as a *set of operations*, as opposed to an individual processing operation. A single processing operation did not constitute "processing" within the meaning of the Act.[1142] Instead, the term "processing" referred to the *entirety of operations undertaken for a particular purpose*.[1143] Robben noted early on the practical difficulties that might arise in determining whether a given series of operations should be considered as being part of the same "processing" or not.[1144] Robben argued that "a reasonable balance" should be struck between the following two extremes:

1136 *Id.*

1137 See Verslag namens de Minister van Justitie uitgebracht door Mevr. Merckx-Van Goey, Wetsontwerp ter bescherming van de persoonlijke levenssfeer ten opzichte van de verwerking van persoonsgegevens, Parl. St. Kamer, 1991–1992 (B.Z.), 2 July 1992, no. 413–12, p. 99–100.

1138 *Ibid*, p. 100. Article 16, §1, 1° of the Act would, however, require controllers to make an inventory of interconnections between the data as well third parties to whom the data might be disclosed (cf. *infra*).

1139 See J. Dumortier, "Privacybescherming en gegevensverwerking. Aantekeningen bij de Wet tot bescherming van de persoonlijke levenssfeer t.o.v. de verwerking van persoonsgegevens", *Vlaamse Jurist* 1993, p. 9 and F. Robben, "Toepassingsgebied en begripsdefinities", *o.c.*, p. 44.

1140 *Id.* See also Verslag namens de Commissie voor de Justitie uitgebracht door de heer Vandenberghe, *Gedr. St., Senaat*, 1991–1992 (B.Z.), 27 October 1992, no. 445-2, p. 20 ("*De term "houder van het bestand – maître du fichier" werd waarschijnlijk als zodanig behouden omdat het een geijkte term is, maar hij slaat in feite op veel meer dan alleen het bestand. Hij slaat op degene die de verwerking houdt of die daarvoor verantwoordelijk is*").

1141 Verslag namens de Minister van Justitie uitgebracht door Mevr. Merckx-Van Goey, Wetsontwerp ter bescherming van de persoonlijke levenssfeer ten opzichte van de verwerking van persoonsgegevens, *Parl. St.* Kamer, 1991–1992 (B.Z.), 2 juli 1992, no. 413–12, p. 17–18.

1142 J. Dumortier, "Privacybescherming en gegevensverwerking. Aantekeningen bij de Wet tot bescherming van de persoonlijke levenssfeer t.o.v. de verwerking van persoonsgegevens", *l.c.*, p. 8.

1143 *Id.*

1144 F. Robben, "Toepassingsgebied en begripsdefinities", *l.c.*, p. 28.

> "On the one hand, a situation in which practically all operations carried out by an entity are considered as a single "processing" with either a highly generic purpose or numerous sub-purposes. The principle of finality, a basic principle of the law, would then risk being undermined in practice because the data could be used without restriction for many different purposes. Moreover, the description of the processing will be so general as to render effective supervision impossible.
>
> On the other hand, a situation in which the entirety of processing operations carried out is heavily divided into numerous processing activities, which would require submission of a separate notification for each processing activity, with a very precise indication of the specific objectives pursued, each time accompanied by the payment of a fee. In this scenario, the strict application of the principle of finality would completely obstruct the efficiency of data processing and supervisory authorities would be overwhelmed with declarations and many amendments thereto."[1145]

Robben concluded that it would be up to the CBPL to articulate the requisite level of precision that would strike the appropriate balance between these two extremes.[1146] The argument made by Robben was based on an argument put forward by Gutwirth, who had previously cautioned against overly broad definitions of purpose.[1147] According to Gutwirth,

> "The delineation of finality thus embodies the key question for the implementation of the Privacy Act. Pleas for the recognition of 'carte blanche' or 'catch all' finalities threaten to undermine the entire substance of the law. In contrast, a requirement for an extensive specialization or limitation of finalities would however be impracticable and run counter to the spirit of the law, which aimed to create a flexible system."[1148]

531. No formal recognition of joint control – Article 1, §6 did not formally recognize the possibility that the decision-making power over the processing might be exercised by more than one actor. To the contrary, the

1145 *Ibid*, p. 28–29 (loose translation).

1146 *Ibid*, p. 29.

1147 S. Gutwirth, "De toepassing van het finaliteitsbeginsel van de Privacywet van 8 december 1992 tot bescherming van de persoonlijke levenssfeer ten opzichte van de verwerking van persoonsgegevens", *Tijdschrift voor Privaatrecht* 1993, vol. 4, p. 1458.

1148 S. Gutwirth, "De toepassing van het finaliteitsbeginsel van de Privacywet van 8 december 1992 tot bescherming van de persoonlijke levenssfeer ten opzichte van de verwerking van persoonsgegevens", *l.c.*, p. 1458 (loose translation). For a more recent discussion see S. Gutwirth, *Privacy and the information age*, Lanham, Rowman & Littlefield Publ., 2002, p. 97 (*"Calls for the recognition of 'catch all' purposes threaten to undermine the whole legislative framework. Such definitions of finalities as "make profit" or "contribute to whatever is of service to a person or corporation" does not impose any limits whatsoever. Any banker insurer-tour operator-salesperson of personal data can do whatever he/she wants. On the other hand, the demand to have stringent specifications of purposes would become paralyzing and unworkable. It would create a massive amount of red tape. In ideal circumstances, the specific purpose of processing should be defined somewhere in between the two extremes, taking into account the constitutional weight of privacy's freedom and the necessity of a catch-up operation."*)

preparatory works clearly indicate that the purpose of the definition was to arrive at a *single* controller for each processing.[1149] Legislative intent notwithstanding, Robben argued that there may well be situations in which it may be impossible to appoint a single controller.[1150] This could occur particularly in cases where different sets of processing activities were wholly or partially integrated with one and other.[1151] In such scenarios, one would have to determine whether it is possible to separate the decision-making power per "sub-processing" (separate control) or it is necessary to view the processing as one "global" processing with joint control.[1152]

532. Processing specified by law – Article 1, §6 explicitly provided that in cases where the purpose of the processing or the types of data to be included were specified by law, the controller of the file would be *"the natural or legal person that is appointed by law to process the data."* In such case, the functional approach described above could be discarded.[1153]

B. *"Processor"*

533. Formal definition – Article 1, §7 defined the "processor" (in Dutch: "*bewerker*")[1154] as

> "the natural or legal person or association entrusted with the organisation and execution of the processing".

534. "Natural or legal person or association" – The processor could be either a natural or legal, as well as an association (in Dutch: "*feitelijke vereniging*").

535. CBPL proposal – The CPBL had proposed to make a further distinction between "processing agents" and "processors". The term "processing agent" would be reserved for entities *outside* the organisation of the controller to whom the processing of personal data has been entrusted. The term "processor", on the other hand, would cover the person *within* the organisation of controller,

---

1149 Verslag namens de Commissie voor de Justitie uitgebracht door de heer Vandenberghe, *Gedr. St., Senaat*, 1991–1992 (B.Z.), 27 October 1992, no. 445–2, p. 52 and 123.

1150 F. Robben, "Toepassingsgebied en begripsdefinities", *o.c.*, p. 45.

1151 *Id.*

1152 *Id.*

1153 *Ibid*, p. 44.

1154 The term "bewerker" could also be translated as "editor", "adaptor", or "redactor". For purposes of simplicity, I have chosen to use the term "processor" here, even though the proper Dutch counterpart for this term is "verwerker" rather than "bewerker". The justification for doing so is the fact the definition of "bewerker" itself refers to the "processing" ("verwerken") of personal data.

appointed by the controller to ensure compliance with data protection requirements.[1155] The government declined to take up the proposal, arguing that the distinction was superfluous.[1156]

536. "Organisation and execution" – The processor was seen as a "mere executor", acting pursuant to the instructions of the controller of the file.[1157] Differentiating between controllers and processors thus required an assessment of who is actually competent to decide about the processing and those who merely executed the processing.[1158]

C. *Civil and criminal liability*

537. Final responsibility with controller – The controller of the file carried the final responsibility for compliance, regardless of how the processing was organised.[1159] Even in cases where the controller relies on a processor to execute processing of personal data, the controller would remain liable in case of non-compliance.[1160]

538. Civil liability – The civil liability of the controller resulted primarily from Article 1382 Civil Code (general liability in tort). In addition, Article 42 of the Data Protection Act provided that the controller of the file shall be liable "*for the payment of fines to which his appointee or agent has been condemned*".

539. Criminal liability – Articles 38 and 39 imposed criminal penalties in case of violation of several provisions of the Act (e.g. violation of the finality principle, failure to register, etc.). Many of the criminal provisions were explicitly targeted at the controller of the file.[1161] Other provisions had a more general

---

1155 Commissie voor de Bescherming van de Persoonlijke Levenssfeer, Advies nr 7/92 betreffende het wetsontwerp tot bescherming van de persoonlijke levenssfeer ten opzichte van de verwerking van persoonsgegevens, 12 May 1992, p. 9–11.

1156 See Verslag namens de Minister van Justitie uitgebracht door Mevr. Merckx-Van Goey, Wetsontwerp ter bescherming van de persoonlijke levenssfeer ten opzichte van de verwerking van persoonsgegevens, *Parl. St. Kamer*, 1991–1992 (B.Z.), 2 July 1992, no. 413–12, p. 100 (stating there would be no added value in such a distinction). See also F. Robben, "Toepassingsgebied en begripsdefinities", *o.c.*, p. 45–46.

1157 Verslag namens de commissie voor de Justitie uitgebracht door de heer Vandenberghe, *Gedr. St., Senaat*, 1991–1992 (B.Z.), 27 October 1992, no. 445–2, p. 80 ("*De bewerker is maar een uitvoerder*").

1158 Verslag namens de commissie voor de Justitie uitgebracht door de heer Vandenberghe, *Gedr. St., Senaat*, 1991–1992 (B.Z.), 27 October 1992, no. 445–2, p. 52.

1159 F. Robben, "Toepassingsgebied en begripsdefinities", *l.c.*, p. 41.

1160 See also Commissie voor de Bescherming van de Persoonlijke Levenssfeer, Advies nr 7/92 betreffende het wetsontwerp tot bescherming van de persoonlijke levenssfeer ten opzichte van de verwerking van persoonsgegevens, 12 May 1992, p. 9.

1161 Verslag namens de commissie voor de Justitie uitgebracht door de heer Vandenberghe, *Gedr. St., Senaat*, 1991–1992 (B.Z.), no. 445–2, p. 37; 54–55 and 80. Although several provisions also

nature ("*he who* ..."), which meant they could in principle extend to entities other than the controller.[1162]

540. Proposal of CBPL – It is worth noting that the CPBL had proposed to extend the scope of several criminal provisions to processors[1163], but the proposal was not followed up.

2.3. CONCLUSION

541. A latecomer to the data protection scene – The Data Protection Act of 1992 has been characterized as a "rush job".[1164] After years of procrastination, the Belgian government suddenly felt an urgent need to adopt general data protection legislation because of growing international pressure. The outcome was a job half done, with many provisions requiring further implementation before they could take effect.[1165]

542. Responsibility and liability – Similar to Convention 108, the Data Protection Act of 1992 designated the "controller of the file" as the entity ultimately responsible for ensuring compliance. The Act additionally recognized the concept of a "processor", but did very little with it in terms of further regulation. The main purpose of the term was seemingly to reinforce the responsibility of the controller, regardless of how the processing was organized.

make reference to the "representative, appointee or agent" of the controller, the preparatory works make clear that it was the general intent of the Belgian legislature not to impose criminal liability upon processors as such. (*Ibid*, p. 80).

1162 *Id.* See also Centrum voor Internationaal Strafrecht, "De Belgische privacy-wetgeving, een eerste analyse", *l.c.*, p. 1154.

1163 Commissie voor de Bescherming van de Persoonlijke Levenssfeer, Advies nr 7/92 betreffende het wetsontwerp tot bescherming van de persoonlijke levenssfeer ten opzichte van de verwerking van persoonsgegevens, 12 May 1992, p. 39–40.

1164 P. De Hert, S. Gutwirth and W. Debeuckelaere, *Anthologie privacy: referentietekst*, *o.c.*, p. 57–58.

1165 *Ibid*, p. 79–80.

CHAPTER 6
DIRECTIVE 95/46/EC

1. ORIGIN AND DEVELOPMENT

543. Economic relevance – On 21 November 1973, the European Commission issued a Communication regarding a "Community Policy on Data Processing".[1166] The Communication stressed the importance of having a flourishing European data processing industry and proposed several measures designed to promote its development.[1167] Although the Communication focused primarily on economic aspects of data processing, it also noted a need to establish "common measures" to protect citizens.[1168]

544. Parliamentary motions – In 1975, the Legal Affairs Committee of the European Parliament prepared an "own initiative" report, which contained a draft Resolution calling for a Directive on "individual freedom and data processing".[1169] A Directive was deemed necessary not only for the protection of citizens, but also to avoid the development of conflicting legislation.[1170] The Resolution was passed[1171], but the European Commission did not put forth any legislative proposals. The call for legislative action was repeated in 1976, 1979 and 1982.[1172] The Commission, however, preferred to

---

1166 Commission of the European Communities, "Community Policy on Data Processing", Communication of the Commission to the Council, SEC(73) 4300 final, 21 November 1973.

1167 *Ibid*, p. 4.

1168 *Ibid*, p. 13.

1169 Legal Affairs Committee, Interim Report on the protection of the rights of the individual in the face of developing technical progress in the field of automatic data processing, 19 February 1975, *European Parliament Working Documents* 1974–1975, Document 487/74, p. 5. See also F. W. Hondius, *Emerging data protection in Europe*, *o.c.*, p. 72–73 and A.C. Evans, "Data Protection Law", *l.c.*, p. 575–576.

1170 *Id.*

1171 European Parliament, Resolution of the European Parliament on the protection of the rights of the individual in the face of the technical developments in data processing, OJ 13 March 1975, C 60/48.

1172 See European Parliament, Resolution of the European Parliament on the protection of the rights of the individual in the face of the technical developments in data processing, OJ 3 May 1976, C100/27; OJ 5 June 1979, C 140/34–38 and OJ 5 April 1982, C87/39–41. See also D. Bainbridge, *EC Data Protection Directive*, *o.c.*, p. 22. See also E. Kosta, *Unravelling consent in European data protection legislation: a prospective study on consent in electronic communications*, Doctoral Thesis, Submitted 1 June 2011, p. 88.

await the completion of Convention 108 and then to urge Member States to ratify it.[1173]

545. The push for harmonisation – As the 1980s progressed, it soon became clear that not all Member States were rushing to ratify Convention 108.[1174] In 1985, the European Commission published a White Paper entitled "Completing the Internal Market", which contained a timetable of completion by 1992.[1175] The continued fragmentation of national approaches to data protection presented a clear risk to the European vision of further integration.[1176] The political push for greater harmonisation provided optimal conditions for further Community action.[1177] In September 1990, the European Commission announced a series of proposed data protection measures, one of which was a proposal for a Council Directive concerning the protection of individuals in relation to the processing of personal data.[1178]

546. Legislative development – The Commission proposal was met with mixed reviews.[1179] After almost two years of debate, the European Parliament published its first reading of the proposal, which contained more than 100 amendments.[1180] The Commission responded swiftly, releasing an amended proposal for the Directive six months later.[1181] The text was then transmitted to the Council, where the further progression of the document was delayed for more than two years due to a blocking minority.[1182] The political climate eventually

---

1173 Commission of the European Communities, Recommendation 81/679/EEC of 29 July 1981 relating to the Council of Europe Convention for the protection of individuals with regard to the automatic processing of personal data, OJ 29 August 1981, L 246/31. The Commission was not, however, completely inactive on the topic: see C. Layton, "Protection of Privacy – Future Prospects at the European Communities Level", in OECD, "Transborder Data Flows and the Protection of Privacy", *Information Computer Communications Policy*, no. 1, 1979, OECD, Paris, p. 213–216.

1174 D. Bainbridge, *EC Data Protection Directive*, *o.c.*, p. 23.

1175 Commission of the European Communities, "Completing the Internal Market", White Paper from the Commission to the European Council, COM(85) 310 final, 14 June 1985.

1176 D. Bainbridge, *EC Data Protection Directive*, *o.c.*, p. 23.

1177 *Id.*

1178 Commission of the European Communities, Commission Communication on the Protection of individuals in relation to the processing of personal data in the Community and information security, COM(90) 314 final, SYN 287 and 288, 13 September 1990.

1179 D. Bainbridge, *EC Data Protection Directive*, *o.c.*, p. 24–25.

1180 European Parliament, Position of the European Parliament on Proposal for a directive I COM(90) 0314 – C3-0323/90 – SYN 287 / Proposal for a Council directive concerning the protection of individuals in relation to the processing of personal data T3-0140/1992, 11 March 1992 (First Reading) OJ 13 April 1992, C 94/173–201.

1181 Commission of the European Communities, Amended proposal for a council directive on the protection of individuals with regard to the processing of personal data and on the free movement of such data, COM(92) 422 final – SYN 287, 15 October 1992, OJ 27 November 1992, C 311/30-61.

1182 See D. Bainbridge, *EC Data Protection Directive*, *o.c.*, p. 26–28.

changed, however, and on 20 February 1995 the Council reached a common position.[1183] The Parliament's second reading followed soon thereafter.[1184] On 18 July 1995, the Commission issued a favourable Opinion on the Parliament's proposed amendments, which had been relatively minor.[1185] The final version of the Directive was officially adopted on 24 October 1995.[1186]

2. ALLOCATION OF RESPONSIBILITY AND LIABILITY

547. Outline – Part II of this book provided an in-depth analysis of the allocation of responsibility and liability under Directive 95/46/EC.[1187] The present chapter is limited to a study of how the controller-processor model evolved during the preparatory works leading up to Directive 95/46/EC.

2.1. LEGISLATIVE DEVELOPMENT

A. Commission proposal

548. "Controller of the file" – The starting point for the definitions contained in the Commission proposal were the definitions of Convention 108.[1188] Article 2(e) of the Commission Proposal defined the "controller of the file" as

1183 Council of the European Union, Common position (EC) No 1/95 adopted by the Council on 20 February 1995 with a view to adopting Directive 95/.../EC of the European Parliament and of the Council of ... on the protection of individuals with regard to the processing of personal data and on the free movement of such data, OJ 13 April 1995, C 93/1–24.

1184 European Parliament, Decision of the European Parliament on the common position established by the Council with a view to the adoption of a European Parliament and Council Directive on the protection of individuals with regard to the processing of personal data and on the free movement of such data, (C4-0051/95 – 00/0287(COD)), OJ 3 July 1995 C 166/105–107.

1185 Commission of the European Communities, Opinion of the Commission pursuant to Article 189 b (2) (d) of the EC Treaty, on the European Parliament's amendments to the Council's common position regarding the proposal for a European Parliament and Council directive on the protection of individuals with regard to the processing of personal data and on the free movement of such data, COM(95) 375 final- COD287, 18 July 1995.

1186 Directive 95/46/EC on the protection of individuals with regards to the processing of personal data and on the free movement of such data, OJ 23 November 1995, L 281/31.

1187 Cf. *supra*, nos. 69 et seq.

1188 Commission of the European Communities, Commission Communication on the Protection of individuals in relation to the processing of personal data in the Community and information security, *l.c.*, p. 19 ("*The definitions are taken from Council of Europe Convention N° 108 with such adjustments and clarifications as are necessary to guarantee a high level of equivalent protection in the Community.*").

> "the natural or legal person, public authority, agency or other body competent under Community law or the national law of a Member State to decide what will be the purpose of the file, which categories of personal data will be stored, which operations will be applied to them and which third parties may have access to them"

This definition is identical to the one contained in Convention 108, save for two adaptations:

> "firstly by referring to Community Law in order to cover the case where specific directives contain substantive provisions on the protection of personal data; and secondly, by specifying that the person who authorizes consultation, notably in the event of direct interrogation, is the controller of the file".[1189]

549. PERSONS WHO "CONTROL THE OPERATIONS" – Article 18 of the Commission Proposal contained a number of provisions designed to promote *data security.* According to Article 18(4), responsibility for compliance with these obligations was not limited to the controller of the file:

> "The obligations referred to in paragraphs 1, 2 and 3 shall also be incumbent on persons who, either de facto or by contract, control the operations relating to a file."

The Explanatory Memorandum clarifies the meaning of Article 18(4) as follows:

> "Article 18(4) assigns responsibility for compliance with the obligations laid down by Article 18(1) to (3). The persons who – de facto or by contract – control the operations relating to a data file are also responsible for ensuring compliance with data security requirements. Those to whom this rule applies are, as the case may be, the controller of the file, the user having access via on-line data retrieval and data processing service bureaux performing data processing on behalf of the controller of the file."[1190]

550. PERSONS WITH ACCESS – Article 18(5) provided that

> "Any person who in the course of his work has access to information contained in files shall not communicate it to third parties without the agreement of the controller of the file."

The aim of this provision was to impose a *duty of professional secrecy* on employees of the controller of a file and other persons who in the course of their professional activity have access to personal information contained in a file.[1191]

1189 Commission of the European Communities, Commission Communication on the Protection of individuals in relation to the processing of personal data in the Community and information security, *l.c.*, p. 20. Compare *supra*, no. 461.

1190 *Ibid*, p. 38.

1191 *Ibid*, p. 39.

551. Processing "on behalf of" – Like Convention 108, the Commission proposal did not define the concept of a "service bureau" or "processor". It did, however, contain a provision dealing specifically with the situation in which the controller enlisted another person to process personal data on its behalf:

> "Article 22
> Processing on behalf of the controller of the file
>
> 1. The Member States shall provide in their law that the controller of the file must, where processing is carried out on his behalf, ensure that the necessary security and organisational measures are taken and choose a person or enterprise who provides sufficient guarantees in that respect.
> 2. Any person who collects or processes personal data on behalf of the controller of the file shall fulfil the obligations provided for in Article 16 and 18 of this Directive.
> 3. The contract shall be in writing and shall stipulate, in particular, that the personal data may be divulged by the person providing the service or his employees only with the agreement of the controller of the file."

The Explanatory Memorandum clarifies the rationale behind Article 22 as follows:

> "The object of this article is to avoid a situation whereby processing by a third party on behalf of the controller of the file has the effect of reducing the level of protection enjoyed by the data subject. To that end, obligations are placed both on the controller of the file and on the third party carrying out the processing."[1192]

552. Liability – Article 21 provided that any individual who suffers damage as result of any act incompatible with the Directive should be entitled to compensation from the controller of the file. The controller of the file would not be liable for any damage resulting from the loss or destruction of data or from unauthorized access if he could prove that he had taken "appropriate measures" to comply with requirements of Articles 18 and 22.[1193]

553. Sanctions – Article 23 called on Member States to provide for "dissuasive sanctions" in order to ensure compliance with the measures taken pursuant to the Directive. The Explanatory Memorandum explicitly envisaged *criminal sanctions*, bearing in mind that "non-compliance with data protection principles constitutes infringement of a fundamental right".[1194]

1192 Commission of the European Communities, Commission Communication on the Protection of individuals in relation to the processing of personal data in the Community and information security, *l.c.*, p. 40.

1193 *Id.*

1194 *Id.*

554. Assessment – The Commission proposal displayed several notable features. The first feature concerns its use of the term "control". The Commission proposal did not consider that the "controller of the file" was the only entity that could exercise "control" over processing operations. "Control over processing operations" could be exercised either by the controller of the file, a person accessing data online, or a service bureau. It seems therefore that the Commission was using the term "control" in an operational sense rather than in a legal sense (i.e. as a legal term of art). A second notable feature of the Commission proposal was the allocation of responsibility contained in Article 22(2). This provision provided that any person collecting or processing personal data "on behalf of" the controller was responsible not only to ensure data security (Article 18), but also to ensure compliance with the basic data protection principles (Article 16) (!). The controller would, however, remain liable for any actions for damages (Article 21).[1195] Finally, it is worth noting that, in comparison to Convention 108, the Commission proposal introduced several new elements, such as the obligation for controllers to exercise due diligence when entrusting the processing of personal data to a third party, as well as the obligation to put in place a contract binding provider of the processing service to the controller's instructions.

B. *First reading European Parliament*

555. Outline – The European Parliament's first reading introduced several important amendments to the original Commission proposal. A first important change was the removal of the old-fashioned concept of the "file", on the grounds that it was outdated and irrelevant given the development of automation and telecommunications.[1196] The "controller of the file" thus became the "controller of the data". A second important change was the formal recognition of the "processor", which had only been implicitly recognized by the Commission's first proposal. Finally, the European Parliament also introduced the definition of a "third party", to designate potential recipients of information that did not belong to the organisation of the controller.

556. "Controller of the data" – In its first reading, the European Parliament proposed to define the "controller of the data" as

> "the natural or legal person, public authority, agency or other body, which processes personal data either on its own account or by a processor and is competent to decide

[1195] See also recital (20): "*Whereas, in the event of non-compliance with this Directive, liability in any action for damages must rest with the controller of the file; whereas dissuasive sanctions must be applied in order to ensure effective protection*".

[1196] See Commission of the European Communities, Amended proposal for a council directive on the protection of individuals with regard to the processing of personal data and on the free movement of such data, COM(92) 422 final – SYN 287, 15 October 1992, p. 3.

the purpose or purposes for which the personal data are processed, which categories of personal data will be stored, which operations will be applied to them and which third parties may have access to them."[1197]

557. "PROCESSOR" – Article 2(ea) defined a processor as

> "a natural or legal person who processes personal data on behalf of the controller of the data".[1198]

Neither Convention 108 nor the OECD Guidelines had adopted the term "processor".[1199] The main reason why the EU legislature decided to introduce this concept was to

> "avoid situations whereby processing by a third party on behalf of the controller of the file has the effect of reducing the level of protection enjoyed by the data subject".[1200]

558. "THIRD PARTIES" – Article 2(hb) defined third parties as

> "natural or legal persons other than the controller of the data. The following shall not be considered third parties: employees of the companies which hold the data, to the exclusion of those in their branches, or in companies belonging to the same holding company, if they receive such data in the course of their work."[1201]

1197 European Parliament, Position of the European Parliament on Proposal for a directive I COM(90) 0314 – C3-0323/90 – SYN 287 / Proposal for a Council directive concerning the protection of individuals in relation to the processing of personal data T3-0140/1992, 11 March 1992 (First Reading) OJ 13 April 1992, C 94/177.

1198 *Ibid*, p. 177.

1199 Although neither Convention 108 nor the OECD Guidelines formally defined the concept of a processor, it is worth observing that the Explanatory Memorandum to the OECD Guidelines did stipulate that a data controller should not be relieved of its obligations merely because the processing of data is carried out on his behalf by another party, such as a "*service bureau*" (see the Explanatory Memorandum to the OECD Guidelines, at paragraph 62). See also *supra*, no. 439. The Explanatory Report accompanying Convention 108 also indicated that concept of the "controller of the file" did not extend to "*persons who carry out the operations according to the instructions given by the controller of the file*". (Explanatory Report, paragraph 32). See also *supra*, no. 465.

1200 Commission of the European Communities, "Proposal for a Council Directive concerning the protection of individuals in relation to the processing of personal data", SYN 287, Explanatory Memorandum, p. 40. The decision to incorporate a separate definition of "processors" was not included in the Commission's initial proposal, but was later introduced pursuant to an amendment proposed by the Committee on Legal Affairs and Citizens' Rights (see Committee on Legal Affairs and Citizens' Rights, Report concerning the proposal by the Commission to the Council for a Directive concerning the protection of individuals in relation to the processing of personal data, European Parliament Session Documents, A3-0010-92, 15 January 1992, 11, amendment no. 18). See also Opinion 1/2010, *l.c.*, p. 24.

1201 *Ibid*, p. 177.

The definition of the term "third parties" was introduced at the same time as the definition of the term "communication", which was defined by Article 2(da) as:

> "the dissemination, disclosure, transmission or making available of personal data to a natural or legal person; communication shall not include the dissemination or making available of personal data to other persons within the organisation or undertaking in which the controller of the data operates, if such persons receive such data in the course of their duties within the framework of the principles laid down in Article 8(1) hereafter."

559. Persons who "control the operations" – Article 18(4) was identical to the initial Commission proposal, except that the reference to the "file" was replaced with a reference to "data".[1202]

560. Persons with access – Article 18(5) likewise remained unchanged save for the substitution of "file" and "data".[1203]

561. Processing "on behalf of" – Article 22 underwent two notable changes. First, Article paragraph 22(1) made reference to the newly coined term "processor" to refer to persons that process personal data on behalf of the controller of the data. Second, Article 22(2) no longer specified that persons acting "on behalf of the controller" were required to fulfil the obligations of former Articles 16 (principles) and 18 (security). Instead, the revised Article 22(2) simply provided that

> "The processor shall only carry out that processing of personal data laid down contractually by the controller of the data and shall take instructions only from the controller."[1204]

Article 22(3) still provided that the contract between the controller of the data and the processor must stipulate that personal data may be divulged only with the agreement of the controller of the data.

562. Liability and sanctions – Article 21 was revised to read as follows:

> "1. The Member States shall provide in their law that any individual whose personal data have been stored and who suffers damage as a result of unlawful processing

1202 *Ibid*, p. 191 ("*The obligations referred to in paragraphs 1, 2 and 3 shall also be incumbent on persons who, either de facto or by contract, control the operations relating to data*").

1203 *Ibid*, p. 191. (""*Any person who in the course of his work has access to information shall not communicate it to third parties without the agreement of the controller of the data*").

1204 *Ibid*, p. 192.

or of any act incompatible with this directive shall be entitled to compensation from the controller of the data.
2. The controller of the data shall compensate the data subject for any damage resulting from storage of his personal data that is incompatible with this directive."[1205]

The Parliament's change had the effect of removing the "escape clause" contained in the first draft of Article 21, which provided that the controller would not be liable for any damage resulting from the loss or destruction of data or from unauthorized access if he could prove that he had taken "appropriate measures" to comply with requirements of Articles 18 and 22 ("security" and "processing on behalf of the controller").[1206]

563. SANCTIONS – Article 23 underwent only minor revisions.[1207]

C. *Amended EC proposal*

564. OUTLINE – The European Commission took on board many of the changes proposed by the European Parliament, but also added a few (minor) changes of its own. First, the definition of a "controller" was simplified. The Commission proposed to simply refer to the "controller" and to omit any reference to either "the file" or the "data".[1208] Second, the amended proposal added the term "objective", as being an additional aspect decided by the controller. The definition of "processor" remained essentially unchanged. Interestingly, Article 17(4) no longer referred to persons "who control the operations", but instead to "persons who share responsibility for carrying out the processing". This change implicitly signalled that the term "control" was no longer being used in an operational sense, but rather as a legal term of art. The most noteworthy change made by the European Commission related to Article 24(2), which now provided that processors were obliged to comply with *all* of the national provisions adopted pursuant to the Directive (!).

565. "CONTROLLER" – Article 2(d) of the amended EC proposal defined the "controller" as

1205 *Ibid*, p. 192.
1206 Cf. *supra*, no. 159.
1207 Article 23 was mainly to underline its applicability to both public and private sector entities: "*Each Member State shall make provision in its law for the application of dissuasive sanctions, applicable to both authorities and organisations governed by public law and other natural or legal persons, in order to ensure compliance with the measures taken pursuant to this directive.*"
1208 The definition was further shortened by referring to the entity "*who processes personal data or causes it to be processed*" (instead of: "*which processes personal data either on its own account or by a processor*") and who "*decides*" (instead of: "*is competent to decide*").

> "any natural or legal person, public authority, agency or other body who processes personal data or causes it to be processed and who decides what is the purpose and objective of the processing, which personal data are to be processed, which operations are to be performed upon them and which third parties are to have access to them".[1209]

The accompanying Explanatory Memorandum clarified the change as follows:

> "[A]s the Directive sets out to regulate the use of data in light of the object being pursued, it is preferable to speak of the "controller", and to drop any reference to a "file" or "data".
>
> The controller is the person ultimately responsible for the choices governing the design and operation of the processing carried out (usually the chief executive of the company), rather than anyone who carries out processing in accordance with the controller's instructions. That is why the definition stipulates that the controller decides the "objective" of the processing. [...] The controller may process data himself, or have them processed by members of his staff or by an outside processor, a legally separate person acting on his behalf."[1210]

566. "PROCESSOR" – The definition of processor remained the same, save for the change in reference to the "controller" instead of the "controller of the data".[1211]

567. "THIRD PARTY" – The definition of "third party" was modified in order to read:

> "any natural or legal person other than the data subject, the controller and any person authorized to process the data under the controller's direct authority or on his behalf".[1212]

According to the Explanatory Memorandum, the definition was reworded in order to clarify which entities should or should not considered as "third parties". As such, persons working for a separate organisation, even if they belong to the same group or holding companies would be considered "third parties". On the other hand, branches processing customer information under the direct authority of their headquarters would not be considered third parties.[1213]

1209 Commission of the European Communities, Amended proposal for a council directive on the protection of individuals with regard to the processing of personal data and on the free movement of such data, COM(92) 422 final – SYN 287, 15 October 1992, OJ 27 November 1992, C 311, p. 39.

1210 *Ibid*, p. 10.

1211 *Ibid*, 39.

1212 *Id.*

1213 Commission of the European Communities, Amended proposal for a council directive on the protection of individuals with regard to the processing of personal data and on the free movement of such data, COM(92) 422 final – SYN 287, 15 October 1992, p. 11.

568. Persons who "carry out the processing" – Article 17(4) [former Article 18(4)] now provided that the obligations regarding security of processing

> "shall also be incumbent on persons who share responsibility for carrying out the processing, and, in particular, on the processor."[1214]

569. Persons with access – Article 17(5) [former Article 18(5)] remained essentially unchanged.[1215]

570. Processing "on behalf of" – Article 24(1) [former Article 22(1)] still imposed the same duty of "due diligence" upon controllers, by stating that the controller

> "must, where processing is carried out on his behalf, ensure that the necessary security and organisational measures are taken and choose a processor who provides sufficient guarantees in that respect."

Article 24(2) [former Article 22(2)] was revised to stipulate that

> "The processor shall carry out only such processing of personal data as is stipulated in his contract with the controller and shall take instructions only from the latter. He shall comply with the national provisions adopted pursuant to this Directive."

The Explanatory Memorandum elaborates as follows:

> "In accordance with Parliament's wishes, paragraph 2 emphasizes that the processor may only act within the terms of his contract with the controller. It is proposed that an express reference should be made to the obligations imposed by the national measures taken under the Directive, which shall also apply to a processor."

Article 24(3) [former Article 22(3)] remained essentially unchanged.[1216]

1214 Commission of the European Communities, Amended proposal for a council directive on the protection of individuals with regard to the processing of personal data and on the free movement of such data, COM(92) 422 final – SYN 287, 15 October 1992, OJ 27 November 1992, C 311/51.

1215 *Ibid*, p. 51. It merely added an exception to the general prohibition of disclosure without authorisation of the controller: "*Any person who, in the course of his work, has access to personal data shall not disclose it to third parties without the controller's agreement, unless he is required to do so under national or Community law.*" See also Commission of the European Communities, Amended proposal for a council directive on the protection of individuals with regard to the processing of personal data and on the free movement of such data, COM(92) 422 final – SYN 287, 15 October 1992, p. 27–28.

1216 Commission of the European Communities, Amended proposal for a council directive on the protection of individuals with regard to the processing of personal data and on the free movement of such data, COM(92) 422 final – SYN 287, 15 October 1992, OJ 27 November 1992, C 311/54 The changes made appear to have been mainly stylistic: "*The contract shall*

571. LIABILITY – Notwithstanding the European Parliament's proposals to amend Article 21, the European Commission still felt that Member States should feel free to exempt the controller from liability where suitable security measures were taken.[1217] Articles 23 [former Article 21] of the amended proposal provided that

> "1. Member States shall provide that any person whose personal data are undergoing processing and who suffers damage as a result of an unlawful processing operation or of any act incompatible with the national provisions adopted pursuant to this directive is entitled to receive compensation from the controller for the damage suffered.
> 2. Member States may provide that the controller may be exempted, in whole or in part, from his liability for damage resulting from the loss or destruction of data or from unauthorized access if he proves that he has taken suitable steps to satisfy the requirements of Articles 17 and 24."[1218]

572. SANCTIONS – Article 24 [former Article 23] underwent minor revisions, which were mainly stylistic in nature.[1219]

D. Council position

573. OUTLINE – After almost three years of deliberation, the Council text brought with it several significant changes. First, the Council shortened the definition of a "controller" considerably, by referring only to the "*purposes and means of the processing of personal data*" as being the defining object of a controller's decision-making power.[1220] The definition of "processor" underwent

---

be in writing and shall state, in particular, that personal data processed there under may be disclosed to a third party by the processor or his employees only with the controller's agreement."

1217 Commission of the European Communities, Amended proposal for a council directive on the protection of individuals with regard to the processing of personal data and on the free movement of such data, COM(92) 422 final – SYN 287, 15 October 1992, p. 33.

1218 Commission of the European Communities, Amended proposal for a council directive on the protection of individuals with regard to the processing of personal data and on the free movement of such data, COM(92) 422 final – SYN 287, 15 October 1992, OJ 27 November 1992, C 311/54. See also Commission of the European Communities, Amended proposal for a council directive on the protection of individuals with regard to the processing of personal data and on the free movement of such data, COM(92) 422 final – SYN 287, 15 October 1992, p. 33.

1219 Article 24 now provided that "*Each Member State shall provide for the imposition of dissuasive penalties on any person who does not comply with the national provisions adopted pursuant to this Directive*". (Commission of the European Communities, Amended proposal for a council directive on the protection of individuals with regard to the processing of personal data and on the free movement of such data, COM(92) 422 final – SYN 287, 15 October 1992, OJ 27 November 1992, C 311/55).

1220 In the amended Commission proposal, the object of the controller's decision-making power extended not only to the purpose of the processing, but also to (1) the objective of the processing; (2) which personal data are to be processed; (3) which operations are to be performed upon them; and (4) which third parties are to have access to them. It would appear that the term "objective" was subsumed by the "purpose" of the processing; whereas the question of which personal data are to be processed, which processing operations are to be

minor revisions, essentially to make clear that a "public authority, agency or any other body" could also act as a "processor". The most drastic changes were introduced via Articles 16 and 17 of the Council text. The Council revised these provisions so that *none* of the obligations contained in the Directive would be directly incumbent upon processors. Instead, the source of the processors obligations would result from a *"contract or legal act binding the processor to the controller"*.[1221] Finally, the Council text expanded the liability escape clause of Article 23(2) to any case where the controller can prove that he is not responsible for the event giving rise to the damage.

574. "CONTROLLER" – In the Council text, Article 2(d) defined the "controller" as

> "the natural or legal person, public authority, agency or any other body which determines the purposes and means of the processing of personal data. Where the purposes and means of processing are determined by national or Community laws or regulations, the controller or the specific criteria for his nomination may be designated by a national or Community law."[1222]

575. "PROCESSOR" – Article 2(e) defined the "processor" as

> "the natural or legal person, public authority, agency or any other body which processes personal data on behalf of the controller".[1223]

576. "THIRD PARTY" – Article 2(f) defined a "third party" as

> "the natural or legal person, public authority, agency or any other body other than the data subject, the controller, the processor and the persons who, under the direct authority of the controller or the processor, are authorized to process the data".[1224]

577. "RECIPIENT" – Article 2(g) defined a "recipient" as

> "the natural or legal person, public authority, agency or any other body to whom data are disclosed, whether a third party or not; however, authorities which may receive data in the framework of a particular inquiry shall not be regarded as recipients"

---

performed and which third parties are to have access to them were subsumed by the "means" of the processing.

1221 By doing so, the Council effectively quashed the notion that a processor might have an independent obligation to assess whether its processing activities were in compliance with the requirements of the Directive.

1222 Council of the European Union, Common position (EC) No 1/95 adopted by the Council on 20 February 1995 with a view to adopting Directive 95/.../EC of the European Parliament and of the Council of ... on the protection of individuals with regard to the processing of personal data and on the free movement of such data, OJ 13 April 1995, C 93/7.

1223 *Ibid*, p. 7.

1224 *Ibid*, p. 7.

The term "recipient" was reportedly introduced primarily to help ensure transparency of processing towards data subjects.[1225]

578. Persons with access – Article 16 [former Article 17(5)] provided that

> "Any person acting under the authority of the controller or of the processor, including the processor himself, who has access to personal data must not process them except on instructions from the controller, unless he is required to do so by law."

579. Due diligence – Article 17(2) [former Article 24(1)] provided that

> "the controller must, where processing is carried out on his behalf, choose a processor who provides sufficient guarantees in respect of the technical security measures and organisational measures governing the processing to be carried out and must ensure compliance with those measures".[1226]

580. Legal binding – Article 17(3) and 17(4) [former Articles 24(2) and 24(3)] provided that

> "3. The carrying out of processing by way of a processor must be governed by a contract or legal act binding the processor to the controller and stipulating in particular that:
> – the processor shall act only on instructions from the controller,
> – the obligations set out in paragraph 1, as defined by the law of the Member State in which the processor is established, shall also be incumbent on the processor.
> 4. For the purposes of keeping proof, the parts of the contract or the legal act relating to data protection and the requirements relating to the measures referred to in paragraph 1 shall be in writing or in another equivalent form."[1227]

581. Liability – Article 23 provided that

> "1. Member States shall provide that any person who has suffered damage as a result of an unlawful processing operation or of any act incompatible with the national provisions adopted pursuant to this Directive is entitled to receive compensation from the controller for the damage suffered.
> 2. The controller may be exempted from this liability, in whole or in part, if he proves that he is not responsible for the event giving rise to the damage."[1228]

1225 *Ibid*, p. 22. Articles 10 and 11, for instance, required controllers to inform data subjects of the "recipients or categories of recipients" of their personal data.
1226 *Ibid*, p. 12.
1227 *Ibid*, p. 12. Article 17(1) concerned the controller's obligation to ensure security of processing.
1228 *Ibid*, p. 14.

The recitals in the Council text made clear that Article 23(2) referred inter alia to situations in which the damages resulted from an "*error on the part of the data subject*" or "*in a case of force majeure*".[1229]

582. Sanctions – Article 24 provided that

> "The Member States shall adopt suitable measures to ensure the full implementation of the provisions of this Directive and shall in particular lay down the sanctions to be imposed in case of infringement of the provisions adopted pursuant to this Directive."

E. *Second reading and final text*

583. Outline – The European Parliament's second reading contained very few amendments. One very important change, however, was the amendment that introduced the notion of "joint control" in the definition of a "controller".

584. Controller – In its second reading, the European Parliament defined the controller as

> "the natural or legal person, public authority, agency or any other body which <u>alone or jointly with others</u> determines the purposes and means of the processing of personal data. Where the purposes and means of processing are determined by national or Community laws or Regulations, the controller or the specific criteria for his nomination may be designated by a national or Community law".[1230]

The accompanying Explanatory Memorandum provided the following rationale for the change:

> "Article 2, sub d) is important, because it allows to establish who is subject to the requirements of the Directive. The text appears to relate only to the most prevalent situation, whereby only one person is considered a controller. In practice it may occur, however, that <u>several different persons decide to process personal data for a particular purpose</u> or in the context of permanent relationship (e.g., within a collaboration framework or a professional association) and provide themselves with the necessary technical means to do so. In such a case, <u>each of these persons, as soon as they do not operate as part of the same legal entity, shall be considered a joint</u>

1229 *Ibid*, p. 6.

1230 European Parliament, Decision of the European Parliament on the common position established by the Council with a view to the adoption of a European Parliament and Council Directive on the protection of individuals with regard to the processing of personal data and on the free movement of such data, (C4-0051/95 – 00/0287(COD)), OJ 3 July 1995 C 166/106.

> controller. This situation may occur more and more in the future, for example in case of an exchange of data between governments or between companies in the context of telematics networks."[1231]

In its Opinion following the Parliament's second reading, the European Commission reasoned that

> "Amendment No 3 provides in Article 2(d) for the possibility that for a single processing operation a number of parties may jointly determine the purpose and means of the processing to be carried out. It follows from this that, in such a case, each of the co-controllers must be considered as being constrained by the obligations imposed by the directive so as to protect the natural persons about whom the data are processed."[1232]

The European Parliament did not propose any further amendments directly affecting the concepts of "controller", "processor", "third party", "recipient" or the relationship between these entities. The amendments proposed by the European Parliament in its second reading were received favourably by both Commission and the Council. The final text of the Directive 95/46 was officially adopted by the Parliament and Council on 24 October 1995.

2.2. CONCLUSION

585. Consolidation and innovation – The main objective of Directive 95/46 was to further harmonize data protection legislation across EU Member States. For the most part, the Directive relied upon the acquis of Convention 108, which had already consolidated the basic architecture for national data protection laws in the EU. However, Directive 95/46 also introduced a number of new elements, in comparison to its predecessor. Important changes included rules on applicable law, the introduction of the concept of processor and the recognition of joint control.

1231 Commissie juridische zaken en rechten van de burger, "Aanbeveling voor de tweede lezing betreffende het gemeenschappelijke standpunt van de Raad met het oog op de aanneming van de richtlijn van het Europese Parlement en de Raad betreffende de bescherming van natuurlijke personen in verband met de verwerking van persoonsgegevens en betreffende het vrije verkeer van die gegevens (C4-00051/95 – 00/0287(COD)), PE 212.057/def, A4-0120/95, 24 mei 1995, p. 15 (own translation of the Dutch official translation).

1232 Commission of the European Communities, Opinion of the Commission pursuant to Article 189 b (2) (d) of the EC Treaty, on the European Parliament's amendments to the Council's common position regarding the proposal for a European Parliament and Council directive on the protection of individuals with regard to the processing of personal data and on the free movement of such data, COM(95) 375 final- COD287, 18 July 1995, p. 3.

586. Responsibility and liability – Within the regulatory scheme of the Directive, the controller carries the primary responsibility for ensuring compliance. At the moment of its enactment, the EU legislature was mindful of the practice whereby one organisation requests another organisation to perform certain processing operations on its behalf. By introducing the concept of a "processor", the EU legislature hoped to be able to address this situation and to ensure a continuous level of protection.

587. Varying degrees of contractual flexibility – Directive 95/46 has devoted several provisions to the relationship between controllers and processors. Article 17(3) obliges controllers to conclude a contract with their processors, which must specify that the processor is obliged (1) to follow the controller's instructions at all times and (2) to implement appropriate technical and organisational measures to ensure the security of processing. In contrast, Directive 95/46/EC in principle does not contain any specific requirements aimed at regulating the relationship among controllers as such.

CHAPTER 7

GENERAL DATA PROTECTION REGULATION

1. ORIGIN AND DEVELOPMENT

588. Review of Directive 95/46 – For almost 15 years, Directive 95/46 stood strong as the central instrument of data protection regulation in the EU. The European Commission assessed its implementation in 2003 and 2007, both times concluding there was no need for revisions.[1233] In 2010, however, the Commission announced that the time for revisions had come.[1234] The Commission argued that while the objectives and principles underlying Directive 95/46 remained sound, revisions were necessary in order to meet the challenges of technological developments and globalisation.[1235]

589. A changing environment – Formal preparations for the review began in July 2009, when the European Commission launched a public consultation "on the legal framework for the fundamental right to protection of personal data".[1236] The consultation revealed concerns regarding the impact of new technologies on data protection, as well as a desire for a more comprehensive and coherent approach to data protection.[1237] Perhaps more significantly, 2009 was also the year when the Lisbon Treaty entered into force.[1238] Article 16 of

---

1233 See European Commission, "Report from the Commission – First Report on the implementation of the Data Protection Directive (95/46/EC)", 15 May 2003, COM(2003) 265 final and European Commission, Communication on the follow-up of the Work programme for a better implementation of the Data Protection Directive, 7 March 2007, COM(2007)87 final.

1234 European Commission, "A comprehensive approach on personal data protection in the European Union", Communication from the Commission to the European Parliament, the Council, the Economic and Social Committee and the Committee of the Regions, 4 November 2010.

1235 *Ibid*, p. 3.

1236 The public consultation ran from 9 July 2009 to 31 December 2009. For a summary see: European Commission, "Summary of replies to the public consultation about the future legal framework for protecting personal data, 4 November 2010.

1237 *Ibid*, p. 4.

1238 Treaty of Lisbon amending the Treaty on European Union and the Treaty establishing the European Community, signed at Lisbon, 13 December 2007, OJ C 306, 17 December 2007.

the Lisbon Treaty provided the EU with a legal basis to enact comprehensive data protection legislation across Union policies (including in the area of police and judicial cooperation in criminal matters).[1239] It also gave the right to data protection renewed prominence: the right to data protection was recognized both by Article 16 of the Treaty and Article 8 of the EU Charter of Fundamental Rights, which became legally binding as the Lisbon Treaty entered into force.[1240]

590. Push for (even) greater harmonisation – A new public consultation ensued following the EC Communication of 4 November 2010.[1241] The Commission concluded that many stakeholders supported the idea of further harmonisation of data protection rules at EU level.[1242] The Commission also felt that despite its aim, Directive 95/46 had failed to ensure an equivalent level of protection throughout the EU.[1243] Persistent fragmentation meant legal uncertainty, administrative burden and an uneven protection for individuals.[1244] A Regulation would provide a strong and uniform legislative framework at EU level.[1245]

591. Central themes of the reform – In 2012, the European Commission indicated that the reform of the EU data protection framework would consist of four main elements, namely:

1239 European Commission, "A comprehensive approach on personal data protection in the European Union", *l.c.*, p. 4 and 13. See also P. Hustinx, "Data Protection in the Light of the Lisbon Treaty and the Consequences for Present Regulations", speech delivered by Peter Hustinx at the 11th Conference on Data Protection and Data Security, Berlin, 8 June 2009 and C. Kuner, "The European Commission's Proposed Data Protection Regulation: A Copernican Revolution in European Data Protection Law", *Bloomberg BNA, Privacy and Security Law Report*, 2 June 2012, p. 2.

1240 *Id.* For a more detailed discussion of the implications of this development see G. González Fuster, *The Emergence of Personal Data Protection as a Fundamental Right of the EU*, Dordrecht, Springer, 2014, p. 230 et seq. and H. Hijmans, *The European Union as a constitutional guardian of internet privacy and data protection*, Academisch proefschrift ter verkrijging van de graad van doctor aan de Universiteit van Amsterdam en de Vrije Universiteit Brussel, 2016, p. 180 et seq.

1241 The public consultation on "the Commission's comprehensive approach on personal data protection in the European Union" ran from 4 November 2010 to 15 January 2011. For a summary of the contributions received see Annex 4 to the Commission's Impact Assessment accompanying its initial proposal for General Data Protection Regulation, p. 54–73.

1242 European Commission, "Summary of Replies to the Public Consultation on the Commission's Communication on comprehensive approach on personal data protection in the European Union, Annex 4, p. 64.

1243 European Commission, "Safeguarding Privacy in a Connected World – A European Data Protection Framework for the 21st Century", Communication from the Commission to the European Parliament, the Council, the European Economic and Social Affairs Committee and the Committee of the Regions, COM(2012) 9 final, 25 January 2012, p. 7.

1244 *Id.*

1245 *Id.*

a) To *provide individuals with control* over their personal data (by reinforcing existing data subject rights and adding new rights such as a "right to be forgotten" and a "right to data portability");
b) To render data protection rules fit for the *digital single market* (by providing full harmonisation by a way of Regulation as well as a "one stop shop" mechanism for business);
c) To enable a smoother exchange of personal data in the *area of police and criminal justice co-operation* (by replacing Framework Decision 2008/977/JHA[1246] with a directive); and
d) To develop updated rules for *cross-border data transfers* (for example, by formally recognizing alternative transfer mechanisms such as Binding Corporate Rules).[1247]

592. Legislative development – The Commission officially released its initial proposal for a General Data Protection Regulation (GDPR) on 25 January of 2012.[1248] The proposed GDPR was accompanied by a proposal for a Directive setting out rules on the protection of personal data processed for the purposes of prevention, detection, investigation or prosecution of criminal offences and related judicial activities (Law Enforcement Directive).[1249] After more than two years of intense lobbying, the European Parliament completed its First Reading of the GDPR on 12 March 2014. The Council of the European Union reached a consensus on a General Approach on 15 June 2015.[1250] The General Approach agreed by the Council formed the basis for its further negotiations with the European Parliament in the context of its so-called "trilogue" discussions, in

1246 Framework Decision 2008/977/JHA of 27 November 2008 on the protection of personal data processed in the framework of police and judicial cooperation in criminal matters, OJ L 350, 30 December 2008, p. 60.

1247 European Commission, "Safeguarding Privacy in a Connected World – A European Data Protection Framework for the 21st Century", *l.c.*, p. 4 et seq.

1248 European Commission, Proposal for a Regulation of the European Parliament and of the Council on the protection of individuals with regard to the processing of personal data and on the free movement of such data (General Data Protection Regulation), COM(2012) 11 final, 2012/0011 (COD), 25 January 2012. An earlier of draft of the proposal was widely leaked in November 2011.

1249 European Commission, Proposal for a Directive of the European Parliament and of the Council on the protection of individuals with regard to the processing of personal data by competent authorities for the purposes of prevention, investigation, detection or prosecution of criminal offences or the execution of criminal penalties, and the free movement of such data, SEC(2012) 72 final, SEC(2012) 73 final, Brussels, 25 January 2012, COM(2012) 10 final, 2012/0010 (COD).

1250 Council of the European Union, "Data Protection: Council agrees on a general approach" (Press Release), 15 June 2015. Actual text: Council for the European Union, Proposal for a Regulation of the European Parliament and of the Council on the protection of individuals with regard to the processing of personal data and on the free movement of such data (General Data Protection Regulation) – Preparation of a general approach", 2012/0011 (COD), 9565/15, 11 June 2015.

which the European Parliament, Council and Commission participate. On 15 December 2015, the political agreement on the proposed data protection reform was announced, thus ending the trilogue process.[1251] On 4 May 2016, the GDPR was published in the Official Journal of the European Union.[1252] The GDPR entered into application on 25 May 2018.[1253]

2. ALLOCATION OF RESPONSIBILITY AND LIABILITY

2.1. LEGISLATIVE DEVELOPMENT

A. *Commission proposal*

593. Preface – The reform package proposed by the European Commission was accompanied by a third evaluation of the implementation of Directive 95/46.[1254] The evaluation highlighted several issues surrounding key concepts of the Directive, including the concepts of "controller" and "processor". First, the Commission observed that divergent national implementations persisted.[1255] According to the Commission, the lack of a harmonized approach

> "has led to uncertainties with regard to responsibility and liability of controllers, co-controllers and processors, the actual or legal capacity to control processing, and the scope of applicable national laws, causing negative effects on the effectiveness of data protection."[1256]

The Commission also noted that the increased complexity of the environment in which controllers and processors operate (e.g. behavioural advertising, cloud computing) rendered it increasingly difficult to apply the concepts in

---

1251 European Commission, Agreement on Commission's EU data protection reform will boost Digital Single Market, Press Release, Brussels, 15 December 2015.

1252 Regulation 2016/679 of the European Parliament and of the Council of 27 April 2016 on the protection of natural persons with regard to the processing of personal data and on the free movement of such data, and repealing Directive 95/46/EC (General Data Protection Regulation), OJ 4 May 2016, L 119/1.

1253 Article 99(2) GDPR.

1254 European Commission, "Evaluation of the implementation of the Data Protection Directive", Annex 2 of Commission Staff Working Paper, *Impact Assessment*, SEC(2012) 72 final, 25 January 2012, p. 5–35.

1255 *Ibid*, p. 8 (noting that while a number of national laws closely follow the definition of the "controller", other laws provide for variations. For instance, certain laws focus on the determination of the "purposes" of the processing, either without any reference to the "means" or make reference to the "contents and use" of processing instead of the "means". The definition of "processor" has also not been implemented consistently across Member States).

1256 *Ibid*, p. 9.

practice.[1257] In the end, however, the Commission arrived at the conclusion that the concepts themselves remain valid.[1258] Legislative changes should focus instead on the obligations and implications associated with each concept:

> "Although the definitions and concepts of "controller" and "processor" remain themselves relevant, they need to be clarified and detailed in specific provisions as regards the obligations, responsibilities and liability of both controllers and processors. Harmonised rules on the responsibilities of data controllers and processors, including the obligation to demonstrate compliance with their obligations, would foster legal certainty. Including in the case of more than one controller and/or processors being involved, it must be clear for the data subject whom to address to in order to exercise his or her rights".[1259]

i. Definitions

594. Minimal change – The initial Commission proposal replicated the definitions of controller and processor quasi verbatim. Only one change was made to the definition of a "controller", which was now defined by Article 4(5) as

> "'controller' means the natural or legal person, public authority, agency or any other body which alone or jointly with others determines the purposes, conditions and means of the processing of personal data; where the purposes, conditions and means of processing are determined by Union law or Member State law, the controller or the specific criteria for his nomination may be designated by Union law or by Member State law"

The only change to the definition of the controller was the addition of the word "conditions". The definition of a processor (Article 4(6)) remained identical to its counterpart under Directive 95/46.

ii. Obligations

595. Outline – Chapter IV of the Commission proposal set forth the obligations of controllers and processors. Article 22(1) began by reaffirming that the controller is the entity which carries responsibility for ensuring

---

1257 *Id.* The difficulties surrounding the application and implications of the controller and processor concepts was also highlighted by certain stakeholder responses to the 2010–2011 public consultation. See e.g. Information Commissioner's Office, "The Information Commissioner's (United Kingdom) response to A comprehensive approach on personal data protection in the European Union", 14 January 2011, p. 9 and BEUC, "A Comprehensive Approach on Personal Data Protection in the European Union – European Commission's Communication", 24 January 2011, p. 12–13.

1258 European Commission, "Evaluation of the implementation of the Data Protection Directive", Annex 2, *l.c.*, p. 10.

1259 *Id.*

compliance. It also described some of the measures which it must implement to ensure compliance, taking into account "*the debate on the "principle of accountability*".[1260] The responsibility of the controller to ensure compliance was further made explicit in several other provisions, including those regarding (a) the principles of data quality (Article 5(f)[1261]; (b) data subject rights (Articles 11–20); and (c) data protection by design and by default (Article 23). Article 24 explicitly addresses the situation of *joint control*. Articles 26 and 27 seek to clarify the position and obligations of processors, mainly by extending upon Articles 16 and 17(2) of Directive 95/46/EC.[1262] Perhaps most significantly, the Commission proposal also specified a range of obligations *relevant to both controller and processor*:

- the obligation to maintain documentation (Article 28)
- co-operation with supervisory authorities (Article 29);
- the obligation to maintain an appropriate level of data security (Article 30);
- the obligation to notify data breaches (Article 31)[1263];
- data protection impact assessments (Article 33);
- prior authorization (Article 34);
- data protection officers (Articles 35–37);
- codes of conduct (Article 38);
- certification (Article 39); and
- international transfers (Articles 40–44).

Interestingly, two sets of obligations were *applicable exclusively to the controller*, namely the obligations regarding data protection by design and by default

1260 European Commission, Proposal for a Regulation of the European Parliament and of the Council on the protection of individuals with regard to the processing of personal data and on the free movement of such data (General Data Protection Regulation), COM(2012) 11 final, *l.c.*, p. 10. See also *infra*, no. 668 et seq.

1261 Article 5(f) provides that personal data must be "*processed under the responsibility and liability of the controller, who shall ensure and demonstrate for each processing operation the compliance with the provisions of this Regulation*" (replacing Article 6(2) Directive 95/46: "it shall be for the controller to ensure that paragraph 1 is complied with"). Difference: "*the controller to ensure*" became "*responsibility and liability of the controller who shall ensure and demonstrate for each processing operation the compliance*")

1262 European Commission, Proposal for a Regulation of the European Parliament and of the Council on the protection of individuals with regard to the processing of personal data and on the free movement of such data (General Data Protection Regulation), COM(2012) 11 final, *l.c.*, p. 10.

1263 As regards the obligation to notify data breaches, a distinction should be made between the obligation to inform breaches to the controller and the obligation to notify breaches to supervisory authorities and data subjects. Only the controller is obliged to notify the data subject and supervisory authorities. The processor is only obliged to notify the controller (Article 31(2)).

(Article 23) and the obligation to notify data breaches to supervisory authorities and data subjects (Articles 31 and 32).[1264]

596. Responsibility of the controller – Article 22 of the Commission proposal provided that

> "1. The controller shall adopt policies and implement appropriate measures to ensure and be able to demonstrate that the processing of personal data is performed in compliance with this Regulation.
> 2. The measures provided for in paragraph 1 shall in particular include:
> (a) keeping the documentation pursuant to Article 28;
> (b) implementing the data security requirements laid down in Article 30;
> (c) performing a data protection impact assessment pursuant to Article 33;
> (d) complying with the requirements for prior authorisation or prior consultation of the supervisory authority pursuant to Article 34(1) and (2);
> (e) designating a data protection officer pursuant to Article 35(1).
> 3. The controller shall implement mechanisms to ensure the verification of the effectiveness of the measures referred to in paragraphs 1 and 2. If proportionate, this verification shall be carried out by independent internal or external auditors."

597. Joint control – Article 24 of the Commission proposal provided that

> "Where a controller determines the purposes, conditions and means of the processing of personal data jointly with others, the joint controllers shall determine their respective responsibilities for compliance with the obligations under this Regulation, in particular as regards the procedures and mechanisms for exercising the rights of the data subject, by means of an arrangement between them."

598. Choice of processor – Article 26(1) of the Commission proposal echoed the obligation of Article 17(2) of the Directive, which requires the controller to choose a processor "providing sufficient guarantees" in respect of the technical security measures and organisational measures governing the processing to be carried out. A notable change, however, was that the choice of processor also needed to guarantee that the processing will be carried out in such a way that it "*will meet the requirements of the Regulation and ensure the protection of the rights of the data subject*".

599. Legal binding – Article 26(2) of the Commission proposal was based on Article 17(3) of the Directive, which provides that the processing carried out by a processor must be governed by a contract or legal act binding the processor

[1264] It should be noted, however, that while Article 31(1) only requires controllers to notify a supervisory authority in case of a security breach, Article 31(2) does require processors to immediately notify controllers in case of a breach.

to certain obligations. The new provision also contained several new elements, however, which must also be included. Specifically, Article 26(2) a required stipulation that the processor shall:

(a) act only on instructions from the controller, in particular, where the transfer of the personal data used is prohibited;
(b) employ only staff who have committed themselves to confidentiality or are under a statutory obligation of confidentiality;
(c) take all required measures pursuant to Article 30 [data security];
(d) enlist another processor only with the prior permission of the controller;
(e) insofar as this is possible given the nature of the processing, create in agreement with the controller the necessary technical and organisational requirements for the fulfilment of the controller's obligation to respond to requests for exercising the data subject's rights laid down in Chapter III;
(f) assist the controller in ensuring compliance with the obligations pursuant to Articles 30 to 34;
(g) hand over all results to the controller after the end of the processing and not process the personal data otherwise;
(h) make available to the controller and the supervisory authority all information necessary to control compliance with the obligations laid down in this Article.

Article 26(3) required the controller and processor to document the controller's instructions and the processor's obligations in writing.

600. Bound by instructions – Article 27 of the Commission proposal was based on Article 16 of Directive 95/46, with the noteworthy change that now the possibility of subprocessing was explicitly recognised[1265]:

> "The processor and any person acting under the authority of the controller or of the processor who has access to personal data shall not process them except on instructions from the controller, unless required to do so by Union or Member State law."

Article 26(4) further clarified that if a processor processes personal data other than as instructed by the controller, the processor would be considered to be a controller in respect of that processing and shall be subject to the rules on joint controllers (as laid down in Article 24).[1266] Article 26(2)d made clear that sub-processing requires prior permission of the controller.

1265 See also P. Blume, "Controller and processor: is there a risk of confusion?", *International Data Privacy Law* 2013, Vol. 3, No. 2, p. 143.

1266 Cf. *supra*, no. 597.

iii. Liability and sanctions

601. Right to compensation and liability – Article 77 of the Commission proposal was based on the liability regime of Article 23 of the Directive, but displays a number of notable differences. A first significant change is that it extended the data subject's right to damages to processors.[1267] It also explicitly addressed the situation where more than one controller or processor is involved in the processing, stipulating that each controller or processor shall be *jointly and severally liable* for the entire amount of the damage:

> "1. Any person who has suffered damage as a result of an unlawful processing operation or of an action incompatible with this Regulation shall have the right to receive compensation from the controller or the processor for the damage suffered.
> 2. Where more than one controller or processor is involved in the processing, each controller or processor shall be jointly and severally liable for the entire amount of the damage."

602. Exemptions – Article 77(3) replicated the escape clause contained in Article 23(2) of the Directive, by providing that

> "The controller or the processor may be exempted from this liability, in whole or in part, if the controller or the processor proves that they are not responsible for the event giving rise to the damage."[1268]

The only difference brought upon by Article 77(3) was that it extended the escape clause to processors as well. In this context, it is worth noting that the Commission proposal also incorporated the intermediary liability exemptions contained in the e-Commerce Directive by way of Article 3(3), which provided that

> "This Regulation should be without prejudice to the application of Directive 2000/31/EC, in particular of the liability rules of intermediary service providers in Articles 12 to 15 of that Directive."

Under the existing framework, the liability exemptions formally did not formally apply to matters regulated by Directive 95/46 pursuant to Article 1(5)b of the e-Commerce Directive.[1269]

1267 Article 75 of the Commission proposal also clearly specifies that individuals have right to judicial remedy against both controllers and processors.

1268 Recital (118) further clarifies the meaning of Article 77(3) in the same way as recital (55) of Directive 95/46.

1269 See Article 1(5)b of Directive 2000/31/EC of the European Parliament and of the Council of 8 June 2000 on certain legal aspects of information society services, in particular electronic

603. Penalties – Article 78(1) of the Commission proposal was based on Article 24 of the Directive and provided that Member States shall lay down the rules on penalties, applicable to infringements of the provisions of this Regulation. It further added that the penalties provided for must be "*effective, proportionate and dissuasive*".[1270]

604. Administrative sanctions – Article 79 empowered supervisory authorities to issue administrative fines for the offences listed in this provision. Relevant offences included *inter alia*: the absence of an appropriate mechanism to respond to data subject requests (Article 79(4)); failure to provide adequate information to data subjects (Article 79(5) and processing personal data without a sufficient legal basis (Article 79(6)a). Article 79 did not differentiate between controllers or processors. In principle, the fines could be imposed against "anyone who" fails to comply with the relevant provisions.[1271] Article 79(2) did provide, however, that the "degree of responsibility" of the natural or legal person shall be taken into account when determining the amount of an administrative fine.

iv. Assessment

605. Concepts intact – The proposal of the European Commission left the concepts of controller and processor intact.[1272] As previously signalled in its evaluation report, the Commission considered the concepts themselves to be largely unproblematic.[1273] The proposed changes instead focused on (a) specifying the obligations of each actor in greater detail; (b) defining additional obligations for processors; and (c) addressing the relationship between joint controllers.[1274]

606. More detailed obligations – The Commission proposal specified the obligations of controllers and processors in much greater detail in comparison to

commerce, in the Internal Market (Directive on electronic commerce), OJ 17 July 2000, L 178/8. For a more detailed discussion of the relationship between the e-Commerce Directive and the Data Protection Directive see *infra*, nos. 1249 et seq.

1270 Recital (19) further clarifies that the penalties should be imposed "*to any person, whether governed by private or public law, who fails to comply with this Regulation*".

1271 Article 73 (right to lodge a complaint) also does not specify whether a complaint might be lodged against either controllers or processors.

1272 The Commission only proposed one minor change to definition of a controller, namely adding the word "conditions". See also P. De Hert and V. Papakonstantinou, "The proposed data protection Regulation replacing Directive 95/46/EC: A sound system for the protection of individuals", *Computer Law & Security Review* 2012, vol. 28, p. 133 and P. Blume, "Controller and processor: is there a risk of confusion?", *l.c.*, p. 143.

1273 Cf. *supra*, no. 593.

1274 See also P. De Hert and V. Papakonstantinou, "The proposed data protection Regulation replacing Directive 95/46/EC: A sound system for the protection of individuals", *l.c.*, p. 133.

Directive 95/46.[1275] Most of the additional obligations (e.g. documentation, data protection impact assessment, designation of a data protection officers) originate from the discussions surrounding the "principle of accountability", which essentially requires controllers to implement appropriate measures to ensure compliance and to demonstrate the measures upon request.[1276] Other provisions, such as the principles of data protection by design and data protection by default (Article 23) and data breach notification (Articles 31 and 32) can be viewed as being complementary to these obligations.

607. PROMINENCE OF THE PROCESSOR – The Commission proposal dealt with processors in a far more detailed way than Directive 95/46.[1277] The obligations incumbent upon processors clearly recognized the important role processors can play, not only in maintaining compliance[1278], but also in assessing the impact of the processing before it is even initiated.[1279] Processors are also directly accountable towards supervisory authorities. For example, processors must (a) maintain and provide appropriate documentation upon request (Article 28); (b) co-operate in case of an investigation (Article 29) and (c) abide by administrative orders (Article 53).[1280] In other words, the Commission proposal clearly afforded the processor an "*independent position*" and a role "*which in some respects seems to equal that of the controller*".[1281]

608. REGULATING JOINT CONTROL – A third significant revision proposed by the Commission concerned the relationship between joint controllers. Article 24 essentially codified the guidance issued by the Article 29 Working Party in Opinion 1/2010, by mandating that joint controllers determine their respective

1275 See also G. Hornung, "A General Data Protection Regulation for Europa? Light and Shade in the Commission's Draft of 25 January 2012", *Scripted 2012*, Volume 9, Issue 1, p. 70.

1276 Article 29 Data Protection Working Party, "Opinion 3/2010 on the principle of accountability", WP 173, 13 July 2010, p. 3. See also *infra*, nos. 669 et seq.

1277 G. Hornung, "A General Data Protection Regulation for Europa? Light and Shade in the Commission's Draft of 25 January 2012", *l.c.* p. 70. See also C. Kuner, "The European Commission's Proposed Data Protection Regulation: A Copernican Revolution in European Data Protection Law", *l.c.*, p. 7 and P. Blume, "Controller and processor: is there a risk of confusion?", *l.c.*, p. 143–144.

1278 See Article 35 of the Commission Proposal (Data Protection Officer).

1279 See Article 33 of the Commission Proposal (Data Protection Impact Assessment).

1280 It is noteworthy that many processor obligations in the proposed Regulation appear to be directly applicable, as opposed to being dependent on a contract or legal act. At the same, the proposed Regulation still maintains the obligation for controllers to legally bind the processor to the same (and other obligations) by way of contract or other legal act in Article 26(2).

1281 P. Blume, "Controller and processor: is there a risk of confusion?", *l.c.*, p. 143. Further indications of the independence of the processor include: the duty to have data protection officer (even in situations where the controller might not be obliged to have one (Article 35); and the fact the legitimate interest of the processor may enable transfers which are neither frequent nor massive (Article 44(1h)). (*Ibid*, p. 144)

responsibilities for compliance by means of an "arrangement" between them, in particular as regards the procedures and mechanisms to accommodate data subject rights.[1282]

609. Ambiguity – The revisions proposed by the Commission regarding the obligations of controllers and processors were met with mixed reviews.[1283] Overall, it seems that the revised allocation of responsibilities proposed by the Commission did not resonate well with the traditional understanding of controller-processor relationships. Moreover, certain commentators felt that by imposing obligations directly on processors, there may be a risk of confusion as to who is ultimately responsible for ensuring compliance.[1284] For example, in relation to the data security obligation (Article 30), the EDPS noted that:

> "In Article 30 on security of processing, reference is made to the controller and the processor. The EDPS welcomes that both actors are mentioned, but recommends the legislator to clarify the provision in such a way that there is no doubt about the overall responsibility of the controller. From the text as it currently stands, both the processor and the controller seem to be equally responsible. This is not in line with the preceding provisions, in particular Articles 22 and 26 of the proposed Regulation."[1285]

1282 Compare *supra*, no. 597.

1283 See in particular European Data Protection Supervisor (EDPS), "Opinion of the European Data Protection Supervisor on the data protection reform package", 7 March 2012, p. 31 (at paragraph 192); Information Commissioner's Office (ICO), "Proposed new EU General Data Protection Regulation: Article-by-article analysis paper", v1.0, 12 February 2013, p. 9 en 35; P. De Hert and V. Papakonstantinou, "The proposed data protection Regulation replacing Directive 95/46/EC: A sound system for the protection of individuals", *l.c.*, p. 133–134; P. Blume, "Controller and processor: is there a risk of confusion?", *l.c.*, p. 143–144; B. Treacy, "Challenging times ahead for data processors", *Privacy & Data Protection Journal* 2012 Vol. 12, Issue 7, p. 3–6; K. Irion and G. Luchetta, "Online Personal Data Processing and EU Data Protection Reform – Report of the CEPS Digital Forum, Centre for European Policy Studies (CEPS), April 2013, p. 46–48; Business Europe, "Commission Proposal on a General Data Protection Regulation", Position Paper, 17 October 2012, p. 11; European Banking Federation, "EBF Position on the European Commission's Proposal for a Regulation on the protection of individual with regard to the processing of personal data and on the free movement of such data (General Data Protection Regulation), 22 May 2015, p. 9–10 and Association of Consumer Credit Information Suppliers (ACCIS), Position paper on proposed Data Protection Regulation, April 2012, p. 21.

1284 See in particular P. Blume, "Controller and processor: is there a risk of confusion?", *l.c.*, p. 143–144 and B. Treacy, "Challenging times ahead for data processors", *l.c.*, p. 5–6.

1285 European Data Protection Supervisor (EDPS), "Opinion of the European Data Protection Supervisor on the data protection reform package", p. 31 (at paragraph 192). See also P. Blume, "Controller and processor: is there a risk of confusion?", *l.c.*, p. 144 ("*Article 30 is a problematic rule as the primary and determining responsibility should be placed solely at controller level [...] There are naturally valid arguments for placing security obligations directly on the processor and against this background it is interesting and somewhat puzzling to notice that the obligations with respect to breach notification (Articles 31–32) rest exclusively on the controller. Security may be breached at many levels and there is no doubt that this will also occur at the processor level. As*

In the same vein, the ICO noted in relation to Article 26 (processor) that

> "[...] we need to be clear about who is responsible for what where a number of organisations are each involved in the processing of personal data, and, as drafted, this Article will not help us here."[1286]

Lack of dogmatic precision could also be found in the provision regarding processors who become joint controllers (Article 26(4)).[1287]

610. Liability – Article 77(2) of the Commission proposal provided that in case where more than one controller or processor is involved in the processing, each controller or processor shall be jointly and severally liable for the entire amount of the damage. The imposition of joint and several liability was welcomed by both the Article 29 Working Party and the EDPS.[1288] The EDPS expressed concerns, however, that the provision could be interpreted as nevertheless requiring the data subject to choose between the controller and processor when seeking compensation:

> "[Article 77] is reasonable and fair from the point of view of the data subject. He or she will usually not be able to do much more than alleging a breach and damage

the processor in Article 30 is made independently responsible for security, it would seem logical that the processor should also report breaches; why this is not the case is uncertain.").

1286 Information Commissioner's Office (ICO), "Proposed new EU General Data Protection Regulation: Article-by-article analysis paper", *l.c.*, p. 34. At the same time, the ICO also reiterated its earlier complaint regarding its difficulties to distinguish between controllers and processors in practice ("*It is fair to say that the ICO can find it difficult to determine which organisations are data controllers and which are processors. The problem arises because, given the collaborative nature of modern business, it is rare for a one organisation (the processor) to only act on instructions from another (the controller). There tends to be a considerable degree of freedom, skill, judgment and the like in terms of the way the first organisation provides services to the second, all against the backdrop of complex collaborative arrangements involving numerous organisations.*") (*Id.*).

1287 See e.g. Information Commissioner's Office (ICO), "Proposed new EU General Data Protection Regulation: Article-by-article analysis paper", *l.c.*, p. 35 ("*We can certainly see why a processor that takes a controller's data and then uses it for its own purposes should take on full data controller responsibility. However, this is different from failing to act on the data controller's instructions. We would have more difficulty with the idea that a processor becomes a controller because it has erased personal data by mistake, for example – this would amount to processing personal data other than as instructed by the data controller -but in a case like this the organisation should just be treated as a 'bad processor' rather than a data controller in its own right.*"). See also B. Treacy, "Challenging times ahead for data processors", *l.c.*, p. 4. In my view, the Commission proposal also errs by implicitly labelling a processor who re-purposes data as a "joint controller", as in the identified scenario the (former) processor does not determine the purposes and means "together with" the (initial) controller. Joint control suggests a joint determination of "purposes conditions and means" under Article 24. (B. Treacy, "Challenging times ahead for data processors", *l.c.*, p. 6). Compare also *supra*, no. 138.

1288 Article 29 Data Protection Working Party, "Opinion 01/2012 on the data protection reform proposals", WP 191, 23 March 2012, p. 23 and European Data Protection Supervisor (EDPS), "Opinion of the European Data Protection Supervisor on the data protection reform package", *l.c.*, p. 44.

sustained from that breach. In contrast, controllers and processors have more access to the relevant facts of the event once they have been established.

However, in view of the responsibility of the controller, a data subject should not have to choose between the controller and the processor. It should be possible always to address the controller, regardless of where and how the damage arose. The Regulation should provide for a subsequent settlement of the damages between the controller and the processor, once the distribution of liability among them has been clarified. The same applies to the case of multiple controllers and processors."[1289]

B. *First Reading European Parliament*

611. Preface – On 16 February 2012, the European Parliament appointed its Committee on Civil Liberties, Justice and Home Affairs (LIBE) as the lead Committee to review the Commission's proposals.[1290] The LIBE Committee, with Jan Philipp Albrecht as its rapporteur, produced its first draft report on the proposed regulation on 16 January 2013.[1291] Following months of intense lobbying (which led to more than 3999 amendments in the LIBE committee alone[1292]), the LIBE committee produced a "comprise" text[1293] which would form the basis of its draft resolution.[1294] The official First Reading of the Parliament took place on 12 March 2014, when the Parliament almost unanimously adopted the resolution prepared by the LIBE Committee.[1295]

612. Prior assessment – The LIBE Committee produced four "working documents" as part of its review of the data protection reform package. In its

---

1289 European Data Protection Supervisor (EDPS), "Opinion of the European Data Protection Supervisor on the data protection reform package", *l.c.*, p. 44.

1290 See the Legislative observatory of the European Parliament, Procedure file 2012/0011(COD).

1291 European Parliament, Committee on Civil Liberties, Justice and Home Affairs, Draft Report on the proposal for a regulation of the European Parliament and of the Council on the protection of individual with regard to the processing of personal data and on the free movement of such data (General Data Protection Regulation), (COM(2012)0011 – C7-0025/2012 – 2012/0011(COD)) 16 January 2013.

1292 See J.P. Albrecht, "EU General Data Protection Regulation – State of play and 10 main issues", 7 January 2015, p. 1.

1293 European Parliament, Committee on Civil Liberties, Justice and Home Affairs, Proposal for a regulation of the European Parliament and of the Council on the protection of individual with regard to the processing of personal data and on the free movement of such data (General Data Protection Regulation) (COM(2012)0011 – C7 0025/2012 – 2012/0011(COD)) Compromise amendments on Articles 1–29, 7 October 2013, p. 4.

1294 Committee on Civil Liberties, Justice and Home Affairs, Report on the proposal for a regulation of the European Parliament and of the Council on the protection of individuals with regard to the processing of personal data and on the free movement of such data (General Data Protection Regulation) (COM(2012)0011 – C7 0025/2012 – 2012/0011(COD)), 21 November 2013.

1295 European Parliament legislative resolution of 12 March 2014 on the proposal for a regulation of the European Parliament and of the Council on the protection of individuals with regard to the processing of personal data and on the free movement of such data (General Data Protection Regulation), (COM(2012)0011 – C7-0025/2012 – 2012/0011(COD)).

second Working Document, the Committee outlined its preliminary views regarding the distribution of responsibilities between controllers and processors contained in the Commission Proposal:

> "The processing of personal data offers many business opportunities to data controllers and processors. However, since personal data protection is a fundamental right, this processing also entails responsibilities. These obligations should be clear and understandable to avoid legal uncertainty for companies and authorities, as well as for the data subjects. Therefore, a much clearer division of duties and responsibilities between data controllers and data processors is needed. More debate is needed on the concept of "joint controllers". Furthermore, we need a clarification on the limits of what a processor can do without being instructed by the controller, including when a processor enlists a sub-contractor for processing."[1296]

The amendments which the LIBE Committee eventually proposed were influenced by the proposals made by the other Committees (ITRE, IMCO, JURI, EMPL), as well as continuous discussions with representatives of the Council, the Commission and other stakeholders.[1297] Prior to issuing its first Draft Report on the proposed Regulation in January 2013, the European Parliament's Directorate-General for Internal Policies published an external report (hereinafter: "External Report").[1298] While the External Report did not contain any official viewpoint of the European Parliament, it served as an additional background document during the further deliberations. Where appropriate, reference will be made to the analysis contained in the External Report.

i. Definitions

613. OUTLINE – In its First Reading, the European Parliament proposed only one change regarding the concepts of controller and processor. Specifically, it proposed to delete the words "and conditions" from the definition of a controller. The definition of a processor remained unchanged. In other words, the European Parliament indirectly took the position that for both concepts the original definitions of Directive 95/46 should be maintained "as is".

1296 European Parliament, LIBE Committee, "Working Document 2 on the protection of individuals with regard to the processing of personal data and on the free movement of such data (General Data Protection Regulation), 8 October 2012, PE497.802v01-00, p. 5.

1297 European Parliament, LIBE Committee, "Report on the proposal for a regulation of the European Parliament and of the Council on the protection of individuals with regard to the processing of personal data and on the free movement of such data (General Data Protection Regulation), 21 November 2013, A7-0402/2013, p. 199. This report contains Opinions issued by the other Committees of The European Parliament (ITRE, IMCO, JURI, EMPL).

1298 See X. Konarski, D. Karwala, H. Schulte-Nölke and C. Charlton, "Reforming the Data Protection Package", Study commissioned by the European Parliament, Directorate-General for Internal Policies, Policy Department A: Economic and Scientific Policy, IP/A/IMCO/ST/2012-02, PE 492.431, September 2012, at p. 33.

614. Deletion of "conditions" – The removal of "conditions" from the definition of a controller was supported by several Committee Opinions and amendments.[1299] The deletion of the term was also supported by the authors of the External Report, who argued that the addition of the term "conditions" was likely to cause more difficulties and uncertainties, rather than eliminate them.[1300]

615. No deletion of "means" – Several Committee Opinions (ITRE, JURI and IMCO) and MEPs proposed to additionally remove the reference to "means" from the definition of a controller.[1301] The IMCO Opinion offered the following rationale for the change:

> "With new technologies and services available such as cloud computing traditional division of entities involved in the processing of personal data may prove difficult, with the processor having in such cases significant influence over the way in which data are being processed. For this reason it seems reasonable to determine the controller as the entity, which decides over the purpose of processing personal data as determination of finality is the most important decision with the other factors serving as means to achieve it."[1302]

The deletion of "means" was also supported by the authors of the External Report, who argued that abandoning the "means" criterion would be advisable because:

1299 See European Parliament, LIBE Committee, "Amendments 602–885", 4 March 2013, PE506.145v01-00, Amendments 744–748). Several proposed amendments went even further, also deleting the word "means" from the definition, but these amendments were not retained by the LIBE Committee. Cf. *infra,* no. 615.

1300 X. Konarski, D. Karwala, H. Schulte-Nölke and C. Charlton, "Reforming the Data Protection Package", *l.c.*, p. 30.

1301 See European Parliament, Opinion of the Committee on Industry, Research and Energy (ITRE), 26 February 2013, Amendment 80; Opinion of the Committee on Internal Market and Consumer Affairs (IMCO), 28 January 2013, Amendment 62; Opinion of the Committee on Legal Affairs (JURI), 25 March 2013, Amendment 38 and European Parliament, LIBE Committee, "Amendments 602–885", 4 March 2013, PE506.145v01-00, amendments 746–48.

1302 European Parliament, Opinion of the Committee on Internal Market and Consumer Affairs (IMCO), 28 January 2013, amendment 62. In the same vein, MEP Adina-Ioana Vălean, Jens Rohde argued that "*The definition of controller should be based on the decision of the purposes for which personal data are processed rather than the conditions or means by which this is achieved. The control over the purpose for processing is the logical basis for allocating different responsibilities between controllers who are responsible for what and why data is processed and processing parties who deal with how data is processed.*" (European Parliament, LIBE Committee, "Amendments 602–885", 4 March 2013, PE506.145v01-00, amendments 746). Other MEP's supported the change for a different reason, namely to clarify that only the controller and not the processor is responsible for compliance (See MEP amendments 748, with justification that: "*The aim of the change is not to lower the level of protection for the individual but to clarify that only the controller and not the processor is responsible. See related Amendments to articles 22, 24, 26 and 77.*").

"– there are substantial doubts as how to understand the term means;
- greater importance is already assigned to the factor of "determining the purposes" rather than "determining the means" of processing;
- Article 29 Working Party even permits the possibility of "delegation" of the competence to determine the means to the processor (at least as defined by the narrow meaning of that term);
- moreover, the general importance of "purposes" of processing is much higher in the personal data protection regulation because – as the legal literature reasonably notes – "the finality pursued by (a set of) processing operations fulfils a fundamental role in determining the scope of the controller's obligations, as well as when assessing the overall legitimacy and/or proportionality of the processing".[1303]

The proposals to delete "means" were, however, received negatively by the European Data Protection Supervisor (EDPS). In particular, the EDPS considered that:

> "Amendments related to controller/processor's roles appear in many parts of the text, including in the definitions. Several amendments would remove the notion that the controller determines not only the purposes but also 'the conditions and means' of the processing, as defined in Article 4(5) of the proposal (e.g. ITRE AM 81; IMCO AM 62; LIBE AM 746, 747, 748). The criteria that the controller determines the 'purposes and means' of the processing were set forth in Directive 95/46/EC and developed in the WP 29 Opinion 1/2010 on the concepts of 'controller' and 'processor'. These criteria have effectively contributed to the understanding and delineation of the roles of controllers and processors and should not be deleted."[1304]

616. Keeping processors – Following the initial proposal by the European Commission, De Hert and Papakonstantinou suggested that the time may have come to "boldly abolish" the concept of processor altogether.1305 In this respect, the External Report mainly expressed caution.1306 It argued that abolition of the controller and processor concepts would effectively render the positions of all actors involved in data processing "equal" and distribute all the obligations

---

1303 X. Konarski, D. Karwala, H. Schulte-Nölke and C. Charlton, "Reforming the Data Protection Package", *l.c.*, p. 31, with reference to B. Van Alsenoy, "Allocating responsibility among controllers, processors, and "everything in between": the definition of actors and roles in Directive 95/46/EC", *Computer Law & Security Review* 2012, Vol. 28, p. 31, footnote 55.

1304 European Data Protection Supervisor (EDPS), "Additional EDPS comments on the Data Protection Reform Package", 15 March 2013, p. 6 (at paragraph 24).

1305 See e.g. P. De Hert and V. Papakonstantinou, "The proposed data protection Regulation replacing Directive 95/46/EC: A sound system for the protection of individuals", *l.c.*, p. 134.

1306 X. Konarski, D. Karwala, H. Schulte-Nölke and C. Charlton, "Reforming the Data Protection Package", *l.c.*, p. 31.

evenly "*without taking into account their individual position, the scope of their tasks, or the expectations of data subjects*".[1307] Moreover, it was argued that "*the removal of such an important class of entities from the regulation could result in a weakening of the level of data protection*".[1308] Finally, it was argued that one can – with proper interpretation – seemingly achieve results similar the ones envisaged by abandoning the processor concept.[1309] The External Report therefore concluded that further proposals should instead elaborate on a precise division and determination of the obligations and responsibilities of data controller and data processor.[1310] As indicated earlier, the LIBE Committee endorsed such an approach in its second Working Document on the general data protection regulation.[1311]

617. No additional actors – Finally, it is worth observing that the LIBE Committee also entertained proposals to introduce additional actors. In its first draft report, for example, the LIBE Committee proposed to introduce the concept of a "producer".[1312] It was argued that

> "producers of automated data processing systems (i.e. hard- and software) should also take into account the principle of privacy by design and by default, even if they do not process personal data themselves. This is especially relevant for widely used standard applications, but also should be respected for niche products)."[1313]

The proposed Amendment did not, however, make it to the First Reading. The same fate would await other proposals to introduce additional actors which were submitted by individual Members of Parliament.[1314]

ii. Obligations

618. Outline – The First Reading introduced only minor changes to the distribution of responsibilities between controllers and processors. As in the

---

1307 *Id.*

1308 *Ibid*, p. 32.

1309 X. Konarski, D. Karwala, H. Schulte-Nölke and C. Charlton, "Reforming the Data Protection Package", *l.c.*, p. 31.

1310 *Ibid*, p. 32.

1311 Cf. *supra*, no. 612.

1312 European Parliament, LIBE Committee, Draft Report on the proposal for a regulation of the European Parliament and of the Council on the protection of individuals with regard to the processing of personal data and on the free movement of such data (General Data Protection Regulation), 2012/0011(COD), PE501.927v04-00, 16 January 2013, p. 66 (Amendment 88).

1313 *Ibid*, p. 71 (Amendment 98).

1314 See European Parliament, LIBE Committee, "Amendments 602–885", 4 March 2013, PE506.145v01-00, amendment 749–750 (proposing a distinction between "direct" and "indirect" controllers) and amendment 751 (proposing the concept of a "publisher").

initial Commission Proposal, the First Reading imposed a range of obligations *upon both controller and processor*, namely in relation to:

- the obligation to maintain documentation (Article 28):
- co-operation with supervisory authorities (Article 29):
- the obligation to maintain an appropriate level of data security (Article 30)[1315];
- the obligation to notify data breaches (Article 31)[1316];
- the obligation to conduct a risk analyses (Article 32a) (new)[1317]:
- data protection impact assessments (Article 33);
- data protection compliance reviews (Article 33a) (new)[1318];
- prior authorization (Article 34);
- data protection officers (Articles 35–37);
- codes of conduct (Article 38);
- certification (Article 39); and
- international transfers (Articles 40–44).

One notable change concerns the requirement of *data protection by design and by default* (Article 23), which under the First Reading also applied to processors.[1319] Still, the First Reading maintained that certain obligations should only apply to the controller. For example, the obligations to notify data breaches to supervisory authorities and data subjects (Articles 31 and 32) still only applied to the controller.

619. Responsibility of the controller – Changes made to Article 22 mainly served to enhance the emphasis on accountability. Not only was the word "accountability" added to the title of the article, several changes were made

1315 The security obligations contained in Article 30 were detailed further in the First Reading.

1316 As regards the obligation to notify data breaches, a distinction should be made between the obligation to inform breaches to the controller and the obligation to notify breaches to supervisory authorities and data subjects. Only the controller is obliged to notify the data subject and supervisory authorities. The processor is only obliged to notify the controller (Article 31(2)).

1317 Article 32a requires both controller and processors to undertake a risk analysis relating to their processing activities in a catalogue of cases. The presence of one or more risks acts as a trigger for additional obligation outlined in Article 32a(3) (appointing representative, designating DPO, conducting data protection impact assessment, consulting DPO or supervisory authority).

1318 Article 33a requires the data controller or processor acting on the controller's behalf to carry out a periodic data protection compliance review.

1319 While Article 23(1) now also mentions processor, Article 23(2) still only mentions controllers. Interestingly, the word "implement" in Article 23(2) was replaced by "ensure", suggesting that the ultimate responsibility for the data protection impact assessment may have remained with the controller.

to expand the controller's obligation to *demonstrate* the adoption of measures to ensure compliance.[1320]

620. Joint control – Article 24 underwent two significant changes. First, it was revised to provide a more precise and accurate description of the concept of "joint control".[1321] Second, the provision was extended to specify that the arrangement between joint controllers must

> "duly reflect the joint controllers' respective effective roles and relationships vis-à-vis data subjects, and the essence of the arrangement shall be made available for the data subject. In case of unclarity of the responsibility, the controllers shall be jointly and severally liable."[1322]

621. Choice of processor – Article 26(1) did not undergo any revisions, save for the substitution of the words "a processing operation" with "processing" (presumably to ensure that the provision can be applied both at the level of an individual processing operation or set of processing operations).

622. Legal binding – Article 26(2) underwent substantial, albeit ambivalent, revisions. On the one hand, the provision was modified to recognize that controllers and processors should have flexibility in deciding how to allocate responsibilities among themselves. On the other hand, it also maintained that certain obligations should still be made applicable processors by way of a contract or other legal act.[1323] Specifically, Article 26(2) provided that

---

1320 Articled 22(1) also adds a specific obligation to implement policies and procedures "*to persistently respect the autonomous choices of data subjects*". Article 22(2) of the Commission Proposal was removed in the First Reading, based on the consideration that it had no added value and failed to mention all obligations required by the Regulation. (See European Parliament, LIBE Committee, "Amendments 1493–1828", 6 March 2013, PE506.164v02-00, Amendment 1666). A similar outline of controller obligations was inserted in Recital (60).

1321 Article 24 now refers to "*several controllers jointly determine purposes and means*" instead of "*a controller determines the purposes, conditions and means of the processing of personal data jointly with others*".

1322 The first part of the revision to Article 24 ("*the arrangement shall duly reflect ...*") had been proposed by ITRE (321/623) and Am 1748 with following justification: "*The arrangement to be entered into by joint controllers should be expressly required to duly reflect the joint controllers' respective roles and relationships with the data subjects. Joint controllers are not necessarily in an equal negotiation position when it comes to contractual agreements. Moreover, not all joint controllers enjoy a direct relationship with the data subject and they do not control the same kind and amount of personal data.*"). The second party of the revision ("*in case of unclarity ...*") was seemingly linked to the revisions made to Article 77(2). Cf. *infra*, no. 625.

1323 The ambivalence stems from the fact that the proposed revision in fact combines two different approaches. ITRE Amendment 223 sought to provide full flexibility in the distribution of roles and responsibilities (and to limit the number of obligations directly incumbent upon processors), whereas the text adopted in First Reading generally still renders processors directly responsible for complying with certain obligations. See also *infra*, no. 630.

"The carrying out of processing by a processor shall be governed by a contract or other legal act binding the processor to the controller. The controller and the processor shall be free to determine respective roles and tasks with respect to the requirements of this Regulation, and shall provide that the processor shall:

(a) process personal data only on instructions from the controller, unless otherwise required by Union law or Member State law;
(b) employ only staff who have committed themselves to confidentiality or are under a statutory obligation of confidentiality;
(c) take all required measures pursuant to Article 30;
(d) determine the conditions for enlisting another processor only with the prior permission of the controller, unless otherwise determined
(e) insofar as this is possible given the nature of the processing, create in agreement with the controller the appropriate and relevant technical and organisational requirements for the fulfilment of the controller's obligation to respond to requests for exercising the data subject's rights laid down in Chapter III;
(f) assist the controller in ensuring compliance with the obligations pursuant to Articles 30 to 34, taking into account the nature of processing and the information available to the processor;
(g) return all results to the controller after the end of the processing, not process the personal data otherwise and delete existing copies unless Union or Member State law requires storage of the data;
(h) make available to the controller all information necessary to demonstrate compliance with the obligations laid down in this Article and allow on-site inspections.[1324]

623. BOUND BY INSTRUCTIONS – No changes were made to Article 27 in First reading. Article 26(4) was revised, however, to provide that:

"If a processor processes personal data other than as instructed by the controller or becomes the determining party in relation to the purposes and means of data processing, the processor shall be considered to be a controller in respect of that processing and shall be subject to the rules on joint controllers laid down in Article 24."

The revision essentially further codified the guidance of the Article 29 Working Party Opinion 1/2010.[1325]

1324 The removal of the reference to "and supervisory authorities" in Article 26(2)h was simply motivated by the fact that the powers of supervisory authorities are dealt elsewhere See European Parliament, LIBE Committee, "Amendments 1493–1828", 6 March 2013, PE506.164v02-00, Amendment 1801).

1325 The revision failed, however, to accommodate the commentary by the Information Commissioner's Office (ICO) regarding the distinction between processors who re-use personal data for a new purpose and processors who simply fail to give effect to certain instructions ("bad" processors). Cf. *supra*, footnote 1288.

iii. Liability and sanctions

624. Right to compensation and liability – Numerous proposals to amend Article 77(1) were made prior to the First Reading. Certain amendments sought to remove liability of processors (e.g. amendments 2818, 2822 and 2825), or to make processor liability contingent upon a disregard of the instructions issued by the controller (amendment 2823). Another proposal sought to exempt both controllers and processors from liability in case of damages caused by unintentional and non-negligent behaviour (amendment 2819).[1326] In the end, the changes to Article 77(1) were relatively minor. The First Reading only substituted the wording "right to receive from" with the words "claim from" and clarified that the right to compensation extends to "non-pecuniary damages".

625. Joint and several liability – A more significant change was made to Article 77(2), which was revised to make joint and several liability conditional upon absence of an "appropriate written agreement". Specifically, revised Article 77(2) provided that

> "Where more than one controller or processor is involved in the processing, each of those controllers or processors shall be jointly and severally liable for the entire amount of the damage, unless they have an appropriate written agreement determining the responsibilities pursuant to Article 24."

The revision essentially consisted of a further codification of the guidance issued by the Article 29 Working Party in 1/2010.[1327] Oddly, Article 24 only referred to *joint controllers* (whereas Article 77(2) imposed solidary liability on both controllers and processors who are "involved" in the processing).[1328]

626. Exemptions – The liability exemption of Article 77(3) was not modified in the First Reading. Likewise, Article 3(3) still incorporated the intermediary liability exemptions contained in the e-Commerce Directive.[1329]

1326 See European Parliament, LIBE Committee, Amendments 2618–2950, 6 March 2013, PE501.927v04-00, amendments 2818–2825.

1327 This rationale is explicitly confirmed by the justification accompanying amendment 2827 ("*Creates an incentive for clarifying the roles and responsibilities in writing in cases where several controllers or processors are involved, in line with Art. 29 Working Party, Opinion 169.*") Likeminded revisions were proposed by way of amendments 2826, 2828–2830. See European Parliament, LIBE Committee, Amendments 2618–2950, 6 March 2013, PE501.927v04-00, amendments 2826–2830.

1328 Several proposals were made to delete Article 24(2) in its entirety (see amendments 2832–2833), but none of these amendments were retained. See European Parliament, LIBE Committee, Amendments 2618 – 2950, 6 March 2013, PE501.927v04-00, amendments 2826–2830.

1329 It is worth noting that in its first draft report, the LIBE Committee seemed inclined to reverse the approach taken by the European Commission, but in the end left it the way it was. See European Parliament, LIBE Committee, "Draft Report on the proposal for a regulation of the

627. Penalties – Article 78 was not modified in First Reading.

628. Administrative sanctions – Article 79 underwent substantive revisions in First Reading, but the revisions did not affect the existing premise that administrative sanctions can be imposed on "anyone who" fails to comply with the relevant provisions.[1330]

iv. Assessment

629. Back to square one – The First Reading made a full return to the definitions of Directive 95/46. The term "conditions" was deleted from the definition of a controller. Despite support by several MEPs to also delete the reference to "means", the LIBE Committee decided to keep the definition of a controller "as is". This was seemingly born out of the recognition that common understanding of both the controller concept could not be disassociated from the existing criteria.[1331] Proposals to introduce additional actors were not accepted. The First Reading thus continued in the same vein as the initial Commission Proposal, leaving existing concepts intact.

630. Processor obligations – Overall, the First Reading proposed only minor changes to the distribution of responsibilities between controllers and processors. Despite several proposals to remove or limit the obligations of processors, the First Reading retained the approach that certain obligations should be directly incumbent upon processors.[1332] In this regard, the LIBE Committee may have felt supported by the additional comments provided by the European Data Protection Supervisor:

> "Many amendments aim at diminishing the responsibility of the processor foreseen in the proposal, for example by removing or weakening the obligations that the processor maintains documentation, carries out a data protection impact assessment (DPIA), or helps the controller comply with security requirements (i.e. ITRE AM 43, 229, 233, 238, 260; LIBE AM 1829, 1832, 1834, 1836, 1837, 2024). However, the extension of certain obligations to processors reflects the current growing role of processors in determining certain essential conditions of the processing (e.g. in the context of cloud computing, where they often decide on transfers and

European Parliament and of the Council on the protection of individual with regard to the processing of personal data and on the free movement of such data (General Data Protection Regulation)", (COM(2012)0011 – C7-0025/2012 – 2012/0011(COD)) 16 January 2013, p. 13.

1330 Article 79(2) still provides, however, that the "degree of responsibility" of the natural or legal person shall be taken into account when determining the amount of an administrative fine.

1331 See also European Data Protection Supervisor (EDPS), "Additional EDPS comments on the Data Protection Reform Package", 15 March 2013, p. 5 (at paragraph 24).

1332 In fact, an additional processor obligation: Article 31(1) (data protection by design) was also made applicable to processors under the First Reading.

sub-processing). In this context, processors should also be accountable for their processing."[1333]

631. Further codification of Opinion 1/2010 – Several amendments which were incorporated in the First Reading can be seen as attempts to further codify the guidance issued by the Working Party in Opinion 1/2010. Clear examples are the amendments proposed to Article 26(4) (processor becomes controller if he processes personal data other than as instructed by the controller or becomes "the determining party" in relation to the purposes and means of data processing) and Article 77(2) (making joint and several liability of joint controllers conditional upon the absence of an arrangement appropriately allocating responsibilities).

632. Ambiguity remains – The First Reading still contained traces of ambivalence with regards to the role of the processor (e.g. in Article 26(2)) as well as a lack of dogmatic precision in several provisions (e.g. the discrepancy between Article 24 and Article 77). It also failed to resolve the basic concerns previously articulated regarding the lack of clarity in the nature of the distribution of responsibilities between controllers and processors.

C. *General approach of the Council*

633. Preface – The Council's approach to adopting a "common position" was an incremental one. Discussions at the level of the Council of the European Union began as early as March of 2012.[1334] The review of the GDPR at the level of the Council was handled by the Working Party on Information Exchange and Data Protection (DAPIX), which conducted a series of article-by-article and chapter-by-chapter discussions, under the auspices of various presidencies.[1335] The European Council finally reached consensus on a General Approach to the GDPR under the Luxembourg Presidency on 15 June 2015, more than three years after discussions had been initiated.[1336]

1333 European Data Protection Supervisor (EDPS), "Additional EDPS comments on the Data Protection Reform Package", *l.c.*, p. 6 (at paragraph 25).

1334 See Council of the European Union, Working Party on Information Exchange and Data Protection (DAPIX), "Outcome of proceedings – summary of discussions on 23–24 February 2012", 2012/0011 (COD), 7221/12, DAPIX 22, 8 March 2012.

1335 Discussion in the DAPIX Council began in March 2012 under the Danish Presidency. Subsequent presidencies were held by Cyprus, Ireland, Lithuania, Greece, Italy, Latvia and Luxembourg.

1336 Council of the European Union (Press release), "Data Protection: Council agrees on a general approach", 15 June 2015 and Council for the European Union, Proposal for a Regulation of the European Parliament and of the Council on the protection of individuals with regard to the processing of personal data and on the free movement of such data (General Data Protection Regulation) – Preparation of a general approach", 2012/0011 (COD), 9565/15, 11 June 2015.

i. Definitions

634. Identical to first reading – Like the European Parliament, the Council rejected the Commission's proposal to add a reference to "conditions" to the definition of controller. The General Approach thus also returned to the 1995 definitions of controller and processor.

ii. Obligations

635. Outline – The General Approach introduced significant changes to the distribution of responsibilities between controllers and processors. Several provisions remained relevant to *both controller and processor*, in particular:

- the obligation to maintain documentation (Article 28)[1337];
- co-operation with supervisory authorities (Article 53 et seq.);
- the obligation to maintain an appropriate level of data security (Article 30);
- the obligation to notify data breaches (Article 31)[1338];
- data protection officers (Articles 35–37);
- codes of conduct (Article 38);
- certification (Article 39); and
- international transfers (Articles 40–44).

An increased number of obligations, however, were rendered *applicable only to controllers*, in particular:

- compliance (and demonstration of compliance) with principles relating to the processing of personal data (Article 5);
- data protection by design and by default (Article 23)[1339];
- notification of data breaches to supervisory authorities and data subjects (Articles 31–32)[1340];

1337 While the both controllers and processors are obliged to maintain certain documentation, Article 28 distinguishes between both actors in terms of the types of documentation they must maintain.

1338 As regards the obligation to notify data breaches, a distinction should be made between the obligation to inform breaches to the controller and the obligation to notify breaches to supervisory authorities and data subjects. Only the controller is obliged to notify the data subject and supervisory authorities. The processor is only obliged to notify the controller (Article 31(2)).

1339 In its First Reading, the European Parliament proposed to extend Article 23 to processors.

1340 As in the Commission Proposal and the First Reading of the Parliament, the obligation to notify the supervisory authority and data subject was exclusively incumbent upon controller. The processor, however, was still under an obligation to notify the controller in case of breach (Article 31(2)).

- data protection impact assessment (Article 33)[1341]; and
- prior consultation (Article 34).[1342]

636. Responsibilty of the controller – Article 22 was revised, primarily to reflect "*a more risk-based*" approach. The Council members generally felt that such an approach was necessary to reduce administrative burden and compliance costs.[1343] As a result, Article 22 was revised to make clear that the controller's obligation to adopt "appropriate measures" shall be determined inter alia on the basis of the "*likelihood and severity*" of the risks presented by the processing.[1344] Similar references to risk considerations were inserted in Articles 30–34.

637. Joint control – Article 24 was extended to further elaborate upon the key elements of the mandatory "arrangement" between joint controllers. The arrangement should cover the information obligations of controllers as well as provide for a "single point of contact" for the exercise of data subject rights.[1345]

638. Legal binding – Like Article 24, Article 26(2) was extended to further elaborate upon the key elements to be included in the arrangement between controllers and processors. In particular, a greater emphasis was placed on addressing subprocessing (see e.g. Article 26(2)a) and the use of standardised contracts.

639. Bound by instructions – The General Approach deleted both Article 26(4) and Article 27 entirely. The requirement to obtain permission from the controller for subprocessing was dealt with in Article 26(2), whereas the consequences of a disregard for instructions was dealt with in Article 77(2).

1341 Contrary to Commission Proposal and First Reading.

1342 Contrary to Commission Proposal and First Reading.

1343 See e.g. "Press Release – 3207th Council meeting – Justice and Home Affairs Brussels – 6 and 7 December 2012", 17315/12 PRESSE 509 PR CO 70, p. 13; Council of the European Union, Note from the Presidency to the Council regarding the General Data Protection Regulation – implementation of risk-based approach – Flexibility for the Public Sector, 2012/0011 (COD), 6607/1/13 REV 1, 1 March 2013, p. 2–4; Council of the European Union, Note from the Presidency to the Working Party on Information Exchange and Data Protection regarding the General Data Protection Regulation – risk-based approach, 2012/0011 (COD), 11481/14, 3 July 2014, p. 1–5.

1344 While the European Parliament in its First Reading also added reference to risks, it did not include the terms "likelihood and severity".

1345 Pursuant to Article 24(2), the data subject would still be able to exercise his or her rights against each of the joint controllers, irrespective of the designation of a single point of contact (unless the data subject was clearly informed of the respective responsibilities of each controller and the arrangement of the respective joint controllers clearly communicated to data subjects in transparent way and said arrangement is not "unfair" with regard to his or her rights – Article 24(3)).

iii. Liability and sanctions

640. Right to compensation and liability – The issue of liability of controllers and processors was discussed extensively by DAPIX.[1346] In the end, Article 77(1) retained the general principle that individuals suffering damages as a result of unlawful processing should be able to receive compensation from the controller or processor. However, Article 77(2) was revised to *differentiate* between the respective liability exposure of each actor:

> "Any controller (...) involved in the processing shall be liable for the damage caused by the processing which is not in compliance with this Regulation. A processor shall be liable for (...) the damage caused by the processing only where it has not complied with obligations of this Regulation specifically directed to processors or acted outside or contrary to lawful instructions of the controller."

The change intended to clarify that a controller should in principle be liable for *any* damages arising from the unlawful processing personal data; whereas a processor would in principle only be liable "*for his segment*".[1347] As a result, the processor would face liability only in case of failure to comply with those obligations of the Regulation which are specifically directly to him or if he acted contrary to or outside of the lawful instructions of the controller.[1348]

641. Exemptions – Article 77(3) was extended to clarify the exemptions shall only be relevant once liability has been established

> "A controller or the processor shall be exempted from liability in accordance with paragraph 2, (...) if (...) it proves that it is not in any way responsible (...), for the event giving rise to the damage."

1346 See e.g. Council of the European Union, Note from Presidency to Working Party on Information Exchange and Data Protection on the proposed General Data Protection Regulation – Chapter IV, 2012/0011 (COD), 12312/14, 1 August 2014, p. 5 and the DAPIX deliberations regarding Chapter VIII cited in the footnotes that follow.

1347 See Council of the European Union, Note from CZ, DE, IE, ES, FR, HR, NL, AT, PL, PT, FI and UK delegations to the Working Group on Information Exchange and Data Protection (DAPIX), 2012/0011 (COD), 7586/1/15 REV 1, 10 April 2015, in particular at p. 11 (Germany); 23–24 (France); p. 27 (Croatia) and 63 (Portugal). See also Council of the European Union, Note from Presidency to JHA Counsellors on the proposed General Data Protection Regulation – Chapter VIII, 9083/15, 27 May 2015, p. 2 (""*As most of the obligations in the Regulation, in particular in Chapter IV, rest with controllers, in many cases the controllers will be primarily liable for damages suffered as a consequence of data protection violations. However, a data subject which has suffered damages due to unlawful processing should also have the possibility to sue directly the processor in case he knows or has strong reasons to believe the processor and not (only) the controller is in fact liable. Paragraph 1 clearly acknowledges that and leaves any person the choice to sue the controller, the processor or both. The controller can thus be the so-called single point of entry, but the data subject may choose another procedural avenue.*")

1348 *Id.*

Article 2(3) of the Commission Proposal, which contained a reference to the liability exemptions contained in the e-Commerce Directive, was deleted. Recital (17) still provided, however that:

> "This Regulation should [...] be without prejudice to the application of Directive 2000/31/EC, in particular of the liability rules of intermediary service providers in Articles 12 to 15 of that Directive."

642. "Cumulative" liability – Because several DAPIX delegations disliked the term "joint and several" liability, the decision was made to drop the terms entirely.[1349] Instead, Article 77(4) would specify in which cases a controller or processor involved in the processing might be held liable "*for the entire damage*":

> "Where more than one controller or processor or a controller and a processor are involved in the same processing and, where they are, in accordance with paragraphs 2 and 3, responsible for any damage caused by the processing, (...) each controller or processor shall be held (...) liable for the entire damage."

The proposed revisions to Article 77(4) significantly limited the instances in which a controller or processor might face cumulative liability. The liability of either controller or processor for the entire damage was made conditional upon a prior finding of responsibility in causing the damage.[1350] Only in cases where the controller or processor could be deemed responsible in accordance with paragraphs 2 and 3 could either of them be held liable for the entire damage.[1351]

643. Joined proceedings – Recital (118) of the General approach clarified that in case of joined proceedings, compensation may be apportioned among the controller and processor who are liable according to their responsibility for the damage caused.[1352] Specifically, recital (118) provided that

1349 Council of the European Union, Note from Presidency to JHA Counsellors on the proposed General Data Protection Regulation – Chapter VIII, 2012/0011 (COD), 9083/15, 27 May 2015, p. 3 ("*Given the fact that the concept of joint and several liability seems to mean different things to different delegations, the new drafting avoids this term altogether.*")

1350 See Council of the European Union, Note from Presidency to JHA Counsellors on the proposed General Data Protection Regulation – Chapter VIII, 2012/0011 (COD), 9083/15, 27 May 2015, p 3.

1351 Council of the European Union, Note from Presidency to JHA Counsellors on the proposed General Data Protection Regulation – Chapter VIII, 2012/0011 (COD), 9083/15, 27 May 2015, p 3 ("*[E]ach non-compliant controller and/or processor involved in the processing are held liable for the entire amount of the damage. However a controller or processor is exempted from this liability if it demonstrates that it is not responsible for the damage (0% responsibility). Thus only controllers or processors that are at least partially responsible for non-compliance (however minor, e.g. 5%) with the Regulation, and/or in case of a processor, with the lawful instructions from the controller, can be held liable for the full amount of the damage.*")

1352 See also the introductory notes by the Presidency accompanying the General Approach: Council for the European Union, Proposal for a Regulation of the European Parliament and

> "Where controllers or processors are involved in the same processing each controller or processor should be held liable for the entire damage. However, where they are joined to the same judicial proceedings, in accordance with national law, compensation may be apportioned according to the responsibility of each controller or processor for the damage caused by the processing, provided that full and effective compensation of the data subject who suffered the damage is ensured. Any controller or processor who has (...) paid full compensation, may subsequently institute recourse proceedings against other controllers or processors involved in the same processing."

644. Recourse – A new paragraph was added to Article 77 to clarify that, in the absence of joined proceedings, a controller or processor who has been held liable "for the entire damage" is entitled to obtain redress from the other actors involved in the processing (insofar as they are may also be deemed responsible the damage). Specifically, Article 77(5) of the General Approach provided that

> "Where a controller or processor has, in accordance with paragraph 4, paid full compensation for the damage suffered, that controller or processor shall be entitled to claim back from the other controllers or processors involved in the same processing that part of the compensation corresponding to their part of responsibility for the damage in accordance with the conditions set out in paragraph 2."

645. Administrative fines – Under the General approach, a supervisory authority can in principle impose fines upon either controller or processor (Article 79a).[1353] Such fines should be effective, proportionate and dissuasive penalties.

646. Penalties – Article 78 was deleted. A new Article 79b was introduced to cover infringements which are not subject to administrative fines pursuant to Article 79a (e.g. violations of Chapter IX – specific data processing situations), calling on Member States to introduce effective, proportionate and dissuasive penalties.

iv. Assessment

647. Significant changes – While the General Approach left the 1995 concepts of controller and processor intact, it introduced significant changes to the distribution of responsibility and liability between controllers and processors. In comparison to the initial Commission Proposal, the General

---

of the Council on the protection of individuals with regard to the processing of personal data and on the free movement of such data (General Data Protection Regulation) – Preparation of a general approach", 11 June 2015, 2012/0011 (COD), 9565/15, p. 2–3.

1353 Article 79a(1) only mentions the controller, but the remaining provisions indicate that both controller and processor might be fined.

approach (a) imposed less obligations directly upon processors and (b) limited the instances in which controllers or processors might be held liable "for the entire damage".

648. Less obligations for processors – During their deliberations, the delegates to the DAPIX Working Party frequently expressed their concerns regarding the lack of clarity in the distribution of responsibilities between controllers and processors.[1354] Many expressed the view that the controller should continue to face "primary" responsibility for compliance.[1355] The obligations incumbent upon processors therefore needed to be limited, as did the corresponding liability exposure.[1356] Although the General Approach did not fully return to the 1995 situation (in which processors were in principle only indirectly accountable), it imposed fewer obligations on processors in comparison to the Parliament's First Reading and the initial Commission proposal.[1357]

649. Less cumulative liability – The issue of cumulative[1358] liability was discussed at length in the DAPIX Working Party.[1359] During the deliberations,

1354 See e.g. Council of the European Union, Note from the Presidency to the Working Group on Information Exchange and Data Protection (DAPIX) – Specific Issues of Chapters I-IV of the General Data Protection Regulation – certain aspects of the relationship between controllers and processors, 2012/0011 (COD), 5345/14, 15 January 2014. Cloud computing was cited as a particular area of concern.

1355 See e.g. Council of the European Union, Note from the Presidency to the Working Group on Information Exchange and Data Protection (DAPIX) on the General Data Protection Regulation – Chapter VIII, 2012/0011 (COD), 7722/15, 13 April 2015, p. 2.

1356 Council of the European Union, Note from the Presidency to the Working Group on Information Exchange and Data Protection (DAPIX) on the General Data Protection Regulation – Chapter VIII, 2012/0011 (COD), 7722/15, 13 April 2015, p. 2–3.

1357 For example, in the initial Commission proposal, the obligation to conduct data protection impact assessments or to undertake prior consultation (Article 33–34) were also relevant to processors.

1358 As indicated earlier, the DAPIX Working Group decided to remove the term "joint and several liability" from the text because the concept meant different things to different delegates.

1359 See in particular Council of the European Union, Note from CZ, DE, IE, ES, FR, HR, NL, AT, PL, PT, FI and UK delegations to the Working Group on Information Exchange and Data Protection (DAPIX), 2012/0011 (COD), 7586/1/15 REV 1, 10 April 2015, p. 73–76 (UK arguing strongly in favour of "liability follows fault"); Council of the European Union, Note from the Presidency to the Working Group on Information Exchange and Data Protection (DAPIX) on the General Data Protection Regulation – Chapter VIII, 2012/0011 (COD), p. 3–4 (outlining 3 possible options); Council of the European Union, Note from the German delegation to the Working Group on Information Exchange and Data Protection (DAPIX) on the Proposal for a General Data Protection Regulation – Chapter VIII, 2012/0011 (COD), 8150/15, 21 April 2015 (Germany seeking to still retain joint and several liability, but to limit to specific instances); Council for the European Union, Note from the Presidency to the JHA Counsellors DAPIX on a Proposal for a General Data Protection Regulation – Chapter VIII, 8371/15, 4 May 2015; Council of the European Union, Note from the German delegation to the JHA Counsellors (DAPIX) on the Proposal for a General Data Protection Regulation – Chapter VIII, 2012/0011 (COD), 8150/1/15, 6 May 2015 (Germany updates its proposals);

the UK delegation argued heavily in favour of a system of "liability follows fault".[1360] In its view, general imposition of joint and several liability regardless of fault (as provided by the Commission Proposal) would have several disadvantages.[1361] Other delegations, the German delegation in particular, sought to retain the principle of joint and several liability, but agreed that it should be limited to instances the controller or processor were liable to the same damage pursuant Article 77(1).[1362] Based on the discussions, the Latvian Presidency was able to narrow the choice down to two options.[1363] Under option 1, each controller and/or processor involved in the processing could be held liable for the entire amount of the damage, provided a shortcoming had been established.[1364] Under option 2, each controller involved in the processing could theoretically be held liable, regardless of fault.[1365] The first option was considered fairer towards the actors involved in the processing, as no actor faced liability if it bore no responsibility at all for the damage.[1366] The second option was considered to be more friendly towards the data subject, but excessive (in particular from the point of view of SMEs).[1367] In the end, the choice was made for option 1.

650. CONSISTENCY WITH PETL – The Council's General Approach regarding "cumulative" liability reflects the general principles of tort law regarding multiple tortfeasors. According to Article 9:101 of the Principles of European Tort Law (PETL), liability is solidary "*where the whole or a distinct part of the damage suffered by the victim is attributable to two or more persons*".[1368] The same provision also stipulates that where persons are subject to solidary

---

Council of the European Union, Note from the Presidency to the Permanent Representatives Committee on the proposal for a General Data Protection Regulation – Chapter VIII, 2012/0011 (COD), 8383/15, 13 May 2015 and Council of the European Union, Note from the Presidency to JHA Counsellor DAPIX on the Proposal for General Data Protection Regulation – Chapter VIII, 2012/0011 (COD), 9083/15, 27 May 2015.

1360 Council of the European Union, Note from CZ, DE, IE, ES, FR, HR, NL, AT, PL, PT, FI and UK delegations to the Working Group on Information Exchange and Data Protection (DAPIX), 2012/0011 (COD), 7586/1/15 REV 1, 10 April 2015, p. 73–76.

1361 *Ibid*, p. 74.

1362 See Council of the European Union, Note from the German delegation to the Working Group on Information Exchange and Data Protection (DAPIX) on the Proposal for a General Data Protection Regulation – Chapter VIII, 2012/0011 (COD), 8150/15, 21 April 2015 and Council of the European Union, Note from the German delegation to the JHA Counsellors (DAPIX) on the Proposal for a General Data Protection Regulation – Chapter VIII, 2012/0011 (COD), 8150/1/15, 6 May 2015.

1363 Council of the European Union, Note from the Presidency to JHA Counsellor DAPIX on the Proposal for General Data Protection Regulation – Chapter VIII, 2012/0011 (COD), 9083/15, 27 May 2015, p. 3–4.

1364 *Ibid*, p. 3.

1365 *Ibid*, p. 19.

1366 *Id.*

1367 *Ibid*, p. 4.

1368 See also *supra*, no. 198.

liability, the victim may claim full compensation from any one or more of them, provided that the victim may not recover more than the full amount of the damage suffered by him.[1369] The main innovation of the General Approach in comparison to Directive 95/46 therefore does not relate to the imposition of "cumulative" or solidary liability (as the General Approach merely clarifies general tort law principles), but rather to the fact that the General Approach also imposes obligations directly upon processors (albeit less extensively than either the initial Commission proposal or Parliament's First Reading).

D. *Trilogue and final text*

651. PREFACE – The trilogue negotiations between the European Commission, Council and Parliament were launched following the Council's adoption of the General Approach. A political agreement among the three bodies was achieved six months later, on 15 December 2015.[1370] The text resulting from the trilogue was made publically available on 28 January 2016.[1371] After making a number of linguistic and numbering edits, the Council adopted its First Reading of the GDPR on 6 April 2016.[1372] The European Commission expressed its support for the Council position at First reading on 11 April 2016.[1373] On 14 April 2016, the European Parliament approved the Council position at first reading, thereby concluding the legislative process.[1374] On 4 May 2016, the final text of GDPR was published in the Official Journal of the European Union.[1375]

1369 *Id.*

1370 European Commission, Agreement on Commission's EU data protection reform will boost Digital Single Market, Press Release, Brussels, 15 December 2015.

1371 Council of the European Union, Proposal for a Regulation of the European Parliament and of the Council on the protection of individuals with regard to the processing of personal data and on the free movement of such data (General Data Protection Regulation) [first reading] – Political agreement", 5455/16, 28 January 2016.

1372 Council of the European Union, Position of the Council at first reading with a view to the adoption of a Regulation of the European Parliament and of the Council on the protection of natural persons with regard to the processing of personal data and on the free movement of such data, and repealing Directive 95/46/EC (General Data Protection Regulation), 5419/16, 6 April 2016.

1373 European Commission, Communication from the Commission to the European Parliament pursuant to Article 294(6) of the Treaty on the Functioning of the European Union concerning the position of the Council on the adoption of a Regulation of the European Parliament and of the Council on the protection of natural persons with regard to the processing of personal data and on the free movement of such data (General Data Protection Regulation) and repealing Directive 95/46/EC, COM(2016) 214 final, 11 April 2016.

1374 European Parliament, "Data protection reform – Parliament approves new rules fit for the digital era", Press Release, 14 April 2016. See also European Commission, "Joint Statement on the final adoption of the new EU rules for personal data protection", 14 April 2016.

1375 Regulation 2016/679 of the European Parliament and of the Council of 27 April 2016 on the protection of natural persons with regard to the processing of personal data and on the free movement of such data, and repealing Directive 95/46/EC (General Data Protection Regulation), OJ 4 May 2016, L 119/1.

i. Definitions

652. Identical to Directive 95/46 – The GDPR replicates the definitions of controller and processor as defined by Directive 95/46. Only minor linguistic edits were made. Article 4 of provides that

> "(7) 'controller' means the natural or legal person, public authority, agency or any other body which, alone or jointly with others, determines the purposes and means of the processing of personal data; where the purposes and means of such processing are determined by Union or Member State law, the controller or the specific criteria for its nomination may be designated provided for by Union or Member State law;"
>
> (8) 'processor' means a natural or legal person, public authority, agency or any other body which processes personal data on behalf of the controller."

ii. Obligations

653. Outline – The GDPR contains the same distribution of responsibilities between controllers and processors as the General Approach of the Council. The following provisions are relevant to *both controller and processor*:

- the obligation to maintain records of the processing (Article 30);
- co-operation with supervisory authorities (Article 58 et seq.);
- the obligation to notify data breaches (Article 33)[1376];
- the obligation to maintain an appropriate level of data security (Article 32);
- data protection officers (Articles 37–39);
- codes of conduct (Article 40);
- certification (Article 42); and
- international transfers (Articles 44–49).

The following obligations apply directly *only to controllers*:

- compliance (and demonstration of compliance) with principles relating to the processing of personal data (Article 5);
- data protection by design and by default (Article 25);
- notification of data breaches to supervisory authorities and data subjects (Articles 33–34);

1376 As regards the obligation to notify data breaches, a distinction should be made between the obligation to inform breaches to the controller and the obligation to notify breaches to supervisory authorities and data subjects. Only the controller is obliged to notify the data subject and supervisory authorities. The processor is only obliged to notify the controller (Article 31(2)).

- data protection impact assessment (Article 35); and
- prior consultation (Article 36).

654. Responsibilty of the controller – Article 24 of the GDPR provides that

> "1. Taking into account the nature, scope, context and purposes of processing as well as the risks of varying likelihood and severity for the rights and freedoms of natural persons, the controller shall implement appropriate technical and organisational measures to ensure and to be able to demonstrate that processing is performed in accordance with this Regulation. Those measures shall be reviewed and updated where necessary.
>
> 2. Where proportionate in relation to processing activities, the measures referred to in paragraph 1 shall include the implementation of appropriate data protection policies by the controller.
>
> 3. Adherence to approved codes of conduct as referred to in Article 40 or approved certification mechanisms as referred to in Article 42 may be used as an element by which to demonstrate compliance with the obligations of the controller."

In comparison to the General Approach, Article 24 was extended to recognise that the likelihood and severity of risks may vary. It now also states explicitly that measures to address risks must be reviewed and updated where necessary.

655. Joint control – Article 26 of the GDPR provides that

> "1. Where two or more controllers jointly determine the purposes and means of processing, they shall be joint controllers. They shall in a transparent manner determine their respective responsibilities for compliance with the obligations under this Regulation, in particular as regards the exercising of the rights of the data subject and their respective duties to provide the information referred to in Articles 13 and 14, by means of an arrangement between them unless, and in so far as, the respective responsibilities of the controllers are determined by Union or Member State law to which the controllers are subject. The arrangement may designate a contact point for data subjects.
>
> 2. The arrangement referred to in paragraph 1 shall duly reflect the respective roles and relationships of the joint controllers vis-à-vis the data subjects. The essence of the arrangement shall be made available to the data subject.
>
> 3. Irrespective of the terms of the arrangement referred to in paragraph 1, the data subject may exercise his or her rights under this Regulation in respect of and against each of the controllers."

A noteworthy change to Article 26(1) *in fine*, in comparison to the General Approach, lies in the fact that the designation of a point of contact for data subjects in the arrangement between joint controllers is no longer mandatory (the word "shall" was substituted with the word "may"). A second noteworthy change is that Article 26(3) no longer provides for an exception to the rule that a data subject may exercise his or her rights against each of the joint controllers involved in the processing.

656. Choice of processor – Article 28(1) of the GDPR provides that

> "Where processing is to be carried out on behalf of a controller, the controller shall use only processors providing sufficient guarantees to implement appropriate technical and organisational measures in such a manner that processing will meet the requirements of this Regulation and ensure the protection of the rights of the data subject."

657. Legal binding – Article 28(3) of the GDPR provides that

> "Processing by a processor shall be governed by a contract or other legal act under Union or Member State law, that is binding on the processor with regard to the controller and that sets out the subject-matter and duration of the processing, the nature and purpose of the processing, the type of personal data and categories of data subjects and the obligations and rights of the controller. That contract or other legal act shall stipulate, in particular, that the processor:
>
> (a) processes the personal data only on documented instructions from the controller, including with regard to transfers of personal data to a third country or an international organisation, unless required to do so by Union or Member State law to which the processor is subject; in such a case, the processor shall inform the controller of that legal requirement before processing, unless that law prohibits such information on important grounds of public interest;
> (b) ensures that persons authorised to process the personal data have committed themselves to confidentiality or are under an appropriate statutory obligation of confidentiality;
> (c) takes all measures required pursuant to Article 32;
> (d) respects the conditions referred to in paragraphs 2 and 4 for engaging another processor;
> (e) taking into account the nature of the processing, assists the controller by appropriate technical and organisational measures, insofar as this is possible, for the fulfilment of the controller's obligation to respond to requests for exercising the data subject's rights laid down in Chapter III;
> (f) assists the controller in ensuring compliance with the obligations pursuant to Articles 32 to 36 taking into account the nature of processing and the information available to the processor;
> (g) at the choice of the controller, deletes or returns all the personal data to the controller after the end of the provision of services relating to processing, and deletes existing copies unless Union or Member State law requires storage of the personal data;
> (h) makes available to the controller all information necessary to demonstrate compliance with the obligations laid down in this Article and allow for and

> contribute to audits, including inspections, conducted by the controller or another auditor mandated by the controller.
>
> With regard to point (h) of the first subparagraph, the processor shall immediately inform the controller if, in its opinion, an instruction infringes this Regulation or other Union or Member State data protection provisions."

In case of sub-processing, the same data protection obligations as set out in the contract or other legal act between the controller and the processor must be imposed on that other processor by way of a contract or other legal act under Union or Member State law. Should the sub-processor fail to fulfil its data protection obligations, the initial processor shall remain fully liable to the controller for the performance of that other processor's obligations (Article 28(4) of the GDPR).

The only notable change to Article 28(3) GDPR, in comparison to the General Approach, is the addition of lit b), which requires the stipulation that persons authorised to process the personal data have committed themselves to confidentiality or are under an appropriate statutory obligation of confidentiality.

658. Bound by instructions – Article 29 of the GDPR provides that

> "The processor and any person acting under the authority of the controller or of the processor, who has access to personal data, shall not process those data except on instructions from the controller, unless required to do so by Union or Member State law."

In addition, Article 28(10) of the GDPR provides that if a processor infringes this Regulation by determining the purposes and means of processing, the processor shall be considered to be a controller in respect of that processing (without prejudice to Articles 82, 83 and 84).

iii. Liability and sanctions

659. Right to compensation and liability – Article 82 of the GDPR provides that

> "1. Any person who has suffered material or non-material damage as a result of an infringement of this Regulation shall have the right to receive compensation from the controller or processor for the damage suffered.
>
> 2. Any controller involved in processing shall be liable for the damage caused by processing which infringes this Regulation. A processor shall be liable for the damage caused by processing only where it has not complied with obligations of this Regulation specifically directed to processors or where it has acted outside or contrary to lawful instructions of the controller."

660. Exemptions – Article 82(3) of the GDPR provides that

> "A controller or processor shall be exempt from liability under paragraph 2 if it proves that it is not in any way responsible for the event giving rise to the damage."

In addition, Article 2(4) of the GDPR provides that

> "This Regulation shall be without prejudice to the application of Directive 2000/31/EC, in particular of the liability rules of intermediary service providers in Articles 12 to 15 of that Directive."

661. Cumulative liability – Article 82(4) of the GDPR provides that

> "Where more than one controller or processor, or both a controller and a processor, are involved in the same processing and where they are, under paragraphs 2 and 3, responsible for any damage caused by processing, each controller or processor shall be held liable for the entire damage in order to ensure effective compensation of the data subject."

662. Joined proceedings – Recital (146) of the GDPR provides that

> "Where controllers or processors are involved in the same processing, each controller or processor should be held liable for the entire damage. However, where they are joined to the same judicial proceedings, in accordance with Member State law, compensation may be apportioned according to the responsibility of each controller or processor for the damage caused by the processing, provided that full and effective compensation of the data subject who suffered the damage is ensured. Any controller or processor which has paid full compensation may subsequently institute recourse proceedings against other controllers or processors involved in the same processing."

663. Recourse – Article 82(5) of the GDPR provides that

> "Where a controller or processor has, in accordance with paragraph 4, paid full compensation for the damage suffered, that controller or processor shall be entitled to claim back from the other controllers or processors involved in the same processing that part of the compensation corresponding to their part of responsibility for the damage, in accordance with the conditions set out in paragraph 2."

664. Administrative fines –Article 83 of the GDPR provides that

> "1. Each supervisory authority shall ensure that the imposition of administrative fines pursuant to this Article in respect of infringements of this Regulation referred to in paragraphs 4, 5 and 6 shall in each individual case be effective, proportionate and dissuasive.

2. Administrative fines shall, depending on the circumstances of each individual case, be imposed in addition to, or instead of, measures referred to in points (a) to (h) and (j) of Article 58(2). When deciding whether to impose an administrative fine and deciding on the amount of the administrative fine in each individual case due regard shall be given to the following:

(a) the nature, gravity and duration of the infringement taking into account the nature scope or purpose of the processing concerned as well as the number of data subjects affected and the level of damage suffered by them;
(b) the intentional or negligent character of the infringement;
(c) any action taken by the controller or processor to mitigate the damage suffered by data subjects;
(d) the degree of responsibility of the controller or processor taking into account technical and organisational measures implemented by them pursuant to Articles 25 and 32;
(e) any relevant previous infringements by the controller or processor;
(f) the degree of cooperation with the supervisory authority, in order to remedy the infringement and mitigate the possible adverse effects of the infringement;
(g) the categories of personal data affected by the infringement;
(h) the manner in which the infringement became known to the supervisory authority, in particular whether, and if so to what extent, the controller or processor notified the infringement;
(i) in case measures referred to in Article 58(2) have previously been ordered against the controller or processor concerned with regard to the same subject-matter, compliance with those measures;
(j) adherence to approved codes of conduct pursuant to Article 40 or approved certification mechanisms pursuant to Article 42; and
(k) any other aggravating or mitigating factor applicable to the circumstances of the case, such as financial benefits gained, or losses avoided, directly or indirectly, from the infringement."

665. Penalties – Article 84(1) of the GDPR provides that

"Member States shall lay down the rules on other penalties applicable to infringements of this Regulation in particular for infringements which are not subject to administrative fines pursuant to Article 83, and shall take all measures necessary to ensure that they are implemented. Such penalties shall be effective, proportionate and dissuasive."

iv. Assessment

666. Minor changes – In comparison to the General Approach of the Council, the changes introduced in the final text of the GDPR were relatively minor. While the concepts of controller and processor underwent linguistic edits, these edits in no way modified the content of the definitions. The provision on joint control was modified to stipulate that the designation of a single point of contact is not mandatory in all instances. It also removed the exception which provided that the data subject might not be able to exercise his rights against every joint controller in cases where "*the data subject has been informed in a transparent and unequivocal manner which of the joint controllers is responsible*". The reference to the liability exemptions contained in Articles 12–15 of the E-Commerce Directive was reinstated in the body of the text, otherwise no substantive changes were made to the provisions concerning liability.[1377]

2.2. CONCLUSION

667. Outline – The GDPR left the concepts of controller and processor intact. Only minor linguistic edits were made to the definitions contained in Directive 95/46. The GDPR did, however, introduce substantial changes as regards the allocation of responsibility and liability between controllers and processors. In comparison to Directive 95/46, the GDPR

(a) increased the emphasis on controller accountability;
(b) increased the number of obligations directly applicable processors and rendered them liable towards data subjects;
(c) explicitly addressed the relationship between joint controllers; and
(d) introduced a "cumulative" liability regime.

A. Controller accountability

668. Background – The GDPR specifies in considerable detail the measures which controllers are expected to put in place in order to ensure compliance. Many of the measures required under Chapter IV of the GDPR can be traced back to policy debates surrounding the principle of "accountability".[1378] From 2009 onwards, data protection authorities regularly met with industry representatives and other stakeholders to explore the potential of accountability as a means to address compliance challenges posed by emerging technologies

[1377] Perhaps an important clarification was introduced in Article 28(10) which specified that if a processor infringes this Regulation by determining the purposes and means of processing, the processor shall not only be considered to be a controller in respect of that processing, but may also be held liable under Articles 82, 83 and 84.

[1378] European Commission, Proposal for a Regulation of the European Parliament and of the Council on the protection of individuals with regard to the processing of personal data and on the free movement of such data (General Data Protection Regulation), COM(2012) 11 final, *l.c.*, p. 10. See also the Revised OECD Privacy Guidelines, which introduced a new part entitled "implementing accountability" (Part Three), which outlined measures similar in nature.

and business models.[1379] The main purpose of these meetings was to determine whether or not the representatives from the various stakeholder groups could reach a consensus position on what it meant for an organisation to be "accountable" and what frameworks of compliance might be.[1380]

669. PRINCIPLE – Accountability is a concept with many dimensions.[1381] It has been characterized by scholars as being an "elusive" and even "chameleon-like" concept, because it can mean very different things to different people.[1382] In its core meaning, accountability refers to the existence of a relationship whereby one entity has the ability to call upon another entity and demand an explanation and/or justification for its conduct.[1383] Over time, different data protection instruments have advanced different types of accountability mechanisms.[1384] In the GDPR, the principle of accountability is mainly used to signal that controllers are not only *responsible* for implementing appropriate measures to comply with the GDPR, but must also be able to *demonstrate* compliance at the request of supervisory authorities.[1385]

1379 J. Alhadeff, B. Van Alsenoy and J. Dumortier, "The accountability principle in data protection regulation: origin, development and future directions", *l.c.*, p. 59.

1380 *Id.* The Center for Information Policy Leadership (CIPL) acted as a driving force behind many of these meetings. In 2010, the Article 29 Working Party issued its own opinion on the principle of accountability (Article 29 Data Protection Working Party, "Opinion 3/2010 on the principle of accountability", 13 July 2010, WP173). Already in 2009, however, the Working Party recommended that the Commission consider "accountability-based mechanisms" and the introduction of an accountability principle in the revised Data Protection Directive in its Opinion on the Future of Privacy (W168, December 2009, paragraph 79).

1381 See e.g. J. Koppell, "Pathologies of Accountability: ICANN and the Challenge of "Multiple accountabilities Disorder"", *Public Administration Review* 2005, vol. 65, p. 94–99 and R. Mulgan, ""Accountability": an ever-expanding concept?", *Public Administration* 2000, vol. 78 p. 555–556.

1382 A. Sinclair, "The Chameleon of Accountability: Forms and Discourses", *Accounting, Organisations and Society* 1995, Vol. 20, p. 219 and M. Bovens, "Analysing and Assessing Accountability: A conceptual Framework", *European Law Journal* 2007, vol. 13, p. 448.

1383 J. Alhadeff, B. Van Alsenoy and J. Dumortier, "The accountability principle in data protection regulation: origin, development and future directions", *l.c.*, p. 71.

1384 *Id.* The principle of accountability made its formal debut in the field of international data protection in the 1980 OECD Privacy Guidelines. For a discussion of the role of the accountability principle in different data protection instruments see J. Alhadeff, B. Van Alsenoy and J. Dumortier, "The accountability principle in data protection regulation: origin, development and future directions", *l.c.*, p. 52–64. When reviewing these instruments, it is apparent where these instruments purport to rely on the same principle of accountability, notable differences exist in terms of the definition of norms, the designation of accountors and accountees, oversight mechanisms and sanctions (*Id.*).

1385 Article 5(2) of the GDPR specifies that the controller shall be responsible for, and be able to demonstrate compliance with the principles relating to the processing of personal data. In the same vein Article 24(1) provides that the controller shall *implement* appropriate technical and organisational measures to ensure and to be able to *demonstrate* that processing is performed in accordance with this Regulation. See also Article 29 Data Protection Working Party, "Opinion 3/2010 on the principle of accountability", 13 July 2010, WP 173, paragraph 34. In the same vein, paragraph 15 of the Revised OECD Privacy Guidelines provide that a

670. Implementing accountability – Article 24(1) of the GDPR confirms that the controller is obliged to implement appropriate technical and organisational measures to ensure compliance. Generally speaking, this will require controllers to put in place internal policies and procedures dedicated to ensure organisational compliance (Article 24(2)). The actual measures adopted by controllers must be tailored to the nature, scope, context and purposes of the processing, as well as the risks presented by the processing.[1386] Beyond these general statements of principle, the GDPR also specifies a number of specific obligations which aim to give further substance to the accountability principle, such as obligations concerning:

(a) data protection by design and by default (Article 25)[1387];
(b) the legal binding of processors (Article 28(3))[1388];
(c) the keeping of appropriate records of the processing (Article 30)[1389];
(d) co-operation with supervisory authorities (Article 31);
(e) personal data breach notification (Articles 33–34);
(f) data protection impact assessments and prior consultation (Articles 35–36);
(g) designation of data protection officer (Articles 37–39); and
(h) codes of conduct and certification (Articles 40–43).

B. *Enhanced obligations for processors*

671. Main obligations – In contrast to Directive 95/46, the GDPR contains a substantial number of provisions which are directly relevant to processors. Whereas processors were in principle only indirectly accountable under Directive 95/46, the GDPR imposes a range of obligations upon processors and renders them liable towards data subjects in case of non-compliance. Processors

---

controller should put in place a privacy management programme which "gives effect" to the Guidelines for all personal data under its control, and should be prepared to demonstrate its privacy management programme as appropriate, in particular at the request of a competent privacy enforcement authority.

1386 Article 24(1) GDPR; Recital (74) GDPR. See also Paragraph 15(a)ii of the Revised OECD Privacy Guidelines (which provides that every controller should have in place a privacy management programme that is tailored "to the structure, scale, volume and sensitivity of its operations" and "provides for appropriate safeguards based on privacy risk assessment".

1387 See also recital (78) ("*In order to be able to demonstrate compliance with this Regulation, the controller should adopt internal policies and implement measures which meet in particular the principles of data protection by design and data protection by default*")

1388 The legal binding of processors is related to the principle of accountability in the sense that it reinforces the notion of controller accountability for all personal data under its control, regardless of whether it is processed by the controller itself or by an agent on its behalf. See also OECD, *Supplementary explanatory memorandum to the revised recommendation of the council concerning guidelines governing the protection of privacy and transborder flows of personal data*, 2013, p. 23.

1389 See in particular also Article 30(4), which provides that the controller or the processor shall make the record available to the supervisory authority on request.

are also accountable to regulators, and can be fined in case of non-compliance with the obligations of the GDPR which are relevant to them. The following table provides a comparative overview of provisions which are directly relevant to processors under Directive 95/46 and the GDPR respectively:

Table 2. Comparison processor provisions Directive 95/46 – GDPR[1390]

Relevant provisions	**Directive 95/45**	**GDPR**
Applicable law	✗	✓
Principles of data quality	✗	✗
Lawfulness of processing	✗	✗
Sensitive data	✗	✗
Transparency	✗	✗
Data subject rights	✗	Indirect application through contract (exceptions)
Co-operation with supervisory authority	Implied	✓
Data protection by design and by default	✗	✗
Documentation	Not specified	✓
Confidentiality	✓	✓
Security	Applicable through contract	✓
Data breach notification[1391]	✗	✓
DPIA, prior authorization	✗	Applicable through contract (exceptions)
Data protection officers	✗	✓
Codes of conduct, certification	Not specified	✓
International transfers	Not Specified	✓
Liability	✗	✓
Administrative fines	Not Specified	✓

1390 Legend: a check mark indicates that the provision in question is directly and expressly applicable to the actor in question; an "X" indicates that it is clear that the provision in question does not directly apply to the actor in question.

1391 As regards the obligation to notify data breaches, a distinction must be made between the obligation to inform breaches to the controller and the obligation to notify breaches to supervisory authorities and data subjects. Only the controller is obliged to notify the data subject and supervisory authorities. The processor is only obliged to notify the controller.

672. Relationship with controller – Despite the increased obligations imposed upon processors, the nature of the relationship between controllers and processors has remained largely the same. As before, the processor is essentially conceived of as an "agent" or "delegate" of the controller, who may only process personal data in accordance with the instructions of the controller (Articles 29 and 28(10)). Considerable detail has been added, however, as regards the legal binding of processors towards controllers (Article 28(3)).

C. *Relationship between joint controllers*

673. Appropriate arrangement – The GDPR introduced a new provision dedicated specifically to situations of joint control. Article 26(1) provides that joint controllers must determine their respective responsibilities for compliance with the GDPR, in particular as regards the exercise of data subject rights and their respective duties to provide information, by means of an "arrangement" between them.[1392] The arrangement must duly reflect the respective roles and relationships of the joint controllers vis-à-vis the data subjects (Article 26(2)).

674. Codification of WP29 Guidance – For the most part, Article 26 of the GDPR can be seen as a codification of guidance provided by the Article 29 Working Party in Opinion 1/2010 as regards the legal implications of joint control.[1393] A notable difference, however, is that joint controllers shall in principle be jointly and severally liable towards data subjects, even if there exists an appropriate arrangement between them (Article 82).

D. *Cumulative liability*

675. Outline – Article 82 of the GDPR retained the basic principle that a controller may be held liable for damages suffered as a result of an unlawful processing activity. Contrary to Directive 95/46, however, the GDPR also recognizes processor liability. In situations involving more than one controller or processor, every controller or processor involved in the processing may in principle be held liable for the entire damage insofar as the damage results from the failure to comply with an obligation for which it is responsible. Finally, the GDPR also explicitly recognizes the eligibility of non-material damages.

676. Controller liability – The liability model for controllers essentially remained the same as under Directive 95/46. A controller shall in principle be liable for any damages arising from the unlawful processing personal data. The

---

1392 Joint controllers are not obliged to put in place such an arrangement in so far as the respective responsibilities of the controllers are determined by Union or Member State law to which the controllers are subject.

1393 Compare *supra*, no. 140–141.

liability of the controller is still "*strict*" in the sense that, once an infringement has been established, the controller cannot escape liability simply by demonstrating the absence of personal fault.[1394] In addition, the controller can still be held liable for unlawful processing activities undertaken by the processor (Article 81(2)). An important clarification, however, is provided by recital (146). Recital (146) specifies that in cases where a controller and processor has been joined to the same judicial proceedings, compensation may be *apportioned* according to the responsibility of each controller or processor for the damage caused by the processing, provided that full and effective compensation of the data subject who suffered the damage is ensured. In cases where the processor is not joined in the same proceeding, the controller is entitled to claim back from the processor any compensation that was paid for damages for which the processor was responsible (Article 82(5)).

677. Processor liability – The liability exposure of processors is more limited in scope than the liability exposure of controllers. Whereas controllers can in principle be held liable for damages arising from *any* infringement of the GDPR, processors can in principle only be held liable in case of failure to comply with obligations of the GDPR specifically directed to processors or where it has acted outside or contrary to lawful instructions of the controller (Article 82(2)). This is essentially a *proportional liability* model, as the processor can only be held liable in relation "for its segment" in the processing.[1395]

678. Cumulative liability – Article 82(4) provides that every controller or processor involved in the processing may be held liable "*for the entire*

1394 As indicated earlier, the characterization of the controller's liability as being a form of "strict" liability is somewhat misleading, given that the data subject must still demonstrate existence of unlawful processing activity, which essentially amounts to a demonstration of "fault" for tort law purposes. Cf. *supra*, no. 149. See also P. Larouche, M. Peitz and N. Purtova, "Consumer privacy in network industries – A CERRE Policy Report", *l.c.*, p. 58 (arguing that "*at the end of the day, the [...] GDPR create[s] little more than a basic fault-based regime for privacy and data protection breaches, with a reversed burden of proof*").

1395 See Council of the European Union, Note from CZ, DE, IE, ES, FR, HR, NL, AT, PL, PT, FI and UK delegations to the Working Group on Information Exchange and Data Protection (DAPIX), 2012/0011 (COD), 7586/1/15 REV 1, 10 April 2015, in particular at p. 11 (Germany); 23–24 (France); p. 27 (Croatia) and 63 (Portugal). See also Council of the European Union, Note from Presidency to JHA Counsellors on the proposed General Data Protection Regulation – Chapter VIII, 9083/15, 27 May 2015, p. 2 (""*As most of the obligations in the Regulation, in particular in Chapter IV, rest with controllers, in many cases the controllers will be primarily liable for damages suffered as a consequence of data protection violations. However, a data subject which has suffered damages due to unlawful processing should also have the possibility to sue directly the processor in case he knows or has strong reasons to believe the processor and not (only) the controller is in fact liable. Paragraph 1 clearly acknowledges that and leaves any person the choice to sue the controller, the processor or both. The controller can thus be the so-called single point of entry, but the data subject may choose another procedural avenue.*")

damage"[1396] insofar as they can be held responsible in accordance with paragraphs 2 and 3. As a result, mere involvement in the processing is not sufficient to give rise to liability: the liability of every controller or processor is conditional upon a prior finding of responsibility in causing the damage. Only in cases where the controller or processor can be deemed responsible in accordance with paragraphs 2 and 3 of Article 82 GDPR can either of them be held liable for the entire damage.[1397]

679. Joint vs. separate control – According to Article 82(2), any controller involved in the processing can in principle be held liable for the damages suffered. Read in isolation, one might assume that both joint and separate controllers can be held equally liable for the entire damage. This is not the case. While joint controllers can in principle always be held liable for damages caused by processing activities under their joint control, separate controllers can only be held liable if the damage was caused by a processing activity which was under the control of that particular controller (Article 82(4)). As a result, separate controllers shall still only be liable for the entire damage in case of "concurring faults".[1398]

680. Exemptions – Article 82(3) GDPR provides that a controller or processor shall be exempt from liability if it proves that it is not in any way responsible for the event giving rise to the damage. Article 82(3) GDPR echoes the escape clause of Article 23(2) of Directive 95/46. Interestingly, the GDPR does not contain a recital similar to recital (55) of Directive 95/46, which provides two examples of how the controller might prove that it is not responsible "*for the event giving rise to the damage*". Nevertheless, it is reasonable to assume that the words "*not in any way responsible for the event giving rise to the damage*" should still be interpreted in the same way. As a result, the escape clause of Article 82(3) in principle refers exclusively to "*events beyond control*", i.e. an abnormal occurrence which cannot be averted by any reasonable measures and which does

---

1396 Due to the apparent confusion among DAPIX delegates regarding the concept of "joint and several" liability, the decision was made to drop the terms entirely. Council of the European Union, Note from Presidency to JHA Counsellors on the proposed General Data Protection Regulation – Chapter VIII, 2012/0011 (COD), 9083/15, 27 May 2015, p. 3 ("*Given the fact that the concept of joint and several liability seems to mean different things to different delegations, the new drafting avoids this term altogether.*")

1397 See also Council of the European Union, Note from Presidency to JHA Counsellors on the proposed General Data Protection Regulation – Chapter VIII, 2012/0011 (COD), 9083/15, 27 May 2015, p 3 ("*[E]ach non-compliant controller and/or processor involved in the processing are held liable for the entire amount of the damage. However a controller or processor is exempted from this liability if it demonstrates that it is not responsible for the damage (0% responsibility). Thus only controllers or processors that are at least partially responsible for non-compliance (however minor, e.g. 5%) with the Regulation, and/or in case of a processor, with the lawful instructions from the controller, can be held liable for the full amount of the damage.*")

1398 Compare *supra*, no. 205.

not constitute the realisation of the risk for which the person is strictly liable.[1399] If anything, the addition of the words "*in any way*" (in comparison to Article 23(2) of Directive 95/46), suggests a desire to tighten the scope of the escape clause even further.[1400] Finally, the incorporation of the intermediary liability exemptions contained in the e-Commerce Directive by way of Article 2(4) makes clear that the exemptions now also apply in cases concerning data protection liability.[1401]

681. NON-MATERIAL DAMAGES – It is worth noting that Article 82(1) GDPR explicitly recognises that data subjects may seek compensation for both material and non-material damages. In doing so, the EU legislature has clarified that the right to compensation extends to "non-pecuniary damages". While this was arguably already the case under Directive 95/46[1402], the clarification is nevertheless welcome with a view of removing doubt and ensuring a harmonised approach among EU Member States.

1399 Cf. *supra*, no. 187.

1400 See also P. Larouche, M. Peitz and N. Purtova, "Consumer privacy in network industries – A CERRE Policy Report", *l.c.*, p. 58.

1401 Pursuant to Article 1(5)b of the e-Commerce Directive, it could be argued that the liability exemptions for intermediary service providers did not apply to cases concerning liability under Directive 95/46.

1402 Cf. *supra*, no. 163.

CHAPTER 8
CONCLUSION

1. INTRODUCTION

682. Outline – The objective of this Chapter is to synthesize how the controller and processor and processor concepts developed over time. While tracing the origin and development of both concepts, special consideration will be given to how the concepts have been used to determine the allocation of responsibility and liability. Three questions in particular shall serve as a guide:

(a) Does the instrument formally define who is responsible for compliance?
(b) How does the instrument deal with situations of outsourcing? Is there a formal recognition of agents "acting on behalf of" the entity responsible for compliance?
(c) How are responsibility and liability allocated? Is every actor subject to its own independent obligations? Or is a contractual approach adopted?

2. DEVELOPMENT OF THE CONTROLLER CONCEPT

2.1. THE MEANING OF "CONTROL"

683. Etymology – According to Sjöblom, the term "control" was brought into the English language in the late middle ages from the French "*contre-rôle*", which meant "duplicate register".[1403] The original meaning of "control" was thus "*to take and keep a copy of a roll of accounts and to look for errors theirein*" or "*to check or verify, and hence to regulate*".[1404] By the 17th century, "control" also referred to the nature of the relationship between the verifier and the verified, signifying "mastery" over something or someone.[1405]

1403 G. Sjöblom, "Control in the History of Computing: Making an Ambiguous concept Useful", *IEEE Annals of the History of Computing* 2011, p. 88.
1404 *Id.*, with reference to the Oxford English Dictionary.
1405 *Ibid*, p. 86.

684. Control in the context of computing – During the 1940s, computers were seen (and often designated) as "control systems".[1406] For example, computers were deployed for purposes of "gunfire control" or "inventory control".[1407] During the late 1950s, the term "control" became increasingly associated with "management control" in the context of organisational theory.[1408] In this context, the concept of "control" has been associated with the generic management process.[1409] The generic management process comprises different elements, such as

> "(1) setting objectives;
> (2) deciding on preferred strategies for achieving those objectives, and then
> (3) implementing those strategies while
> (4) making sure that nothing, or as little as possible, goes wrong".[1410]

Both meanings of "control" also found their application in the context of computing and, eventually, in the context of data protection law. As Sjöblom observes:

> "[C]ontrol suggests agency – that someone is using computer-based systems to control something and achieve a certain objective [...] With its undertone of domination, control helps highlight issues of power relations inherent in computer use [...]."[1411]

In the data protection context, the "controller" is viewed as an entity which processes personal data to achieve a certain objective, deriving outputs from inputs to further its organisational mission. A controller is also the entity "in charge" of the processing, even when he decides to enlist a third party (the processor) to process the personal data on its behalf. Finally, exercising control over the processing of personal data can also serve to exercise control over the individuals concerned (e.g. in the form surveillance, or the granting or withholding of privileges).

2.2. NATIONAL LAWS BEFORE 1980

685. No fixed terminology – Before the term "controller" became a legal term of art, those responsible for ensuring compliance with data protection laws

1406 *Ibid*, p. 88.
1407 *Id.*
1408 *Id.*
1409 K. A. Merchant and D.T. Otley, "A Review of the Literature on Control and Accountability", in C. S. Chapman, A. G. Hopwood and M. D. Shields (eds.), *Handbook of Management Accounting Research*, Vol. 2, 2007, Amsterdam, Elsevier, p. 785.
1410 *Id.*
1411 G. Sjöblom, "Control in the History of Computing: Making an Ambiguous concept Useful", *l.c.*, p. 88.

went by many names. By 1980, more than a third of the then 24 OECD member countries had adopted national data protection legislation.[1412] None of these laws employed a term which etymologically resembled the word "controller". Instead, the laws either did not formally define the actors responsible for compliance (e.g. Hesse[1413], France[1414], Norway[1415], Denmark[1416]), or used varying terminology for doing so (e.g. "responsible keeper"[1417], "storing authority"[1418], "client"[1419], or "owner"[1420]).

686. Recurring elements – Despite the notable differences in terminology, there were two recurring elements in the language used by national legislatures which determined how responsibility should be allocated. The first element is the element of *mastery*: the entity designated for compliance had the ability to exercise power over the processing, in one form or another. Specifically, the entity may be "*entitled to exercise control*" (Hesse), enjoy a "*power of disposal*" (Sweden) or have "*the ability to decide about the creation*" of the processing (France). A second recurring element involves the concept of *gain*: responsibility was bestowed upon the entity which reaps the benefits of the output of the processing. For example, the processing is being carried out *for "the purposes" or "activities" of the entity concerned* (Sweden), or the data are being processed "*for his account*" (Germany, France).

687. Technological mindset – Data protection laws adopted prior to 1981 are characterized by their use of technical jargon.[1421] The laws often referred to rather technical concepts such as "registers" (Sweden), "files" (France) and "databanks" (Luxembourg). A possible explanation for the differences concerns the prevailing perceptions regarding the state of the art in computing at the time the legislation was adopted. Commentators frequently highlight that the mental models and concepts underlying the terminology used by the

1412 Organisation for economic co-operation and development (OECD), "The Evolving Privacy Landscape: 30 Years After the OECD Privacy Guidelines", *l.c.*, p. 8. The countries were: Sweden (1973), the United States (1974), Canada (1976), Germany (1977), Denmark (1978), Norway (1978), France (1978), Austria (1978) and Luxembourg (1979).

1413 Cf. *supra*, no. 310.

1414 Cf. *supra*, no. 397.

1415 See §23 of Act no. 48 of 9 June 1978 relating to personal data filing systems.

1416 See §20 of the Private Register Act ("*lov om private register*") of 8 June 1978 (no. 293).

1417 See section 8 et seq. of the Swedish Data Act (Datalagen) SFS 1973: 289. See also *supra*, nos. 349 et seq.

1418 See paragraph 2(3) of the Federal Data Protection Act of 27 January 1977, *BGBl.* I No. 7 S. 201, which defined the "speicherende Stelle" as "*anyone who stores data on its own account [for its purposes] or has data stored by others*".

1419 See Article 2, §3 of the Federal Act of 18 October 1978 on the protection of personal data, *Bundesgesetzblatt für die Republik Österreich* 1978, 193. Stück, p. 3619.

1420 See Article 2 of the Law of 31 March 1979 regulating the use of personal data in automated data processing, *Journal Officiel du Grand-Duché de Luxembourg* 11 April 1979, no. 29, p. 581.

1421 V. Mayer-Schönberger, "Generational Development of Data Protection in Europe", *l.c.*, p. 224.

legislature are in some way a by-product of its historical context.[1422] According to Mayer-Schönberger, for example, the first generation of data protection laws were tailored regulate the central data processing centres and centralized data banks envisioned at the time.[1423] The same vision permeated the often technical terms and concepts used in these laws, such as "data bank", "data file" or "data record".[1424] Bing similarly points out that early data protection laws reflected a "dated view" of technology, which concerned itself primarily with visions of large mainframes with files maintained by punch cards.[1425]

2.3. INTERNATIONAL INSTRUMENTS

688. First appearance – The term "controller" became a term of art in data protection policy circles in the course of the discussions surrounding the preparation of Convention 108 and the OECD Guidelines.[1426] Speaking at an OECD symposium in 1977, F.W. Hondius, a representative of the Directorate of Legal Affairs of the Council of Europe, commented on the difficulties in developing a common understanding of key concepts as follows:

> "The main difficulty we encountered in preparing this draft was, to use a computer term, to create interfaces between widely different concepts of the various national legal systems. [...] But we found it worth the effort, after having made an analytical survey of the key concepts of national legislation, to try our hand at international standards. Mr. Benjamin will be pleased to recognize, for example, his "beneficial

[1422] See e.g. Home Office (Great Britain), *Report of the Committee on Data Protection*, *o.c.*, p. 14; J. Bing, "A Comparative Outline of Privacy Legislation", *l.c.*, p. 157; N. Lenoir, "La loi 78-17 du 6 janvier 1978 et la Commission national de l'informatique et des libertés: Éléments pour un premier bilan de cinq années d'activité", l.c., p. 464; D.H. Flaherty, Protecting Privacy in Surveillance Societies. The Federal Republic of Germany, Sweden, France, Canada, & the United States, p. 175; Council of Europe, *Legislation and Data Protection. Proceedings of the Rome Conference on problems relating to the development and application of legislation on data protection*, *o.c.*, p. 14–29; J. Bing, "Data Protection in a Time of Changes", in W.F. Korthals Altes a.o. (eds.), *Information law towards the 21st Century*, Information law series 2, Kluwer Law and Taxation Publishers, Deventer, 1992, p. 247 et seq; and V. Mayer-Schönberger, "Generational Development of Data Protection in Europe", *l.c.*, p. 223.

[1423] V. Mayer-Schönberger, "Generational Development of Data Protection in Europe", *l.c.*, p. 223–224.

[1424] *Id.*

[1425] J. Bing, "Data Protection in a Time of Changes", *l.c.*, p. 247 et seq. The impact of terminology should not, however, be overstated. Even when the terminology is updated (e.g. from "controller of the file" to controller of the processing"), the actual impact remains limited if the substantive provisions are not also updated to accommodate new realities.

[1426] The Committee of Experts tasked with preparing Convention 108 also comprised participants from countries outside of Europe, as well as members of the OECD Expert Group on Transborder Data Barriers and Privacy Protection. The suggestion to use the term "controller" may therefore have originated from either forum.

user" concept, which is disguised in our text as "controller of the record", a clumsy English rendering of the marvellous French expression 'maître du fichier'."[1427]

Inspiration for the term was seemingly sourced from computer science literature, in particular the writings of Rein Turn. In his 1975 book, Hondius noted that computer scientist Rein Turn used the term "controller" to refer to what Hondius would refer to as the "user" of a data bank.[1428] Turn had also used the term "controller" in his contribution to the 1974 OECD seminar on Policy issues in data protection and privacy[1429], as well as in anterior publications (dating back at least to 1967).[1430] Turn's use of the term "controller" displayed strong conceptual similarity with the terms "data controller" and "controller of the file". In his contribution to 1974 OECD seminar, for example, Turn defined the "controller" as *"(an agency) with authority over the data-base system, which specifies the population of subjects, type of data collected, and the protection policies"*.[1431] It stands to reason that the terms "controller of the file" and "data controller" were imported from computer science literature.[1432]

689. Subtle differences – Even though strong similarities exist between the definitions of the terms "controller of the file" (Convention 108) and "data controller" (OECD Guidelines), they are not identical. In particular, the terms used to describe the object of a controller's decision-making power are slightly different. Under the OECD Guidelines, the data controller decides about the *"contents and use"* of personal data.[1433] Under Convention 108, the controller of the file decides about the *purposes of the file*, the *categories of personal data* that will be stored, and the *nature of the operations* applied to those data. A second difference between the Convention and the Guidelines concerns the technological imagery that is used. Whereas the OECD Guidelines focussed on the "processing" of personal data, Convention 108 used even more technology-laden terms such as "automated data file", "automatic processing" and "controller of the file". The Convention's reliance on the notion of a "file" would soon be perceived as antiquated. Speaking at a 1982 conference on problems relating to the development and application of data protection law, Paul Sieghart argued that the very notion of a "file" was already out of date:

1427 F.W. Hondius, "The Action of the Council of Europe with regard to International Data Protection", in OECD, *Transborder Data Flows and the Protection of Privacy*, *o.c.*, p. 260 (emphasis added). See also *supra*, no. 438.

1428 See F.W. Hondius, *Emerging data protection in Europe*, *o.c.*, p. 101–103.

1429 See R. Turn, "Data security: costs and constraints", in OECD, *Policy issues in data protection and privacy. Concepts and perspectives*, *o.c.*, p. 244 et seq.

1430 See e.g. H.E. Peterson and R. Turn, "System implications of information privacy", in Proceeding AFIPS '67, (Spring) Proceedings of the April 18–20, 1967, spring joint computer conference, ACM, New York, p. 293.

1431 R. Turn, "Data security: costs and constraints", *l.c.*, p. 244.

1432 See also *supra*, no. 438.

1433 Cf. *supra*, no. 435.

> "What is relevant isn't the file, any more than the computer installation, or indeed even the content of the file or of the installation. What is important is the activity, the task, the application for which the original data are being used, and what one gets to once again is the question of encouraging the right information flows, and seeking to discourage the wrong ones".[1434]

Other commentators similarly observed that the idea of centralized data banks was "an idea which belongs to yesterday"[1435] One should no longer think in "monolithic" and "unitary" terms when it comes to data protection[1436], but instead think in terms of processing operations and information processing systems.[1437]

2.4. NATIONAL LAWS AFTER 1981

690. UK and Belgian Data Protection Acts – Interestingly, the UK Data Protection Act (1984) adopted neither the term "controller of the file" nor the term "data controller". Instead, it employed the term "data user", a term similar to the term "databank user" which had featured in previous Council of Europe documents.[1438] Terminological differences aside, the definition of a data user in the 1984 UK Act was substantively very similar the definitions contained in the OECD Guidelines and Convention 108.[1439] The Belgian Data Protection Act (1992) more closely mirrored both the terminology and definition of the "controller of the file" contained in Convention 108.

691. Recognition of shared control – The 1984 UK Data Protection Act formally recognized that the processing might be controlled by more than one entity. It did so by defining the data user as a person who "*either alone or jointly or in common with other persons*" controls the contents and use of the data. The Act thus immediately distinguished two types of shared control, namely "joint

1434 Council of Europe, *Legislation and Data Protection. Proceedings of the Rome Conference on problems relating to the development and application of legislation on data protection*, o.c., p. 16–17.

1435 *Ibid*, p. 20.

1436 Council of Europe, *Legislation and Data Protection. Proceedings of the Rome Conference on problems relating to the development and application of legislation on data protection*, o.c., p. 14–15.

1437 *Ibid*, p. 27 (noting that the French data protection authority, the CNIL, was increasingly called upon to pronounce itself over the use of networked information systems, rather than over the creation of "files").

1438 See the Explanatory Report accompanying Council of Europe Resolution (73)22 regarding private sector data banks, paragraph 15.

1439 Although the formal definition of a data user referred to the "contents and use" (similarly to the OECD definition), the explanation of these terms mapped with the definition of Convention 108 (item and type of data to be recorded, purposes).

control" (whereby control is exercised by several data users acting together) and "control in common" (whereby several users share a pool of information, but each use the information for his own purposes independently of the other).[1440] The Belgian Data Protection Act of 1992 did not formally recognize the possibility that the decision-making power over the processing might be exercised by more than one entity.[1441] Commentators soon observed, however, that there may be situations in which it is impossible to appoint a single controller (particularly in cases where different sets of processing activities were wholly or partially integrated with one and other).[1442]

2.5. DIRECTIVE 95/46 AND THE GDPR

692. From "file" to "processing" – The initial Commission proposal for a European Data Protection Directive defined its scope in terms of "data files". The continued use of the term "file" was soon criticized, however, by the members of the Economic and Social Committee, who felt that the concept was too narrow.[1443] The Committee felt that the concept of "processing of personal data" rather than "file" should be used to define the scope of the Directive.[1444] The Commission readily agreed on the grounds that the concept of a "file" was outdated and irrelevant given the development of automation and telecommunications.[1445] The amended Commission proposal thus passed from a "static" definition linked to concept of a file to a more "dynamic" definition linked to the processing activity.[1446]

693. From "data, operations and access" to "means" – In the Commission's original proposal, the role of controller would stem from determining four elements: objectives, personal data, operations and third

[1440] Cf. *supra*, no. 497.

[1441] To the contrary, the preparatory works clearly indicate that the purpose of the definition was to arrive at a single controller for each processing.

[1442] Cf. *supra*, no. 531.

[1443] Economic and Social Committee, "Opinion on: the proposal for a Council Directive concerning the protection of individuals in relation to the processing of personal data; the proposal for a Council Directive concerning the protection of personal data and privacy in the context of public digital telecommunications networks, in particular the integrated services digital network (ISDN) and public digital mobile networks; and – the proposal for a Council Decision in the field of information security (91/C 159/14)", OJ 17 June 1991 C 159/40.

[1444] *Id.*

[1445] See Commission of the European Communities, Amended proposal for a council directive on the protection of individuals with regard to the processing of personal data and on the free movement of such data, COM(92) 422 final – SYN 287, 15 October 1992, p. 3. See also D. Bainbridge, *EC Data Protection Directive*, *o.c.*, p. 25.

[1446] Opinion 1/2010, *l.c.*, p. 13.

parties having access to them.[1447] The Council reduced the four elements to two, by referring only to the "purposes and means".[1448] According to the Article 29 Working Party, the practical significance of this change should not be overstated:

> "The final formulation of the provision, referring only to "purposes and means", cannot be construed as being in contradiction to the older version, as there cannot be any doubt about the fact that e.g. the controller must determine which data shall be processed for the envisaged purpose(s). Therefore, the final definition must rather be understood as being only a shortened version comprising nevertheless the sense of the older version. In other words, "means" does not only refer to the technical ways of processing personal data, but also to the "how" of processing, which includes questions like "which data shall be processed", "which third parties shall have access to this data", "when data shall data be deleted", etc."[1449]

694. RELATIONSHIP "PURPOSE" AND "MEANS" – The definition of a controller in Directive 95/46 treats the elements of "purpose" and "means" as equal. Strictly speaking, it does not attach greater weight to either element. Nevertheless, scholars and regulators soon began to emphasize the importance of the element of "purpose" over the element of "means".[1450] This tendency can be explained in part by a desire to be pragmatic (to accommodate the fact that entities that process personal data "on behalf" of other entities often substantially influence the means of the processing). A more compelling justification for this approach is the fact that the finality pursued by (a set of) processing operations fulfils a fundamental role in determining the scope of the controller's obligations, as well as when assessing the overall legitimacy and/or proportionality of the processing (see in particular Article 5(1)b-e and Article 6(1)b-f of the GDPR).[1451] In the end, it is the "purpose" of the processing which establishes whether the collection of personal data is legitimate.[1452]

1447 *Ibid*, p. 14

1448 *Ibid*, p. 13.

1449 *Ibid*, p. 14.

1450 See D. De Bot, *Verwerking van persoonsgegevens*, *o.c.*, p. 46 and Office of the Information Commissioner, "Data Protection Act, 1998 – Legal Guidance", Version 1, not dated, 16. Bainbridge has even raised the question as to whether it might have been better to identify the controller based on who determines the purposes alone (See D. Bainbridge, EC Data Protection Directive, *o.c.*, p. 128.). Proposals in this sense were also made during the legislative process surrounding the GDPR. Cf. *supra*, no. 615.

1451 For a comprehensive analysis of the fundamental role that the finality principle plays within data protection regulation see S. Gutwirth, "De toepassing van het finaliteitsbeginsel van de Privacywet van 8 december 1992 tot bescherming van de persoonlijke levenssfeer ten opzichte van de verwerking van persoonsgegevens", *l.c.*, p. 1409–1477 and S. Gutwirth, *Privacy and the information age*, *o.c.*, p. 97–102.

1452 Economic and Social Committee, "Opinion on: the proposal for a Council Directive concerning the protection of individuals in relation to the processing of personal data; the proposal for a Council Directive concerning the protection of personal data and privacy in the context of public digital telecommunications networks, in particular the integrated

695. Strategic importance of "means" – Despite several proposals to remove the reference to "means" from the definition of controller[1453] in the GDPR, it was decided to keep both elements. The EDPS argued that both elements should be retained, as they have both "contributed to the understanding and delineation of the roles of controllers and processors".[1454] In my opinion, there is also a strategic dimension related to the element of "means". Deleting "means" would arguably make it more difficult to qualify third party service providers as "controllers". Specifically, the deletion of "means" would make it easier for service providers who effectively determine the "means" of the processing (but have limited interest in the purposes pursued by their clients) to argue that their influence over the processing does not warrant a qualification as (co-)controller.[1455] The Working Party's distinction between "essential" and "non-essential" can more readily be understood when viewed in this light.

696. Multiplicity of control – An important characteristic of Directive 95/46 was its recognition of shared or "joint" control. The EU legislature mainly envisioned situations whereby a number of parties jointly determine the purposes and means of the processing as a whole. According to the Article 29 Working Party, however, full joint control, whereby by all controllers equally determine the purposes and means of the processing, is only one of many different kinds "pluralistic" control.[1456] Faced with the increasing complexities of data processing, the Working Party took upon itself the task of differentiating between the different forms in which shared control might manifest itself. Arguably, the Working Party has at times gone farther in its interpretation of the controller concept than initially contemplated by the drafters of Directive 95/46.[1457]

---

services digital network (ISDN) and public digital mobile networks; and – the proposal for a Council Decision in the field of information security (91/C 159/14)", *l.c.*, p. 40.

1453 See European Parliament, Opinion of the Committee on Industry, Research and Energy (ITRE), 26 February 2013, Amendment 80; Opinion of the Committee on Internal Market and Consumer Affairs (IMCO), 28 January 2013, Amendment 62; Opinion of the Committee on Legal Affairs (JURI), 25 March 2013, Amendment 38 and European Parliament, LIBE Committee, "Amendments 602–885", 4 March 2013, PE506.145v01-00, amendments 746–48. The deletion of "means" was also supported by the authors of an External Report commissioned by the European Parliament: see X. Konarski, D. Karwala, H. Schulte-Nölke and C. Charlton, "Reforming the Data Protection Package", *l.c.*, p. 31 and the arguments provided there.

1454 European Data Protection Supervisor (EDPS), "Additional EDPS comments on the Data Protection Reform Package", 15 March 2013, p. 6.

1455 See also MEP amendment 748, which justified the deletion of means as follows: "*The aim of the change is not to lower the level of protection for the individual but to clarify that only the controller and not the processor is responsible. See related Amendments to articles 22, 24, 26 and 77.*"

1456 Opinion 1/2010, *l.c.*, p. 18.

1457 See also L. Moerel, *Binding Corporate Rules: Corporate Self-Regulation of Global Data Transfers*, Oxford, Oxford University Press, 2012, p. 220–222.

697. Approach of the GDPR – The increasing complexity of modern processing operations led several commentators to question the continued viability of both the controller and processor concepts. In the end, however, the EU legislature followed the viewpoint of the Article 29 Working Party who considered that the concepts themselves remained valid.[1458] Legislative changes instead focused on the obligations and implications associated with each concept, resulting in more specific provisions as regards the obligations, responsibilities and liability of both controllers and processors.[1459] The legislative changes also codified parts of the guidance provided by the Article 29 Working Party under Directive 95/46 (e.g. rules on joint control) and confirmed certain general principles of tort law (e.g. rules on "cumulative" liability). The following section, which analyses the development of processor concept, will further clarify how the distribution of responsibility between controllers and processors evolved over time.

3. DEVELOPMENT OF THE PROCESSOR CONCEPT

3.1. NATIONAL LAWS BEFORE 1980

698. Delegation and outsourcing – From the very first data protection laws, policymakers were mindful of the fact that data processing frequently involved outsourcing. Although the Hessian Act of 1970 did not formally define the concept of a "processor", it did refer to the "*operators of data processing centres*" and persons responsible for implementing the processing ("*betrauten personen*"). The Swedish Data Act also made mention of persons and organisations who handled personal registers "on behalf of" a responsible keeper. Nevertheless, the "processor", understood as a third party who processes data as a service to others, was mainly present in the background. It was not until the late 1970s that so-called "computer service bureaux" or "computer service agencies" gained more formal recognition in national data protection laws.[1460]

1458 Opinion 1/2010, *l.c.*, p. 33 ("*In its analysis, it has emphasized the need to allocate responsibility in such a way that compliance with data protection rules will be sufficiently ensured in practice. However, it has not found any reason to think that the current distinction between controllers and processors would no longer be relevant and workable in that perspective.*") and European Commission, "Evaluation of the implementation of the Data Protection Directive", Annex 2, *l.c.*, p. 10.

1459 European Commission, "Evaluation of the implementation of the Data Protection Directive", Annex 2, *l.c.*, p. 10.

1460 The "computer service agency" was formally recognized by §20 of the Danish Act no. 293 concerning private registers of 8 June 1978 ("Lov om private registre m.v."); whereas §22 of Norwegian Act no. 48 of 9 June 1978 relating to personal data filing systems formally regulated "data processing enterprises".

699. Execution vs. Authority – The "power to decide" and the "ability to act" do not necessarily coincide. The early data protection laws differentiated between those entitled to make strategic decisions about the processing of personal data and those who merely execute instructions. For example, section 3 of the Hesse Data Protection Act implied that the decision-making power over the disclosure of data may lie elsewhere than with the actual holders of the data. In the Swedish Data Act, the definition of a "responsible keeper" was designed to target the entity that actually "controlled" the register, as opposed to those who were merely passively following instructions.[1461] The French LIFL repeatedly differentiated between, on the one hand, the entity that "*decided about the creation of data processing*", "*ordered*" or "*had others carry out*" personal data processing, and on the other hand, the entities who might be engaged in the processing of personal data on behalf of others (i.e. the entities "*performing the processing*", the "*holders*" of the files).

700. Accountability of the principal – The early data protection laws implicitly embraced the notion that when someone engages a third party to process personal data on his behalf, he remains responsible for ensuring compliance. For example, the Hesse Data Protection Act, which in principle applied only to the public sector, also found application in situations where a public authority commissioned a private entrepreneur to process data on its behalf.[1462] In the same vein, the Swedish Act Data Act provided for strict liability of the "responsible keeper" in cases where an individual suffered harm because of inaccurate data, regardless of whether the processing of data had been outsourced or not.[1463]

701. Subject to regulation – While the entity possessing the power to decide about the processing may have been "ultimately" responsible for compliance, those involved in the implementation were by no means exempted. The privacy laws of Hesse, Sweden and France all allocated certain responsibilities upon entities acting "on behalf of" the responsible entity, whether they were acting in

---

[1461] In the early stages of the preparation of the Swedish Act, the term "file keeper" had been used in lieu of the term "responsible keeper". The replacement was reportedly made because the term "responsible keeper" made it clearer that the term referred to the party that actually controlled the file and made decisions on its contents. The concept therefore excluded service bureaus and other parties that might have been involved in the processing of a personal register without actually "controlling" it. (see P.G. Vinge, *Swedish Data Act*, *o.c.*, p. 9).

[1462] Hessischer Landtag, *Vorlage des Datenshutzbeauftragten betreffend den Ersten Tätighkeitsbericht*, *l.c.*, p. 11. The Data Protection Commissioner emphasized that in case of outsourcing the public authorities concerned remained responsible and accountable for the implementation of appropriate data protection measures. (*Ibid*, at p. 33). ("*Verantwortlichkeit der Verwaltungen – Entgegen manchen Äusserungen und Erwartungen ist daran zu erinnern, dass die volle verantwortung für die Durchführen des Datenschutzes den Behörden und Stellen obliegt, die mit der maschinellen Datenverarbeitung befasst sind.*")

[1463] Cf. *supra*, no. 342 and 358.

the capacity of a service provider or as an employee.[1464] For the most part, their responsibilities were limited to (a) duties of confidentiality; (b) an obligation to ensure security of processing; as well as (c) a general duty to co-operate with supervisory authorities.[1465]

3.2. INTERNATIONAL INSTRUMENTS

702. PROCESSORS NOT REGULATED – Neither Convention 108 nor the OECD Guidelines formally defined the concept of a "processor", nor did they assign any responsibility to the entities acting "on behalf" of the controller. The Explanatory Memoranda made clear that "service bureaux" or persons who merely carry out the instructions issued by a controller were not targeted by either instrument. In case of the OECD Guidelines, however, the Explanatory Memorandum explicitly noted that Member countries remained free to develop "more complex schemes of levels and types of responsibilities" when implementing the Guidelines[1466]:

> "[...] nothing in the Guidelines prevents service bureaux personnel, "dependent users" [...] and others from also being held accountable. For instance, sanctions against breaches of confidentiality obligations may be directed against all parties entrusted with the handling of personal information [...]."[1467]

703. CONTROLLER ACCOUNTABIILTY – The controller retained his responsibilities, under both Convention 108 and the OECD Guidelines, when engaging a third party to process personal data on his behalf. This premise was

---

1464 Cf. *supra*, no. 314 (Hesse); no. 357 (Sweden) and no. 402 (France).

1465 Still, notable difference existed between the three acts. Under the Hessian Act, responsibility for ensuring compliance with the Hesse Data Protection Act was shared, at least in part, by all entities involved in the preparation and execution of automatic data processing. While the Swedish Data Act imposed fewer obligations upon those who merely executed the processing, two of its provisions explicitly targeted persons or organisations acting "on behalf of" a responsible keeper (duty of confidentiality, duty to co-operation with the Data Inspection Board). The French LIFL imposed a wider range of obligations upon persons or organisations processing personal data on behalf of others, ranging from an obligation to maintain the security of processing, to the duty to co-operate supervisory authorities and the accommodation of data subject rights.

1466 Organisation for economic co-operation and development (OECD), Explanatory Memorandum to the OECD Guidelines on the Protection of Privacy and Transborder Flows of Personal Data, paragraph 40.

1467 Organisation for economic co-operation and development (OECD), Explanatory Memorandum to the OECD Guidelines on the Protection of Privacy and Transborder Flows of Personal Data, paragraph 62. For a detailed discussion of the "processing services" and "data services" offered by "computer service bureaux" at the time see J. Bing, P. Forsberg and E. Nygaard, "Legal problems related to transborder data flows", in OECD, *An Exploration of Legal Issues in Information and Communication Technologies, Information Computer Communication Policy* no. 8, Paris, OECD, 1983, p. 129–131.

most explicit in the definition of a "data controller" in the OECD Guidelines, which defined the data controller as the party who is competent to decide about the contents and use of the data, "*regardless of whether or not such data are collected, stored, processed or disseminated by that party or by an agent on its behalf.*" The principle of accountability (paragraph 14) further reinforced the notion that the data controller remained responsible even when the processing was to be outsourced to a third party.

3.3. NATIONAL LAWS AFTER 1981

704. Formal recognition – Data protection laws after 1981 (e.g. UK, Belgium, and Netherlands) formally recognized "processors" as separate entities, worthy of their own statutory definition. National laws varied significantly, however, as to the extent to which they imposed obligations directly upon these entities.

705. UK Data Protection Act – From its inception, the drafters of the UK Data Protection Act foresaw responsibilities for both "data users" and "computer bureaux". Despite lobbying efforts by the computer services industry, the House of Lords wound up rejecting the notion that computer bureaux should be left outside the scope of the Act. Computer bureaux would be subject to the Act, but would have far fewer responsibilities bestowed upon them. Computer bureaux were mainly obliged to (1) register their activities; (2) act in conformity with instructions of the data user as well as the terms of the relevant register entries; and (3) ensure the security of processing. The remainder of the obligations provided under the Act were directed almost exclusively to data users. Nevertheless, bureaux were subject to the supervision of the Registrar and were exposed to the risk of both civil and criminal liability for activities residing within their sphere of control. A similar approach was adopted in the Netherlands under the Dutch Data Protection Act of 1988.[1468]

706. Belgian Data Protection Act – The Belgian Data Protection Act of 1992 recognized the concept of a "processor", but did very little with it in terms of further regulation. The main purpose of the term was seemingly to reinforce the responsibility of the controller, regardless of how the processing was organized.

707. Agency – The definition of a "computer bureau" in the UK Act made clear that the any processing of personal data by the bureau occurred on an

---

[1468] For more information see A.C.M. Nugter, *Transborder Flow of Personal data within the EC*, *o.c.*, p. 171–172.

agency basis. According to the Data Protection Registrar, however, "agency" in this context merely meant "*a person acting for others*" rather than as an agent in a contractual sense.[1469] Because a computer bureau acted "on behalf" of a data user, it was in principle not allowed to disclose personal data without prior authorization by the data user who controls that data.[1470]

3.4. DIRECTIVE 95/46 AND THE GDPR

A. *Directive 95/46*

708. ROLE OF THE PROCESSOR – Although not defined in the initial Commission proposal, the final version of Directive 95/46 defined the "processor" as a separate entity. The motivation for regulating "processing on behalf of the controller" was to avoid situations whereby processing by a third party on behalf of the controller would have effect of reducing the level of protection enjoyed by the data subject.[1471] According to the Article 29 Working Party, the processor concept wound up serving a dual purpose within the framework of Directive 95/46, namely:

a) to identify the responsibilities of those entities who are closely involved in the processing, but are doing so on behalf of one or more other entities (controller(s));
b) to help distinguish between those entities that are responsible for compliance on the one hand, and those entities that are merely executing the instructions they have been given.[1472]

709. AGENCY – The main substantive component of the processor concept is that a processor acts "on behalf" of a controller. The Article 29 Working Party has approximated this wording with the legal concept of delegation, whereby one entity requests another entity to undertake certain actions on its behalf.[1473] Directive 95/46 implicitly views processors as passive agents, who merely execute instructions received from the controller and have no determinative influence over the processing. This explains why the Directive imposes only the limited obligation of adhering to instructions issued by the controller.

1469 The Data Protection Registrar, "The Data Protection Act 1984: The Definitions", *l.c.*, p. 12.
1470 See also HL Deb, 21 July 1983, vol. 443, at cc 1299–1300 (discussing the exemption to the non-disclosure requirement for access requests by law enforcement and its relationship to computer bureaux).
1471 Cf. *supra*, no. 551.
1472 Opinion 1/2010, *l.c.*, p. 7.
1473 *Id.*

710. Limited accountability – Under Directive 95/46, responsibility for compliance rests entirely with the controller. Processors are in principle only indirectly responsible, by virtue of a contract or other legal act which binds them to the controller. Earlier draft versions of the Directive foresaw a number of obligations that would be directly incumbent upon processors. In the final version, however, only one obligation remained, namely the duty not to process personal data except on instructions from the controller (Article 16). Directive 95/46 also did not afford data subjects with direct recourse against processors (although such recourse could be provided by national law).

711. Contractual safeguards – The extent to which the processor complies with the substantive norms of Directive 95/46 hinges primarily upon the contractual safeguards which are put in place. Article 17(3) of the Directive obliges controllers to put in place a contract or other legal act "binding the processor to the controller", which must specify that the processor is obliged (1) to follow the controller's instructions at all times and (2) to implement appropriate technical and organisational measures to ensure the security of processing. Article 17(3) only mentions the minimum content that should be included in an arrangement between controllers and processors, so it is not excluded that controllers bind their processors to additional data protection principles or safeguards.

B. GDPR

712. Concepts intact – The proposal of the European Commission left the concepts of controller and processor intact.[1474] As indicated earlier, the Commission considered the concepts themselves to be largely unproblematic.[1475] The proposed changes instead focused on (a) specifying the obligations of each actor in greater detail; (b) defining additional obligations for processors; and (c) addressing the relationship between joint controllers.[1476]

713. Direct and indirect accountability – The GDPR retains the general principle that the controller carries "primary" or "overarching" responsibility for ensuring compliance. It also recognizes, however, that processors can play an important role in ensuring compliance. The GDPR

[1474] The Commission only proposed one minor change to definition of a controller, namely adding the word "conditions". See also P. De Hert and V. Papakonstantinou, "The proposed data protection Regulation replacing Directive 95/46/EC: A sound system for the protection of individuals", *Computer Law & Security Review* 2012, vol. 28, p. 133 and P. Blume, "Controller and processor: is there a risk of confusion?", *l.c.*, p. 143.

[1475] Cf. *supra*, no. 593.

[1476] See also P. De Hert and V. Papakonstantinou, "The proposed data protection Regulation replacing Directive 95/46/EC: A sound system for the protection of individuals", *l.c.*, p. 133.

imposes a number of obligations directly upon processors, without necessarily making them dependent on the existence of a "contract or other legal act" between the controller and processor. While contractual safeguards continue to play an important role, the enforceability of certain obligations is no longer contingent upon the existence of such arrangements. For example, with or without a contract, processors are obliged to maintain documentation, ensure an appropriate level of security and co-operate with supervisory authorities. Processors are also directly liable towards data subjects with respect to the activities that fall under their responsibility.

714. More contractual safeguards – The GDPR provides that the relationship between controllers and processors must be governed by a contract or legal act which binds the processor to certain obligation vis-à-vis the controller. In comparison to Directive 95/46, the number of elements to be included in the arrangement between controllers and processors has increased considerably. Under Article 28(3), the arrangement must at a minimum specify the subject-matter and duration of the processing, the nature and purpose of the processing, the type of personal data and categories of data subjects and the obligations and rights of the controller. Other mandatory elements include, but are not limited to: the obligation to process personal data only on instructions of the controller (including in relation to international transfers); the obligation to respect restrictions regarding sub-processing; and the obligation to delete or return all the personal data to the controller after the end of the provision of services.

715. Agency – The GDPR did not deviate from the fundamental premise that the processor should be viewed as an "agent" of the controller and therefore must be bound to adhere to the controller's instructions unless required by law to act otherwise. As a result, the controller in principle remains liable for the actions performed by the processor. The processor faces independent liability, however, in case of failure to comply with its legal obligations or controller instructions (Article 82(2)).

PART IV
USE CASES

CHAPTER 1
INTRODUCTION

"A functional theory does not necessarily translate into a successful practice".
Jonathan Zittrain[1477]

716. Preface – For more than 20 years, the controller-processor model has provided the analytical template for the allocation of responsibility and liability among actors involved in the processing of personal data. While the model itself appears conceptually sound, its application in practice has not always been straightforward. The research objective of this Part of the book is to identify the main issues that surround the practical application of the controller-processor model. To this end, a number of real-life use cases will be examined.

717. Selection criteria – Needless to say, it is impossible to document and analyse every possible use case. A selection needs to be made. In social science research, case selection is generally driven by two objectives, namely (1) *representativeness* (i.e. ensuring that the selected cases are sufficiently representative in light of the research question) and (2) *variety* (i.e. ensuring useful variation on the dimensions of theoretical interest).[1478] A third, sometimes implicit, objective is *relevancy* (i.e. ensuring that the selected use cases are likely to yield insights which can assist in answering the research question).[1479]

718. Relevancy – As the research objective of this Part of the book is to document the issues that arise when applying the controller-processor model in practice, the pool of potentially relevant use cases is limited to instances in which

---

1477 J. Zittrain, "Privacy 2.0", *University of Chicago Legal Forum* 2008, No. 1, article 3, p. 68.

1478 J. Seawright and J. Gerring, "Case Selection Techniques in Case Study Research – A Menu of Qualitative and Quantitative Options", *Political Research Quarterly* 2008, Vol. 61, No. 2, p. 296.

1479 Seawright and Gerring refer to this as "purposeful" (as opposed to "random") selection of case studies. (*Ibid*, p. 295). For additional information regarding criteria for case selection see R.K. Yin, *Case Study Research – Design and Methods*, 2009, London, Sage Publications, Fourth Edition, p. 91–92; R.K. Yin, *Applications of Case Study Research*, 2012, London, Sage Publications, Third Edition, p. 32–39; D.R. Hensler, *Designing Empirical Legal Research: A Primer for Lawyers*, 2011, second revision, p. 101–105 and A.L. George and A. Bennet, *Case Studies and Theory Development in the Social Sciences*, 2005, London, MIT Press, p. 83–84.

such issues occur. In the first phase of selection, a preliminary literature study was undertaken to identify eligible use cases. The threshold for eligibility was the existence of some indication, either in regulatory guidance or doctrine, that the use case in question challenges either the application of the controller and processor concepts or the associated allocation of responsibility and liability.[1480] Each of the retained use cases has been cited by scholars and/or regulators as instances where the application of the controller-processor concepts can be challenging, or where the effective allocation of responsibilities and liability may be undermined.

719. VARIETY – Once the initial screening for relevancy was completed, a further selection was made with the aim of ensuring a sufficient degree of variety. In practice, the control capabilities of actors involved in the processing of personal data are shaped by the social context in which they operate (e.g. public sector, business-to-business, business-to-consumer, consumer-to-consumer). Variations in control capabilities are clearly "variables of interest" in light of the problem statement of this book.[1481] As a result, it was considered desirable to ensure that the selected use cases concern a variety of social contexts which involve different power dynamics and control capabilities among the actors involved in the processing of personal data.

720. REPRESENTATIVENESS – The utility of use case analysis is generally predicated, at least in part, on the proposition that the selected use cases are sufficiently representative.[1482] The analysis conducted in Part V of this book offers some support for the proposition that the selection of use cases made here has in fact been sufficiently representative. Part V of the book will analyse the proposals for change which have been put forward over time in relation the controller-processor model. When comparing the rationale of each of these proposals to the typology of issues derived from the analysis of use cases, it appears that at least one relevant counterpart can be found in each instance.[1483]

1480 It obviously cannot be excluded that there may be other relevant use cases, which have not (yet) been identified by regulators or scholars as presenting issues for the practical application of the controller or processor model. This touches on the issue of representativeness, which will be discussed shortly. Before tackling the question of representativeness, however, it is first of all necessary to ensure relevancy and it is asserted the approach adopted here is a viable (albeit heuristic) method of doing so.

1481 Both the "broken binary" and "threshold for control" problem statements indicate that difficulties in application of the controller-processor model occur, at least in part, due to a misalignment between, on the one hand, the roles and responsibilities of controllers and processors as defined by law and, on the other hand, their effective control capabilities in practice. Cf. *supra*, nos. 8 et seq. The term "variables of interest" has been borrowed from D.R. Hensler, *Designing Empirical Legal Research: A Primer for Lawyers*, *o.c.*, p. 15–17.

1482 See also J. Seawright and J. Gerring, "Case Selection Techniques in Case Study Research – A Menu of Qualitative and Quantitative Options", *l.c.*, p. 306–307.

1483 See also *infra*, no. 1177.

721. Selected use cases – The four use cases which have been selected for analysis are:

(1) e-government identity management;
(2) online social networks;
(3) cloud computing; and
(4) internet search engines.

722. Analysis – Over the following chapters, each of the selected uses cases will be analysed in a structured and focused manner.[1484] First, an overview of the main types of actors and interactions will be provided. Next, the legal status and obligations of each actor shall be analysed, taking into account the different interpretations put forward by courts, regulators and scholars. Finally, at the end of each use case, an evaluation will be made of the main issues that have been identified when applying the controller-processor model to the use case in question. The identified issues will serve as the main input for the typology of issues discussed in Part V.

1484 The analysis will be "structured" in the sense that the analysis of each use case shall be composed of the same subsections and will answer the same questions in relation to each use case. The analysis shall be "focused" in that the analysis will extend only to those aspects which are relevant for purposes of the research question which this Part seeks to address. Based on A.L. George and A. Bennet, *Case Studies and Theory Development in the Social Sciences*, *o.c.*, p. 67 et seq.

CHAPTER 2
E-GOVERNMENT IDENTITY MANAGEMENT

1. INTRODUCTION

723. A DEFINITION OF "E-GOVERNMENT" – Public service delivery is increasingly permeated by information and communication technologies (ICTs). ICTs are deployed for a variety of reasons: cost reduction, convenience, citizen empowerment, fraud prevention, etc.[1485] Historically, the public sector has always shown a strong interest in the use of ICT.[1486] Somewhere in the 1990s, the trend towards increased ICT usage in the public sector received the label of "e-government".[1487] E-government has been defined by the World Bank as

> "the use by government agencies of information technologies (such as Wide Area Networks, the Internet, and mobile computing) that have the ability to transform relations with citizens, businesses, and other arms of government."[1488]

724. APPLICATIONS – At a high level, one can distinguish between five types of e-government applications:

(1) *Access to information* (e.g. dissemination of information to the public through websites);
(2) *Citizen participation* (e.g. online consultations or e-petitions);
(3) *Electronic procurement* (e.g. electronic tender submissions);
(4) *Government-to-government information and service integration* (e.g. re-use of citizen data across governmental departments); and

---

1485 J. Deprest and F. Robben, *eGovernment: the approach of the Belgian federal administration*, 2003, p. 6.

1486 As explained in Part III of this thesis, it was the increased use of ICTs by the public sector that triggered the enactment of the first data protection laws in the early 1970s. Cf. *supra*, nos. 285 et seq.

1487 A. Grönlund and T.A. Horan situate the origin of the term "e-Gov" in the late 1990s, alongside other "e-terms" such as e-Commerce that accompanied the Internet boom. See A. Grönlund and T.A. Horan, "Introducing e-Gov: history, definitions and issues", *Communications of the Association for Information Systems* 2004, Vol. 15, p. 713–729.

1488 The World Bank, *Definition of E-Government*, http://web.worldbank.org (last accessed 30 April 2014).

(5) *Compliance and access to benefits* (e.g. filing of tax returns, requests for permits or social security benefits, etc.).[1489]

725. Role of "identity management" – The relationship between citizens and public administrations is highly personal in nature.[1490] Many governmental services – in particular those belonging to the fifth category above – require identification of their intended recipients. Most of these services also require verification of additional attributes, such as "age", "place of residence", or "professional qualification". Remote delivery of government services requires mechanisms to corroborate the identity and other attributes of the individuals concerned. This is where electronic identity management (eIDM) systems play a role. eIDM systems enable governments both to *identify* and *authenticate* the users of their systems and services.[1491]

726. National strategies – Today, most European countries have developed – or at least launched the development of – a national identity management strategy.[1492] One of the primary objectives of these strategies is to enable remote identification and authentication of citizens. In keeping with this objective, several Member States have moved from purely paper-based identification documents towards electronic identity (eID) cards.[1493] Very often, these electronic identity cards are based on Public Key Infrastructure (PKI).[1494] For transactions which only require a low level of entity authentication assurance,

1489 T.A. Pardo, "Realizing the Promise of Digital Government: It's More than Building a Web Site", *Information Impact Magazine* 2000, p. 3–4. See also Z. Fang, "E-Government in Digital Era: Concept, Practice, and Development", *International Journal of The Computer, The Internet and Management* 2002, Vol. 10, No.2, p. 4.

1490 S.S. Garcia, A.G. Oliva, E.P. Belleboni and I.P. De La Cruz, "Current Trends in Pan-European Identity Management Systems", *IEEE Technology and Society Magazine* 2012, Vol. 31, Issue 3, p. 45.

1491 J.C. Buitelaar, M. Meints and B. Van Alsenoy (eds.), "Conceptual Framework for Identity Management in eGovernment", *FIDIS project*, Deliverable D16.1, 2008, p. 20.

1492 See e.g. Capgemini, IDC, Sogeti, and Politecnico di Milano, "Future-proofing eGovernment for a Digital Single Market", Final Insight Report, June 2015, Study prepared for the European Commission DG Communications Networks, Content and Technology. For a discussion of national identity management strategies among OECD countries see OECD, *Digital Identity Management: Enabling Innovation and Trust in the Internet Economy*, 2011, p. 27 et seq.

1493 It is worth underlining, however, that not all European countries have adopted this approach. Most governments have built upon the existing means for identity verification offline and extended or adapted them to the online world. As a result, eID cards are mainly found in countries which have a tradition with paper-based national identity cards. Countries which do not have such a tradition have developed alternative approaches to introducing digital credentials (e.g. by building on digital credentials provided by banks). (OECD, *Digital Identity Management: Enabling Innovation and Trust in the Internet Economy*, *o.c.*, p. 38–39).

1494 See H. Graux and J. Majava, "eID Interoperability for PEGS. Analysis and Assessment of similarities and differences – Impact on eID interoperability", *IDABC project*, 2007, p. 72 et seq.

alternative mechanisms such as username-password combinations and other non-PKI-based tokens are also accepted.[1495]

727. THE ROLE OF THE EUROPEAN UNION – Since the mid-1990s, the EU has actively sought to promote interoperability among EU public administrations.[1496] The driving force behind these initiatives has been the desire to foster greater co-operation among European public services and to enable cross-border service delivery.[1497] Inevitably, the issue of electronic identity management became increasingly important. Delivery of so-called "Pan-European e-Government Services" (PEGS), would require interoperability between national identity management systems.[1498] To achieve this objective, the EU launched a wide range of initiatives (agendas, roadmaps, action plans, research projects ...) with a strong focus on eID interoperability.[1499] The guiding

---

1495 The Belgian government, for example, issues not only an eID card but also user-name password combinations and a "federal token". Which credential may be used for which transactions depends primarily on the level of assurance required. For a more detailed discussion see D. De Cock, B. Van Alsenoy, B. Preneel and J. Dumortier, "The Belgian eID Approach", in W. Fumy and M. Paeschke, *Handbook of eID Security. Concepts, Practical Experiences, Technologies*, 2011, Publicis, Erlangen, p. 117 et seq.

1496 N.N.G. de Andrade, "'Electronic Identity for Europe': Moving from Problems to Solutions", *Journal of International Commercial Law and Technology* 2013, Vol. 8, No.2, p. 104. One of the first initiatives was the Interchange of Data between Administrations (IDA) programme which was launched in 1995. (Council Decision of 6 November 1995 on a Community contribution for telematic interchange of data between administrations in the Community (IDA) (95/468/EC), OJ L 269/23, 11 November 1995. The IDA programme was eventually followed up by the IDABC and ISA programmes. See Decision 2004/387/EC of the European Parliament and of the Council of 21 April 2004 on interoperable delivery of pan-European eGovernment services to public administrations, businesses and citizens (IDABC), OJ 18 May 2004, L-181 (corrig.), p. 25–35 and Decision No 922/2009/EC of the European Parliament and of the Council of 16 September 2009 on interoperability solutions for European public administrations (ISA), OJ 3 October 2009, L-260/20.

1497 S.S. Garcia, A.G. Oliva, E.P. Belleboni and I.P. De La Cruz, "Current Trends in Pan-European Identity Management Systems", *l.c.*, p. 45.

1498 *Id.*

1499 N.N.G. de Andrade, "'Electronic Identity for Europe': Moving from Problems to Solutions", *l.c.*, p. 104. The increased emphasis on eID interoperability was particularly visible in the i2010 eGovernment Action Plan and the Roadmap for a pan-European eID Framework. See European Commission, *i2010 eGovernment Action Plan: Accelerating eGovernment in Europe for the Benefit of All*, SEC(2006) 511, 24 April 2006 and European Commission, A Roadmap for a pan-European eIDM Framework by 2010, 2006, v1.0. The Roadmap included a list of measurable objectives and milestones for the construction of such framework. It later reconfigured the objectives with the launch of the Digital Agenda, which included two important key actions in the field of eID, namely (1) a proposal for a Council and Parliament Decision on mutual recognition on e-identification and e-authentication across the EU based on online "authentication services" to be offered in all Member States; and (2) a proposal for a revision of the eSignature Directive7 with a view to provide a legal framework for cross-border recognition and interoperability of secure eAuthentication systems. (N.N.G. de Andrade, "'Electronic Identity for Europe': Moving from Problems to Solutions", *l.c.*, p. 104–105.) This eventually led to the adoption of the Regulation (EU) No 910/2014 of the European Parliament and of the Council of 23 July 2014 on electronic identification and trust services

principle in those initiatives has been the construction of a European cross-border eIDM framework, based on interoperability and mutual recognition of national eID resources and management systems.[1500]

728. Outline – The objective of this chapter is to discuss how EU data protection law relates to e-government identity management systems. It will start by identifying the main actors and processes involved in e-government identity management systems. Next, it will analyse the legal status ("role") of each actor, as interpreted by policymakers, regulators and scholars. After that, two real-life examples will be presented to illustrate how responsivity and liability have been allocated in the context of e-government identity management, as well as the issues that arise. The first example concerns the Internal Market Information (IMI) System, one of the very first Pan-European e-government applications. The second example concerns cross-border identification and authentication, in particular the measures taken so far to enable interoperability of identity management systems at pan-European level.

2. ACTORS

729. Selection criteria – The current inventory of actors is based on a literature study of the output of various research projects[1501], academic publications[1502], policy documents[1503] and international standards[1504] concerning identity management and/or e-government. A common denominator among the identified actors is that they participate in the operation of identity management systems, which can be described as

---

for electronic transactions in the internal market and repealing Directive 1999/93/EC (OJ 28 August 2014, L 257/73–114).

1500 N.N.G. de Andrade, "'Electronic Identity for Europe': Moving from Problems to Solutions", *l.c.*, p. 104. See also J.C. Buitelaar, M. Meints and B. Van Alsenoy (eds.), "Conceptual Framework for Identity Management in eGovernment", *l.c.*, p. 61–64.

1501 E.g. the STORK (Secure idenTity acrOss boRders linKed); IDABC (Interoperable Delivery of European eGovernment Services to public Administrations, Businesses and Citizens); FIDIS (Future of Identity in the Information Society) and the LEGAL IST project.

1502 E.g. H. Leitold and B. Zwattendorfer, ""STORK: Architecture, Implementation and Pilots", in N. Pohlmann a.o. (eds.), ISSE 2010 Securing Electronic Business Processes, Springer, 2010, p. 131–142 and D. De Cock, *Contributions to the Analysis and Design of Large-Scale Identity Management Systems*, Dissertation presented in partial fulfilment of the requirements for the degree of Doctor in Engineering, June 2011, 234 p.

1503 E.g. J. Deprest, and F. Robben, *eGovernment: the approach of the Belgian federal administration*, *o.c.*, 57 p.

1504 E.g. ISO/IEC Information technology – Security techniques – Entity authentication assurance framework, ISO/IEC 29115:2013(E), 1 April 2013, 36 p.; International Telecommunication Union (ITU), Entity authentication assurance framework, Recommendation ITU-T X.1254, September 2012, 44 p. and International Telecommunication Union (ITU), Telecommunication Standardization Sector Focus Group on Identity Management, *Report on Identity Management Framework for Global Interoperability*, 30 p.

"the organisational and technical infrastructure used for the definition, designation and administration of identity attributes."[1505]

730. Actors overview – The following types of entities[1506] may be considered as main entities involved in the operation of e-government identity management systems:

(1) Citizen;
(2) Authoritative source;
(3) Credential Service Provider (CSP);
(4) Integrator;
(5) Verifier; and
(6) Relying Party.

731. Visual representation – The aforementioned entities interact with each other in a variety of ways. The following figure provides a – highly simplified – representation of how these entities typically interact in the context of an e-government identity management system. It is intended to be conceptual rather than factual.

Figure 2. Main entities in e-government identity management systems

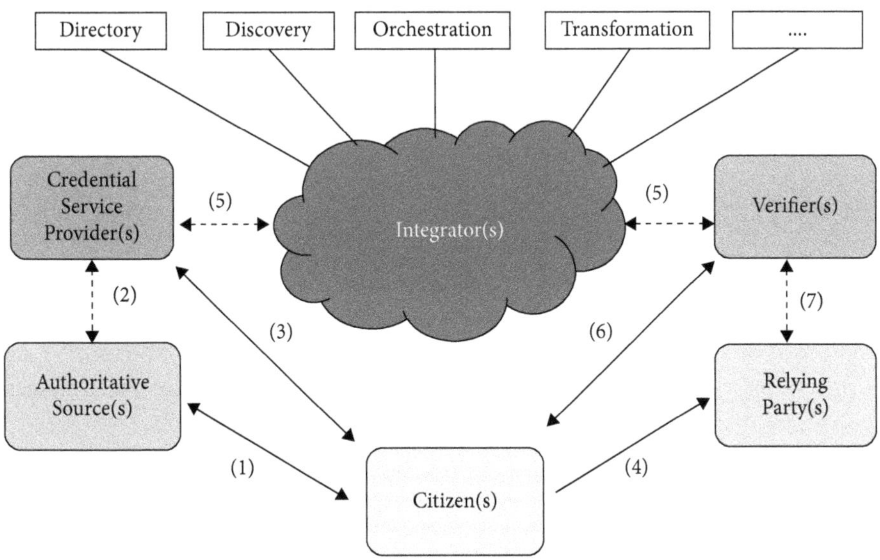

[1505] Modinis project, Common Terminological Framework for Interoperable Electronic Identity Management, Consultation Paper, v2.01, 23 November 2005, p. 12.

[1506] The term "entity" (instead of "actor") is used to signal that each identified "actor" could in principle be either a separate legal entity or a purely technical component operated by the same actor. For example, a Relying Party might operate its own verification service, in which case the "Verifier" depicted in Figure 2 would not be a separate legal entity but rather a component operated by the Relying Party.

732. Legend – The arrows in Figure 2 indicate that an exchange of personal data is taking place. Solid black arrows signify exchanges of personal data which occur primarily "in the foreground", meaning that they can easily be observed or inferred by citizens. They typically imply some form of active involvement by the citizen (e.g. manually entering data, use of an application). Dashed grey arrows were used to signify data exchanges which may be less obvious to citizens. Over the following sections, each of the actors and interactions displayed in Figure 2 will be briefly described.

733. Combinations possible – The reader should note that the categories of entities identified in Figure 2 are by no means mutually exclusive. A given actor may combine multiple roles depending on the circumstances. For example, an Authoritative Source might also act as a CSP, or a Verifier might also operate its own integration service.[1507] The entities identified in Figure 2 should therefore be thought of as conceptual building blocks, which may be provided by one or more actors.

734. Common purpose – As indicated earlier, e-government identity management systems are used to *identify* and *authenticate* individuals who make use of governmental systems or services. They may also be used to corroborate other attributes of the individuals concerned. While the actors depicted in Figure 2 may pursue any range of purposes as part of their daily activities, the following sections will focus on each entity's involvement (or "contribution") in enabling the identification and authentication of citizens' identity attributes.

2.1. CITIZEN

735. Main characteristics – In an identity management context, a citizen is understood primarily as the *subject of a digital identity*.[1508] This identity can be composed of any number of attributes (e.g. name, gender, date of birth,).[1509] As a rule, at least one of these attributes shall consist of an *identifier* which allows

1507 Similarly, a citizen might also operate its own "integrator", e.g. in the form of a middleware software component.

1508 Of course, not only citizens or individuals have digital identities. An identity might also refer to a software component or device. For purposes of conceptual clarity, however, the discussion here focuses only on identities relating to citizens.

1509 From a holistic perspective, the "identity" of an entity can be described as the dynamic collection of all attributes relating to that entity. As such, the identity of an entity is a fluid and evolving concept, rather than a practical one. Identity management systems actually focus on a specific subset of relevant attributes, commonly referred to as "partial" or "digital" identities. (Modinis project, Common Terminological Framework for Interoperable Electronic Identity Management, Consultation Paper, *l.c.*, p. 6 and 12 and the workshops held in the context of the EU FIDIS project).

the citizen to be uniquely recognized within a particular context.[1510] Provided the citizen has also been issued the appropriate credentials, it will be possible to *authenticate* his or her identity remotely.[1511]

736. Related processes – Before creating a digital identity, a government will have collected various data about its citizens. These data are kept in one or more Authoritative Sources (see below). Standard identity data includes information such as first and last name, gender, date of birth and place of residence.[1512]

737. Data flows – The data flows which facilitate identification and authentication of citizens are represented in Figure 2 by arrows (1) through (7). Each of these data flows will be elaborated further over the following sections.

2.2. AUTHORITATIVE SOURCE

738. Main characteristics – In the context of identity management, corroboration of identity information typically involves consultation of one or more "authoritative sources".[1513] An authoritative source can be described as a repository of information which is recognized as being an accurate and up-to-date source of certain information within a particular context.[1514] An example of an authoritative source in the Belgian e-government would be the National Register, which is recognized as being the authoritative source for citizen

1510 An identifier can be described as an attribute or a set of attributes of an entity which uniquely identifies the entity within a certain context. (Modinis project, Common Terminological Framework for Interoperable Electronic Identity Management, Consultation Paper, *l.c.*, p. 12). An entity can be known under more than one identifier. In an e-government context, this identifier is typically assigned by a governmental entity at a very early stage (e.g. the national population register might assign a national identification number at birth).

1511 See also International Telecommunication Union (ITU), Entity authentication assurance framework, Recommendation ITU-T X.1254, *l.c.*, p. 9.

1512 For an example see D. De Cock, B. Van Alsenoy, B. Preneel and J. Dumortier, "The Belgian eID Approach", *l.c.*, p. 123.

1513 See e.g. D. Chadwick, "Federated Identity Management", in Alessandro Aldini, Gilles Barthe and Roberto Gorrieri (eds.), *Foundations of Security Analysis and Design V*, FOSAD 2007/2008/2009 Tutorial Lectures, Springer, 2009, p. 97–99.

1514 See also J.C. Buitelaar, M. Meints and B. Van Alsenoy (eds.), "Conceptual framework for identity management in e-government", *l.c.*, p. 45. In many documents authoritative sources are also referred to as "authentic sources" or "authentic registers" (see e.g. the European Commission Information Society and Media Directorate-General, E-government Unit, "A roadmap for a pan-European eIDM framework by 2010", *l.c.*, p. 5. I have chosen to use of the term "authoritative" as it is more in line with identity management literature and because I believe the term "authoritative" better captures their actual role (it reflects the idea that they are seen as trustworthy within a certain context). Moreover, use of the term "authentic" may also in the long run engender confusion with concepts such as "authentication" or "data authenticity" in the way traditionally used in computer sciences.

attributes such as full name, gender, data of birth, official address, marital status, etc.[1515]

739. Information as a strategic resource – In order to maximize administrative efficiency, several governments have introduced the principle of "single collection" into their e-government policies.[1516] This approach entails that the citizen's personal data is collected only once, and is later shared and re-used by other governmental entities.[1517] The designation of a repository as an authoritative source entails that this repository shall be considered the primary (and perhaps even "sole") source for the information within a particular context.[1518]

740. Related processes – In principle, each item of data shall be subject to *proofing* and *verification* before being registered with an authoritative source.[1519] Once the data have been verified with an appropriate degree of assurance, the data shall be registered with the authoritative source. If not previously assigned, the authoritative source will assign one or more unique identifiers which can be used to identify and recognize the citizen in the future.

741. Data flows – Arrow (1) depicts the process of proofing and verification. Arrow (1) is bi-directional because the authoritative source may assign an identifier to the citizen (in case where it will not rely on a previously assigned identifier).

1515 D. De Cock, B. Van Alsenoy, B. Preneel and J. Dumortier, "The Belgian eID Approach", *l.c.*, p. 125–126.

1516 See e.g. J. Deprest and F. Robben, *eGovernment: the approach of the Belgian federal administration*, *o.c.*, p. 7. The EC eIDM Roadmap developed by the DG Information Society and Media of the European Commission also advocates single collection of personal data (European Commission, A Roadmap for a pan-European eIDM Framework by 2010, 2006, v1.0, Block VIII). See also European Data Protection Supervisor (EDPS), "EDPS Opinion on the proposal for a Regulation establishing a single digital gateway and the 'once-only' principle", Opinion 8/2017, 1 August 2017, p. 7.

1517 The use of authoritative sources is typically justified by the advantages of having single points of contact to update and manage information. Specifically, this approach helps to avoid the existence of multiple copies of the same information in different databases, among which discrepancies may start to develop over time. It is also said to increase convenience for citizens, as they will not be asked to provide the same information over and over again. See J. Deprest and F. Robben, eGovernment: the approach of the Belgian federal administration, *o.c.*, p. 6.

1518 Verification against authoritative sources can take place at various stages of the life-cycle of an identity and can serve different purposes (during enrolment, authentication, authorization, etc.). The generic purpose is typically to confirm the validity of a certain proposition (e.g. an asserted attribute, the revocation status of a credential) in real time (B. Van Alsenoy, N. Vandezande, K. Janssen, a.o., "Legal Provisions for Deploying INDI services", *l.c.*, p. 21).

1519 For example, a citizen declaring a change of address might be required to present a photo ID at the moment of declaration. This declared change of address might subsequently be verified by a police officer visiting the citizen at his or her new home. In practice, the proofing and verification process may be conducted by a separate entity (sometimes referred to as the "Registration Authority").

A subset of data recorded by an authoritative source may be incorporated in a credential which is later issued to the citizen or verifier (see below).

2.3. CREDENTIAL SERVICE PROVIDER

742. Main characteristics – A Credential Service Provider (CSP) is an entity that issues and/or manages credentials.[1520] Classic examples of credentials include passwords and digital signatures.[1521] In a narrow sense, the term "credential" refers only to data and does not include the hardware or software used to produce these data.[1522] However, CSPs may manage these aspects as well.[1523] For purposes of simplicity, this chapter does not further distinguish among the actors who might be involved in the creation and management of credentials.[1524]

743. Related processes – Credential management comprises all processes relevant to the lifecycle management of a credential or the means to produce credentials.[1525] It may involve some or all of the following processes: (1) creation; (2) issuance; (3) activation; (4) storage (5) revocation and/or destruction; (6) renewal and/or replacement and (7) record-keeping.[1526]

1520 International Telecommunication Union (ITU), Entity authentication assurance framework, Recommendation ITU-T X.1254, *l.c.*, p. 2. A credential can be described as a set of data presented as evidence of a claimed identity and/or attribute (*Id.*).

1521 *Ibid*, p. 9 and 30.

1522 Id. The term "credential" is thus used in very narrow sense here: it refers only to the data, not the token which incorporates the credential (e.g. the smart card containing the private key to generate a digital signature). See also Modinis project, Common Terminological Framework for Interoperable Electronic Identity Management, *l.c.*, p. 10.

1523 International Telecommunication Union (ITU), Entity authentication assurance framework, Recommendation ITU-T X.1254, *l.c.*, p. 9.

1524 It is important to realize, however, that the credential management process may involve a plurality of actors. In case of the Belgian eID card, for example, the following actors are involved in the credential management process: (1) the municipalities, which act as the front-office registration and issuance authorities; (2) the National Register, which provides the necessary information for the creation of eID cards; (3) the card manufacturer (Zetes), who also acts as both the Card Initializer (CI) and the Card Personalizer (CP); (4) Certipost, who acts as the Certificate Authority (CA) and (5) Group 4 Securitor, which acts as a secure mail carrier for transportation of the eID cards and card request forms between the municipalities and the card manufacturer. (D. De Cock, B. Van Alsenoy, B. Preneel and J. Dumortier, "The Belgian eID Approach", *l.c.*, p. 126). In this model, Zetes is the credential service provider *strictu sensu* as it generates the cryptographic key pairs which enable the eID card to create digital signatures. It also acts as the card manufacturer. However, the certificates corresponding to the public verification keys are issued by a separate entity, i.e. the Certificate Authority (Certipost). (*Ibid*, p. 129–130).

1525 International Telecommunication Union (ITU), Entity authentication assurance framework, Recommendation ITU-T X.1254, *l.c.*, p. 13 et seq.

1526 *Id.*

744. Levels of assurance – Different credentials support different levels of entity authentication assurance.[1527] The Level of Assurance ("LoA") associated with a particular credential conveys the degree of confidence which a relying party may have that the identity (or other attribute) claimed by a particular entity in fact belongs to that entity.[1528] The type of credentials issued, as well as the safeguards that are implemented by the CSP, are key factors in determining which LoA will be reached during a particular authentication protocol.[1529]

745. Data flows – In principle, a CSP will only collect data emanating from an authoritative source (arrow (2)). Once a credential has been prepared, it can be issued to the citizen in question (arrow (3)). Arrow (3) is bi-directional as a citizen may notify the CSP that a credential should be revoked (e.g. in case of loss or theft). A verifier consults the CSP to request or confirm the validity of a credential concerning a particular citizen (arrow (5)). As shown in Figure 2, the interaction between a CSP and a verifier can also be mediated by an integrator.

2.4. INTEGRATOR

746. Main characteristics – An integrator is an intermediary that facilitates interactions between entities that provide and consume identity-related services. Typical integrator services include (but are not limited to):

1527 Entity authentication assurance can be described as "degree of confidence reached in the authentication process that the entity is what it is, or is expected to be". International Telecommunication Union (ITU), Entity authentication assurance framework, Recommendation ITU-T X.1254, *l.c.*, p. 2.

1528 In recent years, several initiatives have been undertaken in order to develop a common understanding and standardized approach to the issue of EAA. See e.g. W.E. Burr, D. F. Dodson and W.T. Polk, *Electronic Authentication Guideline*, NIST SP800-63, v1.0.2; Graux, H., Majava, J., "eID Interoperability for PEGS – Proposal for a multi-level authentication mechanism and a mapping of existing authentication mechanisms", *IDABC*, December 2007; Glade, B., *Identity assurance framework: Assurance Levels*, v2.0, 24 April 2010, Kantara Initiative; ISO/IEC, Information technology -- Security techniques -- Entity authentication assurance framework, *l.c.*, 36 p. and International Telecommunication Union (ITU), Entity authentication assurance framework, Recommendation ITU-T X.1254, *l.c.*, 44 p. The overall approach of these initiatives is the following. They start by defining a number of assurance levels, typically four (e.g. "low", "moderate", "high" and "very high"). They then define the technical and organisational requirements which must be met in order to meet a certain level of assurance. This approach is designed to help decision-makers assess what type of authentication mechanisms are appropriate for which applications, and whether or not reliance on a particular eID solution is suitable for their purposes. (B. Van Alsenoy, N. Vandezande, K. Janssen, a.o., "Legal Provisions for Deploying INDI services", *l.c.*, p. 32).

1529 International Telecommunication Union (ITU), Entity authentication assurance framework, Recommendation ITU-T X.1254, *l.c.*, p. 12 et seq.

(1) discovery; (2) orchestration; and (3) transformation.[1530] An example of an integrator in the Belgian e-government context would be the Crossroads Bank for Social Security (CBSS).[1531]

747. Role of integrators – Early on, e-Government architects realized that transforming resources and applications into functional products for end-users generally requires putting in place additional building blocks and services. Use of intermediaries or "integrators" was recommended to reduce the potential burden on individual service providers. The services offered by an integrator become part of a common framework, which could be then leveraged when developing applications.[1532] Section 5 will analyse two real-life examples of European e-Government integrators, namely the Internal Market Information (System) and the Pan-European Proxy Service (PEPS).

748. Related processes – In order to facilitate interactions between the providers and consumers of identity related services, an integrator must compile and maintain a directory of relevant resources (e.g. a list of trusted credential service providers). That way, when a verifier requests the attestation of identity information, the integrator will have at its disposal an overview of the sources from which a valid attestation might be obtained. Transformation involves the conversion of information from one format (e.g. the format of in which the attribute is provided by the CSP) to another format (e.g. the format understood by the verifier). Orchestration involves the strategic combination of resources to deliver a composite service (e.g. retrieval and verification of identity information from multiple sources to determine eligibility).[1533]

749. Data flows – As shown in Figure 2, integrators in principle only interact with credential service providers (CSP) and verifiers (arrow 5). As explained earlier, it is perfectly possible for an entity to combine multiple roles. For example, an authoritative source might also act as a CSP, or a relying party might also act as a verifier. If that is the case, the integrator will obviously also interact with the authoritative sources and/or relying parties.

1530 X. Huysmans and B. Van Alsenoy (eds.), D1.3 Conceptual Framework – Annex I. Glossary of Terms, IDEM, v1.07, p. 20–21. See also J.C. Buitelaar, M. Meints, and B. Van Alsenoy (eds.), "Conceptual Framework for Identity Management in eGovernment", *l.c.*, p. 16.

1531 For more information see the homepage of the Crossroadsbank of Social Security. See also B. Van Alsenoy, "E-government Solutions: Trends and Developments in Belgian e-Government", in M. Meints and H. Zwingelberg (eds.), Identity Management Systems – recent developments", FIDIS Deliverable D3.17, 2009, p. 43.

1532 B. Van Alsenoy, "E-government Solutions: Trends and Developments in Belgian e-Government", *l.c.*, p. 40.

1533 For an example see B. Bruegger, *Reference Architecture*, FutureID deliverable D21.4, v1.1. 2014, p. 22 et seq.

2.5. VERIFIER

750. Main characteristics – A verifier is an entity that corroborates identity information.[1534] A typical example of a verifier is an authentication service, which verifies the credentials presented by a citizen before he or she is granted access to a particular resource.[1535] An example of a verifier in the Belgian e-government context would be the Federal Authentication Service (FAS).[1536]

751. Related processes – When a citizen wishes to assert his identity (or other identity attributes) towards a relying party, the verifier will execute an authentication protocol designed to establish confidence in the asserted identity information.[1537] Authentication protocol requirements generally vary depending on the required Level of Assurance (LoA).[1538] For example, for a lower LoA, it may be sufficient for users to present a simple username-password combination. For higher LoAs, authentication may involve use of a cryptographic-based challenge-response protocols (which may in turn involve use of hardware tokens such as smart cards). Verification typically also involves checking the validity and/or revocation status of the presented credentials.

752. Data flows – Authentication services typically perform their functions at the moment where a citizen, holder of a digital identity, interacts with a relying party (e.g. to request access to a service). Arrow (4) depicts the request from the citizen to the relying party. Arrow (6) depicts the subsequent interaction between the citizen and verifier. Arrow (5) represents the communication between to the verifier and the CSP, which may (or may not) be mediated by an integrator. The communication between the verifier and the CSP generally serves to establish the validity and/or revocation status of the presented credentials. Arrow (7) depicts the request for authentication by the relying party, as well as the subsequent response by the verifier regarding the outcome of the authentication process.

1534 International Telecommunication Union (ITU), Entity authentication assurance framework, Recommendation ITU-T X.1254, *l.c.*, p. 10.

1535 In principle, a verifier can be involved in multiple stages of an entity authentication scheme and can perform both credential verification and/or identity information verification functions (International Telecommunication Union (ITU), Entity authentication assurance framework, Recommendation ITU-T X.1254, *l.c.*, p. 10). For purposes of conceptual clarity, the discussion here shall be limited to credential verification as part of an authentication protocol.

1536 See also B. Van Alsenoy, "E-government Solutions: Trends and Developments in Belgian e-Government", *l.c.*, p. 41.

1537 International Telecommunication Union (ITU), Entity authentication assurance framework, Recommendation ITU-T X.1254, *l.c.*, p. 16.

1538 *Id.*

2.6. RELYING PARTY

753. Main characteristics – A relying party is an entity that relies on identity information.[1539] The identity information may be relied on for a variety of purposes, such as account management, access control, authorization decisions, etc.[1540] An example of a relying party in the context of Belgian e-Government is the Tax-on-Web application, a service operated by the Ministry of Finance which enables citizens to submit their tax returns online.

754. Related processes – A relying party can itself perform the operations necessary to retrieve and authenticate identity information, or it may entrust these operations to a third party (verifier).[1541]

755. Data flows – Arrow (4) depicts the interaction between the citizen and relying party. Arrow (7) depicts the interaction between the relying party and verifier who has been requested by relying party to authenticate the citizen on its behalf.

3. ROLES

756. Processing pursuant to a legal basis – In an e-government setting, any participant (authoritative source, credential service provider, integrator, ...) might be acting as a controller, processor or third party depending on the application at hand.[1542] When a legal provision mandates a certain form of processing, it should in principle indicate which entity shall act as a controller. Where legislatures are not explicit in this regard, but merely entrust the processing to a particular body, it may be assumed that the latter will be responsible for the processing operations it performs pursuant to this legal basis.[1543]

757. Application of general criteria – While the legal basis which authorizes the processing may provide clarity, there will still be situations where it is difficult to determine whether a governmental entity is acting as a controller

---

1539 International Telecommunication Union (ITU), Entity authentication assurance framework, Recommendation ITU-T X.1254, *l.c.*, p. 9.

1540 *Id.*

1541 International Telecommunication Union (ITU), Entity authentication assurance framework, Recommendation ITU-T X.1254, *l.c.*, p. 9.

1542 J.C., Buitelaar, M. Meints and E. Kindt, "Towards requirements for privacy-friendly identity management in eGovernment", *l.c.*, p. 16.

1543 D. De Bot, *Privacybescherming bij e-government in België. Een kritische analyse van het Rijksregister, de Kruispuntbank van Ondernemingen en de elektronische identiteitskaart*, o.c., p. 35. See also *supra*, no. 235.

or processor. For instance, several governmental entities might be charged with complementary tasks of public interest. This, in turn, might require multiple governmental entities, each within their respective domain, to carry out certain processing operations. If there is no clear specification in the law as to which entity shall act as a controller and/or processor, their respective roles are determined by the general criteria of the controller and processor concepts.[1544]

758. Outline – The aim of this section is to investigate the potential roles of the actors identified in the previous section, using the general criteria of the controller and processor concepts. This exercise is by no means superfluous, as similar configurations arise in private sector identity management applications. At a practical level, it remains necessary to analyse the specific practices within a particular identity management system in order to determine the responsibilities of each actor involved.[1545] The analysis provided in the following sections is therefore of a high-level nature. Section 5 will go more in-depth by analysing two practical examples. Section 5.1 shall describe how the allocation of roles and responsibilities was addressed in the context of the Internal Market Information (IMI) system. Section 5.2 will explore the guidance provided by a subgroup of the Article 29 Working Party in relation to the Pan-European Proxy Service (PEPS).

3.1. CITIZEN

759. High level analysis – Identity information about citizens typically relates to an identified or identifiable individual.[1546] As a result, citizens shall generally qualify as "data subjects" rather than as "controllers" or "processors".

760. Citizens in "control" of their own data? – Certain identity management applications enable citizens to exercise control over the disclosure of identity information. This raises the question as to whether or not citizens might be considered as (co-)controllers towards the processing of their own personal data. There are essentially two arguments which can be made against such a proposition. First, this interpretation cannot be reconciled with the regulatory scheme of EU data protection law. This scheme is predicated on the

[1544] Cf. *supra*, no. 236.

[1545] T. Olsen, and T. Mahler, "Identity management and data protection law: Risk, responsibility and compliance in 'Circles of Trust' – Part II", *l.c.*, p. 420.

[1546] Legal persons and other entities (e.g. association of fact) may also be holders of digital identity in an e-Government context. In order to engage in online transactions, however, they must be represented by a natural person acting as an agent on their behalf. While legal persons do not qualify as data subjects, their legal representatives do. Moreover, in certain instances, the name of a legal person may also identify a natural person, in which case it may constitute personal data.

notion that the data controller is an entity other than the data subject him- or herself. An individual person might act as a controller of personal data relating to others[1547], but not of his or her own personal data. Accepting that the data subject could act as a controller of the processing of his own personal data would have rather absurd implications: the data subject would have to obtain consent from him- or herself, provide him- or herself with notice, etc.[1548] Second, the fact that the data subject authorizes the disclosure of personal information within a certain context merely signifies his or her agreement towards processing. It does not exclude the presence of another entity who determines the "purposes and means" for the processing of these data. Even where the individual has the ability to "control" the release of his or her personal data (and might even decide the medium that is used), this does not alter the role of the collectors or handlers of the individual's data.

3.2. AUTHORITATIVE SOURCE

761. High level analysis – Storage of personal data by an authoritative source typically results from a business activity (in case of private actors) or public mission (in case of public actors). Sometimes the storage of personal data is the primary activity of the authoritative source. The Belgian National Register, for example, has as its main public mission to collect, record and make available certain types of information regarding the inhabitants of Belgium.[1549] In other cases, storage of information by authoritative sources is a by-product of other activities. For example, a hospital patient registry may act as an authoritative source attesting to the existence of a patient-doctor relationship.[1550] Authoritative sources must in principle be considered as "controllers" within the

---

1547 See the Judgment in *Bodil Lindqvist*, C-101/01, EU:C:2003:596. See also B. Van Alsenoy, J. Ballet, A. Kuczerawy and J. Dumortier, "Social networks and web 2.0: are users also bound by data protection regulations?", *l.c.*, p. 69–70; Article 29 Data Protection Working Party, "Opinion 5/2009 on online social networking", WP163, 12 June 2009; European Network and Information Security Agency (ENISA), "Online as soon as it happens", February 2010, p. 33–34. See also *infra*, no. 880.

1548 Alternatively, one could argue that such processing would be exempted from the application of the GDPR under Article 2(2)c (exemption of processing carried out in the course of a purely personal or household activity) (see references in previous footnote). However, this finding would not undercut the argument that the allocation of responsibilities under the GDPR is structured implies that the data subject and the controller are separate entities.

1549 See Articles 1 and 2 of the Law of 8 August 1983 organising a register of natural persons (B.S., 21 March 1984).

1550 For more information see Commissie voor de Bescherming van de Persoonlijke Levenssfeer (CBPL), Sectoraal Comité van de Sociale Zekerheid en van de Gezondheid, Afdeling «Gezondheid», Beraadslaging nr. 11/088 van 18 oktober 2011, gewijzigd op 9 juni 2015, met betrekking tot de nota betreffende de elektronische bewijsmiddelen van een therapeutische relatie en van een zorgrelatie, SCSZG/15/088, 9 June 2015. See also Commissie voor de Bescherming van de Persoonlijke Levenssfeer (CBPL), Aanbeveling nr 09/2012 van 23 mei

meaning of EU data protection law, as they determine the purposes and means of their own processing activities (or have been explicitly entrusted by law to conduct such processing).

762. Scope of control – The control exercised by an authoritative source extends to all their own processing operations, including acts of disclosure to third parties. The authoritative source in principle does not control any of the subsequent processing operations undertaken by CSPs, integrators, verifiers or relying parties. After all, the purposes pursued by an authoritative source in keeping the data shall in principle be distinct from the specific purposes pursued by the entities to whom the personal data is disclosed. The act of disclosure itself, however, is attributable to the authoritative source. As a result, the authoritative source should only agree to make the information available once it has obtained sufficient assurance of the compatibility and/or legitimacy of the processing which the recipient purports to undertake.[1551]

3.3. CREDENTIAL SERVICE PROVIDER

763. High level analysis – A credential service provider shall generally also be considered a controller within the meaning of EU data protection law. While it cannot be excluded that an entity operates a credential service "on behalf of" another entity, credential services are often dedicated services designed and controlled by the entity which provides them.[1552]

764. Scope of control – A credential service provider shall in principle act as a controller in relation to the collection, adaption, storage and transmission of identity information necessary to deliver the credential service. Its control in principle does not extend to any of the subsequent processing operations undertaken by integrators, verifiers or relying parties.

765. Standardisation – While credential service providers decide for themselves how to provide their services, they will often make use of existing standards. Identity management standards and specifications have been developed by a variety of standardisation bodies, including ISO, ITU-T, ETSI

2012 uit eigen beweging in verband met authentieke gegevensbronnen in de overheidssector (CO-AR-2010-005).

1551 See also B. Van Alsenoy, N. Vandezande, K. Janssen, a.o., "Legal Provisions for Deploying INDI services", *l.c.*, p. 25.

1552 See also Article 29 Data Protection Working Party, "Working Document on on-line authentication services", WP 68, 29 January 2003, p. 14 (considers Microsoft as "data controller" in relation to .NET passport, which is an entity which combines the role of CSP and verifier).

and Liberty Alliance.[1553] The Liberty Alliance protocol for identity federation and single sign-on was studied by the Article 29 Working Party as part of its Working Document on on-line authentication services.[1554] The Working Party considered the Liberty Alliance protocol to be "neutral" from a data protection perspective.[1555] It allows compliance with the Directive but does not require it. As far as the obligation to comply with the Directive is concerned, the Working Party made the following observations[1556]:

- the Liberty Alliance is responsible as far as the technical development of the project is concerned;
- each service provider that implements Liberty specifications bears the responsibility of complying with data protection legislation when operating its "Liberty-enabled" web services;
- service providers within a Circle of Trust become data controllers at the time users visit their websites;
- the different participants should have clear contractual agreements in which the obligations of each party concerning data protection aspects are made explicit.[1557]

766. Asssesment – Even though the Liberty Alliance single sign on protocol was considered to be "neutral" from a data protection perspective, the Working Party stated that the Liberty Alliance should make sure that their specifications allow the organisations that implement and use them to comply with the Directive. The Working Party additionally encouraged them to develop recommendations and guidelines that motivate companies to use the technical specifications in a privacy-compliant or even privacy-enhancing manner. It is unclear, however, on which ground such responsibility is based.[1558] Even if designers take data protection issues into consideration when developing technical specifications, it is primarily the organisations that implement these

---

1553 See also *supra*, at footnote 1529.

1554 Article 29 Data Protection Working Party, "Working Document on on-line authentication services", *l.c.*, p. 11–13. Single sign-on is understood as the ability of the consumer to, after having authenticated once with a particular Identity Provider, to interact with various Service Providers within a "Circle of Trust" (CoT) without needing to re-authenticate. Any time a user account has been federated among Service Providers; the Service Provider managing the federated account will be able to act as an authentication service towards other Service Providers who are part of the same Circle of Trust.

1555 *Ibid*, p. 12.

1556 *Ibid*, p. 12 and p. 14–15.

1557 See also J. Alhadeff and B. Van Alsenoy (eds.), "D6.2 Contractual framework", *l.c.*, p. 38–39

1558 T. Olsen and T. Mahler, "Identity management and data protection law: Risk, responsibility and compliance in 'Circles of Trust' – Part II", *l.c.*, p. 418. Of course, if the developed protocols were to impede compliance this could significantly discourage organisations from implementing those specifications.

specifications that shall be responsible for compliance with data protection legislation, although a case-by-case assessment remains necessary.[1559]

3.4. INTEGRATOR

767. High level analysis – The legal status of integrators can be difficult to determine. By definition, an integrator acts as an intermediary. As a result, the integrator may present itself to some as a processor, who merely facilitates the exchange of information on behalf of others. Others might see integrators as controllers, especially if they act autonomously in the development and provisioning of their services. Finally, it is also possible that the integrator determines the purposes and means of its processing in conjunction with others. A useful parallel might be drawn to the SWIFT case, which involved a financial messaging service that combined both controller and processor characteristics.

768. SWIFT – The Society for Worldwide Interbank Financial Telecommunication ("SWIFT") is a worldwide financial messaging service which facilitates international money transfers. SWIFT was organized in 1973 by a group of European banks that wanted to develop a new method to send payment instructions to correspondent banks in a standardised manner.[1560] Later, SWIFT expanded its service catalogue and began offering its services to other types of financial institutions. Despite the fact that SWIFT had always considered itself to be a mere processor of the instructing financial institutions, the Article 29 Working Party held that SWIFT acted as a data controller.[1561] The main reasons advanced to support this conclusion were that[1562]:

1559 T. Olsen and T. Mahler, "Identity management and data protection law: Risk, responsibility and compliance in 'Circles of Trust' – Part II", *l.c.*, p. 418.

1560 Article 29 Data Protection Working Party, "Opinion 10/2006 on the processing of personal data by the Society for Worldwide Interbank Financial Telecommunication (SWIFT)", WP128, 22 November 2006, p. 10. The SWIFT Opinion had been preceded by an investigation conducted by the Belgian Data Protection authority: see Commissie voor de Persoonlijke Levenssfeer, Advies Nr 37/2006 van 27 september 2006 betreffende de doorgifte van persoonsgegevens door de CVBA SWIFT ingevolge de dwangbevelen van de UST (OFAC). See also the subsequent opinion adopted by the CBPL in 2008: Commissie voor de Persoonlijke Levenssfeer, Decision of 9 December 2008 regarding the Control and recommendation procedure initiated with respect to the company SWIFT, 75 p.

1561 Article 29 Data Protection Working Party, "Opinion 10/2006 on the processing of personal data by the Society for Worldwide Interbank Financial Telecommunication (SWIFT)", *l.c.*, 11. For a more detailed discussion of the factual background to the SWIFT case see G.G. Fuster, P. De Hert and S. Gutwirth, "SWIFT and the vulnerability of transatlantic data transfers", *International Review of Law Computers & Technology* 2008, Vol. 22, p. 191–202.

1562 Article 29 Data Protection Working Party, "Opinion 10/2006 on the processing of personal data by the Society for Worldwide Interbank Financial Telecommunication (SWIFT)", *l.c.*, 11. See also B. C. Treacy, "Lessons from SWIFT: the 'controller' v 'processor' dilemma", Complinet 2008, p. 2.

- SWIFT does more than just act on behalf of its clients. It has taken on specific responsibilities which, by their nature and scope, go beyond the usual set of instructions and duties incumbent on a processor;
- SWIFT management operates in the context of a formal cooperative network which determines both the purposes and means of data processing within the SWIFTNet service;
- SWIFT management decides what personal data is processed via that service, and the level of information that is provided to financial institutions in relation to the processing;
- SWIFT management is able to determine the purposes and means of processing by developing, marketing and changing the existing or new SWIFT services (e.g. by determining the standards applicable to its clients as to the form and content of payment orders without requiring their prior consent);
- SWIFT provides added value to the processing, such as the storage and validation of personal data and the protection of personal data with a high security standard;
- SWIFT management had the autonomy to take critical decisions in respect to the processing, such as determining the security standard to be applied to the data and the location of its operating centers;
- SWIFT management negotiates and terminates with full autonomy its services agreements and drafts and changes its various contractual documents and policies.

While acknowledging that some elements suggest that SWIFT may have acted as a processor in the past, the Article 29 Working party considered that the effective margin of manoeuvre possessed by SWIFT management precluded its qualification as a mere processor. On the other hand, SWIFT was not considered to be as acting as the sole controller.[1563] Rather, there existed a joint responsibility among the financial institutions and the SWIFT cooperative for the processing of personal data via the SWIFTNet FIN service.[1564]

1563 Article 29 Data Protection Working Party, "Opinion 10/2006 on the processing of personal data by the Society for Worldwide Interbank Financial Telecommunication (SWIFT)", *l.c.*, 12

1564 The level responsibility was not considered to the same among all the participants. In particular, the Article 29 Working Party argued that: "*[...] joint responsibility does not necessarily mean equal responsibility. Whilst SWIFT bears primary responsibility for the processing of personal data in the SWIFTNet FIN service, financial institutions also bear some responsibility for the processing of their clients' personal data in the service*". (*Ibid*, 13) (emphasis added). Similarly, in its executive summary the Working Party indicated that "*Both SWIFT and instructing financial institutions share joint responsibility, although in different degrees, for the processing of personal data as "data controllers" within the meaning of Article 2(d) of the Directive.*"

769. Assessment – The SWIFT case illustrates the "hybrid" status of integrators, who can display characteristics of both controllers and processors. In the end, it seems that the qualification of an integrator as either controller or processor will depend on which characteristics are perceived as dominant: factual influence over the processing or the auxiliary nature of the service provided.

3.5. VERIFIER

770. High level analysis – An investigation into the legal status of verifiers presents similar issues as the analysis of integrators. Because identity verification is an auxiliary function, performed in support of some other activity, verifiers can easily be viewed as processors. After all, verifiers processes personal data "on behalf of" relying parties or credential service providers. On the other hand, certain verification services may be sufficiently independent and autonomous, thereby justifying the qualification as "controller". The Pan-European Proxy Service (PEPS) illustrates the conceptual difficulties that may arise in determining the appropriate qualification of verifiers.[1565]

3.6. RELYING PARTY

771. High level analysis – A relying party in principle acts as a controller in relation to its own processing operations. Once the identity information has been verified, the party will proceed to process the data for its own purposes. Each relying party therefore has its own responsibility to comply with data protection legislation.[1566]

772. Scope of control – The scope of control exercised by a relying party extends not only to its own processing operation, but also to its decision to make use of the services provided by credential service providers, integrators and/or verifiers. Even in cases where a relying party has limited options, it shall in principle be obliged to assess the possible implications and privacy risks to data subjects when they make use of such services.

1565 Cf. *infra*, nos. 819 et seq.

1566 See also Article 29 Data Protection Working Party, "Working Document on on-line authentication services", *l.c.*, p. 9 ("*It should be clarified in any case that, apart from of the role that Microsoft plays within the .NET Passport system, all participating sites are to be considered as data controllers in respect of their own processing operations. They have therefore their own responsibility to comply with privacy legislation.*").

4. ALLOCATION OF RESPONSIBILITY AND LIABILITY

773. Legal qualification – According to Olsen and Mahler, most identity management systems consist of "multiple collaborating but single controllers".[1567] The previous section confirmed that several entities indeed act as controllers towards their own processing operations. Nevertheless, it cannot be excluded that certain entities assume the role of processor, nor can it be excluded that several entities jointly determine the purposes and means of a particular processing operation.[1568]

774. Responsibilities to be allocated – There are many responsibilities which need to be allocated within an e-government framework in order to ensure compliance with both legal and policy requirements. The following is by no means an exhaustive list of several of the tasks and responsibilities which will most likely need to be considered[1569]:

- which entities shall act as act as authoritative sources for which data sets;
- which entities shall perform which authentications, authorizations and checks;
- which entities will be charged with the maintenance of logs for which operations;
- which entities will be charged with the updating of technical policies;
- which entities shall serve as a front-office to accommodate the rights of data subjects such as the right of access and correction;
- which entities shall serve as a point-of-contact in the event of a security breach; and
- which entities shall be charged with periodic verification of compliance (audit).

775. Role of legislation and policy – The development of e-government applications does not happen overnight. It requires careful planning and co-ordination, as well as a clear vision for the future. Legislation and policy play a key role in securing the participation of all relevant actors. It should also play a key role in defining and delineating the data protection responsibilities of the actors involved. The following section will analyse how the European

1567 T. Olsen and T. Mahler, "Identity management and data protection law: Risk, responsibility and compliance in 'Circles of Trust' – Part II", *l.c.*, p. 420.

1568 See also S. Deadman (ed.), *Circles of Trust: The Implications of EU Data Protection and Privacy Law for Establishing a Legal Framework for Identity Federation*, Liberty Alliance Project, February 23, 2005, p. 15–16.

1569 J.C. Buitelaar, M. Meints and E. Kindt, "Towards requirements for privacy-friendly identity management in eGovernment", *l.c.*, p. 17.

Commission, and eventually the European legislature, approached this issue in the context of the Internal Market Information System.

5. PRACTICAL EXAMPLES

5.1. INTERNAL MARKET INFORMATION SYSTEM (IMI)

A. *Introduction*

776. WHAT IS IMI? – The Internal Market Information (IMI) system is an ICT tool provided by the European Commission designed to facilitate information exchange for purposes of administrative cooperation. In particular, IMI aims at providing support for the practical implementation of Union acts that require an exchange of personal data among Member States' administrations or among Member States and the Commission or other Union bodies, offices and agencies.[1570] Today, IMI supports the implementation of Union acts in the field of the internal market, which are listed in the Annex to the IMI Regulation 1024/2012.[1571] Since 25 May 2018, it also supports the exchange of information among data protection authorities in the context of cross-border cases on the basis of the GDPR.

777. ORIGIN AND DEVELOPMENT – The IMI project officially started in 2005 in the context of the IDABC program.[1572] IMI was initially built to support one-to-one communication between competent authorities in the implementation of the Professional Qualification Directive and the Services Directive.[1573] Over time, the system was gradually expanded to support other areas of administrative

1570 Article 3(1) of Regulation No 1024/2012 of the European Parliament and of the Council of 25 October 2012 on administrative cooperation through the Internal market Information system and repealing Commission Decision 2008/49/EC, OJ 14 November 2012, L 316/1–11, as amended by Directive 2013/55/EU, Directive 2014/60/EU, Directive 2014/67/EU, Regulation 2016/1628 and most recently by the Regulation 2018/1724 of the European Parliament and of the Council of 2 October 2018 establishing a single digital gateway to provide access to information, to procedures and to assistance and problem-solving services and amending Regulation (EU) No 1024/2012. See also recitals (1) and (2) of Regulation No 1024/2012.

1571 Article 3(1) of Regulation No 1024/2012 and its Annex. Examples include the Professional Qualification Directive (2005/36/EC) and implementing acts, the Patients' Rights Directive (2011/24), etc. The IMI system is also used to carry carry out pilot projects order to assess whether IMI would be an effective tool to implement provisions for administrative cooperation of Union acts not listed in the Annex (Article 4 of Regulation No 1024/2012).

1572 See Article (4).

1573 European Data Protection Supervisor (EDPS), Opinion of the European Data Protection Supervisor on the Commission Proposal for a Regulation of the European Parliament and of the Council on administrative cooperation through the Internal Market Information System ('IMI') 22 November 2011, p. 2.

co-operation and to provide additional functionalities (e.g. one-to-many workflows, repository services).[1574] In 2007, the Article 29 Working Party issued a first Opinion regarding data protection issues related to the IMI System. Shortly thereafter, the Commission published a Decision concerning the implementation of the IMI system as regards the protection of personal data.[1575] The Decision was followed by an Opinion of the European Data Protection Supervisor, which outlined additional steps to be taken.[1576] In 2009, the Commission issued a Recommendation containing data protection guidelines for the IMI system.[1577] In 2012, the European and the Council repealed Commission Decision 2008/49/EC by way of Regulation 1024/2012 on administrative cooperation through the Internal Market Information System ("the IMI Regulation").[1578]

1574 *Id.*

1575 European Commission, Commission Decision of 12 December 2007 concerning the implementation of the Internal Market Information System (IMI) as regards the protection of personal data, OJ 16 January 2008, L 13/18.

1576 European Data Protection Supervisor (EDPS), "Opinion of the European Data Protection Supervisor on the Commission Decision of 12 December 2007 concerning the implementation of the Internal Market Information System (IMI) as regards the protection of personal data" (2008/49/EC) (2008/C 270/01), OJ 25 October 2008, C 270/1.

1577 European Commission, Commission Recommendation of 26 March 2009 on data protection guidelines for the Internal Market Information System (IMI), 2009/329/EC, OJ 18 April 2009, L 100/17.

1578 Regulation No 1024/2012 of the European Parliament and of the Council of 25 October 2012 on administrative cooperation through the Internal Market Information System and repealing Commission Decision 2008/49/EC, OJ 14 November 2012, L 316/1–11, as amended by Directive 2013/55/EU, Directive 2014/60/EU, Directive 2014/67/EU and Regulation 2016/1628. Initially, the European Commission relied primarily upon Decision 2004/387/EC (the "IDABC" decision) in combination with the Professional Qualifications Directive and the Services as justification for the processing of personal data within IMI. Both the Article 29 Working Party and the EDPS expressed multiple reservations as to the adequacy of these instruments towards ensuring the legitimacy of processing. (See in particular Article 29 Data Protection Working Party, "Opinion 7/2007 on data protection issues related to the Internal Market Information System (IMI)", WP 140, 20 September 2007, p. 8–10 and European Data Protection Supervisor (EDPS), "Opinion of the European Data Protection Supervisor on the Commission Decision of 12 December 2007 concerning the implementation of the Internal Market Information System (IMI) as regards the protection of personal data (2008/49/EC) (2008/C 270/01)", *l.c.*, paragraphs 12–28.) In its opinion of 2007, the Article 29 Working Party recommended that the Commission adopt an "ad hoc" solution to support the existing legal basis in the form of a Commission Implementing Decision. Decision 2008/49/EC "concerning the implementation of the Internal Market Information System (IMI) as regards the protection of personal data" was adopted in response to this recommendation. Despite this measure, the EDPS continued to express its reservations as to the presence of a sufficient legal basis, particularly in relation to the requirements that such legal basis must be sufficiently clear and specific, and provide a sufficient degree of legal certainty. European Data Protection Supervisor (EDPS), "Opinion of the European Data Protection Supervisor on the Commission Decision of 12 December 2007 concerning the implementation of the Internal Market Information System (IMI) as regards the protection of personal data (2008/49/EC) (2008/C 270/01)", *l.c.*, paragraphs 18 et seq. It was not until 2012 that IMI was provided a solid and independent legal basis by way of Regulation 1024/2012. See also European Data Protection Supervisor (EDPS), "Opinion of the European Data Protection Supervisor on the Commission Proposal for a Regulation of the European Parliament and of the Council

B. *Functionalities*

778. Structured information exchange – The IMI system is a software application, developed by the Commission in cooperation with the Member States, in order to assist with the practical implementation of information exchange requirements laid down in Union acts.[1579] The IMI system acts as a closed network which, for example, allows the "competent authority" of a particular Member State to identify its counterpart in another Member State and to exchange information using the IMI network.[1580] In addition to its search function, IMI provides users with a set of pre-translated menus, as well as standardised questions and procedures to support the information exchange. IMI now also supports one-to-many workflows (e.g. alert mechanisms, notifications) and repository services. All functionalities of IMI are accessible via web pages.[1581]

779. Example – One of the first IMI functionalities was to assist competent authorities in determining the authenticity of credentials presented by an EU citizen from a different Member State. The 2009 Commission Data Protection Guidelines contain an illustrative example:

> "A German doctor resident in Berlin marries a French man and decides to start a new life in Paris. The German doctor wants to practice her profession in France and therefore submits titles and diplomas to the Order of Doctors in France. The person dealing with the file has doubts about the authenticity of one of the diplomas and uses IMI to check with the competent authority in Berlin."[1582]

780. A federation of authoritative sources – In the example above, the IMI network can be conceptualised as a "federation" of authoritative sources for specific attributes.[1583] The IMI system itself thereby acts as an

---

on administrative cooperation through the Internal Market Information System ('IMI')", 22 November 2011. p. 2–3.
Such as Directive 2005/36/EC, L 255/22–142.

1579 Recital (2) of Regulation No 1024/2012.

1580 See also recital (2) of Regulation No 1024/2012.

1581 See Article 29 Data Protection Working Party, "Opinion 7/2007 on data protection issues related to the Internal Market Information System (IMI)", *l.c.*, p. 4.

1582 European Commission, European Commission, Commission Recommendation of 26 March 2009 on data protection guidelines for the Internal Market Information System (IMI), *l.c.*, p. 28.

1583 One should note, however, that IMI currently does not incorporate national eIDM products in any way: IMI users are provided with credentials (username/passwords/roles) through their national co-ordinators and local administrators. In this sense the IMI model differs from "classic" identity federation models, whereby the mutual reliance on various identity providers is a key aspect. Though managed in a distributed fashion, there is in fact a "centralised" rather than federated IdP model for IMI (only authoritative sources are "federated").

integrator.[1584] It provides a platform through which a relying party (receiving country) may request corroboration of a particular attribute (prerequisite qualification) with the relevant competent authority (authoritative source) in another Member State (country of origin). Upon receipt of a request through IMI, the relevant competent authority will query its own databases in order to return the appropriate response. As indicated earlier, however, the IMI network also allows for other types of information exchange (not related to attribute verification) and also supports information exchanges among other types of IMI actors.

C. *IMI actors*

781. Outline – The four main actors involved in the administration of the IMI system are (1) the European Commission; (2) the IMI coordinators; (3) the competent authorities and (4) the Union bodies, offices and agencies. Jointly they are referred to as the "IMI actors".[1585] The term "IMI user" is used to refer to natural persons working under the authority of an IMI actor.[1586]

782. European Commission – The European Commission hosts and maintains the IMI system in a data centre in Luxembourg.[1587] The Commission also provides the software for IMI, manages the network of national IMI co-ordinators and is involved in the training of and technical assistance to IMI users.[1588] The European Commission can also lay down practical arrangements to facilitate the efficient exchange of information through IMI by way of implementing acts.[1589] The Commission does not participate in administrative cooperation procedures involving the processing of personal data, except where required by the provision of a Union Act listed in the Annex of Regulation No 1024/2012.[1590]

783. IMI Coordinator – An IMI coordinator is a body appointed by a Member States to perform support tasks necessary for the efficient functioning of IMI.[1591] Relevant support tasks include registration of competent authorities, acting as a contact point for IMI actors of the Member State and providing knowledge, training and assistance to IMI actors of that Member State.[1592] Each

---

1584 Compare *supra*, nos. 746 et seq.

1585 Article 5(g) of Regulation No 1024/2012.

1586 Article 5(h) of Regulation No 1024/2012.

1587 European Commission, *The Internal Market Information (IMI) System User Handbook*, Update 2012, Publications Office of the European Union, Luxembourg, 2012, p. 8.

1588 Recital (9) of Regulation No 1024/2012.

1589 Recital (27) of Regulation No 1024/2012.

1590 Article 8(3) of Regulation No 1024/2012.

1591 Article 5(e) of Regulation No 1024/2012.

1592 See Article 6 of Regulation No 1024/2012.

Member State has one National IMI Co-ordinator ("NIMIC"). At the discretion of the Member State, Delegated IMI Coordinators ("DIMICs") may be appointed to take over some or all coordination responsibilities, for example in relation to a particular legislative area or geographical region.[1593]

784. Competent authority – A competent authority is any body which carries responsibilities relating to the application of national law or Union acts in one or more internal market areas.[1594] The competent authorities are the ones actually using the IMI system to exchange information relevant to the performance of their duties. Competent authorities that collaborate through IMI are obliged to provide an adequate response within the shortest possible period of time, in accordance with the applicable Union act.[1595]

785. Union bodies, offices and agencies – In October 2018, the IMI regulation was amended to also include "Union bodies offices and agencies" to the list of "IMI actors".[1596] These actors may now also be involved in exchanges of information, including of personal data, for purposes of administrative cooperation. Such administrative cooperation must also be listed in the Annex to the IMI regulation (unless it is part of an administrative cooperation subject to a pilot project carried out in accordance with Article 4). The addition of this group of actors enables, for example, the EDPS and the EDPB to make use of the IMI system for information exchanges in the context of the GDPR.[1597] As the addition of this type of actor to the IMI system is quite recent, their role will not be further discussed in the sections that follow (although it would seem that their roles towards IMI would ordinarily be comparable to that of a competent authority).

D. Roles

786. Commission Decision 2008/49/Ec – The first effort towards defining the roles and responsibilities of the actors involved in IMI was made in Commission Decision 2008/49/EC.[1598] Article 3, first indent of the Decision simply provided that

---

1593 European Commission, *The Internal Market Information (IMI) System User Handbook*, Update 2012, Publications Office of the European Union, Luxembourg, 2012, p. 8.

1594 Article 5(f)) of Regulation No 1024/2012.

1595 Article 7(1) of Regulation No 1024/2012.

1596 Recital (26) of Regulation No 2018/1724.

1597 See "EDPS Opinion on the proposal for a Regulation establishing a single digital gateway and the 'once-only' principle", Opinion 8/2017, p. 16.

1598 See European Commission, Commission Decision of 12 December 2007 concerning the implementation of the Internal Market Information System (IMI) as regards the protection of personal data, OJ 16 January 2008, L 13/18–23.

"The responsibilities of the controller under Article 2(d) of Directive 95/46/EC and Article 2(d) of Regulation (EC) No 45/2001 shall be jointly exercised by the IMI actors pursuant to Article 6 in accordance with their respective responsibilities within IMI".[1599]

The European Data Protection Supervisor (EDPS), however, considered that the allocation of responsibilities in Article 3 was "unclear and ambiguous".[1600] The EDPS recommended that at least the following specifications be added:

"- each Competent Authority and IMI coordinator is a controller with respect to its own data processing activities as a user of the system;
- the Commission is not a user, but the operator of the system, and it is responsible, first and foremost, for the technical operation, maintenance, and ensuring the overall security of the system, and that
- the IMI actors share responsibilities with respect to notice provision, and provision of right of access, objections, and rectifications [...]".[1601]

The EDPS then proceeded to outline the ways in which the IMI actors might provide notice to data subjects and accommodate data subject rights. It is worth noting, however, that the EDPS did not formally label the European Commission as either a "controller" or "processor". While the role of competent authorities and IMI coordinators as controllers was made explicit, the Commission received the ambiguous label of "operator".

787. Commission Recommendation 2009/329/EC – Following the Opinion of the EDPS, the European Commission issued a Recommendation on data protection guidelines for IMI.[1602] With the recommendation, the Commission sough to give interim effect to the EDPS' recommendations. Regarding the legal qualifications of the actors concerned, the Commission noted that

---

1599 It is worth mentioning that in addition to Directive 95/46, Regulation 45/2001 has also since been replaced, namely by Regulation (EU) 2018/1725 of the European Parliament and of the Council of 23 October 2018 on the protection of natural persons with regard to the processing of personal data by the Union institutions, bodies, offices and agencies and on the free movement of such data, and repealing Regulation (EC) No 45/2001 and Decision No 1247/2002/EC, OJ 21.11.2018, L 295/39.

1600 European Data Protection Supervisor (EDPS), "Opinion of the European Data Protection Supervisor on the Commission Decision of 12 December 2007 concerning the implementation of the Internal Market Information System (IMI) as regards the protection of personal data (2008/49/EC) (2008/C 270/01)", *l.c.*, paragraph 34.

1601 *Ibid*, paragraph 35.

1602 European Commission, Commission Recommendation of 26 March 2009 on data protection guidelines for the Internal Market Information System (IMI), 2009/329/EC, OJ 18 April 2009, L 100/17.

> "IMI is a clear example of joint processing operations and joint controllership. For example, whilst only the competent authorities in the Member States exchange personal data, the storage of these data on its servers is the responsibility of the European Commission. Whilst the European Commission is not allowed to see this personal data it is the operator of the system who physically processes the deletion and rectification of the data."[1603]

788. Regulation 1024/2012 – Article 6(4) of Regulation 1024/2012 confirms that each IMI coordinator shall be considered a controller "*with respect to its own data processing activities as an IMI actor*". Article 7(3) likewise provides that each competent authority shall be a controller with respect to the data processing activities of IMI users acting under its authority. Once again, the European Commission is labelled neither "controller" nor "processor". Article 8 simply lists the responsibilities of the Commission (e.g. ensuring security, operating a helpdesk, etc.), without specifying the Commission's legal status. Only the EDPS, in his Opinion of 22 November 2011 clearly stated that the European Commission should also be considered a "controller".[1604] The label was not carried over, however, to the text of Regulation 1024/2012.

789. Joint controllers?– In contrast to Commission Recommendation 2009/329/EC and the EDPS Opinion of 2007, Regulation 1024/2012 does not refer to joint controllership. Instead, it emphasises that IMI co-ordinators and competent authorities are each considered to act as controller "*with respect to their own data processing activities*". Such language might be indicative of a relationship among collaborating single controllers, rather than a relationship among joint controllers. Regulation 1024/2012 does not clearly specify whether the European Commission is acting as a controller or not. If one takes into account the CJEU judgment in *Jehovah's Witnesses*, the argument can be made that the Commission should be viewed as a joint controller, together with the relevant IMI actor as regards the processing of personal data exchanged via IMI.[1605] After all, IMI is a tool provided by the Commission to facilitate administrative cooperation among the IMI actors.[1606] In addition to ensuring the maintenance and development of the software and IT infrastructure[1607], the Commission also helps to organise and coordinate the processing of personal data that takes place in the context of IMI by providing training and

---

1603 *Ibid*, p. 17.

1604 European Data Protection Supervisor (EDPS), "Opinion of the European Data Protection Supervisor on the Commission Proposal for a Regulation of the European Parliament and of the Council on administrative cooperation through the Internal Market Information System ('IMI')", *l.c.*, paragraph 34.

1605 Judgment in *Jehovah's witnesses*, C-25/17, ECLI:EU:C:2018:551, at paragraph 71 et seq. See also *supra*, no. 230.

1606 Article 5(a) of Regulation 1024/2012.

1607 Article 8(1)a of Regulation 1024/2012.

a helpdesk to assist in the use of IMI and by registering IMI coordinators and granting them access to IMI.[1608] The Commission also has the authority to carry out pilot projects order to assess whether IMI would be an effective tool to implement provisions for administrative cooperation of Union acts not listed in the Annex.[1609] Finally, it should also be taken into account that IMI is a system that seeks to support the objectives of the EU Single Market.[1610] Taken all these elements into account, it seems fair to conclude that the Commission "organises, coordinates and encourages" the processing of personal data within IMI, rending it a joint controller, together with the relevant IMI actor.[1611]

E. *Responsibilities*

790. Outline – Regulation 1024/2012 lays down the basic rules for the use of the IMI system and specifies the main functions and responsibilities of the actors involved in IMI. It also contains several provisions addressing data protection requirements, such as confidentiality[1612], purpose limitation[1613], retention of data[1614], special categories of data[1615], security[1616], transparency[1617], and data subject rights.[1618] The following paragraphs will analyse the allocation of responsibilities among IMI actors.

i. Confidentiality and security

791. European Commission – Regulation 1024/2012 assigns the European Commission primary responsibility for ensuring the security of the IMI system.[1619] Article 17(2) provides that the Commission must put in place the

[1608] Article 8(1)b-c of Regulation 1024/2012.
[1609] Article 4(1) of Regulation 1024/2012.
[1610] Compare with Judgment in *Jehovah's witnesses*, C-25/17, ECLI:EU:C:2018:551, at paragraph 71 ("*Thus, it appears that the collection of personal data relating to persons contacted and their subsequent processing help to achieve the objective of the Jehovah's Witnesses Community, which is to spread its faith and are, therefore, carried out by members who engage in preaching for the purposes of that community. Furthermore, not only does the Jehovah's Witnesses Community have knowledge on a general level of the fact that such processing is carried out in order to spread its faith, but that community organises and coordinates the preaching activities of its members, in particular, by allocating areas of activity between the various members who engage in preaching.*")
[1611] Compare with Judgment in *Jehovah's witnesses*, C-25/17, ECLI:EU:C:2018:551, at paragraph 75.
[1612] Article 10 of Regulation No 1024/2012.
[1613] Article 13 of Regulation No 1024/2012.
[1614] Article 14 of Regulation No 1024/2012.
[1615] Article 16 of Regulation No 1024/2012.
[1616] Article 17 of Regulation No 1024/2012.
[1617] Article 18 of Regulation No 1024/2012.
[1618] Article 19 of Regulation No 1024/2012.
[1619] Article 8(1)a of Regulation No 1024/2012. See also European Data Protection Supervisor (EDPS), "Opinion of the European Data Protection Supervisor on the Commission

necessary measures to ensure security of personal data processed in IMI, including appropriate access control mechanisms and a security plan which shall be kept up-to-date.[1620] The Commission must also ensure that, in the event of a security incident, it is possible to verify what personal data have been processed in IMI, when, by whom and for what purpose (Article 17(3)).

792. Other IMI actors – While the Commission is responsible for a predominant part of the security of IMI, the other IMI actors (i.e. the IMI coordinators the competent authorities, and the Union bodies, offices and agencies) remain obliged to take the necessary procedural and organisational measures to ensure the security of personal data processed by them in IMI (Article 17(4)). Binding IMI users to appropriate confidentiality obligations and limiting the access rights of individual IMI users are examples of measures which other IMI actors can take to help ensure the confidentiality and security of personal data processed by them in IMI.[1621]

793. Assessment – Given that the Commission provides and manages the software and IT infrastructure for IMI, it seems logical that the Commission carries the primary responsibility for ensuring the overall security of the IMI system. Nevertheless, the behaviour of other actors participating in IMI can impact the confidentiality and security of personal data processed within IMI. Moreover, as data controllers, each actor participating retains its own security obligation for information under its control. It is therefore logical that they remain responsible for the security of personal data "processed by them" in IMI.[1622]

Proposal for a Regulation of the European Parliament and of the Council on administrative cooperation through the Internal Market Information System ('IMI')", *l.c.*, paragraph 65.

1620 See also Article 9(4): "*appropriate means shall be put in place by the Member States, the Commission and Union bodies, offices and agencies to ensure that IMI users are allowed to access personal data processed in IMI only on a need-to-know basis and within the internal market area or areas for which they were granted access rights in accordance with paragraph 3.*". IMI uses system of delegated administration to manage access rights. The National IMI Co-ordinators are responsible for ensuring that the relevant competent authorities are registered in IMI and can access (only) the modules correspond to their area of competence. Each competent authority is in turn obliged to appropriately manage the access rights of the IMI users under its authority. See European Commission, *Managing access to IMI*, not dated, p. 2. See also European Commission, *IMI roles and responsibilities*, not dated and European Commission, *Managing my authority and users*, not dated.

1621 See Article 10 of Regulation 1024/2012. See also European Commission, "Data protection guidelines for IMI users", *l.c.*, p. 5–6.

1622 See also Principle 2 of the OECD Recommendation on Digital Security Risk Management, which stipulates that all stakeholders should take responsibility for the management of digital security risks "*based on their roles, the context and their ability to act*" (OECD, Recommendation of the Council on Digital Security Risk Management for Economic and Social Prosperity, 2015).

ii. Data quality

794. European Commission – IMI is based on pre-defined workflows ("administrative cooperation procedures") which allow IMI actors to communicate and interact with each other in a structured manner (Article 11). Each workflow consists of predefined (and pre-translated) questions and answers.[1623] Each of the question sets is based on a specific piece of legislation supported by IMI.[1624] The question sets, like the other functionalities of IMI, have been developed by the Commission in partnership with the Member States.[1625] The Commission also has the authority to adopt implementing acts setting out the essential technical functionality and the procedural arrangements required to enable the operation of the relevant administrative cooperation procedure.[1626]

795. Other IMI actors – Competent authorities requesting information should only provide personal data that is necessary to enable the responding competent authority to respond to the request.[1627] Likewise, competent authorities answering requests are obliged not to provide information that is irrelevant or excessive considering the identified objective of the exchange.[1628] All IMI users should carefully select which questions they include in a request and not ask for more information than is absolutely necessary.[1629] Requests for special categories of data may only be made where the processing of such data is provided for in a Union act and it is absolutely necessary to allow a decision in the particular case which is directly linked to the request.[1630]

1623 European Commission, The Internal Market Information (IMI) System User Handbook, Update 2012, Publications Office of the European Union, Luxembourg, 2012, p. 8.

1624 *Id.*

1625 European Commission, "Communication from the Commission to the European Parliament, the Council, the European Economic and Social Committee and the Committee of the Regions, Better governance of the Single Market through greater administrative cooperation: A strategy for expanding and developing the Internal Market Information System ('IMI')", 21 February 2011, COM(2011) 75 final, p. 3.

1626 Article 11 of Regulation 1024/2012.

1627 European Commission, Commission Decision of 12 December 2007 concerning the implementation of the Internal Market Information System (IMI) as regards the protection of personal data, OJ 16 January 2008, p. 20.

1628 Article 29 Data Protection Working Party, "Opinion 7/2007 on data protection issues related to the Internal Market Information System (IMI)", *l.c.*, p. 11.

1629 European Commission, Commission Decision of 12 December 2007 concerning the implementation of the Internal Market Information System (IMI) as regards the protection of personal data, *l.c.*, p. 20.

1630 *Ibid*, p. 21. See also Article 16 of Regulation 1024/2012. The EC Recommendation goes on to specify that IMI should not be used to conduct systemic criminal background checks (p. 21). See also European Commission, "Data protection guidelines for IMI users", *l.c.*, p. 2.

796. Assessment – While IMI supports "free text" information exchanges[1631], the use of pre-defined workflows can help ensure that exchanged information is "adequate, relevant and not excessive" in relation to the purposes for which it is being processed. Even though the Commission is generally not involved in the administrative cooperation procedures themselves, it defines – in close collaboration with the Member States – which types of information (questions and answers) are relevant to a particular workflow. The Commission thus plays an important role in ensuring that information exchanges (a) have an appropriate legal basis (lawfulness) and (b) are limited to that which is necessary to complete a request (proportionality). The principle of finality is supported by the fact that access rights of individual IMI users shall be limited to the policy areas in which they are active.[1632] Regulation 1024/2012 does not specify how the accuracy of data exchanged through IMI shall be ensured.[1633] It does, however, specify that all IMI actors are obliged to ensure that data subjects can exercise their right to have inaccurate data corrected.[1634]

iii. Retention of data

797. Basic principle – Article 14 provides that personal data processed in IMI shall be "blocked" in IMI as soon as they are no longer necessary for the purposes of administrative cooperation.[1635] Once personal data have been blocked, they may in principle only be processed for the purpose of providing proof of an information exchange through IMI.[1636] Blocked data is automatically deleted in IMI three years after the formal closure of the administrative cooperation procedure.[1637]

1631 European Commission, The Internal Market Information (IMI) System User Handbook, *l.c.*, p. 21.

1632 See Article 9(4)–9(6) of Regulation 1024/2012. See also European Data Protection Supervisor (EDPS), "Opinion of the European Data Protection Supervisor on the Commission Proposal for a Regulation of the European Parliament and of the Council on administrative cooperation through the Internal Market Information System ('IMI')", *l.c.*, paragraph 37.

1633 This is most likely due to the fact that the respective databases are governed also by national data protection regulations, which already require this information to be accurate. The primary responsibility to ensure data accuracy thus rests with the participating competent authorities.

1634 Cf. *infra*, 804 et seq.

1635 The precise timeframe within which personal data is "blocked" is determined in light of the specificities of each type of administrative co-operation. As a general rule, however, personal data should be blocked within six months after the formal closure of an administrative cooperation procedure. However, if a longer period is provided for in the applicable Union act, personal data processed in IMI may be retained up to 18 months after the formal closure of an administrative cooperation procedure (Article 14(1) of Regulation 1024/2012).

1636 Article 14(3) of Regulation 1024/2012.

1637 Article 14(4) of Regulation 1024/2012. 5. At the express request of a competent authority in a specific case and with the data subject's consent, personal data may be deleted before the expiry of the applicable retention period (Article 14(5)).

798. European Commission – The European Commission is responsible for ensuring, by technical means, that personal data are in fact "blocked" once they are no longer necessary for purposes of administrative cooperation between the Member States. It must also ensure their subsequent deletion.[1638]

799. Other IMI actors – IMI actors are encouraged to formally close administrative cooperation procedures as soon as possible after the exchange of information has been completed. Technical means are put place to enable IMI actors to involve the responsible IMI coordinators in any procedure which has been inactive without justification for longer than two months.[1639]

800. Assessment – Given that the Commission provides and manages the software and IT infrastructure for IMI, it is only logical that it provides the technical tools necessary to enable blocking and erasure of data. The IMI Regulation goes one step further, however, by requiring the Commission to actually enforce the policy that blocked data cannot be used for purposes other than providing proof of an information exchange.[1640] It is also responsible for ensuring actual deletion of data. The obligations of the Commission are thus clearly situated at the technical level. In contrast, the responsibilities of other IMI actors seem to be of a more organisational and procedural nature. Competent authorities have a duty to formally "close" administrative cooperation procedures as soon as possible. IMI coordinators, in turn, must follow up on dormant requests to help ensure that personal data is not retained indefinitely.[1641]

iv. Transparency

801. European Commission – Early on, the Commission began publishing on its website the sets of pre-defined questions and data fields corresponding to a particular data exchange. The EDPS immediately applauded this good practice, but also recommended that there be a legal obligation for the Commission to do so.[1642] Article 18 of Regulation 1024/2012 obliges the Commission to make publically available the "*types of administrative cooperation procedures, essential IMI functionalities and categories of data that may be processed in IMI*".[1643] It

[1638] Article 14(6) of Regulation 1024/2012.

[1639] Article 14(7) of Regulation 1024/2012.

[1640] Article 14(6) of Regulation 1024/2012.

[1641] In this regard, the EDPS had recommended that a deadline for automatic deletion be set counting from the start of an exchange, rather than from the formal closure of a procedure. See European Data Protection Supervisor (EDPS), "Opinion of the European Data Protection Supervisor on the Commission Decision of 12 December 2007 concerning the implementation of the Internal Market Information System (IMI) as regards the protection of personal data (2008/49/EC) (2008/C 270/01)", *l.c.*, paragraph 41. The recommendation was not adopted.

[1642] *Ibid*, paragraphs 31–32.

[1643] Article 18(2)d of Regulation 1024/2012.

further requires the Commission to provide data subjects with information on the data protection aspects of administrative cooperation procedures, on top of its basic notice obligation under Articles 11 and 12 of Regulation 45/2001 (now: Articles 15 and 16 of Regulation (EU) 2018/1725).[1644]

802. Other IMI actors – Other IMI actors are responsible for providing data subjects with information regarding their own processing of personal data through IMI, in accordance with Articles 13 and 14 GDPR.[1645] The Commission recommends that competent authorities, when they collect personal data directly from an individual, inform data subjects of the fact that their personal data may be processed through IMI and might be disclosed to the relevant competent authorities of other Member States.[1646] It also recommends to provide a link to information on data protection available on the Commission's IMI website when doing so. The Commission also notes, however, that national laws exempt certain types of public authorities or procedures from the requirement to provide information.[1647] The Commission has committed itself to liaise with national IMI coordinators in order to identify the relevant national rules and to make them publicly available.[1648]

803. Assessment – Article 18 of Regulation 1024/2012 makes clear that the duty to ensure transparency of processing towards data subjects is a joint responsibility of all IMI actors.[1649] The Commission, as "operator" of the system, is best positioned to take a proactive role in providing a "first layer" of information to data subjects on its website.[1650] The active publication of information on the Commission's website allows data subjects to obtain a general overview of the functionalities and legal basis of IMI. It also provides them with an indication of where to turn in case they require more information or wish to exercise their rights as data subjects (see below). Nevertheless, the competent authorities retain their own independent obligation to adequately inform data subjects. As a rule, the competent authority shall be obliged to inform data subjects directly, unless a valid exemption applies.[1651]

1644 See Article 99 of Regulation (EU) 2018/1725.

1645 Previously: Article 10 and 11 of Directive 95/46. See also Article 18(1) of Regulation 1024/2012.

1646 European Commission, "Data protection guidelines for IMI users", *l.c.*, p. 2–3.

1647 *Id.*

1648 *Id.*

1649 *Id.*

1650 European Data Protection Supervisor (EDPS), "Opinion of the European Data Protection Supervisor on the Commission Proposal for a Regulation of the European Parliament and of the Council on administrative cooperation through the Internal Market Information System ('IMI')", 22 November 2011, paragraph 69.

1651 See also Article 29 Data Protection Working Party, "Opinion 7/2007 on data protection issues related to the Internal Market Information System (IMI)", *l.c.*, p. 16 and Judgment in *Smaranda Bara and Others*, C-201/14, EU:C:2015:638.

v. Data subject rights

804. Basic principle – In order to reduce the burden on data subjects (who are unlikely to be familiar with the technicalities of the controller relationships within IMI), Recommendation 2009/329 provided that

> "no competent authority should refuse access, rectification or deletion on the ground that it did not introduce the data in the system or that the data subject should contact another competent authority."[1652]

In other words, the Commission advanced a "no wrong door" policy, to be administered primarily by the Member States. The Commission confirms this approach in its privacy statement on the IMI website.[1653]

805. European Commision – The role of the Commission in actually accommodating data subject rights is limited.[1654] It provides technical support (esp. in cases where the information exchanges have already been "closed") and co-ordination between the competent authorities (in cases where a request for rectification or deletion is received and granted by a competent authority which did not initiate the information exchange).[1655] In 2009, the Commission indicated it is working on a feature that would allow online data rectification and support automatic notifications to those competent authorities involved[1656], but there seem to have been no further updates since.

806. Other IMI actors – IMI actors are obliged to respond within 30 days after the request by the data subject is received by the "responsible" IMI actor.[1657] As indicated above, competent authorities are encouraged to accommodate data subject rights, regardless of whether they initiated the administrative cooperation procedure within IMI or not. In principle, the competent authority receiving the request should examine it and grant or refuse it in accordance with

---

1652 European Commission, European Commission, Commission Recommendation of 26 March 2009 on data protection guidelines for the Internal Market Information System (IMI), *l.c.*, in particular pp. 25–26.

1653 "*If you think that your personal data is in IMI and you would like to have access to it or have it deleted or rectified, you may do so by contacting the administration or the professional body with which you had contacts or any other IMI user that was involved in the administrative cooperation procedure concerning you. If you were not satisfied with the answer received, you may either contact another IMI user involved or lodge a complaint with your data protection authority.*" See also section 9 of Commission Privacy Statement and European Commission, "Data protection guidelines for IMI users", *l.c.*, p. 2–3, question 7.

1654 At least insofar as it concerns personal data involved in an administrative cooperation procedure between Member States, to which the Commission is generally not a party.

1655 See question 8 of the Data Protection guidelines for IMI users, not dated.

1656 See European Commission, Commission Recommendation of 26 March 2009 on data protection guidelines for the Internal Market Information System (IMI), *l.c.*, p. 26.

1657 Article 19 of Regulation 1024/2012.

the merits of the request (and the provisions of its own national data protection law).[1658] If needed, the competent authority may contact other competent authorities before taking a decision.[1659]

807. Assessment – Article 19 confirms that IMI actors are obliged to accommodate data subject rights. It does not, however, specify to whom data subject should direct their requests, nor does it impose a duty on competent authorities to cooperate with one and other in this respect.[1660] The practical approach advanced by the European Commission allows data subjects to exercise their rights with any competent authority who is actually involved in the procedure. The Commission could take its facilitative role one step further, by providing an online form to data subjects who believe that their personal data processed within IMI should be rectified or deleted.

5.2. CROSS-BORDER IDENTIFICATION AND AUTHENTICATION (STORK AND EIDAS)

A. *Introduction*

808. eID interoperability – The EU perceives cross-border delivery of public services a necessary condition for a fully realized single market.[1661] As national eIDM systems matured, the concept of "eID interoperability" gained in political importance.[1662] Through a variety of initiatives, the EU has sought to

---

1658 European Commission, European Commission, Commission Recommendation of 26 March 2009 on data protection guidelines for the Internal Market Information System (IMI), *l.c.*, p. 25.

1659 *Id.*

1660 See in that sense also European Data Protection Supervisor (EDPS), "Opinion of the European Data Protection Supervisor on the Commission Proposal for a Regulation of the European Parliament and of the Council on administrative cooperation through the Internal Market Information System ('IMI')", *l.c.*, paragraphs 71–73.

1661 European Parliamentary Research Service (EPRS), "eGovernment – Using technology to improve public services and democratic participation", July 2015, p. 9.

1662 N.N.G. de Andrade, "'Electronic Identity for Europe': Moving from Problems to Solutions", *l.c.*, p. 104. The increased emphasis on eID interoperability was particularly visible in the i2010 eGovernment Action Plan and the Roadmap for a pan-European eID Framework. See European Commission, *i2010 eGovernment Action Plan: Accelerating eGovernment in Europe for the Benefit of All*, SEC(2006) 511, 24 April 2006 and European Commission, A Roadmap for a pan-European eIDM Framework by 2010, 2006, v1.0. The Roadmap included a list of measurable objectives and milestones for the construction of such framework. It later reconfigured the objectives with the launch of the Digital Agenda, which included two important key actions in the field of eID, namely (1) a proposal for a Council and Parliament Decision on mutual recognition on e-identification and e-authentication across the EU based on online "authentication services" to be offered in all Member States; and (2) a proposal for a revision of the eSignature Directive with a view to provide a legal framework for cross-border recognition and interoperability of secure eAuthentication systems. (N.N.G. de Andrade, "'Electronic Identity for Europe': Moving from Problems to Solutions", *l.c.*, p. 104–105). This

promote the interoperability of national eIDM systems. The guiding principle in those initiatives has been the construction of a European cross-border eIDM framework, based on interoperability and mutual recognition of national eID resources and management systems.[1663]

809. STORK PROJECT – In order to advance the development of practical interoperability solutions, the EU funded a number of Large-Scale Pilot projects (LSPs). Each LSP focused on the development and testing of practical solutions in real-life cross-border public service environments.[1664] As far as eID interoperability is concerned, the most influential project by far was the STORK project.[1665] STORK, which stands for "Secure idenTity acrOss boRders linKed", set out to establish an interoperable system for EU-wide recognition of eIDs that would allow businesses, citizens and government employees to use their national eIDs in any Member State.[1666] The project produced a set of technical specifications for the interoperability of eIDs, which proved to be highly influential for the subsequent regulation of electronic identity authentication services at EU level.

810. REGULATION 910/2014 – On 4 June 2012, the European Commission published a proposal for a Regulation on electronic identification and trust services for electronic transactions in the internal market.[1667] The main objective of the proposal was to ensure the mutual recognition of electronic identification and authentication across the EU and to enhance the existing legal framework on electronic signatures.[1668] In February 2014, a political agreement was reached between representatives of the European Parliament (MEP), the Commission

---

eventually led to the adoption of Regulation No 910/2014 of the European Parliament and of the Council of 23 July 2014 on electronic identification and trust services for electronic transactions in the internal market and repealing Directive 1999/93/EC (OJ 28 August 2014, L 257/73).

1663 N.N.G. de Andrade, "'Electronic Identity for Europe': Moving from Problems to Solutions", *l.c.*, p. 104. See also J.C. Buitelaar, M. Meints and B. Van Alsenoy (eds.), "Conceptual Framework for Identity Management in eGovernment", *l.c.*, p. 61–64.

1664 European Commission, Directorate-General Informatics, "EU activities in the field of eID interoperability", December 2013, p. 2.

1665 The STORK project ended in 2011 and was succeeded by the STORK 2.0 project, which further built on the results of STORK and also sought to develop interoperable solutions for the authentication of legal persons and mandates.

1666 Article 29 Data Protection Working Party, Biometrics & eGovernment Subgroup, Written Report concerning the STORK Project, Ref.Ares (2011) 424406, 15 April 2011, p. 2.

1667 European Commission, Proposal for a Regulation of the European Parliament and of the Council on electronic identification and trust services for electronic transactions in the internal market, COM(2012) 238/2, 4 June 2012.

1668 For more information see J. Dumortier and N. Vandezande, "Trust in the proposed EU regulation on trust services?", *Computer Law and Security Review* 2012, Vol. 28, p. 568–576 and C. Cuijpers and J. Schroers, "eIDAS as guideline for the development of a pan European eID framework in FutureID", *Open Identity Summit* 2014 vol. 237, p.23–38.

and the Council.[1669] The final text of the Regulation on electronic identification and trust services for electronic transactions (commonly referred to as "the eIDAS regulation") was published in the Official Journal on 28 August 2014.[1670]

811. Mutual recognition – Chapter II of the eIDAS regulation governs the mutual recognition of electronic identification schemes among Member States. Provided certain requirements are met, a Member State can notify its national eID scheme to the European Commission. Once an eID scheme has been notified, other Member States shall in principle be obliged to accept the electronic identification means issued under that scheme if they require electronic identification and authentication to access an online service.[1671] Of course, a Member State is only obliged to accept electronic identification means which provide an assurance level which is equal to or higher than the assurance level required by the relevant public sector body to access that service online.[1672]

812. Practical implementation – The eIDAS regulation provides a legal framework for streamlining the mutual recognition of national eID schemes. Specific technical requirements for security and interoperability were left to be specified by way of implementing acts.[1673] On 9 September 2015, the European Commission published two implementing acts relevant to eID recognition, namely the implementing act on the interoperability framework[1674] and the implementing act on levels of assurance.[1675] [1676] Since then, the Commission and the Member States have produced additional documentation regarding the technical interoperability architecture supporting cross-border use of eID

1669 European Commission, "Commission welcomes political agreement on new EU regulation for electronic ID and trust services", 28 February 2014, MEMO/14/151. See also J. Schroers and B. Van Alsenoy, "Making Online Transactions Reliable and Interoperable for Europe", *LSE Media Policy Blog*, 28 May 2015.

1670 Regulation (EU) No 910/2014 of the European Parliament and of the Council of 23 July 2014 on electronic identification and trust services for electronic transactions in the internal market and repealing Directive 1999/93/EC, OJ 28 August 2014, L 257/73–114.

1671 Article 6(1)a of Regulation 910/2014.

1672 Article 6(1)b of Regulation 910/2014. Currently, recognition is only mandatory in cases where the relevant public sector body uses the assurance level "substantial" or "high" in relation to accessing that service online. Recognition of notified electronic identification means which correspond to the assurance level "low" is optional (Article 6(2)).

1673 See also J. Bender, "eIDAS regulation: eID – Opportunities and Risks", *25th SmartCard Workshop*, 4–5 February 2015, p. 157.

1674 European Commission, Commission Implementing Regulation (EU) 2015/1501 of 8 September 2015 on the interoperability framework pursuant to Article 12(8) of Regulation (EU) No 910/2014 of the European Parliament and of the Council on electronic identification and trust services for electronic transactions in the internal market, OJ 9 September 2015, L 235/1–6.

1675 European Commission, Commission Implementing Regulation (EU) 2015/1502 of 8 September 2015 on setting out minimum technical specifications and procedures for assurance levels for electronic identification means pursuant to Article 8(3) of Regulation (EU) No 910/2014 of the European Parliament and of the Council on electronic identification and trust services for electronic transactions in the internal market, OJ 9 September 2015, L 235/7–20.

1676 See also A. Servida, The first big step in eIDAS implementation accomplished, *Digital Agenda for Europe* (blog), 9 September 2015.

under the Connecting Europe Facility (CEF).[1677] The technical interoperability architecture relied heavily upon the STORK architecture.[1678]

B. Functionalities

813. Interoperable identity assurance – When a citizen from one Member State (the "sending Member State") wishes to access an online service offered by a public sector body in another Member State (the "receiving Member State"), the latter may require assurance of the person's identity. Obtaining such assurance requires interoperability among national identity management systems. The Commission's implementing act on the interoperability framework provides for a "network of nodes" to deliver interoperable identity assurance.[1679]

814. A network of "nodes" – Interoperability between different eID schemes is achieved by defining the technical interfaces between so-called "nodes".[1680] A "node" is defined as

> "a connection point which is part of the electronic identification interoperability architecture and is involved in cross-border authentication of persons and which has the capability to recognise and process or forward transmissions to other nodes by enabling the national electronic identification infrastructure of one Member State to interface with national electronic identification infrastructures of other Member States".[1681]

A "node operator" is the entity responsible for ensuring that the node performs correctly and reliably its functions as a connection point.[1682]

815. Integration scenarios – A Member State notifying a national eID scheme can choose between two integration scenarios: a "proxy-based" model or a "middleware-based" model[1683]:

1677 See European Commission, eIDAS – Interoperability Architecture, Version 1.00, 6 November 2015. For more information regarding the Connecting Europe Facility and its role in the implementation of Regulation 910/2014 see European Commission, Introduction to the Connecting Europe Facility eID building block, Version 1.01.

1678 See also Recital (6) of Commission Implementing Regulation 2015/1501: "*Large-scale pilot STORK, including specifications developed by it, and the principles and concepts of the European Interoperability Framework for European Public Services have been taken into the utmost account when establishing the arrangements of the interoperability framework set out in this Regulation.*"

1679 See also L. Reynolds, "The EU approach to identity assurance: an update", GOV.UK Verify (Blog), 20 November 2015.

1680 European Commission, eIDAS – Interoperability Architecture, Version 1.00, *l.c.*, p. 4.

1681 Article 2(1) of Commission Implementing Regulation 2015/1501. There are two types of nodes: eIDAS-Connectors and eIDAS-Services, collectively referred to as "eIDAS-Nodes": European Commission, eIDAS – Interoperability Architecture, Version 1.00, *l.c.*, p. 4.

1682 Article 2(1) of Commission Implementing Regulation 2015/1501.

1683 European Commission, eIDAS – Interoperability Architecture, Version 1.00, *l.c.*, p. 4. See also J. Bender, "eIDAS regulation: eID – Opportunities and Risks", *l.c.*, p. 159.

(1) *Proxy-based*: the sending Member State appoints a proxy (referred to as a "C-PEPS" in the STORK project[1684]) that relays authentication information between the receiving Member State and the eID scheme of the sending Member State;
(2) *Middleware-based*: the sending Member State does not appoint a proxy but instead provides a software component ("middleware") which can be operated in the receiving Member State.

For its part, the receiving Member State can also choose between two integration scenarios: a centralized model or a decentralized model.[1685]

C. *Actors*

816. Outline – Based on the integration scenarios mentioned above, there may be more or less actors involved in the cross-border identification and authentication of citizens. For purposes of clarity, the further analysis shall be limited to two conceptual models: the "PEPS model" and the "middleware model".

817. Middleware model – In the middleware model, the citizen authenticates himself at the relying party in the receiving Member State.[1686] The relying party uses a software component ("SPware") to handle foreign eID tokens. The user experience of the citizen is similar as if he were to access a relying party in his home country, as the components to recognize and verify her eID are integrated by SP.[1687] In this scenario, there are no intermediaries between the citizen and the relying party.[1688]

818. PEPS model – In the PEPS model, the exchange of identification authentication information across Member States takes place through proxies, referred to as "PEPS".[1689] In the figure below, the C-PEPS act as the gateway to

[1684] Cf. *infra*, no. 818.

[1685] European Commission, eIDAS – Interoperability Architecture, Version 1.00, *l.c.*, p. 4. See also J. Bender, "eIDAS regulation: eID – Opportunities and Risks", *l.c.*, p. 159–160.

[1686] H. Leitold, "Challenges of eID Interoperability: The STORK Project", *l.c.*, p. 146. See also H. Leitold and B. Zwattendorfer, ""STORK: Architecture, Implementation and Pilots", in N. Pohlmann a.o. (eds.), *ISSE 2010 Securing Electronic Business Processes*, Springer, 2010, p. 136–137.

[1687] *Id.* Under the eIDAS interoperability architecture, it is envisaged that middleware provided by the sending Member State may also be operated by an external operator (centralized model). See European Commission, eIDAS – Interoperability Architecture, Version 1.00, *l.c.*, p. 4.

[1688] *Id.*

[1689] PEPS stands for "Pan-European Proxy Service". A distinction is made between two types of PEPS: C-PEPS and S-PEPS. The term "C-PEPS" (or "Citizen PEPS") refers to a proxy service located in the country of the citizen (i.e. the "sending" Member State). The term S-PEPS

the eID system of Member State A, whereas the S-PEPS acts as a gateway for service providers in Member State B.

Figure 3. The STORK "PEPS model"[1690]

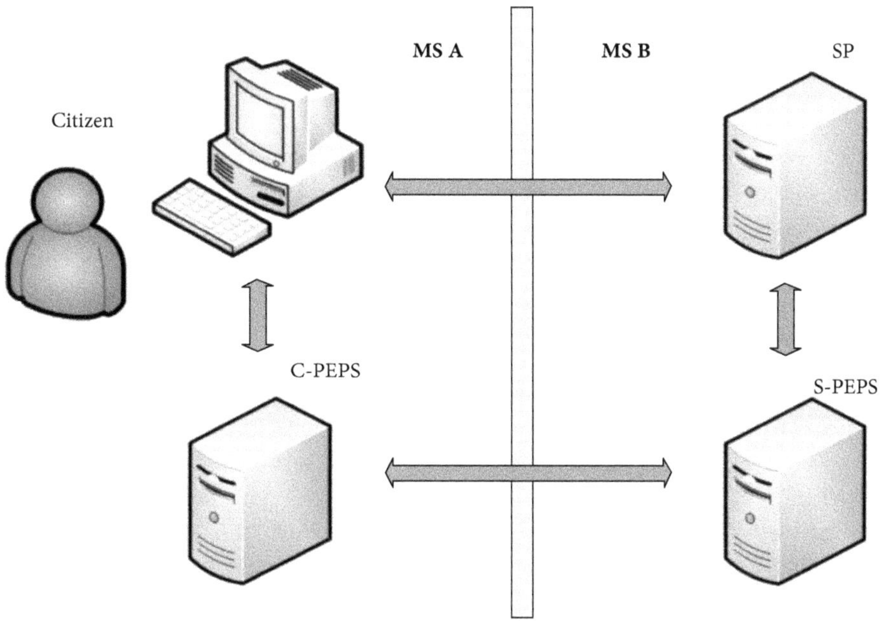

© H. Leitold and B. Zwattendorfer.

When a citizen of Member State A requests access to an online service in Member State B, the service provider requests assistance from the S-PEPS. The S-PEPS communicates an authentication request to the C-PEPS. The C-PEPS then triggers the identification and authentication of the citizen at the credential service provider in Member State A.[1691] Once the citizen has identified and authenticated himself towards the credential service provider, the C-PEPS transmits the relevant identity and authentication information to

---

refers to a proxy service located in the country of the service provider (relying party) (i.e. the "receiving" Member State"). See H. Leitold, "Challenges of eID Interoperability: The STORK Project", in S. Fischer-Hübner a.o. (eds.), *Privacy and Identity Management for Life*, Springer, 2011, p. 147. In the eIDAS interoperability architecture, PEPS are collectively referred to as "eIDAS nodes". The C-PEPS reappears as the "eIDAS-service" node, whereas the S-PEPS has been rebranded as the "eIDAS-connector" node. See European Commission, eIDAS – Interoperability Architecture, Version 1.00, *l.c.*, p. 3–4.

1690 H. Leitold and B. Zwattendorfer, ""STORK: Architecture, Implementation and Pilots", *l.c.*, p. 136.

1691 Based on H. Leitold and B. Zwattendorfer, ""STORK: Architecture, Implementation and Pilots", *l.c.*, p. 136. The credential service provider (referred to as the "identity provider" in the STORK project) is not depicted in this figure.

the S-PEPS, who can then confirm the identity of the citizen towards the service provider.[1692]

The main difference between the Middleware model and the PEPS model is that under the PEPS model the service provider delegates the handling of the identification and authentication process to a PEPS provider, whereas in the MW model the service provider takes care of this himself.[1693]

D. Roles

819. WP29 SUBGROUP – In April 2011, the Biometrics & eGovernment Subgroup of the Article 29 Working Party produced a written report concerning the STORK project.[1694] After describing the basic features of the Middleware and PEPS model, the Subgroup proceeded to analyse the role of the different actors involved. Interestingly, the Subgroup was unable to reach a common position regarding the legal status of the PEPS provider.

820. MIDDLEWARE MODEL – In the middleware model, the legal situation appears to be clear. Because all processing operations, including those related cross-border authentication, are performed by the service provider, the service provider is deemed responsible as the controller "*for all personal data used during the identification and authentification procedures developed and provided by STORK*".[1695]

821. PEPS MODEL – In the PEPS model, however, the legal situation was considered less straight-forward. One the one hand, it could be argued that the PEPS should be deemed a controller as far as its management of electronic identity information is concerned:

> "He processes personal data, transfers them to another PEPS and also handles the replies (signed IDs or rejection). Although the PEPS is a service provided to different institutions (service providers "SP" in the figures above), these are not in control of what happens in the PEPS. The only thing a SP provider is in control of is to either accept or refuse the offer of a PEPS provider."[1696]

On the other hand, it could also be argued that the PEPS is only a processor, acting on behalf of the service providers it serves.[1697] According to the Subgroup,

[1692] Based on Article 29 Data Protection Working Party, Biometrics & eGovernment Subgroup, Written Report concerning the STORK Project, Ref.Ares (2011) 424406, 15 April 2011, p. 4.
[1693] Article 29 Data Protection Working Party, Biometrics & eGovernment Subgroup, Written Report concerning the STORK Project, Ref.Ares (2011) 424406, 15 April 2011, p. 6.
[1694] Article 29 Data Protection Working Party, Biometrics & eGovernment Subgroup, Written Report concerning the STORK Project, Ref.Ares (2011) 424406, 15 April 2011.
[1695] *Ibid*, p. 6.
[1696] *Id.*
[1697] *Ibid*, p. 6–7.

this interpretation had the disadvantage of increasing the number of controllers involved, thereby increasing administrative burdens.[1698] In the end, the Subgroup was not able to come to a common position: "*[s]ome of the subgroup members would consider the PEPS as controller and some as processor.*"[1699]

822. Approach by STORK 2.0 – In STORK 2.0, the follow-up project to STORK, the following position was adopted in relation to the PEPS operators:

> "The PEPS operator acts as a data processor to the SP for the authentication processes conducted on behalf of the SP, with the SP acting as the data controller. This is reasonable, because this processing of personal data is done at the request of the SP, who can thus be said to control the means (it has chosen to use the PEPS) and the purposes (it has a need to authenticate the end user) of the processing. The PEPS operator on the other hand has no own purposes in this processing, and has not chosen the means to be used in the authentication process.
>
> The PEPS operator acts as a data controller for any other processing of personal data, notably any logging of authentication processes that may be done by the PEPS. These are not done for purposes determined by the SP, but rather for public interest purposes (to support accountability). No processors are used for these types of processing of personal data."[1700]

823. Assessment – The approach advanced by the STORK 2.0 project differentiates between processing operations in light of the *interests served* by the processing activity. The service provider has a direct interest in the outcome of an authentication process. He is therefore considered to be the controller in relation to the processing of personal data as part of the authentication process. As far as these operations are concerned, the PEPS operator is considered a mere processor. The PEPS operator is viewed as a controller, however, in relation to "other" processing activity, such as logging. The distinction may seem somewhat artificial, as logging is an integral part of the authentication process designed to help ensure its security. The argument could therefore easily be made that a service provider should also be considered a controller in relation to log entries that correspond with its authentication requests.

E. *Responsibilities*

824. A work in progress – In contrast with the IMI Regulation (cf. *supra*), the eIDAS regulation does not specify how the actors involved should cooperate in order to comply with data protection law. Article 11 of the eIDAS regulation

[1698] *Ibid*, p. 7.
[1699] *Id.*
[1700] H. Graux, "Consolidated Data Protection Report", *STORK 2.0*, Deliverable D3.8, 9 October 2015, p. 22–23.

governs the liability of the "party issuing the electronic identification means" and the "party operating the authentication procedure", but only insofar as its obligations under the eIDAS regulation itself are concerned.

825. WP29 RECOMMENDATIONS – In its written report concerning the STORK project, the subgroup of the Article 29 Working Party recommended the development of (1) common minimum standards for data security; (2) harmonised retention period for log files; (3) procedures to ensure transparency towards data subjects; and (4) specific recommendation on how the principles of data minimisation should be implemented and taken into consideration by service providers.[1701]

826. MEMORANDUM OF UNDERSTANDING – Following the correspondence with the Article 29 Working Party, the STORK 2.0 project developed a Memorandum of Understanding (MoU) which covers certain data protection aspects, namely:

(1) Lawfulness: processing of personal data by PEPS shall require the prior informed consent of the individual concerned following a common approach;
(2) Transparency: a model privacy policy and substandard practice for providing notice to individuals;
(3) Confidentiality and security: PEPS are expected to implement STORK's security guidelines.[1702]

827. OPINION OF THE EDPS – In his Opinion on the draft proposal of the eIDAS regulation, the EDPS recommended a harmonized European approach to data protection issues surrounding crossborder identification and authentication.[1703] In particular, the EDPS emphasized the need to address (1) data security[1704]; (2) transparency and individual control[1705]; (3) the categories of data involved in the identification and authentication of individuals[1706]; (4) use of privacy-enhancing technologies[1707]; (5) requirements for the issuers of national eID schemes.[1708] While certain aspects of the EDPS recommendations were integrated in the final

1701 See also H. Graux, "Initial Data Protection Report", *STORK 2.0*, Deliverable D3.7, 20 November 2012.
1702 H. Graux, "Consolidated Data Protection Report", *l.c.*, p. 25–30.
1703 European Data Protection Supervisor, Opinion of the European Data Protection Supervisor on the Commission proposal for a Regulation of the European Parliament and of the Council on trust and confidence in electronic transactions in the internal market (Electronic Trust Services Regulation), 27 September 2012, at paragraph 14.
1704 *Ibid*, paragraph 19.
1705 *Ibid*, paragraph 21.
1706 *Ibid*, paragraph 27.
1707 *Ibid*, paragraphs 23 and 28.
1708 *Ibid*, paragraph 32.

version of the eIDAS regulation, it is clear that a comprehensive and harmonised approach is yet to emerge.

6. EVALUATION

828. A COMPLEX ENVIRONMENT – eGovernment identity management systems involve a wide range of actors. The preceding sections have illustrated that it can be difficult, even for experts, to determine the precise role of each actor involved. There are at least two factors which complicate the analysis. First, there is the *distribution of influence* over the processing. In eGovernment identity management, different actors influence the processing at different stages and to different degrees. Only rarely does a single actor exercise complete and exclusive control over a given processing activity. Second, eGovernment identity management involves a wide range of *supporting services* (e.g. verification, integration) which are operated independently of the specific information exchanges they facilitate.

829. HYBRID ROLE OF INTERMEDIARIES – Intermediaries, such as IMI or PEPS, promote interoperability among public administrations. While the services they provide mainly benefit the interests of their end-users (the intermediary in principle has no direct interest in the information being exchanged), the end-users have only limited influence over the design and operation of these services. This finding does not, by itself, disqualify end-users from being controllers. It does beg the question, however, when such intermediaries should be considered as mere processors or rather as (joint) controllers. After all, these entities exercise a determinative influence on how the processing shall be organised in order to achieve a particular purpose. The two case studies presented in this chapter illustrate the difficulties surrounding the hybrid role of intermediaries.

830. INTERNAL MARKET INFORMATION SYSTEM – In the case of IMI, the European Commission was labelled a controller for its role in the design and operation of the IMI system.[1709] Its legal relationship with other IMI actors, however, remains blurry. Initially the Commission was labelled a joint controller, more recently it was implied that the Commission acts a separate controller. The controllership status attributed to the Commission for its role in IMI appears similar to the status given by the Article 29 Working Party to the operators of so-called "e-Government portals".

1709 The Commission is not always clearly identified as a "controller". The Commission has more frequently been referred to as the "operator" of the system. Regulation 1024/2012 does not explicitly state whether the Commission is a controller or not.

831. e-Government portals – In Opinion 1/2010, the Article 29 Working Party made the following observations regarding the role of e-Government portals:

> "E-Government portals act as intermediaries between the citizens and the public administration units: the portal transfers the requests of the citizens and deposits the documents of the public administration unit until these are recalled by the citizen. Each public administration unit remains controller of the data processed for its own purposes. Nevertheless, the portal itself may be also considered controller. Indeed, it processes (i.e. collects and transfers to the competent unit) the requests of the citizens as well as the public documents (i.e. stores them and regulates any access to them, such as the download by the citizens) for further purposes (facilitation of e-Government services) than those for which the data are initially processed by each public administration unit."[1710]

832. Critique – Lokke Moerel has extensively criticized the interpretation put forth by the Article 29 Working Party in relation to e-Government portals.[1711] Specifically, she argues that the Working Party mistakenly attributes controllership based on the portal's ability to decide about certain *aspects* of the processing (e.g. security), without also deciding about the purposes and means of the underlying processing operations.[1712] Moerel views the Working Party's construction as a *strategic* interpretation, designed to render the portal provider directly accountable for certain aspects of the processing, which at the time was only possible by attributing controllership:

> "The fact that the third-party provider probably decides also on the security measures for the portal (and is probably best positioned to do so), does not change the fact that he does not have decision-making power as to the purposes and means of the processing. Though I agree with the Working Party 29 that it may be advisable to make data processors (in addition to controllers) responsible for data security, this should be achieved by making (also) the data processor directly responsible for the security of processing in the revised Directive, rather than through a creative interpretation of the concept of controller."[1713]

833. Assessment – In my view, it is not surprising that the Article 29 Working Party considered the operators of e-Government portals as controllers. It is possible to distinguish, at least in theory, between *control over a system* and *control over specific processing activities within that system*.[1714] In practice,

---

1710 Opinion 1/2010, *l.c.*, p. 21.

1711 L. Moerel, *Binding Corporate Rules: Corporate Self-Regulation of Global Data Transfers*, Oxford, Oxford University Press, 2012, p. 221–223.

1712 L. Moerel, *Binding Corporate Rules: Corporate Self-Regulation of Global Data Transfers*, *o.c.*, p. 221.

1713 *Ibid*, p. 222.

1714 See also Tweede Kamer der Staten-Generaal, Regels inzake de bescherming van persoonsgegevens (Wet bescherming persoonsgegevens) – Memorie van Toelichting, *l.c.*, 59

however, it is not always easy to establish when an intermediary "controls a system" or merely "operates a system on behalf of others".[1715] As far as IMI is concerned, the judgment of CJEU in *Jehovah's Witnesses* now offers (additional) support for the argument that the Commission should be viewed as a joint controller as regards the processing of personal data exchanged via IMI, as it effectively "organises, coordinates and encourages" the processing of personal data within IMI.[1716]

834. PAN-EUROPEAN PROXY SERVICE – The example of the Pan-European Proxy Service (PEPS) also illustrates the practical difficulties that may arise when applying the existing concepts to e-Government intermediaries. Despite the additional guidance contained in Opinion 1/2010, the Biometrics & eGovernment Subgroup was unable to come to a common position as to whether the operator of a PEPS should be deemed a controller or a processor. The reasoning of the Subgroup suggests that the final outcome may be more a result of framing rather than the straight-forward application of established criteria. If one emphasises the autonomous design of the service, or the limited choices available to end-users, one winds up concluding that the PEPS operator acts as a controller. Conversely, if one emphasizes the auxiliary nature of the service, designed to serve the interests of others, one winds up concluding that the PEPS operator should be deemed a processor.

835. IMI: A PRAGMATIC APPROACH – Regulation 1024/2012 provides a relatively comprehensive data protection framework for IMI.[1717] After 5 years of incremental progress, the main responsibilities of each actor have been set forth in a binding legal instrument. The final distribution of tasks seems to have been driven more by pragmatic than by formal considerations. The Commission, as co-ordinator and operator of the IMI system, is best placed to assume responsibility for data protection requirements that concern the system as such (e.g. security, transparency regarding the functionalities of IMI). The competent authorities, on the other hand, must remain obliged to use the system responsibly and collaborate in the accommodation of data subject rights. Questions of who is controller, joint controller or processor seem to have had a limited impact in the past. Any lingering conceptual ambiguity was overcome by simply focusing on how responsibilities should be allocated.

---

and M. Overkleeft-Verburg, *De Wet persoonsregistraties – norm, toepassing en evaluatie*, *o.c.*, p. 374.

1715 See also *infra*, no. 1210 et seq.

1716 Cf. *supra*, no. 789.

1717 Certain issues are yet to be addressed, however, such as the use of national unique identifiers.

CHAPTER 3
ONLINE SOCIAL NETWORKS

1. INTRODUCTION

836. The rise of OSNs – One of the most significant developments in the online environment over the past decade has been the rise of social media.[1718] More and more individuals are making use of online social networks (OSNs) to stay in touch with family and friends, to engage in professional networking or to connect around shared interests and ideas. But users are not the only ones who are interested in OSNs. OSNs have come to attract a wide range of actors, which include application developers, web trackers, third-party websites, data brokers and other observers.

837. Outline – The objective of this chapter is to analyse how EU data protection law applies in the context of OSNs. To this end, it will begin by describing the various actors engaging with OSNs and the interactions between them. Next, it will analyse the legal status ("role") of each actor, as interpreted by courts, regulators and scholars. After that, it will describe the main responsibilities assigned to each actor. Once this analysis has been completed, this chapter will critically evaluate the relationship between the current framing of roles and responsibilities in the context of online social networking.

2. ACTORS

838. Overview – The following eight actors may be considered as being particularly relevant to online social networks from a data protection and privacy perspective:

(1) OSN users;
(2) OSN providers;
(3) Page administrators;
(4) (Third-party) Application providers;

1718 O. Tene, "Privacy: The new generations", *International Data Privacy Law* 2011, Vol. 1, No. 1, p. 22.

(5) (Third-party) Trackers;
(6) (Third-party) Data brokers;
(7) (Third-party) Website operators;
(8) Other observers; and
(9) Infrastructure service providers.[1719]

839. Visual representation – The aforementioned actors interact with each other in a variety of ways. The following figure provides a – highly simplified – representation of how these actors typically interact with OSNs and OSN-related data. It is intended to be conceptual rather than factual.

Figure 4. Main OSN actors

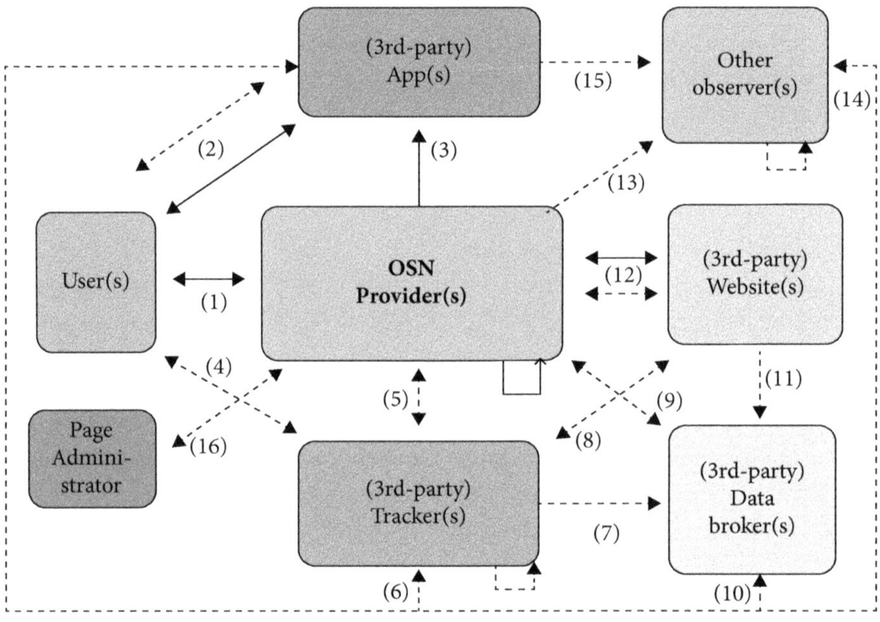

840. Legend – The arrows in Figure 4 indicate that an exchange of personal data is taking place. This exchange can be either uni- or bi-directional. Solid black arrows signify exchanges of personal data which occur primarily "in the foreground", meaning that they can easily be observed or inferred by OSN users. They often imply some form of active involvement by OSN users (e.g. granting

[1719] The inventory of actors provided here was composed on the basis of a literature study of academic publications, regulatory guidance and news articles concerning privacy and data protection in OSNs. A common denominator among the selected entities is that they each process personal data resulting from (a) the usage of OSNs and/or (b) the usage of other services which somehow interact with the OSN.

a permission, manually entering data, use of an application). Dashed grey arrows were used to signify data exchanges which are likely to be less obvious to OSN Users. Some of these exchanges may be detectable (e.g. by monitoring the activities of one's internet browser) or otherwise ascertainable (e.g. by reading the privacy notice of an OSN provider).[1720] Others may occur completely unnoticed. Over the following sections, a brief description is provided of each of the actors and interactions displayed in Figure 4.

841. Combinations possible – The reader should note that the categories of actors identified in Figure 4 are not mutually exclusive. A given actor may combine multiple roles depending on the circumstances (e.g. an OSN provider might also deploy its own tracking mechanisms, or an application provider might also be the operator of a third-party website).

2.1. OSN USER

842. Main characteristics – An OSN user is, as the name suggests, any individual who makes use of an OSN. People can join OSNs in different capacities. Individuals acting in a personal capacity typically join an OSN to stay in touch with friends and family, to exchange information about shared interests, or to seek out employment opportunities.[1721]

843. Data categories – Individuals can disclose a great deal of information about themselves when making use of OSNs. The creation of an OSN account (or "profile") involves disclosure of a number of attributes, which typically include name, date of birth and place of residence. Most OSNs also encourage individuals to upload a picture of themselves.[1722] Depending on the nature of the OSN, individuals might be encouraged to reveal additional information such as relationship status and interests (e.g. Facebook) or current employment (e.g. LinkedIn). Once an individual has signed up, he or she is essentially free to share any information they see fit. This information can range from mundane facts (e.g. "I'm at the mall"), to political views (e.g. "vote 'no' on prop 11"), to highly intimate personal details (e.g. "I'm dating Alice but I think I'm in love with Bob"). Even though the policies of an OSN may impose certain restrictions, individual OSN users are also in a position to disclose information about others. Finally, it is worth

[1720] Even if users are notified of their existence at a certain point in time, they may not be consciously aware of them at a later stage, as these exchanges typically occur "in the background" or do not require active user involvement.

[1721] A. Smith, "Why Americans use social media", *Pew Internet & American Life project*, Pewinternet.org, 15 November 2011.

[1722] d.m. boyd and N.B. Ellison, "Social Networking Sites: Definition, History and Scholarship", *Journal of Computer-Mediated Communication* 2008, vol. 13, p. 211–212.

noting that a significant amount of personal data disclosed via OSNs is relational. Social connections among individual OSN users can be used to create a "social graph", whereby nodes represent users and connections or edges represent the relationships between these users.[1723] In addition, certain OSN features expose additional relational information (e.g. group formation).

844. Data flows – At the end of the day, OSN users disclose considerable amounts of information about themselves. They also access significant amounts of information related to others. This flow of personal data is depicted in Figure 4 as bi-directional arrow (1).

2.2. OSN PROVIDER

845. Main characteristics – An OSN provider is an entity that operates the hard- and software necessary to deliver an OSN service.[1724] According to boyd and Ellison, the key features of social network sites are that they allow individuals to

"(1) construct a public or semi-public profile within a bounded system;
(2) articulate a list of other users with whom they share a connection; and
(3) view and traverse their list of connections and those made by others within the system."[1725]

846. Data categories – OSN providers collect various types of data about their users. Schneier has developed a taxonomy of "social networking data", which distinguishes among the following six categories of data[1726]:

1723 R. Sayaf and D. Clarke, "Access control models for online social networks", in *Social Network Engineering for Secure Web Data and Services*, IGI, 2013, p. 2; G. Pallis, D. Zeinalipour-Yazti and M.D. Dikaiakos in A. Vakali and L.C. Jain (eds.), "Online Social Networks: Status and Trends", *New Directions in Web Data Management*, Studies in Computational Intelligence, Vol. 331, 2011, p. 215.

1724 A reference architecture of OSNs can be found in G. Pallis, D. Zeinalipour-Yazti and M.D. Dikaiakos in A. Vakali and L.C. Jain (eds.), "Online Social Networks: Status and Trends", *l.c.*, p. 217.

1725 d.m. boyd and N.B. Ellison, "Social Networking Sites: Definition, History and Scholarship", *l.c.*, p. 211. This definition has been criticized by Beer as being too broad: see D. Beer, "Social network(ing) sites ... revisiting the story so far: A response to danah boyd & Nicole Ellison", *Journal of Computer-Mediated Communication* 2008, Vol. 13, p. 516 et seq. See also J. Heidemann, M. Klier and F. Probst, "Online social networks: A survey of a global phenomenon", *l.c.*, p. 3867. Like Heidemann, I use the term Online Social Networks to refer to "user-oriented" (as opposed to "content-oriented") social network sites; which emphasize social relationships and communities. The distinction between "content-oriented" and "user-oriented" social networks was proferred by G. Pallis, D. Zeinalipour-Yazti and M.D. Dikaiakos in A. Vakali and L.C. Jain (eds.), "Online Social Networks: Status and Trends", *l.c.*, 2011, p. 220.

1726 B. Schneier, "A Taxonomy of Social Networking Data", *Security & Privacy* 2009, IEEE, Vol. 8, Issue 4, p. 88.

1. *Service data*: data provided to an OSN provider in order to make use the OSN (e.g. legal name, age);
2. *Disclosed data*: data that is posted by OSN users on their own profile pages (e.g. blog entry, picture, video);
3. *Entrusted data*: data that is posted by OSN users on the profile pages of other OSN users (e.g. a wall post, comment);
4. *Incidental data*: data about an OSN user which has been uploaded by another OSN user (e.g. a picture);
5. *Behavioural data*: data regarding the activities of OSN users within the OSN (e.g. who they interact with and how); and
6. *Derived data*: data which is inferred from (other) OSN data (e.g. membership of group X implies attribute Y).

847. DATA USAGE – The data collected by OSN providers are used to enable various forms of social interaction. While the display of user profiles may be considered the "backbone"[1727] of an OSN, many platforms offer an array of additional features and services. OSNs typically provide common messaging services (e.g. chat, email), as well as message board and commenting functions.[1728] An OSN provider can also use the personal data of its users to support its business model. In fact, the primary source of revenue for most OSN providers is derived from advertising.[1729] These business models are based on the principle that "free" services can attract large and diverse audiences, which in turn will attract advertisers.[1730] Popular OSNs, which have a large number of active users, can develop rich sets of demographic and behavioural data.[1731] The profile information of these users, together with information about their activities (e.g. web browsing, app usage, "likes", current location, etc.), can be used to enhance audience segmentation and contextual awareness.[1732] This

1727 d.m. boyd and N.B. Ellison, "Social Networking Sites: Definition, History and Scholarship", *l.c.*, p. 211.

1728 J. Heidemann, M. Klier and F. Probst, "Online social networks: A survey of a global phenomenon", *l.c.*, p. 3867.

1729 For an early analysis of different revenue models for OSN see A. Enders, H. Hungenberg, "The long tail of social networking. Revenue models of social networking sites", *European Management Journal* 2008, Vol. 26, p. 199- 211. For a more recent study see G. Pallis, D. Zeinalipour-Yazti and M.D. Dikaiakos in A. Vakali and L.C. Jain (eds.), "Online Social Networks: Status and Trends", *l.c.*, 2011, pp 213–234. Alternative and/or additional revenue sources include subscription fees (e.g. for "premium" accounts) and platform purchases (e.g. by charging a percentage on the purchase of apps or other products which were bought through the OSN platform).

1730 G. Pallis, D. Zeinalipour-Yazti and M.D. Dikaiakos in A. Vakali and L.C. Jain (eds.), "Online Social Networks: Status and Trends", *l.c.*, p. 221.

1731 *Ibid*, p. 222.

1732 Facebook, for example, enables third parties to target advertisements to its users on the basis of location, gender, age, likes and interests, relationship status, workplace and education. See also R. Heyman and J. Pierson, "An Explorative Mapping of the Belgian Social Media Value Network and its Usage of Personal Identifiable Information", paper presented at

ability is of great interest to advertisers, who are eager to see advertisements presented to users who are likely to be influenced by them.

848. Data flows – The data flows which facilitate behavioural targeting are represented in Figure 4 by arrows (4) through (10). Each of these data flows will be elaborated further in the following sections.

2.3. PAGE ADMINISTRATOR

849. Main characteristics – OSNs are increasingly being used by companies and other organisations to advance commercial, political or humanitarian goals.[1733] A company, for example, might set up a "Page" or other presence on the OSN in order to advertise its products or simply to increase brand awareness. As part of its social media strategy, a company might also use additional services provided by the OSN provider in an effort to increase its engagement with OSN users (e.g. by "boosting" a post[1734] or using other targeting services provided by the OSN).

850. Data categories – Page administrators typically do not disclose large amounts of personal data when creating a presence on an OSN. Depending on the OSN, they may be able to obtain aggregated information (so-called "insights") regarding the interactions individual OSN users have had with their pages or posts. Facebook, for example, offers businesses a service called "Page Insights", which enables page administrators to see demographic data about the people who have liked their page (including gender, age, location and language).[1735]

851. Data flows – The aggregated information disclosed by an OSN provider to a Page administrator in principle does not constitute personal data. In order to create the aggregated information, however, processing of personal data will be necessary. Moreover, the use of additional services offered by the OSN provider

---

IFIP Summerschool on Privacy & Identity Management 2013, p. 2.) For a survey of different targeting methods using social networking information see A. Bagherjeiran, R.P. Bhatt, R. Parekh and V. Chaoji, "Online Advertising in Social Networks", in B. Furht (ed), *Handbook of Social Network Technologies and Applications*, 2010, Springer, New York, p. 653 et seq.

1733 See e.g. J. Heidemann, M. Klier and F. Probst, "Online social networks: A survey of a global phenomenon", *Computer Networks* 2012, vol. 56, p. 3871–3872 (discussing potential usage by businesses); R.D. Waters, E. Burnett, A. Lamm and J. Lucas, "Engaging stakeholders through social networking: How nonprofit organisations are using Facebook", *Public Relations Review* 2009, Vol. 35, Issue 2, p. 102–106. See also Article 29 Working Party, "Opinion 5/2009 on online social networking", WP163, p. 7.

1734 See Facebook Business, "Boost a Facebook Post", https://www.facebook.com/business/pages/boost-post?ref=ens_rdr (last accessed 3 January 2019).

1735 See Facebook Business, Using Page Insights, https://en-gb.facebook.com/business/a/page/page-insights#u_0_2 (last accessed (last accessed 3 January 2019).

to the Page administrator (e.g. the ability reach a particular demographic) may also involve processing personal data. The flow of data from the OSN provider to the Page administrator is depicted in Figure 4 as dashed arrow (16).

2.4. (THIRD-PARTY) APPLICATION PROVIDER

852. MAIN CHARACTERISTICS – Third-party applications (often referred to simply as "apps") have become a popular feature on OSNs.[1736] An app is a standardised piece of software that runs on a computing platform.[1737] In principle, an app can provide just about any functionality: gaming, content streaming, location sharing, crowd funding … the possibilities are endless. Several major OSN providers now allow third-party application developers to offer their apps through the OSN.[1738]

853. DATA COLLECTION – App usage is generally predicated upon the granting of permissions. Permissions requested by application providers typically concern access rights (e.g. the ability to access to profile information, photos, etc.) and/or the ability to act on the user's behalf (e.g. to post on a message board or send an email on behalf of the user).[1739] Once permissions have been granted, the application provider can use these privileges to collect personal data about the user from the OSN provider. It can also collect additional information from users directly (e.g. by monitoring their application usage).

1736 M. Huber, M. Mulazzani, S. Schrittwieser, E.R. Weippl, "AppInspect – Large-scale Evaluation of Social Apps", *Proceedings of ACM Conference on Online Social Networks* (CSON) 2013, p. 1.

1737 OECD, "The App Economy", *OECD Digital Economy Papers* 2013, No. 230, OECD Publishing, p. 8. Apps can be divided among two main categories: "mobile" or "web-based". In case of mobile apps, the "computing platform" that hosts the app is a mobile device, typically a smartphone or a tablet. In case of web-based apps, the app itself is hosted on a webserver which is controlled by the application provider. While mobile apps are stored on a smartphone rather than a webserver, many mobile apps still communicate with a webserver. For purposes of conceptual clarity, we will approach our discussion of third-party applications under the assumption that they are web-based, except when explicitly indicated otherwise. For an in-depth discussion of mobile apps on smart devices see Article 29 Data Protection Working Party, "Opinion 02/2013 on apps on smart devices", WP202, 27 February 2013.

1738 W. De Groef, D. Devries, T. Reynaert and F. Piessens, "Security and Privacy of Online Social Network Applications", in L. Caviglione, M. Coccoli and A. Merlo (eds.), *Social Network Engineering for Secure Web Data and Services*, IGI Global, 2013, p. 207 et seq.

1739 In practice, the OSN user delegates one or more access rights to the application provider using a pre-determined protocol (e.g. OAuth). Once the permissions have been granted, the application provider will query the social network application programming interface (API) to make use the delegated privileges (e.g. access profile information, post to wall). (W. De Groef, D. Devries, T. Reynaert and F. Piessens, "Security and Privacy of Online Social Network Applications", *l.c.*, p. 208). See also M. Huber, M. Mulazzani, S. Schrittwieser, E.R. Weippl, "AppInspect – Large-scale Evaluation of Social Apps", *l.c.*, p. 1–2.

854. DATA USAGE – Third-party application providers may use data about OSN users in a variety of ways. Some apps are "socially aware", meaning that they consume OSN data (e.g. profile data, relationship information) to deliver their functionality. For example, a horoscope application might require the birthdates of you and your contacts in order to create a compatibility chart. Other apps do not require user data to function as such, but use them to incorporate other aspects of social networking.[1740] For example, users might be encouraged to share gaming high scores or to display which music feeds they are listening to on their profile. As in the case of OSN providers, data collected by application providers is often also used to facilitate behavioural advertising, particularly when users are able to use an app without monetary payment.

855. DATA FLOWS – While an app may be accessible through an OSN website, the app itself typically runs on a third-party server (i.e. outside the OSN domain).[1741] In order to make app usage an integral part of the user experience, the OSN provider can embed applications within the OSN website (e.g. as an iframe).[1742] In this approach, the OSN provider effectively acts as a proxy between users and third-party application providers.[1743] Alternatively, the OSN provider can simply direct its users to the websites of the application providers. The data flows among application providers, OSN providers and OSN users are depicted in Figure 4 as arrows (2) and (3). Arrow (2) is bi-directional because application providers may also send their users data about other users (e.g. music feeds or current location).

2.5. (THIRD-PARTY) TRACKER

856. MAIN CHARACTERISTICS – In the context of this chapter, the term "tracker" is used to describe any entity that collects and/or analyses data relating to the internet browsing activities of OSN users across websites.[1744] There are

---

1740 M. Huber, M. Mulazzani, S. Schrittwieser, E.R. Weippl, "AppInspect – Large-scale Evaluation of Social Apps", *l.c.*, p. 2.

1741 *Id.* In earlier implementation models, social applications were deployed on the infrastructure of the OSN itself (this model is sometimes referred to as the "gadget paradigm"). Increasingly, however, a different model is followed, whereby applications are delivered through an Applications Programming Interface (API) (also referred to as the "distributed" paradigm). (W. De Groef, D. Devries, T. Reynaert and F. Piessens, "Security and Privacy of Online Social Network Applications", *l.c.*, p. 208).

1742 M. Huber, M. Mulazzani, S. Schrittwieser, E.R. Weippl, "AppInspect – Large-scale Evaluation of Social Apps", *l.c.*, p. 2. See also W. De Groef, D. Devries, T. Reynaert and F. Piessens, "Security and Privacy of Online Social Network Applications", *l.c.*, p. 211 et seq.

1743 *Ibid*, p. 1.

1744 The term "third party" is bracketed to indicate that several OSN providers deploy their own tracking technologies to monitor user behaviour inside and outside the OSN.

many different ways of tracking individuals online.[1745] The most well-known technique involves the use of "cookies".[1746] Cookies are browser files deployed by website operators in order to keep track of their interactions with a particular visitor.[1747] On many websites, individuals also receive cookies emanating from third party domains ("third-party cookies"), which can be used to monitor their browsing behaviour across different websites.[1748] Other well-known tracking techniques involve use of javascripts and browser fingerprinting.[1749]

857. DATA DISCLOSURE – A 2008 study by Krishnamurthy and Wills found that individuals' activities on OSN may be subject to third-party tracking. Specifically, they found that several user actions (e.g. logging in, viewing a profile page, leaving a message) on OSNs such as Facebook and Myspace resulted in the retrieval of objects from third-party domains.[1750] The access of third-party domains in this context suggested that OSN users may be tracked by third parties even when they are engaged in social networking activities (in addition to being tracked during other browsing activities).[1751] In a follow-up study, the same authors found that many OSNs also leaked additional information about OSN users, such as name, gender or OSN unique ID.[1752] This meant that the browsing behaviour of a particular OSN user – including his or her behaviour outside of the OSN context – might be easily linked to his or her OSN identity.[1753]

1745 See C. Casteluccia, "Behavioural Tracking on the Internet: A Technical perspective", S. Gutwirth et al. (eds.), *European Data Protection: In Good Health?*, 2013, Springer Science+Business Media, p. 21 et seq. for an inventory of prevalent web tracking techniques.

1746 A cookie is an alphanumeric text file which is stored by a web browser. Cookies are typically set by web servers the first time a user visits a particular site. They are then sent back automatically by the browser each time it accesses the web server that placed them. (C. Casteluccia, "Behavioural Tracking on the Internet: A Technical perspective", *l.c.*, p. 23–24 and Article 29 Data Protection Working Party, "Opinion 2/2010 on online behavioural advertising", WP 171, 22 June 2010, p. 7.

1747 This technique may be particularly useful for identifying returning visitors and recording user preferences (e.g. language preferences).

1748 For example, a web page may contain images, links, iframes or other components stored by servers in other domains. When the user accesses the website, these components will be retrieved from the third-party domain, which allows for the placement of third-party cookies. This technique can be used to effectively track users across multiple sites (in particular across all pages where one has placed an advertising image or web bug) (C. Casteluccia, "Behavioural Tracking on the Internet: A Technical perspective", *l.c.*, p. 23–24).

1749 See C. Casteluccia, "Behavioural Tracking on the Internet: A Technical perspective", *l.c.*, p. 21 et seq.

1750 B. Krishnamurthy and C.E. Wills, "Characterizing Privacy in Online Social Networks", *WOSN* 2008, Proceedings of the 1st ACM workshop on Online social networks, 2008 p. 40.

1751 *Ibid*, p. 41.

1752 B. Krishnamurthy and C.E. Wills, "On the Leakage of Personally Identifiable Information Via Online Social Networks", *WOSN 2009*, Proceedings of the 2nd ACM workshop on Online social networks, 2009, p. 7. See also C. Casteluccia, "Behavioural Tracking on the Internet: A Technical perspective", *l.c.*, p. 28.

1753 *Id.* See also J. Cheng, "Social networks make it easy for third parties to identify you", *Ars Technica*, 25 September 2009.

858. Data usage – By monitoring individuals' browsing activities over time, trackers are able to build rich behavioural profiles. These profiles can in turn be used for online behavioural advertising (OBA), which is an important source of revenue for trackers.[1754] In many cases, third-party trackers work on behalf of ad networks, whose goal it is to target ads with the maximum effect possible.[1755]

859. Data flows – The data flows related to tracking of OSN users are depicted in Figure 4 by arrows (4) and (5). Arrow (4) represents tracking which occurs via the browsers of OSN users (arrow (4)). In this scenario, the OSN provider does not directly share information about the user with trackers. Instead, it is sufficient for the OSN provider to embed components which result in the retrieval of third-party objects.[1756] Arrow (5) depicts the data flows which take place in situations where an OSN provider actively collaborates with a tracker. This might occur, for example, in situations where the tracker is working on behalf of the OSN provider (e.g. if the OSN provider wishes to collect data about its users browsing activities outside the OSN).[1757] Many application providers and third-party websites also embed components which facilitate third-party tracking and ad delivery. This is depicted in Figure 4 by arrows (6) and (8).[1758]

1754 The Article 29 Working Party defines behavioural advertising as advertising which is based on the observation of the behaviour of individuals over time. By studying the characteristics of individuals' behaviour over time (repeated site visits, interactions, keywords, etc), trackers can develop specific profiles on individuals, which in turn allows tailoring advertisements to the inferred interests of each individual concerned. (Article 29 Data Protection Working Party, "Opinion 2/2010 on online behavioural advertising", *l.c.*, p. 4).

1755 An ad network is an entity that connects website owners ("publishers") with advertisers. In this model, a website owner simply needs to reserve a certain amount of visual on its website that will serve to display ads and relinquish the rest of the process to one or more ad network providers. The ad network provider is then responsible for distributing advertisements to publishers (on behalf of companies seeking to advertise). (Article 29 Data Protection Working Party, "Opinion 2/2010 on online behavioural advertising", *l.c.*, p. 5). As indicated earlier, the OSN providers may offer targeting options which function independently of third-party trackers, using criteria derived from e.g. the profile information of their users. In this model, the OSN provider uses its own targeting technology and makes its own decisions about ad placement and distribution (in accordance with advertiser demands).

1756 Arrow (4) is bi-directional arrow because every time a user accesses a webpage which links to the tracker's server, the cookie that is stored in the user's browser will be updated with data about the user's latest interactions.

1757 The term "third party" is bracketed to indicate that several OSN provider deploy their own tracking technologies to monitor user behaviour inside and outside the OSN.

1758 Arrows (6) and (8) are misleading to the extent that tracking occurs via the browser or operating system of the user (in which case it would simply coincide with arrow (4). The reason for choosing this form of visual representation is to make clear that users can be tracked across a wide range of activities, i.e. across web browsing, OSN usage and app usage.

2.6. (THIRD-PARTY) DATA BROKER

860. MAIN CHARACTERISTICS – Data brokers (also referred to as "data aggregators" or "information resellers") are entities which collect and sell information. To be more specific, a data broker is a company that collects data, including personal data, from a wide variety of sources with a view of turning these data into marketable commodities.[1759] Among the products offered by data brokers are consumer profiles (which categorize individuals into pre-determined consumer segments) and scoring products (which score the likelihood for certain behaviours, based on inferences drawn from other data).[1760]

861. DATA COLLECTION – Data brokers collect data from a wide variety of sources. Several data brokers also collect data about individuals from OSN sites.[1761] For example, data broker Acxiom reportedly collects data regarding individuals' social media usage to predict whether he or she should be considered a "heavy social media user", "poster", "video sharer", "social influencer", or "social influenced".[1762] Several data brokers reportedly also use click-stream data (i.e. data relating to individuals' browsing behaviour) in developing consumer profiles.[1763]

862. DATA USAGE – Information collected by data brokers is put to a variety of uses. Prominent examples include identity verification, fraud prevention, marketing, credit risk assessments and background checks.[1764] Some data brokers also offer products that enable marketers to use off-line data to target individuals online.[1765] These products can also be put to use in an OSN context. Facebook, for example, has previously partnered with data brokers such as

---

1759 Based on Federal Trade Commission, *Protecting Consumer Privacy in an Era of Rapid Change*, March 2012, p. 68.

1760 U.S. Senate Committee on Commerce, Science and Transportation, "A Review of the Data Broker Industry: Collection, Use, and Sale of Consumer Data for Marketing Purposes", Staff Report for Chairman Rockefeller, 2013, p. 12 and 23.

1761 Other avenues include government records and other public data, purchase or license from other data collectors, cooperative agreements with other companies, self-reporting by consumers (e.g. through surveys or questionnaires). U.S. Senate Committee on Commerce, Science and Transportation, "A Review of the Data Broker Industry: Collection, Use, and Sale of Consumer Data for Marketing Purposes", *l.c.*, p. 15.

1762 *Ibid*, p. 21.

1763 *Id.* See also OECD, "Exploring data-driven innovation as a new source of growth: Mapping the policy issues raised by "big data"", in OECD, Supporting Investment in Knowledge Capital, Growth and Innovation, 2013, OECD Publishing, doi: 10.1787/9789264193307-12-en, p. 328.

1764 Federal Trade Commission, "Protecting Consumer Privacy in an Era of Rapid Change", *l.c.*, p. 68

1765 U.S. Senate Committee on Commerce, Science and Transportation, "A Review of the Data Broker Industry: Collection, Use, and Sale of Consumer Data for Marketing Purposes", *l.c.*, p. 12.

Acxiom, Datalogix and Epsilon so that advertisers can target OSN users on the basis of their purchasing behaviour outside the social network.[1766] Facebook reportedly also partnered with data broker BlueKai to enable further targeting of OSN users on the basis of their browsing activities outside the OSN.[1767]

863. Data flows – Figure 4 visualizes the corresponding data flows as follows: arrow (9) represents the exchange of personal data that takes place between data brokers and social networks. It is important to note that the collection of personal data by data brokers does not necessarily involve "active" disclosure by the OSN provider (e.g. the data might simply be collected from publicly available OSN sites). Arrow (9) is bi-directional as data brokers may also indirectly reveal data about OSN users to the OSN provider (e.g. regarding their inferred interests). Arrows (7), (10) and (11) intend to illustrate that data brokers may also obtain information about individual OSN users from trackers (e.g. browsing history), application providers (e.g. app usage) or third-party website operators (e.g. purchase history).

2.7. (THIRD-PARTY) WEBSITE OPERATOR

864. Main characteristics – A third-party website is, as the name suggests, a website operated by an entity other than the OSN or the OSN user. Third-party websites can interact with OSNs in a variety of ways. For example, OSNs such as Facebook and MySpace allow third parties to leverage their authentication services, so that individuals can make use of their OSN credentials when accessing these websites.[1768] "Social plug-ins" are another prominent way in which third-party websites interact with OSNs. A social plug-in is a website component designed to facilitate the sharing of third-party content within OSNs. Facebook's "Like button", for example, enables users to

---

1766 Specifically, Facebook added "partner categories" as an additional targeting feature, which enables advertisers to target individuals based on the basis of their purchase behaviour outside the social network. See also C. Dello, "Facebook to Partner With Acxiom, Epsilon to Match Store Purchases with User Profiles – Can Facebook Ads Drive Offline Buying?", *Advertising Age*, 22 February 2013.

1767 K. Opshal and R. Reitman, "The Disconcerting Details: How Facebook Teams Up With Data Brokers to Show You Targeted Ads", Electronic Frontier Foundation (EFF), 22 April 2013. In March 2018, Facebook announced that it would be shutting down partner categories: see Facebook, "Shutting Down Partner Categories", Facebook newsroom, 28 March 2018.

1768 M.N. Ko, G.P. Cheek and M. Shebab, "Social-Networks Connect Services", *Computer* 2010, Issue no. 8, IEEE Computer Society, p. 37. The Facebook platform (Facebook's API) also allows third-party sites to obtain authorization tokens from Facebook. This basically works as follows: the user first authenticates herself using Facebook as their identity provider. Next, Facebook issues a token that allows the third-party site to access the user's basic profile information. The third-party site can then request additional permissions, much in the same way as (other) application providers (*Ibid*, p. 38–39). See also *supra*, no. 853.

leave positive feedback for a web page and to share it with others.[1769] Similar tools are offered by other OSNs such as Pinterest ("Pin it") and Linkedin ("in share").[1770]

865. DATA DISCLOSURE – Despite the convenience of plug-ins, their increased presence on third-party websites has also engendered controversy. Specifically, it has been demonstrated that social plug-ins can enable OSN providers to monitor the browsing activities of its users beyond the context of the OSN.[1771] This tracking capability may exist even if the user does not actually click on the plug-in at hand. It is sufficient that the plug-in has been embedded on the website in question in order for the data to be transmitted automatically.[1772] Moreover, the tracking capability offered by plug-ins is not limited to OSN users. Even if an individual does not have an account with a particular OSN provider, the presence of its social plug-ins may allow it to keep track of its visits to other pages in which the plug-in has been embedded.[1773]

866. DATA FLOWS – The data flows between OSN providers and third-party websites are depicted in Figure 4 by two arrows (12): the first is a solid bi-directional arrow which represents those flows which can be easily observed or inferred by OSN users. This is the case, for example, if an OSN user decides to use its OSN credential to log-in to a third-party website or app or to link third-

---

[1769] G. Kontaxis, M. Polychronakis, A.D. Keromytis and E.P. Markatos, "Privacy-Preserving Social Plugins", *Proceedings of the 21st USENIX conference on Security symposium*, 2012, p. 30.

[1770] By embedding social plug-ins the website operator can help increase the visibility of its webpages. It also enriches the data exchanged within OSNs, so these tools are generally considered beneficial for both website operators and OSN providers. For OSN users, the presence of social plug-ins offers convenience, as it enables them to share third-party content within their OSNs almost seamlessly (*Id.*).

[1771] *Id.* See also A.P.C. Roosendaal, "We Are All Connected to Facebook … by Facebook!", in S. Gutwirth et al. (eds), *European Data Protection: In Good Health?*, Springer, 2012, p. 3–19. See also G. Acar, B. Van Alsenoy, F. Piessens, C. Diaz and B. Preneel, "Facebook Tracking Through Social Plug-ins", Technical report prepared for the Belgian Privacy Commission, Version 1.1, 24 June 2015, 24 p. In 2018, the Belgian Privacy Commission conducted new technical findings, documenting the use of so-called "pixels" as an additional means to track the browsing activities of individuals outside of Facebook. See Commission for the Protection of Privacy, "Facebook tracking through social plug-ins", Updated technical report, Version 1.1, 24 February 2017.

[1772] *Id.*

[1773] *Id.* Facebook tracking through social plug-ins and pixels has been the subject of ongoing litigation between the Belgian Data Protection Authority and Facebook: see in particular: Court of First Instance of Brussels, Division of Summary Proceedings, *Willem Debeuckelaere v. Facebook Ireland Ltd., Facebook Inc. and Facebook Belgium BVBA*, Case number 15/57/C, 9 November 2015; Court of Appeal of Brussels, 18th Ch., *Facebook Ireland Ltd., Facebook Inc. and Facebook Belgium BVBA v. Willem Debeuckelaere*, Case number 2016/KR/2, 29 June 2016; Court of First Instance of Brussels, 24th Ch., Civil Matters, *Willem Debeuckelaere v. Facebook Ireland Ltd., Facebook Inc. and Facebook Belgium BVBA*, Case number 2016/153/A, 16 February 2018. At the moment of writing, the judgment of 16 Feburary 2018 is undergoing appeal.

party content to his or her profile. The second arrow is a dashed arrow which is meant to capture the leakage of browsing behaviour through social-plug-ins.[1774] The term "third party" is bracketed to indicate that an OSN provider may also operate websites or apps beyond the OSN context (e.g. Facebook also owns Masquerade).

2.8. OTHER OBSERVERS

867. MAIN CHARACTERISTICS – The previous sections have introduced some of the main players interacting with OSN-related data on a regular basis. An additional category of actors worth identifying is what one might refer to as "other observers". Other observers are entities who, regardless of whether or not they have a formal relationship with an OSN or its users, access data that is processed in the context of an OSN. Such access takes place regularly, and for a plethora reasons: market research, student oversight, law enforcement, intelligence gathering, credit risk assessment, employee background checks, disability verification etc.

868. DATA COLLECTION AND USE – Online news outlets are brimming with reports of how schools, employers, intelligence agencies and other entities are using social media to monitor individuals' activities. For example, school administrators are often cited as reviewing social networking data for inappropriate student behaviour, such as underage drinking.[1775] One Californian high school even hired a firm to monitor public postings on social media to search for possible violence, drug use, bullying, truancy and suicidal threats.[1776] Employers are also known consult OSNs when evaluating job applicants; or to take disciplinary action towards employees (even firing) after learning about unwanted behaviour through social media data.[1777] Last, but definitely not least, recent revelations concerning intelligence operations have indicated that

---

1774 Dashed arrow (12) is misleading – in a way similar to arrows (7) and (9) – to the extent that tracking occurs via the browser or operating system of the user (in which case they would coincide simply with arrow (4). The decision was made to visually represent the data flows in this way in order to make clear that users can be tracked by OSN providers across websites that have their social plug-ins embedded.

1775 See e.g. Associated Press, "District to monitor students MySpace pages", *NBC news*, 23 May 2006; N. Buczek, "Schools discipline students of Internet content", 22 February 2006.

1776 M. Martinez, "California school district hires firm to monitor students' social media", *CNN*, 18 September 2013.

1777 See e.g. C.A. Ciocchetti, "The eavesdropping employer: a twenty-first century framework for employee monitoring", *Future of Privacy Forum*, 2010, p. 45. According to a 2009 study by Proofpoint, an internet security firm, 8 percent of companies with one thousand employees or more have terminated at least one employee for comments posted on a social networking site. See A. Ostrow, "Facebook Fired: 8% of US Companies have Sacked Social Media Miscreants", *Mashable*, 10 August 2009.

national security agencies also use social networking data to evaluate potential national security threats.[1778]

869. Data flows – Arrow (13) represents the data flows which take place in situations where observers access OSN-related data. It is important to note that an observer may also access these data indirectly, e.g. via a data broker or tracker (arrows (14) and (15)). Finally, it is worth underlining that the observation of OSN data is not necessarily limited to data which has been labelled as "public" according to the user's privacy settings (e.g. in case of surreptitious monitoring or co-operation with law enforcement officials).

2.9. INFRASTRUCTURE (SERVICE) PROVIDER

870. Main characteristics – A final category of actors which is worth mentioning are the "infrastructure (service) providers". These are the entities that operate the technical infrastructure which is necessary for OSN providers to offer their services and for OSN users to make use of the OSN. Examples include Internet Service Providers ("ISPs"), hosting service providers, device manufactures, the providers of operating systems, etc. While the role of these entities will not be discussed in detail, it is nevertheless worth noting their essential role in enabling OSN interactions.

3. ROLES

871. Outline – Now that the main actors have been identified, this section will proceed to analyse their legal status under EU data protection law. Specifically, the following sections will evaluate to what extent OSN providers, OSN users, Page administrators, (third-party) application providers, third-party-website operators and other entities may be considered as "controllers" or "processors" within the meaning of the GDPR.

3.1. OSN PROVIDER

872. High-level analysis – OSN providers are generally considered to be "controllers" within the meaning of EU data protection law.[1779] After all, they

---

1778 See e.g. E. MacAskill, J. Borger, N. Hopkins, N. Davies and J. Ball, "GCHQ taps fibre-optic cables for secret access to world's communications", *The Guardian*, Friday 21 June 2013.

1779 See e.g. College Bescherming Persoonsgegevens, "Publicatie van Persoonsgegevens op het Internet", *CBP Richtsnoeren*, December 2007, p. 7–8; B. Van Alsenoy, J. Ballet and A. Kuczerawy, "Social networks and web 2.0: are users also bound by data protection

determine both the *purposes* and *means* of their own processing activities: their *purpose* is to provide a social networking service which generates revenue. They also determine the *means* of their own processing activities: they decide about the nature of the social networking service and how it will be provided – from user registration until account deletion. In addition to those operations that are strictly necessary to provide the OSN service, the provider also decides about a range of additional processing activities; including those designed to enable targeted advertising.[1780]

873. Scope of control – While most would agree that OSN providers should be considered as "controllers", opinions vary as to the boundaries of their control. In certain cases, it is relatively clear whether or not an OSN provider is acting as a controller. For instance, few would dispute that an OSN provider acts as a controller in relation to:

- the collection and use of explicitly solicited data (e.g. information which OSN users are asked to provide when registering to the site, such as their name, age and place of residence)[1781];
- their processing of user data for purposes of targeted advertising (e.g. when analysing "behavioural data"); and
- their processing of user data designed to enhance the quality of the OSN service or to provide additional features (e.g. use of facial recognition techniques to create "tag suggests"[1782]).

874. User-generated content – While the previous examples are relatively straightforward, there are processing activities for which it is more difficult to delineate to the role of the OSN provider. A particular contentious matter, at

regulations?", *l.c.*, p. 70; Article 29 Data Protection Working Party, "Opinion 5/2009 on online social networking", WP 163, 12 June 2009, p. 5; Article 29 Data Protection Working Party, "Opinion 1/2010 on the concepts of controller and processor", *l.c.*, p. 21; P. Van Eecke and M. Truyens, "Privacy and social networks", *Computer Law & Security Review* 2010, Vol. 26, p. 537–538; E. Kosta, C. Kalloniatis, L. Mitrou and S. Gritzalis, "Data protection issues pertaining to social networking under EU law", *Transforming Government: People, Process and Policy* 2010, Vol. 4, No. 2, p. 196; D.B. Garrie, M. Duffy-Lewis, R. Wong and R.L. Gillespie, "Data Protection: the Challenges Facing Social Networking", *International Law & Management Review* 2010, Vol. 6, p. 131; B.J. Koops, "Forgetting Footprints, Shunning Shadows. A Critical Analysis of the "Right to be Forgotten" in Big Data Practice", *Tilburg Law School Legal Studies Research Paper* Series No. 08/2012, p. 10 and Information Commissioner's Office (ICO), "Social networking and online forums – when does the DPA apply?", 24 May 2013, Version 1.0, p. 10–11.

1780 B. Van Alsenoy, J. Ballet and A. Kuczerawy, "Social networks and web 2.0: are users also bound by data protection regulations?", *l.c.*, p. 70.

1781 See also Cour d'Appel de Liège, 7ième Chambre, Bobon Benjamin / SPRL Diablo, 2008/RG/1165, 19 November 2009.

1782 See e.g. S. Curtis, "Facebook defends using profile pictures for facial recognition", *The Telegraph*, 15 November 2013.

least until recently, is whether or not an OSN provider should be considered as a (co-)controller in relation to content shared (spontaneously) by its users. For example, should an OSN provider be considered a "controller" of the processing that takes place when its users share content with one and other (e.g. the sharing of a photograph among friends)? There are essentially four different ways in which this issue has been approached by scholars, courts and regulators, each of which will be elaborated of the following paragraphs.

875. No control – Several authors argue that web 2.0 service providers, such as OSN providers, should not be considered as controllers in relation to user-generated content at all.[1783] After all, these entities exercise little or no influence at the moment content is being uploaded: while OSNs may encourage certain types of sharing, every user decides autonomously whether or not to share specific content. Moreover, it is argued, OSN providers cannot reasonably be expected to fulfil the obligations of controllers in relation to data shared by users (e.g. because they will not know, until after the fact, which data are being shared, about whom, etc.). Furthermore, requiring OSN providers to assume such control would have undesirable consequences, most notably for the freedom of expression of OSN users.[1784] From this perspective, it is argued that only the OSN user who decides to upload certain content should be considered as the controller vis-à-vis this sharing activity. The OSN provider, on the other hand, should be considered a mere "processor"[1785] or "hosting service provider".[1786]

876. Platform control – Other commentators have argued that OSN providers should be considered as controllers in addition to OSN users. Specifically, they argue that the OSN provider should be considered a controller in relation to its social networking service "as a whole".[1787] Once data have been

---

[1783] See e.g. G. Sartor, "Providers' liabilities in the new EU Data Protection Regulation: A threat to Internet freedoms?", *International Data Privacy Law* 2013, Vol. 3, No. 1, p. 9–10.

[1784] *Ibid*, p. 10.

[1785] See e.g. P. Van Eecke and M. Truyens, "Privacy and Social Networks", *l.c.*, p. 537–538. Personally, I consider this interpretation is at odds with 17(3) of Directive 95/46/EC. This provision implies a willingness, on the part of the processor, to only process personal data in accordance with the instructions issued by the controller. Moreover, this provision stipulates that this willingness must be expressed in the form of a legally binding instrument. Given that many OSN providers, in practice, reserve themselves the ability to modify the nature of their services at all times, often without prior consultation of their users, I would argue that they should not be considered as "processors", but rather as separate controllers (whose "control" extends to different aspects of the processing).

[1786] See e.g. G. Sartor, "Providers' liabilities in the new EU Data Protection Regulation: A threat to Internet freedoms?", *l.c.*, p. 5 et seq. Hosting service providers are provided with a (conditional) liability exemption under E-Commerce Directive 2000/31/EC. For purposes of conceptual clarity, the relationship between Directive 95/46/EC and E-Commerce Directive 2000/31/EC will be discussed *infra*, nos. 971 et seq.

[1787] See B. Van Alsenoy, J. Ballet and A. Kuczerawy, "Social networks and web 2.0: are users also bound by data protection regulations?", *l.c.*, p. 70.

uploaded, the OSN provider proceeds to perform operations upon them which enable the actual sharing of information (e.g. storage, analysis[1788], dissemination, access control). And for these processing activities, the provider has determined the "purposes and the means" in advance, independently of the OSN users.[1789] Because the sharing of personal data among contacts is an essential component of its service, these commentators conclude that the OSN provider acts as a (co-) controller vis-à-vis the dissemination of content over its platform (even though the initiative to share this content originated from one of its users).[1790]

877. PIECEMEAL CONTROL – A third approach, which combines elements of the previous two approaches, views both OSN users and OSN providers as controllers, but each "for different combinations of data flows and purposes".[1791] In other words, both entities might act as controllers, but each for different aspects of the processing. They each exercise control, but "at different stages" and "to different degrees".[1792] While this approach allows for greater nuance and flexibility, its practical implications are often not spelled out with great detail.

878. CONTROL UPON "ACTUAL KNOWLEDGE" – Finally, a fourth approach considers that the OSN provider may only be considered a "controller" of personal data shared over its platform once it has obtained actual knowledge of its existence. Under this approach, it is the OSN user who shares the content which is seen as the main (or "primary") controller, while the OSN provider only becomes a ("secondary") controller once it has been notified of specific personal data processing. This appears to have been the reasoning of the Italian Supreme Court in a judgment concerning *Google Video*, where the Court reasoned that

> "[...] as long as the offense is unknown to the service provider, it cannot be regarded as the controller of the processing, because it lacks any decision-making power on

1788 For example, algorithmic analysis carried out by the OSN provider may determine the degree of visibility given to a particular content item. In case of Facebook's "Newsfeed", for instance, Facebook deploys an automated selection mechanism to establish relevancy of content posted by friends, which ultimately determines the degree of visibility a particular item receives. See T. Bucher, "Want to be on top? Algorithmic power and the threat of invisibility on Facebook", *New Media Society* 2012, Vol. 14, p. 1167 et seq.

1789 See B. Van Alsenoy, J. Ballet and A. Kuczerawy, "Social networks and web 2.0: are users also bound by data protection regulations?", *l.c.*, p. 71.

1790 While this approach involves an expansive interpretation of the controller concept, these authors anticipate certain limitations as to the corresponding responsibilities and liabilities of OSN providers. For example, they indicate that OSN providers might be able to escape liability if they can demonstrate having continuously undertaken all reasonable measures to prevent the data protection violation from taking place, and to limit their effects once they have been manifested (see B. Van Alsenoy, J. Ballet and A. Kuczerawy, "Social networks and web 2.0: are users also bound by data protection regulations?", *l.c.*, p. 71).

1791 Van Eecke and M. Truyens, "Privacy and Social Networks", *l.c.*, p. 537–538.

1792 See Opinion 1/2010, *l.c.*, p. 22.

the data itself, and when, instead, the provider is aware of the illegal data and is not active for its immediate removal or makes it inaccessible, however, it takes a full qualification of the data controller".[1793]

879. Assessment – While there are notable differences among the approaches outlined above, these differences are mainly conceptual. To a large extent, the practical implications of each approach may be largely the same, depending on how one interprets the obligations resulting from the qualification of an OSN provider as a "controller". This issue will be revisited later on.[1794]

3.2. OSN USERS

880. Processing data about others – Every OSN user, at least in theory, acts as a "controller" when processing data about others within an OSN.[1795] Private individuals use OSNs for purposes such as social interaction, self-expression, career development and self-education. Organisations, on the other hand, typically use OSNs to further their organisational mission or corporate objectives (e.g. product promotion, membership recruitment, event planning).[1796] In both cases, the OSN user freely determines why it processes personal data relating to others. As to determining the means of the processing, OSN users generally do not have any real decision-making power. While they may have the ability to adapt some minor features or settings, they do not have any real influence as to the manner in which the processing is conducted. They either take it or leave it. But every OSN user does, as a rule, exercise the choice as to whether or not he wishes to share a particular piece of information using an

---

1793 Corte di Cassazione, sez. III Penale, sentenza 17 dicembre 2013 – deposit ail 3 febbraio 2014, sentenza n. 5107/14, at paragraph 7.2. A special word of thanks is owed to Professor Giovanni Sartor for assisting me with this translation.

1794 Cf. *infra*, section 972.

1795 B. Van Alsenoy, J. Ballet and A. Kuczerawy, "Social networks and web 2.0: are users also bound by data protection regulations?", *l.c.*, p. 70; Article 29 Data Protection Working Party, "Opinion 5/2009 on online social networking", *l.c.*, p. 5; R. Wong, "Social networking: a conceptual analysis of a data controller", *Communications Law* 2009, Vol. 14, No. 5, p. 143 et seq.; N. Helberger and J. Van Hoboken, "Little Brother Is Tagging You – Legal and Policy Implications of Amateur Data Controllers", *l.c.*, p. 102 et seq; P. Van Eecke and M. Truyens, "Privacy and social networks", *l.c.*, p. 537–538; and D.B. Garrie, M. Duffy-Lewis, R. Wong and R.L. Gillespie, "Data Protection: the Challenges Facing Social Networking", *l.c.*, p. 131 et seq. An individual cannot act as a controller towards his or her own data. The regulatory scheme of EU data protection law is predicated on the notion that the data controller is an entity other than the data subject him- or herself. An individual person might act as a controller of personal data relating to others, but not of his or her own personal data. See also *supra*, no. 760.

1796 See also Information Commissioner's Office (ICO), "Social networking and online forums – when does the DPA apply?", *l.c.*, p. 4

OSN.[1797] In this sense OSN users still effectively determine the "means" of their processing when entrusting data about others to an OSN.[1798]

881. Scope of control – The control exercised by OSN users in principle extends to any content they choose to provide and any processing operations they undertake of their own accord (i.e. without solicitation).[1799] For example, a company which uses an OSN for purposes of product promotion shall be considered a controller towards:

- any personal data that is included on the company's profile page (including its list of "connections" or "friends");
- any personal data which the company collects through the OSN (e.g. personal attributes of its connections);
- any information about individuals which the company disseminates through the OSN.[1800]

One must, however, be careful not to exaggerate the decision-making power of the individual user. The controllership of the user does not extend to the OSN as a whole, but only to those processing operations for which he can actually determine the purposes and means.[1801]

882. Exemption for "personal use" – The second indent of Article 2(2)c of the GDPR does not apply to the processing of personal data "*by a natural person in the course of a purely personal or household activity*".[1802] This exemption has given rise to the following question: to what extent can OSN usage be considered a "*purely personal or household activity*"? The Court of Justice has provided further guidance regarding the personal use exemption, namely in its *Lindqvist* judgement of 2003.[1803] Here, the Court considered that the exemption for personal use must

[1797] See in the same vein also the Opinion of Advocate General Sharpston in *Buivids*, C-345/17, ECLI:EU:C:2018:780, paragraph 15. The case concerns the making of a video recording by a private individual inside a police station, capturing personal data of police of officers, and its subsequent upload to Youtube, making the video accessible to an indefinite number of people.

[1798] B. Van Alsenoy, J. Ballet and A. Kuczerawy, "Social networks and web 2.0: are users also bound by data protection regulations?", *l.c.*, p. 70.

[1799] *Id.*

[1800] See also Information Commissioner's Office (ICO), "Social networking and online forums – when does the DPA apply?", *l.c.*, p. 3.

[1801] B. Van Alsenoy, J. Ballet and A. Kuczerawy, "Social networks and web 2.0: are users also bound by data protection regulations?", *l.c.*, p. 70. Compare also *infra*, nos. 918 et seq.

[1802] Previously: Article 3(2) of Directive 95/46.

[1803] Judgment in *Bodil Lindqvist*, C-101/01, EU:C:2003:596. The facts of this case were as follows: Mrs. Lindqvist, who worked as a catechist in a local parish, had set up a number of web pages to provide information to fellow parishioners preparing for their confirmation. These pages also included information about several of her colleagues in the parish, who were

"be interpreted as relating only to activities which are carried out in the course of private or family life of individuals, which is clearly not the case with the processing of personal data consisting in publication on the internet so that those data are made accessible to an indefinite number of people".[1804]

883. Criteria for "personal use" – The Court of Justice thus put forward two elements to determine whether the personal use exemption can be applied. In the first place, the processing activity must be carried out "*in the course of private and family life*". Secondly, the exemption shall not apply where the data is published on the Internet and made accessible to an indefinite number of people.[1805] The first criterion suggests that private OSN users, who make use of an OSN for purposes of social interaction, should in principle be able to avail themselves of the personal use exemption. After all, social interaction is an essential component of one's private or family life.[1806] However, one must not lose track of the second element in the reasoning of the ECJ, namely that the exception shall not apply where the data is made accessible to an indefinite number of people. This implies that OSN users might not be able to invoke this exemption once the data in question passes a certain threshold of accessibility.[1807]

---

referenced either by their full names or merely by their first names. In many cases telephone numbers were listed. The pages also described, "in a mildly humorous manner" the jobs held by these colleagues and their hobbies. Other information was also mentioned, such as family circumstances; and of one colleague it was stated that she had injured her foot and was working half-time for medical reasons. Mrs. Lindqvist had not obtained the consent of the individuals referenced on her web pages, nor informed them of the fact that she was mentioning personal information about them. She also had not notified the data protection authority. She was subsequently prosecuted for violation of the Swedish law on personal data.

1804 Judgment in *Bodil Lindqvist*, C-101/01, EU:C:2003:596, paragraph 47.

1805 The Belgian Privacy Commission (CBPL), in a recommendation regarding the sharing of pictures by individuals, also touched upon the question of personal use. It considered that where images are processed for the sole purpose of distribution among a select ("definable") group of friends, family members or acquaintances, such processing could fall under the exception of personal use. As examples it mentioned the transmission of pictures via email to the participants of a family event, or the posting of such pictures on a secured website, which is only accessible to the relevant family members; and which is protected against indexing by search engines. (Commissie voor de Bescherming van de Persoonlijke Levenssfeer, "Aanbeveling uit eigen beweging inzake de verspreiding van beeldmateriaal", Aanbeveling nr. 02/2007, 28 November 2007, p. 21–22). The Dutch Data Protection Authority adopted an almost identical approach shortly thereafter in its Guidance Report relating to the publication of personal data on the internet (See College Bescherming Persoonsgegevens, "Publicatie van Persoonsgegevens op het Internet", *CBP Richtsnoeren*, December 2007, p. 12–13).

1806 B. Van Alsenoy, J. Ballet and A. Kuczerawy, "Social networks and web 2.0: are users also bound by data protection regulations?", *l.c.*, p. 74.

1807 See also N. Helberger and J. Van Hoboken, "Little Brother Is Tagging You – Legal and Policy Implications of Amateur Data Controllers", *l.c.*, p. 103. See in the same vein also the Judgment in *Jehovah's witnesses*, C-25/17, ECLI:EU:C:2018:551, paragraph 42 and 45, as well as the Opinion of Advocate General Sharpston in Buivids, C-345/17, ECLI:EU:C:2018:780, paragraph 40 ("*[T]he second indent of Article 3(2) of Directive 95/46 likewise cannot apply to Mr Buivids' activities. Publishing the video recording on the internet formed no part of his*

884. Article 29 WP – In its 2009 Opinion on social networking, the Article 29 Working Party indicated that the processing activities of private OSN users are generally covered by the personal use exemption.[1808] However, it also identified two situations in which the personal use exemption will not apply. First, the exception will not apply if the individual is acting "*on behalf of a company or association, or uses the [OSN] mainly as a platform to advance commercial, political or charitable goals.*"[1809] Second, the exemption for personal use also will not apply if the individual "*takes an informed decision to extend access beyond self-selected "friends"*".[1810]

885. Recital (18) GDPR – While the GDPR did not modify the drafting of the personal use exemption, it did include an additional recital clarifying its scope. Specifically recital (18) provides that

> "This Regulation does not apply to the processing of personal data by a natural person in the course of a purely personal or household activity and thus with no connection to a professional or commercial activity. Personal or household activities could include correspondence and the holding of addresses, or social networking and online activity undertaken within the context of such activities."

It remains to be seen whether the CJEU will soften its earlier stance and give the personal use exemption a broader interpretation under the GDPR. Given that the language of the exemption itself has not changed, the precedential value of *Lindqvist* and other judgments[1811] interpreting the scope of the personal use exemption in principle remain intact.

886. Conclusion – In conclusion, one can state that OSN users may be considered as "controllers" within the meaning of Article 4(7) of the GDPR when it comes to the disclosure of personal data regarding others via the OSN. Organisations and companies shall in principle be subject to the same set of responsibilities as those incumbent upon controllers in any other context. In case of private individuals, the applicability of the GDPR depends on whether

---

private or family life. On the contrary: publication meant that the data was made available and accessible to an unrestricted number of people."). The case concerns the making of a video recording by a private individual inside a police station capturing personal data of police of officers and its subsequent upload to Youtube, making the video accessible to an indefinite number of people. At the moment of writing, the judgment of the CJEU is still pending.

1808 Article 29 Data Protection Working Party, "Opinion 5/2009 on online social networking", *l.c.*, p. 5.

1809 *Id.*

1810 *Id.*

1811 See in particular Judgment in *František Ryneš*, C-212/13, EU:C:2014:2428 and Judgment in *Wirtschaftsakademie*, C-210/16, ECLI:EU:C:2018:388.

or not the OSN usage falls within the remit of the personal use exemption. The implications of this outcome will be evaluated later on.[1812]

3.3. PAGE ADMINISTRATORS

887. Outline – In *Wirtschaftsakademie*, the CJEU was called upon to assess the legal status of page administrators under EU data protection law. In light of the importance and relevance of the *Wirtschaftsakademie* judgment for the subject matter of this book, this section will present in detail:

(1) the relevant questions referred;
(2) the Opinion of the Advocate-General; and
(3) the holding of the CJEU.

A. *Questions referred*

888. Obligations for non-controllers? – In its request for a preliminary ruling, the *Bundesverwaltungsgericht* (Federal Administrative Court) asked to Court of Justice the following:

> "(1) Is Article 2(d) of Directive [95/46] to be interpreted as definitively and exhaustively defining the liability and responsibility for data protection infringements, or does scope remain, under the "suitable measures" pursuant to Article 24 of Directive [95/46] and the "effective powers of intervention" pursuant to the second indent of Article 28(3) of Directive [95/46], in multi-tiered information provider relationships, for responsibility of an entity that does not control the data processing within the meaning of Article 2(d) of Directive [95/46] when it chooses the operator of its information offering?
>
> (2) Does it follow a contrario from the obligation of Member States under Article 17(2) of Directive [95/46] to provide, where data processing is carried out on the controller's behalf, that the controller must "choose a processor providing sufficient guarantees in respect of the technical security measures and organisational measures governing the processing to be carried out", that, where there are other user relationships not linked to data processing on the controller's behalf within the meaning of Article 2(e) of Directive [95/46], there is no obligation to make a careful selection and no such obligation can be based on national law?"[1813]

With these questions, the referring court essentially sought to learn whether an entity could be held liable in its capacity as administrator of a "fan page" on a

[1812] Cf. *infra*, nos. 966 et seq.

[1813] Judgment in *Wirtschaftsakademie*, C-210/16, ECLI:EU:C:2018:388, paragraph 24. The remaining questions referred concerned the competences of supervisory authorities vis-à-vis an establishment of the controller on its territory.

social network, without being considered a "controller" for the purpose of EU data protection law.[1814]

889. Facts of the case – To properly understand the questions referred, as well as the manner in which the CJEU approached them, it is necessary to briefly outline the factual elements that preceded the reference for preliminary ruling. Wirtschaftsakademie is a private company specialising in the field of education, which made use of a Facebook fan page to offer educational services.[1815] Facebook fan pages (now simply referred to as "pages") are special user accounts that individuals and businesses can set up on Facebook in order to present themselves and to post information of any kind, in particular with a view to developing a business.[1816] One of the additional services available to the administrators of a Facebook page is called "*Facebook insights*", which is available free of charge under the standard terms and conditions of use.[1817] Facebook insights allow page administrators to obtain *statistical information* about the characteristics of people who have visited the fan page (e.g. their age or gender).[1818] To help generate these viewing statistics, Facebook stores at least one cookie containing a unique ID number on the hard disk of every person that visits the fan page.[1819] The ID number, which can be matched with the data of users registered on Facebook, is collected and processed each time Facebook pages are opened.[1820] The statistics which are compiled for the benefit of the page administrator can help the administrator to better target its communications and promote its activities via the social network.[1821]

890. Legal antecedents – In November 2011, the *Unabhängiges Landeszentrum für Datenschutz Schleswig-Holstein* (ULD) ordered Wirtschaftsakademie to deactivate its fan page, on the ground that neither Wirtschaftsakademie nor Facebook[1822] properly informed visitors to the fan

---

1814 See also Judgment in *Wirtschaftsakademie*, C-210/16, ECLI:EU:C:2018:388, paragraph 25.

1815 Opinion of Advocate General Bot in in *Wirtschaftsakademie*, C-210/16, ECLI:EU:C:2017:796, paragraph 2 and the Judgment in *Wirtschaftsakademie*, C-210/16, ECLI:EU:C:2018:388, paragraph 14.

1816 Opinion of Advocate General Bot in in *Wirtschaftsakademie*, C-210/16, ECLI:EU:C:2017:796 paragraph 16.

1817 *Ibid*, paragraph 17.

1818 *Id.*

1819 *Ibid*, paragraph 18.

1820 *Id.*

1821 *Ibid*, paragraph 17. See also Judgment in *Wirtschaftsakademie*, C-210/16, ECLI:EU:C:2018:388, paragraph 17 and 36.

1822 In the judgment, a distinction is made between Facebook Inc. and Facebook Ireland, which are separate legal entities. According to Facebook's policies and terms, it is Facebook Ireland (and not Facebook Inc.) that acts as the (sole) controller for the processing in relation to the processing of personal data. Both the Advocate General and the CJEU took the position that Facebook Ireland and Facebook Inc must be regarded as jointly responsible for the processing of personal data at issue (See Opinion of Advocate General Bot in in *Wirtschaftsakademie*,

page about the fact that Facebook used cookies to process personal data about them.[1823] Wirtschaftsakademie argued, however, that it was not responsible under data protection law for the processing of personal data by Facebook or the cookies which Facebook installed.[1824] After an initial annulment by an administrative court and several appeals by ULD, the case eventually made its way to the referring court.[1825]

891. Analysis by the referring court – When analyzing the case, the referring court took the view that Wirtschaftsakademie could indeed not be considered as a "controller" within the meaning of EU data protection law.[1826] This conclusion was based on the premise that a page administrator has no influence, in law or in fact, over the manner in which personal data are processed by Facebook.[1827] According to the referring court, Wirtschaftsakademie was not in a position to "influence, guide, model or control" the nature and extent of the processing of the data of users of its fan page by Facebook.[1828] The referring court acknowledged, however, that by creating a Facebook page, Wirtschaftsakademie gave Facebook the opportunity to install cookies whenever someone visits its fan page and to collect personal data.[1829] It is against this background that the referring court asked the CJEU whether liability and responsibility for a data protection infringement might be incurred by an entity which is not deemed a "controller" within the meaning of EU data protection law.[1830]

B. *Opinion of the Advocate General*

892. Joint controller – Advocate General Bot disagreed with the position of the referring court that Wirtschaftsakademie could not be considered a "controller". Instead, he argued that Wirtschaftsakademie should be regarded as *jointly responsible* for the phase of the data processing which consists in the *collection* by Facebook of data relating to people who visit the fan page.[1831] The Advocate General considered that a page administrator does in fact exercise a determinative influence over the purposes and means of the processing. First,

C-210/16, ECLI:EU:C:2017:796, paragraphs 47–51 and Judgment in *Wirtschaftsakademie*, C-210/16, ECLI:EU:C:2018:388, paragraphs 55 and 59–60). For readability purposes, reference shall simply be made to "Facebook" rather than each time making the differentiation between Facebook Inc. and Facebook Ireland.

1823 Judgment in *Wirtschaftsakademie*, C-210/16, ECLI:EU:C:2018:388, paragraph 16.

1824 *Id.*

1825 *Ibid*, paragraphs 19–22.

1826 *Ibid*, paragraph 23.

1827 Opinion of Advocate General Bot in *Wirtschaftsakademie*, C-210/16, ECLI:EU:C:2017:796, paragraph 28.

1828 *Ibid*, paragraph 27.

1829 *Id.*

1830 *Ibid*, paragraph 30.

1831 *Ibid*, paragraph 42.

by deciding to create a Facebook page, the administrator enables the data processing to occur.[1832] Second, by adhering to the system put in place by Facebook, he agrees to the purposes and means of the processing, as predefined by Facebook.[1833] Third, while the purposes and means of the 'Facebook Insights' tool, as such, are generally defined by Facebook, a fan page administrator is able to influence the specific way in which that tool is put to use by defining certain criteria[1834]

> "[...] When Facebook invites a fan page administrator to create or modify the audience for his page it indicates that it will do its best to show the page to the people who matter the most to the administrator. Using filters, a fan page administrator can define a personalised audience, which enables him not only to narrow down the group of people to whom information relating to his commercial offer will be published, but also, and most importantly, to designate the categories of people whose personal data will be collected by Facebook. Thus, by defining the audience he wishes to reach, a fan page administrator will also at the same time be identifying which target public is likely to become the subject of Facebook's collection and subsequent use of personal data. In addition to triggering the processing of personal data when he creates a fan page, the administrator of that page consequently plays a predominant role in how that data is processed by Facebook. In this way he participates in the determination of the means and purposes of the data processing, by himself exerting a de facto influence over it."[1835]

893. Related objectives – Advocate General Bot further substantiated the qualification of Wirtschaftsakademie as "joint controller" by pointing out that the administrators of a fan page and Facebook pursue closely related objectives: the administrator wishes to obtain viewing statistics for the purpose of managing the promotion of its activities, and to obtain those statistics the processing of personal data is necessary. That same data processing also enables Facebook better to target the advertising which it publishes on its network.[1836]

894. Take it or leave it – The Advocate General unequivocally rejected the argument that the terms and conditions of a service provider should be determinative in establishing the role of each actor, or that a party who can do no more than to accept or refuse the contract cannot be considered a controller.[1837]

1832 *Ibid*, paragraph 55–56.

1833 *Ibid*, paragraph 56.

1834 *Ibid*, paragraph 57.

1835 *Id.*

1836 *Ibid*, paragraph 59.

1837 *Ibid*, paragraph 60 (""*Any interpretation that is based solely on the terms and conditions of the contract concluded by the Wirtschaftsakademie and Facebook Ireland should, therefore, be rejected. Indeed, the division of tasks indicated in the contract can only suggest the actual roles of the parties to the contract in the processing of personal data. If it were otherwise, the parties would be able artificially to assign responsibility for the data processing to one or other*

895. Partial control may suffice – Moreover, the Advocate General considered that the inability, for the page administrator, to exercise complete control over the processing, did not prevent it from being considered as a controller:

> "[C]omplete control is becoming less and less common in practice. Ever more frequently data processing is complex, comprising several distinct processes which involve numerous parties which themselves have differing degrees of control. Consequently, any interpretation which focusses on the existence of complete control over all aspects of data processing is likely to result in serious lacunae in the protection of personal data."[1838]

In this regard, the Advocate General also noted the fact that the administrator of a page does not have access to the personal data collected by Facebook regarding its visitors, does not preclude it from being considered a (joint) controller.[1839]

896. Broad interpretation – At several points in his Opinion, Advocate General Bot underlined the importance of interpreting the controller concept broadly in order to ensure effective and complete protection of data subjects.[1840]

> "[A] broad interpretation of the concept of 'controller' [...] is likely to prevent abuse. Absent such an interpretation, it would be sufficient for an undertaking to have recourse to the services of a third party in order to escape its obligations in the field of personal data protection. [...] It is therefore necessary to ensure that economic operators that have recourse to a hosting service for their website are not able to evade liability by agreeing to the general terms and conditions of a service provider."[1841]

897. Shared responsibility – As regards the allocation of responsibility, the Advocate General stressed that the fact that *Wirtschaftsakademie* acts as joint

---

of themselves. That is especially true when the general terms and conditions are drawn up in advance by the social network and are not negotiable. The view cannot, therefore, be taken that a person who may do no more than accept or refuse the contract cannot be a controller. Once such a party has concluded the contract of his own volition he may always be regarded as a controller, given his actual influence over the means and purposes of the data processing.")

1838 *Ibid*, paragraph 62.

1839 *Ibid*, paragraph 61.

1840 *Ibid*, at paragraphs 45 and 63–64.

1841 *Ibid*, paragraph 64. The Advocate General also remarked that that, had Wirtschaftsakademie created a website elsewhere than on Facebook and implemented a tool similar to 'Facebook Insights' in order to compile viewing statistics, it would be regarded as the controller of the processing needed to compile those statistics. Wirtschaftsakademie should therefore not be relieved of its obligations under EU data protection law for the sole reason that it uses Facebook's social networking platform to promote its activities. To accept this would create a risk that the rules on the protection of personal data will be circumvented. (*Ibid*, paragraph 65).

controller in no way relieves Facebook from its obligations.[1842] He also added that the existence of shared responsibility does not imply equal responsibility. On the contrary, he argued, different controllers may be involved in the processing of personal data at "different stages and to differing degrees."[1843]

898. Scope of control – The extent to which a page administrator can be deemed a controller appears to be delineated by its ability to influence the processing. According to the Advocate General, a page administrator must be regarded as a controller (along with Facebook) of the processing of personal data that is *carried out for the purpose of compiling viewing statistics for that fan page*.[1844] In his conclusion, he states that the administrator of a fan page must be regarded as being a controller

> "in so far as concerns the phase of personal data processing consisting in the collection by that social network of data relating to people who visit the fan page for the purpose of compiling viewing statistics for that fan page."[1845]

In other words, the responsibility of the page administrator primarily concerns the initial collection of data relating to people who visit the fan page, including through cookies. At the same time, previous elements in the Opinion indicate that the responsibility of the administrator also extends to the additional processing of personal data for the purpose of compiling viewing statistics for that fan page.[1846]

C. *Holding of the CJEU*

899. Joint responsibility[1847] – The CJEU also rejected the statement that Wirtschaftsakademie could not be considered as a "controller" within the meaning of EU data protection law. Like the Advocate General, the CJEU considered that the administrator of a fan page should be regarded as *jointly responsible* for the processing, together with Facebook:

> "While the mere fact of making use of a social network such as Facebook does not make a Facebook user a controller jointly responsible for the processing of personal data by that network, it must be stated, on the other hand, that the administrator

1842 *Ibid*, paragraph 73.
1843 *Ibid*, paragraph 75.
1844 *Ibid*, paragraph 77.
1845 *Ibid*, paragraph 137 (1).
1846 See in particular at paragraphs 17–18, 42, 53 and 57–58 of the Opinion.
1847 It is worth observing that the Judgment does not, in contrast to the Opinion of the Advocate General, use the term "joint controller" as such. The judgment does, however, repeatedly use the terms "jointly responsible". It also refers to the part of the definition of controller which refers to joint controllers ("jointly with others") as part of its reasoning.

of a fan page hosted on Facebook, by creating such a page, gives Facebook the opportunity to place cookies on the computer or other device of a person visiting its fan page, whether or not that person has a Facebook account.

In this context, according to the submissions made to the Court, the creation of a fan page on Facebook involves the definition of parameters by the administrator, depending inter alia on the target audience and the objectives of managing and promoting its activities, which has an influence on the processing of personal data for the purpose of producing statistics based on visits to the fan page. The administrator may, with the help of filters made available by Facebook, define the criteria in accordance with which the statistics are to be drawn up and even designate the categories of persons whose personal data is to be made use of by Facebook. Consequently, the administrator of a fan page hosted on Facebook contributes to the processing of the personal data of visitors to its page.

In particular, the administrator of the fan page can ask for – and thereby request the processing of – demographic data relating to its target audience, including trends in terms of age, sex, relationship and occupation, information on the lifestyles and centres of interest of the target audience and information on the purchases and online purchasing habits of visitors to its page, the categories of goods and services that appeal the most, and geographical data which tell the fan page administrator where to make special offers and where to organise events, and more generally enable it to target best the information it offers.

While the audience statistics compiled by Facebook are indeed transmitted to the fan page administrator only in anonymised form, it remains the case that the production of those statistics is based on the prior collection, by means of cookies installed by Facebook on the computers or other devices of visitors to that page, and the processing of the personal data of those visitors for such statistical purposes. […]

In those circumstances, the administrator of a fan page hosted on Facebook, such as Wirtschaftsakademie, must be regarded as taking part, by its definition of parameters depending in particular on its target audience and the objectives of managing and promoting its activities, in the determination of the purposes and means of processing the personal data of the visitors to its fan page. The administrator must therefore be categorised, in the present case, as a controller responsible for that processing […], jointly with Facebook […]."[1848]

900. Related objectives – Like the Advocate General, the CJEU also pointed out that the objectives pursued by the administrators of a fan page and Facebook are related, at least insofar as the processing is concerned:

"That processing of personal data is intended in particular to enable Facebook to improve its system of advertising transmitted via its network, and to enable the fan page administrator to obtain statistics produced by Facebook from the visits to the page, for the purposes of managing the promotion of its activity, making it aware, for example, of the profile of the visitors who like its fan page or use its applications, so

[1848] Judgment in *Wirtschaftsakademie*, C-210/16, paragraphs 35–39.

that it can offer them more relevant content and develop functionalities likely to be of more interest to them."[1849]

901. Take it or leave it – While the CJEU was quick to point out that the mere fact of making use of a service provided by a social network does not make the user jointly responsible[1850], the CJEU also emphasized that the use of a service provided a social network (and for which the policies and conditions are determined by the latter), does not exempt them from their responsibilities.[1851]

902. Partial control may suffice – The CJEU confirmed that the definition of a (joint) controller does not require each controller involved in the processing to have access to the personal data in question:

> "[...] Directive 95/46 does not, where several operators are jointly responsible for the same processing, require each of them to have access to the personal data concerned."[1852]

As a result, the CJEU did not consider it decisive that the administrator of a fan page only receives statistics in anonymised form, without having access to the underlying personal data.[1853]

903. Broad interpretation – The CJEU similarly recalled that EU data protection law aims to ensure a high level of protection for data subjects[1854] and that the controller concept has been defined broadly, in order to ensure effective and complete protection.[1855]

1849 *Ibid*, paragraph 34.

1850 *Ibid*, paragraph 35.

1851 *Ibid*, paragraph 32 and 38. ("*It appears that any person wishing to create a fan page on Facebook concludes a specific contract with Facebook Ireland for the opening of such a page, and thereby subscribes to the conditions of use of the page, including the policy on cookies, which is for the national court to ascertain. [...] The fact that an administrator of a fan page uses the platform provided by Facebook in order to benefit from the associated services cannot exempt it from compliance with its obligations concerning the protection of personal data.*")

1852 Judgment in Wirtschaftsakademie, C-210/16, paragraph 38.

1853 *Id.*

1854 Judgment in *Wirtschaftsakademie*, C-210/16, paragraph 26.

1855 *Ibid*, paragraph 28. In this regard, the CJEU took special note of the fact that individuals who do not have a Facebook account might be affected by the processing: "*It must be emphasised, moreover, that fan pages hosted on Facebook can also be visited by persons who are not Facebook users and so do not have a user account on that social network. In that case, the fan page administrator's responsibility for the processing of the personal data of those persons appears to be even greater, as the mere consultation of the home page by visitors automatically starts the processing of their personal data. In those circumstances, the recognition of joint responsibility of the operator of the social network and the administrator of a fan page hosted on that network in relation to the processing of the personal data of visitors to that page contributes to ensuring more complete protection of the rights of persons visiting a fan page, in accordance with the requirements of Directive 95/46.*" (*Ibid*, paragraphs 41–42).

904. Shared responsibility – The CJEU confirmed that, as a matter of principle, the exercise of joint control implies that each joint controller shall be subject to the relevant data protection obligations.[1856] The CJEU also confirmed, however, that the existence of *joint responsibility does not necessarily imply equal responsibility* of the various operators involved in the processing of personal data:

> "On the contrary, those operators may be involved at different stages of that processing of personal data and to different degrees, so that the level of responsibility of each of them must be assessed with regard to all the relevant circumstances of the particular case."[1857]

Earlier in its judgment, the CJEU already alluded to the possibility that the level of responsibility of Facebook might in fact be greater than that of the individual fan page administrator:

> "In the present case, [Facebook] must be regarded as primarily determining the purposes and means of processing the personal data of users of Facebook and persons visiting the fan pages hosted on Facebook [...]."[1858]

905. Scope of control – The judgment of the CJEU is less explicit as regards the scope of control exercised by fan page administrators. In its holding, the CJEU focuses primarily on the fact that the concept of "controller" within the meaning of that provision encompasses the administrator of a fan page hosted on a social network (without further specifying the object of the control). From the CJEU's reasoning, however, it is clear that the *definition of parameters* is considered an essential element in order to qualify the administrator as a (joint) controller.[1859] At the same time, however, the CJEU also notes that the

---

1856 *Ibid*, paragraph 29 ("*Furthermore, since, as Article 2(d) of Directive 95/46 expressly provides, the concept of 'controller' relates to the entity which 'alone or jointly with others' determines the purposes and means of the processing of personal data, that concept does not necessarily refer to a single entity and may concern several actors taking part in that processing, with each of them then being subject to the applicable data protection provisions.*")

1857 *Ibid*, paragraph 43.

1858 *Ibid*, paragraph 30.

1859 See in particular at paragraph 39: "*In those circumstances, the administrator of a fan page hosted on Facebook, such as Wirtschaftsakademie, must be regarded as taking part, by its definition of parameters depending in particular on its target audience and the objectives of managing and promoting its activities, in the determination of the purposes and means of processing the personal data of the visitors to its fan page. The administrator must therefore be categorised, in the present case, as a controller responsible for that processing within the European Union, jointly with Facebook [...]*). This language, together with the language at the beginning of paragraph 35 of the judgment, also clearly suggest that for the CJEU that the fact of signing up to service alone may not be sufficient to be deemed a joint controller, rather there must be an additional influence over the purpose and means of the processing.

definition of parameters impacts a range of processing activities[1860], and that the statistics received by the administrator are dependent upon the prior collection and processing of personal data by Facebook.[1861] The responsibility of a Fan page administrator therefore does not appear to be limited to the definition of the parameters itself, but might also extend to the range of processing activities which are determined by the setting of those parameters (as they are also part of the means by which the statistics are drawn up).[1862]

3.4. APPLICATION PROVIDERS

906. High-level analysis – Third-party application providers are generally also considered as "controllers" within the meaning of EU data protection law.[1863] Similar to OSN providers, the objective of most application providers is to provide a certain service which generates revenue, be it directly or indirectly.[1864] The nature of this service will depend on the intended functionality of their application(s): gaming, content streaming, location sharing, crowd funding ...[1865] In this sense, application providers determine the *purposes* of the processing of user data that takes place when they provide their services. Application providers also determine the *means* of their processing:

1860 See in particular at paragraph 36 ("*The administrator may, with the help of filters made available by Facebook, define the criteria in accordance with which the statistics are to be drawn up and even designate the categories of persons whose personal data is to be made use of by Facebook. Consequently, the administrator of a fan page hosted on Facebook contributes to the processing of the personal data of visitors to its page.*") and 37 ("*In particular, the administrator of the fan page can ask for – and thereby request the processing of – demographic data relating to its target audience, including trends in terms of age, sex, relationship and occupation, information on the lifestyles and centres of interest of the target audience and information on the purchases and online purchasing habits of visitors to its page, the categories of goods and services that appeal the most, and geographical data [...]*")

1861 See in particular at paragraph 38 ("*While the audience statistics compiled by Facebook are indeed transmitted to the fan page administrator only in anonymised form, it remains the case that the production of those statistics is based on the prior collection, by means of cookies installed by Facebook on the computers or other devices of visitors to that page, and the processing of the personal data of those visitors for such statistical purposes.*").

1862 After all, the setting of parameters in isolation does not amount to the processing of personal data. It is the interaction between the setting of those parameters, the creation of statistics on the basis of categories of personal data (and the preceding collection of personal data), and the identification of a target audience that involves processing of personal data.

1863 Article 29 Data Protection Working Party, "Opinion 5/2009 on online social networking", *l.c.*, p. 5. See also P. Van Eecke and M. Truyens, "Privacy and Social Networks", *l.c.*, p. 540–541.

1864 As in the case of OSNs, many application providers derive (a portion of) their revenue from targeted advertising (so-called "in-app advertising"). Application providers may also charge money for downloads of their apps, for in-app purchases or for premium subscriptions. For an overview of the different revenue models of mobile apps see OECD, "The App Economy", *l.c.*, p. 22–26.

1865 Cf. *supra*, no. 852.

they stipulate which data shall be collected regarding OSN users and how these data will be subsequently processed. In addition to deciding about the activities which are necessary to deliver the app's functionality, the application provider may also decide about additional processing activities; including those designed to enable targeted advertising.

907. Scope of control – The "control" exercised by application providers in principle extends to any processing which takes place to support the application's functionality. It also extends to any processing undertaken by the application provider to enable targeted advertising (e.g. disclosure of a user's location to support contextual advertising).[1866] Any other subsequent use that is made of the personal data by the application provider will generally also fall within the scope of its control. While application developers have significant freedom in deciding how to organise their own processing of personal data, they are typically constrained by at least two important factors, namely the (1) terms and conditions for application developers and (2) the access control model supported by the OSN.

908. API terms – When collecting data related to OSN users, application providers are not entirely free in deciding how this collection shall be organized. As indicated before, many application providers obtain access to OSN data by soliciting permissions from OSN users. Once these permissions have been granted, the application provider will query the social network's Application Programming Interface (API) to make use of the delegated privileges (e.g. access profile information, post to wall).[1867] Using the API of an OSN is generally subject to a number of terms and conditions, which are stipulated by the OSN provider. As a result, application providers are in principle bound by the limitations and restrictions imposed by the API terms when soliciting, collecting and processing OSN data.[1868]

1866 See also Article 29 Data Protection Working Party, "Opinion 02/2013 on apps on smart devices", WP202, 27 February 2013, p. 12.

1867 W. De Groef, D. Devries, T. Reynaert and F. Piessens, "Security and Privacy of Online Social Network Applications", *l.c.*, p. 208. See also M. Huber, M. Mulazzani, S. Schrittwieser, E.R. Weippl, "AppInspect – Large-scale Evaluation of Social Apps", *l.c.*, p. 1–2. A number of OSN providers, which include Google, Myspace and Yahoo united their efforts to develop a uniform social application programming interface, which is called "*OpenSocial*". The goal of this initiative is to allow application developers to offer their applications to users from various OSNs and to enable their functionality across OSNs. See W. De Groef, D. Devries, T. Reynaert and F. Piessens, "Security and Privacy of Online Social Network Applications", *l.c.*, p. 210. See also F. Le Borgne-Bachschmidt et al., "User-Created-Content: Supporting a participative Information Society", Final Report, 2008, p. 243.

1868 For more information regarding Terms & Conditions of OSN APIs see A. Kuczerawy, "Legal and ethical analysis", *Exploiting Social Networks for Building the Future Internet of Services* (SocIoS), Deliverable D3.5, p. 21–29. While third-party application providers are bound by API terms, they in principle decide autonomously whether they wish to collect certain data

909. Access control models – The access rights of application providers may vary across platforms. In case of Facebook, for example, application providers are granted access to the user's "basic information" by default.[1869] In the past, information available to app developers by default has included user ID, name, picture, gender, locale and friend connections.[1870] Additionally, application developers may also request access to several additional permission classes (e.g. "email permissions", "publish to groups").[1871] These permissions may, for example, enable the application provider to post information on behalf of users or to access private messages.[1872] Other OSN platforms support different access control models; which may be either more granular or more coarse-grained.[1873]

910. Relationship to OSN provider – Third-party application providers are in principle "separate controllers": they determine their own purposes and means for their processing of personal data.[1874] Once access has been granted, an application provider will typically collect the data and export them to its own servers for further processing.[1875] The OSN provider cannot, as a general matter, be considered as a "controller" in relation to the separate processing activities of third-party application developers (unless the latter are acting "on behalf of the" OSN provider). The Opinion of the Article 29 Working Party on data portability supports such interpretation, at least insofar as the transmission of personal data is performed at the (actual) request of the data subject

> "In this respect, the data controller is not responsible for compliance of the receiving data controller with data protection law, considering that it is not the sending data controller that chooses the recipient. At the same time the controller should set

via an OSN and how to use it. Although they too must "take it or leave it", they exercise a choice when deciding to collect data about individuals through an OSN API. In this sense application providers still effectively determine the "means" of their processing when collecting data about OSN users in this way.

1869 M. Huber, M. Mulazzani, S. Schrittwieser, E.R. Weippl, "AppInspect – Large-scale Evaluation of Social Apps", *l.c.*, p. 3.

1870 *Id.* Facebook has since limited the "default public profile fields" to which an application provider is granted access by default. See Facebook for developers, "Permissions Reference – Facebook Login", last accessed 5 January 2019.

1871 *Id.*

1872 *Id.*

1873 See also W. De Groef, D. Devries, T. Reynaert and F. Piessens, "Security and Privacy of Online Social Network Applications", *l.c.*, p. 212–213. For example, "OpenSocial" currently supports only one specific permission: allow or deny the application to access all of the user's data. However, implementers can always enhance this model in their own implementations. (*Id.*).

1874 Cf. *supra*, no. 906.

1875 These servers are outside of the OSN domain, meaning they are beyond the OSN provider's direct control or supervision. (M. Huber, M. Mulazzani, S. Schrittwieser, E.R. Weippl, "AppInspect – Large-scale Evaluation of Social Apps", *l.c.*, p. 2).

safeguards to ensure they genuinely act on the data subject's behalf. For example, they can establish procedures to ensure that the type of personal data transmitted are indeed those that the data subject wants to transmit."[1876]

It should be noted that the OSN provider play an important role in ensuring that application providers (can) comply with data protection requirements (e.g. by supporting sufficiently granular access to user data). Finally, OSN providers are also responsible for ensuring that the personal data of OSN users are not disclosed to unauthorized entities.[1877]

3.5. THIRD-PARTY WEBSITE OPERATORS

911. Outline – The CJEU has recently been requested to assess the legal status of third-party website operators that integrate so-called "plug-ins" made available by OSN providers. At the moment of writing, only the Opinion of the Advocate General has been issued. Nevertheless, in light of the likely importance and relevance of the *Fashion ID* judgment, this section will present in detail:

(1) the relevant questions referred;
(2) the Opinion of Advocate-General Bot; and
(3) the Opinion of Advocate General Bobek.

A. *Questions referred*

912. Facts of the case – Fashion ID, an online retailer for fashion items, embedded a Facebook "Like button" in its website. As result, whenever someone visits Fashion ID's website, that person's IP address and browser string is transferred to Facebook, along with any cookies previously set by Facebook.[1878] The data is transferred automatically when the person's browser loads the website, irrespective of whether he or she has clicked on the button in question and regardless of whether or not he or she has a Facebook account.[1879] The

1876 Article 29 Data Protection Working Party, Guidelines on the right to data portability, WP 242 rev. 01, 5 April 2017, at p. 6–7.

1877 See also *infra*, no. 978 et seq.

1878 In his Opinion, Advocate General Bobek chooses to refer only to Facebook Ireland (rather than Facebook Inc.) on the grounds that Facebook Ireland appears to assume possible liability under Directive 95/46 in the proceedings at issue (and he therefore sees no reason to discuss the potential applicability of Directive 95/46 vis-à-vis Facebook Inc. (Opinion of Advocate General Bobek in Fashion ID, C-40/17, ECLI:EU:C:2018:1039, at footnote 4) Again, for readability purposes, reference shall simply be made to "Facebook" rather than each time making the differentiation between Facebook Inc. and Facebook Ireland.

1879 Opinion of Advocate General Bobek in Fashion ID, C-40/17, ECLI:EU:C:2018:1039, paragraph 1 and 17.

operator of the website embedding a Facebook Like button in principle does not have access to the personal data transferred to the social network provider. Rather, it is by virtue of the integration of the plug-in in its website that the browser of the visitor automatically sends the information to Facebook.[1880]

913. Legal antecedents – A German consumer protection association (*Verbraucherzentrale NRW*) brought legal proceedings against Fashion ID on the ground that its use of the Facebook Like button resulted in a breach of data protection legislation.[1881] Specifically, the association sought an order to force Fashion ID to cease its use of Facebook's Like button because it did not provide the necessary information and/or failed to obtain the consent of website visitors.[1882] The referring court (the Higher Regional Court of Düsseldorf) had doubts, however, as to whether a website operator such as Fashion ID could be considered as a "controller", given its inability to influence the data processing at issue.[1883]

914. Questions referred – Against this background, the referring court asked the CJEU:

> "In a case such as the present one, in which someone has embedded a programming code in his website which causes the user's browser to request content from a third party and, to this end, transmits personal data to the third party, is the person embedding the content the "controller" within the meaning of Article 2(d) of [Directive 95/46] if that person is himself unable to influence this data-processing operation?"[1884]

If not, the referring court wishes to know whether the concept of a controller "definitively" regulates liability and responsibility in such a way that it precludes civil claims against an actor who, although not a "controller", nonetheless creates the cause for the processing operation, but without actually influencing it.[1885] If, on the other hand, the operator of a website integrating can be considered a "controller", the referring court wishes to know how the individual obligations imposed by EU data protection law should be met in such a scenario, in particular as regards the lawfulness of processing (legitimate interest, consent) and the duty to inform.[1886]

1880 See also *supra*, no. 865.

1881 Opinion of Advocate General Bobek in Fashion ID, C-40/17, ECLI:EU:C:2018:1039, paragraph 2.

1882 *Ibid*, paragraph 18.

1883 *Ibid*, paragraph 50–51.

1884 *Ibid*, paragraph 21.

1885 The third question reads as follows: *If Question 2 is answered in the negative: Is Article 2(d) of [Directive 95/46] to be interpreted as meaning that it definitively regulates liability and responsibility in such a way that it precludes civil claims against a third party who, although not a "controller", nonetheless creates the cause for the processing operation, without influencing it?*

1886 *Ibid*, paragraph 3. The remaining two questions are formulated as follows: "*(4) Whose "legitimate interests", in a situation such as the present one, are the decisive ones in the*

B. *Opinion of Advocate General Bot*

915. Fan page analogy – In his Opinion in *Wirtschaftsakademie*, Advocate General Bot also reflected upon the legal status of the operator of a third-party website that embeds social plug-ins. He reasoned that its position is essentially equivalent to that of a page administrator as regards the processing at issue.[1887] As a result, the operator of a third-party website embedding a social plug-in should also be considered a controller:

> "Social plugins enable website operators to use certain social networking services on their own websites in order to increase their website's visibility, for example by embedding in their websites Facebook's 'Like' button. Like fan page administrators, operators of websites with embedded social plugins can benefit from the 'Facebook Insights' service and obtain precise statistical information about the users of their website.
>
> As happens when a fan page is visited, visiting a website that contains a social plugin will trigger the transmission of personal data to the provider in question.
>
> I[n] such circumstances, like the administrator of a fan page, the manager of a website that contains a social plugin should, to the extent that it has a de facto influence over the phase of data processing which involves the transmission of personal data to Facebook, be classified as a 'controller' […]."[1888]

In other words, according to Advocate General Bot, no distinction should be made between an undertaking which equips its website with social plug-ins such as the Facebook Like Button and an undertaking which joins the Facebook social network so as to benefit from the tools which Facebook offers.[1889]

---

balancing of interests to be undertaken pursuant to Article 7(f) of [Directive 95/46]? Is it the interests in embedding third-party content or the interests of the third party?"; "*(5) To whom must the consent to be declared under Articles 7(a) and 2(h) of [Directive 95/46] be made in a situation such as that in the present case?*" and "*(6) Does the duty to inform under Article 10 of [Directive 95/46] also apply in a situation such as that in the present case to the operator of the website who has embedded the content of a third party and thus creates the cause for the processing of personal data by the third party?*" The first question concerned the issue of whether Directive 95/46 precluded a consumer protection association, such as Verbraucherzentrale NRW, from taking action against possible infringements of data protection law, as it did in the current case.

1887 Opinion of Advocate General Bot in in *Wirtschaftsakademie*, C-210/16, ECLI:EU:C:2017:796, paragraph 66 and 69 ("*In my opinion, there is also no need to draw an artificial distinction between the situation in question in the present case and that in Case C-40/17, Fashion ID. […] I fail to see any fundamental difference between the position of a fan page administrator and that of the operator of a website that embeds in its website a programming code of a provider of web tracking services, thus enabling the transmission of data, the downloading of cookies and the collection of data for the benefit of the provider of the web tracking services all without the knowledge of the Internet user*").

1888 *Ibid*, paragraphs 70–72.

1889 *Ibid*, paragraph 64.

C. *Opinion of Advocate General Bobek*

916. Joint control – Advocate General Bobek concluded that, in light of recent CJEU case law[1890], Fashion ID indeed acts as a controller, and is jointly responsible with Facebook for the data processing at issue.[1891] First, like a page administrator, the operator of the website also makes it possible for Facebook to collect data about its visitors by embedding the social plug-in.[1892] Second, it could be argued that the operator of a third-party website also influences the "parameters of the processing"[1893] by doing so:

> "[Fashion ID] could be said to be (co-)determining the parameters of the data collected by the simple act of embedding the plug-in at issue in its website. It is the plug-in itself that provides parameters of the personal data to be collected. Thus, by voluntarily integrating that tool into its website, [Fashion ID] has set those parameters with regard to any visitors to its website."[1894]

As a result, the Advocate General considered that Fashion ID is involved in the determination of both the means and purposes of the processing:

> "First, [...] it seems to be established that [Fashion ID] decides on the use of the plug-in at issue, which serves as a vehicle for the collection and transmission of the personal data. That collection and transmission is triggered by visiting [Fashion ID]'s website. That plug-in was provided to [Fashion ID] by [Facebook]. Both [Facebook] and [Fashion ID] thus appear to have voluntarily caused the collection and transmission stage of the data processing.
>
> Second, looking at the purpose of the data processing, the order for reference does not state the reasons for which [Fashion ID] decided to embed the Facebook 'Like' button in its website. However, and subject to the referring court's verification, that decision appears to be inspired by the wish to increase visibility of [Fashion ID]'s products via the social network. At the same time, it would also appear that the data transferred to [Facebook] are used for the latter's own commercial purposes."

917. Partial control may suffice – In reaching this conclusion, Advocate General Bobek acknowledged that the controller concept should in principle

---

1890 Since the Opinion of Advocate General Bot, the CJEU had handed down its judgment in both *Wirtschaftsakademie* and *Jehovah's Witnesses*.

1891 Opinion of Advocate General Bobek in *Fashion ID*, C-40/17, ECLI:EU:C:2018:1039, paragraph 66.

1892 *Ibid*, paragraph 67.

1893 Advocate General Bobek noted that, the operator a third-party website does not appear to determine the parameters of any processing information about its website users in a manner that is similar to page administors (which would then be returned to it in anonymised or other form). (*Ibid*, paragraph 68).

1894 *Ibid*, paragraph 69.

be interpreted broadly[1895], and recalled that it may be possible to exert factual influence over the processing without having access to the data itself.[1896] It is also not essential, he argued, that the operator of the third party website receive viewing statistics:

> "[I]n the light of Jehovan todistajat, a joint controller can be still classified as such without even having access to any 'fruits of joint labour'. Thus, the fact that the Defendant does not have access to the data passed on to Facebook or that it apparently does not receive any tailored or aggregated statistics in return, does not appear to be decisive."[1897]

It was sufficient, in other words, to have caused the transfer of personal data to take place by embedding the social plug-in, even though the operator of the third-website did not design the social plug-in himself or has no ability to influence the subsequent processing by Facebook.

918. Scope of control – While concluding that Fashion ID must be considered as a controller, Advocate General Bobek was eager to underline that its status as (joint) controller should be limited to the *stages* of the processing for which it effectively (co-)determines the purposes and means:

> "A (joint) controller is responsible for that operation or set of operations for which it shares or co-determines the purposes and means as far as a given processing operation is concerned. By contrast, that person cannot be held liable for either the preceding stages or subsequent stages of the overall chain of processing, for which it was not in a position to determine either the purposes or means of that stage of processing.
>
> In the present case, the relevant stage (operations) of the processing corresponds to the collection and transmission of personal data that occurs by means of the Facebook 'Like' button."[1898]

1895 Opinion of Advocate General Bobek in *Fashion ID*, C-40/17, ECLI:EU:C:2018:1039, paragraph 61. The reference to the "parameters of the processing" was intended to draw an analogy with the reasoning of the CJEU in *Wirtschaftsakademie*. Cf. *supra*, no. 899 and no. 905.

1896 *Ibid*, paragraph 65 ("*In Jehovan todistajat,the Court underlined another important clarification with regard to the notion of joint controller: for there to be joint control and joint responsibility, it is not required that each of the controllers must have access to (all of) the personal data concerned.*)

1897 *Ibid*, paragraph 70.

1898 *Ibid*, paragraph 101 and 102. See also paragraph 108: "*In the light of the above, [...] a person, such as the Defendant, that has embedded a third-party plug-in in its website, which causes the collection and transmission of the user's personal data (that third party having provided the plug-in), shall be considered to be a controller [...]. However, that controller's (joint) responsibility is limited to those operations for which it effectively co-decides on the means and purposes of the processing of the personal data.*"

919. Rationale – In his reasoning, Advocate General Bobek articulates the concern that actors involved in the processing of personal data might, due to the broad interpretation of the controller concept, be subject to excessive liability. From a moral and practical perspective, he considers it highly problematic that an actor should be considered (co-)responsible or jointly liable for activities over which they do not exercise any real control.[1899] In order to limit the risk of excessive liability, the Advocate General does two things: first, he emphasises the importance of breaking the processing down into distinct processing operations. Second, he underlines that "joint control" (and therefore also joint responsibility) only exists insofar as there is a "unity" of purposes and means.

920. Control over distinct operations – As regards the object of a (joint) controller's influence, Advocate General Bobek considers that control should in first instance be assessed with regards to discrete processing operations, rather than a combination (set) of processing operations:

> "Even if the notion of processing is, similar to the notion of controller, rather broad, it clearly underlines and aims at a stage in the processing: it refers to an operation or a set of operations, with an illustrative list of what such individual operations might be. But then logically, the issue of control should rather be assessed with regard to the discrete operation in question, not with regard to an undetermined bundle of everything and anything called processing."[1900]

921. A "unity" of purposes and means – The Advocate General then proceeds to delineate the scope of joint control by emphasizing the need for a "unity" of purposes and means with regard to a certain processing operation:

> "[T]he notion of joint control is not specifically defined by Directive 95/46. But logically, that notion builds on the notion of controller in Article 2(d): the situation of joint control appears when two or more persons determine the means and the purposes of processing of personal data together. In other words, for two (or more) persons to qualify as joint controllers, there must be identity of the purposes and means of the personal data processing between them."[1901]

While he initially refers to an "identity" of purposes and means, his subsequent analysis suggests that it is not necessary that the purposes be completely identical. Instead, it may be sufficient that there exists a "*unity*" or "*mutual complementarity*" between the purposes pursued and the means used:

1899 Opinion of Advocate General Bobek in *Fashion ID*, C-40/17, ECLI:EU:C:2018:1039, in particular at paragraphs 71–75. See also at paragraphs 81, 83 and 85–86.

1900 *Ibid*, paragraph 99.

1901 *Ibid*, paragraph 100.

"[I]n general both [parties] seem to pursue commercial purposes in a way that appears to be mutually complementary. In this way, although not identical, there is unity of purpose: there is a commercial and advertising purpose.

On the facts in the present case, it thus appears that the [parties] co-decide on the means and purposes of the data processing at the stage of the collection and transmission of the personal data at issue."[1902]

In other words: there must exist a unity of 'purposes and means' amongst the (joint) controllers with regard to the respective stage of processing of personal data (data processing operation) in order for joint control to be established.[1903]

922. Subsequent operations – Having delineated the scope of joint control in this case, Advocate General Bobek concludes that the responsibility and possible liability does not extend to the subsequent processing undertaken by the social network, after the data have been transmitted:

"[It] appears that [Fashion ID] and [Facebook] co-decide on the means and purposes of the data processing at the stage of the collection and transmission of the personal data at issue. To that extent, [Fashion ID] acts as a controller and its liability is, to that extent as well, joint with that of [Facebook].

At the same time, [...] the liability of [Fashion ID] has to be limited to the stage of the data processing, in which it is engaged and that it cannot spill over into any potential subsequent stages of data processing, if such processing occurs outside the control and, it would appear, also without the knowledge of [Fashion ID]."[1904]

923. Shared responsibility? – The questions referred in Fashion ID concerned not only the question of whether the operator of a third-party website embedding social plug-ins may be considered as a controller or not. They also concerned how the individual obligations imposed by EU data protection law are to be met in such a scenario, in particular as regards the lawfulness of processing and the duty to inform. For Advocate General Bobek, the responsibilities of a website operator such as Fashion ID should be limited in two ways. First, its responsibilities are to be limited to the scope of its control, i.e. the extent to which it actually co-determines the purposes and means of the processing (delineation). Second, it should only be responsible for obligations which concern processing activities which correspond to the scope of its control (limitation). Moreover, when determining the precise scope of its responsibilities, account should be taken of the stage during which it becomes involved in the processing.

1902 Opinion of Advocate-General Bobek in *Fashion ID*, C-40/17, ECLI:EU:C:2018:1039, paragraphs 105–106.

1903 *Ibid*, paragraph 54. See also *supra*, nos. 128–130.

1904 *Ibid*, paragraph 106–107.

924. Delineation – As indicated earlier, Advocate General Bobek considers that the responsibilities of a website operator only extend to those "aspects" of the processing for which the website operator is jointly responsible, namely the initial collection and transmission of personal data.[1905] They do not extend to subsequent stages in the processing in which the website operator does not determine either the means or purposes.[1906] Second, taking into account the position of the website operator in the sequence of the processing, the website operator does carry the responsibility of ensuring prior information and obtaining the consent of the individuals concerned.[1907] The main reason is because the processing at issue is triggered at the moment when the website is actually visited. In reaching this conclusion, the Advocate General took into account that both the consent of the data subject and the information to be provided must in principle be given *prior* to the initiation of the processing.[1908]

925. Limitation – The obligation to inform data subject comprises several elements.[1909] Under Directive 95/46, such elements included the controller's (or its representative's) identity and the purposes of the processing for which the data are intended. The duty to inform also extends to further information, "*where this is necessary having regard to the specific circumstances in which the data are collected, to guarantee fair processing in respect of the data subject*". Such information might include, for example, information about the recipient of the data or about the existence of the right of access and the right to rectify the data concerning the data subject.[1910] As far as the right of access and rectification is concerned, however, the Advocate General considers that it relates to a

1905 Opinion of Advocate-General Bobek in *Fashion ID*, C-40/17, ECLI:EU:C:2018:1039, paragraph 131 (""*First of all, I consider that both the consent and the information provided must cover all the aspects of the data processing operation(s) for which the joint controllers are jointly liable, namely the collection and the transmission.)*

1906 *Id.* ("*Conversely, those consent and information obligations do not extend to subsequent stages of the data processing in which the Defendant is not involved and for which it logically does not determine either means or purposes.)*

1907 *Ibid*, paragraph 141.

1908 Opinion of Advocate-General Bobek in *Fashion ID*, C-40/17, ECLI:EU:C:2018:1039, paragraph 140 ("consent has to be given and information provided *before* the data are collected and transferred.") See also at paragraphs 132–133 (*[O]ne could suggest that the consent may be provided to either of the joint controllers. However, considering the particular situation at hand, that consent has to be provided to the Defendant, because it is when its website is actually visited that the processing operation is triggered. It would obviously not be in line with efficient and timely protection of data subjects' rights if the consent were to be given only to the joint controller that is involved later (if at all), once the collection and transmission has already taken place. A similar answer is to be given with regard to the information obligation that the Defendant has under Article 10 of Directive 95/46. [...]*").

1909 See also *supra*, no. 55.

1910 Opinion of Advocate-General Bobek in *Fashion ID*, C-40/17, ECLI:EU:C:2018:1039, paragraphs 133.

processing activity beyond the scope of "control" of the website operator and therefore outside the scope of its obligations:

> "Considering that list, the Defendant clearly appears to be in a position to provide information about the identity of the joint controllers, about the purpose of the respective stage of the processing (the operation(s) over which it has joint control); and also about the fact that those data will be transferred.
>
> By contrast, as far as the right of access and the right to rectify are concerned, I understand that [Fashion ID] itself does not have such access to the data being transferred to Facebook Ireland, since it is in no way involved in the storage of data. [...]"[1911]

In other words, because the operator of a website does not itself have access to the data, the Advocate General considers that the operator should not be subject to a related obligation to inform individuals about their rights of access and rectification. He rejects the suggestion that the website operator might conclude an agreement with the social network, which would establish how data subjects shall be enabled to exercise those rights:

> "[...] Thus, it could for instance be suggested that that matter would have to be the subject of an agreement with [Facebook].
>
> But such proposals would, [...] extend the obligations and liability of a (joint) controller(s) to operations for which they are not responsible. If joint control means responsibility for those operation(s) for which there is the unity of purposes and means amongst the controllers, then logically the other ensuing obligations under the directive, such as consent, information, access or rectification ought to correspond to the scope of that original obligation."[1912]

926. No differentation among visitors – Finally, the Advocate General also took the position that it made no difference, as far as the responsibilities of the website operator are concerned, whether or not the visitors to its website have a Facebook account:

> "It was also noted by the Commission at the hearing that those of the visitors who have a Facebook account may have previously consented to such a transfer occurring. That could lead to a differentiated liability of the Defendant, with the Commission apparently suggesting the Defendant's duty to inform and require consent would then apply only to Facebook non-users visiting the website of the Defendant.
>
> I do not agree. I find it difficult to accept the idea that there should be differentiated (less protective) treatment in respect of 'Facebook users' in the circumstances of the present case because they would have already accepted the

---

1911 *Ibid*, paragraphs 134–135.

1912 Opinion of Advocate-General Bobek in *Fashion ID*, C-40/17, ECLI:EU:C:2018:1039, paragraphs 135–136.

> possibility of (any and all of) their personal data being processed by Facebook. Indeed, such an argument implies that upon opening a Facebook account one accepts in advance any data processing with regard to any online activity of such 'Facebook users' by any third party having whatever connection with Facebook. That is so even in a situation in which there is no visible sign of such data processing occurring (as seems to be the case when one simply visits the Defendant's website). In other words, accepting the Commission's suggestion would in effect mean that by opening a Facebook account, a user has actually waived any protection of personal data online vis-à-vis Facebook.
>
> I thus consider that the liability and the ensuing consent and information obligations of the Defendant should be the same vis-a-vis the data subjects irrespective of whether or not they have a Facebook account."[1913]

3.6. OTHER ACTORS

927. High-level analysis – The previous section identified a wide range of additional actors interacting with OSN data, such as trackers, data brokers and other observers. In the interest of brevity, the legal status of each of these actors will only be discussed briefly. Generally speaking, one may start from the assumption that each of these actors will typically also be considered as "controllers" in their own right, at least insofar as their own processing activities are concerned. Only in cases where they clearly process personal data on behalf of and in accordance with their instructions, should they be considered as "processors" rather than "controllers".

928. Third-party trackers – For example, a third-party tracker will in principle be considered a "controller" for its collection and analysis of data related to the web browsing behaviour of OSN users. However, it will only be considered a controller as long as it determines its own purposes and means of the processing. As indicated earlier, trackers can also work on behalf of an ad network.[1914] If a tracker is working on behalf of an ad network, and only processes personal data in accordance with the instructions issued by the ad network provider, the tracker will be considered a "processor" rather than a controller. Another scenario in which a tracker might be considered a "processor" is the scenario in which the tracker processes data on behalf of the OSN provider (e.g. if the OSN provider enlists a third-party tracker to learn more about how its users navigate the OSN).[1915]

1913 *Ibid*, 137–139.

1914 Cf. *supra*, no. 858.

1915 See also Article 29 Data Protection Working Party, "Opinion 02/2013 on apps on smart devices", *l.c.*, p. 13 (indicating that a third party provides analytics services for an application owner, without processing the data for its own purposes or sharing it across developers, it is likely to be acting as a processor).

929. DATA BROKERS – Data brokers in principle act as controllers in their own right. They determine their own purposes when collecting data about individuals (e.g. collect data for purposes of profiling or predictive scoring). They also decide autonomously about how to organize this collection (e.g. which sources to consult, which technical methods to employ). While the product developed by a data broker will (eventually) be consumed by a third party, the data broker will have typically concluded its product development long before it is offered to clients.[1916]

930. OTHER OBSERVERS – Other "observers" of OSN data in principle also collect these data for their own purposes. For example, an employer who accesses the profile of a job applicant is likely to do so in order to assess the fitness of the candidate. Similarly, the intelligence agency mining OSN data in order to detect a potential threat to national security is likewise pursuing its own (statutory) objectives. In certain instances, observers may rely on the assistance of other entities to help achieve its objectives (e.g. a school may hire a private firm to monitor social network usage of its students). In these cases, the extent to which the service provider will be considered a "processor" or a "(co-)controller" will depend largely on (1) how the service provider has defined the purpose(s) of its services up front and (2) the extent to which the service provider acts in accordance with instructions issued by its customers.[1917]

4. ALLOCATION OF RESPONSIBILITY AND LIABILITY

931. OUTLINE – The previous section analysed the legal status of each of the actors introduced in the beginning of this chapter. The purpose of this section is to discuss how the main rights and obligations of each of these entities have been interpreted, in particular by the Article 29 Working Party and national regulatory authorities. In the interest of brevity, the remainder of this chapter will be focused on three actors only, namely the (1) OSN providers; (2) the OSN user and (3) application providers.

4.1. TRANSPARENCY

932. OSN PROVIDER – As a controller, the OSN provider must provide data subjects with certain basic information regarding the processing of their

1916 The third party using the data broker's service will typically also be a controller in its own right, separately from the data broker.

1917 See also B. Van Alsenoy, "Allocating responsibility among controllers, processors, and "everything in between": the definition of actors and roles in Directive 95/46", *l.c.*, p. 36–37

personal data.[1918] According to Article 29 Working party, an OSN provider should inform its users *inter alia* about:

a) the usage of their data for direct marketing purposes (e.g. the use of profile information for purposes of targeting advertisements);
b) any sharing of their data with third parties (e.g. third-party application providers);
c) any profiling to which the users might be subject, including an identification of the main data sources (e.g. personal details submitted during registration, cookies, purchase records); and
d) any use of sensitive data.[1919]

In addition to informing users about its own processing activities, the Working Party also recommends that the OSN provider:

a) provide users with adequate warnings about the privacy risks related to themselves and to others when they upload information to the OSN;
b) remind users that uploading information about other individuals might impinge upon their privacy and data protection rights; and
c) advise users that they should in principle only upload pictures or information about others with the consent of the individuals concerned.[1920]

933. Application providers – Application providers are also obliged as controllers to provide their users with information specified in Articles 13–14 GDPR.[1921] In practice, the provisioning of information to OSN users is often mediated through the OSN provider. Under this approach, the OSN provider communicates the permissions requested by the application provider (e.g. access to certain categories of data). When doing so, the OSN provider may also include links to the privacy notices and terms of the application providers.[1922] In any

1918 See Article 13–14 GDPR (previously: Article 10–11). See also *supra*, no. 55.

1919 Article 29 Data Protection Working Party, "Opinion 5/2009 on online social networking", *l.c.*, p. 7.

1920 *Id.* See also N. Helberger and J. Van Hoboken, "Little Brother Is Tagging You – Legal and Policy Implications of Amateur Data Controllers", *l.c.*, p. 106–107.

1921 Prior to offering its service, the application provider will have to communicate, in one form or another: (1) its identity and contact information; (2) the precise categories of personal data (OSN and other) it will collect; (3) for which specific purposes; and (4) how users may exercise their rights. See also Article 29 Data Protection Working Party, "Opinion 02/2013 on apps on smart devices", *l.c.*, p. 22. For applications installed on smart devices, the Working Party has also recommended that users be informed of the retention periods of their data as well as security measures applied by the controller (*Ibid*, p. 23).

1922 Access to OSN data may also be mediated by the user rather than by the OSN (see Article 29 Data Protection Working Party, "Opinion 5/2009 on online social networking", *l.c.*, p. 9). If that is the case, the application provider must communicate the relevant information itself before obtaining access to personal data of the OSN user.

event, the Article 29 Working Party expects OSN providers to put in place "the means to ensure" that third-party developers comply with their obligations, including the obligation to provide clear and specific information about the processing.[1923]

934. OSN USERS – If the user of an OSN is not covered by the personal use exemption, the user is also obliged to provide data subjects with information in accordance with Articles 13–14 GDPR. Any use of personal data which is not already known to the data subject should be communicated to the data subject either at the moment of collection or prior to their disclosure.

935. ASSESSMENT – In theory, every actor is only obliged to ensure the transparency of processing operations under its control. In practice, however, an actor may be expected to do more than that, taking into account its operational role in the processing. For example, the Article 29 Working Party expects OSN providers to enable third-party application providers to communicate the necessary information to data subjects. In addition, the Working Party also expects OSN providers to warn OSN users about the privacy risks related to themselves and to others when they upload information to the OSN.[1924]

4.2. LEGITIMACY

A. *OSN provider*

936. GROUNDS – Under EU data protection law, processing of personal data may only take place to the extent that there is a "lawful basis" justifying the processing (Article 6 GDPR). There are three grounds in particular which the provider of an OSN might invoke, namely:

a) data subject consent;
b) necessity for the performance of a contract; and
c) an (overriding) legitimate interest.

937. USER DATA – For processing that is strictly necessary to provide the OSN service to its users (e.g. initial creation of profile, offering of basic functionalities),

---

1923 Article 29 Data Protection Working Party, "Opinion 5/2009 on online social networking", *l.c.*, p. 8–9.

1924 The Working Party did not specify whether these warnings were legally required, or whether they were merely a recommended "best practice". At most, an obligation to issue such warnings could be derived from the OSN provider's duty to ensure legitimacy and fairness of its own processing activities. See also *infra*, no. 938.

the OSN provider can in principle rely on the ground of "necessity for the performance of a contract".[1925] For certain operations, the provider may also be able to rely on the "legitimate interest" ground (e.g. processing for purposes of ensuring system security).[1926] For other processing operations, such as the use of users' personal data for purposes of behavioural advertising, the provider will in principle have to obtain the unambiguous consent of its users.[1927]

938. Third-party data – As to the processing of non-user data, the Working Party noted that

> "Many SNS allow users to contribute data about other people, such as adding a name to a picture, rating a person, listing the "people I have met/want to meet" at events. This tagging may also identify non-members. However, the processing of such data about non-members by the SNS may only be performed if one of the criteria laid down in Article 7 of the Data Protection Directive is fulfilled."

The Article 29 Working Party did not specify whether this obligation was directed at OSN users (who upload data relating to non-members) and/or OSN providers (who subsequently process these data). The language employed by the Working Party ("*processing ... by the SNS*") seems to suggest it was directed at the latter. Given that an OSN provider will generally not have a direct relationship with non-users, it seems that Article 7(f) is the only practical basis through which an OSN provider might legitimate its processing of data related to non-members.[1928]

1925 P. Van Eecke and M. Truyens, "Privacy and Social Networks", *l.c.*, p. 542.

1926 *Id.* To be lawful, the processing must respect the appropriate balance between the interests of the controller and the interests of the data subject. For more information see Article 29 Data Protection Working Party, "Opinion 06/2014 on the notion of legitimate interests of the data controller under Article 7 of Directive 95/46/EC", WP217, 9 April 2014.

1927 There are situations in which data subject consent is mandated by law, even though the OSN provider might theoretically be able to invoke another ground to legitimate the processing. For instance, Article 5(3) of the E-Privacy Directive entails that the provider of an OSN must obtain the consent of its users prior to (1) the installation of any software on the device of an end-user (e.g. when offering a mobile application for the OSN); (2) any placement of cookies which are not strictly necessary to provide service (e.g. to monitor web-browsing activities outside the OSN). Consent will also de facto be necessary for the processing of user data for purposes of targeted advertising, as well as any processing of data intending to locate the geographic position of the end-user, regardless of whether it involves any storage of information on the device of the end-user. See also Article 29 Data Protection Working Party, "Opinion 13/2011 on Geolocation services on smart mobile devices", *l.c.*, p. 14.

1928 Whether or not the OSN provider is required to ensure the legitimacy of its processing of non-user data in fact depends on whether or not the OSN provider is (also) considered a "controller" for these activities. See also *infra*, nos. 978 et seq.

B. *Application provider*

939. Grounds – Similar to OSN providers, there are essentially three grounds available to application providers to legitimate their processing of personal data, namely:

a) data subject consent;
b) necessity for the performance of a contract; and
c) an (overriding) legitimate interest.[1929]

940. Implementation – Obtaining the informed consent of OSN users shall in practice be a shared responsibility among application providers and OSN providers (at least where access to OSN data is concerned). Even though an OSN provider may not be considered as a "controller" in relation to the subsequent processing activities of application providers, it is still under an obligation to ensure the legitimacy of its own processing operations (including any disclosure to third parties). After all, technically speaking, obtaining access to data about an OSN user constitutes not only a collection by the recipient, but also a disclosure by the OSN provider.[1930] As a result, OSN providers are obliged take reasonable measures to ensure that meaningful consent is obtained from their users for the disclosure of personal data to application developers.[1931] In practice, the application provider will be responsible for articulating which permissions it requires and for which purposes, while the OSN provider will de facto be responsible for communicating this information to its users and obtaining their authorizations.[1932]

1929 See also P. Van Eecke and M. Truyens, "Privacy and Social Networks", *l.c.*, p. 543 and Article 29 Data Protection Working Party, "Opinion 02/2013 on apps on smart devices", *l.c.*, p. 14–16. 255. Similar to OSN providers, an application provider will be required to obtain consent of its users for (1) the installation of any software on the device of an end-user (e.g. when offering a mobile application) (2) any placement of cookies which are not strictly necessary to provide service (e.g. to monitor web-browsing activities outside the application environment); any use of OSN or other personal data for purpose of targeted advertising; and any processing of data intending to locate the geographic position of the end-user. Cf. *supra*, no. 936.

1930 E. Denham (Assistant Privacy Commissioner of Canada), "Report of Findings into the complaint filed by the Canadian Internet Policy and Public Interest Clinic (CIPPIC) against Facebook Inc. under the Personal Information Protection and Electronic Documents Act, 2009, p. 52.

1931 See also E. Denham, "Report of Findings – CIPPIC v. Facebook Inc.", *l.c.*, p. 3 and D.B. Garrie, M. Duffy-Lewis, R. Wong and R.L. Gillespie, "Data Protection: the Challenges Facing Social Networking", *l.c.*, p. 137. For example, the OSN provider could require its application providers to use a standardised privacy notice. At a minimum, the OSN provider should ensure that the requested permissions and (references to) privacy notices are displayed in a prominent way. See also *supra*, no. 933.

1932 See also *supra*, no. 853.

941. Example: Cambridge Analytica – In October 2018, Facebook was issued a monetary penalty notice by the UK Information Commissioner's Office (ICO) for having allowed a third-party application provider to unlawfully obtain access to the personal data about users of the Facebook platform who did not themselves install the app in question in contravention of the UK Data Protection Act.[1933] Facebook had permitted the application to operate in such a way that it collected the personal data about Facebook friends of users of the App, without those Facebook friends having been informed that such data was being collected, and without them being asked to consent to such collection.[1934]

C. *OSN user*

942. Grounds – In theory, OSN users should in principle only share information about others with the consent of the individuals concerned.[1935] In case of dissemination of one's personal image, the requirement of prior consent for applies regardless of whether or not the OSN user falls within the remit of the personal use exemption.[1936] OSN users who do not benefit from the personal use exemption may rely on their legitimate interest where public figures are concerned.

D. *Assessment*

943. Beyond immediate control – As with transparency, the duty to ensure lawfulness of processing is in principle linked to the scope of one's control. The OSN provider, however, is expected to play a proactive role in ensuring the legitimacy of processing by others. For example, the Article 29 Working Party expects OSN providers to remind OSN users that they should

---

1933 See Information Commissioner's Office (ICO), Monetary Penalty Notice to Facebook Ireland Ltd and Facebook Inc., 24 October 2018, at paragraphs 25 and 45 and following.

1934 *Ibid*, paragraph 46.

1935 P. Van Eecke and M. Truyens, "Privacy and Social Networks", *l.c.*, p. 543. See also N. Helberger and J. Van Hoboken, "Little Brother Is Tagging You – Legal and Policy Implications of Amateur Data Controllers", *l.c.*, p. 106–107.

1936 In principle, anyone seeking to record or use the image of another person must first obtain that person's consent. (D. Voorhoof and P. Valcke, *Handboek Mediarecht*, Larcier, 4^{e} editie, 2014 p. 239–240). In legal terms, the right to control one's image is sometimes also referred to as the "right of personal portrayal" or "portrait right". The term "portrait" should be understood broadly in this context, as any reproduction of the image or likeness of a person, regardless of the technique or carrier used. (Based on P. De Hert and R. Saelens, "Recht op afbeelding", *TPR* 2009, afl. 2, 867. See also L. Dierickx, "Recht op afbeelding" in X., Reeks 'Instituut voor Familierecht en Jeugdrecht KU Leuven, no. 89, Antwerpen, Intersentia, 2005, p. 62. On an international level, the right to control one's image is protected by several human rights instruments, such as the European Convention of Human Rights (Article 8) and the International Covenant of Civil and Political Rights (Article 16). B. Van Alsenoy, V. Verdoodt, R. Heyman, J. Ausloos, E. Wauters and G. Acar, *From social media service to advertising network – A critical analysis of Facebook's Revised Policies*, 25 August 2015, v1.3 p. 86.

only upload pictures or information about others with the consent of the individuals concerned. In practice, the OSN provider also plays an important role in ensuring the legitimacy of processing by application providers by obtaining the relevant permissions from OSN users on behalf of the application provider.

4.3. DATA ACCURACY

944. Basic principle – Every controller is obliged to take "every reasonable step" to ensure to ensure the accuracy of personal data under its control. The precise scope of this duty must be interpreted having regard to the purposes of the processing. For example, the standard of care for ensuring data accuracy will obviously be higher in a medical setting than in the context of OSNs.[1937]

945. OSN provider – The duty to ensure data accuracy in principle only extends to processing of personal data which is under one's control. As indicated earlier, there is some disagreement regarding the extent to which OSN providers should be considered controllers in relation to content shared spontaneously by users. If one accepts that an OSN provider should, at least to some extent, be considered as a "controller" in relation to their processing of user-generated content, the question the becomes: which measures are providers of OSNs obliged to adopt in order promote accuracy of data uploaded by their users?

946. Reasonable measures – The issue of data accuracy was not addressed by the Article 29 Working Party on online social networks. It was, however, explicitly addressed by the UK Information Commissioner's Office (ICO) in its 2013 guidance for online social networks:

> "[In] a situation where the vast majority of the site content is posted directly by third parties, the volume of third party posts is significant, site content is not moderated in advance and the site relies upon users complying with user policies and reporting problems to the site operator, we would not consider that taking 'reasonable steps' requires the operator to check every individual post for accuracy."[1938]

In these situations, the ICO continued, it would be sufficient for the OSN provider to

1937 See also B. Van Alsenoy, A. Kuczerawy and J. Ausloos, "Search Engines after *Google Spain*: Internet@Liberty or Privacy@Peril?", *ICRI Working Paper Series*, Working paper 15/2013, September 2013, p. 36.

1938 Information Commissioner's Office (ICO), "Social networking and online forums – when does the DPA apply?", *l.c.*, paragraph 37 (emphasis added). The ICO did indicate that it might hold otherwise in situations where a data controller plays a more active role in selecting, allowing or otherwise moderating content. (*Ibid*, paragraphs 35–36).

a) have a *clear and prominent policy* for its users about acceptable and non-acceptable posts;
b) have clear and easy to find *procedures* in place for data subjects to dispute the accuracy of posts and ask for them to be removed; and
c) *respond to disputes* about accuracy quickly, and have procedures to remove (or suspend access to) content, at least until such time as the dispute has been settled.[1939]

947. Assessment – The approach by the ICO is clearly a pragmatic approach, which attempts to reconcile the controller's obligation to ensure data accuracy with the "open" nature of online social networks. The OSN provider is not expected to establish the accuracy of personal data prior to dissemination, but is expected to have policies which reduce the risk or, if necessary, remediate the processing of inaccurate data within the OSN. This outcome is not likely to be much different now that the GDPR explicitly incorporates the liability exemptions of E-Commerce Directive 2000/31/EC.[1940]

4.4. CONFIDENTIALITY AND SECURITY

A. *OSN provider*

i. Privacy-friendly default settings

948. Basic principle – Every controller is under a duty to ensure the security and confidentiality of processing.[1941] Applying notions of security and confidentiality in the context of OSNs may seem counter-intuitive at first. After all, OSNs are about sharing data rather than about keeping secrets. Nevertheless, OSN providers are obliged to implement appropriate security measures to prevent "*unauthorized or unlawful access*".[1942]

949. Role of privacy settings – In practice, accessibility of an OSN profile is determined, to greater or lesser extent, by the "privacy settings" associated with that profile.[1943] These settings enable individuals to decide, to a certain extent, about the accessibility of their OSN data (e.g. "friends only", "friends and friends-of-friends", "only me", "public", etc.). Many users wish to limit their disclosure of personal information to people they know, or perhaps even

1939 *Ibid*, paragraph 38.
1940 See also *infra*, no. 971 and following.
1941 Cf. *supra*, no. 59 and following.
1942 Article 17(1) Directive 95/46/EC (emphasis added).
1943 For a comprehensive discussion of privacy settings see J. Ausloos, E. Lievens, Els Kindt and J. Dumortier, "Guidelines for privacy-friendly default settings", *SPION*, Deliverable D6.4, 2012.

to a subset of their contacts. Other users may want to share information with the public at large. Certain types of information will of course also be more intimate then others, which may also influence preferences regarding its accessibility.

950. Default settings – Given that different OSN users may have different preferences regarding the visibility of their personal data, the question arises as to which settings should be set as the default. In its 2009 Opinion, the Article 29 Working Party stated that the OSN provider should offer default settings

> "which allow users to freely and specifically consent to any access to their profile's content that is beyond their self-selected contacts in order to reduce the risk of unlawful processing by third parties".[1944]

In other words, the Working Party considered that access to the profile information of OSN users should be restricted to self-selected contacts (e.g. "friends", "network members") by default. OSN users should be asked for permission before access is extended to any other entity.[1945] For example, information contained in a user's profile should not be made available for indexation by (internal or external) search engines unless the user has explicitly agreed to this.[1946] By restricting access to self-selected contacts by default, OSN providers may also solidify the legitimacy and fairness of their processing activities (as users need to take affirmative action before these data are made available to other third parties).[1947]

951. Data protection by default – Article 25(2) GDPR, which codifies the principle of data protection by default, offers additional support for the position advanced by the Article 29 Working Party:

> "The controller shall implement appropriate technical and organisational measures for ensuring that, by default, only personal data which are necessary for each specific

---

1944 Article 29 Data Protection Working Party, "Opinion 5/2009 on online social networking", *l.c.*, p. 7.

1945 This includes access to personal data by application providers, including when this application has not been downloaded by the OSN user herself, but rather by one of her contacts.

1946 Article 29 Data Protection Working Party, "Opinion 5/2009 on online social networking", *l.c.*, p. 7.

1947 See also J. Ausloos, E. Lievens, Els Kindt and J. Dumortier, "Guidelines for privacy-friendly default settings", *l.c.*, p. 30 et seq. Similar reasoning regarding the controller's duty to ensure the confidentiality and security of processing can also be found in the opinions of the Article 29 Working Party regarding applications for smart devices and location-based services. See in particular Article 29 Data Protection Working Party, "Opinion 02/2013 on apps on smart devices", *l.c.*, p. 11 and 15 and Article 29 Data Protection Working Party, "Opinion 13/2011 on Geolocation services on smart mobile devices", *l.c.*, p. 13–14.

purpose of the processing are processed. That obligation applies to the amount of personal data collected, the extent of their processing, the period of their storage and their accessibility. In particular, such measures shall ensure that by default personal data are not made accessible without the individual's intervention to an indefinite number of natural persons."

ii. Access by third-party apps

952. LAYERED ACCESS – In its 2009 Opinion, the Article 29 Working Party also considered that OSN providers should support "layered access", so that third-party application providers can limit their collection of personal data.[1948] The OSN provider is also obliged, as part of its security obligation, to ensure that application providers do not obtain access to more data than has been authorized by users.[1949]

953. DATA PROTECTION BY DESIGN – Article 25(1) GDPR has made the implementation of appropriate measures to implement data protection principles, such as data minimisation an independent obligation, which exists separately from the obligation to ensure confidentiality and security of processing.

954. COUNTERING MISUSE – The OSN provider is obliged to deploy appropriate measures to detect and remedy apparent misuse by application providers (e.g. complaint handling mechanisms, use of spam detection tools).[1950]

955. ASSESSMENT – OSN providers are obliged to ensure the confidentiality and security of their users' data. In addition, they are obliged to take appropriate measures to implement the principles of data protection by design and by default. In practice, this requires the OSN provider to design its system in such a way that it enables and promotes compliance by third party application providers – even if the subsequent processing activities by those third parties are beyond its (legal) control.

956. DUTY OF CARE – An interesting question to consider is whether OSN providers are under a duty to ensure that data is only being shared with "reliable" entities.[1951] OSNs generally tend to dissociate themselves from

---

1948 Article 29 Data Protection Working Party, "Opinion 5/2009 on online social networking", *l.c.*, p. 9.

1949 See also Data Protection Commissioner, "Report of Audit – Facebook Ireland Ltd.", *l.c.*, p. 88.

1950 See Data Protection Commissioner, "Report of Audit – Facebook Ireland Ltd.", *l.c.*, p. 89–97. See also Article 29 Data Protection Working Party, "Opinion 02/2013 on apps on smart devices", *l.c.*, p. 20–21.

1951 F. Le Borgne-Bachschmidt et al., "User-Created-Content: Supporting a participative Information Society", *l.c.*, p. 243–244.

application providers, who they consider as "third parties".[1952] They typically disclaim any and all responsibility for actions undertaken by these third parties.[1953] Nevertheless, one could argue that OSN providers have a basic duty of care to establish that the recipients of the data under their control are in fact trustworthy (i.e. likely to process it in a lawful manner).[1954] Opponents will argue that this interpretation is excessive, and that it is sufficient for the OSN provider to assume responsibility for its own operations (i.e. the boundaries of its control establish the boundaries of its obligations).

B. *Application provider*

957. Separate obligation – Application providers are also obliged to ensure the security and confidentiality of the personal data which they process. In practice, many application providers will export (a subset of) the data they collect from OSN providers to their own servers for further processing.[1955] This means that they alone shall be capable of (and responsible for) ensuring security of processing. In its Opinion on apps for smart devices, the Article 29 Working Party highlighted a number of security considerations for app developers, including:

a) measures to protect data both in transit and at rest;
b) measures to prevent "buffer overflow" or "injection" attacks;
c) use of low entropy app-specific or temporary device identifiers;
d) use of secure identification and authentication mechanisms.[1956]

C. *OSN user*

958. Limited control – OSN users have very little control over the security of data processed within the OSN – even if they formally act as a controller for their own processing operations and fall outside the scope of the personal use

1952 P. Van Eecke and M. Truyens, "Privacy and Social Networks", *l.c.*, p. 541.

1953 See also F. Le Borgne-Bachschmidt et al., "User-Created-Content: Supporting a participative Information Society", *l.c.*, p. 243–244 and E. Denham (Assistant Privacy Commissioner of Canada), "Report of Findings into the complaint filed by the Canadian Internet Policy and Public Interest Clinic (CIPPIC) against Facebook Inc. under the Personal Information Protection and Electronic Documents Act", *l.c.* paragraphs 166 et seq.

1954 F. Le Borgne-Bachschmidt et al., "User-Created-Content: Supporting a participative Information Society", *l.c.*, p. 244. These authors argue that such an obligation could already be derived from Article 6(1) of Directive 95/46, which requires that personal data must be processed "fairly and lawfully". An alternative way of phrasing this argument would be to say that the OSN provider acts as a "custodian" (or "steward") of data entrusted by its users, who as a result has a certain duty of care before releasing data to third parties. See also *infra*, no. 979.

1955 These servers are outside of the OSN domain, meaning they are beyond the OSN provider's direct control or supervision. (M. Huber, M. Mulazzani, S. Schrittwieser, E.R. Weippl, "AppInspect – Large-scale Evaluation of Social Apps", *l.c.*, p. 2).

1956 Article 29 Data Protection Working Party, "Opinion 02/2013 on apps on smart devices", *l.c.*, p. 18–20.

exemption (e.g. when a company or school decides to make certain information available via an OSN). The OSN user must therefore carefully consider whether the security afforded by the OSN provider are sufficient in light of the risks presented by the processing. If this is not the case, the OSN user should refrain from uploading the data in question.

4.5. DATA SUBJECT RIGHTS

A. *OSN Provider*

959. Problem statement – As a controller, the provider of an OSN must accommodate the exercise of data subject rights. The exercise of these rights vis-à-vis an OSN provider is relatively straightforward in cases where the OSN provider has actively solicited the information in question. Similarly, it seems only natural that the OSN provider accommodate data subject rights in relation to processing activities for which it alone has determined the purposes and means (e.g. use of profile information for advertising purposes, use facial recognition to develop tag suggests). As indicated earlier, however, much of the data shared on OSNs are not actively solicited by the OSN provider, but instead shared spontaneously by its users. An interesting question to consider therefore is whether OSN providers are also obliged to accommodate the exercise of data subject rights in relation to such content. For example, should an individual have a right to ask an OSN provider to take down a photograph posted by one of its users?

960. Relation to control – In principle, individuals can only exercise their rights as data subjects vis-à-vis the "controller" of the processing. The previous sections have made clear that OSNs may involve a multitude of actors, who may each be in "control" of different (aspects of different) processing operations. In principle, each entity is only responsible for those aspects of the processing under its own control, i.e. for which it determines (or co-determines) the "purposes and means".

961. Article 29 WP – While the initiative to share content typically stems from an OSN user (who may therefore be considered as the "primary" controller), most regulators seem to agree that OSN providers should put in place a mechanism to enable individuals to exercise their data subject rights directly towards the OSN provider.[1957] For example, in its Opinion on online social networks, the Article 29 Working Party considered that

[1957] As indicated earlier, there are a number of scholars who have argued that OSN providers (or the providers of similar services) should not be considered as "controllers" in relation to the content shared via their platforms. As a result, these authors question the duty of these

> "Access and rectification rights of users are not limited to the users of the service but to any natural person whose data are processed. Members and non-members of SNS must have a means to exercise their right of access, correction and deletion. The homepage of SNS sites should clearly refer to the existence of a "complaint handling office" set up by the SNS provider to deal with data protection and privacy issues and complaints by both members and non-members."[1958]

Although it is not stated explicitly as such, the quoted text suggests that OSN providers have a duty to accommodate data subject rights in relation to *any* personal data they process. This would imply that individuals can also exercise their rights as data subjects in relation to content shared by OSN users, seeing as these data are also processed by the OSN provider. This interpretation is also in line with guidance issued by national regulators, such as the Dutch Data Protection Authority[1959] and the UK Information Commissioner's Office.[1960] [1961]

962. Open issues – While the guidance issued by the Working Party was most welcome, it refrained from offering any additional guidance as to how OSN providers should actually deal with the exercise of data subject rights. Should they immediately remove any content upon request? Should they query the OSN user from whom the content originated? Should the latter be able to contest the data subject's complaint? The potential implications for other fundamental rights, such as freedom of expression, will be revisited later on.

B. *Application provider*

963. Withdrawal of consent – Application providers must enable users to exercise their rights as data subjects.[1962] Application users should also be provided the ability to withdraw their consent at any time, at least insofar as the

platform providers to accommodate data subject rights vis-à-vis user-generated content. Van Eecke and Truyens, for example, argue that an OSN provider should be considered as a mere processor in relation to content shared by users. In their view, only users should be responsible for accommodating data subject rights. See P. Van Eecke and M. Truyens, "Privacy and Social Networks", *l.c.*, p. 539 and p. 543.

1958 Article 29 Working Party, "Opinion 5/2009 on online social networking", *l.c.*, p. 11.

1959 College Bescherming Persoonsgegevens, "Publicatie van Persoonsgegevens op het Internet", *l.c.*, p. 42.

1960 Information Commissioner's Office (ICO), "Social networking and online forums – when does the DPA apply?", *l.c.*, p. 14.

1961 See also R. Wong, "Social networking: a conceptual analysis of a data controller", *Communications Law* 2009, Vol. 14, No. 5, p. 148. For an example of a recent order issued by the Italian Data Protection Authority see Garante per la protezione dei dati personali, Provvedimento dell'11 febbraio 2016 [doc. web n. 4833448], 11 Feburary 2016.

1962 The Article 29 Working Party recommends that application providers allow their users to exercise these rights by means of a secure online access tool. (Article 29 Working Party, "Opinion 5/2009 on online social networking", *l.c.*, p. 24).

processing is based on consent.[1963] Given their role in facilitating access to OSN data, OSN providers may also be expected to offer tools which allow OSN users to discontinue access to their profile data (unless such access is already limited by default, e.g. to moments at which the application is being used by the OSN users).[1964]

C. *User*

964. LIMITED CONTROL – OSN users who do not fall under the personal use exemption are also obliged to accommodate data subject rights. In practice, every OSN user can only administrate its own profile page. It has little or no ability to influence the subsequent use of data by the OSN provider once it has been uploaded. The OSN user must therefore carefully consider whether the subsequent processing by the OSN provider is compatible with the purposes for which the OSN user collected the data. If this is not the case, the OSN user should in principle refrain from uploading the data in question (or, if the data have already been uploaded, remove it as soon as soon as the individual concerned objects).

5. EVALUATION

965. OUTLINE – For the most part, regulators and scholars have been able to reconcile the regulatory framework of EU data protection law with new social networking realities. But there are also instances in which this framework is beginning to show its limits. There are four areas in particular which merit further consideration, namely (1) the scope of the personal use exemption; (2) the exercise of data subject rights towards user-generated content; (3) the responsibilities of platform providers; and (4) the implications of joint control.

5.1. SCOPE OF THE PERSONAL USE EXEMPTION

966. OSN USERS AS CONTROLLERS – Section 3.2 analysed the extent to which a user of an OSN may be considered as a "controller" within the meaning of Article 4(7) GDPR. The conclusion was that every OSN user, at least conceptually, acts

---

1963 *Ibid*, p. 25. Article 7(3) of the GDPR now explicitly confirms that the data subject shall have the right to withdraw his or her consent at any time.

1964 While not mentioned explicitly by the Article 29 Working Party in its opinion on online social networking, it reached a similar conclusion in its opinion related to apps on smart devices. See Article 29 Data Protection Working Party, "Opinion 02/2013 on apps on smart devices", *l.c.*, p. 25. Further support for this position can now also be found in Articles 24 and 25 of the GDPR.

as a "controller" when processing data relating to others. This implies that OSN users shall in principle be subject to the same requirements and obligations as other controllers, unless they can avail themselves from one of the exemptions recognized by EU data protection law.

967. Personal use? – In its Opinion on social networking, the Working Party considered that the processing activities of private OSN users will generally be covered by the personal use exemption.[1965] Since then, several commentators have contested this view; arguing that in practice there are many situations in which the exemption is inapplicable.[1966] First, it appears to be common ground that the exemption does not apply in situations where data are made accessible to "an indefinite number of people".[1967] As a result, OSN users with "public" profiles will almost certainly fall outside the scope of Article 2(2)c GDPR. Even if a profile is set to "private", however, it is quite possible that the information is still *de facto* accessible to an "indefinite" number of people (e.g. due to access by "friends-of-friends").[1968] Second, a substantial share of individuals does not only (or not exclusively) use OSNs for personal purposes, but also for professional

---

1965 Article 29 Data Protection Working Party, "Opinion 5/2009 on online social networking", *l.c.*, p. 5.

1966 See e.g. P. Van Eecke and M. Truyens, "Privacy and Social Networks", *l.c.*, p. 540; N. Helberger and J. Van Hoboken, "Little Brother Is Tagging You – Legal and Policy Implications of Amateur Data Controllers", *l.c.*, p. 101 et seq. and D.B. Garrie, M. Duffy-Lewis, R. Wong and R.L. Gillespie, "Data Protection: the Challenges Facing Social Networking", *l.c.*, p. 147 et seq. Even before Opinion 5/2009, several authors considered it likely that a substantial number of OSN users might not be able to benefit from the personal use exemption. See e.g. R. Wong, "Social Networking: Anybody is a Data Controller!", Working Paper,(last revised) 2008 and B. Van Alsenoy, J. Ballet and A. Kuczerawy, "Social networks and web 2.0: are users also bound by data protection regulations?", *l.c.*, p. 75.

1967 See also *supra*, nos. 882 et seq.

1968 Previous research has indicated that many users set a relatively low threshold for deciding whether to accept someone as a "friend" (See e.g. R. Gross and A. Acquisti, "Information Revelation and Privacy in Online Social Networks", in *Proceedings of the 2005 ACM Workshop on Privacy in the Electronic Society* (WPES'05), Virginia, 2005. p. 73 and d. boyd, "Friendster and Publicly Articulated Social Networks", in *Conference on Human Factors and Computing Systems* (CHI 2004), Vienna, ACM, April 24–29, 2004, p. 1280. Contra: R. Goettke and J. Christiana, "Privacy and Online Social Networking Websites", Computer Science 199r: Special Topics in Computer Science Computation and Society: Privacy and Technology, 14 May 2007). Given that many profiles are accessible also to "friends of friends", even a profile with a relatively low number contacts may in practice have an extremely large audience. According to a recent study by the Pew Research Institute, the *median* Facebook user can reach *31,170* people through their "*friends-of-friends*". (K. N. Hampton, L.S. Goulet, C. Marlow and L. Rainie, "Why Facebook users get more than they give", *Pew Research Center's Internet & American Life Project*, 2012, p. 5. See also M. Isaac, "On Facebook, There's No Privacy Setting for Your Friends' Bad Judgment", *All things D*, 26 December 2012. Finally, regarding the "blurry-edged" nature of social networks see also L. Gelman, "Privacy, Free Speech, and "Blurry-Edged" Social Networks", *Boston College Law Review* 2009, vol. 50, in particular at p. 1326 et seq.

networking or for political, commercial or charitable ends.[1969] Given that the exemption of Article 2(2)c GDPR only applies to "purely" personal or household activities, those users would find themselves outside its protective remit.[1970]

968. IMPLICATIONS – In cases where the personal use exemption cannot be applied, the OSN user in question shall in principle be subject to the same requirements as those incumbent upon controllers in any other context.[1971] This outcome is warranted where organisations are concerned, who make use of OSNs to realize their commercial, political or other objectives. This outcome is more problematic, however, where private individuals are concerned. If an OSN user is subject to data protection law, it implies, inter alia, that this OSN user is required to ensure:

(1) the lawfulness of processing (e.g. by asking for consent before posting data relating to others);
(2) transparency of processing (e.g. by notifying the individuals concerned of the fact that information about them is now included on an OSN profile);
(3) respect for the data quality principles such as fairness, proportionality, finality and accuracy (e.g. by refraining from posting erroneous statements);
(4) that data subjects have the ability to exercise their rights towards the processing (i.e. right of access, rectification, erasure or blocking); and
(5) the confidentiality and security of processing (e.g. by restricting access to individuals from the same community).

969. ASSESSMENT – At first glance, it seems as if a number of these requirements could be applied to private individuals in a reasonable way. For example, many would agree that "friends" should refrain from uploading pictures of one and other before checking whether it's ok.[1972] Or that they should not post inaccurate or harmful statements about others, regardless of whether or not their profile is set to "private". For other data protection requirements, however, there appears to be a clear mismatch between legal provisions and OSN practices. For example, how does one interpret the requirement of not keeping personal data in identifiable form for longer than is necessary (Article 5(1)e) in relation to OSN users? Is it possible to determine a reasonable time-span as to how long a user should be

---

1969 N. Helberger and J. Van Hoboken, "Little Brother Is Tagging You – Legal and Policy Implications of Amateur Data Controllers", *l.c.*, p. 103.

1970 See also recital (18) GDPR, which specifies that a purely personal or household activity implies that there is "*no connection to a professional or commercial activity*".

1971 Cf. *supra*, nos. 882 et seq.

1972 See also N. Helberger and J. Van Hoboken, "Little Brother Is Tagging You – Legal and Policy Implications of Amateur Data Controllers", *l.c.*, p. 104. Others may find it perfectly acceptable (and even enjoyable) to find themselves "tagged" unexpectedly in a picture uploaded by a shared contact.

allowed to maintain a picture or remark relating to another person on his profile page? Should we be requiring individuals to make such a determination? Another problematic provision is the controller's duty to inform.[1973] Should OSN users be required to formally notify their peers of (1) their identities; (2) the purposes of the processing of their personal data as well as (3) the (categories of) recipients concerned? Or is it sufficient if these things are understood implicitly, as a result of prevailing social norms and common OSN practices?

970. A PRAGMATIC APPROACH – The mismatch between data protection requirements and OSN practices has led several authors to advocate for a pragmatic approach.[1974] Rather than rigid adherence to the provisions of the EU data protection law, they argue, OSN providers and OSN users should share the burdens of compliance in light of their respective roles. The implementation of this approach corresponds, by and large, to the recommendations issued by the Article 29 Working Party in its 2009 Opinion on online social networks. For example, the Working Party already recommended that OSN providers make users aware of the privacy risks involved in uploading information related to others, and that they should obtain their consent before doing so. The use of privacy-friendly default settings may similarly be viewed as an example of a technical measure that supports users when they exercise their responsibilities as "controllers".[1975] While this pragmatic approach seems reasonable (and perhaps even commendable as a matter of practice), one also cannot help but wonder whether the framework of EU data protection law is being stretched too far beyond its intended scope of application.

5.2. CONTROL OVER USER-GENERATED CONTENT

971. DO OSN PROVIDERS "CONTROL" UGC? – Opinions vary on the extent to which OSN providers should be considered as "controllers" in relation to user-generated content.[1976] Some argue that OSN providers should be considered as controllers given the nature of their service. Others consider an OSN provider as a mere "processor", who stores and disseminates content on behalf of its users. Yet others have argued that OSN providers should instead be treated as "hosts" within the meaning of Directive 2000/31/EC.[1977]

1973 See also D.B. Garrie, M. Duffy-Lewis, R. Wong and R.L. Gillespie, "Data Protection: the Challenges Facing Social Networking", *l.c.*, p. 132.

1974 N. Helberger and J. Van Hoboken, "Little Brother Is Tagging You – Legal and Policy Implications of Amateur Data Controllers", *l.c.*, p. 105 et seq.

1975 *Id.*

1976 Cf. *supra*, nos. 874 et seq.

1977 See e.g. G. Sartor, "Providers' liabilities in the new EU Data Protection Regulation: A threat to Internet freedoms?", *l.c.*, p. 5 et seq.

972. Practical implications – While the differences among the approaches outlined above are considerable, they are mainly conceptual. The practical implications of each approach may be largely the same, depending on how one interprets the obligations resulting from the qualification of an OSN provider as a "controller". For example, those who consider OSN providers as "controllers", typically do not expect them to proactively assess the legality of every item shared by users.[1978] The "reasonable measures", which may be expected from OSN providers under this approach, are typically limited to complaint handling once an incident has occurred.[1979] This outcome is quite similar to the "notice-and-take down" mechanisms for hosts resulting from Directive 2000/31/EC. The practical implications in the context of OSNs should therefore not be overstated.[1980] Now that the GDPR explicitly incorporates the liability exemptions of Directive 2000/31/EC, providers of OSN shall generally be able to ward off liability in cases where OSN users unlawfully disseminate personal data, insofar as they are merely (a) storing such information at the request of their users; and (b) do not have knowledge of the illegal activity or information and, upon obtaining knowledge or awareness, acts expeditiously to remove or to disable access to the information.[1981]

973. Benefits – Allowing individuals to exercise their rights vis-à-vis OSN providers offers certain advantages, at least from a privacy perspective. In practice, an individual may encounter several difficulties when trying to exercise her rights towards an OSN user. First off, the OSN user may be acting within the scope of the personal use exemption, which means that they are not obliged to consider data subject rights. Even if the OSN user is acting beyond the scope of Article 2(2)c GDPR, he or she might still refuse to take down the content at issue (e.g. by arguing that its interests in sharing the content supersede the privacy interests of the person concerned). Enforcement can be quite difficult and costly, particularly where the defendant resides in a foreign jurisdiction or if the real identity of the OSN user is concealed.[1982] For each of these reasons, the individual concerned may want to turn to the OSN provider for help.[1983]

1978 See e.g. B. Van Alsenoy, J. Ballet and A. Kuczerawy, "Social networks and web 2.0: are users also bound by data protection regulations?", *l.c.*, p. 71; Information Commissioner's Office (ICO), "Social networking and online forums – when does the DPA apply?", *l.c.*, paragraphs 35–37. See also *supra*, no. 946.

1979 *Id.*

1980 See also B. Van Alsenoy, A. Kuczerawy and J. Ausloos, "Search Engines after *Google Spain*: Internet@Liberty or Privacy@Peril?", *l.c.*, p. 61–62.

1981 See Article 14(1)b Directive 2000/31/EC.

1982 See also N. Helberger and J. Van Hoboken, "Little Brother Is Tagging You – Legal and Policy Implications of Amateur Data Controllers", *l.c.*, p. 108.

1983 See also B. Van Alsenoy, A. Kuczerawy and J. Ausloos, "Search Engines after *Google Spain*: Internet@Liberty or Privacy@Peril?", *l.c.*, p. 5.

974. Risks of over-blocking – While the assistance of OSN providers can offer certain benefits, it also entails certain risks. Without appropriate safeguards, there is a risk that OSN providers might take down content simply because they receive a complaint. After all, the OSN provider may need to decide swiftly about removing or blocking the content at issue in order to exonerate itself from potential liability.[1984] This could easily lead to preventive over-blocking of entirely legitimate content.[1985] Several organisations, including the Council of Europe, have expressed concerns about possible "chilling effects" of such "notice-and-take down" procedures upon individuals' freedom of expression.[1986]

975. No due process – Another concern is that the OSN user from whom the content originated may not even be made aware of the fact that someone objected to it. Or if aware, he or she may not be given the opportunity to defend the use of that content before it is removed. This is at odds with the principles of due process, according to which one should be given the opportunity to be heard before being deprived of one's rights.[1987]

976. Complexity – Finally, there is also the issue of complexity: assessing the legitimacy of a complaint may be difficult in practice.[1988] The evaluation of subjective rights such as the right to privacy is often a delicate exercise; one

---

1984 The liability exposure of OSN providers may stem either from the consideration that (1) the OSN provider is acting as controller in relation to the content at issue; (2) failure to remove the content at issue falls short of a reasonable standard of care (liability in tort); or (3) failure to act expeditiously results in loss of a liability exemption (e.g. the liability exemption accorded to "hosting service providers" under E-Commerce Directive 2000/31/EC).

1985 Similar concerns have been expressed in relation to so-called "notice-and-take down" procedures, such as the ones resulting from EU E-Commerce Directive 2000/31/EC. See also C. Ahlert, C. Marsden and C. Yung, "How Liberty Disappeared from Cyberspace: the Mystery Shopper Tests Internet Content Self-Regulation" ("Mystery Shopper"). For a more detailed discussion of notice-and-take down mechanisms, as well as their relationship to Directive 95/46/EC, see also B. Van Alsenoy, A. Kuczerawy and J. Ausloos, "Search Engines after *Google Spain*: Internet@Liberty or Privacy@Peril?", *l.c.*, p. 58 et seq.

1986 In its document "Declaration on freedom of communications on the Internet", the Council of Europe stated that: *"Member States should, however, exercise caution imposing liability on service providers for not reacting to such a notice. Questions about whether certain material is illegal are often complicated and best dealt with by the courts. If service providers act too quickly to remove content after a complaint is received, this might be dangerous from the point of view of freedom of expression and information. Perfectly legitimate content might thus be suppressed out of fear of legal liability"*. (Council of Europe (Council of Ministers), Declaration on freedom of communications on the Internet, 28 May 2003.

1987 See also A. Kuczerawy and J. Ausloos, "From Notice-and-Takedown to Notice-and-Delist: Implementing the Google Spain Ruling", *CiTiP Working Paper Series* 2015, p. 13.

1988 See also Lievens E., *Protecting Children in the Digital Era – the Use of Alternative Regulatory Instruments*, Martinus Nijhoff Publishers, International Studies in Human Rights, Leiden, 2010, p. 360 (with reference Montéro E., "La responsabilité des prestataires intermediaries sur les réseaux", in: Montéro E. (ed.), *Le commerce electronique européen sur les rails?, Cahiers du CRID*, Brussel, Bruylant, 2001, 289–290).

which is traditionally bestowed upon courts or regulators (rather than upon private actors). Furthermore, perceptions of privacy may also be strongly influenced by cultural factors, which may make it difficult to develop a uniform approach (particularly for OSN providers which have an international user base).

977. Balancing of rights – Over-compliance with removal requests poses a significant threat to freedom of expression. This problem is not, however, limited to matters concerning data protection.[1989] While certain types of content can more readily be identified as "illegal" or "inappropriate", an evaluation will always be necessary.[1990] A number of measures could be devised to help mitigate the risk of unjustified take-downs. For example, one might grant an OSN provider some leeway, by saying that it shall only be responsible for removing if it is sufficiently clear that the interests of the data subject outweigh the interests of others. Furthermore, the OSN user from whom the content originated should in principle be offered the opportunity to defend their use of the content. It is beyond the scope of this book, however, to investigate this matter in greater depth.[1991]

5.3. RESPONSIBILITIES OF PLATFORM PROVIDERS

978. Platform responsibility – The provider of an OSN is uniquely placed to influence the processing of personal data that takes place on its platform. It can influence behaviour both by setting policies for acceptable use (e.g. do not collect user data without consent) and by administering these policies (e.g. by blocking apps containing malware). The previous sections have shown that OSN providers are expected to implement a number of privacy-preserving measures in their role as platform providers. This "platform responsibility"[1992] of OSN

1989 See also B. Van Alsenoy, A. Kuczerawy and J. Ausloos, "Search Engines after *Google Spain*: Internet@Liberty or Privacy@Peril?", *l.c.*, p. 69, with reference to the First Report on the Application of Directive 2000/31 of the European Parliament and of the Council of 8 June 2000 on the Directive on Electronic Commerce, COM(2003) 702 final, Brussels, 21 November 2003; Summary of the results of the Public Consultation on the future of electronic commerce in the Internal Market and the implementation of the Directive on electronic commerce (2000/31/EC); Commission Staff Working Document Online services, including e-commerce, in the Single Market, Brussels, 11 January 2012 SEC(2011) 1641 final.

1990 *Id.*

1991 For a detailed analysis see A. Kuczerawy, *Intermediary Liability and Freedom of Expression in the EU: from Concepts to Safeguards*, KU Leuven Centre for IT & IP Law Series, Intersentia, 2018, p. 425 p.

1992 The concept of "platform responsibility" aims to further stimulate respect of human rights by private companies that manage online platforms. Building on Ruggie's framework "Protect, Respect and Remedy", platform responsibility begins from the finding that online platform providers (such as OSN providers) have the ability to impact different human rights, notably freedom of expression and privacy. For more information see the website of the Dynamic Coalition on Platform Responsibility: http://platformresponsibility.info (last accessed 11 December 2015). See also J. Ruggie, "Protect, Respect and Remedy – A Framework for

providers is not only a corporate social responsibility, it is also part of their fiduciary obligations as data controllers.

979. Fiduciary obligations – Every controller has certain fiduciary obligations in relation to the personal data which have been entrusted to it. For example, every controller must in principle assess the legitimacy of an access request before making data available to third parties.[1993] From a legal perspective, this obligation stems from the fact that every "access" by a third party is also a "disclosure" by the holder of the data, i.e. a processing operation for which the controller is legally responsible.[1994] Through regulatory guidance, the Article 29 Working Party and national authorities have attempted to clarify the fiduciary duties of OSN providers in relation to third-party applications. Specifically, the OSN provider who enables access by third-party applications is obliged to:

a) ensure that access by third-party applications is transparent to users;
b) support layered access, so that the collection of personal data by third-party apps can be limited to that which is necessary;
c) ensure that application providers obtain meaningful consent from OSN users;
d) implement privacy-friendly default settings, in order to reduce the risk of unlawful processing by third parties;
e) remove or block apps that compromise the privacy or security of OSN users;
f) provide tools which allow OSN users to discontinue the access by application providers to their profile data.[1995]

Further support for this position can now also be found in Articles 24 (responsibility of the controller) and 25 (data protection by design and by default) GDPR.

980. Beyond "control"? – In principle, every actor is only responsible for processing under its "control", i.e. for which it determines the purposes and means. In practice, the responsibilities of the OSN provider extend further than its own processing activities. For example, the use of malware technology

Business and Human Rights", Report of the Special Representative of the United Nations Secretary-General on the issue of human rights and transnational corporations and other business enterprises, *innovations* (a United Nations publication), 2008, p. 189–212.

1993 An obvious exception to this rule is, of course, personal data which are legitimately made publically available, e.g. through a publically accessible website.

1994 See also *supra*, no. 953.

1995 While not mentioned explicitly by the Article 29 Working Party in its opinion on online social networking, it reached a similar conclusion in its opinion related to apps on smart devices. See Article 29 Data Protection Working Party, "Opinion 02/2013 on apps on smart devices", *l.c.*, p. 25.

by a third-party application provider is not under the "control" of the OSN provider. Nevertheless, regulators consider it the duty of OSN providers to block or remove misbehaving apps.[1996] While there is a clear legal foundation for this obligation (see now in particular Articles 24–25 GDPR), at times the scope of the responsibilities of OSN providers also appear to extend to areas which are beyond their immediate (legal) control.[1997]

981. Context, role and ability to act – The obligations imposed upon OSN providers in their role as platform providers are consistent with the second principle of the OECD Recommendation on Digital Security Risk Management. The second principle ("responsibility") stipulates that all stakeholders should take responsibility for the management of digital security risks "*based on their roles, the context and their ability to act*".[1998] Data protection authorities expect more from OSN providers in areas where they are best placed to act, even if not every subsequent processing operation is under their immediate control. Conversely, data protection authorities are seemingly willing to relax the obligations in other areas, where the OSN provider is less suited to act. For example, the ICO has interpreted the OSN provider's duty to ensure data accuracy in a pragmatic way, basically limiting its duties to ex post intervention in case of a dispute.[1999]

5.4. JOINT CONTROL, JOINT RESPONSIBILITIES?

982. Limiting joint responsibility – In *Fashion ID*, Advocate General Bobek took the position that the responsibilities of a website operator only extend to those "aspects" of the processing for which it actually (co-)determines the

1996 See e.g. Data Protection Commissioner, "Report of Audit – Facebook Ireland Ltd.", *l.c.*, p. 97. A similar approach was adopted by WP29 in relation to providers of mobile operating systems and app stores (Article 29 Data Protection Working Party, "Opinion 02/2013 on apps on smart devices", *l.c.*, p. p11 and p. 20) For an overview of security measures which app store providers can implement see also M. Decker and G. Hogben, "Appstore security: 5 lines of defence against malware", ENISA, 2011, 20 p. See also See Information Commissioner's Office (ICO), Monetary Penalty Notice to Facebook Ireland Ltd and Facebook Inc., 24 October 2018, in particular at paragraph 50 and following.

1997 A clear example is the recommendation of the Article 29 Working Party to warn OSN users about the privacy risks related to themselves and to others when they upload information to the OSN. Strictly speaking, the decision to upload a particular piece of information is beyond the immediate (legal) control of the OSN provider. Nevertheless, the OSN provider is uniquely placed to educate users and raise awareness about privacy issues involved in sharing information relating to others. For an in-depth discussion of the normative foundation of the responsibility of internet intermediaries see M. Thompson, "Beyond Gatekeeping: The Normative Responsibility of Internet Intermediaries", University of Hong Kong Faculty of Law Research Paper No. 2015/45, 55 p.

1998 See the second principle of the OECD, Recommendation of the Council on Digital Security Risk Management for Economic and Social Prosperity, 2015.

1999 Cf. *supra*, no. 946.

purposes and means.[2000] He then considered that the exercise of joint control in this case was limited to a very specific stage of the processing, namely the initial collection and transmission of data to the OSN provider.[2001] Taking into account the degree of involvement of the website operator, who does not have access to the underlying data, the Advocate General concluded that its obligations did not extend so far as to include the duty to inform visitors of their rights of access and/or rectification in relation to the data being collected.[2002]

983. OBA ANALOGY – The Opinion of Advocate General Bobek appears consistent with the Opinion of the Article 29 Working Party on behavioural advertising.[2003] In this Opinion, the Article 29 Working Party considered the responsibilities incumbent upon website publishers in relation to the redirection of the browsers of visitors to the servers of ad network providers. Similar to a website operator embedding a social plug-in, a website publisher embeds programming code into its website which causes the visitor's browser to automatically make a connection with a third-party server, thereby enabling the collection of personal data, including cookies.[2004] When assessing the scope of obligations of a website publisher in this context, the Working Party considered that:

> "[P]ublishers will have some responsibility as data controllers for these actions. This responsibility cannot, however, require compliance with the bulk of the obligations contained in the Directives. In this regard, it is necessary to interpret the legal framework in a flexible way by applying only those provisions that are pertinent. Publishers do not hold personal information; so obviously, it would not make sense to apply some of the obligations of the Directive such as the right of access. However, as further described below, the obligation to inform individuals of the data processing is fully applicable to publishers."[2005]

2000 Cf. *supra*, no. 918.
2001 Cf. *supra*, no. 922.
2002 Cf. *supra*, no. 925.
2003 Article 29 Data Protection Working Party, "Opinion 2/2010 on online behavioural advertising", WP171, 22 June 2010, p. 11.
2004 *Id.* ("*[I]n a typical scenario where ad network providers serve tailored advertising, publishers contribute to it by setting up their web sites in such a way that when a user visits a publisher's web site, his/her browser is automatically redirected to the webpage of the ad network provider. In doing so, the user's browser will transmit his/her IP address to the ad network provider which will proceed to send the cookie and tailored advertising. In this scenario, it is important to note that publishers do not transfer the IP address of the visitor to the ad network provider. Instead, it is the visitor's browser that automatically transfers such information to the ad network provider. However, this only happens because the publisher has set up its web site in such a way that the visitor to its own web site is automatically re-directed to the ad network provider web site. In other words, the publisher triggers the transfer of the IP address, which is the first necessary step that will allow the subsequent processing, carried out by the ad network provider for the purposes of serving tailored advertising.*")
2005 *Ibid*, p. 11–12.

984. Normative perspective – Earlier in his Opinion, Advocate General Bobek contrasted the inherent conflict that exists between a broad interpretation of the controller concept with the normative foundations of responsibility and liability:

> "[T]here ought to be, perhaps not always an exact match, but at least a reasonable correlation between power, control, and responsibility. Modern law naturally includes various forms of objective liability, which will be triggered merely by certain results occurring. But those tend to be justified exceptions. If, without any reasoned explanation, responsibility is attributed to someone who had no control over the result, such allocation of liability will typically be seen as unreasonable or unjust.
>
> Moreover, […] effective protection of something tends to dramatically decrease if everyone is made responsible for it. Making everyone responsible means that no-one will in fact be responsible. Or rather, the one party that should have been held responsible for a certain course of action, the one actually exercising control, is likely to hide behind all those others nominally 'co-responsible', with effective protection likely to be significantly diluted.
>
> Finally, no good (interpretation of the) law should reach a result in which the obligations provided therein cannot actually be carried out by its addressees. Thus, unless the robust definition of (joint) control is not supposed to turn into a judicially sponsored command to disconnect which is applicable to all actors, and to refrain from using any social networks, plug-ins, and potentially other third-party content for that matter, then in defining the obligations and responsibilities, reality must play a role, again including issues of knowledge and genuine bargaining power and the ability to influence any of the imputed activities."[2006]

Later in his opinion, however, the Advocate General appears to attach the delineation and limitation of a website operators responsibility to the scope of its control in the legal sense (i.e. the extent of co-determination of purposes and means), rather than in the operational sense (ability to comply).[2007]

985. Risks of modulation – The question may asked whether, in the long term, the modulation of data protection responsibilities in cases of joint control would not risk to undermine the effective and complete protection of data subjects. Ordinarily, the obligations incumbent on a controller in principle befall the controller "as a complete set". A controller shall in principle be accountable for every aspect of the data processing: ranging from its obligation to ensure that the data quality principles are complied with, to the obligation to support the exercise of data subject rights, to notification obligations etc.[2008] In practice, the

---

2006 Opinion of Advocate General Bobek in *Fashion ID*, C-40/17, ECLI:EU:C:2018:1039, paragraphs 91–93.

2007 Cf. *supra*, no. 923–925.

2008 Contra: Tweede Kamer der Staten-Generaal, Regels inzake de bescherming van persoonsgegevens (Wet bescherming persoonsgegevens) – Memorie van Toelichting, *l.c.*, p. 59–60.

situation often occurs whereby certain obligations may more easily be fulfilled by entities other than the controller(s) itself (themselves). In Opinion 1/2010, the Working Party emphasized that not being able to directly fulfil all the obligations of a controller does not excuse an entity from its obligations under data protection law.[2009] It may engage other actors to achieve compliance with its obligations, but in principle this does not negate the fact that it is the controller that remains ultimately responsible for them.[2010]

986. Legal vs. Operational control – In the end, the interpretation put forth by Advocate General Bobek results in an approach whereby control in the legal sense and control in an operational sense become integrated with one another. Because the website operator does not have "physical" access to data, and at the same time is generally not involved the subsequent processing activities (after transmission), it is said not be subject to the obligation to inform data subject of their rights of access and rectification. At the same time, Advocate General Bobek concludes that the operator's control, in the legal sense, over the transmission of the data, does not justify any responsibilities vis-à-vis the subsequent processing activities, including the rights of access and rectification, as the website operator is said not to codetermine the purposes and means of those processing activities.[2011]

987. Ripple effects? – At this point, it is interesting to contrast the reasoning of Advocate General Bobek in *Fashion ID* with the reasoning of Advocate General Bot in *Wirtschaftsakademie*. Indeed, while Advocate General Bobek appears keen to limit responsibility to areas in which a party has actual operational control (as well as genuine bargaining power), Advocate General Bot appears to consider that a recognition of broader responsibility is likely to help ensure greater protection:

2009 Opinion 1/2010, *l.c.*, p. 22.

2010 *Id.* (stating "*It may be that in practice those obligations could easily be fulfilled by other parties, which are sometimes closer to the data subject, on the controller's behalf. However, a controller will remain in any case ultimately responsible for its obligations and liable for any breach to them.*").

2011 It could be argued, however, that the co-determination of purposes and means does also extend to certain subsequent processing activities, such as those related to increasing the visibility of the website operator by virtue getting "likes" and/or "insights", as the case may be. In his Opinion in *Wirtschaftsakademie*, Advocate General Bot suggests that third-party website operators might also be able to avail themselves of "insights" similar to those received by fan page administrators. Opinion of Advocate General Bot in *Wirtschaftsakademie*, C-210/16, ECLI:EU:C:2017:796, paragraph 70 ("*Social plugins enable website operators to use certain social networking services on their own websites in order to increase their website's visibility, for example by embedding in their websites Facebook's 'Like' button. Like fan page administrators, operators of websites with embedded social plugins can benefit from the 'Facebook Insights' service and obtain precise statistical information about the users of their website.*") See also *supra*, no. 915

"[R]ecognising that fan page administrators share responsibility for the phase of the data processing which consists in the collection by Facebook of personal data will help ensure greater protection of the rights of those who visit that type of page. Moreover, actively involving fan page administrators in the observance of the rules on the protection of personal data by designating them as controllers is likely to have the ripple effect of encouraging the social networking platform itself to comply with those rules."[2012]

988. Joint controller arrangements – One can debate the extent to which greater recognition of joint control (and responsibility) is likely to increase, in practice, the protection enjoyed by individuals. It seems apparent, however, that a far-reaching modulation of joint control and joint responsibility is likely to complicate the exercise of data subject rights (as data subjects would then carry the onus of determining which actor is responsible for which stage of the processing, which may not be readily apparent, especially if the joint controllers involved were to delineate the scope of their control and corresponding responsibilities in different ways). It is precisely this concern which led the Article 29 Working Party, and later the EU legislature, to stipulate that joint controllers should put in place an arrangement between them, in particular as regards the exercising of the rights of the data subject and their respective duties to provide the information.[2013] The question may therefore be asked whether advanced partitioning and modulation of the legal concept of control would not in practice undermine the intention of the EU legislature to ensure that data subjects are not hindered in the exercise of their rights as data subjects, simply because there are multiple actors who jointly determine the purposes and means of the processing.

989. Outlook – The approach advanced by Advocate General Bobek challenges the assumption that every controller must effectively be able to meet all of the obligations under data protection law. In doing so, it carries the risk of undermining legal certainty. On the other hand, it seems that the number of situations in which it is necessary to support greater flexibility in the application of controller obligations is increasing. In *Google Spain*, for example, the CJEU implicitly acknowledged that there may be practical limits to the ability of a search engine operator to meet all the obligations resulting from EU data protection law.[2014] Likewise, in *Wirtschaftsakademie*, the CJEU also emphasized that responsibilities among joint controllers may be uneven and need to be

2012 Opinion of Advocate General Bot in in *Wirtschaftsakademie*, C-210/16, ECLI:EU:C:2017:796, paragraph 74.

2013 See Opinion 1/2010, *l.c.*, p. 21 and Article 26(1) GDPR. See also *supra*, no. 140.

2014 See *infra*, no. 1115 et seq.

assessed in light of the circumstances.[2015] It may be hoped that, given the broader range of questions referred, the CJEU will provide additional guidance on how the responsibilities of joint controllers should be interpreted in this specific context. It appears inevitable, however, that a case-by-case will remain necessary, in order to tailor the responsibilities and liability of each actor in light of their actual (legal and operational) role towards the processing.

[2015] Cf. *supra*, no. 904. See also Opinion of Advocate General Bobek in Fashion ID, C-40/17, ECLI:EU:C:2018:1039, paragraph 94 ("*Although rather robust in its approach to the definition of joint control in Wirtschaftsakademie Schleswig-Holstein, the Court also hinted at the need to limit the liability of a (joint) controller. More specifically, the Court noted 'that the existence of joint responsibility does not necessarily imply equal responsibility of the various operators involved in the processing of personal data. ... those operators may be involved at different stages of that processing of personal data and to different degrees, so that the level of responsibility of each of them must be assessed with regard to all the relevant circumstances of the particular case'.*")

CHAPTER 4
CLOUD COMPUTING

1. INTRODUCTION

990. What is cloud computing? – Cloud computing has been defined in many ways. Often cited is the definition of the U.S. National Institute for Standards and Technology (NIST), which describes cloud computing as

> "a model for enabling convenient, on-demand network access to a shared pool of configurable computing resources (e.g., networks, servers, storage, applications, and services) that can be rapidly provisioned and released with minimal management effort or service provider interaction."[2016]

The European Network and Information Security Agency (ENISA) has defined cloud computing in slightly more neutral terms, as

> "an on-demand service model for IT provision, often based on virtualization and distributed computing technologies."[2017]

991. Key characteristics – Cloud computing involves the remote consumption of IT resources via a network (e.g. the Internet).[2018] Not every Internet application, however, is deemed worthy of the label of cloud computing.[2019] Most authors also consider "elasticity" and "measured service"

2016 L. Badger, T. Grance, R. Patt-Corner and J. Voas, *Cloud Computing Synopsis and Recommendations*, Special Publication 800-146, National Institute of Standards and Technology (NIST), May 2012, p. 2-1.

2017 D. Catteddu and G. Hogben (eds.), *Cloud computing – Benefits, risks and recommendations for information security*, ENISA, November 2009, p. 14.

2018 While most cloud computing services are delivered via the Internet, cloud computing services may also be offered across a local or private network. (Information Commissioner's Office (ICO), "Guidance on the use of cloud computing", v1.1, 2 October 2012, p. 4.

2019 D. Bigo a.o., "Fighting cyber crime and protecting privacy in the cloud", Study for the European Parliament, Committee on Civil Liberties, Justice and Home Affairs, PE 462.509, 2012, p. 14. It should be noted, however, that certain definitions of cloud computing are so broad that they could potentially include any type of service accessed via the internet. Early critics of the computing hype also eagerly pointed out that, after all is said and done, cloud computing is nothing more than "a computer attached to a network". See R. Leenes, "Who

as defining characteristics of cloud computing.[2020] Cloud providers typically allow customers to expand or decrease their resource consumption almost instantaneously, on a "pay as you go" basis.[2021] Finally, cloud services (especially infrastructure services) are often presented in a "virtualised" manner: providers dynamically assign and reassign resources from a pool which are shared as fungible resources with other customers.[2022]

992. Benefits – When using cloud computing, the customer externalises part of its IT infrastructure and associated maintenance.[2023] Instead of purchasing his own hardware and software, the customer relies on the services of the cloud provider. Because customers normally pay by usage, they can avoid large upfront costs which may otherwise be necessary to set up and operate sophisticated computing equipment.[2024] Moreover, customers can scale up or down rapidly as their needs increase or decrease.[2025] Put differently, cloud computing promises "computing power on demand", with limited or no expense beyond actual consumption.[2026] Providers, in turn, are able to leverage economies of scale, by

---

Controls the Cloud?", *Revista D'Internet, Dret I Política (IDP)* 2010, no. 11, p. 2 (quoting Larry Ellison, CEO of Oracle).

2020 See e.g. L. Badger, T. Grance, R. Patt-Corner and J. Voas, Cloud Computing Synopsis and Recommendations, o.c., p. 2-1; Information Commissioner's Office (ICO), Guidance on the use of cloud computing, o.c., p. 4 and S.Y. Esayas, "A walk in to the cloud and cloudy it remains: The challenges and prospects of 'processing' and 'transferring' personal data", Computer, Law & Security Review 2012, Vol. 28, p. 663.

2021 D. Catteddu and G. Hogben (eds.), *Cloud computing – Benefits, risks and recommendations for information security*, *o.c.*, p. 14.

2022 W.K. Hon, C. Millard and I. Walden, "Who is Responsible for 'Personal Data' in Cloud Computing? The Cloud of Unknowing, Part 2", Queen Mary University of London, School of Law Legal Studies Research Paper No. 77/2011, 2011, p. 6 and L. Badger, T. Grance, R. Patt-Corner and J. Voas, *Cloud Computing Synopsis and Recommendations*, *o.c.*, p. 2-1. A cloud provider typically manages a pool of hardware resources for resource efficiency: during periods of reduced consumer demand, the cloud provider may power off unused components. (L. Badger, T. Grance, R. Patt-Corner and J. Voas, *Cloud Computing Synopsis and Recommendations*, *o.c.*, p. 4-1).

2023 J.-M. Van Gyseghem, "Cloud computing et protection des données à caractère personnel: mise en ménage possible?", *Revue du Droit des Technologies de l'Information* 2011, no. 42, p. 36 and B. Docquir, "Le 'cloud computing' ou l'informatique dématérialisée: la protection des données au coeur de la relation contractuelle", *Revue de Droit Commercial* 2011, Vol. 10, p. 1001. Strictly speaking, cloud computing services can also be implemented on-site, on the customer's preferences (see L. Badger, T. Grance, R. Patt-Corner and J. Voas, *Cloud Computing Synopsis and Recommendations*, *o.c.*, p. 4-4). The remainder of this chapter will approach the topic of cloud computing with the assumption that the cloud is hosted and operated in an offsite location (i.e. outside the organisation of the customer).

2024 European Commission, "Unleashing the Potential of Cloud Computing in Europe", Communication of the Commission to the European Parliament, the Council, the European Economic and Social Committee and the Committee of the Regions, COM(2012) 529 final, 27 September 2012, p. 4.

2025 L. Badger, T. Grance, R. Patt-Corner and J. Voas, *Cloud Computing Synopsis and Recommendations*, *o.c.*, p. 2-1.

2026 European Commission, "Unleashing the Potential of Cloud Computing in Europe", *l.c.*, p. 2. It should be noted, however, that the term cloud computing is used in reference to a

pooling their resources and reaching large volumes of customers with relatively low overhead.[2027]

993. Risks – The risks of cloud computing mirror its benefits. By externalising portions of IT infrastructure, the customer invariably gives up a certain degree of control.[2028] Servers, data and applications are no longer kept within the organisation, but on the premises of one or more external providers.[2029] As a result, customers are by definition dependent on the cloud provider to implement appropriate measures to ensure the confidentiality and security of processing.[2030] Cloud customers may also lack sufficient information regarding the processing operations that take place.[2031] For example, cloud computing is typically associated with a sense of geographic indeterminacy:

> "the use of hardware is dynamically optimised across a network of computers, so that the exact location of data or processes, as well as the information which piece of hardware is actually serving a particular user at a given moment, does not in principle have to concern the user, even though it may have an important bearing on the applicable legal environment."[2032]

---

variety of systems and technologies and business models. Claims about the benefits of cloud computing are in fact only true for some kinds of cloud systems. For a more detailed discussion see L. Badger, T. Grance, R. Patt-Corner and J. Voas, *Cloud Computing Synopsis and Recommendations*, *o.c.*, p. 4-1 et seq.

2027 European Commission, "Unleashing the Potential of Cloud Computing in Europe", *l.c.*, p. 4. This statement mainly holds true in case of public clouds, which are offered to the public at large. See L. Badger, T. Grance, R. Patt-Corner and J. Voas, *Cloud Computing Synopsis and Recommendations*, *o.c.*, p. 8-4.

2028 Article 29 Data Protection Working Party, "Opinion 05/2012 on Cloud Computing", *l.c.*, p. 5–6.

2029 B. Docquir, "Le 'cloud computing' ou l'informatique dématérialisée: la protection des données au coeur de la relation contractuelle", *l.c.*, p. 1001. It should be noted that there also exist on-site cloud solutions, in which case the cloud infrastructure is hosted on the customer's premises. For more information see L. Badger, T. Grance, R. Patt-Corner and J. Voas, *Cloud Computing Synopsis and Recommendations*, *o.c.*, p. 4-4.

2030 Article 29 Data Protection Working Party, "Opinion 05/2012 on Cloud Computing", *l.c.*, p. 5.

2031 *Ibid*, p. 5.

2032 European Commission, "Unleashing the Potential of Cloud Computing in Europe", *l.c.*, p. 3. See also L. Badger, T. Grance, R. Patt-Corner and J. Voas, *Cloud Computing Synopsis and Recommendations*, *o.c.*, p. 2-1 and P. Balboni, "Data Protection and Data Security Issues Related to Cloud Computing in the EU", in N. Pohlmann, H. Reimer and W. Schneider (eds.), *ISSE 2010 Securing Electronic Business Processes*, Springer, 2010, p. 164–165. One might argue that the very metaphor of "cloud" computing, in fact, encourages a vision of something elusive, beyond control or regulation. See also T. McMullan, "How we talk about the cloud shapes the way we perceive internet privacy", *The Guardian* (online edition), 7 October 2015, (*"As a name, the cloud is at once a fluffy, approachable means to digest a global network of servers. It is also a vague, formless entity that grows and shrinks above our heads. In terms of privacy, it represents an important change in how we think about our data; stored in the arms of an invisible force, at once everywhere and nowhere."*).

From a business perspective, migrating to the cloud increases the customer's dependency on the availability and continuity of external services.[2033] Moreover, if the cloud provider uses proprietary technology, it may prove difficult for customers to shift data and documents between different cloud-based systems, which could lead to vendor lock-in.[2034]

994. Old wine, new business model? – Cloud computing is simply one of the latest evolutionary steps in the delivery of IT.[2035] In a sense, there is really "nothing new" about cloud computing. As noted by Marchini:

> "the idea of obtaining use of a software application remotely is as old as computing; early software use involved access to mainframes with distributed dumb terminals or to data processing power through bureau services."[2036]

The main distinction, Marchini continues, is scale: it has simply become more prevalent.[2037] Once again, a wide range of processing operations is taking place outside the walls of the organisation itself, in principle leaving the organisation with more time to focus on its own core activities.[2038] Another major difference concerns the technical foundation and organisation of cloud computing services, which cause data and data processing to be distributed dynamically among data centres located around to world.[2039]

995. Types of cloud services – Cloud services are typically divided into three categories, depending on which IT resource forms the main object of the service (software, platforms, or infrastructure)[2040]:

2033 P. Balboni, "Data Protection and Data Security Issues Related to Cloud Computing in the EU", *l.c.*, p. 165–166.

2034 Article 29 Data Protection Working Party, "Opinion 05/2012 on Cloud Computing", *l.c.*, p. 5. See also D. Svantesson and R. Clarke, "Privacy and consumer risks in cloud computing", *Computer Law & Security Review* 2010, Vol. 26, p. 391 et seq.

2035 A. Joint and E. Baker, "Knowing the past to understand the present – issues in the contracting for cloud based services", *Computer Law & Security Review* 2011, Vol. 27, p. 408.

2036 R. Marchini, *Cloud computing: A Practical Introduction to the Legal Issues, BSI Standards Institution*, London, 2010, p. 2.

2037 *Id.*

2038 P. Schwartz, "Information Privacy in the Cloud", *University of Pennsylvania Law Review* 2013, Vol. 161, p. 1649. See also B. Docquir, "Le 'cloud computing' ou l'informatique dématérialisée: la protection des données au coeur de la relation contractuelle", *l.c.*, p. 1003.

2039 International Working Group on Data Protection in Telecommunications, Working Paper on Cloud Computing – Privacy and data protection issues – "Sopot Memorandum", adopted 23–24 April 2012, p. 6.

2040 L. Badger, T. Grance, R. Patt-Corner and J. Voas, *Cloud Computing Synopsis and Recommendations*, *o.c.*, p. 2-1/2. See also Leenes R. Leenes, "Who Controls the Cloud?", *l.c.*, p. 3; D. Catteddu and G. Hogben (eds.), *Cloud computing – Benefits, risks and recommendations for information security*, *o.c.*, p. 15; D. Bigo a.o., "Fighting cyber crime and protecting privacy in the cloud", *l.c.*, p. 13; B. Docquir, "Le 'cloud computing' ou l'informatique dématérialisée: la protection des données au coeur de la relation contractuelle", *l.c.*, p. 1001; and Article 29

- *Software as a Service (SaaS)*: customers are able to remotely use the software applications offered by the provider, running on a cloud infrastructure;
- *Platform as a Service (PaaS)*: customers are able to deploy onto a cloud infrastructure (which acts as a "platform") consumer-created or -acquired applications (as long as they use the programming languages and tools supported by the provider);
- *Infrastructure as a Service (IaaS)*: customers are able to use processing, storage, networks, and other fundamental computing resources offered by the provider, whereby the consumer is free to deploy and run arbitrary software (which can include both operating systems and applications).

996. A SPECTRUM OF CONTROL – The three service models described above can be seen as a "spectrum" or "continuum", which ranges from low-level functionality (IaaS) to high-level functionality (SaaS), with PaaS in the middle.[2041] One could argue that the higher the functionality, the greater the control exercised by the cloud provider.[2042] In case of IaaS, the customer is essentially renting storage and processing capabilities, retaining full freedom to deploy whichever applications he sees fit. In case of SaaS, the functionality offered by the technology is pre-defined by the provider. All the customer is expected to do is to access and consume the final product, no assembly required.

997. LAYERS OF CLOUDS – It should be noted that there may be layers of cloud providers involved in providing a service, sometimes without the customer's knowledge.[2043] For example, a SaaS provider might rely on an external IaaS and/or PaaS provider when offering its services to customers.[2044] In addition, both cloud providers and cloud customers can also combine cloud services from

---

Data Protection Working Party, "Opinion 05/2012 on Cloud Computing", *l.c.*, p. 26. Another frequent classification is based on the *target user* of the service offered, which distinguishes between public, private, community or hybrid clouds. See e.g. S.Y. Esayas, "A walk in to the cloud and cloudy it remains: The challenges and prospects of 'processing' and 'transferring' personal data", *l.c.*, p. 663.

2041 W.K. Hon, C. Millard and I. Walden, "Who is Responsible for 'Personal Data' in Cloud Computing? The Cloud of Unknowing, Part 2", *l.c.*, p. 6. See also S.Y. Esayas, "A walk in to the cloud and cloudy it remains: The challenges and prospects of 'processing' and 'transferring' personal data", *l.c.*, p. 663.

2042 S.Y. Esayas, "A walk in to the cloud and cloudy it remains: The challenges and prospects of 'processing' and 'transferring' personal data", *l.c.*, p. 663.

2043 W.K. Hon, C. Millard and I. Walden, "Who is Responsible for 'Personal Data' in Cloud Computing? The Cloud of Unknowing, Part 2", *l.c.*, p. 6.

2044 *Id.* See also B. Docquir, "Le 'cloud computing' ou l'informatique dématérialisée: la protection des données au coeur de la relation contractuelle", *l.c.*, p. 1002. ("*caractéristique marquante du cloud computing est la multiplicité et, subséquemment, l'opacité relative des acteurs auxquelles l'utilisateur peut se trouver confronté: ainsi, un service de stockage de documents ou de photos qui développe sa propre application et la commercialise en mode software as a service peut utiliser l'infrastructure d'un autre fournisseur (infrastructure as a service ou platform as a service*").

different cloud providers.[2045] For example, the customer of a PaaS provider might consume the services of multiple SaaS providers, whereas the PaaS provider itself might be a customer of multiple IaaS providers.

998. Outline – The objective of this chapter is to analyse how EU data protection law relates to the context of cloud computing. To this end, it will begin by describing the various actors involved in cloud computing and the interactions between them. Next, it will analyse the legal status ("role") of each actor, as interpreted by regulators and scholars. After that, it will describe the main responsibilities assigned to each actor, as interpreted in particular by the Article 29 Working Party and national regulatory authorities. Once this analysis has been completed, this chapter will critically evaluate the relationship between the current framing of roles and responsibilities in the context of cloud computing.

999. Scope – For purposes of conceptual clarity, the remainder of this chapter limits itself to the discussion of public, offsite cloud services which involve the processing of personal data.[2046]

2. ACTORS

1000. Overview – The following types of entities[2047] may be considered as the main entities involved in the operation of cloud computing services:

(1) Cloud customer, including end-users.
(2) Cloud providers, including
    (a) Application providers;
    (b) Platform providers; and
    (c) Infrastructure providers.[2048]

1001. Visual representation – The aforementioned entities interact with each other in a variety of ways. The following figure provides a – highly simplified

2045 W.K. Hon, C. Millard and I. Walden, "Who is Responsible for 'Personal Data' in Cloud Computing? The Cloud of Unknowing, Part 2", *l.c.*, p. 6,

2046 In other words onsite, private or community cloud services are outside the scope of the present analysis.

2047 The term "entity" (instead of "actor") is used to signal that each identified "actor" could in principle be either a separate legal entity or a purely technical component operated.

2048 The inventory of actors provided here was composed on the basis of a literature study of academic publications and regulatory guidance concerning privacy and cloud computing. A common denominator among the selected entities is that they each process personal data resulting in the context of cloud computing services.

– representation of how these entities might interact in the provisioning of cloud computing services. It is intended to be conceptual rather than factual.

Figure 5. Main entities involved in cloud computing

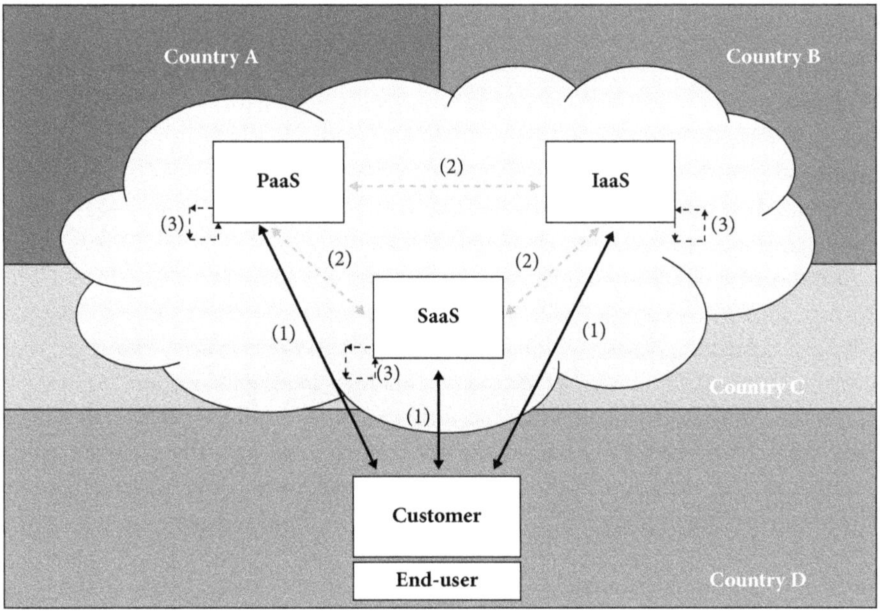

1002. Legend – The arrows in Figure 5 indicate that an exchange of personal data is taking place. Exchanges of personal data in the context of cloud computing are in principle bi-directional, as data is in principle disclosed with a view of further processing by the entity who disclosed it. Solid black arrows were used to depict data exchanges which may be actively initiated by the customer, depending on the service model (SaaS, PaaS or IaaS). Dashed grey arrows signify data exchanges which might be less obvious to cloud customers, depending on the service model and information provided by the cloud provider. The coloured segments were added to signal that that each entity might be located in a different jurisdiction. Over the following sections, a brief description is provided of each of the actors and interactions displayed in Figure 5.

1003. Combinations possible – The reader should note that the categories of actors identified in Figure 5 are not mutually exclusive. A given actor may combine multiple roles depending on the circumstances (e.g. a SaaS provider might also operate PaaS and/or IaaS services).

2.1. CLOUD CUSTOMER AND END-USER

1004. MAIN CHARACTERISTICS – The cloud customer is the subscriber of a cloud computing service. It may be either a natural or legal person, or a group of natural and/or legal persons. Typical cloud customers include companies and self-employed businessmen who use cloud services in the exercise of their commercial activities (e.g. for purposes of customer relations management), as well as private individuals who use cloud services in a purely private capacity (e.g. to back-up personal photos).[2049] The end-user is the natural person who actually uses the cloud computing service in a specific context.[2050] The end-user may coincide with the cloud customer, but may also be a separate entity (e.g. an employee within the organisation of the cloud customer).[2051] Finally, it is worth noting that cloud customers may combine cloud services from different cloud providers.[2052]

1005. DATA DISCLOSURE – Cloud customers and end-users access cloud services under a client-server model, which means that they send messages over a network to server computers, which then perform work in response to the messages received.[2053] The data disclosed to the service provider typically includes "first-party data" (e.g. data relating to the cloud customer or his employees) as well as "third-party data" (e.g. data relating to the clients of the cloud customer).

1006. DATA FLOWS – The interaction between cloud customers and cloud providers is depicted in figure 5 by way of arrows (1). The customer may be in direct communication with all three types of cloud providers, or only with a subset of them, depending on service model. In the latter case, the contracted cloud provider may enlist one or more other cloud providers to obtain the auxiliary services necessary to provide the functionality requested by the customer (arrows (2)).

2.2. CLOUD PROVIDER

A. *Application provider (SaaS)*

1007. MAIN CHARACTERISTICS – Cloud application providers (SaaS) provide their customers with (1) the ability to use specific software applications on

---

2049 See also J.-M. Van Gyseghem, "Cloud computing et protection des données à caractère personnel: mise en ménage possible?", *l.c.*, p. 36.

2050 R. Leenes, "Who Controls the Cloud?", *l.c.*, p. 3.

2051 *Id.*

2052 W. Kuan Hon, C. Millard and I. Walden, "Who is Responsible for 'Personal Data' in Cloud Computing? The Cloud of Unknowing, Part 2", *l.c.*, p. 6.

2053 L. Badger, T. Grance, R. Patt-Corner and J. Voas, *Cloud Computing Synopsis and Recommendations*, *o.c.*, p. 4-1.

demand and (2) application data management services (e.g. backup and data sharing between consumers).[2054] The software applications offered by SaaS providers are often meant to replace conventional applications to be installed by users on their local systems.[2055] Commonly cited examples of SaaS services include: Microsoft's Office 365 (which includes office applications such as Word, Excel, etc.), Salesforce.com (which provides customer relations management applications), Google Docs (a collaborative word processing application), and Dropbox (a storage and sharing application).[2056]

1008. DATA COLLECTION – Cloud application providers may collect various types of personal data. For example, the following types might be collected:

1. *Contact information* (e.g. such as name, company name, address, phone number, and email address);
2. *Billing information* (e.g. billing name and address, credit card number, and the number of employees within the organisation that will be using the services);
3. *Optional information* (e.g. company annual revenues, number of employees, or industry);
4. *Website navigational information* (e.g. Cookies, Web Beacons and IP Addresses);
5. *Submitted data* (e.g. data submitted to public forums, as part of a friend referral or as part of a testimonial);
6. *(Third-party) Customer data*: data submitted by customers for storage and processing purposes (e.g. contact information of current and recurring customers, accounts, emails, calendars, and tasks); and
7. *Data collected through mobile applications* (e.g. call records, pictures, geographic location, contact information).[2057]

1009. DATA USAGE – Cloud application providers use the data collected from their customers and end-users in a variety of ways. Here too, a distinction should be made between "first-party data" and "third-party data". For example, a cloud provider might use data about its customers and end-users ("first-party data") to communicate with them, enforce access privileges, market new products and

---

2054 L. Badger, T. Grance, R. Patt-Corner and J. Voas, *Cloud Computing Synopsis and Recommendations*, *o.c.*, p. 5-1.

2055 Article 29 Data Protection Working Party, "Opinion 05/2012 on Cloud Computing", *l.c.*, p. 26.

2056 See R. Leenes, "Who Controls the Cloud?", *l.c.*, p. 3, P. Schwartz, "Information Privacy in the Cloud", *l.c.*, p. 1633. Several authors also consider Facebook as an example of a SaaS application (see e.g. R. Leenes, "Who Controls the Cloud?", *l.c.*, p. 3). Contra: D. Bigo a.o., "Fighting cyber crime and protecting privacy in the cloud", *l.c.*, p. 15.

2057 This overview of categories of data was based on a previous version of the Salesforce.com privacy notice.

improve its sites and services. Data submitted by cloud customers concerning their clients ("third-party data") may mainly be processed for the purposes of providing the services requested by customers. Services offered by Salesforce.com, for example, include customer relations management, customer service, marketing and analytics services.[2058] It is not excluded, however, that cloud application providers also process data submitted by customers for purposes beyond the services requested.

1010. Data flows – Arrow (1) depicts the flow of data between cloud application providers and their customers. As indicated earlier, there may be layers of cloud providers involved in providing a service. Arrow (2) signals the potential interaction between cloud application providers and cloud platform and/or cloud infrastructure providers. Arrow (3) intends to illustrate that cloud customers may combine the services of multiple cloud application providers.

B. *Platform provider (PaaS)*

1011. Main characteristics – Cloud platform providers (PaaS) provide their customers with tools and execution resources to develop, test, deploy and administer applications.[2059] Typical features include software development tools (e.g. programming languages, run-time environments), configuration management, and deployment platforms.[2060] PaaS services are usually addressed to market players that use them to develop and host applications either to meet in-house requirements or to deploy them as services to third parties.[2061] Commonly cited examples are Microsoft's "Azure", and Google's "App engine".[2062]

1012. Data collection – Cloud platform providers may collect various types of personal data. Similar to SaaS providers, the following types might be collected:

1. *Customer data*: all data that are provided to the cloud provider through use of its online service but excluding Administrator Data, Payment Data, or Support Data (e.g. text, sound, image or video files);

2058 See www.salesforce.com.

2059 L. Badger, T. Grance, R. Patt-Corner and J. Voas, *Cloud Computing Synopsis and Recommendations*, *o.c.*, p. 6-1.

2060 D. Catteddu and G. Hogben (eds.), *Cloud computing – Benefits, risks and recommendations for information security*, *o.c.*, p. 15 and L. Badger, T. Grance, R. Patt-Corner and J. Voas, *Cloud Computing Synopsis and Recommendations*, *o.c.*, p. 6-1.

2061 Article 29 Data Protection Working Party, "Opinion 05/2012 on Cloud Computing", *l.c.*, p. 26

2062 D. Catteddu and G. Hogben (eds.), *Cloud computing – Benefits, risks and recommendations for information security*, ENISA, November 2009, p. 15 and P. Schwartz, "Information Privacy in the Cloud", *l.c.*, p. 1633.

2. *Administrator data*: information provided during sign-up, purchase, or administration of services (e.g. name, address, phone number, and email address, as well as aggregated usage information and account controls);
3. *Access control data*: data that is used to manage access to other types of data or functions within the cloud (e.g. passwords, security certificates, and other authentication-related data);
4. *Metadata*: data concerning configuration and technical settings (e.g. disk configuration settings for a virtual machine);
5. *Payment data* (e.g. credit card number, name and billing address, security code associated with the payment instrument, organisational tax ID);
6. *Support data* (e.g. information submitted in a support request form, chat sessions, information about hardware or software used, error-tracking files);
7. *Cookies & similar technologies* (e.g. web beacons, analytics cookies); and
8. *Data collected through local software* (e.g. data about the use or performance of software agents or device management applications installed on a device).[2063]

1013. Data use – Cloud platform providers use the data collected from their customers and end-users in a variety of ways. Once again, a distinction should be made between "first-party data" and "third-party data". For example, a cloud provider might use data about its customers and end-users ("first-party data") to communicate with its customers, to complete transactions and to ensure quality of service. Data submitted by cloud customers concerning their clients ("third-party data") may mainly be processed for the purposes of providing the services as requested by customers. Azure platform services, for example, include app development and testing, API management and application insights.[2064] Finally, it should be noted that while Azure was conceived of as a cloud platform service (PaaS), it also enables customers to host external, already existing applications (IaaS) and to run software written by Microsoft itself (SaaS) (e.g. analytics).[2065]

1014. Data flows – Arrow (1) depicts the flow of data between cloud platform providers and their customers. Arrow (2) signals the potential interaction between cloud platform providers and cloud application and/or cloud infrastructure providers. Arrow (3) intends to illustrate that cloud customers may combine the services of multiple cloud platform providers.

2063 This overview of categories of data is based on a previous version of Microsoft's Azure service.

2064 See Microsoft, "Microsoft Azure", accessible at https://azure.microsoft.com/en-us (last accessed 3 May 2016).

2065 See A. Chauhan, V. Fontama, M. Har a.o., "Introducing Microsoft Azure HDInsight Technical Overview", Microsoft Press, 2014, p. 24.

C. *Infrastructure provider (IaaS)*

1015. Main characteristics – Cloud infrastructure providers (IaaS) provide their customers with access to virtual computers, storage, infrastructure components and configuration services.[2066] Customers typically rely on IaaS to replace corporate IT systems at the company's premises and/or use the leased infrastructure alongside the corporate systems.[2067] Hardware resources are typically allocated to customers in the form of "virtual machines" (or "instances") which they can consume on demand ("dynamic resource renting").[2068] Customers are in principle able to install the operating system(s) and applications of their choosing.[2069] Commonly cited examples of IaaS include Amazon's Elastic Compute Cloud (EC2) and Simple Storage Service (S3) and Rackspace Cloud.[2070]

1016. Data collection – Cloud infrastructure providers may collect various types of personal data. A broad distinction can once again be made between the two types of data: account information and customer content. Account information concerns information that customers provide to the cloud provider in connection with the creation or administration of their account (i.e. "first-party data"). Customer content is data stored by end-users on the cloud provider's systems, which may (but does not necessarily) include personal data relating to third parties (i.e. "third-party data").[2071]

1017. Data use – The Amazon AWS privacy policy, for example, outlines the several forms of data use, including customer communication (e.g. promotional offers), analytics, advertising (including advertising on third-party websites),

---

2066 L. Badger, T. Grance, R. Patt-Corner and J. Voas, *Cloud Computing Synopsis and Recommendations*, *o.c.*, p. 7-1.

2067 Article 29 Data Protection Working Party, "Opinion 05/2012 on Cloud Computing", *l.c.*, p. 26

2068 L. Badger, T. Grance, R. Patt-Corner and J. Voas, *Cloud Computing Synopsis and Recommendations*, *o.c.*, p. 7-1/3. For a description of "virtualisation" see L. Badger, T. Grance, R. Patt-Corner and J. Voas, *Cloud Computing Synopsis and Recommendations*, *o.c.*, p. 7–2; W. Kuan Hon, C. Millard and I. Walden, "Who is Responsible for 'Personal Data' in Cloud Computing? The Cloud of Unknowing, Part 2", *l.c.*, p. 17 and S. Marston a.o., "Cloud computing – The business perspective", *Decision Support Systems* 2011, Vol. 51, p. 178.

2069 L. Badger, T. Grance, R. Patt-Corner and J. Voas, *Cloud Computing Synopsis and Recommendations*, *o.c.*, p. 7–2.

2070 D. Catteddu and G. Hogben (eds.), *Cloud computing – Benefits, risks and recommendations for information security*, ENISA, November 2009, p. 15. See also S. Marston a.o., "Cloud computing – The business perspective", *Decision Support Systems* 2011, Vol. 51, p. 178.

2071 Amazon, for example, defines "customer content" as "*customer content as software (including machine images), data, text, audio, video or images that a customer or any end user transfers to us for processing, storage or hosting by AWS services in connection with that customer's account and any computational results that a customer or any end user derives from the foregoing through their use of AWS services.*" http://aws.amazon.com/compliance/data-privacy-faq/ (last accessed 5 January 2019).

personalisation and recommendation, service improvement, fraud and abuse prevention and managing credit risks. The Amazon AWS privacy policy in principle only applies to customer's account information and not to content stored by customers on Amazon systems.[2072] Amazon states it does not access or use customer content *"except as necessary to maintain or provide the Service Offerings, or as necessary to comply with the law or a binding order of a governmental body"*.[2073]

1018. Data flows – Arrow (1) depicts the flow of data between cloud infrastructure providers and their customers. Arrow (2) signals the potential interaction between cloud infrastructure providers and cloud platform providers and/or cloud software providers. Arrow (3) intends to illustrate that cloud customers may combine the services of multiple cloud infrastructure providers.

3. ROLES

3.1. CLOUD CUSTOMERS AND END-USER

1019. High-level analysis – Cloud customers are generally viewed as "controllers" in relation to the processing of (third-party) personal data they entrust to cloud providers.[2074] Cloud customers determine both the "purposes" and "means" of the processing, in that they decide

(1) for which purposes to use cloud services (e.g. in furtherance of their commercial or other objectives);
(2) which cloud services to use and, by extension, how personal data shall be processed; and
(3) which cloud provider to enlist.

2072 Amazon Web Services, "AWS Privacy", accessible at https://aws.amazon.com/privacy (last accessed 5 January 2019).

2073 Amazon Web Services, "AWS customer agreement", accessible at https://aws.amazon.com/agreement/ (last accessed 5 January 2019).

2074 See e.g. J.G.L. van der Wees, "De verantwoordelijke en de bewerker in de cloud", *Computerrecht* 2011, Afl. 3, p. 110; B. Docquir, "Le 'cloud computing' ou l'informatique dématérialisée: la protection des données au coeur de la relation contractuelle", *l.c.*, p. 1009; A. Mantelero, "Cloud computing, trans-border data flows and the European Directive 95/46/EC: applicable law and task distribution", *European Journal for Law and Technology* 2012, Vol. 3, No. 2, available at http://ejlt.org/article/view/96/253; Article 29 Data Protection Working Party, "Opinion 05/2012 on Cloud Computing", *l.c.*, p. 8; Information Commissioner's Office (ICO), "Guidance on the use of cloud computing", *l.c.*, p. 7; Commission Nationale de l'Informatique et Libertés (CNIL), "Recommendations for companies planning to use Cloud computing services", 25 June 2012, p. 5.

To the extent that the end-user and cloud customer coincide, he or she will be considered the controller of the processing. Employees who process personal data on behalf of the cloud customer are "persons acting under the authority of the controller" within the meaning of Article 29 GDPR.[2075]

It is also possible that a cloud customer contracts a cloud service in order to process personal data on behalf of a third party (who may actually be the controller or simply another entity in the supply chain).[2076] In such cases, it is possible that the cloud customer acts only as a processor.[2077]

1020. Scope of control – In practice, the degree of control exercised by the cloud customer regarding the means of the processing may be limited. More often than not, cloud services are offered under standard terms, on a "take it or leave it basis".[2078] Depending on the nature of the cloud service (SaaS, PaaS or IaaS), the cloud customer will be able to exercise greater or lesser control over the manner in which the processing is operated[2079]:

- *SaaS*

In case of SaaS, the cloud customer essentially only has control over the application-specific resources which the SaaS application makes available.[2080] The processing capabilities of the cloud customer are dependent on the features and services supported by the software offered by the cloud provider. For example, if the cloud provider offers an email application, the customer will typically have the ability to create, edit or send messages.[2081] Depending on the service, the customer may also enjoy limited administrative control over the application. For example, in the case of the email application, the cloud customer may have the ability to create new accounts for end-users and/or review the activities of end-users.[2082] It should be noted, however, that the processing capabilities (and thus also the scope of control of cloud customers) may vary widely across SaaS applications (compare e.g. Salesforce.com with Dropbox services).

2075 Cf. *supra*, nos. 217 et seq.

2076 Amazon Web Services, "Whitepaper on EU Data Protection", October 2015, p. 11, available at http://d0.awsstatic.com/whitepapers/compliance/AWS_EU_Data_Protection_Whitepaper.pdf (last accessed 5 January 2019).

2077 See also *infra*, no. 1052 and *supra*, no. 252 et seq. for a discussion of the requirements in case of sub-processing.

2078 See also L. Badger, T. Grance, R. Patt-Corner and J. Voas, *Cloud Computing Synopsis and Recommendations*, *o.c.*, p. 3-1.

2079 See also *infra*, nos. 1027 et seq.

2080 L. Badger, T. Grance, R. Patt-Corner and J. Voas, *Cloud Computing Synopsis and Recommendations*, *o.c.*, p. 5-3.

2081 *Id.*

2082 *Id.*

- *PaaS*

In case of PaaS, the cloud customer in principle has complete control over which applications shall be implemented and deployed (as long as he uses the programming languages and tools supported by the provider).[2083] The customer is granted access to programming and utility interfaces, which provide him with an execution environment to run his applications and access to the necessary computing resources (e.g. memory, persistent storage, data stores, data bases and network connections).[2084] The cloud customer in principle enjoys complete administrative control over the applications deployed, which may be either consumer-created or acquired. It should be noted, however, that the provider of the PaaS service may offer its customers the ability to run applications written by the provider (in which case this portion of the service corresponds to a SaaS model) or to host external, already existing applications (in which case this portion of the service corresponds to an IaaS model).[2085]

- *IaaS*

In case of IaaS, the cloud customer enjoys complete control over the computing resources offered by the provider, which are typically presented in the form of "virtual machines" (VMs). The customer has full control over the operation of the guest operating system in each VM and is free to deploy and run arbitrary software.[2086] Under the IaaS service model, the customers typically carries the burden of operating, updating and configuring the rented computer resources for security and reliability.[2087] It should be noted, however, that the provider of an IaaS service may also offer its customers applications written by the provider (in which case this portion of the service corresponds to a SaaS model) or to host external, already existing applications (in which case this portion of the service corresponds to an IaaS model).

The amount of control which cloud customers enjoy in determining the "means" of the processing thus varies significantly across service models. In case of SaaS, the ability for the customer to influence the means of the processing shall be significantly reduced. In case of IaaS, the customer enjoys practically the same level of privileges as if the owned computing resources himself. Even in case of SaaS, however, the cloud customer still determines the means of the

2083 *Ibid*, p. 6-3.
2084 *Id.*
2085 See also *supra*, no. 1013.
2086 L. Badger, T. Grance, R. Patt-Corner and J. Voas, *Cloud Computing Synopsis and Recommendations*, *o.c.*, p. 7–2.
2087 *Id.* In case of PaaS and Saas, these aspects are typically taken care of by the cloud provider (*Id.*).

processing by choosing to process personal data through a particular cloud service.

1021. Personal use exemption – Cloud computing services are consumed not only by businesses and governments, but also be individuals acting in the course of personal or household activity. The latter shall in principle be exempted from compliance in accordance with Article 2(2)c of the GDPR, unless the data is made available to an indefinite number of people.[2088]

3.2. CLOUD PROVIDER

1022. Preliminary distinction – Section 2 illustrated that cloud providers may provide a wide variety of services, each of which may involve the processing of personal data. While there is agreement among scholars and regulators as to the legal status of the cloud customer, the legal status of the cloud provider appears to be less clear-cut. At the outset, a distinction must be made between data about the customers themselves ("first party-data") and data submitted by customers to the cloud provider for further processing ("third-party data").[2089]

1023. First-party data – Every cloud provider, regardless of service model, acts as a controller when processing personal data about its customers for purposes of account creation, administration and billing (first party-data). The same applies also in relation to data processing undertaken by the cloud provider to improve its services (e.g. use of site analytics to monitor performance) or to market new products. For those sets of processing operations, the cloud provider clearly determines the purposes and means of the processing.

1024. Third-party data – As far as the processing of third-party data is concerned (i.e. data entrusted to the cloud provider for further processing), many scholars and regulators seem inclined to assign the cloud provider the role of processor.[2090] Others point out that there may be situations in which the cloud

2088 Cf. *supra*, nos. 967 et seq.

2089 W. Kuan Hon, C. Millard and I. Walden, "Who is Responsible for 'Personal Data' in Cloud Computing? The Cloud of Unknowing, Part 2", *l.c.*, p. 11–12.

2090 A. Mantelero, "Cloud computing, trans-border data flows and the European Directive 95/46/EC: applicable law and task distribution", *l.c.*; D. Catteddu and G. Hogben (eds.), *Cloud computing – Benefits, risks and recommendations for information security*, *o.c.*, p. 46; L. Determann, "Data Privacy in the Cloud–Myths and Facts", Institute for IT Law, 10 April 2012, online publication at http://www.iitr.us/publications/40-data-privacy-in-the-cloud-a-dozen-myths-and-facts.html; Article 29 Data Protection Working Party, "Opinion 05/2012 on Cloud Computing", *l.c.*, p. 7–8 (but there may be exceptions: Article 29 Data

provider should be considered as a (joint) controller.[2091] Finally, certain scholars defend the viewpoint that there may be situations in which the cloud provider should be viewed as neither a controller nor processor.[2092] But almost all agree that the legal status of the cloud provider must be assessed in light of the actual services provided, the interactions between the parties and the set of data or operations at issue.[2093]

1025. Heterogenous concept – The divergent viewpoints regarding the legal status of the cloud provider may be explained, at least in part, because of heterogeneous nature of the concept of "cloud computing". The concept of cloud computing encompasses many different service models (SaaS, PaaS and IaaS), which each have different properties and foresee varying degrees of control for customers and providers respectively. Second, the concept is sometimes understood so broadly that it becomes difficult to conceive of any internet application which would not be considered a cloud service.[2094] Finally, there is a great variety among cloud computing services, even within a particular service model (compare e.g. Salesforce.com with Dropbox services).

1026. Outline – The main objective of this section is to provide an inventory of the arguments advanced by scholars and regulators regarding specific cloud service models in support of the view that the provider should be considered as either a controller, joint controller or processor. Given the heterogeneous nature of cloud services the analysis of the roles of cloud providers in the sections that follow should be reviewed with great caution. This section does not seek to provide a definitive qualification of the role of the providers of different types of

---

Protection Working Party, "Opinion 05/2012 on Cloud Computing", *l.c.*, p. 20); Information Commissioner's Office (ICO), *Guidance on the use of cloud computing*, *o.c.*, p. 7–10.

2091 See e.g. R. Leenes, "Who Controls the Cloud?", *l.c.*, p. 8; J.G.L. van der Wees, "De verantwoordelijke en de bewerker in de cloud", *l.c.*, p. 110–111; De Hert, P., Papakonstantinou, V. and Kamara, I., "The new cloud computing ISO/IEC 27018 standard through the lens of the EU legislation on data protection", *l.c.*, p. 17–18; F. Gilbert, "Cloud service providers as joint-data controllers", *Journal of Internet law* 2011, p. 3–12; European Data Protection Supervisor (EDPS), "Opinion of the European Data Protection Supervisor on the Commission's Communication on 'Unleashing the potential of Cloud Computing in Europe'", 16 November 2012, paragraphs 46–48 and Commission Nationale de l'Informatique et Libertés (CNIL), *Recommendations for companies planning to use Cloud computing services*, *o.c.*, p. 6.

2092 W. Kuan Hon, C. Millard and I. Walden, "Who is Responsible for 'Personal Data' in Cloud Computing? The Cloud of Unknowing, Part 2", *l.c.*, p. 14 et seq.

2093 See e.g. B. Docquir, "Le 'cloud computing' ou l'informatique dématérialisée: la protection des données au coeur de la relation contractuelle", *l.c.*, p. 1002; J.G.L. van der Wees, "De verantwoordelijke en de bewerker in de cloud", *l.c.*, p. 110–111; P. Balboni, "Data Protection and Data Security Issues Related to Cloud Computing in the EU", *l.c.*, p. 168 and P. De Hert, V. Papakonstantinou and I. Kamara, "The new cloud computing ISO/IEC 27018 standard through the lens of the EU legislation on data protection", *l.c.*, p. 18.

2094 For example, several authors consider OSNs as an example of cloud computing. See e.g. R. Leenes, "Who Controls the Cloud?", *l.c.*, p. 6.

cloud services. A case-by-case analysis remains indispensable.[2095] For purposes of conceptual clarity, the analysis shall be limited the processing of third-party data by cloud providers.

A. *Application providers (SaaS)*

1027. Relevant characteristics – In case of SaaS, the cloud provider offers its customers the ability to consume software applications remotely. A typical SaaS provider manages the underlying cloud infrastructure (including network, servers, operating systems, storage), decides which applications to offer, and may also decide about individual application capabilities.[2096] The SaaS provider configures and manages the operation of the application so that it provides expected service levels to consumers.[2097] At a technical level, the SaaS provider retains ultimate authority over the application.[2098] While the customer may enjoy a certain level of administrative control, such control exists only at the discretion of the provider.[2099]

1028. Legal status – The legal status of SaaS providers appears to be the most ambiguous of all cloud service models. There are essentially three different ways in which this issue has been approached by scholars and regulators, each of which will be elaborated of the following paragraphs.

1029. Provider as processor – A first group of scholars and regulators seem predisposed to consider all cloud providers as processors.[2100] While acknowledging that there may be exceptions, these authors emphasize that (a) the initiative to use the cloud service lies with the cloud customer and (b) the customer has ability to choose which cloud service best suits its needs.[2101]

2095 Moreover, the reader should note that several of the sources cited here predate the GDPR (and therefore also Article 28(3)). One could argue that Article 28(3) provides additional "safeguards for the controller-processor relationship", meaning that in light of the additional elements which must now be included in the "contract or other legal act", the qualification of the actors might become more straightforward in practice. At the same time, it should be noted that the addition of contractual provisions alone is generally insufficient to determine an entity's legal status under data protection law, if it does not correspond with the ability to exercise control over the processing.

2096 L. Badger, T. Grance, R. Patt-Corner and J. Voas, *Cloud Computing Synopsis and Recommendations*, *o.c.*, p. 2-1/2.

2097 L. Badger, T. Grance, R. Patt-Corner and J. Voas, *Cloud Computing Synopsis and Recommendations*, *o.c.*, p. 5-3.

2098 *Id.*

2099 *Id.*

2100 Cf. *supra*, footnote 2091. It should be noted, however, that these scholars and regulators do not necessarily distinguish among cloud service models (SaaS, PaaS or IaaS) when assessing the legal status of cloud providers.

2101 Information Commissioner's Office (ICO), *Guidance on the use of cloud computing*, *o.c.*, p. 7–9; Article 29 Data Protection Working Party, "Opinion 05/2012 on Cloud Computing", *l.c.*,

Certain authors also point out that the cloud customer is usually the entity who collected information from data subjects and therefore already subject to data protection law.[2102] Alessandro Mantelero additionally argues that the decision-making power of cloud providers is not sufficient to consider them autonomous data controllers.[2103] Finally, Lothar Determann argues that cloud providers tend to offer platforms and software "*without any interest, knowledge, or influence regarding data types and processing purposes*".[2104]

1030. Provider as separate controller – A second group of commentators view SaaS providers as controllers in their own right, but only with respect to the additional uses determined by the cloud provider.[2105] For example, the SaaS provider which authorizes itself to use data entrusted by customers for purposes of marketing or delivery of value-added services, should be considered as controllers in respect of these processing operations.[2106] If the activities of the provider remain limited, however, to the "processing mandate" given by the cloud customer, the SaaS provider would be deemed a mere processor.[2107]

1031. Provider as joint controller – A third group argues that certain SaaS providers should be considered as joint controllers rather than processors.[2108] These authors emphasize that SaaS providers effectively determine the "means" of the processing, often on a unilateral basis. SaaS providers design, operate and maintain software services with specific uses in mind.[2109] They determine the

p. 7–8; A. Mantelero, "Cloud computing, trans-border data flows and the European Directive 95/46/EC: applicable law and task distribution", *l.c.*, section 3.1.

2102 A. Mantelero, "Cloud computing, trans-border data flows and the European Directive 95/46/EC: applicable law and task distribution", *l.c.*, section 3.1.

2103 *Id.*

2104 L. Determann, "Data Privacy in the Cloud–Myths and Facts", *l.c.*, Myth 10.

2105 B. Docquir, "Le 'cloud computing' ou l'informatique dématérialisée: la protection des données au coeur de la relation contractuelle", *l.c.*, p. 1009 and J.-M. Van Gyseghem, "Cloud computing et protection des données à caractère personnel: mise en ménage possible?", *l.c.*, p. 44–45.

2106 B. Docquir, "Le 'cloud computing' ou l'informatique dématérialisée: la protection des données au coeur de la relation contractuelle", *l.c.*, p. 1009. See also Article 29 Data Protection Working Party, "Opinion 05/2012 on Cloud Computing", *l.c.*, p. 8

2107 *Id.*

2108 European Data Protection Supervisor (EDPS), "Opinion of the European Data Protection Supervisor on the Commission's Communication on "Unleashing the potential of Cloud Computing in Europe", *l.c.*, p. 12–14; Commission Nationale de l'Informatique et Libertés (CNIL), *Recommendations for companies planning to use Cloud computing services*, *o.c.*, p. 5–6; F. Gilbert, "Cloud service providers as joint-data controllers", *l.c.*, p. 7–8; J.G.L. van der Wees, "De verantwoordelijke en de bewerker in de cloud", *l.c.*, p. 110–111.

2109 European Data Protection Supervisor (EDPS), "Opinion of the European Data Protection Supervisor on the Commission's Communication on "Unleashing the potential of Cloud Computing in Europe", *l.c.*, p. 13; F. Gilbert, "Cloud service providers as joint-data controllers", *l.c.*, p. 10 *("[...] a SaaS model where the SaaS provider has developed an*

features and processing capabilities of the services they offer and choose which tools to use, whereas customers can only decide about certain settings.[2110] As a result, SaaS customers may have little or no influence over how (or where) personal data are processed.[2111] Moreover, cloud services are offered through standard contracts, with little or no possibility to negotiate special terms.[2112] Finally, it is also pointed out that SaaS providers typically enjoy much greater technical expertise than their customers.[2113]

B. Platform provider (PaaS)

1032. Relevant characteristics – In case of PaaS, the cloud provider offers its customers the ability to develop, test, deploy and administer applications.[2114] PaaS providers manage the underlying cloud infrastructure (e.g. operating system, servers, networks) and determine the programming models that

---

application for which it has determined the features and proposed uses, and the customer is only able to assert its control over the use of the data hosted by the SaaS by deciding some specific settings. In this case, it would seem likely that at least some SaaS offerings might qualify as "data controllers.")

2110 F. Gilbert, "Cloud service providers as joint-data controllers", *l.c.*, p. 10. See also European Data Protection Supervisor (EDPS), "Opinion of the European Data Protection Supervisor on the Commission's Communication on "Unleashing the potential of Cloud Computing in Europe", *l.c.*, p. 12 ("*When looking at SaaS solutions like cloud-based office productivity tools or business intelligence tools, the cloud client usually has no possibility to influence the type of service offered by the provider. In addition, the relationship between provider and client may not involve any direct negotiation and may amount to a simple registration process. As a consequence, the level of control over the means of the processing operations by the cloud client may be extremely limited. In this scenario, the EDPS considers that the qualification of the cloud service provider as co-controller might be more appropriate.*")

2111 J.G.L. van der Wees, "De verantwoordelijke en de bewerker in de cloud", *l.c.*, p. 110 and European Data Protection Supervisor (EDPS), "Opinion of the European Data Protection Supervisor on the Commission's Communication on "Unleashing the potential of Cloud Computing in Europe", *l.c.*, p. 13.

2112 European Data Protection Supervisor (EDPS), "Opinion of the European Data Protection Supervisor on the Commission's Communication on "Unleashing the potential of Cloud Computing in Europe", *l.c.*, p. 13 and Commission Nationale de l'Informatique et Libertés (CNIL), *Recommendations for companies planning to use Cloud computing services*, *o.c.*, p. 5.

2113 F. Gilbert, "Cloud service providers as joint-data controllers", *l.c.*, p. 9 ("*The "expertise of the parties" test may also be crucial in the case of cloud services. Indeed, in many cases the customer uses the service because it does not have the expertise to run these functions in-house. This is especially the case for SaaS providers, and it is indeed one of the primary selling points used by these service providers. They provide the technical expertise to achieve a particular goal, for example the operation of a CRM system, so that the customer may focus on the important activities that are directly related to the unique expertise of the customer, such as the development, marketing, and sale of its own products and services. Would not a cloud service provider that flaunts its expertise at a particular task (such as the design and operation of a CRM database) be in a position similar to that of the accountant [as described in WP169]?*")

2114 L. Badger, T. Grance, R. Patt-Corner and J. Voas, *Cloud Computing Synopsis and Recommendations*, *o.c.*, p. 6-1.

customers can use.[2115] PaaS providers in principle have no role (administrative or otherwise) in relation to the applications which are developed or run over their infrastructure.[2116]

1033. Legal status – Compared to SaaS, the influence of the provider of a PaaS service is much more limited. Its sphere of influence is confined to the lower levels of the software stack (hardware, operating system), with the exception of the programming and utility interfaces which the provider makes available to customers.[2117] It is therefore not surprising that many authors would consider PaaS providers as processors rather than controllers.[2118] Nevertheless, at least one regulator has previously signalled that there may be instances in which PaaS providers might nevertheless be considered controllers.[2119]

1034. Provider as processor – Microsoft has positioned itself as a processor in relation to its PaaS service "Azure" as well as other Microsoft cloud services. In April 2014, the Article 29 Working Party acknowledged that Microsoft's data processing agreement is in line with Commission Decision 2010/87/EU (standard contractual clauses for transfers to processors).[2120] Strictly speaking, the finding of conformity between Microsoft's contracts and the EU model clauses did not formally confirm Microsoft's status as processor. It does confirm, however, that at least from a contractual perspective the relationship between Microsoft and its Azure customers was consistent with a controller-processor relationship. In addition, it is also worth noting that the British Standards Institution (BSI) has validated that Azure is compliant with the ISO/IEC 27018 code of practice for the protection of Personally Identifiable Information (PII) in public clouds acting as PII processors.[2121]

1035. Provider as joint controller – In its 2012 guidance, the CNIL noted that certain PaaS providers may be considered as joint controllers. Specifically, it reasoned that in some cases of public PaaS, customers have no real power to give

---

2115 *Ibid*, p. 6-3.

2116 *Id.* As indicated earlier, it is possible that that the provider of the PaaS service may offer its customers the ability to run applications written by the provider (in which case this portion of the service corresponds to a SaaS model) or to host external, already existing applications (in which case this portion of the service corresponds to an IaaS model). Cf. *supra*, no. 1020.

2117 L. Badger, T. Grance, R. Patt-Corner and J. Voas, *Cloud Computing Synopsis and Recommendations*, *o.c.*, p. 6-3.

2118 See e.g. L. Determann, "Data Privacy in the Cloud–Myths and Facts", *l.c.*, Myth 10.

2119 Commission Nationale de l'Informatique et Libertés (CNIL), *Recommendations for companies planning to use Cloud computing services*, *o.c.*, p. 5–6.

2120 Article 29 Data Protection Working Party, Email to Ms Dorothee Belz, 2 April 2014.

2121 See L. Woehler, "Microsoft Azure: The first cloud computing platform to conform to ISO/IEC 27018, the only international set of privacy controls in the cloud", *Microsoft Azure Blog*, 16 February 2015.

the provider instructions and are not in a position to monitor the effectiveness of the security and confidentiality guarantees given by the cloud provider.[2122] The CNIL considered that in such circumstances it may be appropriate to consider the cloud provider as joint controller.[2123]

C. *Infrastructure provider (IaaS)*

1036. Relevant characteristics – In case of IaaS, the cloud provider provides its customers with access to virtual computers.[2124] The IaaS provider uses a Virtual Machine Monitor (VMM) or "hypervisor" to synthesize one or more virtual machines from its pool of hardware resources.[2125] The cloud provider manages only the underlying cloud infrastructure (hardware, networks) and hypervisor.[2126] A typical IaaS provider has no role (administrative or otherwise) in relation to either the applications or operating systems which are run over its infrastructure.[2127]

1037. Legal status – The provider of an IaaS services in principle has no control over the processing activities that take place on its virtual machines. The IaaS customer typically enjoys complete control over its virtual machine, the guest operating system and all software application layers above it.[2128] IaaS providers can nevertheless process (store, copy, delete) personal data "on behalf" of their customers. Many authors would therefore consider IaaS providers as "processors". Certain authors argue, however, that the provider of an IaaS service should not even be considered a processor.[2129]

2122 Commission Nationale de l'Informatique et Libertés (CNIL), *Recommendations for companies planning to use Cloud computing services*, *o.c.*, p. 5–6.

2123 *Ibid*, p. 6. Van der wees likewise indicates that there may be situations in which the PaaS provider acts as a (joint) controller, but its actual legal status should be determined in light of the services being offered and underlying contractual arrangements. (J.G.L. van der Wees, "De verantwoordelijke en de bewerker in de cloud", *l.c.*, p. 111).

2124 L. Badger, T. Grance, R. Patt-Corner and J. Voas, *Cloud Computing Synopsis and Recommendations*, *o.c.*, p. 7-1.

2125 *Id.*

2126 *Id.*

2127 *Id.* Again, it should be noted that the provider of an IaaS service may also offer its customers applications written by the provider (in which case this portion of the service corresponds to a SaaS model) or offers a programming environment that enable customers develop and run new applications (in which case this portion of the service corresponds to an PaaS model). In such situations, the analysis regarding SaaS and PaaS providers applies rather than the analysis concerning IaaS.

2128 *Id.*

2129 W. Kuan Hon, C. Millard and I. Walden, "Who is Responsible for 'Personal Data' in Cloud Computing? The Cloud of Unknowing, Part 2", *l.c.*, p. 14 et seq.

1038. PROVIDER AS PROCESSOR – Amazon has positioned itself as a processor in relation to its Amazon Web Services (AWS).[2130] AWS offers its customers a "data processing addendum" which, similar to Microsoft's data processing agreement, has been considered to be in line with Commission Decision 2010/87/EU (standard contractual clauses for transfers to processors).[2131] AWS has also been validated for compliance with ISO 27018.[2132] AWS's data processing addendum states that Amazon Web Services acts as a processor (or sub-processor) in relation to customer data (i.e. any personal data that is uploaded to AWS under the customer's AWS account).

1039. "NOT EVEN A PROCESSOR" – Kuan Hon and others have argued that there are several instances in which the provider of a cloud service should not be considered as processors, but rather as neutral intermediaries within the meaning of the E-Commerce Directive.[2133] These authors point out that many cloud providers, especially infrastructure providers, may not have any knowledge or awareness of the fact that their systems are used to process personal data.[2134] They also argue that there are situations where the cloud provider may not even be able to determine whether the data processed using its infrastructure is personal in nature (e.g. in case of encrypted or anonymised data).[2135] Moreover, they consider that it is the customer who actually "processes" the data, whereas the cloud provider merely provides the technical infrastructure to do so.[2136]

2130 See Amazon Web Services, AWS GDPR Data Processing Addendum, available at https://d1.awsstatic.com/legal/aws-gdpr/AWS_GDPR_DPA.pdf (last accessed 6 January 2019).

2131 See Commission Nationale pour la Protection des Données (Luxembourg), Letter to Mr. Dubois regarding the AWS data processing addendum, 6 March 2015.

2132 See Amazon Web Services, "Data Privacy", accessible at http://aws.amazon.com/compliance/data-privacy-faq (last accessed 3 May 2016).

2133 W. Kuan Hon, C. Millard and I. Walden, "Who is Responsible for 'Personal Data' in Cloud Computing? The Cloud of Unknowing, Part 2", *l.c.*, p. 14 et seq.

2134 *Ibid*, p. 18–19 and 27.

2135 *Ibid*, p. 19 (""*[I]t is arguable that infrastructure providers are not even 'processors', particularly where they are used only for processing power. It is more difficult to do so where the service provided consists of or includes persistent storage of data, in other words where the provider acts as a data host. However, the provider will often not know the nature of data stored with it, so it seems problematic that its status should depend on what data its customer decides to store and how well the customer encrypts or anonymises the data.*").

2136 *Ibid*, p. 16 and p. 19–20 ("*It should be borne in mind that when cloud services, whether IaaS, PaaS or SaaS, comprise 'pure' passive, infrastructure-like data storage facilities ('utility storage'), it is the user who chooses what kind of data to store on the provider's equipment, and in what form. The provider has no control over the user's actions here. Utility storage providers are unlikely to know whether the user is storing personal data or non-personal data, unless and until they inspect the data. This strengthens the argument that incidental access should not render these kinds of utility providers 'processors'.*")

4. ALLOCATION OF RESPONSIBILITY AND LIABILITY

1040. Outline – In its Opinion on cloud computing, the Article 29 Working Party analysed the allocation of responsibilities between cloud customers and cloud providers from the perspective of a controller-processor relationship.[2137] The analysis in the sections that follow takes a similar point of departure. Where appropriate, however, reference shall also be made to situations in which the cloud provider acts as a joint controller. As was the case with the analysis of the role of the cloud provider (section 3.2), the analysis here shall be limited the processing of third-party data by cloud providers.

4.1. TRANSPARENCY

1041. Cloud customer – As a controller, the cloud customer is obliged to ensure transparency of processing of data subjects. At a minimum, the data subject must be informed of the identity of the controller and the purposes of the processing. The Article 29 Working Party considers that cloud customers should inform data subjects about the identity of the cloud provider and all subcontractors (if any), as well as about locations in which data may be stored or processed by the cloud provider and/or its subcontractors.[2138]

1042. Cloud provider – The cloud customer can only acquit its transparency obligations towards data subjects if it receives sufficient information from the cloud provider.[2139] According to the Article 29 Working Party, the cloud provider should therefore inform the customer of all subcontractors contributing to the provision of the respective cloud service as well as of the locations of all data centres where personal data may be processed at.[2140] In the meantime,

---

2137 Article 29 Data Protection Working Party, "Opinion 05/2012 on Cloud Computing", *l.c.*, p. 4 ("*This opinion focuses on the situation, where the relationship is assumed to be a controller-processor relationship, with the customer qualifying as controller and the cloud provider qualifying as processor. In cases where the cloud provider acts as a controller as well, they have to meet additional requirements.*")

2138 Article 29 Data Protection Working Party, "Opinion 05/2012 on Cloud Computing", *l.c.*, p. 20. Such information shall be deemed mandatory in case where it is necessary to ensure fairness of processing. (*Ibid*, p. 10–11) See also J.-M. Van Gyseghem, "Cloud computing et protection des données à caractère personnel: mise en ménage possible?", *l.c.*, p. 46. While at the time the recommendation to inform data subjects of the locations in which the data was issued "as a matter of good practice", it should be noted that Articles 13–14 GDPR now require controllers to inform data subjects of transfers where applicable.

2139 Article 29 Data Protection Working Party, "Opinion 05/2012 on Cloud Computing", *l.c.*, p. 11.

2140 *Ibid*, p. 11. See also Article 29 Data Protection Working Party, "Opinion 02/2015 on C-SIG Code of Conduct on Cloud Computing", WP 232, 22 September 2015, p. 6 and Commission

this recommendation has essentially been codified by way of Article 28 GDPR. In cases where the cloud provider acts as a joint controller, the provider is also responsible for ensuring compliance. In such situations, the CNIL recommends that the information be provided by the entity to whom the data subjects have communicated their data.[2141]

4.2. DATA QUALITY

A. *Purpose specification and use limitation*

1043. Cloud customer – The cloud customer is under an obligation to ensure that personal data are not processed for purposes which are incompatible with the purpose for which the data were collected.[2142] To this end, the cloud customer should obtain appropriate commitments from the cloud provider (including technical and organisational safeguards, such as access control, logging and auditing), which should in turn be captured in appropriate contractual safeguards.[2143]

1044. Cloud provider – In order to retain its status as processor, the cloud provider may not process personal data for any purpose not authorized by the controller. Any processing of personal data beyond the controller's instructions shall in principle render the cloud provider a controller.[2144] Article 28(3) GDPR additionally provides that the processor may process the personal data only on documented instructions from the controller. In order to stay within the confines of its role as processor, the cloud provider

Nationale de l'Informatique et Libertés (CNIL), *Recommendations for companies planning to use Cloud computing services*, *o.c.*, p. 8–9.

2141 Commission Nationale de l'Informatique et Libertés (CNIL), *Recommendations for companies planning to use Cloud computing services*, *o.c.*, p. 6 ("*Although the customer and the service provider, both data controllers, are responsible for the provision of information, in practice it is preferable that the entity to which the data subjects have communicated their data informs them of the processing means used by the service provider. Consequently, the service provider must give the customer all the information necessary to meet his obligation of provision of information. However, the service provider must remain the contact to whom the data subject must refer to obtain more information on the processing for which the service provider acts as joint controller.*")

2142 Article 6(1)b of Directive 95/46/EC.

2143 Article 29 Data Protection Working Party, "Opinion 05/2012 on Cloud Computing", *l.c.*, p. 11 and p. 20.

2144 See also Article 29 Data Protection Working Party, "Opinion 02/2015 on C-SIG Code of Conduct on Cloud Computing", *l.c.*, p. 8 ("*The CSP may cease to be considered a processor, with all its consequences especially in terms of liability, in cases where the actions taken by the CSP exceeds by far the normal capacities of a data processor in viewed of its supposed absence of autonomy with respect to the instructions of the controller*".).

> "should configure its role as a mere leverage in the hands of the controller, with no involvement in the semantics of the processing and no margin of maneuver for any sort of further processing".[2145]

If the cloud provider uses personal data in a way that breaches the contract, it will be considered a controller in relation to these activities and may be held liable accordingly.[2146]

B. Retention of data

1045. Cloud customer – The cloud customer is under an obligation to ensure that personal data are not kept in identifiable form for longer than is necessary.[2147] Insecure or incomplete deletion of personal data is a real concern in cloud environments, as data may be kept redundantly on different servers at different locations.[2148] The cloud customer should therefore obtain adequate guarantees, in particular through contractual measures, that data shall be deleted securely by the cloud provider once the cloud customer has requested deletion.[2149]

1046. Cloud provider – The cloud customer is dependent on the cloud provider to implement deletion of data. According to the Article 29 Working Party, secure erasure of personal data requires that either the storage media are destroyed or demagnetized or the stored personal data are deleted effectively through overwriting.[2150] The cloud provider should therefore document its deletion practices and make available tools which allow the cloud customer to easily request deletion.

1047. Contract or other legal act – Article 28(3)g GDPR requires the stipulation, in the contract or other legal act governing the processing, that the processor shall at the choice of the controller, delete or return all the personal data to the controller after the end of the provision of services relating

2145 Article 29 Data Protection Working Party, "Opinion 02/2015 on C-SIG Code of Conduct on Cloud Computing", *l.c.*, p. 9.

2146 Article 29 Data Protection Working Party, "Opinion 05/2012 on Cloud Computing", *l.c.*, p. 14.

2147 Article 5(1) GDPR (previously article 6(1)e of Directive 95/46).

2148 Article 29 Data Protection Working Party, "Opinion 02/2012 on Cloud Computing", *l.c.*, p. 12. See also D. Catteddu and G. Hogben (eds.), *Cloud computing – Benefits, risks and recommendations for information security*, ENISA, November 2009, p. 10 and 40.

2149 *Id.* The CNIL additionally recommends including a clause in the contract between the cloud provider and customer which enable an of audit deletion logs either by the customer or by a trusted third party of the customer's choosing (Commission Nationale de l'Informatique et Libertés (CNIL), *Recommendations for companies planning to use Cloud computing services*, *o.c.*, p. 14).

2150 *Id.*

to processing, and deletes existing copies unless Union or Member State law requires storage of the personal data.

4.3. CONFIDENTIALITY AND SECURITY

1048. Cloud customer – As a controller, the cloud customer is responsible for ensuring the confidentiality and security of processing.[2151] The cloud customer must therefore choose a cloud provider providing sufficient guarantees to implement appropriate technical and organisational measures in such a manner that processing will meet the requirements of the GDPR and ensure the protection of the rights of the data subject.[2152] The cloud customer is also obliged to ensure compliance with those measures.[2153] In practice, this requires cloud customers to perform a comprehensive *risk assessment*.[2154] Article 28(3)h also requires the controller to secure an *audit clause*, which either entitles the cloud customer to initiate its own audit (performed either by himself or by another auditor mandated by the controller).[2155]

1049. Cloud provider – In practice, the cloud provider will often determine the security features of his services in advance. The cloud provider will therefore need to render these features transparent towards potential cloud customers, so that they can make an informed decision about whether or not to use the service.[2156] The information provided should be sufficiently detailed as to allow the customer to determine whether technical and organisational measures taken

2151 Article 32 GDPR (previously: Article 17(1) of Directive 95/46).

2152 Article 28(1) GDPR (previously: Article 17(1) Directive 95/46).

2153 Cf. *supra*, no. 88–90.

2154 See also Article 24 GDPR. This risk assessment must cover not only risks presented by the processing itself (e.g. nature of the data, impact on data subject), but must also cover risks relating specifically to use of cloud computing services (e.g. loss of control or transparency). The risk analysis should also address specific data protection compliance risks, which concern mainly security obligation and international transfers (Article 29 Data Protection Working Party, "Opinion 05/2012 on Cloud Computing", *l.c.*, p. 19). For a detailed discussion of typical security objectives to be assessed: Article 29 Data Protection Working Party, "Opinion 05/2012 on Cloud Computing", *l.c.*, 14–16 and D. Catteddu and G. Hogben (eds.), *Cloud computing – Benefits, risks and recommendations for information security*, *o.c.*, p. 21 et seq.

2155 See also Article 29 Data Protection Working Party, "Opinion 05/2012 on Cloud Computing", *l.c.*, p. 22 and Article 29 Data Protection Working Party, "Opinion 02/2015 on C-SIG Code of Conduct on Cloud Computing", *l.c.*, p. 11 and Sopot p. 5–6 for a more detailed discussion of audit requirements. See also Commission Nationale de l'Informatique et Libertés (CNIL), *Recommendations for companies planning to use Cloud computing services*, *o.c.*, p. 15 for a template audit clause.

2156 B. Docquir, "Le 'cloud computing' ou l'informatique dématérialisée: la protection des données au coeur de la relation contractuelle", *l.c.*, p. 1013.

by the controller provide will provide appropriate guarantees.[2157] In addition, the cloud provider should offer *"a sufficient level of information on the threats on and vulnerabilities of the CSP service and infrastructure and on the risk management decisions taken by the CSP."*[2158] Finally, the cloud provider is also under an obligation to notify the cloud customer in case of any security breach which affects the customer's data.[2159]

1050. Shared responsibility in practice – At a practical level, ensuring the confidentiality and security of personal data in the cloud is typically a shared responsibility between cloud providers and cloud customers.[2160] Different cloud providers have put forward different models of task distribution. Microsoft, for example, in its Whitepaper on Protecting Data and Privacy in the Cloud argues that:

> "While providers are responsible for building services and features that facilitate compliance with applicable data protection and privacy regulations and standards, it is up to the customer to configure services and train their workers to use those services in a way that maintains compliance requirements for its industry and location. Also, though it is up to the provider to create strong operational controls to protect customer data in the cloud, it is up to the customer to use those controls in a way that limits unintended data sharing and access. Finally, the provider is responsible for demonstrating its commitment to data protection by obtaining certifications, sharing attestation reports, and signing agreements. However, it is the cloud customer's responsibility to verify that the provider's audit reports, certifications and other evidence meet its organisational data protection expectations."[2161]

Amazon Web Services proposes a slightly different task model. A distinction is made between "security *of* the cloud", which concerns the security of the underlying cloud infrastructure (hardware, networks, servers, location) and "security *in* the cloud", which concerns the security of applications, platforms and operating systems that run in the cloud.[2162] While the former is considered

2157 See also Article 29 Data Protection Working Party, "Opinion 02/2015 on C-SIG Code of Conduct on Cloud Computing", *l.c.*, p. 10.

2158 Id. The Working Party considers that without such information, the background for the customer to perform its own data protection risk management would not be adequate. (*Id.*).

2159 Article 33(2) GDPR. See also Article 29 Data Protection Working Party, "Opinion 05/2012 on Cloud Computing", *l.c.*, p. 21; D. Catteddu and G. Hogben (eds.), *Cloud computing – Benefits, risks and recommendations for information security*, ENISA, November 2009, p105 ENISA.

2160 See also European Data Protection Supervisor (EDPS), "Opinion of the European Data Protection Supervisor on the Commission's Communication on "Unleashing the potential of Cloud Computing in Europe", *l.c.*, p. 20.

2161 Microsoft, "Protecting Data and Privacy in the Cloud", *Reactive Security Communications*, 2014, p. 10.

2162 Amazon Web Services, *Whitepaper on EU Data Protection*, October 2015, p. 3–4. See also C. Woolf, "AWS Shared Responsibility Model and GDPR", 15 May 2018, available at https://aws.

the responsibility of the cloud provider, the latter is considered the responsibility of the cloud customer. In the end, the actual distribution of tasks will depend to a large extent on the type of cloud service offered (SaaS, PaaS or IaaS), as this determines the level of control which each party has over each layer of the software stack (hardware, operating system, middleware, software). ENISA has developed an overview of the division of security-relevant roles and responsibilities in relation to each service model, noting that the actual division of responsibilities may vary widely between SaaS offerings and IaaS offerings.[2163]

1051. CONTRACTUAL BINDING – Article 28(3) states that processing by a processor shall be governed by a contract or other legal, which must at a minimum stipulate that the processor:

(a) only processes the personal data only on *documented instructions* from the controller[2164];
(b) ensures that persons authorised to process the personal data are bound to *confidentiality*[2165];
(c) takes all appropriate measures to ensure *security of processing*;
(d) respects the *conditions for engaging another processor* ("sub-processing")[2166];
(e) assists the controller, insofar as this is possible and taking into account the nature of the processing, for the fulfilment of the controller's obligation to accommodate *data subject rights*;
(f) assists the controller in ensuring compliance with the obligations regarding *security* of processing (Article 32), *data breach* notification and communication (Articles 33–34) and *data protection impact assessment* and prior consultation (Articles 35–36), taking into account the nature of processing and the information available to the processor;
(g) at the choice of the controller, *deletes or returns* all the personal data to the controller after the end of the provision of services relating to processing,

amazon.com/blogs/security/the-aws-shared-responsibility-model-and-gdpr (last accessed 6 January 2019).

2163 See D. Catteddu and G. Hogben (eds.), *Cloud computing – Benefits, risks and recommendations for information security*, ENISA, November 2009, p. 66–68. A visual representation of a similar distribution of responsibilities is provided by Microsoft's "a data protection responsibility spectrum" (Microsoft, "Protecting Data and Privacy in the Cloud", *l.c.*, p. 10). See L. Badger, T. Grance, R. Patt-Corner and J. Voas, *Cloud Computing Synopsis and Recommendations*, *o.c.*, p. 5-1 et seq. for a detailed discussion of the control enjoyed the level of control which each party has over each layer of the software stack (hardware, operating system, middleware, software). Appendix A offers an outline of the distribution of responsibilities between cloud providers and customers depending on the service model.

2164 See *supra*, no. 95.

2165 The duty of confidentiality may result either from the fact the persons in question have committed themselves to confidentiality or are under an appropriate statutory obligation of confidentiality (Article 28(3)b GDPR).

2166 See *infra*, no. 1052.

and deletes existing copies unless Union or Member State law requires storage of the personal data;

(h) makes available to the controller all information necessary to *demonstrate compliance* with the obligations laid down in Article 28 GDPR and allow for and *contribute to audits, including inspections*, conducted by the controller or another auditor mandated by the controller.[2167]

Already under Directive 95/46, the Article 29 Working Party recommended that cloud contracts include similar range of provisions as "*contractual safeguards for the controller-processor relationship*".[2168] Indeed, as discussed in Part II, Article 28(3) GDPR seeks inter alia to ensure that the controller remains capable of exercising "control" over the processing notwithstanding the fact that it has decided to outsource the processing. In addition, it also foresees that the processor shall be bound by a *duty to assist* the controller with respect to certain obligations. Finally, Article 28(3) also contains provisions designed to promote the *accountability* of both controllers and processors.[2169]

1052. Sub-processing – Cloud providers that act as processors may in practice subcontract certain services out to sub-processors.[2170] Article 28(2) GDPR stipulates that the processor shall not engage another processor without prior specific or general written authorisation of the controller. In the case of general written authorisation, the processor must inform the controller of any intended changes concerning the addition or replacement of other processors, thereby giving the controller the opportunity to object to such changes.[2171] Already under Directive 95/46, the Article 29 Working Party considered that the cloud provider (processor[2172]) may only engage with the agreement of the customer after informing the customer of "*the type of service subcontracted, the characteristics of current or potential sub-contractors and guarantees that these entities offer to the provider of cloud computing services to comply with Directive 95/46/EC*".[2173]

2167 Article 28(3) GDPR in fine adds that with regard to point (h) of the first subparagraph, the processor shall immediately inform the controller if, in its opinion, an instruction infringes this Regulation or other Union or Member State data protection provisions.

2168 Article 29 Data Protection Working Party, "Opinion 05/2012 on Cloud Computing", *l.c.*, p. 12–14

2169 Cf. *supra*, no. 102.

2170 Article 29 Data Protection Working Party, "Opinion 05/2012 on Cloud Computing", *l.c.*, p. 9.

2171 Cf. *supra*, no. 94.

2172 According to the CNIL, if the cloud provider controller acts as a joint controller, the provider is not required to obtain prior authorization from the customer but only has to inform the customer: see Commission Nationale de l'Informatique et Libertés (CNIL), *Recommendations for companies planning to use Cloud computing services*, *o.c.*, p. 8.

2173 *Ibid*, p. 9.

1053. Recourse – Pursuant to Article 28(4) GDPR, the same data protection obligations as set out in the contract or other legal act between the controller and the processor must be imposed on the sub-processor.[2174] If the sub-processor fails to fulfil its data protection obligations as set out in the contract or other legal act between the cloud customer and (initial) cloud provider, the latter shall remain fully liable to the controller for the performance of that other processor's obligations.[2175]

4.4. DATA SUBJECT RIGHTS

1054. Cloud customer – The cloud customer must ensure that it is able to accommodate data subjects' rights of access, correction or deletion or blocking. The cloud customer must therefore verify the cloud provider offers sufficient guarantees in terms of technical and organisational measures to ensure the protection of data subject rights, including in cases when data is further processed by subcontractors.[2176]

1055. Cloud provider – A cloud provider (as processor) is not obliged to accommodate data subject rights. Pursuant to Article 28(3)e GDPR, however, the contract or other legal act between the controller and processor shall stipulate that the processor shall assist the controller for the fulfilment of its obligation to respond to requests for exercising the data subject's rights by appropriate technical and organisational measures, insofar as this is possible and taking into account the nature of the processing., In cases where the provider acts as co-controller, the cloud provider is also directly responsible for accommodating data subject rights. If that is the case, the responsibilities for exercise of data subject rights should also be clearly allocated between the cloud provider and cloud customer by means of an arrangement between them.[2177]

4.5. INTERNATIONAL TRANSFERS

1056. Cloud customer – EU data protection law takes as a point of departure that personal data should only be transferred outside the EU if the country to

---

2174 See also Article 29 Data Protection Working Party, "Opinion 05/2012 on Cloud Computing", *l.c.*, p. 9–10. See also *supra*, nos. 252 et seq.

2175 Article 28(4) *in fine* GDPR. See also Article 29 Data Protection Working Party, "Opinion 05/2012 on Cloud Computing", *l.c.*, p. 10.

2176 Article 28(1) GDPR. See also Article 29 Data Protection Working Party, "Opinion 05/2012 on Cloud Computing", *l.c.*, p. 16.

2177 Article 26 GDPR. See also Article 29 Data Protection Working Party, "Opinion 02/2015 on C-SIG Code of Conduct on Cloud Computing", *l.c.*, p. 9.

where the data shall be transferred ensures an adequate level of protection.[2178] Absent a finding of adequacy, the controller must adduce "appropriate safeguards" to ensure a continuous level of protection.[2179] In cases where the cloud provider is established outside the EU, has data centres outside the EU, or subcontracts to other processors established outside the EU, the cloud customer shall in principle be obliged to put in place additional safeguards (or ensure that safeguards are in place). Such safeguards may take the form of contractual clauses or binding corporate rules.[2180]

1057. Cloud provider – With the entry into application of the GDPR, processors have become directly subject to the requirements concerning international transfers. In addition, Article 28(3)a provides that the arrangement between controllers and processors must stipulate that the processor shall only process the personal data only on *documented instructions* from the controller, including with regard to transfers. The cloud provider must therefore, at minimum, be transparent towards the cloud customer regarding all jurisdictions in which personal data may be processed (either by the cloud provider itself or its subprocessors).[2181] In practice, the contract between cloud provider and customer is likely to incorporate a list of locations in which the cloud service may be provided in order to satisfy this requirement.[2182] A cloud provider that engages in international transfers without the prior authorization of the cloud customer shall be in risk of being considered a controller.[2183] In this regard, the Working Party has stated that:

> "The CSP may cease to be considered as a processor, with all its consequences especially in terms of liability, in cases where the actions taken by the CSP exceeds by far the normal capacities of a data processor in view of its supposed absence of autonomy with respect to the instructions of the controller. This may be the case, for example, where CSPs autonomously organise international transfers of data to respond to a law enforcement authority or state security's requests without seeking any involvement of the respective controllers."[2184]

2178 See Article 45 GDPR (previously Article 25 Directive 95/46).

2179 See Article 46 GDPR (previously: Article 26 Directive 95/46).

2180 See Article 29 Data Protection Working Party, "Opinion 05/2012 on Cloud Computing", *l.c.*, p. 17 et seq. For more information regarding BCR's for processors see Article 29 Data Protection Working Party, "Explanatory Document on the Processor Binding Corporate Rules", WP 204 rev.01, adopted 19 April 2013, revised 22 May 2015.

2181 See also Article 29 Data Protection Working Party, "Opinion 05/2012 on Cloud Computing", *l.c.*, p. 20 and Article 29 Data Protection Working Party, "Opinion 02/2015 on C-SIG Code of Conduct on Cloud Computing", *l.c.*, p. 7.

2182 See also Article 29 Data Protection Working Party, "Opinion 05/2012 on Cloud Computing", *l.c.*, p. 21.

2183 Article 29 Data Protection Working Party, "Opinion 02/2015 on C-SIG Code of Conduct on Cloud Computing", *l.c.*, p. 8.

2184 *Id.*

5. EVALUATION

1058. Outline – For some, cloud computing can be viewed as simply the next evolutionary step in IT outsourcing.[2185] Nevertheless, the cloud computing paradigm has put considerable pressure on the controller-processor model. First, the specialized nature of certain cloud services can make it difficult to determine whether the cloud provider should be considered a controller or processor. Second, the cloud customer shall generally be unable to influence the design of the cloud services on offer. Third, the growing diversification in cloud computing services increases the number of actors involved in the processing of personal data, which may dilute the distribution of roles and responsibilities among the actors involved. Fourth, the argument has been made that certain actors in the cloud value chain should be labelled neither controller nor processor, especially in cases where the provider has no knowledge of the personal data being processed on its infrastructure.

5.1. THRESHOLD FOR CONTROL

1059. Conceptual ambiguity – Most scholars and regulators take the view that, at least as a point of departure, the provider of a cloud service should be considered a processor.[2186] Nevertheless, other scholars and regulators seem inclined to attribute certain cloud providers the role of controller, especially where SaaS providers are concerned.[2187] The confusion surrounding the status of certain cloud providers is attributable, at least in part, to the nature of the two criteria that give rise to control: purposes and means.

1060. Clarification of "purpose" – According to the Article 29 Working Party, a processor by definition cannot be involved in the determination of the purposes of the processing.[2188] In case of SaaS, however, the service offered by the provider is usually designed with a particular use (i.e. "purpose") in mind.[2189] Certain applications, such as customer service management, intrinsically involve processing of personal data. Does the offering of a standard service intended for processing personal data amount to a definition of "purpose"? The Working Party's guidance on cloud computing is essentially silent on this issue.[2190] Scholars have answered this question in different ways. Mantelero and

---

2185 Article 29 Data Protection Working Party, "Opinion 05/2012 on Cloud Computing", *l.c.*, p. 4.

2186 Cf. *supra*, footnote 2091.

2187 Cf. *supra*, footnote 2092.

2188 Cf. *supra*, no. 109.

2189 See also F. Gilbert, "Cloud service providers as joint-data controllers", *l.c.*, p. 10.

2190 The Working Party merely notes that a cloud provider shall be deemed a controller if it uses personal data for its "own purposes". This reference to the "own purposes" of the cloud

Determann, for example, argue that one of the reasons why cloud providers should not be viewed as controllers is because they offer their services without any *interest* in the data being processed or the uses made of these data.[2191] Gilbert, on the other hand, points to a number of Working Party opinions in which service providers have been deemed controllers even if they do not have a direct interest in the outcome of the underlying processing activities.[2192]

1061. "PURPOSE" VS. "INTEREST" – The historical-comparative analysis of data protection law (undertaken in Part III of this book) offers some support to the argument that the concept of "purpose" is closely related to the concept of "interest". Traditionally, the controller has always been conceived of as the "beneficiary" of the processing: the data processing is carried out "on his behalf", "for his activities", or "for his purposes".[2193] Salom points out that the existence of an "interest" in the processing would almost automatically exclude that the entity concerned may be considered a processor:

> "Since data processors act on behalf of controllers, they have no personal interest in the outcome of the process they carry out (except the economic interest relating to the compensation agreed with the controller for the services provided, and their liability for the quality of these services); in fact, if data processors had any personal interest in the purposes sought in data processing, they would lose their status as data processor because they would stop acting on behalf of the data controller to act on their own behalf, for their own interest and, therefore, would not fit the definition of data processor [...]".[2194]

1062. PURPOSE AS FINALITY – While there exists a close relationship between the concepts of "purpose" and "interest", the two are by no means identical.[2195]

---

provider implicitly seem to refer to purposes other than the delivery of the service explicitly requested by the customer.

2191 A. Mantelero, "Cloud computing, trans-border data flows and the European Directive 95/46/EC: applicable law and task distribution", *l.c.*, section 3.1 ("*[...] the cloud provider receives the information to be processed in the interest of the user*") and L. Determann, "Data Privacy in the Cloud-Myths and Facts", *l.c.*, Myth 10 ("*[...] providers tend to offer a platform or software functionality as a service, without any interest, knowledge, or influence regarding data types and processing purposes*").

2192 F. Gilbert, "Cloud service providers as joint-data controllers", *l.c.*, p. 9 et seq. (analyzing the Working Party's opinions on applicable law (WP 179), online social networks (WP 163), and SWIFT (WP 128).

2193 Cf. *supra*, no. 686.

2194 J.A. Salom, "'A third party to whom data are disclosed': A third group among those processing data", *l.c.*, p. 178. See also T. Léonard and A. Mention, "Transferts transfrontaliers de données: quelques considérations théorique et pratiques", in B. Docquir and A. Puttemans (eds.), *Actualités du droit de la vie privée*, Bruxelles, Bruylant, 2008, p. 101 ("*L'utilité et le bénéfice du traitement ne le concernent pas directement*").

2195 J.A. Salom, "'A third party to whom data are disclosed': A third group among those processing data", *l.c.*, p. 181. An additional argument against equating "interest" with "purpose" is that

The purpose of the processing refers to the finality of the processing, i.e. the *aims* or *objectives* pursued by the processing. Establishing the purpose of the processing can be achieved by asking the following questions: "*To what end are personal data being processed?*" "*What is the output of the processing and what is the intended use of this output?*" Determining the purpose of the processing is therefore not the same as having an interest in the processing. The subtle distinction between "purpose" and "interest" is summarized eloquently again by Salom:

> "The purpose of data processing refers to the objective or material result pursued through processing the personal data it focuses on, the information or the conclusion targeted as a result of processing the data of interest, or in the inferences made based on the personal data that are being processed. [...] In contrast, the interests that are intended to be fulfilled through the data processing reveal an entirely subjective aspect, namely the project, business, or activity being developed and for which data processing is essential. The interests pursued by data processing are based on an intention, and are a completely volitional and abstract element for which data processing operations can be used as a necessary tool."[2196]

If a cloud provider has an interest in the outcome processing, it almost invariably means that the provider is also involved in the determination of the purposes of the processing (at least for those operations whereby it has an interest in the outcome of the processing). It can also be argued, however, that the cloud provider should be deemed a controller even where he has no direct interest in the processing, simply by virtue of its involvement in determining the output or material result of the processing.

1063. Clarification of "means" – Cloud providers often determine large portions of the "means" of the processing (e.g. the hardware, operating system, and software applications).[2197] But is this sufficient to consider them controllers? The Article 29 Working Party accepts that processor(s) may enjoy a certain "margin of manoeuvre" in specifying how the processing shall be

Article 7(f) of Directive 95/46 mentions both purpose and interest in the same sentence, thereby clearly indicating that they carry a distinct meaning.

2196 *Ibid*, p. 181. Salom further observes that Directive 95/46 consistently employs the terms purpose and interests with this subtle distinction in mind ("*In this sense, the Directive refers to the purposes of the data processing when regulating the information obligation in Articles 10 (c) and 11 (b), not obliging the data controller to inform about its interest in the data processing, and also makes several references to the purpose of different kinds of data processing in recitals (28), (30), and (37), and Article 4.1 (c). [...] The Directive never refers to the 'interest of the processing' but to the 'interest of 'an entity or individual, referring always to a subjective intention in recitals 30, 42, 45, and Articles 7 (f), 8 (b), 13.1 (e), and 26.1 (c) and (e).*")

2197 W. Kuan Hon, C. Millard and I. Walden, "Who is Responsible for 'Personal Data' in Cloud Computing? The Cloud of Unknowing, Part 2", *l.c.*, p. 10.

organized.[2198] Only if the processor determines the "essential" means of the processing would this imply its status of controller.[2199] The Working Party does not consider the choice for a particular hardware or software as determining "essential" means per se. Nevertheless, other aspects of the processing which are often determined by cloud providers (e.g. security measures, location of data, use of subcontractors, deletion processes, new service features, synchronisation services) may be considered as "essential" means.[2200] Yet deciding about these aspects of the processing apparently is not enough for the Working Party to consider the cloud provider as a controller. Indeed, the analysis in section 4 suggests that as long as the cloud provider clearly outlines the essential elements of the processing in advance (and does not draw outside these lines without additional agreement from the customer), the provider may retain its status as processor.

1064. Balancing test – To help distinguish between controllers and processors, the Article 29 Working Party has provided a range of additional criteria.[2201] In practice, the approach advanced by the Working Party seems to be more of a "balancing test" or "sliding scale" rather than a rigid adherence to existing criteria. As noted by Gilbert:

> "The opinions issued by the Working Party show a sliding scale. The more the service provider follows the specific instructions of the client, the more chance it has to be deemed a data processor. On the other hand, the more the service provider has autonomy, and has the ability to make decisions regarding the data, the more likely it

---

2198 Opinion 1/2010, p. 13–14.

2199 *Ibid*, p. 14.

2200 See also F. Gilbert, "Cloud service providers as joint-data controllers", *l.c.*, p. 9; W. Kuan Hon, C. Millard and I. Walden, "Who is Responsible for 'Personal Data' in Cloud Computing? The Cloud of Unknowing, Part 2", *l.c.*, p. 11. See also European Data Protection Supervisor (EDPS), "Opinion of the European Data Protection Supervisor on the Commission's Communication on "Unleashing the potential of Cloud Computing in Europe", *l.c.*, p. 12 ("... *the complexity of the technical means used in the cloud environment has now reached such a stage that it is necessary to add that the cloud client/data controller may not be the only entity that can solely determine the "purposes and means" of the processing. More and more often, the determination of the essential elements of the means, which is a prerogative of the data controller, is not in the hands of the cloud client. In this respect, the cloud service provider typically designs, operates and maintains the cloud computing IT infrastructure*").

2201 For example in Opinion 1/2010, the Working Party mentions: level of prior instructions given (the greater the level of instruction, the more limited the margin of manoeuvre of the processor; monitoring of the execution of the service (a constant and careful supervision of compliance provides an indication of being in control of the processing operations); image given to the data subject; and expertise of the parties (if the expertise of the service provider plays a predominant role in the processing, it may entail its qualification as data controller) (Opinion 1/2010, *l.c.*, p. 28). See also CNIL, "Les transferts de données à caractère personnel hors Union européenne", not dated, p. 11–12 and CNIL, "Les questions posées pour la protection des données personnelles par l'externalisation hors de l'Union européenne des traitements informatiques", September 2010, p. 14–15. See also *supra*, no. 114.

is that, at least with respect to these specific activities, the service provider would be deemed a data controller."[2202]

Based on an analysis of key opinions of the Article 29 Working Party, Gilbert has developed a list of questions to help determine whether the cloud provider should, on the whole, be deemed a controller or processor.[2203] While the additional guidance of the Working Party is useful, it also demonstrates that a number of grey areas remain, which may lead to divergent interpretations in practice.[2204]

5.2. DESIGN OF CLOUD SERVICES

1065. Pre-defined services – As indicated in the previous section, cloud providers often determine large portions of the "means" of the processing. Public cloud services are typically offered on a "take it or leave" it basis, whereby the customer has little ability to influence the design or operation of the system.[2205] As a result, many of the design decisions concerning the processing have already been made by the cloud provider, which may constrain the customer's ability to comply with certain requirements under EU data protection law, notably requirement of data protection by design.[2206]

1066. Data protection by design – Article 25(1) GDPR requires controllers to put in place appropriate technical and organisational measures designed to implement data protection principles, such as data minimisation. Controllers must take the requirement into account, not just during the processing itself, but "*already at the time of the determination of the means of the processing*". The concept of data protection by design was borne out of the recognition that technological design choices may have considerable impact on data protection

---

2202 F. Gilbert, "Cloud service providers as joint-data controllers", *l.c.*, p. 8. Later, Gilbert continues: "*The opinions issued by the Working Party show a sliding scale. At one end of the spectrum, a service provider that provides only basic services is a data processor. At the other end, a service provider that is "in control," e.g., has autonomy, retains the power to draft and change its contracts and policies, or provides added value for the processing of the data, should be deemed a "data controller," and should share with the customer the liability and risks associated with the processing of personal data.*" (*Ibid*, p. 12).

2203 F. Gilbert, "Cloud service providers as joint-data controllers", *l.c.*, p. 12.

2204 W. Kuan Hon, C. Millard and I. Walden, "Who is Responsible for 'Personal Data' in Cloud Computing? The Cloud of Unknowing, Part 2", *l.c.*, p. 11.

2205 See e.g. R. Leenes, "Who Controls the Cloud?", *l.c.*, p. 8–9. See however also D. Catteddu and G. Hogben (eds.), *Cloud computing – Benefits, risks and recommendations for information security*, ENISA, November 2009, p. 98.

2206 See in the same vein: P. Tsormpatzoudi and F. Coudert, "Technology providers' responsibility in protecting privacy... dropped from the sky?", *Paper presented at the Amsterdam Privacy Conference* (APC), 23–26 October 2015, p. 1.

and the idea that new technologies and services should therefore be developed with data protection in mind from the start, rather than as an afterthought:

> "When developing, designing, selecting and using applications, services and products that are based on the processing of personal data or process personal data to fulfil their task, producers of the products, services and applications should be encouraged to take into account the right to data protection when developing and designing such products, services and applications and, with due regard to the state of the art, to make sure that controllers and processors are able to fulfil their data protection obligations."[2207]

1067. Indirect incentives – Several authors have already pointed out that the controller-processor model relies on the implicit assumption that controllers shall in fact have both the ability and the incentive to determine the design and operation of a data processing system:

> "Within this logic underlying the law, the controller is the main architect of an information system and decides the why and how of the system's operations. In building the system, the controller might use/integrate the systems and services of other organizations, but this happens under the controller's control and responsibility."[2208]

The requirement of data protection by design is only imposed upon controllers, not on processors. There appears to an expectation that this will lead to an increase the demand for privacy preserving applications and services, which will in turn create an incentive for service providers to incorporate data protection considerations into the design of their services.[2209] As Tsormpatzoudi and Coudert point out, however, this outcome is dependent on the premise that controllers have both sufficient incentives and market power to create pressure in the supply market to incorporate privacy preserving features.[2210]

1068. Market dynamics – Cloud computing providers can offer processing services at reduced costs based on economies of scale.[2211] In order to maximise economies of scale, a provider will design and offer its services in a manner that is likely to satisfy the widest possible range of customers. Data protection by design, however, is based on the notion that services and application should

2207 Recital (78) GDPR.

2208 R. Mahieu, J. van Hoboken, H. Asghari, "Responsibility for Data Protection in a Networked World. On the question of the controller, "effective and complete protection" and its application to data access rights in Europe", *l.c.*, p. 7.

2209 P. Tsormpatzoudi and F. Coudert, "Technology providers' responsibility in protecting privacy… dropped from the sky?", *l.c.*, p. 7.

2210 *Id.*

2211 Cf. *supra*, no. 992.

be designed in order to give effect to data protection principles, such as data minimisation, transparency and use limitation. The correct application of those principles is very context-specific. While certain technical measures (e.g. anonymisation) may work well for certain types of applications (e.g. analytics), they may work less well for others (e.g. customer relations management). At the same time, the extent of data protection by design obligations depend on several criteria, most notably the state of the art and the cost of implementation. As a result, a "chicken-or-egg" problem emerges: in the absence of reasonably priced, off-the-shelf solutions with proven track record, it is difficult to imagine a generally enforceable obligation of data protection by design, save perhaps for very high risk applications.[2212]

1069. Take it or leave it? – In 2012, the European Data Protection Supervisor noted that

> "T]he contractual asymmetry between service providers and clients [...] may make it very difficult or even impossible for cloud clients acting as data controllers to comply with the requirements for personal data processing in a cloud computing environment. The asymmetry could also lead to an undesirable allocation of responsibility in relation to compliance with data protection law. If the qualification of data controller and processor does not appropriately reflect the level of control over the means of processing, the responsibility for the protection of personal data even risks to evaporate with the use of cloud computing"[2213]

While the GDPR has done a lot to address issues resulting from the *contractual* asymmetry that exists between cloud providers and cloud customers, it has done little address the limited level of control a cloud customer may have over the means of the processing. The requirement of data protection by design has been placed squarely upon the shoulders of the controller. In theory, the issue might be overcome by providing incentives through regulatory enforcement (e.g. for failure to choose a processor offering sufficient guarantees in terms of data protection by design). In practice, however, that would mean imposing liability upon actors who, as a matter of fact, might have limited or no capability to comply with the obligation themselves.[2214]

2212 See also B. Van Alsenoy, E. Lievens, K. Janssen, a.o., "A Regulatory Framework for INDI Operators", Global Identity Networking for Individuals (GINI), Deliverable D3.2, 2012, p. 43.

2213 European Data Protection Supervisor (EDPS), "Opinion of the European Data Protection Supervisor on the Commission's Communication on "Unleashing the potential of Cloud Computing in Europe", *l.c.*, p. 6. See also W. Kuan Hon, C. Millard and I. Walden, "Who is Responsible for 'Personal Data' in Cloud Computing? The Cloud of Unknowing, Part 2", *l.c.*, p. 12–14 (noting that many providers do not even acknowledge processor status).

2214 Compare *supra*, no. 984. Gürses and van Hoboken note that notwithstanding the principle that end-users of processing services have significant responsibility over their choice of processor, there has not been much progress in enforcing this principle (S. Gürses and J. van

5.3. NETWORKED DATA PROCESSES

1070. Multiplication of actors – Cloud computing services are characterized by what Schwartz has termed "networked data processes".[2215] The cloud service offered by one provider might be produced by combining services from a range of other providers, which together realise a particular outcome.[2216] Another way to think about cloud services is in terms of "modular units", whereby different functions and operations can be assembled, pulled apart and reassembled as needed.[2217] The result is an environment which involves a growing number of actors, whereby each actor is involved in the processing to varying degrees, possibly at different levels of the software stack (hardware, operating system, middleware, software).[2218]

1071. Multiplication of controllers? – One way to respond to the increased diversification of processing services is to apply the concept of control more granularly. Instead of trying to squeeze certain cloud providers into the (ill-fitting) jacket of "processor", both provider and customer are treated as a "controllers" – but only with respect to those decisions and operations over which it has effective control.[2219] One benefit of this approach is that it could lead to an allocation of responsibilities that reflects the actual influence over processing activities.[2220] An immediate consequence of such an approach, however, is a multiplication in the number of "controllers" involved whenever cloud services are used.

1072. Unintended consequences? – The multiplication of controllers was an issue considered by the Article 29 Working Party in its Opinion 1/2010:

> "[...] multiplication of controllers may [...] lead to undesired complexities and to a possible lack of clarity in the allocation of responsibilities. This would risk making the entire processing unlawful due to a lack of transparency and violate the principle of fair processing."[2221]

Hoboken, "Privacy After the Agile Turn", in J. Polonetsky, O. Tene and E. Selinger (eds.), *Cambridge Handbook of Consumer Privacy*, Cambridge University Press, 2017, p. 17).

2215 P. Schwartz, "Information Privacy in the Cloud", *l.c.*, p. 1630.

2216 Article 29 Data Protection Working Party, "Opinion 05/2012 on Cloud Computing", *l.c.*, p. 5

2217 P. Schwartz, "Information Privacy in the Cloud", *l.c.*, p. 1634.

2218 See also *supra*, nos. 1020 et seq.

2219 See also European Data Protection Supervisor (EDPS), "Opinion of the European Data Protection Supervisor on the Commission's Communication on "Unleashing the potential of Cloud Computing in Europe", *l.c.*, paragraph 55.

2220 *Id.*

2221 Opinion 1/2010, *l.c.*, p. 24.

The principle of transparency of processing is a core principle of EU data protection law. The more controllers involved, the more difficult it may become for data subjects to ascertain who is responsible for which aspect of the processing. But is this really an issue of how the concept of "controller" is applied? Or is the issue caused by the manner in which the duties regarding transparency towards data subjects have been framed? It seems that Article 26 of the GDPR seeks to remedy this issue, at least where joint controllers are concerned. Article 26(1) requires joint controllers to conclude an arrangement between them, in particular as regards the exercise of data subject rights.[2222] Article 26(2), moreover, provides that the essence of this arrangement shall be made available to the data subject. Finally, Article 26(3) provides that notwithstanding the terms of the arrangement, the data subject shall be able to exercise his or her rights in respect of and against each of the controllers.

1073. Delineating (joint) control – In today's networked world, almost no system in which personal data is processed stands on its own.[2223] While some would argue that greater recognition of joint control is likely to offer greater protection to data subjects, others have argued the opposite.[2224] In any event, it appears that the framework for assigning responsibilities to different stages of the processing still requires further development and clarification, in particular in cases of joint control.[2225] While case law and regulatory guidance can go a long way in clarifying the boundaries of joint control and joint responsibility, legal uncertainty will often remain until the right qualification of each actor in a particular case has been established by a judicial authority.

5.4. HOSTING SERVICES

1074. Cloud providers as hosts? – Article 14 of the E-Commerce Directive describes "hosting services" as services consisting of the storage of information provided by the recipient of the service. Seeing as the majority of cloud providers

2222 Strictly speaking, the GDPR does not specify a similar obligation for separate controllers (although each controller shall still be bound by a duty to ensure that the processing remains transparent towards data subjects).

2223 R. Mahieu, J. van Hoboken, H. Asghari, "Responsibility for Data Protection in a Networked World. On the question of the controller, "effective and complete protection" and its application to data access rights in Europe", *l.c.*, p. 3.

2224 Contra: Opinion of Advocate General Bobek in *Fashion ID*, C-40/17, ECLI:EU:C:2018:1039, paragraph 92 ("*[...] Making everyone responsible means that no-one will in fact be responsible. Or rather, the one party that should have been held responsible for a certain course of action, the one actually exercising control, is likely to hide behind all those others nominally 'co-responsible', with effective protection likely to be significantly diluted.*")

2225 R. Mahieu, J. van Hoboken, H. Asghari, "Responsibility for Data Protection in a Networked World. On the question of the controller, "effective and complete protection" and its application to data access rights in Europe", *l.c.*, p. 23–24.

store personal data on behalf of their customers, Kuan Hon and others have argued that cloud providers (especially PaaS and IaaS providers) should be considered as "hosts".[2226] The main rationale for their argument appears to be the favourable liability regime which has been granted to hosts. Under Article 14, hosts are in principle exempted from liability in relation to information stored at the request of their customers, as long as the provider does not have actual or constructive knowledge of the unlawful character of the information stored at the request of the recipient of the service.[2227]

1075. The "cloud of the unknowing" – To support their argument, Kuan Hon and others point out that many cloud providers, especially infrastructure providers, do not have any knowledge or awareness of the fact that their systems are used to process personal data.[2228] They also point out that there are situations where the cloud provider may not even be able to determine whether the data processed using its infrastructure is personal in nature (e.g. in case of encrypted or anonymised data).[2229] In such situations, they argue that a cloud provider should not even be considered a "processor", but should instead be exempted from compliance with data protection requirements altogether:

> "A cloud provider whose services are used to process data on behalf of a consumer or business customer, but who does not know that the data are 'personal data', or who knows the data's status but has no access to the data it processes, should not be a 'processor' for the purposes of the DPD, because a processor, according to the definition, 'processes personal data'. Thus such a provider should not be subject to any data protection obligations."[2230]

The hosting exemption would only apply, however, insofar as the necessary conditions are met:

> "Any such exemptions should of course be subject to similar provisions as to the loss of immunity, and corresponding imposition of data protection obligations as

2226 W. Kuan Hon, C. Millard and I. Walden, "Who is Responsible for 'Personal Data' in Cloud Computing? The Cloud of Unknowing, Part 2", *l.c.*, in particular at p. 17 et seq.

2227 See Article 14(1)a of Directive 2000/31/EC

2228 *Ibid*, p. 18–19 and p. 27.

2229 *Id.* (""*[I]t is arguable that infrastructure providers are not even 'processors', particularly where they are used only for processing power. It is more difficult to do so where the service provided consists of or includes persistent storage of data, in other words where the provider acts as a data host. However, the provider will often not know the nature of data stored with it, so it seems problematic that its status should depend on what data its customer decides to store and how well the customer encrypts or anonymises the data.*").

2230 *Ibid*, p. 28. See also p. 18 ("*We therefore suggest that mere hosting of data, without knowledge as to its 'personal data' nature, should not render the provider a processor, and even more so with encrypted data: the cloud of unknowing should not be the cloud of 'processing'. We believe an exemption or exception to data protection laws is justified here.*")

controller or processor, should the service provider acquire the relevant knowledge and/or access."[2231]

1076. Assessment – A cloud provider that stores personal data on behalf of its customers could, as a matter of principle, be considered a hosting provider. But the question of whether or not cloud providers can be qualified as "hosts" may, in many cases, be of only limited practical relevance. There are mainly two reasons for this. The first reason is that the liability exemption for hosts is predicated upon an absence of knowledge. Certain cloud services (especially SaaS) services are simply intended to process personal data. As a result, the cloud provider cannot reasonably claim to be unaware of the fact that processing of personal data is taking place. Moreover, if the cloud customer complies with his obligation to ensure an appropriate legal binding of the provider[2232], the latter will by definition have knowledge of the fact that his service is used to process personal data (even in case of PaaS or IaaS services). Hence the cloud provider would no longer be "unknowing" of the nature of the content or activity. Second, in situations where the cloud provider does not have actual or constructive knowledge of the fact that personal data are being processed (e.g. if the cloud customer failed to obtain appropriate safeguards), the provider should be able to argue that the event giving rise to the damage cannot reasonably be attributed to him.[2233] Therefore, the practical impact in terms of actual liability exposure of most cloud providers may be quite limited.[2234] From the provider's perspective, however, the formal recognition of the applicability of the hosting regime via Article 2(2)c of the GDPR provides additional legal certainty and help it to assess its legal risks when offering cloud services to EEA-based cloud customers.

2231 *Id.*

2232 Cf. *supra*, no. 1051.

2233 See Article 82(3) of the GDPR.

2234 In the same vein (regarding search engines): B. Van Alsenoy, A. Kuczerawy and J. Ausloos, "Search Engines after *Google Spain*: Internet@Liberty or Privacy@Peril?", *l.c.*, 60–62.

CHAPTER 5
INTERNET SEARCH ENGINES

1. INTRODUCTION

1077. INFORMATION LOCATION TOOLS – Internet search engines facilitate the location and retrieval of information. Specifically, they help their users to find relevant content amidst the abundance of content that is available online.[2235] Without these services, locating relevant information on the web would often be a challenge.[2236] With the help of search engines, however, information on just about any topic can be retrieved with considerable ease.

1078. BENEFITS – The societal benefits of internet search engines are tremendous. On a daily basis, people all over the world use search engine services for various activities, such as shopping, research and entertainment. People also use search engines to get in touch with new ideas or to stay abreast of global developments. It is fair to say that search engines play a pivotal role in today's information society. They also promote fundamental values such as freedom of expression and access to information. As observed by the Committee of Ministers of the Council of Europe:

> "Search engines enable a worldwide public to seek, receive and impart information and ideas and other content in particular to acquire knowledge, engage in debate and participate in democratic processes."[2237]

1079. PRIVACY IMPACT – At the same time, internet search engines have also raised numerous privacy concerns. A distinction can be made between two sets of concerns: those relating to (1) the users of search engine services

---

2235 B. Van Alsenoy, A. Kuczerawy and J. Ausloos, "Search Engines after *Google Spain*: Internet@ Liberty or Privacy@Peril?", *l.c.*, p. 5.

2236 As Solove put it: "*Without search engines, the Internet would be an endless expanse of digital babble, and finding any particular piece of information would be akin to locating a specific grain of sand in the Sahara Desert.*" (D.J. Solove, *The Future of Reputation: Gossip, Rumor and Privacy on the Internet*, 2007, New Haven, Yale University Press, p. 9).

2237 Council of Europe, Recommendation of the Committee of Ministers to member States on the protection of human rights with regard to search engines, CM/Rec(2012)3, Adopted by the Committee of Ministers on 4 April 2012 at the 1139th meeting of the Ministers' Deputies, paragraph 1.

and those relating to (2) search targets.[2238] The first set focuses on the privacy interests of people who use internet search engines. Individuals reveal a lot of information about themselves when searching for information online: about their personal interests, their travel plans, their political beliefs, their sexual preferences, their medical conditions, etc. In fact, the data contained in a search-query log can be far more revealing than the contents of a private email or telephone conversation.[2239] The second set of concerns focuses on the privacy interests of "search targets". Internet search engines have made it relatively easy to find out information about just about anyone. By using a search engine, one can easily aggregate personal data which would otherwise remain dispersed across company websites, newspaper articles, social networking pages, blogs, etc. Internet search engines have, in other words, significantly reduced the transaction costs of compiling a comprehensive profile about a specific person.[2240] As a result, people have become increasingly concerned with the information to which search engines refer.

1080. A RIGHT TO BE DELISTED? – Due to their impact, the providers of internet search engines are often confronted with requests to remove certain references from their search results. For example, private individuals might ask a search engine to stop referring to one or more web pages which contain personal data about them. The removal of references to harmful or privacy-intrusive content from search results can offer considerable relief for the affected individuals. At the same time, such a mechanism would give rise to a number of questions: do search engine providers have an obligation to accommodate such requests? Does it make any difference whether the content in question was lawfully published or not? Should a search engine operator be charged with drawing the balance between freedom of expression and privacy? These questions were at the heart of *Google Spain*[2241], a case decided by the Court of Justice on 13 May 2014.

1081. SCOPE LIMITATION – The objective of this chapter is to analyse how the EU data protection framework relates to the activities of internet search engines. In the interest of brevity, this chapter will limit itself to analysis of the processing of personal data found on web pages and in search results. Personal data which is collected by internet search engines directly from their users are outside the scope of this chapter. This issue has already been treated extensively by

---

2238 See e.g. O. Tene, "What Google Knows: Privacy and Internet Search Engines", *Utah Law Review* 2008, no. 4, p. 1440 et seq.

2239 *Ibid*, p. 1442–1443.

2240 *Ibid*, p. 1440. Without search engines, the visibility of much of these data would remain limited: even though they might be publicly accessible, uncovering and compiling all of these data would often be difficult and resource-intensive. (*Id.*).

2241 Judgment in *Google Spain* C-131/12, EU:C:2014:317.

scholars[2242] and regulators[2243], and is also less relevant to the research question of this book.

1082. TERMINOLOGY – For purposes of simplicity, the terms "search engine" and "search engine provider" shall be used as synonyms for the terms "internet search engine" and "internet search engine provider" respectively. The reader should note, however, that the term "search engine" is also used in a more generic sense, i.e. to refer to any technical component designed to facilitate discovery of resources within an (open or closed) information system. In the context of this chapter, the term "search engine" is used to refer to information retrieval systems designed to facilitate the location and retrieval of content which is publicly accessible via the Internet.

1083. OUTLINE – This chapter will begin by identifying the main actors involved in the publication and retrieval of online information. Next, it will analyse the legal status ("role") of each actor, as interpreted by regulators, scholars and courts. After that, we will describe the main responsibilities of each of these actors in relation to their processing of personal data found on webpages.[2244]

2. ACTORS

1084. ACTORS OVERVIEW – The following five actors may be considered as being particularly relevant to the availability, location and retrieval of personal data online:

(1) Search engine providers;
(2) Website publishers;

2242 See e.g. O. Tene, "What Google Knows: Privacy and Internet Search Engines", *l.c.*, p. 1140–1464 and E. Kosta, C. Kalloniatis, L. Mitrou and E. Kavakli, "Search Engines: Gateway to a New 'Panopticon'?", in S. Fischer-Hübner a.o. (eds.), *Trust, Privacy and Security in Digital Business*, Lecture Notes in Computer Science Volume 5695, 2009, p. 11–21.

2243 See e.g. International Data Protection and Privacy Commissioners' Conference: Resolution on Privacy Protection and Search Engines, 28th edition, 2–3 November 2006, London; Agencia Española de Protección de Datos (Spanish Data Protection Agency), "Statement on Internet Search Engines", p. 4 et seq, 1 December 2007; Article 29 Data Protection Working Party, "Opinion 1/2008 on data protection issues related to search engines", WP 148, 4 April 2008, p. 7 et seq.

2244 Substantial portions of this chapter consist of parts of a joint research paper written together with two of my former colleagues, Aleksandra Kuczerawy and Jef Ausloos (B. Van Alsenoy, A. Kuczerawy and J. Ausloos, "Search Engines after *Google Spain*: Internet@Liberty or Privacy@ Peril?", *ICRI Working Paper Series*, Working paper 15/2013, September 2013, 74 p.) The parts reproduced here correspond, for the most part, with my personal contributions to this paper. However, the entire paper was a joint work and therefore their contributions should be duly noted. Explicit references to the joint paper are therefore also made throughout this chapter.

(3) Content providers;
(4) End-users; and
(5) Infrastructure Service providers.[2245]

1085. Visual representation – The aforementioned actors interact with each other in a variety of ways. The following figure provides a – highly simplified – representation of how these actors typically interact with one and other to facilitate the retrieval of data contained on publicly available websites. It is intended to be conceptual rather than factual.

Figure 6. Main actors internet search engines

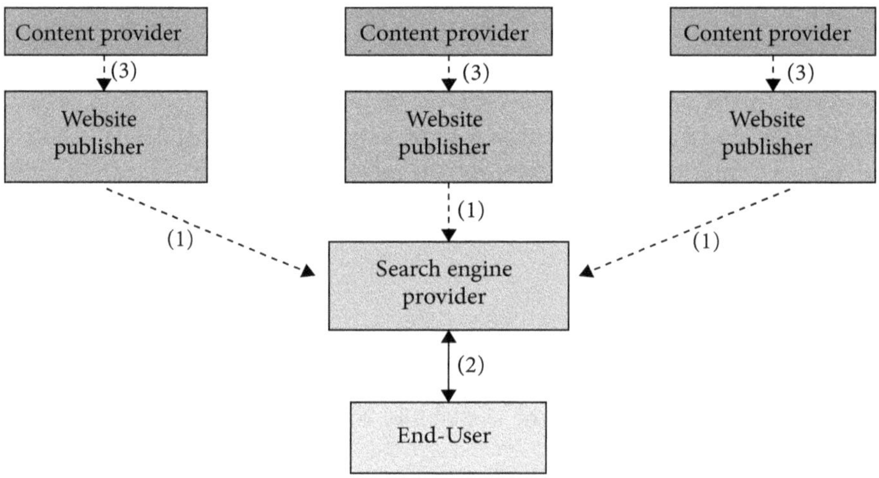

1086. Legend – The arrows in Figure 6 indicate that an exchange of personal data is taking place. Exchanges of personal data which are relevant to the current analysis our mainly uni-directional (with the exception of the interaction between end-users and the search engine provider). Solid black arrows were

[2245] The inventory of actors provided here was composed on the basis of a literature study of academic publications and regulatory guidance concerning internet search engines. The primary sources of reference were: J. Van Hoboken, *Search engine freedom. On the implications of the right to freedom of expression for the legal governance of Web search engines*, Academisch Proefschrift ter verkrijging van de graad van doctor aan de Universiteit van Amsterdam, defended on 23 March 2012, 357 p.; M.L. Boonk, *Zeker over zoeken? Naar een juridisch kader voor verichtingen van zoeksystemen met betrekking tot via internet beschikbare open content*, 2013, Zutphen, Uitgeverij Paris, 466 p.; Agencia Española de Protección de Datos, "Statement on Internet Search Engines", *l.c.*, 15 p. and Article 29 Data Protection Working Party, "Opinion 1/2008 on data protection issues related to search engines", *l.c.*, 29 p. A common denominator among the selected entities is that they (1) process personal data which is (being) made publicly accessible via the Internet and/or (2) are instrumental in the retrieval of such data.

used to depict data exchanges in which the end-user is actively involved at the moment of delivery of the search engine service. Dashed grey arrows depict the transfers of personal data prior to delivery of the search engine service to the end-user. Over the following sections, a brief description is provided of each of the actors and interactions displayed in Figure 6.

2.1. SEARCH ENGINE PROVIDER

1087. Main characteristics – In the context of this chapter, a search engine provider is understood as an entity that offers an information retrieval service for online content.[2246] These services are typically made available to the public at large at no monetary cost. The primary source of revenue for the providers of such search engines is derived from advertising.[2247]

1088. Processing activities – Search engine providers undertake a range of technical operations in order to provide their users with the search functionality. The following paragraphs will outline, by way of illustration, how search engine provider Google has described the operation of its search engine service. Similar operations are, however, undertaken by other search engine providers. Google identifies the following sets of operations[2248]:

(1) crawling;
(2) indexing;
(3) algorithmic analysis;
(4) retrieval;
(5) ranking; and
(6) fighting spam.

1089. Crawling – "Crawling" is generally understood as the use of software programs that make requests for online material.[2249] These programs, also referred to as "crawlers" or "spiders", are configured to look for information on

[2246] Based on J. Van Hoboken, *Search engine freedom. On the implications of the right to freedom of expression for the legal governance of Web search engines*, *o.c.*, p. 41. See also the definition provided by M.L. Boonk, who defines a search engine as "*a system which assists end-users in finding relevant information on the internet*" (personal translation) (M.L. Boonk, *Zeker over zoeken?*, *o.c.*, p. 36).

[2247] OECD, *The Economic and Social Role of Internet Intermediaries*, 2010, Paris, OECD Publishing, p. 12.

[2248] See Google, "How search works – the Story", available at http://www.google.com/insidesearch/howsearchworks/thestory/ (last accessed 19 January 2019). See also B. Van Alsenoy, A. Kuczerawy and J. Ausloos, "Search Engines after *Google Spain*: Internet@Liberty or Privacy@Peril?", *l.c.*, p. 11–12.

[2249] J. Van Hoboken, *Search engine freedom. On the implications of the right to freedom of expression for the legal governance of Web search engines*, *o.c.*, p. 41.

the Internet, "*according to a set of criteria which tell it where to go and when*".[2250] According to Google, its spiders

> "start by fetching a few web pages, then they follow the links on those pages, and fetch the pages they point to, and follow all the links on those pages [...] and so on [...] until we've indexed a pretty big chunk of the Web".[2251]

1090. Indexing – Once the relevant web pages have been fetched (i.e. a copy has been collected), the content of these pages is analysed and "parsed"[2252] for purposes of indexation.[2253] Google compares its search engine index to an index found in the back of a book, in that it "*includes information about words and their locations*".[2254] It is this index which is consulted when a search engine user enters a search query.[2255]

1091. Algorithmic analysis – As a user enters a search term, the search engine provider may try to gain a better understanding of what the user is looking for by analysing the search terms. For example, the provider might compare the entered search terms not only to keywords, but also to synonyms of that word. It may also check for common spelling mistakes or consider

---

2250 *Ibid*, p. 42–42.

2251 Matt Cutts (Google Quality Group Engineer), *How Search Works*, s30-s44, available at http://www.youtube.com/watch?v=BNHR6IQJGZs (last accessed 19 January 2019).

2252 See J. Van Hoboken, *Search engine freedom. On the implications of the right to freedom of expression for the legal governance of Web search engines*, o.c., p. 43 ("*The parser is the processing tool between the crawler and the index. [...] The pieces of content the crawler finds are not the same in size, sort, language, code, and other characteristics, so the parser need to normalize them for the index. It also extracts a number of related data and meta-data that can be useful for the search engine's technology*").

2253 See also U. Kohl, "Google: the rise and rise of online intermediaries in the governance of the Internet and beyond (Part 2)", *International Journal of Law and Information Technology* 2013, p. 5. Google states that it uses a "knowledge graph" to sort pages "*by their content and other factors*" (http://www.google.com/intl/en/insidesearch/howsearchworks/thestory/index.html). For more information on knowledge graphs and structural parsing see L. Zhang, *Knowledge Graph Theory and Structural Parsing*, PhD Thesis, University of Twente, 2002, 232 p.

2254 See http://www.google.com/intl/en/insidesearch/howsearchworks/crawling-indexing.html (last accessed 17 May 2013). This is of a course a somewhat simplified representation: while keywords and references may be the basic elements of the index, a search engine's index also contains additional (meta-)information, which may for example be used to apply the ranking algorithms (J. Van Hoboken, *Search engine freedom. On the implications of the right to freedom of expression for the legal governance of Web search engines*, o.c., p. 43).

2255 "*[W]hen you do a Google search, you aren't actually searching the web, you're searching Google's index of the web*" (Matt Cutts (Google Quality Group Engineer), *How Search Works*, o.c., s17–23). See also the Opinion of Advocate General Jääskinen in Google Spain, C-131/12, ECLI:EU:C:2013:424, paragraph 34: "*[S]earch results displayed by an internet search engine are not based on an instant search of the whole World Wide Web, but they are gathered from content that the internet search engine has previously processed. This means that the internet search engine has retrieved contents from existing websites and copied, analysed and indexed that content on its own devices. This retrieved content contains personal data if any of the source web pages do.*"

translations. A feature advertised by Google is its so-called "Knowledge Graph", a tool designed to map out the relationships between real-world objects (e.g. "Benjamin Franklin" and "Philadelphia") with a view of enhancing users' search experiences.[2256] Google also provides an "autocomplete" function, whereby it suggests possible search queries based on the information users have begun typing in the search box (e.g. a user typing "New York" might see suggestions for "New York Times" or "New Yorker").[2257]

1092. Retrieval and ranking – The search query, together with the provider's "interpretation" of it, is then used to consult the search engine's index. This exercise typically yields a large number of possible results. Not all results are equal, however. In determining the order of results, search engine providers apply what is commonly referred to as a "ranking algorithm". Google's ranking algorithm reportedly has included over two hundred factors, such as "site and page quality"[2258], "freshness", "user context" (e.g. location, web history), etc.[2259] A search engine provider might also, either autonomously or on the basis of user settings, filter out certain results based on their content (e.g. by filtering out what it believes to be "adult" images or content which has been reported as being "offensive").[2260] In addition, a search engine provider might also have a policy to "downgrade" certain types content, either manually or automatically (e.g. because it considers the website to be engaged in "spam").[2261]

1093. User data vs. third-party data – Personal data processed by search engines are typically divided into two categories: user data and third-party data.[2262] *User data* comprises all data relating to the individuals who use a particular search engine – in their capacity of users. These data are either (a)

2256 See e.g. Google, "Introducing the knowledge graph", 2012, available at http://www.youtube.com/watch?v=mmQl6VGvX-c (last accessed 19 January 2019).

2257 See Google, "Autocomplete", accessible at https://support.google.com/websearch/answer/106230?hl=en (last accessed 6 January 2019).

2258 The "quality" of a website or page is determined by a variety of "signals" which are used to infer the trustworthiness, reputability or authority of a site (http://www.google.com/intl/en/insidesearch/howsearchworks/thestory/index.html). One of these signals is "PageRank", an algorithm which determines the relevancy of a webpage by looking inter alia at the number of times it is linked to by other web pages. (U. Kohl, "Google: the rise and rise of online intermediaries in the governance of the Internet and beyond (Part 2)", *l.c.*, p. 5).

2259 http://www.google.com/intl/en/insidesearch/howsearchworks/thestory/index.html (last accessed 17 May 2013).

2260 For an example see Google's "SafeSearch" https://support.google.com/websearch/answer/510?hl=nl (last accessed 19 January 2019).

2261 See e.g. http://www.google.com/intl/en/insidesearch/howsearchworks/fighting-spam.html. For a more general overview of Google's policies affecting the search results it yields see http://www.google.com/intl/en/insidesearch/howsearchworks/policies.html (last accessed 17 May 2013).

2262 Agencia Española de Protección de Datos (Spanish Data Protection Agency), "Statement on Internet Search Engines", *l.c.*, p. 1.

actively provided by the user to the search engine provider; (b) derived from his or her use of the service; or (c) obtained from other sources.[2263] *Third-party data*, on the other hand, refers to data about individuals which is drawn from (other) websites and displayed in the results pages of search engines.[2264] For example, if a newspaper article or blog post references an individual by name, this name might be included in a page description (or "snippet"[2265]) displayed on the results page. As explained earlier, this chapter will only analyse the processing of such third-party data.[2266]

1094. Data flows – Arrows (1) in figure 6 depict the collection of personal data that takes place when internet search engines crawl the web. Arrow (1) is uni-directional as crawling in principle involves only the collection of personal data, not disclosure of personal data. Arrow (2) depicts the interaction between the end-user and the provider of the search engine service. Arrow (2) is bi-directional because (a) the results presented by the search engine operator may include personal data and (b) the search queries entered by the user may include personal data.

2.2. WEBSITE PUBLISHERS AND CONTENT PROVIDERS

1095. Main characteristics – In the context of this chapter, a website publisher is understood as the natural or legal person that makes one or more webpages publically accessible through the internet. Content included in a publically accessible webpage may be authored by the website publisher, by a third-party ("content provider"), or both. In other words, it is possible that the role of publisher and content provider coincide, but this is not necessarily the case.

2263 Examples include IP addresses, user preferences, clickstream data, user names (where applicable), etc.

2264 Agencia Española de Protección de Datos (Spanish Data Protection Agency), "Statement on Internet Search Engines", *l.c.*, p. 2–3.

2265 Google describes "snippets" as "*small previews of information, such as a page's title and short descriptive text, about each search result*" (http://www.google.com/intl/en/insidesearch/howsearchworks/algorithms.html). See also the Opinion of Advocate General Jääskinen in *Google Spain*, C-131/12, ECLI:EU:C:2013:424, paragraph 35 ("*internet search engines often display additional content alongside the link to the original website. There can be text extracts, audiovisual content or even snapshots of the source web pages. This preview information can be at least in part retrieved from the devices of the internet search engine service provider, and not instantly from the original website. This means that the service provider actually holds the information so displayed*").

2266 In other words: the analysis of the role and responsibilities of search engines under data protection law only concerns the processing at issue in *Google Spain* and does not pertain to the data protection obligations which search engines have in relation to their users (in their capacity as users).

1096. DATA DISCLOSURE – There are several ways in which website content can wind up in the index of a search engine. The most common way is by simply posting the content online and waiting for the search engine's crawlers to come by and include it.[2267] In this regard, it is important to note that the publisher of a website can signal to search engines it does not wish for its pages to be indexed.[2268] The publisher can do this through the so-called *Robots Exclusion Protocol*, a protocol whereby the administrator of a website stores a file ("robots. txt") on the website's server specifying an access policy for web robots (e.g. web crawlers used by search engines).[2269] Specifically, the robots.txt file can be used to specify for which types of robots ("user-agent") the website publisher wishes to "disallow" access.[2270] Absent such specification, it is assumed that the website publisher wishes for all its pages to be indexed.[2271] Website publishers can actually also try to optimise the way in which search engines include them in their search results, for example by using page description metatags.[2272]

1097. DATA FLOWS – Arrow (1) depicts the disclosure of data by website publishers to internet search engines. Arrow (3) depicts the disclosure of data from content providers to website publishers.

2.3. END-USERS

1098. MAIN CHARACTERISTICS – End-users are natural persons who make use of internet search engines to locate relevant information online. Search queries performed by end-users can be categorized into three broad categories,

---

2267 J. Van Hoboken, *Search engine freedom. On the implications of the right to freedom of expression for the legal governance of Web search engines*, *o.c.*, p. 53. Other ways include participation in paid placement programs or other contracts between website publishers and search engine providers. (*Id.*).

2268 X. "About /robots.txt", not dated, accessible at http://www.robotstxt.org/robotstxt.html (last accessed 12 January 2019).

2269 M. Koster, "A Standard for Robot Exclusion", not dated, available at http://www.robotstxt.org/orig.html (last accessed 12 January 2019).

2270 *Id.* See also Opinion of Advocate General Jääskinen in *Google Spain*, C-131/12, ECLI:EU:C:2013:424, paragraphs 41–42. ("*Source web pages are kept on host servers connected to internet. The publisher of source web pages can make use of 'exclusion codes' for the operation of the internet search engines. Exclusion codes advise search engines not to index or to store a source web page or to display it within the search results. Their use indicates that the publisher does not want certain information on the source web page to be retrieved for dissemination through search engines.*")

2271 In this regard, it is important to note that the Robots Exclusion Protocol is a de facto standard, which is not enforced by anybody and there are no guarantees that all web robots will abide by it. M. Koster, "A Standard for Robot Exclusion", not dated, available at http://www.robotstxt.org/orig.html (last accessed 12 January 2019).

2272 For more information see Google, "Search Engine Optimization (SEO) – Starter Guide", available at https://support.google.com/webmasters/answer/7451184?hl=en (last accessed 12 January 2019).

namely "informational", "navigational" and "transactional".[2273] When the user simply wants to find information about particular topic which is presumed to be available online, the search query is considered "informational".[2274] A search query is considered "navigational" if the end-user makes use of a search engine to find a specific website which he or she knew (or assumed) to be present on the web.[2275] Finally, a search query is "transactional" if the end-user aims to reach a destination where further interaction would take place, such as making a purchase.[2276]

1099. DATA DISCLOSURE AND COLLECTION – In order to be provided with the most relevant search results, the end-user will enter the search terms it considers most relevant to his or her topic of interest. If the object of the search is to find out more information about a specific person, the end-user will typically enter that person's name as a search term. Once the search term has been entered, the provider of the search engine will provide a list of results which the provider deems might relevant for the user. If the search term was a name, the list of search results will typically include links to websites which include the name of the person that was used as a search query.

1100. DATA FLOWS – Arrow (2) depicts the information flow between end-users and search engine providers. The arrow is bi-directional as end-users can both disclose personal data to search engine providers (through search terms) and collect personal from search engine providers (through search engine results and the accompanying "snippets").

2.4. INFRASTRUCTURE (SERVICE) PROVIDERS

1101. MAIN CHARACTERISTICS – Infrastructure (service) providers are the entities that operate the technical infrastructure which is necessary to support the interaction between web publishers, search engines and end-users. Examples include Internet Service Providers ("ISPs"), hosting service providers, device manufactures, the providers of operating systems, etc. While the role of these entities will not be discussed in detail, it is nevertheless worth noting their important role in supporting the dissemination and retrieval of information online.

2273 J. Van Hoboken, *Search engine freedom. On the implications of the right to freedom of expression for the legal governance of Web search engines*, *o.c.*, p. 50.

2274 *Id.*

2275 *Id.*

2276 *Id.*

3. ROLES

3.1. SEARCH ENGINE PROVIDER

1102. Outline – In *Google Spain*, the Court of Justice was asked to assess the legal status of search engine providers under Directive 95/46. In light of the importance and relevance of *Google Spain* for the research question of this book, this section will present

(1) the question referred in *Google Spain*;
(2) the oral arguments of the parties in *Google Spain*;
(3) the 2008 Opinion by the Article 29 Working Party;
(4) the opinion of the Advocate-General in *Google Spain*; and
(5) the holding of the CJEU.

A. *Question referred in Google Spain*

1103. Control over "third-party data" – In its request for a preliminary ruling[2277], the Spanish *Audencia Nacional* asked the CJEU to determine whether

> "Article 2(d) of Directive 95/46 [must] be interpreted as meaning that the undertaking managing [Google Search] is to be regarded as the 'controller' of the personal data contained in the web pages that it indexes".

For purposes of clarity, it should be noted that this question only concerned the processing undertaken by Google itself (i.e. the location, indexation, temporary storage and making available of third-party content).[2278] In other words, the question did not extend to the processing activities undertaken by website publishers, content providers and/or end-users of the search engines service.

B. *Oral arguments*[2279]

1104. Arguments by Google – Google's counsel advanced several arguments as to why the search engine provider should not be considered as a "controller" within the meaning of Article 2(d). To be considered a "controller", it was argued, it is first and foremost required that the entity concerned has the objective ("purpose") of processing personal data. Google's search engine, on the

2277 Judgment in *Google Spain* C-131/12, EU:C:2014:317.
2278 See questions 2.1 and 2.2 of the Reference for a preliminary ruling.
2279 The account of the oral arguments presented here is based on personal notes made while attending the public hearing in *Google Spain*. It is not based on the written submissions of the parties to the CJEU.

other hand, indexes websites "*indiscriminately*" (i.e. without targeting personal data per se). Therefore, the search engine provider cannot be considered to be acting as a "controller" for its processing of personal data contained on those websites.[2280] Instead, it is the publisher of the information who should be labelled as the sole controller of this data. After all, it was argued, Google's intervention is *purely accessory* in nature: it is merely making information published by others more readily accessible. If a publisher, for whatever reason, decided to remove certain information from its website, this information would (eventually) be removed from Google's index and no longer appear in its search results. As a result, Google's counsel continued, the role of a search engine should be thought of as that of an "intermediary" as described in Articles 12–14 of the Directive 2000/31 or that of a telecommunications service provider as described in recital (47) of Directive 95/46.[2281]

1105. Opposing arguments – Quite a different line of argumentation could be heard coming from the European Commission and the Member States. They emphasized the need to distinguish between the processing activities of publishers on the one hand, and the processing activities of search engines on the other hand. Search engines, it was argued, carry out many operations (collection of website content, storage, analysis, ranking, etc.) which are completely distinct from those carried out by the publisher of the information.[2282] For these operations, search engine providers exclusively determine both the purposes and the means.[2283] As a result, search engines should not be considered as mere "intermediaries", but rather as the providers of a value-added service for which they carry their own responsibilities.[2284] To strengthen the argument, it was

---

2280 A similar line of argument was also put forth in relation to question 2.1, which essentially asked whether Google's location, indexation, temporary storage and making available of personal data should be considered as processing within the meaning of Article 2(b) of the Directive. See B. Van Alsenoy, A. Kuczerawy and J. Ausloos, "Search Engines after *Google Spain*: Internet@Liberty or Privacy@Peril?", *l.c.*, p. 12–13.

2281 Recital (47) of Directive 95/46 states that "*Whereas where a message containing personal data is transmitted by means of a telecommunications or electronic mail service, the sole purpose of which is the transmission of such messages, the controller in respect of the personal data contained in the message will normally be considered to be the person from whom the message originates, rather than the person offering the transmission services; whereas, nevertheless, those offering such services will normally be considered controllers in respect of the processing of the additional personal data necessary for the operation of the service*".

2282 See also Agencia Española de Protección de Datos (Spanish Data Protection Agency), "Statement on Internet Search Engines", *l.c.*, p. 7 ("*Internet search engines carry out information processing of their own, distinct from that of the websites to which they facilitate access*").

2283 According to this view, Google's "purpose" is to list (references to) relevant website content in its search results with a view of generating revenue from advertising. Its "means" include the use of web crawlers, indexation techniques, caches, ranking algorithms, etc., all of which are controlled exclusively by Google.

2284 It is worth noting that Google's opponents explicitly acknowledged that the search engine provider cannot be considered a controller for the initial act of publication (i.e. the uploading

asserted that the harm at issue mainly resulted from Google's activities: if the content at issue would not be (so readily) available through its search engine, the damage to the plaintiff's reputation would be considerably less.[2285]

C. *Opinion of the Article 29 Working Party*

1106. Ambiguous approach – In 2008, the Article 29 Working Party adopted an Opinion on data protection issues related to search engines. The Opinion addressed the role of search engine provider in relation to third-party data, albeit in somewhat cryptic terms. Specifically, the Working Party reasoned that

> "The principle of proportionality requires that to the extent that a search engine provider acts purely as an intermediary, it should not be considered to be the principal controller with regard to the content related processing of personal data that is taking place. In this case the principal controllers of personal data are the information providers. The formal, legal and practical control the search engine has over the personal data involve is usually limited to the possibility of removing data from its servers. With regard to the removal of personal data from their index and search results, search engines have sufficient control to consider them as controllers (either alone or jointly with others) in those cases [...]".[2286]

This language appeared to help both sides in *Google Spain*: on the one hand, it offered support to Google's claim that it should not be considered a ("principal") controller of the personal data contained in the web pages that it indexes, at least in so far as it acts as an intermediary. On the other hand, the Opinion also offered support to the claim that a search engine does act as a controller towards its own processing operations, including indexation and the inclusion of content in its search results.

1107. Proportionality test – Perhaps the most striking element of the Working Party's reasoning is its reference to the principle of proportionality. Instead of limiting itself to a mechanical application of the "controller" concept,

---

of content and/or subsequent display on the website). Rather, they argued that the collection, aggregation and dissemination of personal data undertaken by the search engine provider should be perceived as a distinct set of processing operations for which Google carries a responsibility independent from that of the publisher.

2285 See also Article 29 Data Protection Working Party, "Opinion 1/2008 on data protection issues related to search engines", WP 148, 4 April 2008, p. 5 ("*Some search engines republish data in a so-called 'cache'. By retrieving and grouping widespread information of various types about a single person, search engines can create a new picture, with a much higher risk to the data subject than if each item of data posted on the internet remained separate. The representation and aggregation capabilities of search engines can significantly affect individuals, both in their personal lives and within society, especially if the personal data in the search results are incorrect, incomplete or excessive*") (emphasis added).

2286 Article 29 Data Protection Working Party, "Opinion 1/2008 on data protection issues related to search engines", *l.c.*, p. 14 (emphasis added).

the Article 29 Working Party used the principle of proportionality as a means to delineate the obligations of search engines under data protection law. In my opinion, the approach advanced by the Working Party may have resulted in the right outcome, but could have benefited from a more detailed discussion. In particular, Opinion 1/2008 failed to explain the relationship between the criteria in the legal definition of controller on the one hand, and the nature and scope of an entity's obligations under data protection law on the other hand. This point will be further developed later on.[2287]

D. *Opinion of the Advocate-General*

1108. Preliminary observations – The Opinion of Advocate General Jääskinen started by highlighting the many changes that have occurred since the enactment of Directive 95/46 and in particular "the emergence of the internet and the various related phenomena".[2288] Given this radical change in environment, the Advocate General argued that one should avoid a "blind literal interpretation"[2289] of the controller concept. Instead,

> "the principle of proportionality, the objectives of the Directive and the means provided therein for their attainment must be taken into account in order to achieve a balanced and reasonable outcome".[2290]

1109. Knowledge and intent – Having set forth his preliminary observations, the Advocate General argued that

> "[T]he general scheme of the Directive, most language versions and the individual obligations it imposes on the controller are based on the idea of responsibility of the controller over the personal data processed in the sense that the controller is aware of the existence of a certain defined category of information amounting to personal data and the controller processes this data with some intention which relates to their processing as personal data."[2291]

2287 See *infra*, nos. 1162 et seq.

2288 Opinion of Advocate General Jääskinen in *Google Spain*, C-131/12, ECLI:EU:C:2013:424, paragraph 77. Search engines were still "*at their nascent stage*", he continued, and "*the provisions of the Directive simply do not take into account the fact that enormous masses of decentrally hosted electronic documents and files are accessible from anywhere on the globe and that their contents can be copied and analysed and disseminated by parties having no relation whatsoever to their authors or to those who have uploaded them onto a host server connected to the internet.*" (*Ibid*, paragraph 78).

2289 *Ibid*, paragraph 81.

2290 *Ibid*, paragraph 79.

2291 *Ibid*, paragraph 82 (original emphases modified).

It therefore followed, according to the Advocate General, that the entity concerned must be "*aware of what kind of personal data he is processing and why*"[2292] in order to be considered a "controller". Specifically

> "the data processing must appear to him as processing of personal data, that is 'information related to an identifiable person in some semantically relevant way and not a mere computer code."[2293]

1110. No control over third-party pages – Based on the foregoing considerations, the Advocate General concluded that search engines cannot be considered a "controller" of personal data on third-party source web pages. After all, he reasoned, a search engine provider

> "is not 'aware' of the existence of personal data in any other sense than as a statistical fact web pages are likely to include personal data. In the course of processing of the source web pages for the purposes of crawling, analysing and indexing, personal data does not manifest itself as such in any particular way."[2294]

The Advocate General further substantiated his argument by pointing to the fact that a search engine provider "*has no relationship with the content of third-party source web pages*", nor does it "*have any means of changing the information in the host servers*".[2295] He also pointed to recital (47) of the Directive, which stipulates that it is in principle the originator of a message (and not the provider of the communications service) which is to be considered as the controller of its content.[2296] Finally, the finding that search engine providers cannot "*in law or in fact*" fulfil the obligations of a controller in relation to the personal data on source web pages, mandated the conclusion that a search engine provider cannot be considered as a controller in this regard.[2297]

2292 *Ibid*, paragraph 83.

2293 *Ibid*, paragraph 83.

2294 *Ibid*, paragraph 84.

2295 *Ibid*, paragraph 86.

2296 *Ibid*, paragraph 87. The AG continued by saying that "*[t]his recital, as well as the exceptions to liability provided by the eCommerce Directive 2000/31 [...] builds on the legal principle according to which automated, technical and passive relationships to electronically stored or transmitted content do not create control or liability over it*" (*Id.*). In this regard, it is worth observing that recital (47) also considers that the providers of telecommunications and electronic mails services "*will normally be considered controllers in respect of the processing of the additional personal data necessary for the operation of the service*".

2297 *Ibid*, paragraph 89–90. According to the Advocate General, this absence of control also extends to data contained in the cache memory of an internet search engine ("*because the cache is the result of completely technical and automated processes producing a mirror image of the text data of the crawled web pages*") – except where the search engine provider decided not to comply with the exclusion codes. (*Ibid*, paragraphs 92–93).

1111. Control over the index – The foregoing observations made by the Advocate General seemed mainly to support the position of Google, at least in relation to their crawling activities. The index of a search engine, however, is a different matter. The Advocate General was quite resolute in his affirmation that search engine providers do "control" their indexes, which link key words to the relevant URL addresses.[2298] This conclusion was warranted because

> "[t]he service provider determines how the index is structured and may technically block certain search results [...] [and] decides whether exclusion codes on source web are to be complied with or not."[2299]

The Advocate General thus appeared to be of the opinion that the structuring and population of a search engine index does involve processing of personal data "in a semantically relevant way".[2300] The outcome of this approach is that search engine providers are not considered controllers with respect to their initial collection and use of personal data (i.e. "for the purposes of crawling, analysing and indexing"[2301]), but are considered controllers in relation to their index once it is established.[2302]

1112. Assessment – While the distinction made by the Advocate General seems logical at first, it is also a bit artificial.[2303] After all, EU data protection law arguably intends to cover all stages of the data processing life cycle, from its initial collection through to its eventual deletion.[2304] By differentiating between the moment of collection and the later use of this data, the Advocate General appears to place the initial processing activities of search engines outside of data protection law.[2305] Be that as it may, the Advocate General embraced the premise

---

2298 *Ibid*, paragraph 91.

2299 *Id.*

2300 *Ibid*, paragraph 83.

2301 *Ibid*, paragraph 84.

2302 See also B. Van Alsenoy, A. Kuczerawy and J. Ausloos, "Search Engines after *Google Spain*: Internet@Liberty or Privacy@Peril?", *l.c.*, p. 17–18.

2303 By using a similar line of reasoning, one could also argue that someone who sends out a drone mounted with a video camera to canvas certain areas or conducts an analysis of internet traffic should not be considered a controller for the data he collects (seeing as much of the collected data may be of a non-personal nature) until he actually watches (or otherwise analyses) this data and determines that personal data was in fact recorded.

2304 See also the definition of "processing" contained in Article 4(2) GDPR (previously: Article 2(b) Directive 95/46).

2305 The conclusion of the AG on this point appears to have been fuelled mainly by pragmatic considerations. For example, how can a controller provide a data subject with (prior) information in accordance with Article 13 or 14 if it does not yet know which data subjects it is dealing with? How can it ascertain accuracy? How can it ensure proportionality? Of course, nobody can be obliged to do the impossible (*impossibilium nulla est obligatio*). A more relevant question, however, is whether data controller obligations must indeed be interpreted in such a way that they actually prohibit data collection in situations where personal data

that the providers of search engine services carry out a distinct set of processing operations for which they carry their own data protection responsibilities. While one can disagree as to the precise moment at which these providers may be considered "in control" of the processing of personal data, the basic premise still stands.[2306]

E. *Holding of the CJEU*

1113. Purposes and means – In relation to the activities of locating information on the internet, indexing it automatically, storing it temporarily and making it available to internet users, the CJEU embraced the arguments put forward by the European Commission and the Member States. The Court considered that:

> "It is the search engine operator which determines the purposes and means of that activity and thus of the processing of personal data that it itself carries out within the framework of that activity and which must, consequently, be regarded as the 'controller' in respect of that processing [...]."[2307]

1114. Separate activities – The Court of Justice also recognized that the processing activities of search engines should be distinguished from those carried out by the publishers of websites.[2308]

> "the processing of personal data carried out in the context of the activity of a search engine can be distinguished from and is additional to that carried out by publishers of websites, consisting in loading those data on an internet page."

1115. Privacy impact – Finally, the Court of Justice also explicitly considered the impact of search engine services upon individual's privacy, acknowledging that search engines play a decisive role in the overall dissemination of information online:

> "[I]t is undisputed that that activity of search engines plays a decisive role in the overall dissemination of those data in that it renders the latter accessible to any internet user making a search on the basis of the data subject's name, including to internet users who otherwise would not have found the web page on which those data are published.

---

cannot be readily identified as such in advance. This issue will be investigated later on (cf. *infra*, nos. 1162 et seq).

2306 B. Van Alsenoy, A. Kuczerawy and J. Ausloos, "Search Engines after *Google Spain*: Internet@ Liberty or Privacy@Peril?", *l.c.*, p. 18–19.

2307 Judgment in *Google Spain*, C-131/12, EU:C:2014:317, paragraph 33.

2308 *Ibid*, paragraph 35.

Also, the organisation and aggregation of information published on the internet that are effected by search engines with the aim of facilitating their users' access to that information may, when users carry out their search on the basis of an individual's name, result in them obtaining through the list of results a structured overview of the information relating to that individual that can be found on the internet enabling them to establish a more or less detailed profile of the data subject.

Inasmuch as the activity of a search engine is therefore liable to affect significantly, and additionally compared with that of the publishers of websites, the fundamental rights to privacy and to the protection of personal data, the operator of the search engine as the person determining the purposes and means of that activity must ensure, within the framework of its responsibilities, powers and capabilities, that the activity meets the requirements of Directive 95/46 in order that the guarantees laid down by the directive may have full effect and that effective and complete protection of data subjects, in particular of their right to privacy, may actually be achieved."[2309]

3.2. WEBSITE PUBLISHERS AND CONTENT PROVIDERS

1116. WEBSITE PUBLISHER – The act of loading content on a publically accessible webpage constitutes "processing" of personal data within the meaning of EU data protection law.[2310] In cases where the content has been authored or selected by the website publisher, the publisher shall in principle be deemed a controller in relation to this processing activity.[2311] The scope of control of the website publisher in principle extends to (1) the decision to include personal data on website; (2) the decision to render personal data accessible via the internet and (3) allowing indexation by search engines (unless robots.txt is used in such a way to indicate the wish not to be indexed).[2312] In cases where the content was not authored or selected by the website publisher, but instead stored at the request of the recipient of the service, the legal status of the website publisher is similar to that of the OSN provider in relation to third-party data.[2313]

2309 Judgment in *Google Spain*, C-131/12, EU:C:2014:317, paragraph 36–38. See also paragraph 34 ("*Furthermore, it would be contrary not only to the clear wording of that provision but also to its objective – which is to ensure, through a broad definition of the concept of 'controller', effective and complete protection of data subjects – to exclude the operator of a search engine from that definition on the ground that it does not exercise control over the personal data published on the web pages of third parties.*").

2310 See Article 4(2) GDPR (previously: (see Article 2(b) Directive 95/46). See also Judgment in *Bodil Lindqvist*, C-101/01, EU:C:2003:596, paragraph 25.

2311 See also Opinion of Advocate General Jääskinen in Google Spain, C-131/12, ECLI:EU:C:2013:424, paragraph 40 ("*It follows from the above findings in Lindqvist that the publisher of source web pages containing personal data is a controller of processing of personal data within the meaning of the Directive. As such the publisher is bound by all the obligations the Directive imposes on the controllers.*")

2312 See also Opinion of Advocate General Jääskinen in Google Spain, C-131/12, ECLI:EU:C:2013:424, paragraph 41–42.

2313 Cf. *supra*, nos. 874 et seq.

1117. Content provider – Individuals posting content on a website shall in principle also be considered as controllers within the meaning of Article 2(d) of Directive 95/46 (unless they are acting on behalf of or under the authority of someone else).[2314]

3.3. END-USER

1118. Opinion advocate general – Few commentators have explicitly reflected upon the legal status of the end-users of search engines. Although the CJEU was not asked to assess the legal status of end-users, the Advocate General nevertheless indirectly reflected upon this issue as follows:

> "Let us think of a European law professor who has downloaded, from the Court's website, the essential case-law of the Court to his laptop computer. In terms of the Directive, the professor could be considered to be a 'controller' of personal data originating from a third party. The professor has files containing personal data that are processed automatically for search and consultation within the context of activities that are not purely personal or household related."[2315]

1119. Purposes and means – The example used by the Advocate General was mainly intended to caution the Court against an overly broad interpretation of the controller concept. Strictly speaking, however, the end-user does determine his own "purposes and means" when processing personal data by means of a search engine. As a result, end-users of search engines can be considered as controllers in relation to their own processing activities, namely (1) the entering of search terms containing personal data and (2) any further processing of personal data obtained through search results.

1120. Personal use exemption – Individuals who make use of internet search engines in a purely personal capacity shall in principle be exempted from compliance in accordance with Article 3(2) of Directive 95/46.[2316]

1121. Assessment – Many would agree with the Advocate General that applying EU data protection law to the end-users of search engines, even when they act outside of a context which is purely personal or household related, may lead to excessive and unreasonable legal consequences.[2317] On the other hand,

---

2314 See also *supra*, no. 880.

2315 Opinion of Advocate General Jääskinen in Google Spain, C-131/12, ECLI:EU:C:2013:424, paragraph 29.

2316 Cf. *supra*, nos. 966 et seq.

2317 See e.g. House of Lords, European Union Committee, "EU Data Protection Law: A 'right to be forgotten'?", HL Paper 40, London, The Stationairy Office Limited, 30 July 2014, at paragraph 41.

few would disagree that a prospective employer that uses search engines to obtain more information about job applicants should be viewed as a controller in relation to his collection and subsequent processing of information. Whether or not the qualification of an entity as controller in fact leads to excessive and unreasonable consequences, depends mainly on the responsibilities and other consequences associated with this qualification. This issue will be revisited later on.[2318]

3.4. INFRASTRUCTURE (SERVICE) PROVIDERS

1122. ISPs AND HOSTS – Infrastructure service providers, such as Internet Service Providers ("ISPs") and hosting service providers, act as controllers in relation to the processing of personal data they undertake in order to provide their services. The scope of control exercised by these entities in principle only extends to the processing of additional personal data (e.g. traffic data) necessary for the operation of the service and not to content stored on their servers or transmitted through their networks.[2319] In any event, they cannot be held liable for information stored or transmitted insofar as they meet the conditions for liability exemption contained in Articles 12–14 of the E-Commerce Directive.[2320]

4. ALLOCATION OF RESPONSIBILITY AND LIABILITY

1123. OUTLINE – The previous section concluded that each of the actors identified in section 2 can be considered as a "controller" within the meaning of EU data protection law, at least in relation to certain processing operations. This section will elaborate upon the legal implications of this conclusion.[2321] Rather than discuss the obligations of each entity separately, the analysis will be structured according to a number of basic data protection requirements. For each requirement, it will then be analysed how the obligations of each actor are currently interpreted. This approach will allow for a better evaluation regarding the extent to which the current allocation of responsibility and liability promotes effective implementation of data protection requirements. It will also enable reflection as to whether or not EU data protection law enables

---

2318 Cf. *infra*, nos. 1229 et seq.

2319 See recital (47) of Directive 95/46/EC.

2320 Article 2(4) GDPR.

2321 As noted above, this analysis only concerns the allocation of responsibility and risk in relation to the processing personal data included on websites. It does not pertain to the data protection obligations which search engines have in relation to their users (in their capacity as users).

the taking into account of other basic principles of EU law, such as the principle of proportionality.

4.1. LAWFULNESS

1124. Search engine provider – Search engines can in principle legitimate their processing of third-party data on Article 6(1)f GDPR.[2322] In his Opinion in *Google Spain*, the Advocate General identified three separate legitimate interests justifying the provision of search engine services:

> "(i) making information more easily accessible for internet users;
> (ii) rendering dissemination of the information uploaded on the internet more effective; and
> (iii) enabling various information society services supplied by the internet search engine service provider that are ancillary to the search engine, such as the provision of keyword advertising."[2323]

1125. Balance of interests – Article 6(1)f GDPR only legitimates the processing of personal data for as long as the interests served are not overridden by the interests or fundamental rights and freedoms of the data subject which require the protection of personal data (in particular where the data subject is a child). It is worth noting that Article 6(1)f also refers to the legitimate interests of third parties. Hence, the interests of search engine users – specifically their right to freedom of expression and information – may also be taken into account when considering the legitimacy of processing.[2324]

1126. Website publishers and content providers – Website publishers and content providers may have various legitimate reasons for posting personal data online. In his opinion, the Advocate General noted that web publication "*is a means for individuals to participate in debate or disseminate their own content or content uploaded by others on internet*".[2325] Website publishers and

---

2322 Previously: Article 7(f) Directive 95/46.

2323 Each of these legitimate interests correspond to three fundamental rights protected in the Charter: freedom of information and freedom of expression (both in Article 11) and freedom to conduct a business (Article 16). See Opinion of Advocate General Jääskinen in Google Spain, C-131/12, ECLI:EU:C:2013:424, paragraph 95. During oral arguments, the counsel for the European Commission also explicitly confirmed that the providing of a search engine service can be considered a legitimate interest within the meaning of Article 7(f) of Directive 95/46. See also Spanish Data Protection Agency (AEPD), "Statement on Internet Search Engines", *l.c.*, 6.

2324 B. Van Alsenoy, A. Kuczerawy and J. Ausloos, "Search Engines after *Google Spain*: Internet@ Liberty or Privacy@Peril?", *l.c.*, p. 30. See also *infra*, no. 1146.

2325 Opinion of Opinion of Advocate General Jääskinen in Google Spain, C-131/12, ECLI:EU:C:2013:424, paragraph 122.

content providers can therefore in principle also legitimate their processing activities on the basis of Article 6(1)f, provided also that the interests served are not overridden by the interests or fundamental rights and freedoms of the data subject.[2326] Depending on the circumstances, web publishers and content providers might also be to invoke other grounds of Article 6 GDPR, such as data subject consent.

1127. End-users – Internet users have the right to seek and receive information made available on the internet, both by consulting the source web pages or by using internet search engines.[2327] The processing of personal data undertaken by end-users when using a search engine may therefore also, as a matter of principle, be justified on the basis of Article 6(1)f (unless the search results are used in manner which constitutes an excessive interference with the interests, rights or fundamental freedoms of the individual concerned).

4.2. PRINCIPLES RELATING TO THE PROCESSING OF PERSONAL DATA

A. *Purpose specification and use limitation*

1128. Search engine provider – The purpose specification principle implies that search engines may only index personal data for pre-defined purposes. The stated mission of Google is "*to organize the world's information and make it universally accessible and useful*".[2328] In other words, the primary purpose of the search engine provider is to deliver the search engine service, at least as far as its processing of third-party data is concerned.

1129. Web publisher and content provider – Web publishers and content providers must also have a specific and legitimate purpose for making information available online. There are many such purposes imaginable:

[2326] B. Van Alsenoy, A. Kuczerawy and J. Ausloos, "Search Engines after *Google Spain*: Internet@ Liberty or Privacy@Peril?", *l.c.*, p. 30. In this regard, the Court of Justice noted that the ground justifying the publication of a piece of personal data on a website does not necessarily coincide with that which is applicable to the activity of search engines. Moreover, even where that is the case, the outcome of the weighing of the interests at issue may differ according to whether the processing carried out by the operator of a search engine or that carried out by the publisher of the web page. (Judgment in *Google Spain*, C-131/12, EU:C:2014:317, paragraph 86).

[2327] Opinion of Advocate General Jääskinen in *Google Spain*, C-131/12, ECLI:EU:C:2013:424, paragraph 121.

[2328] Google, "Our mission is to organize the world's information and make it universally accessible and useful", Google Company, not dated, available at https://www.google.com/about (last accessed 19 January 2019).

provisioning of information, news reporting, literary expression, etc. Regardless of the actual purposes pursued by a web publisher or content provider, the act of dissemination will generally constitute an exercise of his or her right to freedom of expression.[2329] In case of processing for "journalistic, literary or artistic" purposes, the content provider and/or web publisher may benefit from certain exemptions or derogations.[2330]

1130. END-USER – End-users may pursue various objectives when using internet search engines. As indicated earlier, search queries performed by end-users can generally be categorized into three broad categories, namely "informational", "navigational" and "transactional".[2331] The specific purpose for which an end-user makes use of a search engine may vary from one search query to another.

B. *Data minimisation*

1131. SEARCH ENGINE PROVIDER – In his Opinion in *Google Spain*, the Advocate General dealt rather succinctly with the principles of data quality. In his view, the index of a search engine complies with the criteria of adequacy, relevancy and proportionality "inasmuch as [...] the data corresponding to the search term really appears or has appeared on the linked web pages [...]".[2332] In other words: as long as the data corresponding to the search term really appears or has appeared on the linked web pages, it complies with the principle of data minimisation.[2333] As to the requirement that personal data should not be stored longer than necessary[2334], the Advocate-General was similarly succinct. He merely stated that this requirement should (also) be assessed "from the point of view of the processing in question that is provision of information location service, and not as an issue relating to the content of the source web pages."[2335]

1132. ASSESSMENT – Although brief, the reasoning of the Opinion of the Advocate General underlines an important point: controller obligations must be evaluated in light of the scope of their "control" as well as the purposes pursued by the processing. Given the stated purpose of search engines (to

2329 B. Van Alsenoy, A. Kuczerawy and J. Ausloos, "Search Engines after *Google Spain*: Internet@ Liberty or Privacy@Peril?", *l.c.*, p. 32.
2330 See Article 85 GDPR (previously: Article 9 Directive 95/46). See also *infra*, no. 1147.
2331 J. Van Hoboken, *Search engine freedom. On the implications of the right to freedom of expression for the legal governance of Web search engines*, *o.c.*, p. 50.
2332 Opinion of Advocate General Jääskinen in Google Spain, C-131/12, ECLI:EU:C:2013:424, paragraph 98.
2333 Article 5(1)c GDPR (previously: Article 6(1)c Directive 95/46).
2334 Article 5(1)e GDPR (previously: Article 6(1)e Directive 95/46).
2335 *Id.* In the context of search engines, this seems to imply that (personal) data will have to be removed when the original data is removed as well (or when exclusion codes are put in place).

help make online information more easily accessible), the Advocate General argued that the requirements of relevancy and adequacy are met as long as data corresponding to the search term actually appears or has appeared on the linked web pages.[2336] The Opinion of the Advocate General failed to consider, however, that the impact of the processing towards the individual concerned may be excessive in a particular situation. Arguably, it would be unreasonable to require the search engine provider to assess the potential impact of every search result on a proactive basis. Once the search engine is made aware, however, of the fact that the display of certain search results following a name search has a significant adverse impact on the privacy interests of the individuals concerned, the proportionality of processing must be reassessed.[2337]

1133. Website publishers and content providers – Website publishers and content providers must assess the potential impact of making personal data publically available prior to loading it onto a public webpage. In principle, they should also reassess, from time to time, whether it is still necessary to keep the personal data online in light of the purposes pursued by the processing. If appropriate, the website publisher should remove or anonymize personal data if it is no longer necessary to keep the data online in identifiable form, or consider the use of the robots.txt exclusion protocol.[2338]

1134. End-users – As a rule, it is impossible for end-users to determine in advance whether the search results retrieved by consulting an internet search engine shall be "adequate, relevant and limited to what is necessary in relation to the purposes for which they are collected". Only once the results have been retrieved can the end-user actually determine whether this is the case. As a result, the end-user can effectively only comply with the principle of proportionality after collection (e.g. by limiting further storage or subsequent use of personal data which has been retrieved using a search engine).

1135. Assessment – The previous paragraphs illustrate that the principle of data minimisation may impact different actors in different ways. Whereas website publishers and content providers are in principle obliged to assess the proportionality of disclosure ex ante, the provider of a general internet search

---

2336 In the same vein: M. Peguera, "The Shaky Ground of the Right to Be Delisted", (Draft, August 2015), *l.c.*, p. 37–39.

2337 See also *infra*, no. 1146.

2338 See also Tribunal Supremo. Sala de lo Civil, *A and B v Ediciones El Pais*, Judgment number 545/2015, ECLI:ES:TS:2015:4132. For a discussion see H. Tomlinson, "Case Law, Spain: A and B v Ediciones El Pais, Newspaper archive to be hidden from internet searches but no 're-writing of history'", *Inforrm's Blog*, 19 November 2015. See also Cour de Cassation, Arrêt C.15.0052.F, 29 April 2016 (upholding a decision of the Court of Appeal of Liège requiring the publisher of a newspaper to anonymise the litigious article online version of its digital archive).

engine can generally only be expected to assess proportionality ex post (once it has been made aware of the impact of its activities in a particular situation). These discrepancies result not only from the fact that each actor pursues different purposes, but also from the nature of their operations and the assessment of what constitutes a reasonable obligation "within the framework of its responsibilities, powers and capabilities".[2339]

C. *Accuracy*

1136. Search engine provider – Every controller is obliged to take "every reasonable step" to ensure the accuracy of personal data under its control.[2340] During oral arguments in *Google Spain*, the counsel for the European Commission indicated that search engines generally cannot be expected to (proactively) verify the accuracy of the information they reference.[2341] Given the volume of personal data processed by internet search engines, as well as the purposes they pursue, it would indeed be unreasonable to require search engines to establish the accuracy of personal data prior to including it in their index or search results.[2342] It is reasonable, however, to require search engines to assess the accuracy of information reactively (e.g. upon notification of its inaccuracy). Even though a search engine is not directly responsible for the accuracy of third-party content as such, its continued referral to inaccurate after notification may be excessive.

1137. Website publishers and content providers – Website publishers and content providers must take every reasonable step to ensure the accuracy of personal data prior to uploading it to a publically available webpage. They must also take every reasonable step to keep personal data up to date and to ensure that inaccurate data are rectified.

2339 See also *infra*, nos. 1162 et seq.

2340 Article 5(1d) GDPR (previously: Article 6(1)d Directive 95/46).

2341 In his Opinion, the Advocate General went even further in stating that the personal data contained in Google's index or cache cannot be regarded as incomplete or inaccurate. (Opinion of Advocate General Jääskinen, Case C-131/12, paragraph 105). The conclusion advanced by the Advocate General builds upon his earlier assessment that the principles of data quality may be deemed satisfied as long as the search term really appears or has appeared on the linked web pages. This interpretation is at odds with an earlier Opinion of another Advocate General, namely the Opinion drawn up by Advocate General Kokkot in the *Satamedia* case. In this case, the Advocate General specified that "further processing of personal information which is proved to be false cannot be justified by the fact that it has been published" (Opinion of Advocate-General Kokott in *Satamedia*, Case C-73/07, EU:C:2008:266, paragraph 124). Even though the personal data is publicly available already, the data subject will still maintain a right to prevent the "*perpetuation and intensification of interference by means of the further processing of information, for instance, in the case of erroneous information [...].*" (*Ibid*, paragraph 122).

2342 B. Van Alsenoy, A. Kuczerawy and J. Ausloos, "Search Engines after *Google Spain*: Internet@ Liberty or Privacy@Peril?", *l.c.*, p. 36.

1138. End-users – End-users cannot determine the accuracy of personal data retrieved through search results in advance. Only once the results have been retrieved can the end-user actually determine whether this is the case. As a result, the end-user can effectively only comply with the principle of accuracy after collection (e.g. by consulting additional sources and rectifying or deleting local copies of retrieved data as needed).

1139. Assessment – The principle of data accuracy, similarly to the principle of data minimisation, may impact different actors in different ways. Which measures may be considered as "reasonable" will vary in light of the purposes pursued by the processing and the powers and capabilities of each actor.

4.3. TRANSPARENCY

1140. Search engine provider – The collection of third-party data by search engines is by definition indirect. Article 14 GDPR specifies that in case of indirect collection, the data subject should in principle still be provided with certain minimum information, including a.o. the identity of the controller and the purposes of the processing. Article 14(5) GDPR adds, however, that the controller shall not be obliged to inform the data subject if the provision of such information "proves impossible or would involve a disproportionate effort". Given the scale of their operations and the purposes pursued, it can be argued that actively notifying each data subject of every collection constitutes a disproportionate effort.[2343]

1141. Website publishers and content providers – Website publishers and content providers may collect personal data either directly from the data subject or indirectly. In case of direct collection, the data subject must in principle be provided with the necessary information at the moment of collection (except where he already has this information or if another derogation or exemption applies).[2344] If it is envisaged that personal data shall be made available online, the data subject should in principle also be informed thereof.[2345]

2343 B. Van Alsenoy, A. Kuczerawy and J. Ausloos, "Search Engines after *Google Spain*: Internet@ Liberty or Privacy@Peril?", *l.c.*, p. 37.

2344 E.g. in case of processing for journalistic, artistic or literary purposes.

2345 In case of indirect collection, the website publisher is not obliged to inform the data subject when the provisioning of information proves impossible or would involve a disproportionate effort. In addition, website publishers may be exempted from the obligation to inform data subject pursuant to the journalistic exemption of Article 9 (which permits exceptions for both direct and indirect collection).

1142. End-users – The collection of third-party data by end-users is by definition also indirect. End-users shall typically also be exempted from notice obligation, though there may be situations where it arguably would not require disproportionate effort for end-users to inform the individual concerned (e.g. during a recruitment process, if information collected through search engines is used to assess a job applicant).

4.4. CONFIDENTIALITY AND SECURITY

1143. Search engine provider – As the processing of third-party data is concerned, it seems that the obligation to ensure confidentiality and security of processing holds only limited meaning for search engines. After all, third-party data processed by internet search engines will – by definition – already be publicly available (otherwise it would not be indexed by the search engine).[2346] The main obligation for search engines in this respect is to ensure the integrity of personal data contained in its index (i.e. guard against unauthorized alterations).[2347]

1144. Website publishers and content providers – Website publishers and content providers should implement appropriate technical and organisational security measures to ensure the confidentiality and security of personal data which is placed online but is not authorized for public disclosure. Even if the information is intended to be accessible the public, it may nevertheless be appropriate in certain cases to take appropriate measures to limit indexing by search engines (e.g. a website operated by a public authority which publishes a list of recipients of agricultural subsidies).

1145. End-users – End-users in principle do not need to implement any measures to ensure the confidentiality and security of personal data collected through search engines, unless the data is subsequently brought in combination with other (non-public) personal data.

2346 Consequently, a duty of confidentiality understood as a prohibition of unauthorized disclosure or access seems nonsensical in a search engine context, because it can be assumed that data that is placed online (without putting in place exclusion codes or other tools to obscure data) is intended for viewing by an indefinite audience). (B. Van Alsenoy, A. Kuczerawy and J. Ausloos, "Search Engines after *Google Spain*: Internet@Liberty or Privacy@ Peril?", *l.c.*, p. 38).

2347 B. Van Alsenoy, A. Kuczerawy and J. Ausloos, "Search Engines after *Google Spain*: Internet@ Liberty or Privacy@Peril?", *l.c.*, p. 38.

4.5. RIGHT TO OBJECT AND TO ERASURE

1146. Search engine provider – In *Google Spain*, the CJEU recognized that the provider of a search engine must, as a matter of principle, accommodate the data subject's rights to object and to erasure.[2348] Specifically, the Court held that – insofar as the conditions to exercise these rights are in fact satisfied – the operator of a search engine is obliged

> "to remove from the list of results displayed following a search made on the basis of a person's name links to web pages, published by third parties and containing information relating to that person".[2349]

The data subject's "right to be delisted" applies only to search results that show up following a name search. The search engine provider must in principle accommodate a request for delisting unless there is a preponderant interest on the part of the general public in having access to the information in question by way of a name search.[2350] It is not required that the data are erased simultaneously or beforehand from the source web page, nor that the publication of the data on the source webpage is unlawful.[2351]

1147. Website publishers and content providers – Website publishers and content providers must also, as a matter of principle, accommodate the data subject's right to object and to erasure. It should be noted, however, that the assessment may result in a different outcome:

> "[N]ot only does the ground, under Article 7 of Directive 95/46, justifying the publication of a piece of personal data on a website not necessarily coincide with that which is applicable to the activity of search engines, but also, even where that is the case, the outcome of the weighing of the interests at issue to be carried out under

---

2348 For a discussion of the rights of access and rectification see B. Van Alsenoy, A. Kuczerawy and J. Ausloos, "Search Engines after *Google Spain*: Internet@Liberty or Privacy@Peril?", *l.c.*, p. 38–41.

2349 Judgment in *Google Spain*, C-131/12, EU:C:2014:317, paragraph 88.

2350 *Ibid*, paragraph 97–99. Relevant criteria include the nature of the information in question, its sensitivity for the data subject's private life and on the interest of the public in having unbridled access to that information (an interest which may vary, in particular, according to the role played by the data subject in public life). (*Ibid* paragraph 81). For a further elaboration of the criteria to be considered by search engine operators implementing *Google Spain* see Article 29 Data Protection Working Party, "Guidelines on the implementation of the Court of Justice of the European Union judgment on 'Google Spain and Inc. v. Agencia Española de Protección de Datos (AEPD) and Mario Costeja González' C-131/12", WP 225, 26 November 2014, p. 12–20; X., "The Advisory Council to Google on the Right to be Forgotten", 6 February 2015, p. 7–14 and J. Ausloos and A. Kuczerawy, "From Notice-and-Takedown to Notice-and-Delist: Implementing the Google Spain ruling", *CiTiP Working Paper Series*. 5 October 2015, p. 27–37.

2351 Judgment in *Google Spain*, C-131/12, EU:C:2014:317, paragraph 81.

Article 7(f) and subparagraph (a) of the first paragraph of Article 14 of the directive may differ according to whether the processing carried out by the operator of a search engine or that carried out by the publisher of the web page is at issue, given that, first, the legitimate interests justifying the processing may be different and, second, the consequences of the processing for the data subject, and in particular for his private life, are not necessarily the same."[2352]

Moreover, the processing of personal data by the publisher of webpage may, in some circumstances be carried out "solely for journalistic purposes" and thus benefit from an exemption.[2353] As a result, it cannot be ruled out that in certain circumstances the data subject may be capable of exercising his right to object and to erasure against that operator but not against the publisher of the web page.[2354]

1148. End-users – End-users who are not covered by the exemption for purely personal or household activities, or any other derogation or exemption, must in principle also accommodate data subjects' right to object and to erasure.

5. EVALUATION

1149. Outline – The *Google Spain* decision may fairly be characterized as a milestone in European data protection law. In addition to settling important issues of applicable law and data subject rights, it also dealt extensively with the core concepts of the Directive. The aim of this section is to assess the interpretation put forward by the CJEU as well as its implications for other actors involved in the processing of personal data.

5.1. TRUE TO BOTH LETTER AND SPIRIT

1150. A literal and teleogical approach – In his advisory opinion, the Advocate General cautioned against a "blind literal interpretation" of the controller concept.[2355] Too much had changed since the Data Protection

2352 Judgment in *Google Spain*, C-131/12, EU:C:2014:317, paragraph 86. The Court of Justice continued as follows: "*Indeed, since the inclusion in the list of results, displayed following a search made on the basis of a person's name, of a web page and of the information contained on it relating to that person makes access to that information appreciably easier for any internet user making a search in respect of the person concerned and may play a decisive role in the dissemination of that information, it is liable to constitute a more significant interference with the data subject's fundamental right to privacy than the publication on the web page.*" (*Ibid*, paragraph 87).

2353 *Ibid*, paragraph 85.

2354 *Id.*

2355 Opinion of Advocate General Jääskinen in *Google Spain*, C-131/12, ECLI:EU:C:2013:424, paragraph 81.

Directive was enacted.[2356] A literal interpretation would render EU data protection law applicable to a wide range of situations unanticipated by the Community legislature. This, in turn, would lead to unreasonable and excessive legal consequences.[2357] At first glance, it appears as if the CJEU simply brushed aside these words of caution. It opted for a formal approach, sticking close to the literal wording of the legal definition of a controller. But the Court also invoked a teleological argument[2358]:

> "it would be contrary not only to the clear wording of that provision but also to its objective – which is to ensure, through a broad definition of the concept of 'controller', effective and complete protection of data subjects – to exclude the operator of a search engine from that definition on the ground that it does not exercise control over the personal data published on the web pages of third parties."[2359]

Later on, the CJEU expanded at some length to consider the impact of internet search engines on individuals' privacy. Specifically, it noted that search engines render personal data accessible to internet users "*who otherwise would not have found the web page on which those data are published*".[2360] The Court also noted that "*the organisation and aggregation of information [...] effected by search engines [...] may, when users carry out their search on the basis of an individual's name, result in [...] a more or less detailed profile of the data subject.*"[2361] The reasoning of the Court of Justice recalls two of the main privacy concerns associated with internet search engines, namely the decline of "practical obscurity" and "aggregation".

1151. Practical obscurity – Practical obscurity exists where information is technically available, but can only be found by spending a considerable amount of time and effort.[2362] Such would be the fate of most online information were

---

2356 *Ibid*, paragraph 77.

2357 *Ibid*, paragraph 30.

2358 See also G. Sartor, "Search Engines as Controllers – Inconvenient implications of a Questionable Classification", *Maastricht Journal of European and Comparative Law* 2014, Vol. 21, No. 3, p. 568; O. Lynskey, "Control over Personal Data in a Digital Age: Google Spain v AEPD and Mario Costeja Gonzalez", *The Modern Law Review* 2015, Vol. 78, no. 3, p. 524 ("*Resorting to both a literal and teleological interpretation of the Directive, the Court held that a search engine should not be excluded from the definition of controller and, in this way, the Court preserved the broad personal scope of application of the Directive.*") and D. Sancho-Villa, "Developing Search Engine Law: It Is Not Just about the Right to Be Forgotten", *Legal Issues of Economic Integration* 2015, Vol. 42, no. 4, p. 369 (arguing that the Court of Justice relied primarily on a teleological interpretation rather than a formal analysis).

2359 Judgment in *Google Spain*, C-131/12, EU:C:2014:317, paragraph 34.

2360 *Ibid*, paragraphs 36–37.

2361 *Ibid*, paragraphs 36–37.

2362 See W. Hartzog and F. Stutzman, "The Case for Online Obscurity", *California Law Review* 2013, Vol. 101, No. 1, p. 21. Hartzog and Stutzman attribute term "practical obscurity" to the 1989 U.S. Supreme Court judgment *U.S. Department of Justice v. Reporters Committee*

it not for search engines. Search engines make it easy to locate information which would otherwise, from a practical perspective, be too difficult to locate. Ordinarily speaking, this is precisely the added value of search engines. But when the search target is a private individual, the efficiency gains offered by search engines may entail a privacy cost.[2363]

1152. Aggregation – The second privacy concern identified by the CJEU relates to what Solove has termed "aggregation".[2364] In the context of information privacy, *aggregation* refers to the gathering together of information about a person.[2365] While a single piece of information by itself may not be so revealing, several pieces combined together can be quite telling.[2366] As more and more life events are logged online (e.g. a high school graduation, a change in job, the participation in a charity drive, etc.), search engines are capable of collating increasingly detailed biographical pictures. If one carries out a search on the basis of an individual's name, the ensuing list of results may offer a (seemingly) comprehensive profile of the individual concerned. This profile may have a profound impact on a person's reputation, livelihood and personal development. Or, as the saying now goes: "*You are what Google says you are.*"[2367]

1153. Change of context – While the drafters of Directive 95/46 may not have envisaged the Web as we know it today, they were mindful of the privacy concerns highlighted by the CJEU. In fact, similar concerns had triggered the

---

for Freedom of the Press [489 U.S. 749 (1989)]. In this case the Supreme Court recognized that individuals have a privacy interest in maintaining the practical obscurity of so-called "rap sheets". Rap sheets are aggregated criminal records compiled by the FBI on the basis of state and local records. Even though the underlying information is ostensibly part of "the public record" (each item can in principle be found after a diligent search of local courthouse files, county archives, etc.), the Supreme Court considered this information to be "practically obscure" (because of the extremely high cost and low likelihood of the information being compiled by the public). The difference between, on the one hand, distributed, decentralized and hard-to-locate information, and, on the other hand, a centralized computer file was considered significant enough to justify non-disclosure under Article 7c of the Freedom of Information Act (which excludes from disclosure records or information compiled for law enforcement purposes which constitute an "unwarranted invasion of personal privacy").

2363 See also See O. Tene, "What Google Knows: Privacy and Internet Search Engines", *l.c.*, p. 1441. Or, as Grimmelmann has put it: "*from a victim's perspective [...] search works best when it works the least*" (J. Grimmelmann, "Speech engines", *Minnesota Law Review* 2014, Vol. 98, p. 907).

2364 D. Solove, "A taxonomy of privacy", *University of Pennsylvania Law Review* 2006, Vol. 154, No. 3, p. 506. See also O. Tene, What Google Knows: Privacy and Internet Search Engines", *l.c.*, p. 1458.

2365 D. Solove, "A taxonomy of privacy", *l.c.*, p. 506.

2366 *Id.*

2367 M. Angelo, "You Are What Google Says You Are", *Wired*, 11 February 2009. See also Meg Leta Ambrose, "You Are What Google Says You Are: The Right to be Forgotten and Information Stewardship", *International Review of Information Ethics* 2012, Vol. 17 (pointing out that much online information is in fact more ephemeral than commonly portrayed).

enactment of the very first EU data protection laws back in the 1970s.[2368] In this sense, the Court's ruling is true to both the letter and spirit of EU data protection law. At the same time, one should not lose sight of the context in which the Data Protection Directive emerged. Even if its concepts and principles are, for the most part, "technology neutral", the Directive was still enacted within a particular socio-technical context. This context was composed of implicit assumptions about technology and how it will be used.[2369] In other words: while being true to the values pursued by the Community legislature, the CJEU arguably applied them to a context unanticipated at the time of enactment.

5.2. ABSENCE OF KNOWLEDGE OR INTENT

1154. Issue at stake – In his Opinion, the Advocate General argued that in order to be considered a controller, the entity concerned should at least be aware of the fact that he is processing personal data.[2370] Moreover, the entity should process the data "*with some intention which relates to their processing as personal data.*"[2371] The Court of Justice implicitly rejected this argument, however, when interpreting the definition of "processing". Specifically, the Court considered that it does not matter that the provider of the search engine "*also carries out the same operations in respect of other types of information and does not distinguish between the latter and the personal data*".[2372] As a result, a search engine provider

2368 See e.g. A.R. Miller, "Personal Privacy in the Computer Age: The Challenge of a New Technology in an Information-Oriented Society", *Michigan Law Review* 1969, vol. 67, p. 1105 And F. W. Hondius, *Emerging data protection in Europe*, *o.c.*, p. 101. See also V. Mayer-Schönberger, "Generational Development of Data Protection in Europe", *l.c.*, p. 222; C.J. Bennet, *Regulating privacy. Data Protection and Public Policy in Europe and the United States*, *o.c.*, p. 14; L.A. Bygrave, *Data Protection Law. Approaching its Rationale, Logic and Limits*, *o.c.*, p. 97–98.

2369 See M. Birnhack, "Reverse Engineering Information Privacy Law", *Yale Journal of Law and Technology* 2012, Vol. 24, p. 68 et seq. and C. Reed, "The Law of Unintended Consequences – Embedded Business Models in IT Regulation", *l.c.*, paragraph 36 et seq.

2370 Opinion of Advocate General Jääskinen in Google Spain, C-131/12, ECLI:EU:C:2013:424, paragraph 83. The mere "statistical fact" that web pages are likely to include personal data was deemed insufficient (*Ibid*, paragraph 84).

2371 *Ibid*, paragraph 82. See in the same vein also C. Mitchell-Rekrut, "Search engine liability under the Libe Data Regulation Proposal: interpreting third party responsibilities as informed by Google Spain", *Georgetown Journal of International Law* 2014, Vol. 45, p. 883–884 ("*It remains true that search engines do not "determine[] the purpose[] and means of the processing of personal data" as personal data. As the AG suggested, it would be improper to conflate a search engine's broad "purpose" of indiscriminately cataloguing content on the internet with the myriad individual purposes for which people and organisations throughout the world publish data on the internet as controllers.*") (original emphasis).

2372 Judgment in *Google Spain*, C-131/12, EU:C:2014:317, paragraph 28 (" … *regardless of the fact that the operator of the search engine also carries out the same operations in respect of other types of information and does not distinguish between the latter and the personal data.*").

can be considered a "controller" even if he does not deliberately target personal data as such.[2373]

1155. Implications – Sartor argues that the approach adopted by the CJEU may lead to an overly broad application of the controller concept:

> "[I]f choosing to process a data set would entail being the controller for the processing of any personal data in that data set, then whoever is running any machine that processes data passing through the internet (for instance a router, pushing forward data towards their destination) would count as a [controller] of the personal data transmitted by that machine, and would be liable for letting through any personal data that should not have been made accessible. The same would hold for providers caching internet data, or hosting them in the cloud."[2374]

1156. Assessment – The argument advanced by Sartor is essentially a "slippery slope" argument. If knowledge or intent are not required to consider an entity a controller, every entity interacting with personal data might potentially be considered a controller, thereby exposing them to unwarranted liability risks. The risks would be particularly troublesome in cases where passive intermediaries are involved, such as the providers of mere conduit or hosting services. In my view, Sartor's argument omits two important considerations. Specifically, the argument fails to acknowledge that (a) different actors may be in control of different aspects of the processing, even when processing the same personal data[2375]; and (b) search engines do not merely transmit or store information at the request of the recipient of the service. Search engine services involve a distinct set of processing activities for which the search engine provider exclusively determines the purposes and means.[2376]

2373 In the same vein: P. De Hert and V. Papakonstantinou, "Comment – Google Spain – Addressing Critiques and Misunderstandings One Year Later", *Maastricht Journal of European and Comparative Law* 2015, Vol. 22, No. 4, p. 627 ("*'Knowledge' of the data controller or 'alteration' of the data, as Google contested, are not necessary conditions to this end.*"). See also D. Sancho-Villa, "Developing Search Engine Law: It Is Not Just about the Right to Be Forgotten", *l.c.*, p. 371.

2374 G. Sartor, "Search Engines as Controllers – Inconvenient implications of a Questionable Classification", *l.c.*, p. 570. (Note: in the original version of this article, the word "processor" appears instead of the word "controller" in the fourth line of the quote. As the remainder of the quote suggests, however, that the author in fact intended to use the word "controller". This has been confirmed separately with the author via email correspondence).

2375 This is explicitly confirmed by recital (47) of Directive 95/46, as well as guidance by the Article 29 Working Party. See also *supra*, no. 127.

2376 See also B. Van Alsenoy, A. Kuczerawy and J. Ausloos, "Search Engines after *Google Spain*: Internet@Liberty or Privacy@Peril?", *l.c.*, p. 16; E. Defreyne and R. Romain, "L'arrêt «Google Spain»: commentaire et mise en perspective", *Revue du Droit des Technologies de l'Information* 2014, no. 56, p. 80–84; H. Hijmans, "Right to Have Links Removed – Evidence of Effective Data Protection", *Maastricht Journal of European and Comparative Law* 2014, Vol. 21, No. 3, p. 558–559 and P. De Hert and P. Papakonstantinou, "Comment – Google Spain – Addressing Critiques and Misunderstandings One Year Later", *l.c.*, p. 627.

1157. Purpose as "finality" – The reasoning of the CJEU lends further support for the proposition that the concept of "purpose" should be understood as "finality" rather than "interest".[2377] Even if the provider of a search engine has no personal interest in the content or outcome of a specific search query (other than providing the most relevant search results), it still determines the finality of the processing required to deliver the search engine service.

5.3. SHOOTING THE MESSENGER?

1158. Search engines as intermediaries – In *Google Spain*, Google portrayed itself as a "neutral intermediary" between content providers and content seekers. Search engines, it was argued, merely help individuals find content placed online by others. As a result, any harm suffered should be attributed directly to the content provider. Moreover, if one were to allow data subjects to exercise their rights towards search engines, this would shift the burden of compliance from the original content provider to the provider of the search engine service. It would, in other words, be the equivalent of "shooting the messenger".[2378]

1159. Active involvement – Google's opponents, on the other hand, claimed that the privacy harm suffered by the plaintiff is a direct result of the search engine service. They rejected the notion that Google acts as a "neutral intermediary", arguing that it actively directs the flow of information from one party to another.[2379] Moreover, the harm suffered by the plaintiff was a consequence, not so much of the initial publication, but rather of its remaining readily accessible through search engines. Without Google's intervention, it was argued, the publication in question would be far less likely to cause harm to the plaintiff's privacy interests.[2380]

1160. Neutral or biased? – The arguments made in *Google Spain* are similar to those often heard in discussions regarding the alleged "neutrality"

2377 Compare *supra*, no. 1060 et seq.

2378 B. Van Alsenoy, A. Kuczerawy and J. Ausloos, "Search Engines after *Google Spain*: Internet@ Liberty or Privacy@Peril?", *l.c.*, p. 67.

2379 See in the same vein also the statements by Chris Scott and Steve Wood before the House of Lords European Union Committee "*Google does not merely passively deliver information; Google sculpts the results.*" (Chris Scott) and "*[...] we did not agree with the analogy of a search engine as a mere conduit, if you like, of the information just passing through it. Given the level of interaction a search engine has and the interest it takes using algorithms when it is interacting with personal information and spidering the internet, we felt that the way in which the court advanced that issue was correct.*" (Steve Wood) (House of Lords, European Union Committee, "EU Data Protection Law: A 'right to be forgotten'?", *l.c.*, p. 13–14).

2380 B. Van Alsenoy, A. Kuczerawy and J. Ausloos, "Search Engines after *Google Spain*: Internet@ Liberty or Privacy@Peril?", *l.c.*, p. 67.

of Internet search engines.[2381] Grimmelmann points out that there are two diametrically opposed theories regarding the nature of search engines.[2382] For some, a search engine ought to be viewed as a passive and neutral "conduit" between websites and users. For others, a search engine should be seen an active and opinionated "editor", who sifts through the internet and uses experts judgment to identify items of importance and interest.[2383] According to Grimmelmann, these two opposing theories "*form the rhetorical backdrop to the ongoing legal battles over search*".[2384] However, as Grimmelmann also points out, neither extreme is particularly satisfying. In practice search engines combine elements of both theories; acting both as conduits and editors at the same time.[2385]

1161. Hybrid role of search engines – In *Google Spain*, the conflict concerned the crawling, indexing, storage and making available of personal data mentioned on a third-party web page. Given that the purposes and means of these processing operations are determined exclusively by the search engine itself, it seems only natural to qualify them as a "controller" for these activities. The difficulty lies, however, in separating those activities from the intermediary function performed by search engines. Some might argue that search engines act both as "content selectors" (i.e. "controllers") and "messengers" (i.e. "intermediaries") when making content accessible to end-users.[2386] In this light, it is difficult to maintain a strict separation between the "intermediary" function of search engines and the operations for which they act as "controllers". Any allocation of responsibility in relation to the latter activity will inevitably have implications upon the former. Whether or not one considers such allocation to be appropriate, however, may simply depend on one's perception as to which aspect of the search engine service is dominant (selection or messaging).[2387]

2381 For a critical analysis of the arguments regarding the "neutrality" of search engines and their role as "innocent messengers" see U. Kohl, "Google: the rise and rise of online intermediaries in the governance of the Internet and beyond (Part 2)", *l.c.*, p. 4–11.

2382 J. Grimmelmann, "Speech engines", *l.c.*, p. 871

2383 Grimmelmann's own metaphor portrays search engines as "trusted advisors" in attempt to combine the best of both worlds (*Ibid*, p. 895 et seq.).

2384 *Ibid*, 871.

2385 *Ibid*, 873–874. See also B. Van Alsenoy, Kuczerawy, and Ausloos, "Search Engines after *Google Spain*: Internet@Liberty or Privacy@Peril?", *l.c.*, p. 68.

2386 A search engine's referencing (i.e. rendering accessible) of content is intrinsically linked to its indexation and analysis of such content: cf. *supra*, nos. 1088 et seq.

2387 B. Van Alsenoy, A. Kuczerawy and J. Ausloos, "Search Engines after *Google Spain*: Internet@ Liberty or Privacy@Peril?", *l.c.*, p. 68. Compare also M. Peguera, "The Shaky Ground of the Right to Be Delisted", (Draft, August 2015), p. 31 et seq.

5.4. SCOPE OF OBLIGATIONS OF SEARCH ENGINE PROVIDERS

1162. Problem statement – Critics of *Google Spain* have argued that the CJEU was wrong in considering search engines as "controllers", because such a categorization has unreasonable consequences.[2388] Their argument is based, at least in part, on the premise that search engines are unable to comply with all of the obligations and restrictions that EU data protection law typically imposes upon controllers.[2389] A similar line of reasoning had also led the Advocate General to conclude that search engines should not be considered as controllers in relation to the personal data on source web pages hosted on third-party servers.[2390]

1163. Tailoring obligations – Most provisions of EU data protection law allow for flexibility in their application. Several provisions have explicit "safety-valves" built in, which allow for derogations in cases where strict compliance would be disproportionate or unreasonable.[2391] For provisions that do not have such explicit safety-valves built in, practitioners can fall back on the general

---

[2388] G. Sartor, "Search Engines as Controllers – Inconvenient implications of a Questionable Classification", *l.c.*, p. 570 and M. Peguera, "The Shaky Ground of the Right to Be Delisted", *l.c.*, p. 29–30).

[2389] See e.g. M. Peguera, "The Shaky Ground of the Right to Be Delisted", *l.c.*, p. 29: "*the question arises as to whether this characterization can be seen as a proportionate outcome in terms of the legal duties that stem from it. Considering search engines as controllers is not without consequences, as they are unable to comply with most of the obligations the Directive imposes on data controllers.*"

[2390] Opinion of Advocate General Jääskinen in Google Spain, C-131/12, ECLI:EU:C:2013:424, paragraph 89–90 ("*In my view the internet search engine service provider cannot in law or in fact fulfil the obligations of controller provided in Articles 6, 7 and 8 of the Directive in relation to the personal data on source web pages hosted on third-party servers. Therefore a reasonable interpretation of the Directive requires that the service provider is not generally considered as having that position. An opposite opinion would entail internet search engines being incompatible with EU law, a conclusion I would find absurd. Specifically, if internet search engine service providers were considered as controllers of the personal data on third-party source web pages and if on any of these pages there would be 'special categories of data' referred to in Article 8 of the Directive (e.g. personal data revealing political opinions or religious beliefs or data concerning the health or sex life of individuals), the activity of the internet search engine service provider would automatically become illegal, when the stringent conditions laid down in that article for the processing of such data were not met.*")

[2391] See also Article 29 Data Protection Working Party, "Opinion 4/2007 on the concept of personal data", WP 136, 20 June 2007, p. 4–5 ("*Even where processing of personal data within the scope of the Directive is involved, not all the rules contained therein may be applicable in the particular case. A number of provisions of the Directive contain a substantial degree of flexibility, so as to strike the appropriate balance between protection of the data subject's rights on the one side, and on the other side the legitimate interests of data controllers, third parties and the public interest which may be present*"")

principle of proportionality, which is a basic principle of EU law.[2392] As the Court of Justice observed in *Lindqvist*:

> "it is for the authorities and courts of the Member States not only to interpret their national law in a manner consistent with Directive 95/46 but also to make sure they do not rely on an interpretation of it which would be in conflict with the fundamental rights protected by the Community legal order or with the other general principles of Community law, such as inter alia the principle of proportionality."[2393]

1164. "Responsibilities, powers & capabilities" – In *Google Spain*, the Court of Justice took care to interpret EU data protection law in such a way that it would not unduly restrict the offering of search engine services. In qualifying search engine providers as controllers, the Court also immediately indicated that there may be limits to the obligations of search engine providers:

> "[...] the operator of the search engine as the person determining the purposes and means of that activity must ensure, within the framework of its responsibilities,

---

2392 For more information regarding the principle of proportionality as a basic principle of EU law see F.G. Jacobs, "Recent Development in the Principle of Proportionality in European Community Law", in E. Ellis (ed.), *The Principle of Proportionality in the Laws of Europe*, 1999, Hart Publishing, Oxford, p. 1–22 and C. Kuner, "Proportionality in European Data Protection Law And Its Importance for Data Processing by Companies", *Privacy & Security Law Report* 2008, Vol. 7, no. 44, p. 2.

2393 Judgment in *Bodil Lindqvist*, C-101/01, EU:C:2003:596, paragraph 87. In this regard, it is worth drawing attention to attention to *Volker und Markus Schecke*, a case decided by the CJEU in 2010. This case concerned the publication of information about the beneficiaries of certain agricultural funds. Pursuant to the relevant EU Regulations, Member States were required to publish the names of the beneficiaries of such aid, as well as the amounts received by each beneficiary. Two beneficiaries challenged this publication, one of whom was a private person, whereas the other was a legal person. The Court of Justice agreed with the referring Court that the drafters of the Regulation at issue had, at least insofar as the publication concerned private persons, insufficiently balanced the interests at stake. Where the information concerned legal persons, however, the Court of Justice considered that the publication of such information was in fact proportionate. The Court of Justice went on to observe that "*Furthermore, the obligation on the competent national authorities to examine, before the data in question are published and for each legal person which is a beneficiary of [agricultural] aid, whether the name of that person identifies natural persons would impose on those authorities an unreasonable administrative burden*". (Judgment in *Volker und Markus Schecke*, Joined Cases C-92/09 and C-93/09, EU:C:2010:662, paragraph 87). This cursory consideration by the CJEU illustrates a very important point, namely that a controller's obligations need to be interpreted within reason. While the Court of Justice recognized that data relating to a legal person might also (indirectly) constitute personal data, it stated that it would be unreasonable to oblige public sector bodies to investigate this in each instance prior to publication. By analogy, one can argue that search engines cannot be expected to conduct this analysis prior to undertaking its automated collection ("crawling") of webpages. To hold otherwise would require search engine providers to conduct a manual review of each website intended for indexation. Taking into account the scale of search engine operations, the ratio of personal to non-personal data, as well as the purposes of the processing, such a burden would arguably be unreasonable. See also B. Van Alsenoy, A. Kuczerawy and J. Ausloos, "Search Engines after *Google Spain*: Internet@Liberty or Privacy@Peril?", *l.c.*, p. 29–30.

powers and capabilities, that the activity meets the requirements of Directive 95/46 in order that the guarantees laid down by the directive may have full effect and that effective and complete protection of data subjects, in particular of their right to privacy, may actually be achieved."[2394]

By explicitly referring to the "powers and capabilities" of the search engine operator, the Court of Justice implicitly acknowledged that there may be practical limits to the ability of a search engine operator to meet all the obligations resulting from EU data protection law.[2395] In particular, it can be argued that *Google Spain* does not oblige search engine providers to exercise preventative control over the information it disseminates.[2396] In fact, the reasoning of the CJEU suggests that the obligations of search engine providers concerning third-party data essentially only "reactive": only after the provider has been made aware of the fact that the display of specific search results following a name search adversely impacts the data subject, must the provider assess whether or not delisting is necessary.[2397]

1165. Critique – Peguera and Sartor have called into question the approach of the CJEU by offering two critiques. The first critique is that this approach does not comport with the language of EU data protection law.[2398] While EU data protection law does exempt controllers from fulfilling certain obligations which would require disproportionate efforts, it does not do so in all instances, most notably in relation to special categories of data.[2399] The second critique is that the approach of the Court of Justice may easily lead to inconsistent outcomes and therefore give rise to legal uncertainty.[2400] Sartor eloquently summarizes as follows

"The very need to use broad principles or questionable distinctions to pre-empt apparently straightforward implications of the Court's approach should lead us

[2394] Judgment in *Google Spain*, C-131/12, EU:C:2014:317, paragraph 38.

[2395] For a more narrow reading see M. Thompson, "Beyond Gatekeeping: The Normative Responsibility of Internet Intermediaries", *l.c.*, p. 26.

[2396] H. Hijmans, "Right to Have Links Removed – Evidence of Effective Data Protection", *l.c.*, p. 559 ("*For me, it is obvious that this judgment does not mean that a search engine provider should exercise preventive control over the information it disseminates, nor that it is in any other manner limited in its essential role of ensuring a free internet. In essence, the Court confirms that a search engine – which has as its core activity the processing of large amounts of data with potentially important consequences for the private life of individuals – cannot escape from responsibility for its activities.*")

[2397] See also Article 29 Working Party, Guidelines on the Implementation of the Court of Justice of the European Union Judgment on "Google Spain and Inc. v Agencia Española de Protección de Datos (AEPD) and Mario Costeja González" C-131/12, p. 6 ("*The ruling does not oblige search engines to permanently carry out that assessment in relation to all the information they process, but only when they have to respond to data subjects' requests for the exercise of their rights.*")

[2398] M. Peguera, "The Shaky Ground of the Right to Be Delisted", *l.c.*, p. 29.

[2399] *Ibid*, 30.

[2400] *Id.*

to question that very approach, and to doubt that it provides a sustainable legal framework, which may adequately support legal practice."[2401]

The critique of Peguera and Sartor should not be taken lightly. If "reasonable" interpretations de facto exempt controllers from complying with certain obligations, there is a risk of undermining the effectiveness of the data protection framework as a whole.[2402]

1166. Assessment – The precise scope of data protection obligations must always be assessed in context. A controller's obligations might indeed be lighter – or more onerous – depending on the purposes pursued by the processing and the risks for data subjects.[2403] The critiques of Peguera and Sartor illustrate that certain provisions of EU data protection law fail to provide adequate flexibility in all contexts. Such a finding does not, however, undermine the validity of the controller concept as such, but rather requires us to reconsider how to the obligations associated with that concept should be formulated. The formulation of the Court of Justice ("*within the framework of its responsibilities, powers and capabilities*") may be considered a useful addition in this respect.[2404]

1167. Special categories of data – The CJEU has recently been requested to determine whether the restrictions concerning special categories of data are in fact applicable to search engine providers, having regard to their specific "responsibilities, powers and capabilities".[2405] At the moment of writing, only the Opinion of Advocate General has been issued.[2406] Nevertheless, it is worth taking note of his analysis, as it deals specifically with one of the issues highlighted by Peguera and Sartor. In his Opinion, Advocate General Szpunar begins his analysis by considering that one should take into account historical context in which Directive 95/46 was enacted when determining to what extent an obligation shall apply to search engine operator:

2401 G. Sartor, "Search Engines as Controllers – Inconvenient implications of a Questionable Classification", *l.c.*, p. 575.

2402 B. Van Alsenoy, A. Kuczerawy and J. Ausloos, "Search Engines after *Google Spain*: Internet@ Liberty or Privacy@Peril?", *l.c.*, p. 44–45. During oral arguments in Google Spain, the Advocate General asked the Commission whether it thinks that there is such a thing as a "light version" of the controller concept. In other words, is it appropriate to qualify an entity as a "controller" if many of its basic responsibilities are interpreted in such a lenient way? The European Commission responded by saying that the search engine's obligations should be assessed on a case-by-case basis, and only in the context of specific requests (*Ibid*, p. 44).

2403 B. Van Alsenoy, A. Kuczerawy and J. Ausloos, "Search Engines after *Google Spain*: Internet@ Liberty or Privacy@Peril?", *l.c.*, p. 44.

2404 Cf. *infra*, nos. 1325 et seq.

2405 Request for a preliminary ruling from the Conseil d'État (France) lodged on 15 March 2017 – G.C., A.F., B.H., E.D. v Commission nationale de l'informatique et des libertés (CNIL), Case C-136/17, question 1.

2406 Opinion of Advocate General Szpunar, *G. C., A. F., B. H., E. D. v. Commission nationale de l'informatique et des libertés (CNIL)*, C-136/17, ECLI:EU:C:2019:14.

"44. [...] Étant donné que la directive 95/46, qui date de l'année 1995, et dont les destinataires des obligations qu'elle prévoit sont en principe les États membres, n'avait pas été rédigée en ayant à l'esprit les moteurs de recherche tels qu'ils existent à l'heure actuelle, ses dispositions ne se prêtent pas à une application intuitive et purement littérale à de tels moteurs de recherche. C'est précisément pour cette raison que les juridictions de renvoi avaient, tout comme dans la présente affaire, des doutes dans l'affaire ayant donné lieu à l'arrêt Google Spain et Google et se sont adressées à la Cour.

45. Par conséquent, l'on ne saurait adopter une approche de «tout ou rien» concernant l'applicabilité des dispositions de la directive 95/46 aux moteurs de recherche. Selon moi, il convient d'examiner chaque disposition du point de vue de son aptitude à être appliquée à un moteur de recherche.»

The Advocate General then turns to the question of "responsibilities, powers and capabilities". He considers that the language of the *Google Spain* judgment allows for two consequences to be drawn:

"51. Il est possible de tirer deux conclusions de ce passage. Tout d'abord, comme le soutient la Commission dans ses observations, la directive 95/46 part du principe que tout responsable du traitement doit satisfaire à l'ensemble des exigences qu'elle édicte, y compris celles prévues à son article 8.

52. Ensuite, et même si ce passage est formulé comme une obligation incombant à l'exploitant d'un moteur de recherche, un tel exploitant **ne peut agir** que dans le cadre de ses responsabilités, de ses compétences et de ses possibilités. En d'autres termes, un tel exploitant peut ne pas être en mesure d'assurer le plein effet des dispositions de la directive 95/46, justement en raison de ses responsabilités, de ses compétences et de ses possibilités limitées.

53. Il convient donc d'interpréter l'article 8 de la directive 95/46 de façon à tenir compte des responsabilités, des compétences et des possibilités d'un exploitant d'un moteur de recherche.

54. À cet égard, il convient d'exclure une application ex ante de l'article 8, paragraphe 1, de la directive 95/46 à un exploitant d'un moteur de recherche. Un contrôle ex ante de pages Internet qui sont référencées en tant que résultat d'une recherche ne relève pas de la responsabilité ni des possibilités d'un moteur de recherche. La tâche d'un exploitant d'un moteur de recherche est, comme le signale son titre, de rechercher, de trouver, de relever et de mettre à disposition, et ce grâce à un algorithme qui permet de trouver les informations de la manière la plus efficace. En revanche, ce n'est pas à l'exploitant d'un moteur de recherche de contrôler, voire de censurer. L'exploitant d'un moteur de recherche agit aux fins de la recherche et réagit aux fins du déréférencement d'un résultat de recherche. C'est en tout cas ainsi que je comprends l'arrêt Google Spain et Google.

> 55. Dans un même ordre d'idées, et ainsi que le souligne également la Commission, les interdictions et les restrictions édictées à l'article 8, paragraphe 1, de la directive 95/46 ne peuvent pas s'appliquer à un exploitant d'un moteur de recherche comme s'il avait lui-même fait figurer les données sensibles dans les pages Internet référencées. Logiquement, l'activité d'un moteur de recherche n'intervient qu'après la mise en ligne de données (sensibles) et a un caractère secondaire.
>
> 56. Partant, les interdictions et les restrictions prévues à l'article 8, paragraphe 1, de la directive 95/46 ne peuvent s'appliquer à un moteur de recherche qu'en raison de ce référencement et, donc, par l'intermédiaire d'une vérification ex post, sur la base d'une demande de déréférencement formée par la personne concernée."

Having outlined the extent to which search engine providers shall be subject to the restrictions related to the processing of special categories of data, the Advocate General proceeds to assess whether the restrictions shall be applied as such, or whether additional considerations (e.g. the freedom to access information) may soften their application.[2407]

1168. A THREE-PART TEST – The Opinion of Advocate General Szpunar is interesting in that it offers further insight as to how the CJEU might further develop the principle that each controller is obliged to comply with EU data protection law "*within the framework of its responsibilities, powers and capabilities*". "Responsibilities" in first instance refers to the obligations and restrictions imposed by EU data protection law upon controllers. The starting point is that the *entirety* of obligations and restrictions imposed by EU data protection law must be met. Nevertheless, limits upon the controller's ability to influence the processing, either in law or in fact, may limit the extent to which the controller shall actually be held responsible. "Powers" appears to refer in first instance to decision-making power, the ability to influence the processing by virtue of an *implicit or explicit authority* over the processing.[2408] "Capabilities", on the other hand, appears to refer to the technical capabilities of the controller, taking into his *operational role* in the processing, including the stage at which the controller becomes involved in the (sequence of) processing activities.[2409]

[2407] See Opinion of Advocate General Szpunar, *G. C., A. F., B. H., E. D. v. Commission nationale de l'informatique et des libertés (CNIL)*, C-136/17, ECLI:EU:C:2019:14, paragraphs 59 et seq.

[2408] It is interesting to note that the word "powers" in French is translated by the word "compétences". As described in Part II, earlier definitions of the controller concept explicitly referred to as a party who was "competent to decide" about the processing. Cf. *infra*, no. 1180. See also Opinion 1/2010, *l.c.*, p. 9–10.

[2409] In this regard, the reasoning of Advocate General Szpunar bears some resemblance to the Opinion of Advocate General Bobek in Fashion ID (cf. *supra*, nos. 918 et seq.) An important difference, however, is that Advocate General Bobek seeks to delineate the responsibilities of controllers by delineated the scope of their control, whereas Advocate General Szpunar appears to delineate the responsibilities of controllers on the basis of their "responsibilities, powers and capabilities" as set forth in *Google Spain.*

5.5. IMPACT ON FREEDOM OF EXPRESSION

1169. Risks of over-compliance – In his Opinion in *Google Spain*, the Advocate General argued that allowing data subjects to exercise their rights vis-à-vis search engines would negatively impact freedom of expression. Specifically, he reasoned that:

> "Such 'notice and take down procedures', if required by the Court, are likely either to lead to the automatic withdrawal of links to any objected contents or to an unmanageable number of requests handled by the most popular and important internet search engine service providers".[2410]

Over-compliance with removal requests poses a significant threat to freedom of expression online.[2411] This problem is not, however, limited to matters concerning data protection.[2412] While certain types of content can more readily be identified as "illegal" or "inappropriate", an evaluation will always be necessary. And as long as intermediaries face an immediate threat of liability, the most cautionary approach is to act upon any indication of illegality, without engaging in any balancing of rights.[2413]

1170. Mitigation strategies – A number of measures could be devised to help mitigate the risk of over-compliance with delisting requests. For example, one might grant the search engine provider some leeway, by saying that it shall only be obliged to delist if it is sufficiently clear that the interests of the data subject outweigh the interests of others.[2414] It is beyond the scope of this book, however, to investigate this matter in greater depth.[2415]

2410 Opinion of Advocate General Jääskinen in Google Spain, C-131/12, ECLI:EU:C:2013:424, paragraph 133 (emphasis added).

2411 B. Van Alsenoy, A. Kuczerawy and J. Ausloos, "Search Engines after *Google Spain*: Internet@ Liberty or Privacy@Peril?", *l.c.*, p. 69.

2412 European Commission, First Report on the Application of Directive 2000/31 of the European Parliament and of the Council of 8 June 2000 on the Directive on Electronic Commerce, COM(2003) 702 final, Brussels, 21 November 2003; European Commission, Summary of the results of the Public Consultation on the future of electronic commerce in the Internal Market and the implementation of the Directive on electronic commerce (2000/31/EC); European Commission, Commission Staff Working Document Online services, including e-commerce, in the Single Market, Brussels, 11 January 2012 SEC(2011) 1641 final.

2413 B. Van Alsenoy, A. Kuczerawy and J. Ausloos, "Search Engines after *Google Spain*: Internet@ Liberty or Privacy@Peril?", *l.c.*, p. 69. See also *supra*, no. 974.

2414 In the same vein: G. Sartor, "Search Engines as Controllers – Inconvenient implications of a Questionable Classification", *l.c.*, p. 572–574 and M. Thompson, "Beyond Gatekeeping: The Normative Responsibility of Internet Intermediaries", *l.c.*, p. 25 et seq.

2415 For a discussion of possible measures to mitigate risks of over-compliance see: J. Ausloos and A. Kuczerawy, "From Notice-and-Takedown to Notice-and-Delist: Implementing the Google Spain ruling", *l.c.*, p. 17–25.

PART V
RECOMMENDATIONS

CHAPTER 1
INTRODUCTION

1171. Objective – In the final part of this book, the insights developed over the three preceding parts shall be used as a basis for policy recommendations. The policy recommendations address the question of how the current allocation of responsibility and liability among actors involved in the processing of personal data might be modified in order to increase legal certainty while maintaining at least an equivalent level of data protection.

1172. Methodology – The policy recommendations shall be developed in four stages. First, the issues identified in Part IV shall be summarised and presented in a structured manner ("typology of issues"). Second, an inventory will be made of ways in which these issues might be remedied ("typology of solutions"). Third, an evaluation will be made of the extent to which the proposed remedies are capable of addressing each of the identified issues. Finally, in the fourth phase, the approach adopted by the European legislature in the context of the GDPR will be compared with the outcome of the preceding evaluations. Where relevant, recommendations for possible further improvements will be made.

1173. Sources – The typology of issues will be developed by categorising the issues identified in Part IV and presenting them in a structured manner. The typology of solutions, on the other hand, will be developed on the basis of proposals put forward by various stakeholders, particular in the context of the review of Directive 95/46 and run-up to the GDPR. The evaluation of possible solutions shall, for the most part, be based on the typology of issues. Each proposal will be evaluated on the basis of whether, and if so, to what extent, it is capable of addressing each of the identified issues. If multiple solutions have been proposed, an internal comparison will be made. Where appropriate, insights from the field of law and economics will be applied to assist the internal comparison of the proposed solutions.[2416]

2416 In other words, the typology of issues shall serve as the positive assessment framework to evaluate the proposed solutions. No additional assessment criteria will be used to evaluate the proposed solutions. Only in the context of the internal comparison of possible solutions, shall the insights from the field of law and economics be applied in order to enhance the evaluation process.

CHAPTER 2
TYPOLOGY OF ISSUES

1. INTRODUCTION

1174. Preface – Part IV of this book demonstrated that applying the concepts of controller and processor can be difficult in practice. Practitioners often disagree as to whether an entity should be considered a controller or processor, or struggle to make an unambiguous determination. The objective of this Chapter is to provide a structured overview of the main issues that emerge in practice. To this end, a typology of issues shall be developed which categorizes the issues identified in Part IV and presents them in a structured manner.

1175. Categorisation – The typology of issues shall be structured according to four traditional methods of legal interpretation, namely: (1) grammatical; (2) teleological; (3) systemic; and (4) historical. The chosen methods were retained simply because they are the methods of legal interpretation that have been relied upon – either explicitly or implicitly – by scholars, regulators and courts when evaluating the use cases documented in Part IV.[2417] Applying this categorisation, the following typology of issues can be developed:

(1) *Grammatical issues*: issues that concern the words chosen to define the concepts of controller and processor;
(2) *Teleological issues*: issues that concern the policy objectives that underlie the allocation of responsibility and liability between controllers and processors;
(3) *Systemic issues*: issues that arise in light of the functions fulfilled by the controller and processor concepts within the regulatory scheme of EU data protection law; and
(4) *Historical issues*: issues that arise when applying the regulatory framework of EU data protection law to situations which were not envisaged by the European legislature.

2417 For an overview of methods of legal interpretation see L. Kestemont, *Methods for traditional legal research*, Reader Research Master in Law: Methods of Legal Research. KU Leuven – University of Tilburg (Leuven/Tilburg), 2015, 36 p. See also W. Brugger, "Legal Interpretation, Schools of Jurisprudence, and Anthropology: Some Remarks from a German Point of View", *American Journal of Comparative Law* 1994, Vol. 42, No. 2, p. 395–421 and N. MacCormick, "Argumentation and Interpretation in Law", *Ratio Juris* 1993, Vol. 6, No. 1, p. 16–29.

1176. Justification – The development of a typology of issues according to traditional methods of legal interpretation is motivated by the assumption that conflicts of interpretation, as well as interpretative guidelines provided by courts and regulators, can help to uncover the main issues at stake.

1177. Limitations – The utility of the exercise undertaken over the following sections is predicated on the assumption that the selection of use cases analysed in Part IV offers a sufficiently representative account of the main issues that arise when applying the controller and processor concepts in practice.[2418] In other words, there can be no pretence at being exhaustive. Be that as it may, the analysis of proposals put forward by different stakeholders[2419] suggests that the typology of issues presented here is rather comprehensive. While the issues documented here do not provide a definitive normative framework on the basis of which proposals for legislative change should be accepted or discarded, they nevertheless provide a useful framework for an informed and structured evaluation of competing policy options.

2. GRAMMATICAL

1178. Preface – The first category of issues arises from the grammatical interpretation of the controller and processor concepts. The grammatical interpretation method consists of *isolating the essential words* used in a legal provision and *clarifying their meaning* by reference to either the literal meaning of the words or their meaning in common parlance.[2420] The analysis of use cases in Part IV has revealed that the criteria (i.e. "essential words") to determine whether a party is acting as a controller or processor may be subject to multiple interpretations. The aim of this section is to detail how the existing criteria can be understood in different ways and to clarify how this may affect the interpretation of the concepts of controller and processor.

2.1. "DETERMINES"

1179. Decision-making power – To "determine", according to the Article 29 Working Party, means to exert factual influence by exercising decision-making power.[2421] The notion of "decision-making power" can be understood in different ways. The first meaning is formal, or normative in nature, and refers to

2418 See also *supra*, no. 720.
2419 Cf. *infra*, nos. 537 et seq.
2420 L. Kestemont, *Methods for traditional legal research*, *o.c.*, p. 7.
2421 Opinion 1/2010, *l.c.*, p. 8–9.

the decision-making power of persons which are *authorized* to lead and manage an organisation's activities.[2422] The second meaning is descriptive, or non-normative in nature, and refers to *factual influence*.[2423]

1180. AUTHORITY TO DECIDE – Traditionally, the legal status of controller has been attached to a party's *authority to decide* about the processing, rather than its involvement in the processing itself. Previous iterations of the controller concept in fact contained an explicit reference to authority: both the definition of the 1980 OECD Guidelines and Convention 108 describe the controller as the entity that is "*competent to decide*" about the processing.[2424] In Opinion 1/2010, the Working Party still attached considerable importance to the notion of "competence". While recognizing the functional nature of the controller concept, the Working Party also tried to link the question of decision-making power to both formal criteria (explicit competences) and traditional roles (implicit competences) as much as possible.[2425]

1181. FACTUAL INFLUENCE – The apparent emphasis on authority (explicit and implicit competences) may be contrasted with the increasing emphasis on *factual influence* over the processing. Even in Opinion 1/2010, the Working Party repeatedly underlined the "functional nature" of controller concept, which aims to allocate responsibility where factual influence is. As a result, it would appear that the word "determine" is used to convey a dual meaning: it can refer both to the (implicit or explicit) authority to decide about the processing as well as the exercise of factual influence over the processing.

1182. ISSUE – The dual meaning ascribed to the notion of decision-making power can give rise to difficulties when applying the controller concept in practice. While the two meanings may coincide, in practice this is not necessarily

2422 In her 1995 thesis, Overkleeft-Verburg also identifies two distinct meanings of the concept of "decision-making power". One the one hand, it can be understood in the "operational" sense, referring to an exercise of decision-making power by subordinates who have been tasked with undertaking the processing of personal data. On the other hand, it can also be understood in the "managerial" sense, referring to the decision-making power of persons which are authorized to lead and manage an organisation's activities. Overkleeft-Verburg points out that the Dutch legislature used both meanings interchangeably during the preparation of the Dutch Data Protection Act of 1989. This implied that the concept of a "controller" could refer to a wide variety of entities: a natural or legal person, a public body, the management board of an institution, the head of an administrative department, branch directors, etc. The ambiguous nature of the term resulted in considerable legal uncertainty in practice. See M. Overkleeft-Verburg, *De Wet persoonsregistraties – norm, toepassing en evaluatie*, *o.c.*, p. 369 et seq.

2423 Regarding the difference between "power" (as factual influence) and "authority" (as normative influence) see also M. Thompson, "Beyond Gatekeeping: The Normative Responsibility of Internet Intermediaries", *l.c.*, p. 11–12.

2424 Cf. *supra*, no. 432 and no. 461.

2425 Opinion 1/2010, *l.c.*, p. 9–10.

the case. A discrepancy between the "authority to decide" about the processing of personal data and "factual influence" over the processing of personal data is particularly likely to occur in cases where those engaged in the processing at an operational level exercise considerable influence in deciding how the processing shall be organised. The cloud computing use case analysed in Part IV clearly supports this proposition.[2426]

2.2. "PURPOSE"

1183. FINALITY VS. INTEREST – A controller determines the "purposes" of the processing. The notion of "purpose" can be understood in different ways. The first meaning is subjective, or personal in nature, and results from a personal project, business, or activity for which data processing is essential (*purpose as interest*).[2427] The second meaning is objective, or non-personal in nature, and refers to the aims or objectives pursued by the processing itself (*purpose as finality*).

1184. INTEREST – Traditionally, the controller has been conceived of as the "main beneficiary" of the processing: the data processing is carried out "on his behalf", "for his activities", or "*for his purposes*".[2428] As a result, the absence of a personal interest in the outcome of the processing is often invoked as an argument to disqualify a particular actor as controller. In the case of cloud computing, for example, several authors argue that the absence of interest in the outcome of the processing implies that cloud providers should generally be viewed as processors rather than as controllers.[2429] A similar argumentation was also put forward in the context of the Pan-European Proxy Service envisioned by STORK and STORK 2.0.[2430]

1185. FINALITY – The "purpose" of the processing can also be understood in an objective sense, i.e. without reference to the subjective interests of the parties involved in the processing. Establishing the purpose of the processing then involves an analysis of the *aims or objectives* of the processing itself. To

---

2426 Cf. *supra*, nos. 1065 et seq.

2427 Based on J.A. Salom, "'A third party to whom data are disclosed': A third group among those processing data", *l.c.*, p. 181.

2428 Cf. *supra*, no. 1061.

2429 Mantelero, A., "Cloud computing, trans-border data flows and the European Directive 95/46/EC: applicable law and task distribution", *l.c.*, section 3.2 ("*[...] the cloud provider receives the information to be processed in the interest of the user*") and L. Determann, "Data Privacy in the Cloud–Myths and Facts", *l.c.*, Myth 10 ("*[...] providers tend to offer a platform or software functionality as a service, without any interest, knowledge, or influence regarding data types and processing purposes*"). Cf. *supra*, 1029.

2430 Cf. *supra*, 823.

determine the finality of processing, one might ask questions such as "*What is the objective or material end of the processing?*" "*What is the output of the processing and what is the envisioned use of this output?*"[2431] Authors who consider cloud providers as (joint) controllers typically emphasize the role of the provider in (pre)determining the material ends of the processing services they offer (e.g. a SaaS application designed for CRM).[2432]

1186. Interplay and overlap – The distinction between finality and interest can be difficult to make in practice. The main reason is that finality and interest often go hand in hand. If a party involved in the processing of personal data also has an interest in the outcome of the processing, he or she will typically also be involved in deciding the finality of processing. This is logical, seeing as the pursuit of an interest will involve the use of functionalities (i.e. instruments which yield certain outputs) that actually advance the interests of the actor concerned. The end-user of a service which involves the processing of personal data will therefore almost invariably be considered as a controller. On the other hand, it is possible for an actor to be involved in determining the finality of processing without having a personal interest in the outcome processing as such. The Article 29 Working Party's analysis of e-Government portals clearly supports this proposition.[2433]

1187. Issue – The distinction between finality and interest is relevant in situations where an entity does not have an interest in the outcome of the processing, but is nevertheless involved in determining the finality of processing. Practitioners who understand purpose as finality (rather than interest) are more likely to consider service providers as controllers (or joint controllers) insofar as they autonomously design their processing services with a specific use in mind (e.g. a purpose-built SaaS application). Conversely, practitioners who understand purpose as interest are less likely to do so.

2.3. "AND"

1188. Cumulative requirement – Article 4(7) GDPR provides that the controller determines the purposes *and* means of the processing. The use of the word "and" implies the existence of a cumulative requirement: an actor must be involved in determining both the finality (purpose) and modalities (means) of the processing in order to be considered a controller.

2431 See also on J.A. Salom, "'A third party to whom data are disclosed': A third group among those processing data", *l.c.*, p. 181.

2432 Cf. *supra*, no. 1031.

2433 Cf. *supra*, no. 831.

1189. Interpretation by WP29 – In Opinion 1/2010, the Working Party took the position that decisions about the technical and organisational means of the processing can be delegated by the controller to the processor.[2434] Against this background, the Working Party considered that the technical and organisational means of the processing might even be determined exclusively by the data processor.[2435] Only in cases where the determination of means concerns the "essential means" of the processing, or if the actor is involved in the determination of purposes, shall the actor concerned be deemed a (joint) controller rather than processor.[2436]

1190. Issue – Van Eecke and Truyens point out that the Working Party's distinction between "essential" and "non-essential" means (see also *infra*) is at odds with the literal wording of the legal definition of a controller.[2437] Specifically, they argue that the approach of the Working Party reduces a dual legal requirement ("and") to a single requirement ("or"), by stating that it is sufficient for a party to determine either the purpose or the essential aspects of the means in order to qualify as a data controller.[2438]

1191. Caveats – In theory, one could derive two premises from the guidance provided by the Article 29 Working Party. The first premise is that it is possible for an actor to determine the "means" of the processing without being involved in the definition of the "purpose" of the processing. Conversely, the second premise is that it is possible for an actor to determine the "purpose" of the processing without being involved in the determination of "means". While both premises would be valid, conceptually speaking, a number of caveats must be made. The first caveat is that every choice of "means" can be viewed as involving a determination of *the purpose of those means*. Means are not chosen in the abstract, but rather with a view of achieving a certain outcome or functionality (i.e. as "means to an end").[2439] The second caveat is that a choice of means might be as simple as a decision to make use of a service provided by a third party.[2440] Even if the entity concerned does not have the power to influence how the

2434 Opinion 1/2010, *l.c.*, p. 15.

2435 Opinion 1/2010, *l.c.*, p. 14. See in the same vein also Tweede Kamer der Staten-Generaal, Regels inzake de bescherming van persoonsgegevens (Wet bescherming persoonsgegevens) – Memorie van Toelichting, *l.c.*, p. 61–62.

2436 *Ibid*, p. 19.

2437 P. Van Eecke and M. Truyens, "Privacy and social networks", *l.c.*, p. 539.

2438 *Id.*

2439 In the same vein: T. Léonard and A. Mention, "Transferts transfrontaliers de données: quelques considérations théorique et pratiques", *l.c.*, p. 107 ("*[...] le sous-traitant détermine évidemment la finalité même d'utilisation de ses services. Ainsi par exemple, le système de traitement qu'il offre en service est conçu pour permettre des analyses de marché, pour communiquer des messages, pour dresser le profil de clients, etc.*")

2440 In the same vein: Opinion of Advocate General Bobek in *Fashion ID*, C-40/17, ECLI:EU:C:2018:1039, paragraph 69 (cf. *supra*, no. 916) and Opinion of Advocate General Bot

service is designed or organized, it can at a minimum decide whether or not to use the service. In this sense, a controller still effectively determines the means of the processing when he entrusts the processing of personal data to a particular service provider, even if the only choice that is made in relation to the modalities of the processing is simply to "take it or leave it".[2441]

1192. Assessment – One should take care not to lose sight of the specific context in which the Working Party provided its guidance regarding "essential" and "non-essential" means of the processing. The aim of the Working Party was to clarify situations in which a processor can no longer be considered a mere "processor" but must instead be considered a controller (or joint controller). In other words, the primary objective of the Working Party was to clarify the "tipping point" at which a service provider's involvement is such that it becomes justified to subject the service provider to the obligations and responsibilities ordinarily incumbent upon controllers. The Working Party's distinction between "essential" and "non-essential" means should therefore be viewed primarily in this light. While certain language in Opinion 1/2010 can effectively be read as suggesting that the determination of (certain) means is optional in certain cases, earlier opinions (e.g. SWIFT, social networks) and other sections of Opinion 1/2010[2442] confirm that both a determination of both purposes and the means are (and remain) constitutive elements for control. Nevertheless, Van Eecke and Truyens rightfully draw attention to the inherent ambiguity in the approach developed by the Working Party, which will be elaborated further in the following section.

2.4. "MEANS"

1193. Means to an end – A controller must decide not only about the purposes of the processing of personal data, but must also decide about the means that shall be used to realise these purposes.

1194. "Essential" vs. "Non-essential" means – As indicated above, the Article 29 Working Party has introduced a distinction between "essential"

in in *Wirtschaftsakademie*, C-210/16, ECLI:EU:C:2017:796, paragraph 61 (cf. *supra*, nos. 892 et seq.).

2441 B. Van Alsenoy, J. Ballet, A. Kuczerawy and J. Dumortier, "Social networks and web 2.0: are users also bound by data protection regulations?", *l.c.*, 70. Léonard and Mention point out that in such cases the controller's determination of means is only *indirect*: it is the processor who effectively determines the means of the processing, the controller only indirectly determines the means by choosing a particular processor. (T. Léonard and A. Mention, "Transferts transfrontaliers de données : quelques considérations théorique et pratiques", *l.c.*, p. 105).

2442 See e.g. Opinion 1/2010, *l.c.*, 26.

and "non-essential" means.[2443] "Essential means", according to the Working Party, are those elements which are traditionally and inherently reserved to the determination of the controller, such as "*which data shall be processed*?", "*for how long shall they be processed*?", and "*who shall have access to them*?".[2444] "Non-essential means" concern more practical aspects of implementation, such as the choice for a particular type of hard- or software.[2445]

1195. Relevance of the distinction – The Working Party attaches considerable weight to the distinction between essential and non-essential means. According to the Working Party, a determination of "means" only implies control when the determination concerns the essential elements of the means.[2446] Under this approach, the Working Party considers it possible that the technical and organisational means of the processing are determined exclusively by the data processor.[2447]

1196. Rationale – The distinction between "essential" and "non-essential" means appears to have been motivated by practical considerations. In practice entities providing processing services often, at least to a certain extent, have a determinative influence over the means of the processing. As one scholar puts it, the determination of the "means" of the processing *is* the service offered by a processor.[2448] One of the reasons why a controller may decide to enlist a processor is precisely because the controller lacks the technical expertise necessary to design and develop a processing system which is suited to his objectives.[2449] Absent any further threshold, *every* service provider offering

---

2443 See also *supra*, nos. 110 et seq.

2444 The Article 29 Working Party derived these criteria from the legislative development of the controller and processor concepts. As indicated earlier, previous iterations of the controller concept referred to four elements ("purpose and objective", "which personal data are to be processed", "which operations are to be performed upon them" and "which third parties are to have access to them"). According to the Working Party, the word "means" should be understood as comprising these elements. ("*[T]he final definition must rather be understood as being only a shortened version comprising nevertheless the sense of the older version.*") (*Ibid*, p. 14).

2445 *Id.*

2446 *Id.*

2447 *Id.*

2448 T. Léonard, "'Data processor' and 'Data controller' – Are these concepts still adequate?", presentation held at the conference: "*Reinventing data protection*", Brussels, 12–13 October 2007, slide 9. See also T. Léonard and A. Mention, "Transferts transfrontaliers de données: quelques considérations théorique et pratiques", *l.c.*, p. 105 («*Les moyens du traitement deviennent l'objet même du service fourni par les différents sous-traitants qui interviennent dans le processus de traitement. Ils sont déterminés par le seul sous-traitant comme élément essentiel de son service.*») See also P. Van Eecke, M. Truyens et al. (eds.), "The future of online privacy and data protection", *l.c.*, 33.

2449 See also A. Joint and E. Baker, "'Knowing the past to understand the present' – issues in the contracting for cloud based services", *Computer Law & Security Review* 2011, Vol. 24, Issue 4, 408.

standardised processing services which involve the processing of personal data might effectively be considered a controller.

1197. Issue – Although the Working Party provided several examples to clarify the distinction between "essential" and "non-essential" means, the distinction can be difficult to apply in practice. After all, every choice of "means" serves to achieve a particular objective and may, depending on one's point of view, be considered "essential" in achieving that objective. This issue was implicitly acknowledged by the Working Party itself in Opinion 1/2010, in relation to the choice of security measures:

> "In some legal systems decisions taken on security measures are particularly important, since security measures are explicitly considered as an essential characteristic to be defined by the controller. This raises the issue of which decisions on security may entail the qualification of controller for a company to which processing has been outsourced."[2450]

Cloud computing services have put further pressure on the distinction between "essential" and "non-essential" means. Certain aspects of cloud computing services that are often determined by cloud providers (e.g. security measures, location of data, use of subcontractors, deletion processes, new service features, synchronisation services) may be considered as "essential" means.[2451] In this regard, the EDPS observed that

> "More and more often, the determination of the essential elements of the means, which is a prerogative of the data controller, is not in the hands of the cloud client. In this respect, the cloud service provider typically designs, operates and maintains the cloud computing IT infrastructure."[2452]

In its Opinion on cloud computing, the Article 29 Working Party did not, however, consider that the cloud provider's influence concerning essential

---

2450 Opinion 1/2010, *l.c.*, p. 15.

2451 See also F. Gilbert, "Cloud service providers as joint-data controllers", *l.c.*, p. 9; W. Kuan Hon, C. Millard and I. Walden, "Who is Responsible for 'Personal Data' in Cloud Computing? The Cloud of Unknowing, Part 2", *l.c.*, p. 11. See also European Data Protection Supervisor (EDPS), "Opinion of the European Data Protection Supervisor on the Commission's Communication on "Unleashing the potential of Cloud Computing in Europe", *l.c.*, p. 12 ("*... the complexity of the technical means used in the cloud environment has now reached such a stage that it is necessary to add that the cloud client/data controller may not be the only entity that can solely determine the "purposes and means" of the processing. More and more often, the determination of the essential elements of the means, which is a prerogative of the data controller, is not in the hands of the cloud client. In this respect, the cloud service provider typically designs, operates and maintains the cloud computing IT infrastructure*")

2452 European Data Protection Supervisor (EDPS), "Opinion of the European Data Protection Supervisor on the Commission's Communication on "Unleashing the potential of Cloud Computing in Europe", *l.c.*, p. 12.

elements of the processing automatically renders him controller. Rather, the Opinion indicated that as long as the cloud provider clearly outlines the essential elements of the processing in advance (and does not draw outside these lines without additional agreement from the customer), the provider may retain its status as processor.[2453] While the guidance of the Working Party is pragmatic, it also demonstrates that a number of grey areas remain, which may lead to divergent interpretations in practice.[2454]

2.5. "ALONE OR JOINTLY WITH OTHERS"

1198. Together or alone – The legal definition of a controller contains a distinction between "joint" and "separate" control. Joint control exists where two or more actors jointly determine the purposes and means of the processing in question. If the parties do not pursue the same purposes, or do not rely upon the same means for achieving their respective objectives, they are likely to be considered as "separate controllers" rather than "joint controllers".[2455]

1199. Relevance of the distinction – The distinction between joint and separate control has significant practical importance with regard to liability exposure.[2456] In principle, collaborating separate controllers are only responsible for ensuring compliance of their own processing activities. A separate controller is generally not liable for acts or omissions committed by the other controller.[2457] In case of joint control, however, each controller may be considered responsible for ensuring compliance of the processing as a whole (at least insofar as it falls within the scope of his (joint) control). As a result, each joint controller can in principle be held liable for any damages resulting from non-compliance, unless it is able to demonstrate that it is not in any way responsible for the event giving rise to the damage.[2458] The distinction between joint and separate control is also

2453 Cf. *supra*, no. 1063.

2454 W. Kuan Hon, C. Millard and I. Walden, "Who is Responsible for 'Personal Data' in Cloud Computing? The Cloud of Unknowing, Part 2", *l.c.*, p. 11.

2455 Cf. *supra*, no. 126. See also Opinion 1/2010, *l.c.*, 25.

2456 In addition, Article 24 of the draft GDPR requires that the respective responsibilities of joint controllers be determined by way of an arrangement between them (unless, and in so far as, the respective responsibilities of the controllers are determined by Union or Member State law).

2457 T. Olsen and T. Mahler, "Privacy – Identity Management Data Protection Issues in Relation to Networked Organisations Utilizing Identity Management Systems", *l.c.*, p. 41.

2458 In Opinion 1/2010, the Article 29 Working Party considered that joint and several liability should only be imposed insofar as an alternative, clear and equally effective allocation of obligations and responsibilities has not been established by the parties involved or does not clearly stem from factual circumstances. (Opinion 1/2010, *l.c.*, p. 24.) As mentioned earlier, I do not consider the limitation provided by the Article 29 Working Party to be entirely correct if one takes into account the general principles of European tort law (cf. *supra*, no. 180). In

relevant in relation to basic controller obligations more generally, including the accommodation of data subject rights.

1200. Issue – The distinction between "joint" and "separate" control may be difficult to draw in practice. Joint and separate control reside at opposite ends of a continuum, with many possible variations between them. The notion of "partial joint control", as well as the recognition that joint control may be exercised "asymmetrically", at "different stages" and "to different degrees" clearly illustrate this point. Further confounding the analysis is the suggestion that control may be exercised only over certain *aspects* of the processing.[2459] While a granular application of the concept of "control" promotes flexibility, it also complicates matters. Establishing where the control of one party ends and another begins becomes increasingly difficult. Moreover, it increases the risk of confusion between two distinct issues: the legal status of an entity (as either controller or joint controller) and the legal implications associated with this status (i.e. the scope of its obligations).[2460]

2.6. "THE PROCESSING"

1201. Operation or set of operations – The decision-making power of a controller extends to the "processing" of personal data. The term "processing" is defined by Article 4(2) as "any operation or set of operations" which is performed upon personal data. As a result, the concept of a controller can be linked either to a single processing operation or to a set of operations.[2461]

1202. Subject to framing – In situations where personal data is exchanged among multiple actors, the assessment of which actor (or actors) control(s) the processing hinges on the vantage point of the assessor. If "the processing" is considered from a very high level, i.e. as the entirety of operations that are needed to realize a particular service or output, one is likely to reach a different conclusion than if one were to "zoom in" on the individual processing operations which are performed to realize that service or output.[2462] As a result, practical

any event, Article 26(3) of the GDPR explicitly confirms that a data subject may exercise his or her rights under this Regulation in respect of and against each joint controllers irrespective of the terms of the arrangement between them.

2459 Cf. *supra*, no. 832.

2460 See also *infra*, nos. 1229 et seq.

2461 See also *supra*, no. 920.

2462 J. Alhadeff and B. Van Alsenoy, "Legal and Policy handbook for TAS³ implementations", *Trusted Architecture for Securely Shared Services* (TAS³), Deliverable 6.1–6.2, v1.0, 2012, p. 101. See also International Chamber of Commerce (ICC), ICC Task Force on Privacy and the Protection of Personal Data, "Summary of the Workshop on the Distinction between Data Controllers and Data Processors", Paris, Thursday, 25 October, 2007, p. 2 ("*Level of detail in*

difficulties might arise in determining whether a given series of operations should be considered as being part of the same "processing" or not.[2463]

1203. Guidance – According to the Article 29 Working Party, the question of which entity is acting as a controller should be looked at "both in detail and in its entirety".[2464] Specifically:

> "In some cases, various actors process the same personal data in a sequence. In these cases, it is likely that at micro-level the different processing operations of the chain appear as disconnected, as each of them may have a different purpose. However, it is necessary to double check whether at macro-level these processing operations should not be considered as a "set of operations" pursuing a joint purpose or using jointly defined means."[2465]

The Working Party did not explicitly state when control should be assessed either at the level of a specific operation or set of operations. Its language suggests that the presence of a jointly defined purpose or use of jointly defined means should be determinative in deciding whether or not the processing should be assessed together or in isolation. An alternative approach would be to look at general perception. Given the central importance of the purpose specification principle to the regulatory scheme of EU data protection law, however, the delineation of "the processing" should be made in light of the purposes pursued.[2466] As Gutwirth argues:

> "[T]he delineation and separation of purposes is decisive in the establishment of the number of processing operations. Finality is the key to pinpoint what the processing operation is. And since the whole protection system is engrafted onto the processing operation, it will succeed or fail based on the way in which processing is delineated. Personal data processing is each processing operation or series of operations with personal data which aims to realize one purpose, one finality."[2467]

1204. Assessment – The definition of processing as being either an operation or set of operations is beneficial. It promotes adaptability and allows a reasonable balance to be struck between two extremes: a separate controller for every

---

analyzing the purposes and means of processing: Some participants indicated that decisions on the purposes and means of processing should be evaluated at each stage of the data processing chain, while others found that the overall picture of a data processing situation should be examined to determine whether a party was a data controller or a data processor.")

2463 See also *supra*, nos. 116 et seq. (noting that the delineation of "the processing" should in principle be made in light of the purposes pursued).

2464 Opinion 1/2010, *l.c.*, p. 3.

2465 Opinion 1/2010, *l.c.*, p. 20.

2466 Gutwirth, S., *Privacy and the information age*, *o.c.*, p. 97.

2467 *Id.*

processing operation and a single controller for all processing operations.[2468] Less straightforward, however, is the situation where personal data is not processed "as part of a chain", but rather as part of an integrated system (e.g. the IMI system).[2469] In such cases, control over "the processing" may be more difficult to determine, as different actors may control different *aspects* of the processing.[2470]

2.7. "OF PERSONAL DATA"

1205. Object of control – If an actor determines the purposes and means of the processing, but no personal data are involved, he or she will not be considered a controller. At least some of the data processed under the authority of a controller must relate to an identified or identifiable individual.

1206. Knowledge or intent – The question may be asked whether it is necessary that the actor controlling the processing is *aware* of the fact that he or she is processing personal data. One could argue that in order to be considered a controller, the actor must exercise decision-making power towards the processing of data which it knows to be personal in nature.[2471] The CJEU has implicitly rejected this argument, however, when interpreting the definition of "processing" in the context of *Google Spain*.[2472] As a result, an actor can be considered a "controller" even if he or she does not deliberately target personal data as such or is not a priori aware which data relate to identified or identifiable individual.[2473] This finding has implications not only for search engines, but also for other service providers such as online social networks and certain cloud providers.

1207. With or without access – The CJEU has also repeatedly stated that it is not necessary for every entity involved in the processing to have access the personal data concerned in order to be considered a (joint) controller.[2474]

2468 See also *supra*, no. 530.
2469 Cf. *supra*, nos. 786 et seq.
2470 Cf. *supra*, nos. 831 et seq.
2471 Google Spain SSRN paper, p. 16. See also Opinion of Advocate General Jääskinen in Google Spain, C-131/12, ECLI:EU:C:2013:424, paragraph 83.
2472 Judgment in *Google Spain*, C-131/12, EU:C:2014:317, paragraph 28 (" ... *regardless of the fact that the operator of the search engine also carries out the same operations in respect of other types of information and does not distinguish between the latter and the personal data.*").
2473 In the same vein: P. De Hert and P. Papakonstantinou, "Comment – Google Spain -Addressing Critiques and Misunderstandings One Year Later", *Maastricht Journal of European and Comparative Law* 2015, Vol. 22, No. 4, p. 627 ("'*Knowledge' of the data controller or 'alteration' of the data, as Google contested, are not necessary conditions to this end.*").
2474 Judgment in *Wirtschaftsakademie*, C-210/16, ECLI:EU:C:2018:388, paragraph 38; Judgment in *Jehovah's witnesses*, C-25/17, ECLI:EU:C:2018:551, paragraph 69.

1208. Issue – If an actor can be considered a (joint) controller without active knowledge of or access to the personal data involved, the question arises as to how the absence of such knowledge or access may affect the scope of his obligations. At a practical level, the actor may not be able to comply with all controller obligations until he or she becomes (or is made) aware of the fact that personal data are involved. This issue was implicitly recognized in *Google Spain*, where the CJEU recognized that there may be practical limits to the ability of a search engine operator to meet all the obligations resulting from EU data protection law.[2475] Even after becoming aware, however, the actor in question may not have (operational) capability to give effect to certain requirements or obligations, instead being dependant on the involvement of other entities involved in the processing. How the inability to implement, at an operational level, specific requirements or obligations should (or should not) affect the scope responsibility (or liability) of an actor involved in the processing has been subject to divergent interpretations.[2476]

2.8. "ON BEHALF OF"

1209. Agency – The definition of a processor states that a processor acts "on behalf of" a controller. The processor concept is frequently linked to the concepts of delegation and agency, understood as the process whereby one person (the principal) enlists another person (the "delegate" or "agent") to act on his behalf.[2477]

1210. Cumulation possible? – The criteria to determine whether an entity is acting as a controller or processor are not, by their nature, mutually exclusive. From a linguistic perspective, an actor can be involved in determining the purposes and means of the processing while at the same time acting "on behalf of" someone else. It is true that the legal definition of a processor implies that the processor is an entity separate from the controller, which would imply that the two roles cannot coincide (or at least not simultaneously). The linguistic criteria contained in the definitions of controller and processor, however, do not by themselves prevent cumulation.

2475 In qualifying search engine providers as controller, the Court of Justice also immediately indicated that there may be limits to the obligations of search engines: "*[...] the operator of the search engine as the person determining the purposes and means of that activity must ensure, within the framework of its responsibilities, powers and capabilities, that the activity meets the requirements of Directive 95/46 in order that the guarantees laid down by the directive may have full effect and that effective and complete protection of data subjects, in particular of their right to privacy, may actually be achieved.*" (Judgment in *Google Spain*, C-131/12, EU:C:2014:317, paragraph 38). Advocate General Szpunar has confirmed this approach more explicitly: Opinion of Advocate General Szpunar, *G. C., A. F., B. H., E. D. v. Commission nationale de l'informatique et des libertés (CNIL)*, C-136/17, ECLI:EU:C:2019:14, paragraph 54. Cf. *supra*, no. 1167.

2476 See for example *supra*, no. 982 et seq.

2477 Cf. *supra*, no. 84.

1211. Hybrid actors – Two of the use cases analysed in Part IV illustrate how certain actors combine the characteristics of both controllers and processors. In the e-Government setting, for example, the Pan-European Proxy Service could be viewed as either a controller or processor.[2478] Similar considerations apply in relation to certain cloud providers, who process personal data on behalf of their customers, while still exercising decision-making power regarding the purposes and/or means of the processing.[2479]

1212. Subject to framing – In principle, once an actor is involved in determining the purposes and means of the processing, he or she must be deemed a (joint) controller – even if the processing itself is performed mainly to serve the interests of another party. In practice, however, regulators and scholars appear willing to accept that an entity may still be viewed as a "processor" even if it enjoys considerable latitude in deciding how the processing shall be organized.[2480] This has resulted in a situation where the assessment of the legal status of an entity may vary depending on which characteristics are perceived as dominant. If one emphasises the autonomy of the entity concerned (e.g. in designing and operating the service), or the limited choices available to end-users, one winds up concluding that the entity acts as a controller. Conversely, if one emphasizes the auxiliary nature of the service, designed to serve the interests of others, one winds up concluding that the entity should be deemed a processor. In other words: the final outcome of the analysis may be more a result of framing rather than the straight-forward application of established criteria.

1213. Additional criteria – To help distinguish between controllers and processors, the Article 29 Working Party has developed a range of additional criteria. In Opinion 1/2010, for example, the Working Party mentions:

- level of prior instructions given (the greater the level of instruction, the more limited the margin of manoeuvre of the processor);
- monitoring of the execution of the service (a constant and careful supervision of compliance provides an indication of being in control of the processing operations);
- image given to the data subject; and
- expertise of the parties (if the expertise of the service provider plays a predominant role in the processing, it may entail its qualification as data controller).[2481]

[2478] Cf. *supra*, nos. 819 et seq.
[2479] Cf. *supra*, nos. 1022 et seq.
[2480] Cf. *supra*, no. 1063.
[2481] Opinion 1/2010, *l.c.*, p. 28. See also *supra*, no. 114.

1214. Balancing test – None of the additional criteria developed by the Article 29 Working Party are by themselves determinative. Instead, the approach advanced by the Working Party seems to be more of a balancing test: the more elements there are pointing in favour of a particular qualification, the more likely it is that the "official" criteria (i.e. "purposes", "means", "on behalf") will be applied in a way that supports this qualification.

1215. Caveats – While the additional criteria provided by the Article 29 Working Party are helpful, a number of caveats can be made. First, not all of the additional criteria are anchored in the legal definitions of controller and processor. Second, the additional criteria can (also) be distributed among different actors. For example, even though the service provider might play a predominant role in the processing, the image given to the data subject might suggest another actor is in charge of the processing. Finally, the use of additional, non-determinative, criteria is likely to increase the role of framing.

1216. Practical implications – The assessment of whether an entity is acting as a controller or processors requires careful appreciation of all the factual elements surrounding the processing. The criteria provided by the legal definitions of controller and processor may not always allow for a straight-forward determination. More often than not, the assessment will be driven by an overall assessment of the totality of circumstances, to determine the entity "should" be viewed as a controller or processor. The outcome of this assessment will inevitably be influenced by the teleological assumptions held by the adjudicator. This aspect will be developed further in the course of the following section.

3. TELEOLOGICAL

1217. Preface – The second category of issues arises from the teleological interpretation of the controller and processor concepts. The teleological method of interpretation involves interpreting a legal provision in light of the *original objectives* of the legislature (e.g. protecting certain interests, imposing a specific kind of behaviour).[2482] Applied to the controller-processor model, one can say that a teleological issue occurs when one or more of the objectives that underlie the controller and processor concepts are not fully realised in practice.

1218. Three related objectives – The preparatory works suggest that the primary aim of the differentiation between controllers and processors is to ensure a *continuous level of protection* in case of outsourcing. A secondary

2482 L. Kestemont, *Methods for traditional legal research*, *o.c.*, p. 12. See also and N. MacCormick, "Argumentation and Interpretation in Law", *l.c.*, p. 24–26.

objective of the differentiation between controllers and processors is to provide *legal certainty* to the actors involved in the processing as regards the scope of their obligations. Finally, the case law of the CJEU indicates that the concept of a controller also seeks to ensure *effective and complete protection* of data subjects.

3.1. CONTINUOUS LEVEL OF PROTECTION

1219. Commission proposal – While the initial Commission proposal for a Data Protection Directive did not contain a formal distinction between "controllers" and "processors", it did include a specific provision referring to persons or enterprises who process personal data "on behalf of" the controller. Article 22 of the Commission proposal provided that the controller may only outsource the processing of personal data to persons or enterprises which provide sufficient guarantees as regards the implementation of security measures.[2483] It also required the controller to conclude a contract which specified the person or enterprise providing the processing service (as well as their employees) to confidentiality.[2484]

1220. Explanatory memorandum – The Explanatory Memorandum accompanying the Commission proposal clarified the rationale behind Article 22 as follows:

> "The object of this article is to avoid a situation whereby processing by a third party on behalf of the controller of the file has the effect of reducing the level of protection enjoyed by the data subject. To that end, obligations are placed both on the controller of the file and on the third party carrying out the processing."[2485]

On the basis of this text, it seems reasonable to conclude that the primary rationale for introducing the distinction between controllers and processors was to ensure a continuous level of protection in case of outsourcing.[2486] While the initial Commission proposal foresaw imposing obligations directly upon processors, the final text of Directive 95/46 envisaged that continuous protection would be ensured by way of contractual safeguards, coupled with the liability of a controller for the actions of its processor.

2483 Article 22(1) of the Commission Proposal.

2484 Article 22(3) of the Commission Proposal. Interestingly, Article 22(2) provided that any person who collects or processes personal data on behalf of the controller must comply with the basic principles of data protection, suggesting that processors were equally responsible for compliance. Article 21, however, which concerned the issue of liability, only provided for liability of the controller.

2485 Commission of the European Communities, "Proposal for a Council Directive concerning the protection of individuals in relation to the processing of personal data", SYN 287, Explanatory Memorandum, p. 40.

2486 See also Opinion 1/2010, *l.c.*, p. 25–26.

1221. Accountability – An important element of ensuring a continuous level of protection concerns the liability of controllers for the actions of their processors. Even in case of outsourcing, the controller shall in principle remain accountable for any harm suffered as a result of unlawful processing. While the initial Commission proposal provided that the controller might be exempted from liability if he could demonstrate having taken appropriate measures (e.g. contractual binding, due diligence in choosing processors), the final text considerably narrowed the exemption (imposing strict liability).[2487] As a result, one could argue that an additional rationale underlying the distinction between controllers and processors was to reinforce the accountability of the controller of the processing towards data subjects, regardless of how the processing was organized. The imposition of liability upon the controller for the actions of its processor allows individuals to exercise their rights as data subjects with a single entity (the controller). By rendering a single actor responsible for ensuring compliance for the processing as a whole, the data subject is, at least in theory, spared the burden of determining the precise nature of the task allocation between the controller and processor. In case of harm, data subjects are in theory also protected against the risk of being unable to determine whether the harm should be attributed to the controller or processor.[2488]

1222. Staying in control – There is an additional rationale behind the differentiation between controllers and processors, which is closely related to the desire to ensure a continuous level of protection. Part of the aim of the controller-processor model is to ensure that the controller in fact remains "in control" of the processing.[2489] The obligation of the processor to abide by the instructions of the controller clearly illustrates this proposition.[2490]

2487 Cf. *supra*, no. 159.

2488 In my opinion, this also explains why the Article 29 Working Party and national regulators consider "image given to data subjects" as a relevant factor in determining whether an entity should be considered as a controller or processor. Cf. *supra*, no. 114.

2489 See in particular T. Léonard and A. Mention, "Transferts transfrontaliers de données: quelques considérations théorique et pratiques", *l.c.*, p. 101–102 ("*La régime mise en place par la Loi à l'égard du sous-traitant vise à neutraliser les risques de l'intervention d'un tiers dans le traitement des données, et a perte potentielle de contrôle sur les données qui peut en résulter pour le responsable: le sous-traitant ne peut agir que sur instruction du responsable du traitement*") and P. Blume, "An alternative model for data protection law: changing the roles of controller and processor", *International Data Privacy Law* 2015, Vol. 5, No. 4, p. 294 ("*The well-known starting point is that the processor acts on behalf of the controller and that there must be a contract regulating the duties of the processor who furthermore has to be instructed by the controller. The processor has no independence and resembles an employee. This system is intended to ensure that the controller so to speak is in control and that there in principal is no difference between the use of internal and external helps.*")

2490 See also the Judgment in *Probst*, C-119/12, ECLI:EU:C:2012:748, paragraph 25. See also *supra*, no. 100.

1223. Issue – An implicit assumption of the controller-processor model of EU data protection law is that the controller is able to exercise control over the processing.[2491] The model assumes that whoever determines the "purposes and means" of the processing is effectively able to "take the lead" and ensure compliance with data protection requirements.[2492] After all, the idea of ensuring continuous protection by imposing strict liability upon controllers only makes sense if controllers can effectively adduce adequate safeguards.[2493] The processor, on the other hand, is implicitly viewed as being "non-autonomous", i.e. as merely executing instructions issued by a controller without substantially influencing the manner in which the processing shall be organized.[2494] In practice, however, the decision-making power of controllers is often constrained by the decisions made by processors, who autonomously design their services and offer them under standardised terms. The cloud computing use case analysed in Part IV clearly supports this proposition.[2495] The objective of ensuring continuous

---

2491 See also P. Blume, "An alternative model for data protection law: changing the roles of controller and processor", *International Data Privacy Law* 2015, Vol. 5, No. 4, p. 292. ("*Data protection is founded on a fiction, at least to a large degree. The fiction is that the data controller is in control and is able to meet the obligations set out in the law. [...] In order to believe in data protection law, it is necessary to believe that the controller is capable of performing the leading role in the play and act this role as it is written and thought.*")

2492 M. Thompson, "Beyond Gatekeeping: The Normative Responsibility of Internet Intermediaries", *l.c.*, p. 26 ("*The notion of control [...] does not belong to the granular reality of being in control but rather comes up as an expectation directed to whoever happens to "determine the purposes and means of the processing of personal data*"). One might also argue that definition of controller combines both factual ("is") and normative ("ought") components: the definition extends the object of the decision-making power to include elements over which the entity concerned should (normatively speaking) exercise decision-making power and take responsible decisions. Compare also *supra*, no. 528 (discussing the CBPL proposal to extend the definition of controller under the Belgian data protection act, which was based on the consideration that certain aspects of the processing are important therefore the controller of the file "*should*" also have the power to decide about them).

2493 P. Blume, "An alternative model for data protection law: changing the roles of controller and processor", *l.c.*, p. 292.

2494 See also Information Commissioner's Office (ICO), "The Information Commissioner's response to the European Commission's consultation on the legal framework for the fundamental right to protection of personal data", p. 2. ("*The definitions assume that a processor is an essentially passive entity, acting on behalf of a controller, with no independent influence over the way the processing takes place.*") and P. De Hert and V. Papakonstantinou, "The proposed data protection Regulation replacing Directive 95/46/EC: A sound system for the protection of individuals", *l.c.*, p. 133–134 ("*[...] the Commission appears to uphold in its draft Regulation the aforementioned traditional personal data processing scheme, whereby roles are expected to be distinguishable and data processors are expected to be passive and of an executionary only function*").

2495 See also P. Blume, "An alternative model for data protection law: changing the roles of controller and processor", *l.c.*, p. 294. See also See also Article 29 Data Protection Working Party, "Opinion 02/2015 on C-SIG Code of Conduct on Cloud Computing", *l.c.*, p. 8 ("*The CSP may cease to be considered a processor, with all its consequences especially in terms of liability, in cases where the actions taken by the CSP exceeds by far the normal capacities of a data processor in viewed of its supposed absence of autonomy with respect to the instructions of the controller*"). Cf. *supra*, nos. 1044 et seq.

protection may therefore be undermined in practice in situations where controllers lack a sufficiently strong bargaining position or do not have the ability to choose from services which are compliant with EU data protection law.

3.2. LEGAL CERTAINTY

1224. Clarifying roles and responsibilities – A second objective of the controller and processor concepts is to clarify the responsibilities of actors involved in the processing as regards the scope of their obligations.[2496] The concept of a processor, in particular, serves to identify the responsibilities of those processing personal data under the authority of the controller.[2497] This is closely related to the principle of legal certainty.[2498] By differentiating between controllers and processors, the EU legislature was able to delineate the (more limited) legal obligations incumbent upon those processing "on behalf of others". At the same time, it also allowed the legislature to clarify which measures controllers are expected to undertake when outsourcing data processing in order to ensure a continuous level of protection (i.e. due diligence, legal binding, oversight).[2499]

1225. Issue – The aspirations of legal certainty motivating the distinction between controllers and processors have not been realised in practice. The current uncertainty is attributable in part to the nature of the existing concepts, but also – and perhaps to a larger extent – to the fact that the controller-processor model fits only a portion of the processing relationships that occur in practice.[2500] The controller processor-model only provides legal certainty in cases where the factual circumstances surrounding the processing can easily

2496 Opinion 1/2010, *l.c.*, p. 5.

2497 Opinion 1/2010, *l.c.*, p. 5.

2498 The principle of legal certainty is a general principle of EU law, which expresses the fundamental premise that those subject to the law must be able to ascertain what the law is so as to be able to plan their actions accordingly. (T. Tridimas, *The General Principles of EU Law*, 2nd edition, Oxford University Press, Oxford, 2006, p. 242 et seq.). See also J. Raitio, "The Expectation of Legal Certainty and Horizontal Effect of EU Law", in U. Bernitz, X. Groussot and F. Schulyok (eds.), *General Principles of EU Law and European Private Law*, Kluwer Law International, Croyden, p. 199–211.

2499 Cf. *supra*, nos. 87 et seq.

2500 Several authors have argued that the controller-processor relationship reflects an outdated processing paradigm. Kuner, for example, has noted that the distinction between controllers and processors was far clearer the time the Directive was adopted. C. Kuner, *European Data Protection Law – Corporate Compliance and Regulation*, *o.c.*, p. 71–72. In the same vein, Moerel observes that "*At the time the first outsourcing transactions were concluded, it was indeed the controller who was in the driving seat as to imposing all terms relating to the outsourcing, including security requirements and whether data were transferred to non-EU countries or not. Today, with more commoditized outsourcing services [...] contractual terms on security and whether data transfers are taking place or not are (as much) dictated by the*

be mapped to the model and its implicit assumptions regarding autonomy and control. In other cases, the controller-processor model may actually create uncertainty, especially if the parties involved in the processing are unable to make an unambiguous determination regarding the legal status of each actor.[2501] Legal uncertainty increases, moreover, when the formal qualification established by parties involved in the processing does not withstand regulatory scrutiny and leads to requalification.[2502]

3.3. EFFECTIVE AND COMPLETE PROTECTION

1226. Principle – The teleological method of interpretation has also been central to the reasoning of the CJEU in interpreting EU data protection law.[2503] According to the CJEU, one of the objectives EU data protection law is to ensure the "effective and complete" protection of the fundamental rights and freedoms of natural persons, and in particular their right to privacy, with respect to the processing of personal data.[2504] In *Google Spain*, for example, the Court explicitly referred to considerations of effectiveness in its interpretation of the controller concept:

> "it would be contrary not only to the clear wording of that provision but also to its objective – which is to ensure, through a broad definition of the concept of 'controller', effective and complete protection of data subjects – to exclude the operator of a search engine from that definition on the ground that it does not exercise control over the personal data published on the web pages of third parties."[2505]

1227. Limitations – The objective of ensuring "effective and complete" protection of individuals does not imply that each party involved in the processing of personal data must be subject to the same obligations. In *Google*

---

outsourcing supplier." (L. Moerel, *Binding Corporate Rules: Corporate Self-Regulation of Global Data Transfers*, *o.c.*, p. 216)

2501 See for example the discussion of the Pan-European E-Government service *supra*, nos. 819 et seq.

2502 See also L. Moerel, *Binding Corporate Rules: Corporate Self-Regulation of Global Data Transfers*, *o.c.*, p. 223.

2503 See also D. Sancho-Villa, "Developing Search Engine Law: It Is Not Just about the Right to Be Forgotten", *l.c.*, p. 369.

2504 Judgment in *Google Spain* C-131/12, EU:C:2014:317, paragraph 53. See also G. Fuster, "Beyond the GDPR, above the GDPR", *Internet Policy Review* (blog), 30 November 2015.

2505 Judgment in *Google Spain*, C-131/12, EU:C:2014:317, paragraph 34. The principle of effectiveness, like the principle of legal certainty, is a general principle of EU law. The principle of effectiveness requires the effective protection of Community rights, including the effective enforcement of Community law in national courts. For a discussion see T. Tridimas, *The General Principles of EU Law*, *o.c.*, p. 418 et seq. See also N. Reich, "The Principle of Effectiveness and EU Private Law", in U. Bernitz, X. Groussot and F. Schulyok (eds.), *General Principles of EU Law and European Private Law*, Kluwer Law International, Croyden, p. 301–326.

Spain, for example, the Court of Justice also indicated that the burden incumbent upon search engines may be limited in light of their effective control capabilities:

> "[...] the operator of the search engine as the person determining the purposes and means of that activity must ensure, within the framework of its responsibilities, powers and capabilities, that the activity meets the requirements of Directive 95/46 in order that the guarantees laid down by the directive may have full effect and that effective and complete protection of data subjects, in particular of their right to privacy, may actually be achieved."[2506]

1228. Issue – The approach of the Court of Justice in *Google Spain* has attracted considerable criticism. A first critique is that search engines are unable to comply with all of the obligations and restrictions that EU data protection law ordinarily imposes upon controllers.[2507] The second critique is that the approach of the Court of Justice may easily lead to inconsistent outcomes and therefore give rise to legal uncertainty.[2508] Strictly speaking, however, these critiques do not concern the concepts of controller and processors themselves, but rather the implications associated with the concepts of controller and processor. This matter will be discussed further under the following section.

4. SYSTEMIC

1229. Preface – The third category of issues arises from the systemic interpretation of the controller and processor concepts. According to the CJEU, provisions of Community law must be interpreted not only in light of its objectives, but also *in light of the "system" it establishes.*[2509] Where multiple interpretations are possible, practitioners must take into account the logic of the regulatory scheme established by the legislature.[2510] The systemic interpretation method involves taking into consideration the normative context in which a legal provision is placed and to derive logical consequences from other legal

2506 Judgment in *Google Spain*, C-131/12, EU:C:2014:317, paragraphs 36–38. See also paragraph 34 (*"Furthermore, it would be contrary not only to the clear wording of that provision but also to its objective – which is to ensure, through a broad definition of the concept of 'controller', effective and complete protection of data subjects – to exclude the operator of a search engine from that definition on the ground that it does not exercise control over the personal data published on the web pages of third parties."*).

2507 While most of the provisions of Directive 95/46 allow for flexibility in their application, this is not always the case. See e.g. M. Peguera, "The Shaky Ground of the Right to Be Delisted", *l.c.*, p. 29 (*"Considering search engines as controllers is not without consequences, as they are unable to comply with most of the obligations the Directive imposes on data controllers."*

2508 *Id.*

2509 Judgment in *Satamedia*, Case C-73/07, EU:C:2008:266, paragraph 51.

2510 See also G. Itzcovich, "The Interpretation of Community Law by the European Court of Justice", *German Law Journal* 2009, Vol. 10, No. 5, p. 549–557 and N. MacCormick, "Argumentation and Interpretation in Law", *l.c.*, p. 22–23.

norms belonging to the same normative text.[2511] Systemic issues occur when the *functions* fulfilled by the controller and processor concepts give rise to unintended or undesirable consequences in practice, which in turn have an undue influence on the interpretation of the controller and processor concepts in specific instances ("strategic interpretations").

1230. Outline – Part II of this book identified the various functions of the controller and processor concepts.[2512] As a matter of principle, each of the functions of the controller and processor concepts play a role in shaping their interpretation. Most relevant to the present analysis, however, is the function of these concepts in relation to (a) the transparency and data subject rights; (b) the scope of the obligations incumbent upon controllers; (c) the implications of joint control; and (d) the degree of contractual flexibility in the relationship among actors involved in the processing of personal data.

4.1. TRANSPARENCY AND DATA SUBJECT RIGHTS

1231. The duty to inform – Every controller is in principle under an obligation to identify himself towards the data subject.[2513] One of the underlying objectives of this provision is to ensure that the data subject is aware of which entity is responsible for the processing, in order to allow him to exercise his rights as a data subject. The more controllers involved, the more difficult it may become for data subjects to ascertain who is responsible for which aspect of the processing. But is this really an issue of how the concept of "controller" is applied? Or is the issue caused by the manner in which the duties regarding transparency towards data subjects have been framed?[2514]

1232. Joint control – It seems that Article 26 of the GDPR offers a partial remedy to this issue, at least where joint controllers are concerned. Article 26(1) requires joint controllers to conclude an arrangement between them, in particular as regards the exercise of data subject rights.[2515] Article 26(2), moreover, provides that the essence of this arrangement shall be made available to the data subject. Finally, Article 26(3) provides that notwithstanding the terms of the arrangement, the data subject shall be able to exercise his or her rights in respect of and against each of the controllers.

2511 *Ibid*, p. 549.

2512 Cf. *supra*, nos. 261 et seq.

2513 See Articles 13-14 GDPR.

2514 See also *supra*, no. 1072.

2515 Strictly speaking, the GDPR does not specify a similar obligation for separate controllers (although each controller shall still be bound by a duty to ensure that the processing remains transparent towards data subjects).

1233. Separate control – Article 26 GDPR provides only a partial solution. In practice, not every collaboration between controllers takes the form of a joint controller relationship.[2516] There may, however, also be situations in which a collaboration between separate controllers requires a mutual arrangement to ensure implementation of adequate data protection safeguards, not least as regards transparency of processing and the exercise of data subject rights.

4.2. SCOPE OF OBLIGATIONS

1234. All or nothing? – The obligations incumbent on a controller in principle befall the controller "as a complete set".[2517] A controller shall in principle be accountable for every aspect of the data processing: ranging from its obligation to ensure that the data quality principles are complied with, to the obligation to support the exercise of data subject rights, to notification obligations etc.[2518] In practice, the situation often occurs whereby certain obligations may more easily be fulfilled by entities other than the controller(s) himself (themselves). In Opinion 1/2010, the Working Party clearly emphasized that not being able to directly fulfil all the obligations of a controller does not excuse an entity from its obligations under data protection law.[2519] It may engage other actors to achieve compliance with its obligations, but this does not negate the fact that it is the controller that remains ultimately responsible for them.[2520] In other opinions, however, the Working Party has indicated that certain data controllers might be dispensed from complying with certain provisions in situations where these provisions are "not pertinent".[2521]

1235. Illustration – Perhaps the best illustration is provided by the Opinion of the Article 29 Working Party on behavioural advertising.[2522] In this Opinion,

2516 Cf. *supra*, nos. 122 et seq.

2517 See also R. Mahieu, J. van Hoboken, H. Asghari, "Responsibility for Data Protection in a Networked World. On the question of the controller, "effective and complete protection" and its application to data access rights in Europe", *l.c.*, p. 8.

2518 Contra: Tweede Kamer der Staten-Generaal, Regels inzake de bescherming van persoonsgegevens (Wet bescherming persoonsgegevens) – Memorie van Toelichting, *l.c.*, p. 59–60.

2519 Opinion 1/2010, *l.c.*, p. 22.

2520 *Id.* (stating "*It may be that in practice those obligations could easily be fulfilled by other parties, which are sometimes closer to the data subject, on the controller's behalf. However, a controller will remain in any case ultimately responsible for its obligations and liable for any breach to them.*").

2521 Article 29 Data Protection Working Party, "Opinion 2/2010 on online behavioural advertising", WP171, 22 June 2010, p. 11.

2522 *Id.*

the Article 29 Working Party considered the scope of the obligations incumbent upon website publishers in relation to the redirection of the browsers of internet users to the webpages (servers) of ad network providers. In this regard, the Working Party considered that:

> "[…] publishers will have some responsibility as data controllers for these actions. This responsibility cannot, however, require compliance with the bulk of the obligations contained in the Directives. In this regard, it is necessary to interpret the legal framework in a flexible way by applying only those provisions that are pertinent. Publishers do not hold personal information; so obviously, it would not make sense to apply some of the obligations of the Directive such as the right of access. However, as further described below, the obligation to inform individuals of the data processing is fully applicable to publishers."[2523]

The guidance of the Working Party has far-reaching implications. It suggests that, in addition to the many different forms in which control might manifest itself (separate control, joint control, partial joint control), there may also be variation in terms of the scope of a controller's obligations. In other words, the Working Party's guidance could be read as suggesting that not every actor acting as a "controller" is necessarily bound to ensure compliance with all the obligations otherwise incumbent upon controllers.

1236. Issue – The aforementioned guidance of the Working Party further challenges the assumption that every controller must effectively be able to meet all of the obligations incumbent upon controllers.[2524] It also creates risk of undermining legal certainty.[2525] On the other hand, it seems that the number of situations in which it is necessary to support greater flexibility in the application of controller obligations is increasing. In *Google Spain*, for example, the CJEU implicitly acknowledged that there may be practical limits to the ability of a search engine operator to meet all the obligations under EU data protection law.[2526]

4.3. IMPLICATIONS OF JOINT CONTROL

1237. Joint control, joint responsibility? – Determining the precise scope of an entity's obligations may be even more difficult in cases of joint control. Indeed, the *Fashion ID* case illustrates that different approaches are imaginable

2523 *Ibid*, p. 11–12.
2524 Compare *supra*, no. 1223.
2525 Cf. *supra*, no. 1224.
2526 For a more narrow reading see M. Thompson, "Beyond Gatekeeping: The Normative Responsibility of Internet Intermediaries", *l.c.*, p. 26.

when it comes to the allocation of responsibilities among joint controllers.[2527] One could argue that in case of joint control, the scope of obligations of each entity should also be assessed "*within the framework of their responsibilities, powers and capabilities*", i.e. the standard advanced by the CJEU in *Google Spain* when assessing the responsibilities of search engine operators. Even then, however, several approaches may still be possible. As noted by Mahieu, van Hoboken and Asghari:

> "When we apply this limiting principle "within the framework of their responsibilities, powers and capabilities", developed in a situation of independent control to a situation of joint control, two interpretations are possible: each controller is responsible for what it is able to do even without proper coordination with other joint controllers. For example, a publisher could inform data subjects about the fact that personal data processing, through the use of cookies, is happening. Alternatively, it could mean that whenever one of the controllers is able to prevent any infringement of the data protection laws, they should do so, either by persuading their joint controller to commit to all data protection obligations or by not integrating the infringing service."[2528]

The authors go on to consider that the existing frameworks for assigning responsibilities are inconclusive with respect to the question of how far the responsibility extends in case of joint control.[2529] For example, the framework developed by the Working Party does not allocate specific responsibilities, but instead relies on the active collaboration of joint-controllers to distribute responsibilities, but does not determine what to do when this coordination does not take place.[2530] The GDPR also does not explicitly clarify how to delineate responsibility and liability among joint controllers, if it is to be accepted that joint control does not automatically amount to joint responsibility and liability.

4.4. LEGAL BINDING

1238. Minimum requirements – Article 28(3) GDPR requires processing by a processor to be governed by "contract or other legal act" with their processors,

[2527] See Opinion of Advocate-General Bobek in *Fashion ID*, C-40/17, ECLI:EU:C:2018:1039, at paragraphs 131 et seq. (cf. *supra*, nos. 922 et seq.) and Opinion of Advocate General Szpunar, *G.C., A.F., B.H., E.D. v. Commission nationale de l'informatique et des libertés (CNIL)*, C-136/17, ECLI:EU:C:2019:14, at paragraphs 51 et seq. (cf. *supra*, nos. 1167).

[2528] R. Mahieu, J. van Hoboken, H. Asghari, "Responsibility for Data Protection in a Networked World. On the question of the controller, "effective and complete protection" and its application to data access rights in Europe", *l.c.*, p. 22–24.

[2529] *Ibid*, p. 22

[2530] Id.

which must contain a considerable number of stipulations.[2531] In contrast, the GDPR contains only limited requirements as regards the "arrangement" to be concluded among joint controllers and none at all aimed at regulating the relationship among separate controllers.[2532] The Article 29 Working Party has previously stated that controllers are free to determine how to best allocate responsibility amongst each other, "*as long as they ensure full compliance*".[2533] The result is that collaborating (co-)controllers are in principle free to assign responsibilities, whereas controller-processor relationships must be modelled according to a pre-defined format.

1239. Negative incentive – The regulatory model of the EU data protection law incentivises service providers to structure their contractual relationships with customers as controller-processor relationships, because the status of processor entails fewer responsibilities and less liability exposure.[2534] In theory, following the controller-processor model also provides greater legal certainty for customers, who know exactly which contractual assurances must at a minimum be in place. The downside of this situation is that it may prevent actors involved in the processing from defining and allocating responsibilities in a way that more accurately reflects their respective effective control capabilities over (different aspects of) the processing. In other words, induces the creation of artificial

2531 Under Article 28(3), the arrangement must at a minimum stipulate that the processor: (a) only processes the personal data only on documented instructions from the controller; (b) ensures that persons authorised to process the personal data are bound to confidentiality; (c) takes all appropriate measures to ensure security of processing; (d) respects the conditions for engaging another processor ("sub-processing"); (e) assists the controller, insofar as this is possible and taking into account the nature of the processing, for the fulfilment of the controller's obligation to accommodate data subject rights; (f) assists the controller in ensuring compliance with the obligations regarding security of processing (Article 32), data breach notification and communication (Articles 33–34) and data protection impact assessment and prior consultation (Article 35–36), taking into account the nature of processing and the information available to the processor; (g) at the choice of the controller, deletes or returns all the personal data to the controller after the end of the provision of services relating to processing, and deletes existing copies unless Union or Member State law requires storage of the personal data; (h) makes available to the controller all information necessary to demonstrate compliance with the obligations laid down in Article 28 GDPR and allow for and contribute to audits, including inspections, conducted by the controller or another auditor mandated by the controller.

2532 One notable exception has resulted from the administrative practice surrounding international transfers. Cf. *supra*, footnote 300.

2533 Opinion 1/2010, *l.c.*, 24.

2534 It has been pointed out that with the entry into application of the GDPR, certain service providers now actually seek to be designated as controllers rather than processors. Doing so offers them greater contractual flexibility (less onerous terms) and increases their ability to process the data for their own purposes. Moreover, as processors are now directly subject to their own obligations and liability exposure, the incentive to "hide behind" the processor role has been significantly reduced. See in particular P. Lee, "Every vendor wants to be… a data controller?!", LinkedIn, 20 September 2018, available at https://www.linkedin.com/pulse/every-vendor-wants-data-controller-phil-lee/ (last accessed 19 January 2019).

contract clauses that exists primarily to sustain a legal fiction which does not necessarily correspond with reality.

1240. One size fits all? – The controller-processor model works well in situations where the relationship between the parties is consistent with the assumptions of autonomy and control that surround controller-processor relationship. The template is less useful, however, in cases where the relationship between actors is less "binary".[2535] In practice, only a portion of the processing relationships can easily be fitted into the controller-processor model. Relationships of joint control, separate control and partial joint control are becoming increasingly common.[2536]

1241. Implications – The issue of contractual flexibility does not directly concern the concepts of controller and processor as such. Instead, it concerns the degree of prescription in regulating the relationship between controllers and processors. A possible remedy to the issue might consist of relaxing the rigidity of controller-processor template (e.g. by merely requiring controllers to "adduce adequate safeguards" when outsourcing personal data processing).[2537]

5. HISTORICAL

1242. Preface – The fourth and final category of issues arises from the historical method of interpretation of the controller concept. When applying the historical method, the interpreter tries to identify what the legislature wanted to regulate when using certain words and sentences, by *taking into account the historical elements that motivated the legislature's intervention.*[2538] Historical issues emerge when legal rules are applied to new actors or situations which were not envisaged by the legislature and which do not merit similar treatment.[2539]

2535 See also *supra*, no. 1225.

2536 For a discussion of why controller may need to seek out similar contractual assurances even in case of separate controllers and joint controllers see M. Hintze, "Data Controllers, Data Processors, and the Growing Use of Connected Products in the Enterprise: Managing Risks, Understanding Benefits, and Complying with the GDPR", *l.c.*, p. 10 et seq. ("*[I]t is almost always advisable and in the commercial interest of the enterprise to ensure that providers acting as controllers are subject to binding contractual commitments to protect the data and to use it only for legitimate and appropriate purposes.*).

2537 Cf. *infra*, nos. 1330 et seq.

2538 W. Brugger, "Legal Interpretation, Schools of Jurisprudence, and Anthropology: Some Remarks from a German Point of View", *l.c.*, p. 397; L. Kestemont, *Methods for traditional legal research*, *o.c.*, p. 11.

2539 For an example of an historical method of interpretation of the controller concept see Opinion of Advocate General Jääskinen in Google Spain, C-131/12, ECLI:EU:C:2013:424, paragraphs 77–81.

1243. Outline – Over time, the processing capabilities of individuals have expanded considerably. Today, individuals enjoy processing capabilities which were initially the prerogative of large organisations, governments, and universities.[2540] This new reality has put considerable pressure on the framing of roles and responsibilities in EU data protection law. Two issues in particular have come to the fore, namely:

(1) the rise of "amateur" data controllers, who process personal data relating to others outside a professional or organisational context ("democratisation of control"); and
(2) the legal status of online service providers in relation to user-generated content.

5.1. THE DEMOCRATISATION OF "CONTROL"

1244. "Privacy 2.0" – The role of individuals has shifted. In less than 30 years, individuals have transcended their role as passive "data subjects" to become actively involved in the creation, distribution and consumption of personal data.[2541] Individuals share pictures, post videos and tweet reviews. Unless an exemption or derogation applies, individuals are – at least in theory – subject to EU data protection law. This hypothesis was confirmed early on by the *Lindqvist*[2542] ruling and more recently in *Ryneš*.[2543] Central to both cases was the question of whether the processing activities of an individual fell within the scope of the exemption provided for processing "*by a natural person in the course of a purely personal or household activity*".[2544]

1245. Lindqvist – In *Lindqvist*, the Court of Justice put forth two criteria to determine whether the personal use exemption applies. In the first place the processing activity must be carried out "*in the course of private and family life*". Secondly, the exemption shall not apply where data are published on the internet and made accessible to an "*indefinite number of people*". The first component of the *Lindqvist* test is perhaps the most striking. Whereas Article 3(2) of Directive 95/46 referred to data processing in the context of "*purely personal or household*" activities, the Court of Justice referred to activities carried out "*in the course of private or family life*". The latter wording is nowhere to be found in the text of Directive 95/46. The word choice instead seems to have been inspired by

2540 See e.g. J. Bing, "Data protection in a time of changes", *l.c.*, p. 247–248.
2541 OECD, *Supplementary explanatory memorandum to the revised recommendation of the Council concerning guidelines governing the protection of privacy and transborder flows of personal data*, 2013, Paris, p. 32.
2542 Judgment in *Bodil Lindqvist*, C-101/01, EU:C:2003:596.
2543 Judgment in *František Ryneš*, C-212/13, EU:C:2014:2428.
2544 Article 2(2)c GDPR (previously: of Article 3(2) Directive 95/46).

the language of Article 7 of the EU Charter and/or Article 8 of the European Convention of Human Rights.[2545] The allusion to this terminology appears to have been intentional. If so, it arguably has important ramifications for the scope of the personal use exemption. It has long been established that the protection of "private life" under Article 8 ECHR is not restricted to that which has historically been dubbed "the private sphere". Rather, the European Court of Human Rights has repeatedly underlined that it also protects a right to identity and personal development, and the right to establish and develop relationships with others.[2546] The second part of the *Lindqvist* test precludes its application in cases where data are made available to an "indefinite" number of people, yet does not specify a limit or threshold. The second part of the *Lindqvist* test is arguably most problematic.[2547] It implies, for example, that users of online social networks may be unable to invoke the personal use exemption once the data in question passes a certain threshold of accessibility.[2548]

1246. RYNEŠ – The Court of Justice was called upon to interpret the scope of the personal use exemption for a second time in *Ryneš*, which concerned the use of video surveillance for home security purposes.[2549] The *Ryneš* Court held that

---

2545 Article 8(1) ECHR provides that "Everyone has the right to respect for his *private and family life*, his home and his correspondence". Article 7 of the EU Charter provides that "Everyone has the right to respect for his or her *private and family life*, home and communications."

2546 See e.g. European Court of Human Rights, *P.G. and J.H. v. United Kingdom*, 25 September 2001, application no. 44787/98 at 56 and European Court of Human Rights, *Niemietz v. Germany*, 16 December 1992, application no. 13710/88, at 29.

2547 See also R. Wong and J. Savirimuthu, "All or Nothing: This is the Question? The Application of Article 3(2) Data Protection Directive 95/46/EC to the Internet", *The John Marshall Journal of Information Technology and Privacy Law* 2008, Vol. 25, Issue 2. p. 246 ("*The ECJ's decision clarifies the extent to which individuals may be able to benefit from Article 3(2), when placing personal information on the Internet, however, it raises several questions. If it is accepted that limiting access of an individual's Web page to family members will be exempt from Article 3(2) DPD, such that the Data Protection Directive 95/46/EC does not apply, where does one draw the line for individuals whose web pages may extend beyond family members?*"); E. C. Harris, "Personal Data Privacy Tradeoffs and How a Swedish Church Lady, Austrian Public Radio Employees, and Transatlantic Air Carriers Show That Europe Does Not Have All the Answers", 22 *Am. U. Int'l L. Rev.* 2007, p. 787 and F.J. Garcia, "Bodil Lindqvist: A Swedish Churchgoer's Violation of the European Union's Data Protection Directive Should Be a Warning to U.S. Legislators", *Fordham Intell. Prop. Media & Ent. L.J.* 2005, Vol. 15, p. 1232 et seq.

2548 Cf. *supra*, no. 967 et seq. See also N. Helberger and J. Van Hoboken, "Little Brother Is Tagging You – Legal and Policy Implications of Amateur Data Controllers", *l.c.*, p. 103. See in the same vein also the Judgment in *Jehova's witnesses*, C-25/17, ECLI:EU:C:2018:551, paragraph 42 and 45; Opinion of Advocate General Sharpston in Buivids, C-345/17, ECLI:EU:C:2018:780, paragraph 40.

2549 Judgment in *František Ryneš*, C-212/13, EU:C:2014:2428. The facts in Ryneš were as follows: For a number of years, Mr. Ryneš had been plagued by attacks by unknown persons. The windows of the family home had been broken on several occasions. In order to protect his family and home, Mr. Ryneš decided to install a camera system. It consisted of one fixed camera which monitored the entrance to his home, as well as the public footpath and the entrance to the house opposite. Almost immediately, the camera system served its purpose. On the second night after its installation, one of the windows of Mr. Ryneš's home was broken by a shot from a catapult. The video recording made it possible to identify two suspects, which eventually led to criminal

continuous video surveillance of a public space cannot be regarded as a "purely personal or household" activity. According to the Court, the monitoring of a public space meant that the surveillance system was "*directed outwards from the private setting*" and therefore did not fall within the scope of the personal use exemption.[2550] In reaching its conclusion, the CJEU also took into account that (a) the objective of EU data protection law to ensure a high level of protection[2551]; (b) any derogations and limitations must apply only in so far as is strictly necessary[2552]; and (c) the very wording of the personal use exemption ("purely") also suggests it should be narrowly construed.[2553]

1247. Issue – Data protection law has traditionally targeted governmental and commercial institutions as the main subjects of regulation.[2554] Although data protection law has evolved over time, it still reflects an organisational mindset.[2555] The highly technical manner in which many provisions have been drafted makes them a "poor fit" for regulating the activities of private individuals.[2556] The analysis of online social networks conducted in Part IV clearly illustrates this proposition.[2557]

---

proceedings. When petitioned by one of suspects, the Czech Data Protection Authority (DPA) held that Mr. Ryneš's camera system violated the Czech data protection act. The main reasons were that (1) the camera system had captured, without consent of the individuals concerned, the images of people moving along the street or entering the house opposite; (2) Mr. Ryneš had failed to provide the individuals concerned any information regarding the processing of their personal data; and (3) Mr. Ryneš had failed to report the camera system to the DPA. Further legal proceedings ensued, resulting in a reference for a preliminary ruling to the ECJ. Could the processing carried out by Mr. Ryneš be classified as the processing of personal data "by a natural person in the course of a purely personal or household activity"?

2550 Judgment in *František Ryneš*, C-212/13, EU:C:2014:2428, paragraph 33. Specifically, the Court reasoned that "*To the extent that video surveillance such as that at issue in the main proceedings covers, even partially, a public space and is accordingly directed outwards from the private setting of the person processing the data in that manner, it cannot be regarded as an activity which is a purely 'personal or household' activity for the purposes of the second indent of Article 3(2) of Directive 95/46.*" (*Id.*).

2551 *Ibid*, at paragraph 27

2552 *Ibid*, at paragraph 28–29.

2553 *Ibid*, at paragraph 30.

2554 J. Zittrain, *The Future of the Internet- And How to Stop It*, *o.c.*, p. 200. The reason is simple: computer usage started out as a prerogative of large companies, governments, and universities. See e.g. J. Bing, "Data protection in a time of changes", *l.c.*, p. 247–248. For discussion of the availability and main forms of usage of computer systems in the 1970s see Commission des Communautés Européens, "Systèmes à grande puissance de traitement automatique de l'information. Besoins et applications dans la Communauté européenne et au Royaume-Uni vers les années soixante-dix", *Études*, Série Industrie, no. 6, 1971, p. 39–57. See also V. Mayer-Schönberger, "Generational Development of Data Protection in Europe", *l.c.*, p. 223 and C. Reed, "The Law of Unintended Consequences – Embedded Business Models in IT Regulation", *Journal of Information Law and Technology* 2007, vol. 2, paragraph 33.

2555 See also M. Birnhack, "Reverse Engineering Information Privacy Law", *l.c.*, p. 64 et seq. and C. Reed, "The Law of Unintended Consequences – Embedded Business Models in IT Regulation", *l.c.*, in particular paragraphs 26 through 39.

2556 For a detailed discussion see B. Van Alsenoy, "The evolving role of the individual under EU data protection law", ICRI Working Paper Series, Working paper 23/2015, August 2015, p. 14 et seq.

2557 Cf. *supra*, no. 969.

5.2. CONTROL OVER USER-GENERATED CONTENT

1248. The question of "control" – Online platforms enable individuals to share information with essentially unlimited audiences. The role and responsibility of platform providers, such as online social networks or micro-blogging sites, has been a topic of much debate.[2558] A particular contentious matter is whether or not these providers should be considered as a "controllers" in relation to content shared spontaneously by their users. The analysis of online social networks in Part IV discussed the different ways in which this issue has been approached by scholars, courts and regulators.[2559]

1249. Relationship directive 2000/31 – Article 2(4) states that the GDPR shall be without prejudice to the liability rules of intermediary service providers contained in Articles 12–15 of Directive 2000/31/EC. From the perspective of a data subject seeking to obtain removal of online content, it matters little whether the takedown is performed because the intermediary is deemed a "controller" or "host". Insofar as the unlawful dissemination of personal data is considered as "illegal content or activity" within the meaning of Article 12 of Directive 2000/31/EC, the data subject should be able to request removal under both instruments. From the perspective of the provider, however, the applicability of the liability exemptions contained in the E-Commerce Directive may be considered as beneficial. Keller, for example, has argued that the standard of care incumbent upon "controllers" is more onerous (and therefore more likely to give rise to liability) than the standard of care incumbent upon internet intermediaries.[2560]

[2558] See e.g. D. Keller, "Intermediary Liability and User Content under Europe's New Data Protection Law", *Center for Internet and Society (CIS) Blog*, Stanford Law School, 8 October 2015.

[2559] Cf. *supra*, nos. 971 et seq. The *Google Spain* ruling offers further support for proposition that certain OSN providers should be considered as "controllers" in relation to user-generated content, as they are actively involved in determining visibility of content (e.g. through so-called "timelines" or "newsfeeds" and by offering search functionalities).

[2560] See D. Keller, "Intermediary Liability and User Content under Europe's New Data Protection Law", *l.c.*, FAQ 2 ("*[...] parts of the GDPR seemingly create liability for intermediaries even when they are unaware that they are processing content unlawfully. Such a departure from the eCommerce Directive's knowledge standard would be a sea change for intermediary liability, and make the operation of open platforms for users to receive and impart information a much riskier business.*") Keller also points out that the size of possible penalties under the GDPR may provide an added incentive for intermediaries to "overcomply" with removal requests.

CHAPTER 3
TYPOLOGY OF SOLUTIONS

1. INTRODUCTION

1250. PREFACE – Over the past decade, a number of solutions have been put forward to remedy the issues that surround the application of the controller-processor model. The aim of this Chapter is to introduce and discuss the proposed solutions in light of the issues identified in the previous chapter. Where appropriate, additional solutions, not previously put forward, will be discussed as well.

1251. CATEGORISATION – In order to facilitate the comparison of possible solutions in relation to the issues identified in Chapter 2, the solutions will be categorized in the same manner as the typology issues presented in the previous chapter:

(1) *Grammatical solutions*: proposals that involve changing the words chosen to define the concepts of controller and processor;
(2) *Teleological solutions*: proposals that present alternative ways in which the policy objectives underlying the controller and processor concepts might be realized;
(3) *Systemic solutions*: proposals that involve modifying the implications associated with the concepts of controller and processor;
(4) *Historical solutions*: proposals that seek to confine the scope of application of the controller and processor concepts to actors and situations envisaged by the legislature.

1252. INTERDEPENDENCIES – While maintaining the categorisation above promotes consistency in presentation, it is obvious that a proposed solution might seek to address multiple issues. It is equally possible that a solution seeking to address one issue may indirectly ameliorate or exacerbate other issues, without deliberately seeking to do so. With this in mind, the potential solutions will be categorized according to the type of issue that is the *focal point* of the proposed solution. Where interdependencies exist, the discussion of each solution will involve an assessment of whether the solution is likely to improve or aggravate other issues.

1253. Methodology – The solutions analysed in this Chapter have been sourced from literature concerning the application controller and processor concepts, as well as from the stakeholder responses and legislative proposals put forward in the context of the review of Directive 95/46 and run-up to the GDPR. Not every issue identified in Chapter 2, however, has been explicitly addressed by scholars or stakeholders. Where no remedy has been put forward, possible solutions will be developed in light of the lessons learned from historical-comparative analysis and by drawing inspirations from approaches adopted by other national and international privacy frameworks.[2561]

1254. Positive assessment framework – The typology of issues set forth in Chapter 2 shall serve as the *positive assessment framework* to evaluate the proposed solutions.[2562] Each proposal will be evaluated in light of issue it seeks to remedy, simply by asking the following questions: how likely is the proposed solution to solve the identified issue? What are the advantages and disadvantages of this approach? In principle, no additional assessment criteria will be used to evaluate the proposed solutions. Only in the context of the internal comparison between different possible solutions, shall insights from the field of law and economics be applied in order to enhance the evaluation process.

2. GRAMMATICAL

1255. Outline – Grammatical solutions consist of modifying or clarifying the words that have been used to define the concepts of controller or processor. The point of departure is that if the current wording gives rise to difficulties of interpretation, the remedy is to modify this wording. Proposed solutions include (a) removing words from the definition of controller; (b) adding words to the definition of controller; and (c) substantively modifying the definition of controller.

2.1. DELETION OF "MEANS"

1256. Proposals – Prior to the First Reading of the General Data Protection Regulation, several Parliamentary Committees proposed to remove the word

2561 For reasons of accessibility, analysis has been limited to privacy frameworks available in English. In the end, the German *Bundesdatenschutzgesetz* of 1977 and the Canadian Personal Information Protection and Electronic Documents Act (PIPEDA) of 2000 acted as additional sources of inspiration, as they contain interesting alternative approaches to the identification of responsible actors and regulation of outsourcing arrangements.

2562 According to Kestemont, a "positive assessment framework" can be described as "*a set of criteria that are being formulated in a 'positive way'. This implies that the outcome of the evaluation will be positive or favourable when the legal phenomenon meets (nearly) all criteria.*" (L. Kestemont, *Methods for traditional legal research*, o.c., p. 31).

"means" from the definition of a controller.[2563] The IMCO Committee explained the proposal as follows:

> "With new technologies and services available such as cloud computing traditional division of entities involved in the processing of personal data may prove difficult, with the processor having in such cases significant influence over the way in which data are being processed. For this reason it seems reasonable to determine the controller as the entity, which decides over the purpose of processing personal data as determination of finality is the most important decision with the other factors serving as means to achieve it."[2564]

The deletion of "means" was also supported by the authors of an External Report commissioned by the Parliament, who argued that abandoning the "means" criterion would be advisable because:

- "there are substantial doubts as how to understand the term "means";
- greater importance is already assigned to the factor of "determining the purposes" rather than "determining the means" of processing;
- Article 29 Working Party even permits the possibility of "delegation" of the competence to determine the means to the processor (at least as defined by the narrow meaning of that term);
- moreover, the general importance of "purposes" of processing is much higher in the personal data protection regulation because – as the legal literature reasonably notes – "the finality pursued by (a set of) processing operations fulfils a fundamental role in determining the scope of the controller's obligations, as well as when assessing the overall legitimacy and/or proportionality of the processing".[2565]

2563 See European Parliament, Opinion of the Committee on Industry, Research and Energy (ITRE), 26 February 2013, Amendment 80; Opinion of the Committee on Internal Market and Consumer Affairs (IMCO), 28 January 2013, Amendment 62; Opinion of the Committee on Legal Affairs (JURI), 25 March 2013, Amendment 38 and European Parliament, LIBE Committee, "Amendments 602–885", 4 March 2013, PE506.145v01-00, amendments 746–48.

2564 European Parliament, Opinion of the Committee on Internal Market and Consumer Affairs (IMCO), 28 January 2013, amendment 62. In the same vein, MEP Adina-Ioana Vălean, Jens Rohde argued that "*The definition of controller should be based on the decision of the purposes for which personal data are processed rather than the conditions or means by which this is achieved. The control over the purpose for processing is the logical basis for allocating different responsibilities between controllers who are responsible for what and why data is processed and processing parties who deal with how data is processed.*" (European Parliament, LIBE Committee, "Amendments 602–885", 4 March 2013, PE506.145v01-00, amendments 746). Other MEP's supported the change for a different reason, namely to clarify that only the controller and not the processor is responsible for compliance (See MEP amendments 748, with justification that: "*The aim of the change is not to lower the level of protection for the individual but to clarify that only the controller and not the processor is responsible. See related Amendments to articles 22, 24, 26 and 77.*")

2565 X. Konarski, D. Karwala, H. Schulte-Nölke and C. Charlton, "Reforming the Data Protection Package", *l.c.*, p. 31, with reference to B. Van Alsenoy, "Allocating responsibility among

1257. Rationale – The reasoning of the IMCO Committee reveals a dual motivation behind the proposal to delete the word "means" from the definition. The first motivation is that it would clarify that the determination of "purpose" is what really matters (primacy of purpose).[2566] The second motivation stems from the finding that providers of processing services often exercise significant influence over the way in which data are being processed. Removal of the word "means" would signal a desire to exclude such service providers from the scope of the controller concept. In other words, it would imply that service providers who effectively determine the "means" of the processing (but have limited interest in the purposes pursued by their clients) should no longer be qualified as (co-)controllers.[2567]

1258. Counterarguments – Despite its many supporters, the proposal to delete the word "means" was received negatively by the European Data Protection Supervisor (EDPS). In particular, the EDPS considered that the word "means" should not be deleted as it "*effectively contributes to the understanding and delineation of the roles of controller and processor*".[2568] A second counterargument may be derived from the guidance of the Article 29 Working Party, which emphasizes the *functional nature* of the controller concept. According to the Working Party, the aim of the controller is to allocate responsibility upon those actors who exercise factual influence over the processing. Retaining the word "means" would make it easier to keep actors who exercise significant influence over the way in which data are being processed within the scope of the controller concept.[2569] The need to hold service providers accountable for aspects of the processing which are effectively under their control was also highlighted by report of the CEPS Digital Forum on the data protection reform.[2570]

2.2. ADDING "CONDITIONS"

1259. Proposal – In its draft proposal of the GDPR, the European Commission extended the definition of controller to include a reference to

---

controllers, processors, and "everything in between": the definition of actors and roles in Directive 95/46/EC", *l.c.*, p. 31, footnote 55.

2566 See also *supra*, nos. 109 et seq.

2567 See also MEP amendment 748, which justified the deletion of means as follows: "*The aim of the change is not to lower the level of protection for the individual but to clarify that only the controller and not the processor is responsible. See related Amendments to articles 22, 24, 26 and 77.*"

2568 European Data Protection Supervisor (EDPS), "Additional EDPS comments on the Data Protection Reform Package", 15 March 2013, p. 6 (at paragraph 24).

2569 See also *supra*, no. 695.

2570 K. Irion and G. Luchetta, "Online Personal Data Processing and EU Data Protection Reform – Report of the CEPS Digital Forum, Centre for European Policy Studies (CEPS), *l.c.*, p. 47–48.

"conditions". The controller would be the entity who not only determines the "purposes and means" of the processing, but also the "conditions" of the processing. Neither the Commission Communication nor the Explanatory Memorandum offered any further clarification regarding the underlying rationale for this proposal.

1260. Counterarguments – The authors of the External Report commissioned by the Parliament put forward a number of arguments against the Commission Proposal. First, it is unclear how the term "conditions" should be understood, if it were expected to have a different meaning or connotation what is already covered by the word "means".[2571] Second, the use of the conjunction "and" would imply a requirement of cumulative satisfaction. This might actually trigger greater difficulties and uncertainties of interpretation, rather than eliminate them.[2572]

2.3. "BENEFIT-BASED" APPROACH

1261. Proposal – A third proposal consists of substantively modifying the definition of the controller concept. In 2008, authors Léonard and Mention proposed to define the controller as the entity that *benefits from the use of data*, rather than as the entity who "determines purposes and means" of the processing.[2573] The proposal is closely tied to the observation that the constitutive element of the processor concept is that this entity processes personal data *on behalf of* the controller:

> "If the processor only processes data on behalf of the controller, it may be appropriate to focus the distinguishing criterion for the controller the identification of he who benefits from the use of data and in this sense really decides about the purposes of their use. The processor certainly profits and benefits from the treatment that is the very purpose of his service, but he does not draw as such profit from the use itself of data for the information they contain."[2574]

1262. Rationale – Léonard and Mention depart from the observation that the existing criteria no longer work in practice. The "means" criterion is deemed inadequate, because in practice almost every processor exercises a determinative influence over the manner in which the processing is organised.[2575] The

2571 X. Konarski, D. Karwala, H. Schulte-Nölke and C. Charlton, "Reforming the Data Protection Package", *l.c.*, p. 30.
2572 *Id.*
2573 T. Léonard and A. Mention, "Transferts transfrontaliers de données: quelques considérations théorique et pratiques", *l.c.*, p. 109.
2574 *Id.* (original emphasis)
2575 *Ibid*, p. 105

"purpose" criterion is likewise deemed inadequate, because in practice every processor designs and offers his services with a particular finality in mind (and in that sense can always be seen as determining the "purpose" of the processing).[2576] By differentiating on the basis of "who receives the benefit from the use of the data", it is argued, it is possible to operate a much neater distinction between controllers and processors.

1263. Counterarguments – While the proposal of Léonard and Mention was not formally discussed in the context of the GDPR negotiations, its rationale and intended effect are similar to the proposal to delete the "means" criterion.[2577] As a result, similar countervailing arguments can be made. If adopted as such, the proposal would entail that the providers of processing services would effectively be excluded from the concept of a controller, even if they exercise a determinative influence over the manner in which the processing is organised (including the "essential elements" of the processing). Absent additional measures, there could be a risk that the providers of processing services may lack appropriate incentives to organise their services in a manner which sufficiently takes into account the interests of data subjects.[2578]

2.4. ASSESSMENT

1264. Internal comparison – Of the three proposals presented discussed above, the "benefit-based" approach seems most apt to introduce greater clarity in the distinction between controllers and processors. It is indeed difficult to imagine how the proposal to add "conditions" would assist in disambiguating the controller concept.[2579] Merely deleting the "means" criterion would likewise be too subtle a change, especially in light of the fact that scholars continue to associate multiple meanings to the "purpose" criterion.[2580] The "benefit-based" approach would support a relatively clear distinction between actors

2576 *Ibid*, p. 107.

2577 The main difference is that the proposal of Léonard and Mention would further substitute the "purpose" criterion with a reference to "who benefits from the use of the data". However, the rationale offered by proponents of the proposal to delete the "means" criterion implicitly suggests these proponents also understand the "purpose" criterion as referring to "interest in" or "benefit from" the processing. For a more detailed discussion of the interpretation of purpose as "interest" vs. "finality" see *supra*, nos. 1060 et seq.

2578 See also K. Irion and G. Luchetta, "Online Personal Data Processing and EU Data Protection Reform – Report of the CEPS Digital Forum, Centre for European Policy Studies (CEPS), *l.c.*, p. 47–48.

2579 First, as indicated earlier, it is unclear how the word "conditions" would add meaning beyond what is already included by the word "means". In addition, the more cumulative criteria are enumerated in a single definition, the more likely one is to find that they are not united in a single entity (compare also *supra*, no. 528)

2580 Cf. *supra*, nos. 1060 et seq.

who provide processing services ("processors") on behalf of others and actors who consume them in the pursuit of their own organisational objectives ("controllers"). An additional advantage of the benefit-based approach is that it would introduce a mutually exclusive criterion in the definitions of controller and processor.[2581]

1265. Interdependencies – Adoption of the "benefit-based approach" would affect the teleological issues identified in Chapter 2. On the one hand, by offering a clearer basis for differentiation between controllers and processors, the benefit-based approach would arguably improve legal certainty. On the other hand, the benefit-based approach could adversely affect the objective of the EU legislature to ensure a continuous level of protection by responsibilizing actors who exercise a determinative influence over the manner in which the processing is organized. By excluding the providers of processing services from the scope of the controller concept, such service providers may be insufficiently accountable for their decisions regarding how the processing should be organized. Additional measures may therefore be necessary to address this issue. Finally, it is worth noting that the benefit-based approach would leave unaffected the systemic and historical issues identified in Chapter 2.

1266. Accountability gap – A benefit-based approach would only be acceptable if additional measures are put in place to ensure the providers of processing services are accountable for the manner in which they decide to organise their processing services. As noted by the Report of the CEPS Digital Forum on the data protection reform:

> "[T]he means of data processing carries a stand-alone risk for the protection of personal data; important procedural aspects and decisions are deployed, such as algorithms. Regulation should therefore not be blind to the means even if this aspect of data processing is no longer under the exclusive control of the controller. Here, parallel to reducing the level of responsibility on the part of the controller, accountability on the part of the processor would need to be stepped up."[2582]

In other words, it would be necessary for the EU legislature to ensure that certain obligations remain directly applicable to the providers of processing services to ensure accountability in relation to those aspects of the processing which are effectively under their control. Failure to do so would make it increasingly

---

2581 As indicated earlier, the current criteria to distinguish between controller and processors are not mutually exclusive. Cf. *supra*, no. 1210.

2582 K. Irion and G. Luchetta, "Online Personal Data Processing and EU Data Protection Reform – Report of the CEPS Digital Forum, Centre for European Policy Studies (CEPS), *l.c.*, p. 47–48. While these observations were made in relation to the proposal to remove the word "means" from the definition of controller, similar considerations also apply in relation to the interest-based approach. Compare also *supra*, no. 488.

difficult for regulators to exert influence over essential elements of the processing which can otherwise create stand-alone data protection risks. Relevant obligations include: the obligation to implement appropriate security measures, the obligation to implement data protection by design and by default, the duty to respect international transfer restrictions, and the obligation to co-operate with supervisory authorities.[2583]

1267. Remaining issues – While the "benefit-based" approach makes it easier to differentiate between controllers and processors in most cases, its application may not always be equally straight-forward. Considering the fact pattern in *Google Spain*, for example, it could be argued that the provider of a search engine service is not the ultimate "beneficiary" of the service he provides. Under a purely benefit-based approach, it might be argued that the provider of a search engine service should no longer be considered as a "controller". Such an outcome would stand in stark contrast with the reasoning of the Court of Justice, who considered it necessary to qualify search engines as controllers in order to ensure "effective and complete" protection of data subjects.[2584] Similar objections might also be made in relation to data brokers, whose data processing activities have the potential to significantly affect the privacy interests of data subjects, but are the ultimate "beneficiaries" of the data services they offer to their customers.[2585]

1268. Final text GDPR – The final text of the GDPR left the controller and processor concepts "as is". Given the extremely broad scope ratione materiae of the Directive, a certain amount of legal uncertainty appears inevitable.[2586] Even if the criteria contained in the legal definition of the controller concept were to be rephrased, the need for continuous adaptability would most likely lead to wording which still leaves room for legal uncertainty in some cases. Practitioners may therefore simply have to accept a certain amount of ambiguity in the criteria set forth by the regulatory framework, and plan accordingly.[2587] Chapter 4

2583 It is worth noting that each of the obligations mentioned here were included in the list of obligations which would be imposed upon processors under the First Reading of the European Parliament. Under the General Approach of the Council, however, the number of obligations directly incumbent upon processors was reduced (in particular as regards data protection by design and by default).

2584 Cf. *supra*, no. 1150.

2585 A possible remedy might be to specify that, in order to be considered a processor, the party must process the data "exclusively on the instructions of" or "exclusively at the request of" another party (in addition to processing the data exclusively on his behalf). Cf. *infra*, no. 1356.

2586 See also Judgment in *Bodil Lindqvist*, C-101/01, EU:C:2003:596, paragraph 86: "*As regards Directive 95/46 itself, its provisions are necessarily relatively general since it has to be applied to a large number of very different situations.*"

2587 See also C. Kuner, *European data protection law: corporate compliance and regulation*, o.c., p. 72.

will nevertheless present a proposal for possible revisions to the controller and processor concepts, based on the solution proposed by Léonard and Mention.

3. TELEOLOGICAL

1269. Outline – Teleological solutions are solutions which propose alternative ways in which policy objectives underlying the controller and processor concepts might be realized. The point of departure is that if the current approach fails to achieve important policy objectives, it is necessary to consider alternative approaches to realise those objectives. Proposed solutions include (a) abolishing the distinction between controllers and processors or (b) increasing the number of obligations directly incumbent upon processors.

3.1. ABOLITION OF THE DISTINCTION

1270. Proposal – Proposals to abolish the distinction between controllers and processors can be traced back as early as 2007, to a workshop organized by the ICC Task Force on Privacy and the Protection of Personal Data.[2588] The summary report of the workshop notes that:

> "Abolition of the distinction between controller and processor: Some participants stated that the distinction between data controller and data processor is artificial, and it would be preferable to have a single category of party processing personal data whose rights and obligations are determined under the facts in each case and in accordance with general legal principles; other participants disagreed with this proposal."[2589]

While not all the workshop participants shared the view that the distinction between controllers and processors should be abolished, the proposal was further developed by the ICC itself in its response to the European Commission consultation on the Legal Framework for the Fundamental Right to Protection of Personal Data:

> "The distinction between "data controller" and "data processor" should be abolished, and each party that processes personal data should be responsible and liable based on its own role in the data processing. [...] Existing concepts of agency law and tort law already provide a sufficient legal framework for assessing the responsibility of parties

[2588] International Chamber of Commerce (ICC), ICC Task Force on Privacy and the Protection of Personal Data, "Summary of the Workshop on the Distinction between Data Controllers and Data Processors", Paris, Thursday, 25 October, 2007, 6 p.

[2589] *Ibid*, p. 2.

involved in data processing, without forcing them into a limited set of categories that does not fit reality."[2590]

1271. Variations – Proposals to abolish the distinction between controllers and processors were also made by other respondents to the aforementioned EC consultation, as well as by academics.[2591] There are, however, notable variations among the proponents of this approach, not least as regards the question of how responsibility and liability should be allocated under the revised model. The ICC, for example, advocated that each party involved in the processing of personal data should only be responsible and liable "*based on its own role*" in the processing. The law firm of Bird & Bird argued that the liability exposure of an organisation involved in the processing of personal data should be limited "*to the extent of its legal right to control the data and to the extent necessary to secure the fundamental rights of the individual*".[2592] De Hert and Papakonstantinou, on the other hand, implied that each entity involved in the processing might be held equally accountable:

> "perhaps the preferable way forward would be for the Commission to boldly abolish the notion of "data processors" from its Regulation altogether, and vest the data controller title, rights and obligations upon anyone processing personal information, regardless of its means, conditions or purposes."[2593]

The International Pharmaceutical Privacy Consortium considered that parties involved in the processing of personal data should be free to *designate* which party will be legally accountable, as long as the designated party has a

2590 International Chamber of Commerce (ICC), ICC Commission on E-business, IT and Telecoms, "ICC Response to the European Commission Consultation on the Legal Framework for the Fundamental Right to Protection of Personal Data", December 2009, p. 4.

2591 See Bird & Bird, "Response to European Commission Consultation on the Legal Framework for the Fundamental Right to Protection of Personal Data", *l.c.*, at paragraph 19; European Privacy Officers Forum (EPOF), "Comments on the Review of European Data Protection Framework", *l.c.*, p. 5 and P. De Hert and V. Papakonstantinou, "The proposed data protection Regulation replacing Directive 95/46/EC: A sound system for the protection of individuals", *l.c.* p. 134.

2592 Specifically, Bird & Bird advocated "*to replace the distinction of controllers and processors with a principle that any organisation processing personal data should be liable to comply with the data protection principles but only to the extent of its legal right to control the data and to the extent necessary to secure the fundamental rights of the individual.*" (Bird & Bird, "Response to European Commission Consultation on the Legal Framework for the Fundamental Right to Protection of Personal Data", *l.c.*, at paragraph 22. The European Privacy Officers Forum similarly reasoned that "*[p]robably the only practical approach is to make any party processing personal data liable for compliance with the rules, but only to the extent necessary to safeguard personal information in respect to a particular processing operation, and to the extent of that person's legal right to control the data.*" (European Privacy Officers Forum (EPOF), "Comments on the Review of European Data Protection Framework", *l.c.*, p. 9.

2593 P. De Hert and V. Papakonstantinou, "The proposed data protection Regulation replacing Directive 95/46/EC: A sound system for the protection of individuals", *l.c.*, 133–134.

European presence or has appointed a European representative.[2594] Finally, the UK Information Commissioner's Office suggested that general liability might be assigned to the organisation(s) that *initiate* the processing, whereas anyone *subsequently involved* in the processing of personal data at a later stage would only be liable "*for their own aspect*" of the processing.[2595]

1272. RATIONALE – One of the objectives underlying the controller-processor distinction was to clarify the obligations of each actor involved in the processing of personal data.[2596] Each of the proponents cited above elaborated at length as to why they believe this objective is no longer realised in practice. In general, most proponents argued that the distinction reflects an outdated paradigm, which is overly simplistic and has become increasingly difficult to apply in practice.[2597] Some even suggested that, because of its decreased relevance and applicability, the distinction actually *creates* confusion and imposes excessive interpretation costs.[2598] Abolishing the controller-processor distinction mainly seeks to

---

2594 International Pharmaceutical Privacy Consortium, "Comments in Response to the Consultation on the Legal Framework for the Fundamental Right to Protection of Personal Data", *l.c.*, p. 7.

2595 Specifically, the ICO reasoned that "*Rather than trying to keep rigid definitions, better data protection is achieved by making sure that any new legal framework clearly identifies the persons responsible for the various aspects of the processing of the data, and that the responsibility remains in place throughout the information life cycle. Liability could be assigned to the organisation, or organisations, that initiate the processing, whereas anyone processing personal data at any stage of the information life cycle should be responsible for dealing with it properly and securely, and be accountable for their own aspect of the processing. This could mean being accountable to whoever initiated the processing; to individuals; to regulators; or all three.*" (Information Commissioner's Office (ICO), "The Information Commissioner's response to the European Commission's consultation on the legal framework for the fundamental right to protection of personal data", 2009, p. 2–3.

2596 Cf. *supra*, nos. 1224 et seq.

2597 See e.g. Information Commissioner's Office (ICO), "The Information Commissioner's response to the European Commission's consultation on the legal framework for the fundamental right to protection of personal data", *l.c.*, p. 2–3; P. De Hert and V. Papakonstantinou, "The proposed data protection Regulation replacing Directive 95/46/EC: A sound system for the protection of individuals", *l.c.*, 133–134 and European Privacy Officers Forum (EPOF), "Comments on the Review of European Data Protection Framework", *l.c.*, p. 5.

2598 European Privacy Officers Forum (EPOF), "Comments on the Review of European Data Protection Framework", *l.c.*, p. 5; Bird & Bird, "Response to European Commission Consultation on the Legal Framework for the Fundamental Right to Protection of Personal Data", *l.c.*, at paragraph 19 ("*The SWIFT case also demonstrates the amount of time and effort that is required to determine who is a controller and who is a processor (with organisations potentially having different roles depending on each individual act of processing). This diverts resources away from more substantive compliance requirements*"). See also International Pharmaceutical Privacy Consortium, "Comments in Response to the Consultation on the Legal Framework for the Fundamental Right to Protection of Personal Data", *l.c.*, p. 7 ("*A great deal of time and effort is spent trying to determine the appropriate categorization of the parties involved in a data processing activity, and it is reasonable to question whether this time might be better spent actually ensuring that appropriate data privacy and security safeguards are in place.*")

remedy this situation. In addition, it could also provide greater flexibility to the parties involved in the processing of personal data to determine how to mutually allocate responsibilities.

1273. Counterarguments – The proposal to abolish the distinction between controllers and processors was met with caution. For example, the External Report commissioned by the European Parliament stated that:

> "Such solutions, however, also entail certain far-reaching consequences in the form of, for example, making the positions of all entities involved in data processing equal and distributing all the obligations evenly, without taking into account their individual position, the scope of their tasks, or the expectations of data subjects. Therefore, the possible adoption of such solutions requires far-reaching prudence."[2599]

The authors of the External Report did not explore the possibility of combining the abolition of the controller-processor concepts with alternative criteria for allocating responsibility and liability. It was implied, however, that it may be possible to achieve similar outcomes, provided the current framework is interpreted properly:

> "[I]t seems that, on the basis of the dichotomy adopted in EU law, one can – with proper interpretation – achieve results similar to those found in regulations [which do not make a distinction between controllers and processors]."[2600]

3.2. OBLIGATIONS FOR PROCESSORS

1274. Proposal – Under Directive 95/46, processors were in principle only indirectly accountable for compliance.[2601] The Directive itself specified only one obligation directly towards the processor, namely in Article 16. Article 16 provided that the processor may only process personal data pursuant to the instructions of the controller.[2602] In its draft proposal for the GDPR, the

---

2599 X. Konarski, D. Karwala, H. Schulte-Nölke and C. Charlton, "Reforming the Data Protection Package", *l.c.*, p. 31.

2600 *Id.* One of the regulations referred to by the authors is the Canadian Personal Information Protection and Electronic Documents Act (PIPEDA), according to which responsible organisations must take all reasonable steps to protect personal information under their control, regardless of where it is processed. For a discussion see also B. Van Alsenoy, "Allocating responsibility among controllers, processors, and "everything in between": the definition of actors and roles in Directive 95/46/EC", *l.c.*, p. 41–42 and J. Alhadeff, B. Van Alsenoy and J. Dumortier, "The accountability principle in data protection regulation: origin, development and future directions", *l.c.*, p. 55–56.

2601 Cf. *supra*, nos. 145 et seq.

2602 In addition, the processor shall in principle be obligated to observe all relevant aspects of data protection law by virtue of the contract which must be concluded among controllers

Commission significantly expanded the number of obligations incumbent upon processors. Specifically, the Commission envisaged that the following provisions would also be directly applicable to processors: (a) the obligation to maintain documentation; (b) the duty of co-operation with supervisory authorities; (c) the obligation to maintain an appropriate level of data security; (d) data protection impact assessments; (e) prior authorization; (f) data protection officers; (g) codes of conduct; (h) certification; and (i) international transfers.[2603]

1275. Rationale – The Commission's proposal was grounded in the view that, despite the increased complexity of the environment in which controllers and processors operate, the concepts themselves remain valid.[2604] Rather than abolish the distinction, the Commission would "clarify and detail" the responsibilities and liability of both controllers and processors.[2605] While the Commission's stated intent was to enhance legal certainty, it would appear that the approach proposed by the Commission was motivated by other factors as well. In its detailed analysis of impacts accompanying the proposal, the Commission reasoned that

> "New and harmonised provisions which clarify the legal obligations for the processor, irrespective of the obligations laid down in the contract or the legal act with the controller, as well as the application of the "data protection by design" principle, the need for data protection impact assessments in some cases, and an obligation to cooperate with supervisory authorities will bring about benefits for the individual, as this will ensure that outsourcing and delegation by controllers to processors do not result in lowering the standard of data protection."[2606]

As noted by the EDPS, imposing obligations directly upon processors more accurately reflected the "*growing role of processors in determining certain essential conditions of the processing*".[2607] In addition, doubts had been expressed whether the "contractual approach" of Directive 95/46 (whereby processors are obligated to observe relevant aspects of data protection law by virtue of their contract with the controller) actually created the right incentives for compliance.[2608] The

---

and processors (Article 17(3)).See also Opinion 1/2010, *l.c.*, 26 and T. Olsen and T. Mahler, "Identity management and data protection law: Risk, responsibility and compliance in 'Circles of Trust' – Part II", *l.c.*, p. 418.

2603 Cf. *supra*, no. 595.

2604 European Commission, "Evaluation of the implementation of the Data Protection Directive", Annex 2, *l.c.*, p. 10.

2605 *Id.*

2606 European Commission, "Detailed analysis of impacts", Annex 5, *l.c.*, p. 91.

2607 European Data Protection Supervisor (EDPS), "Additional EDPS comments on the Data Protection Reform Package", *l.c.*, at paragraph 25.

2608 L. Moerel, *Binding Corporate Rules: Corporate Self-Regulation of Global Data Transfers*, *o.c.*, p. 216–218 ("*Thought should be given to the question whether the present set-up of the Directive where the controller is the sole bearer for all data protection obligations is indeed the best*

finding that certain organisations who are traditionally viewed as controllers (e.g. the customers of cloud services), often have a weak bargaining position in practice, undoubtedly provided additional motivation for the decision to increase the number of obligations directly incumbent upon processors.[2609] Finally, as indicated earlier, it has been argued that the choice of "means" of the processing creates a stand-alone risk for data protection for which processors should also be accountable.[2610]

1276. Counterarguments – The approach put forward by the European Commission was not entirely well received. Certain commentators felt that by imposing obligations directly on processors, there may be a risk of confusion as to who is ultimately responsible for ensuring compliance.[2611] For example, in relation to the data security obligation (Article 30), the EDPS noted that:

> "In Article 30 on security of processing, reference is made to the controller and the processor. The EDPS welcomes that both actors are mentioned, but recommends the legislator to clarify the provision in such a way that there is no doubt about the overall responsibility of the controller. From the text as it currently stands, both the processor and the controller seem to be equally responsible. This is not in line with the preceding provisions, in particular Articles 22 and 26 of the proposed Regulation."[2612]

In the same vein, the ICO noted in relation to Article 26 of the Commission Proposal (processor) that

---

incentive to achieve compliance in case of complex data processing operations. In light of the diminishing contracting power of multi-nationals vis-à-vis their multinational outsourcing suppliers, an obligation on all parties involved in the data processing (whether controller or data processor) to achieve accountability as to the end result, may ultimately prove the better stick. This may work as an incentive for all parties to come to a proper allocation of obligations in relation to the network. By separating the contractual form from the liability regime, it is left to the parties to allocate responsibilities where they are best placed." (original emphasis) Moerel goes on to advocate in favour of allocating responsibility *at the source of the risk*, rather than through a chain of contracts along the supply chain. The obligation to ensure data security should in particular be imposed directly upon processors (in addition to data controllers (*Ibid*, p. 222).

2609 *Ibid*, p. 216. Blume even goes so far as to suggest that, in light of the increased dominance and effective control capabilities of processors, it should be considered whether the current roles of controllers of processors might be reversed. See P. Blume, "An alternative model for data protection law: changing the roles of controller and processor", *l.c.*, p. 295–297.

2610 K. Irion and G. Luchetta, "Online Personal Data Processing and EU Data Protection Reform – Report of the CEPS Digital Forum, Centre for European Policy Studies (CEPS), *l.c.*, p. 47–48. Cf. *supra*, no. 1266.

2611 See in particular P. Blume, "Controller and processor: is there a risk of confusion?", *l.c.*, p. 143–144 and B. Treacy, "Challenging times ahead for data processors", *l.c.*, p. 5–6.

2612 European Data Protection Supervisor (EDPS), "Opinion of the European Data Protection Supervisor on the data protection reform package", *l.c.*, p. 31 (at paragraph 192). See also P. Blume, "Controller and processor: is there a risk of confusion?", *l.c.*, p. 144.

> "[...] we need to be clear about who is responsible for what where a number of organisations are each involved in the processing of personal data, and, as drafted, this Article will not help us here."[2613]

While supporting the idea of directly imposing the obligations upon processors, Moerel has argued that the approach of the European Commission failed to provide adequate flexibility as far as the mutual allocation of responsibility and liability is concerned.[2614]

3.3. ASSESSMENT

A. *Abolition of the distinction*

1277. ADVANTAGES – The proposal to abolish the distinction between controllers and processors has considerable appeal. It would eliminate from the legal framework an artificial construct which has given rise to considerable difficulties of interpretation. From a purely practical perspective, the need to appropriately divide responsibilities exists regardless of whether the relationship between the actors involved is a relationship between controller and processor, separate controllers or (partial) joint controllers. By abolishing these distinctions, parties can focus immediately on how to best allocate responsibilities.

1278. DISADVANTAGES – There are, however, a number of disadvantages to this approach. First, while parties no longer need to invest time and energy debating their formal legal status, there is still a need to allocate responsibilities. Removing the distinction between controllers and processors would remove an

---

2613 Information Commissioner's Office (ICO), "Proposed new EU General Data Protection Regulation: Article-by-article analysis paper", *l.c.*, p. 34. At the same time, the ICO also reiterated its earlier complaint regarding its difficulties to distinguish between controllers and processors in practice ("*It is fair to say that the ICO can find it difficult to determine which organisations are data controllers and which are processors. The problem arises because, given the collaborative nature of modern business, it is rare for a one organisation (the processor) to only act on instructions from another (the controller). There tends to be a considerable degree of freedom, skill, judgment and the like in terms of the way the first organisation provides services to the second, all against the backdrop of complex collaborative arrangements involving numerous organisations.*") (*Id.*).

2614 L. Moerel, *Binding Corporate Rules: Corporate Self-Regulation of Global Data Transfers*, *o.c.*, p. 218 ("*I agree that the imposing of direct obligations on processors is a good way to ensure that processors in complex processing operations do not "hide" behind their processorship in order to avoid liability. However, if the Proposed Regulation allows joint controllers to divide responsibilities between them, I do not see why this possibility would not be extended to a division of responsibilities between joint processors (or between main and sub-processors) and further between (joint) controllers and such (joint or sub-) processors. If individuals keep their rights against any of them, there seems little to be said against such possibility to divide responsibilities.*")

important "guidepost" as to what an appropriate allocation of responsibilities might look like.[2615] Moreover, one should not lose sight of the fact that the controller-processor relationship is in fact a *normative* construct: by regulating the relationship between controllers and processors, the EU legislature has not merely indicated what the contractual relationship might look like, it is also an indication of what the relationship *should* look like.[2616] Finally, allocating responsibility and liability may prove more difficult in practice. As indicated earlier, there are different opinions as regards the question of how responsibility and liability should be allocated in absence of the controller-processor model. Some appear to favour an equal distribution among those involved in the processing, others argue that responsibility and liability should be allocated in function of the specific "role" assumed by the actor in question. The benefits and drawbacks specific to each approach will be analysed over the following paragraphs.

i. Equal distribution (joint and several liability)

1279. Basic principle – Equal distribution of responsibility and liability would imply that each party involved in the processing is subject to liability exposure for the whole of the processing, regardless of its specific function. It closely resembles a "strict" liability regime, whereby mere "involvement" in an unlawful processing activity may be sufficient to trigger liability exposure towards data subjects. While the party who is thus held liable may be able to take recourse against another party pursuant to the their internal distribution of liabilities, any party who is thus held liable is obliged to indemnify the data subject and might potentially be subject to administrative penalties.[2617]

1280. Advantages – From the perspective of the data subject, equal distribution of responsibility and liability offers a number of benefits. First, it provides data subjects with maximum protection against insolvency of any of

[2615] Of course, data protection authorities could still provide similar guideposts when interpreting other provisions which contain open-ended obligations (e.g. the duty to take "all appropriate measures" to ensure confidentiality and security of processing). Such guidance, however, would not enjoy the same legal weight as a statutory provision.

[2616] Under the controller-processor model, service providers who act as processors are contractually bound to limit the further use of data to purposes specified by the customer. Controllers, on the other hand, are in principle free to reuse data for their own purposes provided those purposes are compatible or they have consent. In other words, the controller-processor model may help to slow down function creep.

[2617] In principle, the liability exposure of each party under the equal distribution model may be either proportional (each party's liability exposure is limited to their proportional share in causing the damages or in light of the severity of their faults) or joint and several (each party's liability exposure towards the data subject is for the whole amount of the damages, regardless of the nature of fault or contribution). For purposes of conceptual clarity, the proportional liability model shall be discussed separately. Cf. *infra*, nos. 1282 et seq.

the parties involved in the processing. Second, it completely removes the burden from data subjects to ascertain who is "ultimately" responsible for the damage. In situations where there is no clear indication of which party should be accountable to data subjects, this is a significant advantage. Third, imposing liability upon any actor involved in the processing could also provide data subjects with considerable economies of scale. For example, if a data subject would be able to exercise the right to object with the major providers of processing services (who offer their processing services to a large number of customers), the data subject would be relieved from the burden of contacting customers of the processing service individually.

1281. Disadvantages – For all its advantages, equal distribution also displays considerable disadvantages. First, imposing the same obligations and liability exposure upon every actor "involved" in the processing, no matter how remotely, is likely to be excessive in many cases.[2618] Second, the transaction cost for the providers of processing services would increase exponentially, given their increased liability exposure. The probability of litigation, with the attendant negative publicity, is likely to induce certain service providers to become highly selective with their clientele.[2619] Third, an equal imposition of responsibility and liability would effectively force providers of processing services to become more involved in the processing they would otherwise be.[2620] Service providers might even be called upon to interfere in the internal relationship between their customers and the data subjects involved, a relationship which is essentially foreign to them.[2621] Moreover, there is the risk that the parties hold different views as to how compliance should be achieved, or as to how a data subject request should be resolved. Such differences in opinion between the parties involved in the processing may put a considerable strain on their commercial

---

2618 For example, a telecom provider is strictly speaking also "involved" in the processing conducted using a cloud service, but the provider may not have actual or constructive knowledge of the processing of personal data taking place, nor have any relationship with the data subjects concerned. In the same vein, a PaaS cloud provider may strictly speaking also be "involved" in the processing undertaken by third-party application providers, but may have no knowledge or relationship with the data subjects concerned. See also W. Kuan Hon, C. Millard and I. Walden, "Who is Responsible for 'Personal Data' in Cloud Computing? The Cloud of Unknowing, Part 2", *l.c.*, p. 18 et seq. See also the Opinion of Advocate General Bobek in *Fashion ID*, C-40/17, ECLI:EU:C:2018:1039, paragraphs 91–93.

2619 This may make it more difficult for smaller and less-established companies to find processing partners.

2620 For example, the staff of a cloud provider might de facto be required, in the context of an exercise of data subject rights, to access and scrutinize information they otherwise would not seek access to.

2621 See also T. Léonard and A. Mention, "Transferts transfrontaliers de données: quelques considérations théorique et pratiques", *l.c.*, p. 108. Not being a direct party to the commercial, legal or other relationship between the customer and the data subject, the providers of processing service may be ill-placed to judge the propriety of the processing or determine whether or not to accommodate a particular request made by a data subject,

relationship. While the authority to make decisions on data subject requests may be allocated internally between the parties, the risk of liability exposure may render certain providers uncomfortable with leaving such decisions in the hands of their customers.[2622]

ii. Role-based accountability (proportional liability)

1282. Basic principle – An alternative to the equal distribution model is the model of "role-based accountability". Instead of imposing equal responsibility and liability upon each of the actors involved in the processing, proponents of this approach advocate allocating responsibility and liability in function of the "role" of each party involved in the processing.[2623] Under this model, liability can be either strict or negligence-based, but it is in any event "proportional" rather than joint and several or vicarious.[2624]

1283. Advantages – A major benefit of the role-based model is that every party involved in the processing shall only be accountable in light of its *actual* role in the processing. The scope of a party's responsibilities can be determined completely in light of the degree of control each party exercises in practice. In theory, it is also possible to differentiate according to different aspects of the processing: one party might, for example, be functionally responsible for security, while another might be responsible for ensuring data accuracy. From a fairness perspective, this is a significant improvement over the equal distribution model, as in principle each party shall only be exposed to liability in light of its effective control capabilities.

1284. Disadvantages – While the role-based model provides advantages over the equal distribution model, it also displays a number of flaws. First, it is worth observing that proponents of the role-based model often fail to provide

---

2622 There is also the question of how meaningful transparency can be ensured in a model where every actor involved in the processing would in principle be obliged to disclose its identity and purposes pursued when processing the data. In principle, the parties involved could designate a party among themselves, as suggested by the International Pharmaceutical Privacy Consortium (cf. *supra*, no. 1271). However, granting parties the same flexibility as regards liability exposure and the duty to accommodate data subject rights is less straightforward. If the parties are given complete freedom to designate who shall be responsible, the stronger party will almost inevitably seek to transfer responsibility to the weaker party, which may not appropriately reflect their respective control capabilities.

2623 Cf. *supra*, no. 1271.

2624 Under proportional liability, each party's liability exposure is limited to their proportional share in causing the damages. If one party proves insolvent, the loss shall in principle be borne by the data subject. By contrast, in case of joint and several liability, each party can be held liable by data subjects for the full amount. See also J. Boyd and D.E. Ingberman, "The 'Polluter pays principle'": Should Liability be Extended When the Polluter Cannot Pay?", *The Geneva Papers on Risk and Insurance* 1996, Vol. 21, No. 79, p. 184

a clear alternative standard for allocating responsibility. It is simply envisaged that the scope of a party's responsibility should be determined in light of its "role" or "control". The role-based model therefore does not solve the difficulties regarding the concept of "control", it simply moves the question to a later stage in the analysis.[2625] *Chassé par la porte, il revient par la fénêtre.* One could even argue that the role based-model is not actually a solution, but simply a restatement of the policy objectives underlying the controller-processor model (i.e. to allocate responsibility with those entities that exercise factual influence over the processing). The role-based model also raises questions as regards incentives: if the scope of a party's obligations are determined purely in light of its actual role, there is a risk that parties will "do less" to ensure compliance with data protection responsibilities.[2626] Last but not least, the role-based model is unlikely to provide effective remedy for data subjects. On the contrary, data subjects may experience greater difficulties in obtaining redress, as they risk carrying the burden of demonstrating that a party should have done more in light of its "role" or "degree of control" (which may be more onerous than demonstrating the exercise of a determinative influence over the purpose and means" of the processing).

iii. Combined approach (general and proportional liability)

1285. Basic principle – The "combined approach" consists of assigning general liability to one party (for the processing as a whole), whereas anyone involved in the processing of personal data at a later stage is accountable for their own aspect of the processing.[2627] The party that is assigned general liability might, for example, be the party that "*initiates*" the processing[2628] or, alternatively, the party who has the "*primary relationship*" with the data

[2625] In other words: while the concept of "control" is no longer applied as a factor to determine the formal status of an actor, it remains equally relevant to establishing the scope of each party's obligations.

[2626] After all, the more they do, the more likely they are in considered to be in control of those aspects of the processing.

[2627] See e.g. W. Kuan Hon, C. Millard and I. Walden, "Who is Responsible for 'Personal Data' in Cloud Computing? The Cloud of Unknowing, Part 2", *l.c.*, p. 24–25 ("*we advocate a more flexible approach, which may impose primary liability on one party, but assign different degrees of responsibility and liability to other actors in proportion to the individual parts they each play in the processing chain*")

[2628] The ICO proposed assigning liability "to the organisation, or organisations, that initiate the processing, whereas anyone processing personal data at any stage of the information life cycle should be responsible for dealing with it properly and securely, and be accountable for their own aspect of the processing. This could mean being accountable to whoever initiated the processing; to individuals; to regulators; or all three." (Information Commissioner's Office (ICO), "The Information Commissioner's response to the European Commission's consultation on the legal framework for the fundamental right to protection of personal data", *l.c.*, p. 2–3.

subject.[2629] The party who is assigned general liability is liable for any processing activities undertaken on its behalf, whereas the other parties shall only be proportionally liable in light of their role. Liability in principle is not joint and several, except possibly in cases of jointly committed faults or where different faults contribute to the same damage.[2630]

1286. ADVANTAGES – The combined approach displays a number of advantages over the previous two models. It incorporates, for the most part, the benefits of the role-based approach (proportional liability), but also ensures that the data subject is in a position to seek remedy from a single actor in relation to every aspect of the processing. The combined approach also has the advantage that it is consistent with the general principles of tort law.[2631] Finally, the combined approach would represent only a minor change in relation to the controller-processor model. The data subject would enjoy the same recourse capabilities vis-à-vis the party who is assigned general liability as it would against controllers and joint controllers. In addition, there is an explicit recognition that the data subject may also hold other parties accountable for those aspects of the processing for which they are responsible.

1287. DISADVANTAGES – The limitations of the combined approach are similar to those of the role-based model. First, proponents of the combined approach fail to provide a clear alternative standard that could realistically replace the current criteria for control. While the concept of "initiation" has a strong appeal (reference to initiation has also been made in the interpretation of the controller concept[2632]), it may not scale well in the case of multiple collaborating controllers, whereby one controller independently decides to re-use data for a separate purpose.[2633] Imposing general liability upon the party who has the "primary relationship" with the data subject works relatively well in the business-to-consumer (B2C) context, but presents difficulties in situations where the party behind the processing does not have a direct relationship with the data

---

2629 Bird & Bird, "Response to European Commission Consultation on the Legal Framework for the Fundamental Right to Protection of Personal Data", *l.c.*, at paragraph 20 (the authors themselves immediately dismissed the proposal as it inapplicable in contexts such as law enforcement) (*Ibid*, at paragraph 21).

2630 As we will be discussed later, the combined approach closely resembles the approach ultimately taken by the EU legislature under the GDPR. The main difference is that the GDPR retained both the concepts of controller and processor, which enables it to differentiate among the obligations incumbent upon each party involved in the processing. Cf. *infra*, 1310.

2631 Cf. *supra*, nos. 150 et seq.

2632 Cf. *supra*, no. 76.

2633 If it is argued that such re-purposes is tantamount to "initiating" a new form of processing, it is clear that the "initiation" approach is in fact equivalent to the current approach (which hinges on the decision to process personal data for a particular purpose).

subject (e.g. law enforcement agencies, data brokers, search engines).[2634] Second, the combined approach does not specify how the obligations of other parties involved in the processing of personal data shall be determined. It is simply envisaged that each party shall be accountable in relation to its "own aspect" of the processing, without specifying which data protection obligations may be viewed as relevant in relation to a particular aspect of the processing.

iv. Interdependencies

1288. Grammatical issues – Abolishing the distinction between controllers and processors would theoretically solve the grammatical issues associated with the concepts of controller and processor. As indicated earlier, however, it would create a need for alternative criteria – and hence vocabulary – to determine which obligations apply to which party. Alternatively, the same vocabulary and criteria might be implemented in a later stage of the analysis (e.g. by using the criterion of "control" when assessing the scope of liability of a party involved in the processing as opposed to determining whether the party falls within the remit of the controller concept).

1289. Systemic issues – Abolishing the distinction between controllers and processors would have implications for provisions which hinge (or have hinged) upon the distinction between controllers and processors, namely (a) applicable law; (b) scope of obligations; (c) transparency; (d) data subject rights; (e) interest balancing and (f) legal binding. For purposes of conceptual clarity, the relationship with systemic issues will discussed in the next section.

1290. Historical issues – Abolishing the distinction between controllers and processors could potentially aggravate certain historical issues. Absent additional measures, it would increase the likelihood of directly imposing the full panoply of controller obligations upon actors who fulfil an intermediary role or otherwise facilitate the dissemination of content shared by their customers.

B. *Obligations for processors*

1291. Advantages – The benefits of imposing obligations directly on processors are essentially three-fold. First, in comparison with the proposal to abolish the distinction between controllers, this approach represents a much less radical departure from the current framework. Existing case law and regulatory

---

2634 See also Bird & Bird, "Response to European Commission Consultation on the Legal Framework for the Fundamental Right to Protection of Personal Data", *l.c.*, at paragraph 22 ("*It would also be unlikely to translate easily outside the consumer arena because if, for example, data are processed by law enforcement agencies without the individual's knowledge, then talk of a 'primary relationship' would seem strained*").

guidance concerning the controller and processor concepts remain relevant. Second, imposing additional obligations directly upon processors renders the obligation to comply with (certain) data protection requirements independent of the prior conclusion of a contract between controllers and processors. As indicated earlier, this is especially relevant in situations where controllers are in a relatively weak bargaining position. Third, this approach partially reduces the practical importance of the distinction between controllers and processors. As a result, establishing whether a party to the processing is acting as a controller or processor becomes less of an "all or nothing" exercise. Regardless of legal status, certain basic obligations are directly applicable to both controllers and processors.

1292. LIMITATIONS – Two of the three advantages outlined in the previous paragraph only apply insofar as obligations are in fact imposed directly upon processors. If an obligation is not imposed upon processors (e.g. data protection by design and by default), there shall be limited or no possibility of holding processors accountable for those aspects of the processing (unless the obligations are imposed by way of contract). Any discrepancies may still influence the interpretation of the controller and processor concepts. A second limitation (or benefit, depending on one's perspective) is that the approach does not completely remove the need to further specify distribution of tasks. For example, if both controllers and processors are subject to obligation to ensure security, in practice there is still a need for further task distribution as to which party will take care of which security requirements (e.g. enforcing access control privileges vs. assigning access control privileges).[2635] Finally, it is worth noting that it might not always be appropriate to impose the same obligations on all providers of processing services.[2636]

1293. INTERDEPENDENCIES – Imposing obligations directly upon processors reduces certain systemic issues, as the applicability of certain obligations is no longer contingent upon legal status. Absent further measures, however, other systemic issues remain unaffected. Grammatical issues regarding the distinction between controllers and processors remain the same, as do the historical issues that arise when applying the controller and processor concept to contexts not anticipated by the EU legislature.

C. *Internal comparison*

1294. PROBLEM STATEMENT – Each of the proposals presented above has its merits and limitations. Abolishing the distinction between controllers and

---

[2635] One could argue that this limitation also exists under Directive 95/46 and therefore does not constitute a disadvantage compared to the current state of affairs.

[2636] Cf. *infra*, no. 1303.

processors would theoretically decrease the associated interpretation costs, but requires an alternative mechanism to allocate responsibility and liability. The question of which approach is best suited for purposes of data protection law is (at least in part) a question as to the *optimal degree of differentiation and specificity* of data protection law. To develop this point further, it is necessary to first clarify the distinction between two types of legal pronouncements, namely "standards" and "rules".[2637]

i. Standards vs. rules

1295. Basic properties – A *rule* is a legal pronouncement which states a determinate legal result that follows from one or more well-specified triggering facts.[2638] A *standard*, in contrast, puts forward a legal or social criterion that legal decision-makers ("adjudicators") use in order to judge actions under particular circumstances.[2639] Standards indicate the types of circumstances that are relevant to a decision on legality, but remain relatively open-ended.[2640] Rules, on the other hand, withdraw from the consideration of the decision-maker one or more circumstances that would be relevant to decision-making according to a standard.[2641] An example may serve to better illustrate the distinction between standards and rules. The legal pronouncement that "*in case of outsourcing, every controller must bind its processors by way of a contract or legal act specifying at a minimum [xyz]*" is essentially a rule. It clearly specifies the situation in which the rule is to take effect and enumerates its consequences. On the other hand, the legal pronouncement that "*every actor involved in the processing of personal data shall take every reasonable measure to ensure adequate protection of personal data, including in case of outsourcing*" is a standard rather than a rule.

2637 See also B. Coene, *De wenselijkheid van de investeringsbescherming geboden door de sui generis intellectuele rechten rond chips, computerprogramma's en databanken*, Proefschrift aangeboden tot het behalen van de titel van Doctor in de Rechten aan de KU Leuven en de UGent, Academiejaar 2015–2016, p. 221–249 and p. 347–362.

2638 R.B. Korobkin, "Behavioural analysis and legal form: Rules vs. Standards Revisited", *Oregon Law Review* 2000, Vol. 79, No. 1, p. 23.

2639 V. Fon and F. Parisi, "Codifications and the optimal specificity of legal rules", Law and Economics Working Paper Series 04–32, George Mason University School of Law, 2007, p. 4. See also R.B. Korobkin, "Behavioural analysis and legal form: Rules vs. Standards Revisited", *l.c.*, p. 23. ("*Standards [...] require legal decision makers to apply a background principle or set of principles to a particularized set of facts in order to reach a legal conclusion*").

2640 I. Ehrleich and R. A. Posner, "An Economic Analysis of Legal Rulemaking", *The Journal of Legal Studies* 1974, Vol. 3, No. 1, p. 258.

2641 *Ibid*, p. 258. See also V. Fon and F. Parisi, "Codifications and the optimal specificity of legal rules", *l.c.*, p. 4. Another way to distinguish rules from standards is by looking at the extent to which "*efforts to give content to the law are undertaken before or after individuals act*". See L. Kaplow, "Rules versus Standards: An Economic Analysis", *Duke Law Journal* 1992, Vol. 42, p. 560. See also R.B. Korobkin, "Behavioural analysis and legal form: Rules vs. Standards Revisited", *l.c.*, p. 32 (observing that the public costs of administrating rules will tend to be "front-loaded", whereas the costs of administering standards tend to be "backloaded").

1296. A FALSE DICHOTOMY – Rules and standards reside at opposite ends of a continuum.[2642] In practice, the difference between rules and standards is a question of degree rather than a binary distinction.[2643] The greater its specificity, the more a legal pronouncement approximates a rule. The more it allows for flexibility in its application (e.g. through qualifications, exceptions, or criteria), the more a legal pronouncement resembles standard.[2644] A multi-factor balancing test can display both rule- and standard-like properties. Depending on the degree of specificity with which the facts relevant to the legal determination are specified in advance, it shall resemble a rule to a greater or lesser extent.[2645]

1297. BENEFITS AND COSTS – Rules and standards each have associated benefits and costs.[2646] Generally speaking, detailed rules are often considered inflexible, unable to cope with change, and quickly outdated.[2647] Broad standards, on the other hand, support flexibility and adaptability, but can result in uncertainty, inconsistent application and concerns regarding unfettered discretion of enforcement officials.[2648] Conversely, rules are generally considered to provide greater legal certainty and consistency in application. When promulgating (or updating) a legal norm, lawmakers must consider the degree of precision or specificity with which they will issue their legal pronouncement. Which approach is likely to yield the best result? A rule or a standard? In the field of law and economics, a considerable body of scholarship has been developed which deals precisely with this issue. While said scholarship does not provide a definitive answer to the question of whether or not the distinction between controllers and processors should be maintained, it does provide an interesting analytical framework which merits discussion.

ii. Optimal specificity of legal rules

1298. ECONOMIC APPROACH – Scholars in the field of law and economics approach the issue of specificity of rule-making in terms of economic efficiency.

2642 I. Ehrleich and R. A. Posner, "An Economic Analysis of Legal Rulemaking", *l.c.*, p. 258; L. Kaplow, "Rules versus Standards: An Economic Analysis", *l.c.*, p. 561–562; R.B. Korobkin, "Behavioural analysis and legal form: Rules vs. Standards Revisited", *l.c.*, p. 25–30; B. Coene, *De wenselijkheid van de investeringsbescherming geboden door de sui generis intellectuele rechten rond chips, computerprogramma's en databanken*, *o.c.*, p. 349–358.

2643 R.B. Korobkin, "Behavioural analysis and legal form: Rules vs. Standards Revisited", *l.c.*, p. 25–26.

2644 *Ibid*, p. 27–28.

2645 *Ibid*, p. 28

2646 I. Ehrleich and R. A. Posner, "An Economic Analysis of Legal Rulemaking", *l.c.*, p. 259.

2647 B.M. Hutter, *Regulation and Risk. Occupational Health and Safety on the Railways*, Oxford, Oxford University Press, 2001, p. 76.

2648 *Id.* See also R. Baldwin and M. Cave, *Understanding regulation – Theory Strategy and Practice*, *o.c.*, p. 119 (who refer to rules as "specification" or "design" standards, whereas standards in the sense above are referred to as "performance" or "output" standards). On the benefits of principles see also N. Sethi, "Reimagining Regulatory Approaches: on the Essential Role of Principles in Health Research Regulation", *Scripted* 2015, Vol. 12, Issue 2, p. 91–116.

They essentially ask themselves the following question: given the activity to be regulated, what is the optimal level of differentiation and precision?[2649] Ehrleich and Posner have extensively catalogued the benefits and costs associated with the promulgation of rules and standards respectively.[2650] They take into account benefits and costs not only at the moment of promulgation, but also at the moment of application (e.g. costs of interpretation, risks of over- or underinclusion).[2651] Since then, other scholars have built upon these insights and identified additional considerations that can influence the cost-benefit analysis (e.g. the degree of specialisation of decision-makers[2652]) or incorporated insights from other disciplines (e.g. behavioural analysis[2653]).[2654] It is beyond the scope of this book to evaluate each of these approaches in detail. Nevertheless, it is worth introducing the main insights they offer and to consider their potential implications for data protection law.

1299. Rules of thumb – Whether rules or standards yield the best outcome depends on a number of factors. A general rule of thumb, supported by several scholars, is that rules are likely to be preferable over standards if the primary behaviour (i.e. the regulated activity) is factually homogenous, stable, and occurs frequently.[2655] Standards, on the other hand, are likely to be preferable

---

2649 I. Ehrleich and R. A. Posner, "An Economic Analysis of Legal Rulemaking", *l.c.*, p. 261 et seq. (who define the optimum choice as the option which maximises the excess of benefits over costs). See also B. Coene, *De wenselijkheid van de investeringsbescherming geboden door de sui generis intellectuele rechten rond chips, computerprogramma's en databanken*, *o.c.* p. 224 et seq and 349 et seq (who argues, as regards the question of whether further specificity and differentiation is desirable, test is whether further differentiation increases likelihood of realising policy objectives, as long as the cost of differentiation does not exceed the benefits; or that optimal when the legislative measures contributes to the greatest possible realisation of the policy objective which exceeds the cost of formulation and application). See e.g. also V. Fon and F. Parisi, "Codifications and the optimal specificity of legal rules", *l.c.*, p. 6 (who consider the optimal degree of specificity of legal rules as that which maximises the value of the law net of the fixed cost of lawmaking and the variable cost of adjudication).

2650 I. Ehrleich and R. A. Posner, "An Economic Analysis of Legal Rulemaking", *l.c.*, p. 262–271.

2651 *Id.* Another way to think of the choice between rules and standards is as a choice regarding the extent to which a given aspect of a legal command should be resolved in advance or left to an enforcement authority to consider. (L. Kaplow, "Rules versus Standards: An Economic Analysis", *l.c.*, p. 561–562).

2652 V. Fon and F. Parisi, "Codifications and the optimal specificity of legal rules", *l.c.*, p. 7 et seq.

2653 R.B. Korobkin, "Behavioural analysis and legal form: Rules vs. Standards Revisited", *l.c.*, p. 44–57.

2654 See also J. Black, "The Rise, Fall and Fate of Principles Based Regulation", *LSE Law Society and Economy Working Papers* 17/2010, 2010, 26 p.

2655 I. Ehrleich and R. A. Posner, "An Economic Analysis of Legal Rulemaking", *l.c.*, p. 272–273; R.B. Korobkin, "Behavioural analysis and legal form: Rules vs. Standards Revisited", *l.c.*, p. 42–43 ("*If disputes are frequent and factually homogeneous, rules are likely to have lower administrative costs, and thus are more desirable than standards on that score. If disputes are infrequent and/or factually heterogeneous, standards are preferable because they will likely be more cost effective for lawmakers to administer. Whether rules or standards have higher advice costs depends on whether the standard requires a complex investigation or merely a reference to*

in situations where the primary behaviour is heterogeneous, evolves rapidly over time, or occurs infrequently. The underlying rationale is that the benefits of detailing a rule will be greater the more often it is applied.[2656] The cost of detailing a rule, however, is likely to be higher as the heterogeneity or complexity of the regulated activity increases.[2657] Moreover, if the social, economic or technical factors shaping the problem evolve rapidly over time, crafting detailed rules may yield insufficient return on investment.[2658] Finally, (certain) rules are more likely to create risks of over- or underinclusion than standards.[2659] Standards, on the other hand, are less likely to be affected by changes over time in the circumstances to which they are applied.[2660]

1300. LIMITATIONS – Before discussing how these rules of thumb might be applied in the context of data protection law, it is worth underlining that they do not always provide a clear-cut solution. As noted by Korobkin:

> "Although a thorough economic analysis of the comparative costs of rules and standards provides a variety of relevant insights into the ultimate choice of legal form, it provides no clear prescription for how to balance the various competing factors, some of which favour rules and others of which favour standards. Consequently, economic analysis of the choice of legal form does not provide lawmakers with a rule, even a complex one, for choosing between rules and standards in a particular factual situation."[2661]

a widely-shared social norm and the complexity of the comparable rule."). See also B. Coene, *De wenselijkheid van de investeringsbescherming geboden door de sui generis intellectuele rechten rond chips, computerprogramma's en databanken*, *o.c.*, p. 359–361.

2656 See e.g. L. Kaplow, "Rules versus Standards: An Economic Analysis", *l.c.*, p. 563.

2657 I. Ehrleich and R. A. Posner, "An Economic Analysis of Legal Rulemaking", *l.c.*, p. 274.

2658 Von and Parisi refer to this as "the problem of obsolescence"; arguing that as the rate of obsolescence increases, the value of the legal rule decreases (V. Fon and F. Parisi, "Codifications and the optimal specificity of legal rules", *l.c.*, p. 10)

2659 R.B. Korobkin, "Behavioural analysis and legal form: Rules vs. Standards Revisited", *l.c.*, p. 42–43 "Overinclusion" refers to the situation whereby a rule prohibits or otherwise limits socially desirable behavior. Underinclusion refers to situation whereby the rule permits socially undesirable conduct (*Ibid*, p. 36). However, as Korobkin also notes, the lack of ex ante clarity associated with standards will lead to some well-intentioned undesirable behavior on the part of citizens, and errors in applying standards might cause them to be over- or underinclusive as applied (*Ibid*, p. 44). See also L. Kaplow, "Rules versus Standards: An Economic Analysis", *l.c.*, p. 565 (arguing that the suggestion that rules are more prone to over- or under-inclusiveness is misleading because typically it implicitly compares a complex standard and a relatively simple rule, whereas both rules and standards can in fact be quite simple or highly detailed in their operation).

2660 I. Ehrleich and R. A. Posner, "An Economic Analysis of Legal Rulemaking", *l.c.*, p. 277. See also V. Fon and F. Parisi, "Codifications and the optimal specificity of legal rules", *l.c.*, p. 10.

2661 R.B. Korobkin, "Behavioural analysis and legal form: Rules vs. Standards Revisited", *l.c.*, p. 43. Korobkin goes on to note that "*One view of this state of affairs is that economic reasoning has failed to resolve the question of whether lawmakers should make legal pronouncements in the form of rules or standards. Another view is that selecting a legal form is an activity more suited to being guided by a standard than by a rule.*" See also V. Fon and F. Parisi, "Codifications

iii. Implications for data protection law

1301. A MIX OF STANDARDS AND RULES – European data protection law consists of a mix of standards and rules. The principle of data accuracy, for example, promulgates a standard for determining which measures controllers should adopt to ensure data accuracy. The regulation of the relationship between controllers and processors, on the other hand, is closer to a "rule" than a standard. As soon as the relationship between two parties is qualified as a controller-processor relationship, certain specified legal results follow. Of course, not every implication (legal pronouncement) that follows from the qualification of a party as either a controller or processor is itself a rule.[2662] Nevertheless, I would argue that the differentiation between controllers and processors was introduced primarily to facilitate the promulgation of rule-like requirements (i.e. the need to ensure legal binding which contains certain minimum elements and the obligation for processors to only act on the instructions of the controller).[2663] The rule-like quality of the controller-processor model stands in stark contrast with the standard-like approach which has been developed in relation to separate and joint control. Separate controllers enjoy a considerable flexibility when allocating responsibility amongst each other, as long as "*as long as they ensure full compliance*".[2664] In case of joint control, the controllers are obliged to determine their respective responsibilities "*in a transparent manner*" and in manner which "*duly reflect[s] the joint controllers' respective effective roles and relationships vis-à-vis data subjects*".[2665]

1302. PRIMARY ACTIVITY – As a general matter, it is clear that type of activities regulated by data protection law are highly heterogeneous and evolve rapidly. Based on this observation, the use of standards might appear preferable over the use of rules.[2666] On the other hand, data processing activities are a part of daily

---

and the optimal specificity of legal rules", *l.c.*, p. 7 et seq (observing that each of the variables above, do not necessarily reinforce each other / can work in opposite directions)

2662 Moreover, it should be observed that, over time, the *distinction* between controllers and processors itself has come to resemble more of a standard than a rule. The criteria to distinguish between controllers and processors are increasingly applied in a flexible and more open-ended fashion. Regulators have supplemented the statutory criteria (purpose, means, on behalf) with additional criteria (e.g. image given to data subject, level of instruction, degree of expertise), whereby none of these criteria themselves is considered determinative. As observed by Gilbert, the approach of the Working Party seems to have become a "balancing test" or "sliding scale" rather than a rigid adherence to existing criteria. Cf. *supra*, no. 1064).

2663 The question of whether it is desirable to maintain the distinction between controllers and processors should be viewed primarily in this light.

2664 Opinion 1/2010, *l.c.*, p. 24.

2665 Article 26(1) GDPR.

2666 Regarding the desirability of detailed rules vs. general principles in data protection regulation see Home Office (Great Britain), Computers and Privacy, Cmnd. 653, Her Majesty's Stationary Office (HMSO), London, 1975; reproduced by Home Office (Great Britain), Report of the Committee on Data Protection, Cmnd. 7341, HMSO, London, 1978, p. 455–456; G.

life and occur on a massive scale. This would suggest that the promulgation of certain rules might nevertheless offer economies of scale. What is relevant for our current analysis, however, is not whether the primary activity regulated by data protection law *as a whole* is homogenous or heterogeneous, stable or unstable, frequent or infrequent. What is relevant is whether the *primary activity regulated by the controller-processor model* – i.e. outsourcing – is homogenous or heterogeneous, stable or unstable, frequent or infrequent.

iv. Implications for the controller-processor model

1303. Over- and under-inclusion – The use cases presented in Part IV offered a small glimpse of the increasingly complex manner in which organisations collaborate, including in case of outsourcing. The cloud computing use case illustrated that there are a variety of ways in which one organisation might process personal data "on behalf of" another entity. In this context, the "rule-like" approach of the controller-processor model creates risks of both over- and under-inclusion.[2667] Hon and Millard, for example, have argued that considering all PaaS and IaaS providers as "processors" is essentially *overinclusive*, particularly in cases where the personal data processed by them is rendered unintelligible through encryption.[2668] Conversely, the argument can also be made that the controller-processor model is *underinclusive* in cases where the service providers exercise significant influence over either the purposes or means of the processing.[2669]

1304. Assessment – Overinclusion is generally considered acceptable as long as the adverse impact on socially desirable behaviour is minimal.[2670]

Dworkin, "The Younger Committee Report on Privacy", *l.c.*, p. 402 and F. Robben, F., "Toepassingsgebied en begripsdefinities", *l.c.*, p. 24.

2667 Regarding the distinction between over- and underinclusion see *supra*, footnote 2660. Generally speaking, problems of overinclusion and underinclusion are more frequent the greater the heterogeneity of the conduct intended to be affected by a rule (I. Ehrleich and R. A. Posner, "An Economic Analysis of Legal Rulemaking", *l.c.*, p. 270).

2668 Cf. *supra*, no. 1075.

2669 Of course, cloud providers who determine either the purposes or «essential» means of the processing are considered as (joint) controllers rather than processors, and therefore fall outside the controller-processor model all together. Nevertheless, the primary activity being regulated in such a cases is still the activity of outsourcing, which is the intended remit of controller-processor model.

2670 Based on R.B. Korobkin, "Behavioural analysis and legal form: Rules vs. Standards Revisited", *l.c.*, p. 37 ("*Rules also have lower undesirable behavior costs when the behavior deterred by an overinclusive rule is not highly valuable or when the behavior permitted by an underinclusive rule is not highly costly*"). See also V. Fon and F. Parisi, "Codifications and the optimal specificity of legal rules", *l.c.*, p. 5 (arguing that imperfections of a rule are more or less significant depending on the relative size of the value of the regulate activity and the gravity of negative effects absent legal constraints). It should be noted however, that imposing a fixed model may also have hidden costs, such as deterring development of more innovative which

Arguably, unnecessary transaction costs (e.g. the conclusion of controller-processor agreements in cases where its added value is minimal) is only significantly detrimental once it reaches a certain scale. From the perspective of the provider of a processing service, however, issues of overinclusion become significant once the obligations directly applicable to processors require substantial additional effort.[2671] Problems of overinclusion can be mitigated by either allowing enforcement officials to wave application of a rule in specific instances or by adding specific exceptions to the rule.[2672] The problem of underinclusion, on the other hand, can be remedied by backing the rule up with a standard.[2673] The regulatory guidance regarding joint and separate control has essentially done just this: in situations where the provider of a processing service is considered a controller rather than a processor, the parties are expected to put in place "clear and equally effective allocation of obligations and responsibilities".[2674]

1305. Interpretation costs – In theory, rules offer greater *ex ante* certainty to both private actors and regulators. As soon as the fact pattern arises which triggers the application of the rule, the legal consequences of this fact pattern are already determined.[2675] From this perspective, rules have the potential to result in lower interpretation costs than standards.[2676] The controller-processor model

---

might be more effective in practice (see R. Baldwin and M. Cave, *Understanding regulation – Theory Strategy and Practice*, *o.c.*, p. 119 (who note that the use of detailed specification standards [rules] may inhibit innovation and the development of new, perhaps safer and more efficient modes of operation).

2671 Cf. *infra*, nos. 1316 et seq.

2672 I. Ehrleich and R. A. Posner, "An Economic Analysis of Legal Rulemaking", *l.c.*, p. 268: "*The problem of overinclusion is frequently dealt with by delegation to enforcement officials of authority to wave application of the rule. [...] In principle one could rewrite the rule to specify all the possible exceptions; but in practice it may be cheaper to allow ad hoc exceptions to be made at the enforcement level – as recognized by even the severest critics of official discretion. Again, however, some benefits of governance by rules are sacrificed by recognizing exceptions based on implicit use of an overriding standard*".) Accommodating factually different situations can in principle also be accommodated through more detailed rules, but this will generally increase the complexity of the rule by introducing multiple exceptions and sub-rules (R.B. Korobkin, "Behavioural analysis and legal form: Rules vs. Standards Revisited", *l.c.*, p. 36. As we will see later, the EU legislature has mitigated the issue of overinclusion primarily by adding exceptions (in particular by incorporating the liability exemptions of the E-Commerce Directive). Cf. *infra*, nos. 1343 et seq.

2673 I. Ehrleich and R. A. Posner, "An Economic Analysis of Legal Rulemaking", *l.c.*, p. 268 ("*The problem of underinclusion can be solved by backing up the rule with a standard. [...] The result of adding a standard is, however, to sacrifice some of the benefits of the rule.*")

2674 Opinion 1/2010, *l.c.*, p. 24

2675 R.B. Korobkin, "Behavioural analysis and legal form: Rules vs. Standards Revisited", *l.c.*, p. 32

2676 Rules do not always result in lower interpretation costs than standards. For example, if a rule is very complex, it is likely to require subject-matter expertise in its interpretation. Moreover, if the application of standard is intuitive and straightforward even to laymen, a standard may still have lower interpretation costs (I. Ehrleich and R. A. Posner, "An Economic Analysis of Legal Rulemaking", *l.c.*, p. 270–271).

offers a relatively clear set of rules in situations where the factual circumstances can easily be mapped to the model and its implicit assumptions regarding autonomy and control.[2677] For those cases, the model results in decreased interpretation costs for both private actors and regulators. In situations where the factual circumstances do not neatly map the controller-processor model, however, the opposite is true. Interpretation costs increase as both private actors and regulators have to invest more time and resources analysing and debating the legal status of each actor. The desirability of abolishing (option A) or retaining the controller-processor model (option B) therefore depends, at least in part, on whether the model is still readily applicable in a sufficiently large number of circumstances. As noted by Ehrlich and Posner:

> "a point is eventually reached at which the social costs generated by its imperfect fit with current reality exceed the benefits of having minimized uncertainty as to which rule would be followed."[2678]

1306. Assessment – Whether the interpretation costs associated with the controller-processor model have come to exceed its benefits is essentially an empirical question.[2679] It is beyond the scope of this book to make such an assessment. Several responses to the Commission consultation suggest that interpretation costs of the controller-processor model already exceed its benefits, but an empirical analysis would be necessary in order to make a definitive assessment (e.g. by posing this particular question to a large number and representative sample of stakeholders). It should be noted, however, that many objections concerning the controller-processor model concern the *concepts* of controller and processor, as well as the *implications* associated with these concepts, rather than the *differentiation* among parties involved in the processing of personal data as such. In fact, most stakeholders advocating in favour of abolishing the distinction between controllers and processors still advocate in favour of differentiating between parties involved in the processing and tailoring their obligations in light of their "actual role".[2680]

2677 Regarding the implicit assumptions of autonomy and control underlying the controller-processor model see *supra*, no. 1223.

2678 I. Ehrleich and R. A. Posner, "An Economic Analysis of Legal Rulemaking", *l.c.*, p. 278. The authors make this point in relation to the rule of "stare decisis" (which requires courts to adhere to precedent), but in my view similar point can be made in relation to the controller processor model, which is essentially a codification of past regulatory guidance regarding appropriate measures in case of outsourcing.

2679 See also V. Fon and F. Parisi, "Codifications and the optimal specificity of legal rules", *l.c.*, p. 10–11, who refer to this as the "obsolescence problem" and discusses its relationship to economies of scale in adjudication.

2680 Cf. *supra*, nos. 1270 et seq. By definition, this implies differentiation among the actors involved in the processing, even if concepts of "controller" and "processor" were themselves to be abolished.

D. *Final text GDPR*

1307. Outline – The final text of the GDPR retained the controller-processor model. Significant changes were introduced however, as regards the allocation of responsibility and liability. Specifically, the GDPR imposes a considerable number of obligations directly upon processors and renders them liable in case of violations.

1308. Obligations for processors – Under the GDPR, processors are obliged to ensure confidentiality and security of processing, independently of the existence of a contractual arrangement to that effect between controllers and processors (Articles 29 and 32). Processors are also obliged to maintain appropriate records of all processing activities which they carry out on behalf of a controller, and to present such records to a supervisory authority upon request (Article 30). Processors must also designate a data protection officer in the same cases where this is required from controllers (Article 37). Restrictions regarding international transfers now also apply directly to processors (Article 44). Finally, it is also envisaged that codes of conduct and certification mechanisms be developed for processors (Articles 40–42).

1309. Data protection by design – The EU legislature chose not to assimilate controllers and processors as regards the obligation of data protection by design.[2681] This is regrettable, given substantial influence processors have in determining the means of the processing. In my view, it would have been reasonable to impose a similar obligation upon processors, as long as one takes into account the intended purpose of the services they offer.[2682]

1310. Liability model – Article 82(2) GDPR provides that any controller and processor involved in the processing shall be liable for the damage caused by the processing which is not in compliance with the GDPR. The processor, however, shall only be liable only if he failed to comply with the obligations of the GDPR directed specifically to processors or if he acted outside or contrary to lawful instructions of the controller. Article 82 GDPR is conceptually similar to the

2681 Article 23 provides that "*having regard to the state of the art and the cost of implementation and taking account of the nature, scope, context and purposes of the processing as well as the risks of varying likelihood and severity for rights and freedoms of individuals posed by the processing, the controller shall, both at the time of the determination of the means for processing and at the time of the processing itself, implement appropriate technical and organisational measures, such as pseudonymisation, which are designed to implement data protection principles, such as data minimisation, in an effective way and to integrate the necessary safeguards into the processing in order to meet the requirements of this Regulation and protect the rights of data subjects.*"

2682 See also Microsoft, "Protecting Data and Privacy in the Cloud", *Reactive Security Communications*, 2014, p. 3–5 (arguing that it is responsibility of cloud providers to design services in such a way that enables compliance).

"combined approach" described earlier (general and proportional liability).[2683] The main difference is that the GDPR retained both the concepts of controller and processor in order to further differentiate among the obligations incumbent upon each party involved in the processing.

1311. Escape clause – Article 82(3) provides that a controller or processor may be exempted from liability provided it proves that it is not in any way responsible for the event giving rise to the damage. This provision echoes Article 23(2) of Directive 95/46, with the important difference that its scope of application now also extends to processors.[2684] Another change is the introduction of the words "in any way", which clarifies that faults contributing indirectly to the damage may still constitute grounds for liability. At the end of the day, however, the liability regime contained in the GDPR is still essentially a fault-based regime as regards privacy and data protection breaches, albeit with a reversed burden of proof.[2685]

1312. Risks of under- and overinclusion? – Despite the changes made in relation to the obligations incumbent upon processors, the controller-processor model is still not able to accommodate all forms of outsourcing. The risk of *underinclusion* has been addressed – in part – by addressing the implications of joint control.[2686] As will be seen in the next section, the GDPR has essentially codified the standard put forward by the Article 29 Working Party in Opinion 1/2010. The GDPR does not, however, explicitly address the situation of collaborating single controllers. In other words, the GDPR may still be underinclusive in practice in relation to situations of separate control.[2687] Risks resulting from *overinclusion* have arguably become more significant now that processors are directly subject to certain obligations. The incorporation of the liability exemptions of the E-Commerce Directive significantly mitigates the risks of overinclusion. Nevertheless, there may still be service providers whose services do not neatly map to the exemptions, which may result in overinclusion in specific instances.

1313. Evaluation – Every legal norm, whether it be a standard or a rule, is imperfect in the sense that it cannot operate without costs.[2688] Rules are attempts

---

2683 Cf. *supra*, nos. 1285 et seq. For a discussion of the ratio legis underlying this provision see also *supra*, no. 649.

2684 For an analysis of the escape clause contained in Article 23(2) of Directive 95/46 see *supra*, nos. 158 et seq.

2685 P. Larouche, M. Peitz and N. Purtova, *Consumer privacy in network industries – A CERRE Policy Report*, Centre on Regulation in Europe, 25 January 2016, p. 58. The only exception of course is in cases where the GDPR imposes an obligation of result.

2686 See also *infra*, no. 1319.

2687 Regarding the difference between joint control, partial joint control and separate control see *supra*, nos. 131 et seq.

2688 D. Schmidtchen a.o., "The Internalisation of External Costs in Transport: From the Polluter Pays to the Cheapest Cost Avoider Principle", *l.c.*, p. 111.

to model and rationalize human behavior, and every form of rationalization implies a certain loss.[2689] Especially in highly dynamic environments, there will always be cases where the regulatory paradigms and concepts which underlie rules do not neatly map reality or lead to suboptimal outcomes.[2690] On the other hand, complexity does not justify inaction. As noted by Schmidtchen

> "Human behaviour is complex and not always easy to predict. However, if one seeks to make problems tractable enough to provide for some illumination, we need to make simplifying assumptions which do not capture reality. The optimal scale of a map depends on the context that is going to be used in; a map with a scale of 1:1 is clearly of no use at all. The same applies to modelling human behaviour."[2691]

On balance, the desirability of abolishing or retaining the controller-processor model is a question of the optimal degree of differentiation and specificity of legal norms. Determining optimality is an extremely complicated exercise, as it requires balancing the costs and benefits of many different variables. Obtaining an accurate and detailed picture of each of these variables is extremely difficult in practice.[2692] In practice, the approach adopted by legislatures may not be a purely rational choice, but rather the result of lengthy rounds of negotiation and revision, compromise and accommodation.[2693] In the GDPR, the EU legislature decided to retain the controller-processor model. It also provided greater recognition to situations of joint control, to clarify that the controller-processor model is by no means the only model of collaboration. Finally, by imposing additional obligations directly upon processors, the GDPR at least partially alleviates some of the systemic issues which previously plagued the controller processor-model. Taken together, this is likely to be an adequate approach, at least for the time being. In the long term, however, it may become necessary to revisit the current approach. Chapter 4 will therefore outline an alternative approach, which omits the problematic concepts of controller and processor,

2689 *Id.* ("*[A]ll institutions – here broadly understood as rules and norms – are imperfect in the sense that they do not operate without costs: opportunity costs in terms of a misallocation of resources and risks, setup and operating costs. Consequently, rationality requires taking all costs into account when making an institutional choice*").

2690 See also I. Ehrleich and R. A. Posner, "An Economic Analysis of Legal Rulemaking", *l.c.*, p. 268 "*Greater specificity of legal obligation generates allocative inefficiency as a result of the necessarily imperfect fit between the coverage of a rule and the conduct sought to be regulated [...] The inherent ambiguity of language and the limitations of human foresight and knowledge limit the practical ability of the rule maker to catalog accurately and exhaustively the circumstances that should activate the general standard. Hence the reduction of a standard to a set of rules must in practice create both overinclusion and underinclusion*".

2691 D. Schmidtchen a.o., "The Internalisation of External Costs in Transport: From the Polluter Pays to the Cheapest Cost Avoider Principle", *l.c.*, p. 118.

2692 R. Baldwin and M. Cave, *Understanding regulation – Theory Strategy and Practice*, *o.c.*, p. 122–124. See also B. Coene, *De wenselijkheid van de investeringsbescherming geboden door de sui generis intellectuele rechten rond chips, computerprogramma's en databanken*, *o.c.*, p. 232 et seq.

2693 *Ibid*, p. 124.

while supporting differentiation and greater flexibility in terms of the allocation of responsibility and liability.[2694]

4. SYSTEMIC

1314. Preface – Systemic solutions are solutions that involve modifying the implications associated with the controller and processor concepts. The point of departure is that certain functions fulfilled by the controller and processor concepts within the regulatory scheme of EU data protection law can give rise to unintended or undesirable consequences in practice. Systemic solutions seek to address these issues by adjusting the function of the controller and processor concepts in relation to one or more provisions.

1315. Outline – Proposed systemic measures include:

(1) associating the same or similar legal consequences to both the controller and processor concepts (partial assimilation);
(2) providing greater recognition of situations of joint control;
(3) using alternative means of securing transparency and accommodation of data subject rights;
(4) use of standards to determine the scope of obligations incumbent upon each party involved in the processing; and
(5) enhancing the degree of contractual flexibility in the relationship between controllers and processors.

4.1. PARTIAL ASSIMILATION

1316. Proposal – The legal status of a party as controller or processor has significant ramifications under EU data protection law.[2695] First, it may have a determinative influence on the extent to which EU law applies to the processing. Second, it determines to what extent the party shall be accountable towards supervisory authorities and data subjects. In its draft proposal for the GDPR, the Commission proposed to reduce the systemic importance of the distinction in several ways. First, it provided that the territorial scope of EU law would no longer be completely dependent on controller or processor status. Second, it made processors directly accountable to supervisory authorities and data subjects for those aspects of the processing for which they are responsible. Finally, it rendered a substantial number of provisions directly applicable to

---

2694 Cf. *infra*, nos. 1353 et seq.
2695 Cf. *supra*, nos. 261 et seq.

processors.[2696] The following table provides a comparative overview of the main changes introduced by the EC draft proposal:

Table 3. Comparison Directive 95/46 – EC proposal GDPR

Relevant provisions	**Directive 95/46**		**EC Draft GDPR**	
	Controllers	Processors	Controllers	Processors
Applicable law	✓	✗	✓	✓
Principles of data quality	✓	✗	✓	✗
Legitimacy of processing	Implied	✗	Implied	✗
Sensitive data	Implied	✗	Implied	✗
Transparency	✓	✗	✓	✗
Data subject rights	✓	✗	✓	Applicable through contract (with exceptions)
Co-operation with supervisory authority	Implied	Implied	✓	✓
Data protection by design and by default	Implied	✗	✓	✗
Documentation	Implied	Not specified	✓	✓
Confidentiality	✓	✓	✓	✓
Security	✓	Applicable through contract	✓	✓
Data breach notification[2697]	✗	✗	✓	✓
DPIA, prior authorization	✓	✗	✓	✓
Data protection officers	✓	✗	✓	✓
Codes of conduct, certification	✓	Not specified	✓	✓
International transfers	✓	Not Specified	✓	✓
Liability	✓	✗	✓	✓
Administrative fines	Implied	Not Specified	✓	✓

2696 See also *supra*, no. 595.

2697 As regards the obligation to notify data breaches, a distinction should be made between the obligation to inform breaches to the controller and the obligation to notify breaches to supervisory authorities and data subjects. Only the controller is obliged to notify the data subject and supervisory authorities. The processor is only obliged to notify the controller.

1317. Rationale – As indicated earlier, the stated objective of the European Commission was to "clarify and detail" the responsibilities and liability of controllers and processors with a view of establishing legal certainty.[2698] Be that as it may, by imposing the same or similar legal consequences to the legal status of both controller and processor, the Commission proposal also reduced the systemic importance of the distinction.

1318. Counterarguments – As indicated earlier, certain commentators felt that by imposing the same or similar obligations directly upon processors, there may be a risk of confusion as to who is ultimately responsible for ensuring compliance.[2699]

4.2. GREATER RECOGNITION OF JOINT CONTROL

1319. Proposal – In its draft proposal for the GDPR, the Commission introduced a provision requiring joint controllers to determine their respective responsibilities for compliance, in particular as regards the procedures and mechanisms for exercising the rights of the data subject, by means of an arrangement between them.[2700] In addition, the proposal also stipulated that in situations where more than one controller is involved in the processing, each controller shall be jointly and severable liable for the damages as a whole.

1320. Rationale – While Directive 95/46 already recognised the possibility of joint control, it did not spell out its legal implications. The absence of guidance by the EU legislature led to uncertainty and divergent opinions in practice.[2701] Providing greater recognition of joint control signals more clearly that the controller-processor model is by no means the only manner in which parties involved in the processing of personal data can structure their collaboration. It also provides more stable legal footing for parties who choose to do so, thereby increasing legal certainty.

1321. Counterarguments – The main counterargument against this approach is that it provides only a partial solution. In practice, not every collaboration between controllers takes the form of joint control.[2702] There may, however, also be situations in which a collaboration between separate controllers

---

2698 Cf. *supra*, no. 1275.

2699 Cf. *supra*, no. 1276.

2700 Cf. *supra*, no. 597.

2701 See also European Privacy Officers Forum (EPOF), "Comments on the Review of European Data Protection Framework", *l.c.*, p. 5 ("*This is not helped by the fact that the concept of joint controller is not well acknowledged by European data protection law and supervisory authorities.*")

2702 Cf. *supra*, nos. 122 et seq.

requires a mutual arrangement to ensure implementation of adequate data protection safeguards, not least as regards transparency of processing and the exercise of data subject rights. This issue will be elaborated further under the next subsection.

4.3. "NO WRONG DOOR" AND "SINGLE POINT OF CONTACT"

1322. Proposal – The General Approach of the Council provided that in case of joint control, joint controllers should in principle designate among themselves a *single point of contact* for data subjects to exercise their rights.[2703] Irrespective of such an arrangement, however, the data subject would still be able to exercise his or her rights in respect of and against each of the joint controllers ("*no wrong door*").[2704]

1323. Rationale – The introductory text accompanying the General Approach did not specify why the Council imposed the obligation to provide for a single point of contact, combined with a "no wrong door" policy. One might speculate, however, that the proposal was motivated by the finding that the processing of personal data may involve an increasing number of controllers. The multiplication of controllers involved in the processing can make it difficult for data subjects to know who to turn to in order to exercise their rights. By providing that joint controllers should put in place a single point of contact, the data subject is relieved from the burden of determining who is responsible for which aspect of the processing. By further stipulating that the data subject is able to exercise his or her rights against each of the joint controllers, the data subject retains maximum recourse avenues in case of harm.

1324. Counterarguments – The main disadvantage of this approach is the same as the one identified under the previous section, i.e. that it provides only a partial solution. It does not address the case where the processing involves a large number of collaborating single controllers (i.e. "separate controllers" or "controllers in common"). Moreover, in case of joint control, data subjects were in principle already in a position to exercise their rights in full vis-à-vis every joint controller involved in the processing.[2705] From this perspective, one could argue that the "no wrong door" policy did not really add anything new.

2703 See Article 24(1) of the General Approach. Under the General Approach, joint controllers would be exempted from this obligation in cases where the respective responsibilities of the controllers are determined by Union or Member State law to which the controllers are subject.

2704 Article 24(2) of the General Approach.

2705 In case of joint control, each joint controller is in principle responsible and liable for the processing as a whole. As a result, the data subject should already be able to exercise his rights vis-à-vis any of the (joint) controllers involved in the processing. Even if the specific

4.4. TAILORING OBLIGATIONS

1325. Proposal – A proposal which has not yet been put forward is to introduce language which would allow adjudicators to further tailor the obligations of controllers and/or processors in light of their specific role in the processing. One way to do this would be to codify the language used by the Court of Justice in *Google Spain* to indicate the limits of the obligations incumbent upon search engines ("*within the framework of its responsibilities, powers and capabilities*"[2706]). An alternative formulation can be found in the OECD Recommendation on Digital Security Risk Management. The second principle ("responsibility") stipulates that all stakeholders should take responsibility for the management of digital security risks "*based on their roles, the context and their ability to act*".[2707]

1326. Rationale – The precise scope of data protection obligations must always be assessed in context. A party's obligations might indeed be lighter – or more onerous –depending on the purposes pursued by the processing and the risks for data subjects.[2708] Certain provisions of EU data protection law fail to provide adequate flexibility in all contexts.[2709] By incorporating additional standards into the legal framework, it may be possible to soften the adverse impact of certain rule-like ("all or nothing") features of the current framework.[2710] On the one hand, it would enable adjudicators limit the scope of a party's obligations in cases where ensuring compliance of certain aspects (or for certain stages) of

controller approached by the data subject is not internally responsible for that element of the processing, he in principle remains accountable as joint controller for operations performed by his fellow joint controllers (or processors). See also *supra*, nos. 174–180.

2706 Judgment in *Google Spain*, C-131/12, EU:C:2014:317, paragraph 38. See also *supra*, no. 1163 et seq.

2707 See the second principle of the OECD, Recommendation of the Council on Digital Security Risk Management for Economic and Social Prosperity, 2015. Such language could be introduced either after the specific provision in question (e.g. by specifying that "*it shall be for the controller [and/or processor] to ensure that paragraph 1 is complied with, taking into account its responsibilities, powers and capabilities [alternative: taking into account context role and ability to act]*"), or when determining the scope of liability exposure (e.g. by specifying that "*any party who has contributed to the harm suffered may be exempted from liability insofar as it has implemented every reasonable measure to prevent and remove harm, taking into account its responsibilities, powers and capabilities [alternative: taking into account context role and ability to act]*)".

2708 B. Van Alsenoy, A. Kuczerawy and J. Ausloos, "Search Engines after *Google Spain*: Internet@ Liberty or Privacy@Peril?", *l.c.*, p. 44. See also Tweede Kamer der Staten-Generaal, Regels inzake de bescherming van persoonsgegevens (Wet bescherming persoonsgegevens) – Memorie van Toelichting, *l.c.*, p. 59–60.

2709 For example, the restrictions regarding sensitive data in the context of processing of personal data by search engines. Cf. *supra*, no. 1165.

2710 Cf. *supra*, no. 1234. It should be noted, however, that by imposing additional obligations directly on processors, the differentiation between controllers and processors becomes less stark (less of an "all or nothing" exercise).

the processing is beyond its actual control capabilities.[2711] On the other hand, it would enable adjudicators to impose heightened responsibilities on other actors where this is reasonable in light of their role, even if the processing at issue does not strictly reside within their sphere of "direct control".[2712]

1327. COUNTERARGUMENTS – Introducing standards to mitigate the adverse consequences of rules implies sacrificing some of the benefits which rules otherwise provide.[2713] While introducing a standard may enhance flexibility and adaptability, it is likely to increase the interpretation and administration costs in situations where this would otherwise not be necessary (i.e. where simple application of the rule would lead to the socially desirable outcome). Moreover, the argument can be made that most of the provisions of EU data protection law do already allow for flexibility in their application.[2714] As a result, flexibility should only be enhanced where needed, which may also be achieved by adding exceptions as opposed to a general standard. This could be done either by introducing (blanket) exemptions for certain types of processing activities (e.g. as was done by incorporating the liability exemptions contained in the E-Commerce Directive[2715]), or by adding (more limited) exceptions to specific provisions. Finally, as illustrated by the jurisprudence of the CJEU and

---

2711 Cf. *supra*, nos. 1234 et seq.

2712 See also *supra*, no. 978. See also the critique of Ruggie regarding use of concept of "control" to delineate responsibilities (J. Ruggie, "Clarifying the Concepts of "Sphere of influence" and "Complicity"", Report of the Special Representative of the Secretary-General on the Issue of Human Rights and Transnational Corporations and other Business Enterprises, A/HRC/8/16, 15 May 2008, at paragraphs 16–17 Ruggie explicitly discards the use of concepts of "control" and "causation" as means to assign responsibility: "*Furthermore, the concepts of control or causation could wrongly limit the baseline responsibility of companies to respect rights. The responsibility to respect requires that companies exercise due diligence to identify, prevent and address adverse human rights impacts related to their activities. If the scope of due diligence were defined by control and causation this could imply, for example, that companies were not required to consider the human rights impacts of suppliers they do not legally control, or situations where their own actions might not directly cause harm but indirectly contribute to abuse.*" Ruggie goes on to posits alternative model of "due diligence" and complicity, which requires "a process whereby companies not only ensure compliance with national laws but also manage the risk of human rights harm with a view to avoiding it. *The scope of human rights related due diligence is determined by the context in which a company is operating, its activities, and the relationships associated with those activities.*"

2713 I. Ehrleich and R. A. Posner, "An Economic Analysis of Legal Rulemaking", *l.c.*, p. 268 ("*The problem of underinclusion can be solved by backing up the rule with a standard. [...] The result of adding a standard is, however, to sacrifice some of the benefits of the rule.*")

2714 See also Article 29 Data Protection Working Party, "Opinion 4/2007 on the concept of personal data", *l.c.*, p. 4–5 ("*Even where processing of personal data within the scope of the Directive is involved, not all the rules contained therein may be applicable in the particular case. A number of provisions of the Directive contain a substantial degree of flexibility, so as to strike the appropriate balance between protection of the data subject's rights on the one side, and on the other side the legitimate interests of data controllers, third parties and the public interest which may be present.*"). See also *supra*, no. 1163.

2715 This approach has been advocated by Sartor and will be discussed later on. Cf. *infra*, no. 1343.

guidance of the Article 29 Working Party, the adverse effects caused by the strict application of rules can also be softened when interpreting them.[2716]

1328. Analytical framework – At the very least, regulators and courts should strive to contribute to the development of a common analytical framework to assess the scope of the obligations of actors involved in the processing of personal data. While a case-by-case assessment is likely to be necessary[2717], legal certainty is likely to increase insofar as the same criteria are used consistently and in a systematic fashion. In *Google Spain*, the CJEU concluded that the obligations of a search engine provider should be assessed in light of its "responsibilities, powers and capabilities". "Responsibilities" in first instance refers to the obligations and restrictions imposed by EU data protection law upon controllers. The starting point is that the *entirety* of obligations and restrictions imposed by EU data protection law must be met. Nevertheless, limits upon the controller's ability to influence the processing, either in law or in fact, may limit the extent to which the controller shall actually be held responsible. "Powers" appears to refer in first instance to decision-making power, the ability to influence the processing by virtue of an *implicit or explicit authority* over the processing.[2718] "Capabilities", on the other hand, appears to refer to the technical capabilities of the controller, taking into his *operational role* in the processing, including the stage at which the controller becomes involved in the (sequence of) processing activities.[2719] When applying these criteria, regulators and courts should take into account objective of ensuring effective and complete protection of data subjects. In my view, this means that in cases where it is not completely unreasonable to allocate responsibility (or liability), taking into account the aforementioned criteria, then responsibility (and liability) should be attributed, even if the actor involved is not in a position to exercise complete control over every aspect the processing. Holding otherwise would undermine the intention of the EU legislature, both under Article 8 of the Charter and under Article 26 GDPR.

1329. Outlook – There exists an inherent conflict between the aim of ensuring effective and complete protection of data subjects, through a broad interpretation of the concept of a (joint) controller, and the objective of allocating

---

2716 See also *supra*, no. 1164. Critics of this approach argue that this approach fails to provide adequate guidance for practitioners: cf. *supra*, no. 1165.

2717 See also R. Mahieu, J. van Hoboken, H. Asghari, "Responsibility for Data Protection in a Networked World. On the question of the controller, "effective and complete protection" and its application to data access rights in Europe", *l.c*, p. 22 ("*national courts will have to fill this interpretative void*").

2718 It is interesting to note that the word "powers" in French is translated by the word "compétences". As described in Part II, earlier definitions of the controller concept explicitly referred to as a party who was "competent to decide" about the processing. Cf. *infra*, no. 1180 See also Opinion 1/2010, *l.c.*, p. 9–10.

2719 Cf. *supra*, no. 1168.

responsibility primarily on the basis of factual influence.[2720] A certain trade-off may be inevitable. One way to help ensure a fair allocation of responsibility and liability would be to apply the three-factor test established by the CJEU in *Google Spain* when assessing whether an entity is or is not "in any way responsible for the event that give rise to the damage" (Article 82(3) GDPR) or when assessing the "degree of responsibility" of the controller or processor (Article 83(2)d). In any case, it will be interesting to see whether the CJEU continues to employ the same factors in its analysis, in particular when assessing the obligations of each actor in case of joint control.

4.5. CONTRACTUAL FLEXIBILITY

1330. Proposal – Another possible measure, which is similar in nature (but more narrow in scope) than the previous one, is to enhance the degree of contractual flexibility in the relationship between controllers and processors. Specifically, rather than prescribe mandatory elements which must be included in every contract between controllers and processors, one could simply require controllers to "adduce adequate safeguards" when outsourcing personal data processing.[2721]

1331. Rationale – The main argument in favour of enhancing contractual flexibility is to remedy situations in which the controller-processor template is ill-suited to govern a particular outsourcing arrangement. Hon and Millard, for example, have argued that there are situations in which considering certain cloud providers as processors is excessive (e.g. in cases where the cloud provider has neither knowledge nor control of the fact that his services are used to process personal data).[2722] An additional argument, put forward by Moerel, is non-discrimination: if joint controllers enjoy full flexibility in mutually allocating responsibility, so should controllers and processors.[2723]

2720 See also *supra*, no. 984. As observed at footnote 2410, however, there exists an important conceptual distinction between the delineation of "control" and the delineation of the responsibilities associated with the legal qualification of an actor's role as "controller".

2721 This approach could be applied in conjunction with abolishing the distinction between controllers and processors (cf. *supra*, nos. 1270 et seq.) and would closely resemble the approach of the Canadian Privacy Act (PIPEDA), which simply requires responsible organisations to take all reasonable steps to protect personal information under their control, regardless of where it is processed. See B. Van Alsenoy, "Allocating responsibility among controllers, processors, and "everything in between": the definition of actors and roles in Directive 95/46/EC", *l.c.*, p. 41–42.

2722 W. Kuan Hon, C. Millard and I. Walden, "Who is Responsible for 'Personal Data' in Cloud Computing? The Cloud of Unknowing, Part 2", *l.c.*, p. 27–28. See also *supra*, no. 1304.

2723 L. Moerel, *Binding Corporate Rules: Corporate Self-Regulation of Global Data Transfers*, *o.c.*, p. 218 ("*I agree that the imposing of direct obligations on processors is a good way to ensure that processors in complex processing operations do not "hide" behind their processorship in*

1332. Counterarguments – A first argument in favour of prescribing which elements should at a minimum be included in the contract between controllers and processors is that those elements in fact operate as "contractual safeguards" of the controller-processor relationship.[2724] By introducing these elements, the parties actually define their mutual relationship in such a way that corresponds with the controller-processor model. An additional argument is that the controller-processor model is in fact a normative construct, from which parties should not have the ability to derogate freely.[2725]

4.6. ASSESSMENT

1333. Internal comparison – The solutions outlined over the previous sections are by no means mutually exclusive. Each of them can be used to reduce the systemic role of the distinction between controllers and processors. Of course, substantial differences will remain, which may continue to shape the interpretation of these concepts. By assimilating the systemic role of each concept as much as possible, however, the risk can be minimised.

1334. Interdependencies – The partial assimilation of the role of controllers and processors, as well as the decision to provide greater recognition of joint control, has helped to alleviate certain teleological issues regarding continuous protection and legal certainty. By imposing similar obligations upon controllers and processors, processors have been made directly accountable towards regulators and data subjects. By providing greater recognition of joint control, greater legal certainty is provided for actors whose collaboration does not neatly map with the controller-processor model. The grammatical and historical issues, however, remain the same.

1335. Final text GDPR – For the most part, the proposal of the European Commission to partially assimilate the functions fulfilled by the controller and processor concepts was retained in the final text of the GDPR. One notable difference concerns the modification of the reference to processors in the provisions regarding data protection impact assessments and prior authorisation.[2726] The

---

order to avoid liability. However, if the Proposed Regulation allows joint controllers to divide responsibilities between them, I do not see why this possibility would not be extended to a division of responsibilities between joint processors (or between main and sub-processors) ad further between (joint) controllers and such (joint or sub-) processors. If individuals keep their rights against any of them, there seems little to be said against such possibility to divide responsibilities.")

2724 See also Article 29 Data Protection Working Party, "Opinion 05/2012 on Cloud Computing", *l.c.*, p. 12. Cf. *supra*, no. 1051.

2725 See also *supra*, no. 1278.

2726 Contrary to the initial proposal put forward by the European Commission, the final version of the GDPR does not render these provisions directly applicable to processors.

final text of the GDPR also elaborates upon the implications of joint control, but does not specifically address the implications of separate control.

1336. Possible remedy – The situation of separate control is less straightforward than the situation of joint control. In case of separate control, each controller pursues his own distinct purpose(s) in processing personal data.[2727] Separate controllers shall in principle only be accountable for those processing activities which are effectively under their control. As a result, they have no formal obligation to accommodate data subject rights in relation to those stages or aspects of the processing which are under the exclusive control of another party. In situations where a large number of separate controllers are involved, the risk of lack of transparency towards data subjects increases. A possible mitigation strategy could be to also require separate controllers to designate a single point of contact and implement a "no wrong door" policy, in cases where this is necessary in order to ensure fairness of processing. Interpreting the principle of fairness in this way would allow for a case-by-case assessment as to whether such a measure is necessary in light of the circumstances.[2728]

1337. Standards vs. rules – The proposals regarding the tailoring of obligations and contractual flexibility are related to the question of the optimal degree of specificity of data protection norms. The use cases analysed in Part IV illustrated that there are situations in which it is necessary to support greater flexibility in the application of controller obligations. The incorporation of standards, either as complements or replacements to rules, may help to achieve this.[2729] Other approaches are also possible, however, such as the adding of specific exceptions or the use of blanket exemptions. The optimal approach will depend on whether one considers that the adding of rules will be sufficient to stand the test of time, or that instead standards are needed to ensure adequate flexibility and adaptability. Similar considerations apply in relation to the proposal to allow for greater contractual flexibility in the relationship between controllers and processors.[2730]

2727 Cf. *supra*, no. 126.

2728 The requirement to implement such a policy may depend on an appreciation of the facts of the case, including the image given to data subjects. Not every set of processing activities involving collaborating single controllers would require putting in place a "no wrong door policy". Take for example an online purchase. The average data subject is likely able to discern the distinction between processing activities for which the merchant acts as controller and those for which the card provider and/or payment service provider acts as controller. In such situations, the data subject may be expected to approach each controller separately for those processing activities which clearly belong to the sphere of control for either party.

2729 See also *supra*, no. 1304.

2730 It should be noted that the final text of the GDPR has substantially increased the number of elements to be included in the contracts between controllers and processors. Cf. *supra*, nos. 98–99.

5. HISTORICAL

1338. OUTLINE – Historical solutions are solutions which seek to limit the scope of application of the controller and processor concepts to the actors and situations for which they were created. The point of departure is that the application of the controller and processor to circumstances unanticipated by the European legislature leads to unintended or undesirable consequences, at least in certain situations. Historical solutions include (1) expanding the scope of the personal use exemption and (2) applying the liability exemptions contained in the E-Commerce Directive.

5.1. PERSONAL USE EXEMPTION

1339. PROPOSAL – In February of 2013, the Article 29 Working Party issued a Statement on the "current discussions" surrounding the data protection reform. The second annex accompanying the Statement concerned the future of the personal use exemption.[2731] In the Statement, the Working Party considered that

> "the current Directive's approach to personal or household processing has an unrealistically narrow scope that no longer reflects individuals' capacity to process data for personal and household activities and has therefore become anachronistic."[2732]

To remedy this issue, the Working Party proposed using the following five criteria to determine whether or not the personal use exemption applies[2733]:

(1) *Publicity*: is the data disseminated to an indefinite number of persons or to a limited community of friends, family members or acquaintances?
(2) *Data subjects involved* is the data about individuals who have a personal or household relationship with the person posting it?
(3) *Scale and frequency*: does the scale and frequency of the processing suggest a professional or full-time activity?
(4) *Concerted action*: is the individual acting alone or is there evidence of individuals acting together in a collective and organized manner?
(5) *Adverse impact*: what is the potential adverse impact on individuals, including intrusion in their privacy?

2731 Article 29 Data Protection Working Party, "Statement of the Working Party on current discussions regarding the data protection reform package – Annex 2 Proposals for Amendments regarding exemption for personal or household activities", 27 February 2013, p. 2.
2732 *Ibid*, p. 2.
2733 *Ibid*, p. 4.

None of these criteria would, by themselves, necessarily exclude application of the personal use exemption.[2734] Instead, one should look at them in combination to determine whether, on the whole, the personal use exemption applies.[2735] The proposed criteria would afford data protection authorities a certain degree of discretion when deciding whether or not to take action against a particular processing activity. At the same time, using the identified criteria would promote objectivity in this decision-making process.[2736]

1340. VARIATIONS – The Article 29 Working Party proposed introducing the criteria above by way of a recital, without substantively modifying the actual language of the personal use exemption.[2737] The General Approach of the Council, however, suggested to go further by omitting the word "purely".[2738] Earlier proposals made by the European Commission focused on introducing negative criteria, using phrases such as "without any gainful interest" and "thus without any connection with a professional or commercial activity".[2739]

1341. RATIONALE – The proposal of the Article 29 Working was motivated by a historical interpretation of the personal use exemption: at the time the exemption was conceived, the processing capabilities of individuals where much more limited. With the rise of Internet connectivity, new forms of communication and social interaction have emerged:

> "[A]ccess to the internet – uncommon for natural persons in the mid 1990's – and more functional information and communications technology (ICT) has opened the way for a range of personal processing activities that the current Directive could not have been expected to anticipate."[2740]

2734 *Id.*

2735 *Id.*

2736 *Id.*

2737 *Ibid*, p. 10. The only change proposed by the Article 29 Working Party would be to change the word "purely" by the word "exclusively".

2738 See Council for the European Union, Proposal for a Regulation of the European Parliament and of the Council on the protection of individuals with regard to the processing of personal data and on the free movement of such data (General Data Protection Regulation) – Preparation of a general approach", 11 June 2015, 2012/0011 (COD), 9565/15, p. 76.

2739 See European Commission, Proposal for a Regulation of the European Parliament and of the Council on the protection of individuals with regard to the processing of personal data and on the free movement of such data (General Data Protection Regulation), COM(2012) 11 final, *l.c.*, p. 40. The Commission proposals were rejected, however, by both the Article 29 Working Party and the legislative bodies.

2740 *Ibid*, p. 2 See also OECD, "The Evolving Privacy Landscape: 30 Years After the OECD Privacy Guidelines", *l.c.*, p. 20–21 and 27–28 and also N. Xanthoulis, "Negotiating the EU Data Protection Reform: Reflections on the Household Exemption", in A.B. Sideridis a.o. (eds.), *E-Democracy, Security, Privacy and Trust in a Digital World*, 5th International Conference, E-Democracy 2013, Springer, Communications in Computer and Information Science, 2014, p. 138.

The justification of the Article 29 Working Party may be complemented with the arguments advanced by scholars who have also advocated in favour of revising the personal use exemption. Garrie a.o., for example, have argued that it would be very burdensome and unrealistic to apply several of the provisions of EU data protection law to private individuals.[2741] Wong and Savirimuthu point out that it may be impossible for supervisory authorities to secure compliance in relation to private individuals.[2742] Finally, it has also been suggested that any attempts to do so might itself constitute an interference with individuals' fundamental right to privacy.[2743]

1342. COUNTERARGUMENTS – Data protection advocates are cautious when it comes to expanding the notion of "personal use". For all its benefits, the widespread availability of ICTs also enables individuals to inflict considerable privacy harms. Outing a sexual preference[2744], broadcasting a traumatic experience[2745], public shaming[2746] or posting "revenge porn" are all just a few clicks away. While traditional civil law remedies (e.g. defamation, breach of confidence, right to control the use of one's image, misuse of private information) may offer a solution, certain remedies show limitations when applied to the online context.[2747] Data protection laws could provide an

---

2741 D.B. Garrie, M. Duffy-Lewis, R. Wong and R.L. Gillespie, "Data Protection: the Challenges Facing Social Networking", *l.c.*, 131 et seq. and p. 149. See also N. Helberger and J. Van Hoboken, "Little Brother Is Tagging You – Legal and Policy Implications of Amateur Data Controllers", *l.c.*, p. 104; P. Roth, "Data Protection Meets Web 2.0 – Two Ships Passing in the Night", *UNSW Law Journal* 2010, Vol. 33, p. 534 and 560 and J. Zittrain, *The Future of the Internet– And How to Stop It*, *o.c.*, p. 221, ("*[...] the sorts of administrative burdens we can reasonably place on established firms exceed those we can place on individuals--at some point, the burden of compliance becomes so great that the administrative burdens are tantamount to an outright ban.*")

2742 R. Wong and J. Savirimuthu, "All or nothing: this is the question? The application of Art. 3(2) data protection directive 95/46/EC to the internet". *l.c.*, p. 244. See also N. Xanthoulis, "Negotiating the EU Data Protection Reform: Reflections on the Household Exemption", *l.c.*, p. 138.

2743 Article 29 Data Protection Working Party, "Statement of the Working Party on current discussions regarding the data protection reform package – Annex 2 Proposals for Amendments regarding exemption for personal or household activities", *l.c.*, p. 3 ("*It is certainly the case that an inappropriate level of scrutiny and regulation of natural persons' personal or household processing activities by DPAs could inhibit individuals' freedom of speech and could in itself constitute a breach of the individual's right to privacy.*"). See also J. Zittrain, *o.c.*, p. 222; R. Wong and J. Savirimuthu, "All or nothing: this is the question? The application of Art. 3(2) data protection directive 95/46/EC to the internet". *L.c.*, p. 244 and N. Xanthoulis, "Negotiating the EU Data Protection Reform: Reflections on the Household Exemption", *l.c.*, p. 138.

2744 See e.g. High Court of Justice, *Applause Store Productions Limited and Matthew Firsht v. Grant Raphael*, 24 July 2008, [2008] EWHC 1781 (QB).

2745 See e.g. Corte di Cassazione, sez. III Penale, sentenza 17 dicembre 2013 – deposit ail 3 febbraio 2014, sentenza n. 5107/14.

2746 High Court of Justice, Stephen Robins and Gabbitas Robins v. Rick Kordowski and Tim Smee, 22 July 2011, [2011] EWHC 1912 (QB).

2747 See e.g. D. Erdos, "Filling Defamation's Gaps: Data Protection and the Right to Reputation", *Oxford Legal Studies Research Paper* 2013, No. 69.

important legal backstop in such cases. Perhaps a more compelling argument against extending the scope of the personal use exemption concerns the potential role of data protection authorities. The GDPR requires Member States to provide an independent supervisory authority which is dedicated to monitoring compliance.[2748] It also stipulates that every individual should have the right to file a complaint if they feel their rights and freedoms are being harmed by personal data processing.[2749] From the perspective of an aggrieved individual, filing a complaint with a national DPA constitutes a much lower threshold than the initiation of formal legal proceedings. While the former can often be done online, free of charge, the latter is likely to entail considerable legal expense.

5.2. LIABILITY EXEMPTIONS OF THE E-COMMERCE DIRECTIVE

1343. Proposal – In its proposal for the GDPR, the European Commission incorporated the intermediary liability exemptions contained in the E-Commerce Directive.[2750] While the Commission did not explicitly motivate its decision for doing so, scholars who had advocated in favour of applying the liability exemptions of the E-Commerce Directive had provided several reasons. Hon and Millard, for example, simply argued that it would be "appropriate" or "justified" to do so in cases where the provider of a (cloud-based) processing service has no knowledge or control over the processing of personal data.[2751] In support of their argument, they also invoked considerations of non-discrimination.[2752] Sartor, on the other hand, mainly argued in favour of applying the exemptions to avoid otherwise unreasonable outcomes in relation

---

2748 Article 29 Data Protection Working Party, "Statement of the Working Party on current discussions regarding the data protection reform package – Annex 2 Proposals for Amendments regarding exemption for personal or household activities", *l.c.*, p. 1

2749 *Ibid*, p. 3.

2750 Article 3(3) of the Commission proposal provided that "*This Regulation should be without prejudice to the application of Directive 2000/31/EC, in particular of the liability rules of intermediary service providers in Articles 12 to 15 of that Directive.*"

2751 W. Kuan Hon, C. Millard and I. Walden, "Who is Responsible for 'Personal Data' in Cloud Computing? The Cloud of Unknowing, Part 2", *l.c.*, p. 24 (""*it makes sense for pure infrastructure cloud providers to be treated as neutral intermediaries, unless and until they have the requisite knowledge and control over that data (in the form of access to it, at least for more than incidental purposes*").

2752 *Ibid*, p. 27 ("*there seems no good reason why cloud providers who are neutral intermediaries, akin to hosting or caching providers under the ECD, should not benefit from similar liability defences, while also benefitting from a prohibition on having a general duty to monitor actively any data transmitted or stored by them*").

to the dissemination of content via the Internet[2753] and to ensure a uniform approach as regards the liability of internet service providers.[2754]

1344. Counterarguments – A first argument against the incorporation of the liability exemptions contained in the E-Commerce Directive is that a reasonable interpretation of the obligations of controllers and processors, which takes into account the principle of proportionality, would not result in the imposition of excessive liability. The decision of the Court of Justice in *Google Spain*, as well as the decision of the Italian Supreme Court in *Google Video*, clearly support this proposition.[2755] A second argument is that the incorporation of the liability exemptions may result in reduced protection for data subjects, particularly if the standard of care applied to intermediaries is lower than the standard that would otherwise be applied to controllers.[2756] Third, the interpretation of the concepts employed by the E-Commerce Directive (i.e. "hosting, "mere conduit" and "caching") have also given rise to a fair degree of legal uncertainty.[2757]

5.3. ASSESSMENT

1345. Internal comparison – The two historical solutions described above are complementary. Both represent attempts to limit the adverse effects which may arise when applying the controller and processor concepts to contexts unanticipated by the EU legislature.

1346. Expanding personal use – The Court of Justice has consistently held that EU data protection law does not, by itself, unduly restrict legitimate uses

---

2753 G. Sartor, "Search Engines as Controllers – Inconvenient implications of a Questionable Classification", *l.c.*, p. 570. A similar line of reasoning had also led the AG to conclude that search engines should not be considered as controllers in relation to the personal data on source web pages hosted on third-party servers.

2754 G. Sartor, "Providers' liabilities in the new EU Data Protection Regulation", *l.c.*, p. 5 (arguing against "data protection exceptionalism") and M. V. de Azevedo Cunha, L. Marin and G. Sartor, "Peer-to-peer privacy violations and ISP liability: data protection in the user-generated web", *l.c.*, p. 57 (arguing in favour of a uniform approach).

2755 Cf. *supra*, no. 878 (*Google Video*) and no. 1164 (*Google Spain*).

2756 Keller, for example, argues that the standard of care incumbent upon "controllers" is more onerous (and therefore more likely to give rise to liability) than the standard of care incumbent upon internet intermediaries. See D. Keller, "Intermediary Liability and User Content under Europe's New Data Protection Law", *l.c.*, FAQ 2.

2757 See e.g. P. Van Eecke, "Online service providers and liability: a plea for a balanced approach", *Common Market Law Review* 2011, Vol. 48, p. 1481 et seq.; E. Montéro, "Les responsabilités liées au web 2.0", *Revue du Droit des Technologies de l'Information* 2008, no. 32, p. 364 et seq. and B. Van der Sloot, "Welcome to the Jungle: the Liability of Internet Intermediaries for Privacy Violations in Europe", *JIPITEC* 2015, Vol. 6, p. 214–216.

of technology. While both the Directive and GDPR support a certain degree of flexibility, it is clear that the existing notion of "purely personal or household activities" is overly narrow. Absent further derogations, there is a risk that data protection law will unduly interfere with individual freedom.

1347. Final text GDPR – Despite the many arguments and constructive proposals in favour of expanding the personal use exemption, the current scope of the exemption was retained in the final version of the GDPR. Interestingly, recital (18) of the GDPR stipulates that "social networking" and "online activity" undertaken in the context of a personal or household activity falls within the remit of the personal use exemption, thus suggesting that the scope of the personal use exemption might have been implicitly widened after all.[2758] It remains to be seen whether the CJEU will soften its earlier stance and give the personal use exemption a broader interpretation under the GDPR. Given that the language of the exemption itself has not changed, the precedential value of Lindqvist and other judgments[2759] interpreting the scope of the personal use exemption in principle remain intact.

1348. Liability exemptions – The question of whether or not to incorporate the liability exemption of the E-Commerce directive concerned, once again, the optimal specificity of legal rules.[2760] It would be possible to limit liability exposure by adopting a standard-based approach, along the lines described in the previous section.[2761] On the other hand, incorporating the rule-like liability exemptions contained in the E-Commerce Directive may well prove to yield additional benefits. First, it might further the development of a more horizontal and uniform approach to the issue of platform responsibility.[2762] In addition, Article 15 of the E-Commerce Directive clearly provides that Member States may not impose general monitoring obligations upon internet intermediaries.

2758 See also Council of the European Union, Position of the Council at first reading with a view to the adoption of a Regulation of the European Parliament and of the Council on the protection of individuals with regard to the processing of personal data and on the free movement of such data (General Data Protection Regulation) – Draft Statement of the Council's reasons, 5419/16 ADD 1, 17 March 2016, p. 6 (noting that final version of the personal use exemption was motivated by the desire to "*avoid setting rules that would create unnecessary burden for individuals*").

2759 See in particular Judgment in *František Ryneš*, C-212/13, EU:C:2014:2428 and Judgment in *Wirtschaftsakademie*, C-210/16, ECLI:EU:C:2018:388.

2760 See also *supra*, nos. 1298 et seq.

2761 In particular by determining liability exposure in light of the "powers, responsibilities and capabilities" or in light of "context, role and ability to act". Cf. *supra*, no. 1325.

2762 M. V. de Azevedo Cunha, L. Marin and G. Sartor, "Peer-to-peer privacy violations and ISP liability: data protection in the user-generated web", *International Data Privacy Law* 2012, Vol. 2, No. 2, p. 57–58. This may also help to more consistently address concerns regarding the negative implications of so-called "notice and take down" mechanisms with regards to freedom of expression.

While most would agree that internet intermediaries should not be expected to proactively monitor whether the personal data disseminated through their platform is being processed lawfully, the formal applicability of Article 15 of Directive 2000/31/EC would offer certain providers greater legal certainty.

1349. Caveats – To be clear, the applicability of the liability exemptions of Directive 2000/31/EC to actors involved in the processing of personal data is not a panacea: the concepts of "hosting, "mere conduit" and "caching" are subjects of continuous debate and have themselves given rise to a fair degree of legal uncertainty.[2763] Moreover, the liability exemptions of Directive 2000/31/EC only affect the liability exposure of controllers in relation to mere distribution or storage activities. An absence of liability for mere distribution or storage does not, however, imply an absence of responsibility with regard to other operations performed on that content. Many service providers perform additional operations which go beyond a purely "intermediary", "passive", or "neutral" capacity.[2764] As a result, it may still be necessary to interpret the obligations of internet intermediaries as controllers in light of their "responsibilities, powers and capabilities".[2765]

1350. Final text GDPR – The proposal to incorporate the liability exemptions contained in the E-Commerce directive was retained in the final text of the GDPR. While this approach may provide greater legal certainty to certain actors, it is equally clear that many service providers will still need to assess their liability exposure in light of the liability provisions of the GDPR itself, as well as the interpretative guidance provided by the CJEU and the European Data Protection Board.

1351. Interdependencies – The historical solutions presented here leave the grammatical issues entirely unaffected. The incorporation of the liability exemptions of the E-Commerce Directive does, however, alleviate certain teleological issues (legal certainty) as well as certain systemic issues (scope of obligations).

2763 Cf. *supra*, at footnote 2759.

2764 B. Van Alsenoy, J. Ballet, A. Kuczerawy and J. Dumortier, "Social networks and web 2.0: are users also bound by data protection regulations?", *l.c.*, p. 62.

2765 Compare *supra*, nos. 1325 et seq. See also K. Hon, E. Kosta, C. Millard and D. Stefanatou, "White paper on the proposed data protection regulation", Cloud Accountability Project, 28 February 2014, p. 21.

CHAPTER 4
RECOMMENDATIONS

1352. Outline – The aim of this Chapter is to outline possible avenues for further improving the allocation of responsibility and liability among actors involved in the processing of personal data. The following recommendations shall be presented:

(1) abolish the concepts of controller and processor or revise the definitions;
(2) use standards and exemptions to mitigate risks of overinclusion;
(3) require the providers of processing services to implement data protection by design;
(4) enhance contractual flexibility in the relationship between controllers and processors; and
(5) expand the scope of the personal use exemption.

1. ABOLISH THE CONCEPTS OR REVISE THE DEFINITIONS

1353. Supporting differentiation – As indicated earlier, many issues associated the controller-processor model relate to the *concepts* of controller and processor, rather than the policy choice of *differentiating* between parties involved in the processing.[2766] For this reason alone, it is worth considering whether it is possible to omit the problematic concepts of controller and processor, while still supporting differentiation as regards the allocation of responsibility and liability. Using the liability provisions of the GDPR as the point of departure, the following paragraphs will outline how the GDPR might be revised to support such differentiation whilst omitting the concepts of controller and processor. Next, a proposal for possible revisions to the controller and processor and concepts will be presented.

2766 Cf. *supra*, no. 1306.

1.1. ABOLISHING THE CONCEPTS

1354. Article 82 GDPR – Article 82 of the GDPR provides that

> "1. Any person who has suffered material or immaterial damage as a result of an infringement of the Regulation shall have the right to receive compensation from the controller or processor for the damage suffered.
> 2. Any controller involved in the processing shall be liable for the damage caused by the processing which is not in compliance with this Regulation. A processor shall be liable for the damage caused by the processing only where it has not complied with obligations of this Regulation specifically directed to processors or acted outside or contrary to lawful instructions of the controller.
> 3. A controller or processor shall be exempted from liability in accordance with paragraph 2 if it proves that it is not in any way responsible for the event giving rise to the damage."[2767]

1355. Alternative – It would be perfectly possible to omit the concepts of controller and processor from Article 82 GDPR while still retaining the same liability model. Under such an approach, a revised Article 82 might read as follows:

> "1. Any person who has suffered material or immaterial damage as a result of an infringement of the Regulation shall have the right to receive compensation [...].
> 2. Every party involved in the processing shall be liable for the damaged caused by his own processing activities as well as processing undertaken by others on its behalf, taking into account the following limitations:
>   (a) a party who exclusively processes the data in accordance with the instructions of another party and on his behalf shall only be liable insofar as the damages are a result of a failure to comply with articles [list of provisions otherwise relevant to processors].
>   (b) any party involved in the processing may be exempted from liability insofar as he can prove that the damages are the result of an event which cannot in any way be attributed to him."

[2767] Article 82 goes on to provide that where more than one controller or processor or a controller and a processor are involved in the same processing and, where they are, in accordance with paragraphs 2 and 3, responsible for any damage caused by the processing, each controller or processor shall be held liable for the entire damage, in order to ensure effective compensation of the data subject (Article 82(4)). In addition Article 82(5) provides that where a controller or processor has, in accordance with paragraph 4, paid full compensation for the damage suffered, that controller or processor shall be entitled to claim back from the other controllers or processors involved in the same processing that part of the compensation corresponding to their part of responsibility for the damage in accordance with the conditions set out in paragraph 2. While these provisions essentially codify general principles of tort law, they could be incorporated mutatis mutandis under the proposed alternative approach. For purposes of conceptual clarity, only the first 3 paragraphs of Article 82 are presented here.

The main advantage of this approach is that it does not require parties to consider the formal legal status of each actor, but the outcome is essentially the same. Moreover, it resolves the grammatical issue which occurs by virtue of the fact that the criteria contained in the controller and processor concepts are not by nature mutually exclusive.[2768] The two substantive criteria determining the scope of a party's liability exposure are "*on behalf of*" and "*in accordance with instructions*". The proposal to use the words "on behalf of" as the main criterion to determine the scope of a party's liability exposure is based on the proposal put forward by Léonard and Mention (i.e. the "benefit-based approach").[2769] The words "*exclusively*" and "*in accordance with the instructions of another party*" were added to clarify that a party shall only be subject to fewer data protection obligations insofar as the processing of the data in question is undertaken purely on an agency basis.[2770] To strengthen the latter point, the wording "at his request" might additionally be inserted.

1.2. REVISING THE DEFINITIONS

1356. Alternative criteria – An alternative approach would be to retain the controller and processor concepts whilst modifying their respective definitions. Using the same criteria as outlined in the previous paragraph, a controller would be defined as "*a natural or legal person, public authority, agency or any other body who processes personal data for himself or causes personal data to be processed by others on his behalf*"[2771] and the processor would be defined as "*a natural or legal person, public authority, agency or any other body which processes personal data on behalf of a controller, at its request and in accordance with its instructions*". The benefits of revising the concepts of controller and processor in this way are essentially the same as the ones outlined in the previous subsection, with the additional advantage that it requires fewer drafting changes to other provisions of the GDPR.

2768 Cf. *supra*, no. 1210.

2769 Cf. *supra*, no. 1261.

2770 If the party concerned processes (or has processed) the data in question on his own initiative, i.e. outside the instructions of another party, it would in principle be subject to full panoply of data protection requirements. By adding this clarification, it is envisaged that service providers such as data brokers or the providers of search engine services shall in principle be subject to the same obligations as would otherwise be incumbent upon controllers.

2771 The formulation "his own processing activities as well as processing undertaken by others on his behalf" was inspired by paragraph 2(3) of the German *Bundesdatenschutzgesetz* of 27 January 1977 which defined the "speicherende Stelle" as "*anyone who stores data on its own account [for its purposes] or has data stored by others*". Similar formulations were used in the French Law on Informatics, Files and Liberties (LIFL) (cf. *supra*, nos. 400 et seq.); in the context of the preparations of the UK Data Protection Act (cf. *supra*, no. 484) as well as in an early draft of Directive 95/46 (cf. *supra*, no. 556).

2. USE OF STANDARDS AND EXEMPTIONS

1357. Tailoring obligations – The liability model outlined in the previous section coincides with the liability model for controllers and processors under the GDPR. This model could easily be supplemented by a standard to support the tailoring of obligations, e.g. by adding the following provision:

> "(c) any party who has contributed to the damages suffered may be exempted from liability insofar as it demonstrates that it has implemented every reasonable measure to prevent and remove damages, taking into account its responsibilities, powers and capabilities."

As indicated earlier, there are benefits and costs associated with the introduction of an additional standard which supports tailoring obligations.[2772] In the end, however, the addition of this standard would merely constitute a further codification of the reasoning of the CJEU in *Google Spain*.[2773] As a result, one could argue that the addition of this standard would not provide added value as such. Nevertheless, it may still be beneficial to introduce the standard into the statutory text, if only to validate the approach taken by the CJEU and to explicitly recognise it as a valid limitation of the liability exposure to which parties involved in the processing might otherwise be subject.

1358. Liability exemptions – The revised liability model outlined above could additionally be supplemented with a reference to the liability exemptions contained in the E-Commerce Directive by simply adding a provision which reads:

> "(d) The liability exemptions contained in E-Commerce Directive shall apply to damages suffered as a result of an infringement of the Regulation."

As the EU legislature has already decided to incorporate a reference to the liability exemptions of the E-Commerce Directive in the GPDR, the proposal here is mainly aesthetic (i.e. to incorporate a reference to liability exemptions in the article concerning liability as opposed to the scope section).

3. REQUIRE DATA PROTECTION BY DESIGN FROM "PROCESSORS"

1359. Data protection by design – Under the GDPR, processors are not subject to the obligation to implement data protection by design. This is regrettable, given the substantial influence processors exercise in determining

[2772] Cf. *supra*, no. 1297.
[2773] Cf. *supra*, no. 1164.

the means of the processing.[2774] In my view, it would be reasonable to impose a similar obligation upon the providers of processing services, as long as one takes into account the intended purpose (finality) of the services they offer.[2775]

1360. Article 25 GDPR – Article 25 GDPR provides that

> "Having regard to the state of the art and the cost of implementation and taking account of the nature, scope, context and purposes of the processing as well as the risks of varying likelihood and severity for rights and freedoms of individuals posed by the processing, the controller shall, both at the time of the determination of the means for processing and at the time of the processing itself, implement appropriate technical and organisational measures, such as pseudonymisation, which are designed to implement data protection principles, such as data minimisation, in an effective way and to integrate the necessary safeguards into the processing in order to meet the requirements of this Regulation and protect the rights of data subjects."

Extending the obligation to implement data protection by design to the providers of processing services could be realised either simply by inserting the words "*and processor*" behind the word controller, or by revising the text to reflect a passive form ("*appropriate technical and organisational measures shall be implemented*").

2774 See also P. Tsormpatzoudi and F. Coudert, "Technology providers' responsibility in protecting privacy... dropped from the sky?", *Paper presented at the Amsterdam Privacy Conference* (APC), 23–26 October 2015 (noting that "*Privacy and data protection challenges stemming from the development of ICT are often related to the fact that certain data processing-related decisions are already made during the development phase. This limits the ability of the data controller to comply with the data protection framework which is only applicable from the moment that personal data are collected and processed, thus at the very end of the supply chain.*")

2775 See also Microsoft, "Protecting Data and Privacy in the Cloud", *Reactive Security Communications*, 2014, p. 3–5 (arguing that it is responsibility of cloud providers to design services in such a way that enables compliance). As early as 1972, the Younger Committee already considered that the design of a service to meet a customer's needs was an area of joint involvement and responsibility among the provider and customer of the service. See Home Office (Great Britain), *Report of the Committee on Privacy*, *o.c.*, p. 182 et seq. Cf. *supra*, no. 482. After the Younger Committee, the Lindop Committee likewise considered that it should be a requirement for computer bureaux to avoid taking on applications if it was unable to provide the relevant safeguards identified in the relevant Codes of Practice. The Committee even foresaw an advisory role for bureaux, especially towards small users who may not be aware of the contents of the relevant Codes of Practice. Cf. *supra*, no. 489. Under the 1984 UK data protection act, not all computer bureaux needed to know what was contained in the register entry of the data user to whom it was providing services. A computer bureau which only performed the limited service of "causing data to be processed automatically" would not do anything which constituted an offence under section 5(3). If the computer bureaux provided a wider service, however, which involved collecting information on behalf of the data user or disclosing it in accordance with its instructions, it would run the risk of committing an offence if departed from the particulars contained in the user's register entry. See The Data Protection Registrar, "The Data Protection Act of 1984: Questions and Answers on the Act (1–20)", *l.c.*, p. 6 (Question 9). Cf. *supra*, no. 509. Today, an equivalent approach would be to impose upon the providers of value-added services a duty to of care to ensure that the legitimacy of processing has been ensured (e.g. by requiring a web analytics company to check the privacy notice of its customers to make sure that third-party analytics are covered).

Under this approach, the provider of a processing service ("processor") would be responsible for designing its services and features in such a way that they facilitate compliance with data protection requirements, whereas it would be up to the customer of the processing service ("controller") to configure the services and features in the appropriate manner.[2776] Providers of processing services may also be required by regulators to demonstrate compliance with the principle of privacy by design.[2777]

4. ENHANCE CONTRACTUAL FLEXIBILITY

1361. Legal binding – The GDPR has significantly increased the number of provision to be included in the contract or other legal act binding the processor to the controller. Specifically, Article 28(3) GDPR provides that

> "Processing by a processor shall be governed by a contract or other legal act under Union or Member State law, that is binding on the processor with regard to the controller and that sets out the subject-matter and duration of the processing, the nature and purpose of the processing, the type of personal data and categories of data subjects and the obligations and rights of the controller. That contract or other legal act shall stipulate, in particular, that the processor:
> (a) processes the personal data only on documented instructions from the controller, including with regard to transfers of personal data to a third country or an international organisation, unless required to do so by Union or Member State law to which the processor is subject; in such a case, the processor shall inform the controller of that legal requirement before processing, unless that law prohibits such information on important grounds of public interest;
> (b) ensures that persons authorised to process the personal data have committed themselves to confidentiality or are under an appropriate statutory obligation of confidentiality;
> (c) takes all measures required pursuant to Article 32;
> (d) respects the conditions referred to in paragraphs 2 and 4 for engaging another processor;
> (e) taking into account the nature of the processing, assists the controller by appropriate technical and organisational measures, insofar as this is possible, for the fulfilment of the controller's obligation to respond to requests for exercising the data subject's rights laid down in Chapter III;
> (f) assists the controller in ensuring compliance with the obligations pursuant to Articles 32 to 36 taking into account the nature of processing and the information available to the processor;

[2776] See also Microsoft, "Protecting Data and Privacy in the Cloud", *Reactive Security Communications*, 2014, p. 10.
[2777] *Id.*

(g) at the choice of the controller, deletes or returns all the personal data to the controller after the end of the provision of services relating to processing, and deletes existing copies unless Union or Member State law requires storage of the personal data; and
(h) makes available to the controller all information necessary to demonstrate compliance with the obligations laid down in this Article and allow for and contribute to audits, including inspections, conducted by the controller or another auditor mandated by the controller."

Article 28(3) GDPR clearly echoes the guidance of the Article 29 Working Party in relation to cloud computing.[2778] For many outsourcing scenarios, the inclusion of each of these elements in the contract or other legal act binding the processor to the controller may well be appropriate. As indicated earlier, however, there may be situations in which the inclusion of each of these elements in every type of outsourcing arrangement may be excessive. For example, the provider of an IaaS service, who hosts encrypted data on behalf of a SaaS or PaaS provider, may not need to know which types of personal data are being stored on its servers.[2779] Its ability to assist the controller in accommodating data subject rights may, for the same reason, be non-existent. In other words, the rules contained in Article 28(3) may be overinclusive.[2780]

1362. Alternative – The duty to ensure appropriate legal binding of parties processing personal data on behalf of others should be replaced by a more flexible standard (e.g. "*any party who enlists another party to process personal data on his behalf shall adduce adequate safeguards*").[2781] The inclusion of such a standard, as an alternative to the rule contained in Article 28(3), would closely resemble the approach of the Canadian Privacy Act (PIPEDA).[2782] Schedule 5 of PIPEDA sets forth the basic data principles with which a "responsible organisation" must comply. The first of these principles is the principle of accountability. Clause 4.1

2778 Cf. *supra*, no. 947.

2779 See also K. Hon, E. Kosta, C. Millard and D. Stefanatou, "White paper on the proposed data protection regulation", *l.c.*, p. 19 ("*The Council would require the controller-processor contract to cover 'the subject-matter and duration of the contract, the nature and purpose of the processing, the type of personal data and categories of data subjects'. This echoes WP196 but does not suit self-service infrastructure cloud services, where the provider would not know the subject matter, nature or purpose of processing, etc, unless it inspected data or monitored processing, which the controller would positively not wish the provider to do; nor would the controller wish to give such information to the provider, let alone be required to do so in the contract.*")

2780 It should be noted, however, that Article 28(3)e and 28(3)f both contain standards to mitigate risks of overinclusiveness (e.g. "*taking into account the nature of the processing*", "*insofar as this is possible*", and "*taking into account the information available to processors*").

2781 Cf. *supra*, no. 1330.

2782 Canadian Personal Information Protection and Electronic Documents Act (PIPEDA), S.C. 2000, c. 5. See also W. Kuan Hon, C. Millard and I. Walden, "Who is Responsible for 'Personal Data' in Cloud Computing? The Cloud of Unknowing, Part 2", *l.c.*, p. 28.

identifies a variety of measures that responsible organisations must implement in order to comply with this principle.[2783] The accountability principle requires, inter alia, that responsible organisations take all reasonable steps to protect personal information under their control, regardless of where it is processed.[2784] In particular, organisations are considered to remain responsible for the actions by third parties to whom data has been "transferred".[2785] In other words, while PIPEDA does not make a formal distinction between controllers and processors, it does contain provisions aimed at achieving a similar effect, namely ensuring that personal information is guaranteed a comparable level of protection while the information is being processed by a third party.[2786] This approach has a number of advantages. The first is that it enables greater flexibility, while at the same time reinforcing the notion that the responsible organisation is obligated to adduce adequate safeguards when engaging other actors to help achieve its objectives. A second advantage is that it does not rely upon the formal qualification of the actor to whom the information has been transferred; thus having the potential to mitigate some of the adverse impacts resulting from the underinclusive nature of the controller-processor model.[2787]

1363. Role of regulatory guidance – Replacing the rule of Article 28(3) with a standard would imply sacrificing certain benefits, in particular as regards specificity and legal certainty. I would submit, however, that additional

---

[2783] The principle of accountability received considerable attention in the context of the review of Directive 95/46. See e.g. Article 29 Data Protection Working Party, "Opinion 3/2010 on the principle of accountability", WP 173, 13 July 2010, p. 3; European Commission, Communication from the Commission to the European Parliament, the Council, the Economic and Social Committee and the Committee of the Regions, "A comprehensive approach on personal data protection in the European Union", November 2010, Brussels, COM(2010) 609 final, p. 12. For more information on the different meanings associated with accountability, as well as the role that the accountability principle has played in various instruments of data protection over time see J. Alhadeff, B. Van Alsenoy and J. Dumortier, "The accountability principle in data protection regulation: origin, development and future directions", *l.c.*, p. 50 et seq.

[2784] Office of the Privacy Commissioner of Canada, "PIPEDA – Processing Personal Data Across Borders Guidelines", 2009, p. 8.

[2785] J. Alhadeff, B. Van Alsenoy and J. Dumortier, "The accountability principle in data protection regulation: origin, development and future directions", *l.c.*, p. 55. Note that the term "transfer" has a very specific meaning in PIPEDA, which is to be contrasted with "disclosure". See Office of the Privacy Commissioner of Canada, "PIPEDA – Processing Personal Data Across Borders Guidelines", *l.c.*, 5. A "transfer" is understood as an exchange of information whereby its use is confined to the purpose for which it was collected (*Ibid*, 5). A "disclosure", on the other hand, concerns an exchange of information for a purpose which was previously not yet identified. This distinction bears considerable resemblance to some of the guidance provided by the Working Party in Opinion 1/2010, where it is indicated that when a processor either re-uses data it for a different purpose or otherwise acts beyond the instructions given by a controller, its qualification as a processor will change to that of controller for these processing operations (see Opinion 1/2010, *l.c.*, in particular p. 14).

[2786] See also clause 4.1.3 of Section 5 of PIPEDA.

[2787] Cf. *supra*, no. 1303.

specificity and legal certainty could be provided through regulatory guidance, as was already being done under Directive 95/46.

5. EXPAND THE SCOPE OF THE PERSONAL USE EXEMPTION

1364. Article 2(2)c GDPR – Article 2(2)c of the GDPR specifies that the Regulation shall not apply to the processing of personal data "*by a natural person in the course of a purely personal or household activity*". This wording is identical to the wording of Article 3(2) of Directive 95/46/EC. Interestingly, recital (18) of the GDPR stipulates that "social networking" and "online activity" undertaken in the context of a personal or household activity fall within the remit of the personal use exemption, thus suggesting that the scope of the personal use exemption might have been widened ever-so-slightly after all.[2788]

1365. Derogations possible – The conceptual approach outlined by the Court of Justice in *Ryneš* suggested that EU data protection law can (and should) be implemented in such a way that it does not unduly restrict individuals' ability to pursue a legitimate objective. Under the GDPR, Member States have retained similar abilities to restrict the application of certain provisions by means of national legislation. It is up to the Member States, however, to actually provide for appropriate derogations. A significant number of Member States have already introduced specific rules governing the use of CCTV, including by private individuals.[2789] Beyond CCTV, however, it seems only few States have introduced

---

[2788] See also the Council of the European Union, Position of the Council at first reading with a view to the adoption of a Regulation of the European Parliament and of the Council on the protection of individuals with regard to the processing of personal data and on the free movement of such data (General Data Protection Regulation) – Draft Statement of the Council's reasons, 5419/16 ADD 1, 17 March 2016, p. 6 (noting that the final version of the personal use exemption was motivated by the desire to "avoid setting rules that would create unnecessary burden for individuals"). See also, however, the (modified) position of the Article 29 Working Party, as expressed prior to the trilogue negotiations: Article 29 Data Protection Working Party, "Letter from the Art. 29 WP to MEP Jan Philipp Albrecht in view of the trilogue – Appendix Core topics in the view of trilogue", 17 June 2015, p. 3. ("*The Working Party recognizes the Council of the EU's aim to slightly broaden the scope of the household exemption in order to limit the scope of the Regulation but feels that any exceptions to the rules shall be formulated and interpreted restrictively. [...] The Working Party is in favour of a limited and carefully balanced household exemption applying to "purely" household activities as provided for in Directive 95/46/EC and interpreted by ECJ case law.*") The ultimate return to the original wording of Article 3(2) of Directive 95/46 suggests a desire not to call into question previous case law of the Court of Justice regarding the scope of the personal use exemption.

[2789] See D. Korff, *EC Study on Implementation of Data Protection Directive 95/46/EC*, Study Contract ETD/2001/B5-3001/A/49, 2002, 135 et seq.

specific derogations.[2790] Without ruling out the possibility such derogations may still be introduced, it is likely they will lag behind technical and societal developments. Moreover, as this measure is not harmonized at Community level, the risk of fragmentation is considerable.[2791]

1366. Expanding personal use – In my opinion, the personal use exemption should apply to all activities which may reasonably be construed as taking place in the course of an individual's private or family life. In addition, an individual should be able to benefit from the personal use exemption regardless of the recipients involved.[2792] Instead, the terms "private and family life" should (continue to) be interpreted broadly, extending to any activities related to the development of one's personal identity or the establishment of relationships with others.[2793] Only when the risk of excessive interference in the privacy interests of others is evident (e.g. due to the scale or frequency of the processing, combined with the recipients and nature of the data), might it be proportionate to bring the activities of private individuals within the scope of data protection law. In order to promote legal certainty, additional criteria establishing the boundaries of the personal use exemption should be anchored in the law.

1367. Alternative – Article 2(2)c of the GDPR should be revised to specify that the Regulation shall not apply to the processing of personal data "*by a natural person in the context of his or her private or family life*". Omitting the word "purely" encourages a broader understanding of the personal use exemption, thereby considerably mitigating risks of overregulation. In addition, by explicitly

---

2790 Idem.

2791 Of course, one might argue that the use of a general standard to delineate the scope of the personal use exemption, as opposed to introducing a rule, will also give rise to an absence of legal certainty. While it is recognized that there will still be some legal uncertainty and national differences due to potential for different weighting of different criteria, it can also be argued that with further guidance from Court of Justice, WP29 and EDPS eventually a consistent application will emerge. See also N. Xanthoulis, "Negotiating the EU Data Protection Reform: Reflections on the Household Exemption", *l.c.*, p. 148–149. ("*The vast variety of users' online activities, particularly the ones that involve UGC and participation in SNS, prevent the EU legislator from sufficiently providing for a clear-cut definition of private conduct (as opposed to activity done in public), thus, leading us to conclude that a fair, efficient and practical solution would only be achieved if the matter is left to be subsequently determined on case by case basis, by national courts and competent authorities and eventually the CJEU. Such long process might result to the initial fragmentation of the interpretation of proposed Regulation's scope, at least in the short term, before a homogenous application of the proposed exemption is achieved.*")

2792 This would effectively require reversing the second part of personal use test advanced by *Lindqvist*.

2793 The European Court of Human Rights has underlined that it also protects a right to identity and personal development, and the right to establish and develop relationships with others. (European Court of Human Rights, *P.G. and J.H. v. United Kingdom*, 25 September 2001, application no. 44787/98, paragraph 56 and European Court of Human Rights, *Niemietz v. Germany*, 16 December 1992, application no. 13710/88, paragraph 29).

referring to the terms "private and family life", as the Court of Justice did in *Lindqvist*[2794], it would be made clear that that any activities related to the development of one's personal identity or the establishment of relationships with others should in principle fall within the remit of the personal use exemption. The revision of Article 2(2)c GDPR might additionally be complemented by the criteria proposed by the Article 29 Working Party in its 2013 Statement.[2795] After all, the criteria proposed by the Article 29 Working Party would offer useful guidance when determining whether an activity might no longer be considered as taking place "*in the context of his or her private of family life*". In other words: the Working Party criteria would help to promote legal certainty, while still preserving a much needed degree of flexibility.

2794 The first part of the "personal use" test promulgated by the ECJ in *Lindqvist* also refers to "in the course of private or family life of individuals" (Judgment in *Bodil Lindqvist*, C-101/01, EU:C:2003:596, paragraph 74).

2795 Cf. *supra*, no. 1339.

CHAPTER 5
CONCLUSION

1368. Main research question – The distinction between controllers and processors is central to EU data protection law. Unfortunately, certain technological and social developments have rendered it increasingly difficult to apply this model in practice, thereby leading to legal uncertainty. The main research question this book set out to answer is whether the allocation of responsibility and liability among actors involved in the processing of personal data could be revised in a manner which increases legal certainty while maintaining at least an equivalent level of data protection.[2796] In order to answer this question, four sub-questions helped guide the research, namely[2797]:

1. What is the nature and role of the controller and processor concepts under European data protection law?
2. What is the origin of the controller-processor model and how has it evolved over time?
3. What are the types of issues that arise when applying the controller-processor model in practice?
4. Which solutions have been proposed to address the issues that arise in practice and to what extent are they capable of addressing the issues?

1369. Nature and role of concepts – The concept of a controller is a *functional* concept: it enumerates a set of criteria with a view of allocating responsibilities upon those actors who exercise significant factual influence over the processing. The processor concept likewise serves to allocate responsibility, but is dependent primarily on a decision of a controller to enlist a separate actor to process personal data on its behalf. The primary role of both the controller and processor concepts is to allocate responsibility. In addition, both the controller and processor concepts play an important role in the determination of which law(s) applies (apply) to the processing, and in the determination of what is required in order to comply with certain substantive provisions of European data protection law.

[2796] Cf. *supra*, no. 15.
[2797] Cf. *supra*, no. 20.

1370. Origin and development – Before the term "controller" became a term of art, those responsible for ensuring compliance with data protection laws went by many names. Despite notable differences in terminology, two recurring elements can be distinguished. The first element is the element of *mastery*: the actor designated as being responsible for compliance had the ability to exercise power over the processing, in one form or another. A second recurring element involves the concept of *gain*: responsibility was bestowed upon the entity which reaps the benefits of the output of the processing. From the very first data protection laws, policymakers were also mindful of the fact that data processing frequently involved outsourcing. Nevertheless, the concept of a "processor", understood as a third party who processes data as a service to others, was mainly present in the background. It was not until the late 1970s that the providers of processing services received formal recognition, worthy of their own statutory definitions. Central to each of these definitions was the notion of *agency*: the "processor" was always understood as an entity acting on behalf of someone else, without personal interest in the output of the processing activity. Once created, the controller-processor model served mainly to ensure a continuous level of protection for data subjects in cases of outsourcing. While the controller was generally deemed "ultimately" responsible for compliance, several national laws also imposed obligations directly upon processors. At EU level, a similar pattern emerged: while processors were mainly indirectly accountable under Directive 95/46, the GDPR imposes a host of requirements directly upon processors and renders them accountable towards regulatory authorities and data subjects.

1371. Typology of issues – Experts frequently disagree as to whether an actor should be considered a "controller" or "processor", or struggle to make an unambiguous determination. Four categories of issues can be distinguished: (1) issues that concern the words chosen to define the concepts of controller and processor (*grammatical issues*); (2) issues that concern the policy objectives that underlie the allocation of responsibility and liability between controllers and processors (*teleological issues*); (3) issues that arise in light of the functions fulfilled by the controller and processor concepts (*systemic issues*); and (4) issues that arise when applying the controller-processor model to situations which were not envisaged by the European legislature (*historical issues*). The teleological issues are perhaps the most troubling, as they imply that the policy objectives underlying the distinction between controllers and processors may be difficult to realise in practice. The grammatical, systemic and historical issues have merely amplified the call for legislative change over time.

1372. Proposed solutions – The review of Directive 95/46 triggered a variety of proposals to remedy the shortcomings of the existing framework. While changing the definitions themselves might have been beneficial, none of the proposed solutions appeared satisfactory. Other proposals went to the heart of the controller-processor model, advocating either its abolition or partial assimilation of the functions fulfilled by both concepts. In addition, a number of modifications were proposed to address the need for increased flexibility when applying the existing framework to current processing realities.

1373. Approach of the GDPR – With the new General Data Protection Regulation, European legislature made a number of significant changes to the controller-processor model. While it retained the basic concepts of controller and processor, it considerably reduced the systemic importance of the distinction between the two, in particular by providing greater recognition to situations of joint control and by imposing a number of obligations directly upon processors. The incorporation of the liability exemptions of the E-Commerce Directive additionally helps to mitigate risks of unintended consequences when applying data protection law in cases where personal data are processed through the Internet.

1374. Recommendations – The changes introduced by the GDPR are likely to be sufficient for the time being. In the long run, however, it may become necessary to introduce further changes. This book has outlined a number of avenues for possible improvements. First, the possibility of abolishing the distinction between controllers and processors should receive further consideration. It is possible to implement the same policy choices without retaining these problematic concepts. Alternatively, the definitions of each concept could be revised to include less ambiguous and mutually exclusive criteria. Second, the legislature should consider the use of standards (as opposed to rules) to mitigate certain risks of overinclusion. Third, I believe the obligation to implement data protection by design should eventually also be made directly applicable to the providers of processing services, given their important role in determining the means of the processing. Fourth, the legal framework should allow for contractual flexibility in the relationship between "controllers" and "processors", leaving room for greater specificity in the form of regulatory guidance. Finally, the scope of the personal use exemption should be expanded. Other legal constructs, such as tort law and personality rights, are better suited to regulate conflicts between private individuals. It is up to all of us to develop these constructs further, and to inform them with data protection considerations as needed.

BIBLIOGRAPHY

1. LEGISLATION AND IMPLEMENTING ACTS

COUNCIL OF EUROPE

Council of Europe, Convention for the Protection of Human Rights and Fundamental Freedoms, 4 November 1950.
Council of Europe, Convention for the Protection of Individuals with regard to Automatic Processing of Personal Data, 28 January 1981.

EUROPEAN UNION

Convention implementing Schengen agreement of 14 June 1985 between the Governments of the States of the Benelux Economic Union, the Federal Republic of Germany and the French Republic on the gradual abolition of checks at their common borders, 19 June 1990, OJ 22 September 2000, L 239/19.
Directive 95/46/EC on the protection of individuals with regards to the processing of personal data and on the free movement of such data, OJ 23 November 1995, L 281/31.
Council Decision of 6 November 1995 on a Community contribution for telematic interchange of data between administrations in the Community (IDA) (95/468/EC), OJ 11 November 1995, L 269/23.
Directive 1999/93/EC of the European Parliament and of the Council of 13 December 1999 on a Community Framework for electronic signatures, OJ 19 January 2000, L 13/12.
Directive 2000/31/EC of the European Parliament and of the Council of 8 June 2000 on certain legal aspects of information society services, in particular electronic commerce, in the Internal Market, OJ 17 July 2000, L 178/1.
Regulation (EC) No 45/2001 of the European Parliament and of the Council of 18 December 2000 on the protection of individuals with regard to the processing of personal data by the Community institutions and bodies and on the free movement of such data, OJ 12 January 2001, L 8/1.
Directive 2002/58/EC of the European Parliament and of the Council of 12 July 2002 concerning the processing of personal data and the protection of privacy in the electronic communications sector, OJ 31 July 2002, L 201/37.
Decision 2004/387/EC of the European Parliament and of the Council of 21 April 2004 on interoperable delivery of pan-European eGovernment services to public administrations, businesses and citizens (IDABC), OJ 18 May 2004, L-181/25 (corrig.).

Treaty of Lisbon amending the Treaty on European Union and the Treaty establishing the European Community, signed at Lisbon, 13 December 2007, OJ 17 December 2007, C 306.

European Commission, Commission Decision of 12 December 2007 concerning the implementation of the Internal Market Information System (IMI) as regards the protection of personal data, OJ 16 January 2008, L 13/18.

Framework Decision 2008/977/JHA of 27 November 2008 on the protection of personal data processed in the framework of police and judicial cooperation in criminal matters, OJ 30 December 2008, L 350/60.

European Commission, Commission Recommendation of 26 March 2009 on data protection guidelines for the Internal Market Information System (IMI), 2009/329/EC, OJ 18 April 2009, L 100/17.

Decision No 922/2009/EC of the European Parliament and of the Council of 16 September 2009 on interoperability solutions for European public administrations (ISA), OJ 3 October 2009, L-260/20.

Commission Decision of 5 February 2010 on standard contractual clauses for the transfer of personal data to processors established in third countries under Directive 95/46/EC of the European Parliament and of the Council (notified under document C(2010) 593), 2010/87/EU, OJ 12 February 2010, L 39/5.

Regulation No 1024/2012 of the European Parliament and of the Council of 25 October 2012 on administrative cooperation through the Internal market Information system and repealing Commission Decision 2008/49/EC, OJ 14 November 2012, L 316/1.

Regulation (EU) No 910/2014 of the European Parliament and of the Council of 23 July 2014 on electronic identification and trust services for electronic transactions in the internal market and repealing Directive 1999/93/EC, OJ 28 August 2014, L 257/73.

European Commission, Commission Implementing Regulation (EU) 2015/1501 of 8 September 2015 on the interoperability framework pursuant to Article 12(8) of Regulation (EU) No 910/2014 of the European Parliament and of the Council on electronic identification and trust services for electronic transactions in the internal market, OJ 9 September 2015, L 235/1.

European Commission, Commission Implementing Regulation (EU) 2015/1502 of 8 September 2015 on setting out minimum technical specifications and procedures for assurance levels for electronic identification means pursuant to Article 8(3) of Regulation (EU) No 910/2014 of the European Parliament and of the Council on electronic identification and trust services for electronic transactions in the internal market, OJ 9 September 2015, L 235/7.

Regulation 2016/679 of the European Parliament and of the Council of 27 April 2016 on the protection of natural persons with regard to the processing of personal data and on the free movement of such data, and repealing Directive 95/46/EC (General Data Protection Regulation), OJ 4 May 2016, L 119/1.

Regulation (EU) 2018/1725 of the European Parliament and of the Council of 23 October 2018 on the protection of natural persons with regard to the processing of personal data by the Union institutions, bodies, offices and agencies and on the free movement of such data, and repealing Regulation (EC) No 45/2001 and Decision No 1247/2002/EC, OJ 21 November 2018, L 295/39.

NATIONAL LEGISLATION

Law of 16 December 1969 establishing the data processing centre of the State of Hesse and regarding the data processing centres of local communities, *HE GVBI*, 22 December 1969, No. 32, Part I, p. 304 (Hesse).
Data Protection Act of 7 October 1970, *HE GVBI.* 12 October 1970, no. 41, Part I, p. 625 (Hesse).
Law of 4 September 1974, *HE GVBl.* 9 September 1974, no. 27, I, p. 365 (Hesse).
Law of 31 January 1978, *HE GVBl.* 7 February 1978, no. 4, I, p. 96 (Hesse).
Law of 11 November 1986, *HE GVBl.* 20 November 1986, no. 25, I, p. 309 (Hesse).
Law of 5 November 1998, *HE GVBl.* 9 November 1998, no. 22, I, p. 421(Hesse).
Data Act of 11 May 1973 ("*Datalagen*"), *SFS* 1973: 289 (Sweden).
Private Register Act ("*Lov om private register*") of 8 June 1978 (no. 293) (Denmark).
Act no. 48 of 9 June 1978 relating to personal data filing systems (Norway).
Law no. 70-643 of 17 July 1970 seeking to reinforce the protection of the rights of individuals and citizens, *J.0.* 19 July 1970, p. 6755 (France).
Decree no. 74-938 of 8 November 1974 establishing the Committee on Informatics and Liberties, *J.O.* 13 November 1974, p. 11403 (France).
Federal Data Protection Act of 27 January 1977, *BGBl.* I No. 7 S. 201 (Germany).
Law no. 78-17 of 6 January 1978 concerning informatics, files and liberties, *J.O.*7 January 1978, p. 227 (corr. 25 January 1978) (France).
Federal Act of 18 October 1978 on the protection of personal data, *Bundesgesetzblatt für die Republik Österreich* 1978, 193. Stück, p. 3619 (Austria).
Law of 31 March 1979 regulating the use of personal data in automated data processing, *Journal Officiel du Grand-Duché de Luxembourg* 11 April 1979, no. 29, p. 581 (Luxembourg).
Law no. 94-548 of 1 July 1994 concerning the processing of personal data for purposes of medical research purposes modifying the law no. 78-17 of 6 January 1978 concerning informatics, files and liberties, *J.O.* 2 July 1994, p. 25 (France).
Law no. 2004-801 of 6 August 2004 concerning the protection of natural persons with regards to the processing of personal data and modifying Law no. 78-17 of 6 January 1978 concerning informatics, files and liberties, *J.O.* 7 August 2004, p. 24 (France).
Right to Privacy Bill, *HC Deb* 26 November 1969, vol. 792, c. 430 (United Kingdom)
Act No. 101/2000 Coll. Of 4 April 2000 on the Protection of Personal Data (Czech Republic).
Law of 8 August 1983 organising a register of natural persons, *B.S.*, 21 March 1984 (Belgium).
Law of 15 January 1990 establishing and organising a Crossroadsbank for Social Security, *B.S.* 22 February 1990 (Belgium).
Law of 17 June 1991 approving the Convention for the Protection of Individuals with regard to Automatic Processing of Personal Data, drawn up in Strasbourg on 28 January 1981, *B.S.* 30 December 1993 (Belgium).
Law of 8 December 1992 on the protection of privacy in relation to the processing of personal data, *B.S.* 18 March 1993 (Belgium).

Law of 6 July 2000 containing rules regarding the protection of personal data (Data Protection Act), *Staatsblad* 302 (Netherlands).
Personal Information Protection and Electronic Documents Act (PIPEDA), S.C. 2000, c. 5, (Canada).

2. PREPARATORY WORKS

DIRECTIVE 95/46

Debates of the European Parliament, Report of Proceedings from 12 to 16 November 1973, 1973–1974 Session, OJ November 1973, Annex No. 168p. 104 (reply to Oral Question 122/73).
Legal Affairs Committee, Interim Report on the protection of the rights of the individual in the face of developing technical progress in the field of automatic data processing, 19 February 1975, *European Parliament Working Documents* 1974–1975, Document 487/74.
European Parliament, Resolution of the European Parliament on the protection of the rights of the individual in the face of the technical developments in data processing, OJ 13 March 1975, C 60/48.
European Parliament, Resolution of the European Parliament on the protection of the rights of the individual in the face of the technical developments in data processing, OJ 3 May 1976, C100/27; OJ 5 June 1979, C-140/34-38 and OJ 5 April 1982, C87/39-41.
Commission of the European Communities, Recommendation 81/679/EEC of 29 July 1981 relating to the Council of Europe Convention for the protection of individuals with regard to the automatic processing of personal data, OJ 29 August 1981, L 246/31.
Commission of the European Communities, Commission Communication on the Protection of individuals in relation to the processing of personal data in the Community and information security, COM(90) 314 final, SYN 287 and 288, 13 September 1990.
European Parliament, Committee on Economic and Monetary Affairs and Industrial Policy, Working Document on data protection (COM(90) 314 fin.), drafted by Mr. F. Herman, 26 February 1991, PE 148.204, 11 p.
Economic and Social Committee, "Opinion on: the proposal for a Council Directive concerning the protection of individuals in relation to the processing of personal data; the proposal for a Council Directive concerning the protection of personal data and privacy in the context of public digital telecommunications networks, in particular the integrated services digital network (ISDN) and public digital mobile networks; and – the proposal for a Council Decision in the field of information security (91/C 159/14), OJ 17 June 1991 C 159/38.
European Parliament, Position of the European Parliament on Proposal for a directive I COM(90) 0314 – C3-0323/90 – SYN 287 / Proposal for a Council directive concerning the protection of individuals in relation to the processing of personal data T3-0140/1992, 11 March 1992 (First Reading) OJ 13 April 1992, C 94/173-201.

Commission of the European Communities, Amended proposal for a council directive on the protection of individuals with regard to the processing of personal data and on the free movement of such data, COM(92) 422 final - SYN 287, 15 October 1992, OJ 27 November 1992, C 311/30-61.

Commission of the European Communities, Amended proposal for a council directive on the protection of individuals with regard to the processing of personal data and on the free movement of such data, COM(92) 422 final - SYN 287, 15 October 1992, OJ 27 November 1992, C 311/39.

Council of the European Union, Common position (EC) No 1/95 adopted by the Council on 20 February 1995 with a view to adopting Directive 95/.../EC of the European Parliament and of the Council of ... on the protection of individuals with regard to the processing of personal data and on the free movement of such data, OJ 13 April 1995, C 93/1-24.

Commissie juridische zaken en rechten van de burger, "Aanbeveling voor de tweede lezing betreffende het gemeenschappelijke standpunt van de Raad met het oog op de aanneming van de richtlijn van het Europese Parlement en de Raad betreffende de bescherming van natuurlijke personen in verband met de verwerking van persoonsgegevens en betreffende het vrije verkeer van die gegevens (C4-00051/95 - 00/0287(COD)), PE 212.057/def, A4-0120/95, 24 mei 1995.

European Parliament, Decision of the European Parliament on the common position established by the Council with a view to the adoption of a European Parliament and Council Directive on the protection of individuals with regard to the processing of personal data and on the free movement of such data, (C4-0051/95 - 00/0287(COD)), OJ 3 July 1995 C 166/105–107.

Commission of the European Communities, Opinion of the Commission pursuant to Article 189 b (2) (d) of the EC Treaty, on the European Parliament's amendments to the Council's common position regarding the proposal for a European Parliament and Council directive on the protection of individuals with regard to the processing of personal data and on the free movement of such data, COM(95) 375 final- COD287, 18 July 1995.

GENERAL DATA PROTECTION REGULATION

European Commission, Communication from the Commission to the European Parliament, the Council, the Economic and Social Committee and the Committee of the Regions, A comprehensive approach on personal data protection in the European Union, Brussels, COM(2010) 609 final, November 2010.

European Commission, Proposal for a Regulation of the European Parliament and of the Council on the protection of individuals with regard to the processing of personal data and on the free movement of such data (General Data Protection Regulation), COM(2012) 11 final, 2012/0011 (COD), 25 January 2012.

European Commission, "Evaluation of the implementation of the Data Protection Directive", Annex 2 of Commission Staff Working Paper, Impact Assessment, SEC(2012) 72 final, 25 January 2012.

Council of the European Union, Working Party on Information Exchange and Data Protection (DAPIX), "Outcome of proceedings – summary of discussions on 23–24 February 2012", 2012/0011 (COD), 7221/12, DAPIX 22, 8 March 2012.

European Commission, Proposal for a Regulation of the European Parliament and of the Council on electronic identification and trust services for electronic transactions in the internal market, COM(2012) 238/2, 4 June 2012.

European Parliament, LIBE Committee, "Working Document 2 on the protection of individuals with regard to the processing of personal data and on the free movement of such data (General Data Protection Regulation), PE497.802v01-00, 8 October 2012.

European Parliament, Committee on Civil Liberties, Justice and Home Affairs, Draft Report on the proposal for a regulation of the European Parliament and of the Council on the protection of individual with regard to the processing of personal data and on the free movement of such data (General Data Protection Regulation), (COM(2012)0011 – C7-0025/2012 – 2012/0011(COD)) 16 January 2013.

European Parliament, Committee on Civil Liberties, Justice and Home Affairs, Proposal for a regulation of the European Parliament and of the Council on the protection of individual with regard to the processing of personal data and on the free movement of such data (General Data Protection Regulation) (COM(2012)0011 – C7 0025/2012 – 2012/0011(COD)) Compromise amendments on Articles 1–29, 7 October 2013.

Committee on Civil Liberties, Justice and Home Affairs, Report on the proposal for a regulation of the European Parliament and of the Council on the protection of individuals with regard to the processing of personal data and on the free movement of such data (General Data Protection Regulation) (COM(2012)0011 – C7 0025/2012 – 2012/0011(COD)), 21 November 2013.

Council of the European Union, Note from the Presidency to the Working Group on Information Exchange and Data Protection (DAPIX) – Specific Issues of Chapters I-IV of the General Data Protection Regulation – certain aspects of the relationship between controllers and processors, 2012/0011 (COD), 5345/14, 15 January 2014.

European Parliament legislative resolution of 12 March 2014 on the proposal for a regulation of the European Parliament and of the Council on the protection of individuals with regard to the processing of personal data and on the free movement of such data (General Data Protection Regulation), (COM(2012)0011 – C7-0025/2012 – 2012/0011(COD)), 12 March 2014.

Council of the European Union, Note from Presidency to Working Party on Information Exchange and Data Protection on the proposed General Data Protection Regulation – Chapter IV, 2012/0011 (COD), 12312/14, 1 August 2014.

Council of the European Union, Note from CZ, DE, IE, ES, FR, HR, NL, AT, PL, PT, FI and UK delegations to the Working Group on Information Exchange and Data Protection (DAPIX), 2012/0011 (COD), 7586/1/15 REV 1, 10 April 2015.

Council of the European Union, Note from the Presidency to the Working Group on Information Exchange and Data Protection (DAPIX) on the General Data Protection Regulation – Chapter VIII, 2012/0011 (COD), 7722/15, 13 April 2015.

Council of the European Union, Note from the German delegation to the Working Group on Information Exchange and Data Protection (DAPIX) on the Proposal for a General Data Protection Regulation – Chapter VIII, 2012/0011 (COD), 8150/15, 21 April 2015.

Council for the European Union, Note from the Presidency to the JHA Counsellors DAPIX on a Proposal for a General Data Protection Regulation – Chapter VIII, 8371/15, 4 May 2015.

Council of the European Union, Note from the German delegation to the JHA Counsellors (DAPIX) on the Proposal for a General Data Protection Regulation – Chapter VIII, 2012/0011 (COD), 8150/1/15, 6 May 2015.

Council of the European Union, Note from the Presidency to the Permanent Representatives Committee on the proposal for a General Data Protection Regulation – Chapter VIII, 2012/0011 (COD), 8383/15, 13 May 2015.

Council of the European Union, Note from Presidency to JHA Counsellors on the proposed General Data Protection Regulation – Chapter VIII, 2012/0011 (COD), 9083/15, 27 May 2015.

Council for the European Union, Proposal for a Regulation of the European Parliament and of the Council on the protection of individuals with regard to the processing of personal data and on the free movement of such data (General Data Protection Regulation) – Preparation of a general approach", 2012/0011 (COD), 9565/15, 11 June 2015.

Council of the European Union, Proposal for a Regulation of the European Parliament and of the Council on the protection of individuals with regard to the processing of personal data and on the free movement of such data (General Data Protection Regulation) [first reading] – Political agreement", 5455/16, 28 January 2016.

Council of the European Union, Position of the Council at first reading with a view to the adoption of a Regulation of the European Parliament and of the Council on the protection of individuals with regard to the processing of personal data and on the free movement of such data (General Data Protection Regulation) – Draft Statement of the Council's reasons, 5419/16 ADD 1, 17 March 2016.

Council of the European Union, Position of the Council at first reading with a view to the adoption of a Regulation of the European Parliament and of the Council on the protection of natural persons with regard to the processing of personal data and on the free movement of such data, and repealing Directive 95/46/EC (General Data Protection Regulation), 5419/16, 6 April 2016.

European Commission, Communication from the Commission to the European Parliament pursuant to Article 294(6) of the Treaty on the Functioning of the European Union concerning the position of the Council on the adoption of a Regulation of the European Parliament and of the Council on the protection of natural persons with regard to the processing of personal data and on the free movement of such data (General Data Protection Regulation) and repealing Directive 95/46/EC, COM(2016) 214 final, 11 April 2016.

NATIONAL LEGISLATION

Assemblé Nationale, Projet de loi relatif à l'informatique et aux libertés, Enregistré à la Présidence de l'Assemblée national le 9 aout 1976, Annexe au procès-verbal de la séance du 2 octobre 1976, *Document Parl.* no. 2516, p. 1–18 (France).
HL Deb 21 December 1982, vol. 437 c. 926 (United Kingdom).
HL Deb 20 January 1983 vol. 437 cc 1551 (United Kingdom).
HL Deb 10 March 1983 vol. 440, at cc 373 (United Kingdom).
HL Deb, 24 March 1983, vol. 440, at cc 1275 (United Kingdom).
HL Deb, 5 July 1983, vol. 443, at cc 509 (United Kingdom).
HL Deb, 19 July 1983, vol. 443, cc 1068 (United Kingdom).
HL Deb, 21 July 1983, vol. 443, cc 1299 (United Kingdom).
Voorstel van wet betreffende de bescherming van het privé-leven en de persoonlijkheid, *Parl. St.* Senaat, 1970–1971, 19 juli 1971, no. 706 (Belgium).
Wetsontwerp tot bescherming van de persoonlijke levenssfeer ten opzichte van de verwerking van persoonsgegevens, *Parl. St. Kamer*, 1990–1991, 6 May 1991, no. 1610–1 (Belgium).
Memorie van Toelichting, Wetsontwerp ter bescherming van de persoonlijke levenssfeer ten opzichte van de verwerking van persoonsgegevens, *Parl. St. Kamer*, 1990–1991, 6 May 1991, no. 1610–1 (Belgium)
Verslag namens de Minister van Justitie uitgebracht door Mevr. Merckx-Van Goey, Wetsontwerp ter bescherming van de persoonlijke levenssfeer ten opzichte van de verwerking van persoonsgegevens, *Parl. St. Kamer*, 1991–1992 (B.Z.), 2 July 1992, no. 413–12 (Belgium).
Verslag namens de commissie voor de Justitie uitgebracht door de heer Vandenberghe, *Gedr. St.* Senaat, 1991–1992 (B.Z.), 27 October 1992, no. 445-2 (Belgium).
Raad van State, Advies van de Raad van State bij het voorontwerp van wet tot omzetting van de Richtlijn 95/46/EG van 24 oktober 1995 van het Europees Parlement en de Raad betreffende de bescherming van natuurlijke personen in verband met de verwerking van persoonsgegevens en betreffende het vrij Verkeer van die gegevens, 2 February 1998, *Parl. St. Kamer* 1997–1998, no. 1566/1 (Belgium).
Tweede Kamer der Staten-Generaal, Regels inzake de bescherming van persoonsgegevens (Wet bescherming persoonsgegevens) – Memorie van Toelichting, Vergaderjaar 1997–1998, 25 892, no. 3 (Netherlands).

3. CASE LAW

EUROPEAN COURT OF HUMAN RIGHTS

European Court of Human Rights, P.G. and J.H. v. United Kingdom, 25 September 2001, application no. 44787/98.
European Court of Human Rights, Niemietz v. Germany, 16 December 1992, application no. 13710/88.

COURT OF JUSTICE OF THE EUROPEAN UNION

Judgment in *Bodil Lindqvist*, C-101/01, EU:C:2003:596.
Judgment in *Kalliopi Nikolaou*, T-259/03, EU:T:2007:254.
Judgment in *Satamedia*, Case C-73/07, EU:C:2008:266.
Judgment in *Fotios Nanopoulos*, F-30/08, EU:F:2010:43.
Judgment in *Volker und Markus Schecke*, Joined Cases C-92/09 and C-93/09, EU:C:2010:662.
Judgment in *Probst*, C-119/12, ECLI:EU:C:2012:748.
Judgment in *Google Spain*, C-131/12, EU:C:2014:317.
Judgment in *František Ryneš*, C-212/13, EU:C:2014:2428.
Judgment in *Smaranda Bara and Others*, C-201/14, EU:C:2015:638.
Judgment in *Weltimmo*, C-230/14, EU:C:2015:639.
Judgment in *Breyer*, C-582/14, ECLI:EU:C:2016:339.
Judgment in *Wirtschaftsakademie*, C-210/16, ECLI:EU:C:2018:388.
Judgment in *Jehova's witnesses*, C-25/17, ECLI:EU:C:2018:551.
Opinion of Advocate General Sharpston in Buivids, C-345/17, ECLI:EU:C:2018:780.
Opinion of Advocate General Bobek in *Fashion ID*, C-40/17, ECLI:EU:C:2018:1039.
Opinion of Advocate General Szpunar, *G. C., A. F., B. H., E. D. v. Commission nationale de l'informatique et des libertés (CNIL)*, C-136/17, ECLI:EU:C:2019:14.

NATIONAL CASE LAW

Kh. Kortrijk, 1ste Kamer, 19 June 2003, *T.G.R.* 2007, p. 96 (Belgium).
Gent, 6 January 2005, *T.G.R.* 2007, p. 92 (Belgium).
Cour d'Appel de Liège, 7ième Chambre, Bobon Benjamin / SPRL Diablo, 2008/RG/1165, 19 November 2009 (Belgium).
Court of First Instance of Brussels, Division of Summary Proceedings, *Willem Debeuckelaere v. Facebook Ireland Ltd., Facebook Inc. and Facebook Belgium BVBA*, Case number 15/57/C, 9 November 2015 (Belgium).
Cour de Cassation, Arrêt C.15.0052.F, 29 April 2016 (Belgium).
Court of Appeal of Brussels, 18th Ch., *Facebook Ireland Ltd., Facebook Inc. and Facebook Belgium BVBA v. Willem Debeuckelaere*, Case number 2016/KR/2, 29 June 2016 (Belgium).
Court of First Instance of Brussels, 24th Ch., Civil Matters, *Willem Debeuckelaere v. Facebook Ireland Ltd., Facebook Inc. and Facebook Belgium BVBA*, Case number 2016/153/A, 16 February 2018 (Belgium).
Bundesverfassungsgericht, Decision of 15 December 1983 regarding Volkzählungsgesetz 83, *BVerfGE* vol. 65, p. 1 (Germany).
Corte di Cassazione, sez. III Penale, sentenza 17 dicembre 2013 – deposit ail 3 febbraio 2014, sentenza n. 5107/14 (Italy).
High Court of Justice, *Applause Store Productions Limited and Matthew Firsht v. Grant Raphael*, 24 July 2008, [2008] EWHC 1781 (QB) (United Kingdom).
High Court of Justice, *Stephen Robins and Gabbitas Robins v. Rick Kordowski and Tim Smee*, 22 July 2011, [2011] EWHC 1912 (QB) (United Kingdom).

Court of Appeal (Civil Division), *Google Inc v Vidal-Hall & Ors* [2015] EWCA Civ 311 (United Kingdom).
High Court of Justice, *Various Claimants v Wm Morrisons Supermarket PLC*, [2017] EWHC 3113 (United Kingdom).
Court of Appeal, *Various Claimants v Wm Morrisons Supermarket PLC*, [2018] EWCA Civ 2339 (United Kingdom).
Tribunal Supremo. Sala de lo Civil, A and B v Ediciones El Pais, Judgment number 545/2015, ECLI:ES:TS:2015:4132 (Spain).
United States Supreme Court, *U.S. Department of Justice v. Reporters Committee for Freedom of the Press*, 489 U.S. 749 (1989) (United States).

4. REGULATORY OPINIONS AND GUIDANCE

ARTICLE 29 WORKING PARTY AND EUROPEAN DATA PROTECTION BOARD

Article 29 Data Protection Working Party, "Working document on determining the international application of EU data protection law to personal data processing on the Internet by non-EU based web sites", WP 56, 30 May 2002.
Article 29 Data Protection Working Party, "Working Document on on-line authentication services", WP 68, 29 January 2003.
Article 29 Data Protection Working Party, "Working document on E-Government", WP 73, 8 May 2003.
Article 29 Data Protection Working Party, "Opinion 10/2006 on the processing of personal data by the Society for Worldwide Interbank Financial Telecommunication (SWIFT)", WP 128, 22 November 2006.
Article 29 Data Protection Working Party, "Working Document on the processing of personal data relating to health in electronic health records (EHR)", WP 131, 15 February 2007.
Article 29 Data Protection Working Party, "Opinion 4/2007 on the concept of personal data", WP 136, 20 June 2007.
Article 29 Data Protection Working Party, "Opinion 7/2007 on data protection issues related to the Internal Market Information System (IMI)", WP 140, 20 September 2007.
Article 29 Data Protection Working Party, "Opinion 1/2008 on data protection issues related to search engines", WP 148, 4 April 2008.
Article 29 Data Protection Working Party, "Opinion 5/2009 on online social networking", WP 163, 12 June 2009.
Article 29, "The Future of Privacy – Joint contribution to the Consultation of the European Commission on the legal framework for the fundamental right to protection of personal data", WP 168, 1 December 2009.
Article 29 Data Protection Working Party, "Opinion 1/2010 on the concepts of 'controller' and 'processor'", WP 169, 16 February 2010.
Article 29 Data Protection Working Party, "Opinion 2/2010 on online behavioural advertising", WP 171, 22 June 2010.

Article 29 Data Protection Working Party, "Opinion 3/2010 on the principle of accountability", WP 173, 13 July 2010.

Article 29 Data Protection Working Party, "FAQs in order to address some issues raised by the entry into force of the EU Commission Decision 2010/87/EU of 5 February 2010 on standard contractual clauses for the transfer of personal data to processors established in third countries under Directive 95/46/EC", WP 176, 12 July 2010.

Article 29 Data Protection Working Party, "Opinion 8/2010 on applicable law", WP 179, 16 December 2010.

Article 29 Data Protection Working Party, Biometrics & eGovernment Subgroup, "Written Report concerning the STORK Project", Ref.Ares(2011)424406, 15 April 2011.

Article 29 Data Protection Working Party, "Opinion 01/2012 on the data protection reform proposals", WP 191, 23 March 2012.

Article 29 Data Protection Working Party, "Opinion 05/2012 on Cloud Computing", WP 196, 1 July 2012.

Article 29 Data Protection Working Party, "Opinion 02/2013 on apps on smart devices", WP 202, 27 February 2013.

Article 29 Data Protection Working Party, "Statement of the Working Party on current discussions regarding the data protection reform package – Annex 2 Proposals for Amendments regarding exemption for personal or household activities", 27 February 2013.

Article 29 Data Protection Working Party, "Opinion 03/2013 on purpose limitation", WP 203, 2 April 2013.

Article 29 Data Protection Working Party, "Working document 01/2014 on Draft Ad hoc contractual clauses 'EU data processor to non-EU sub-processor'", WP 214, 21 March 2014.

Article 29 Data Protection Working Party, "Opinion 06/2014 on the notion of legitimate interests of the data controller under Article 7 of Directive 95/46/EC", WP 217, 9 April 2014.

Article 29 Data Protection Working Party, "Guidelines on the implementation of the Court of Justice of the European Union judgment on 'Google Spain and Inc. v. Agencia Española de Protección de Datos (AEPD) and Mario Costeja González' C-131/12", WP 225, 26 November 2014.

Article 29 Data Protection Working Party, "Opinion 02/2015 on C-SIG Code of Conduct on Cloud Computing", WP 232, 22 September 2015.

Article 29 Data Protection Working Party, "Update of Opinion 8/2010 on applicable law in light of the CJEU judgment in Google Spain, WP 179 update", 16 December 2015.

Article 29 Data Protection Working Party, "Guidelines on the right to data portability", WP 242 rev. 01, 5 April 2017.

Article 29 Data Protection Working Party, "Guidelines on Personal data breach notification under Regulation 2016/679", WP250 rev.01, 6 February 2018.f

Article 29 Data Protection Working Party, "Guidelines on transparency under Regulation 2016/679", WP260 rev.01, 11 April 2018.

European Data Protection Board, "Guidelines 3/2018 on the territorial scope of the GDPR (Article 3) – Version for public consultation", 16 November 2018.

EUROPEAN DATA PROTECTION SUPERVISOR

European Data Protection Supervisor (EDPS), "Opinion of the European Data Protection Supervisor on the Commission Decision of 12 December 2007 concerning the implementation of the Internal Market Information System (IMI) as regards the protection of personal data (2008/49/EC) (2008/C 270/01)", OJ 25 October 2008, C 270/1.

European Data Protection Supervisor (EDPS), "Opinion of the European Data Protection Supervisor on the Commission Proposal for a Regulation of the European Parliament and of the Council on administrative cooperation through the Internal Market Information System ('IMI')", 22 November 2011.

European Data Protection Supervisor (EDPS), "Opinion of the European Data Protection Supervisor on the data protection reform package", 7 March 2012.

European Data Protection Supervisor, "Opinion of the European Data Protection Supervisor on the Commission proposal for a Regulation of the European Parliament and of the Council on trust and confidence in electronic transactions in the internal market (Electronic Trust Services Regulation)", 27 September 2012.

European Data Protection Supervisor (EDPS), "Opinion of the European Data Protection Supervisor on the Commission's Communication on 'Unleashing the potential of Cloud Computing in Europe'", 16 November 2012.

European Data Protection Supervisor (EDPS), "Additional EDPS comments on the Data Protection Reform Package", 15 March 2013.

European Data Protection Supervisor, "Assessing the necessity of measures that limit the fundamental right to the protection of personal data: A Toolkit", 11 April 2017.

European Data Protection Supervisor (EDPS), "EDPS Opinion on the proposal for a Regulation establishing a single digital gateway and the 'once-only' principle", 1 August 2017.

NATIONAL DATA PROTECTION AUTHORITIES

Data Protection Registrar, "The Data Protection Act 1984: An introduction to the act and guide for data users and computer bureaux", Data Protection Registrar, Wilmslow, 1985.

The Data Protection Registrar, "The Data Protection Act of 1984: Questions and Answers on the Act (1–20)", Office of The Data Protection Registrar, Wilmslow, 1985.

Data Protection Registrar, "The Data Protection Act 1984: The Definitions", Great Britain. Office of the Data Protection Registrar, Wilmslow, 1989.

Information Commissioner's Office (ICO), "Data Protection Act, 1998 – Legal Guidance", Version 1, not dated.

Information Commissioner's Office (ICO), "Outsourcing – A guide for small and medium-sized businesses", v1.0, 28 February 2012.

Information Commissioner's Office (ICO), "Guidance on the use of cloud computing", v1.1, 2 October 2012.

Information Commissioner's Office (ICO), "Proposed new EU General Data Protection Regulation: Article-by-article analysis paper", v1.0, 12 February 2013.

Information Commissioner's Office (ICO), "Social networking and online forums – when does the DPA apply?", version 1.0, 24 May 2013.
Information Commissoner's Office (ICO), Monetary Penaty Notice to Facebook Ireland Ltd and Facebook Inc., 24 October 2018.
Commissie voor de Persoonlijke Levenssfeer, Advies Nr 37/2006 van 27 september 2006 betreffende de doorgifte van persoonsgegevens door de CVBA SWIFT ingevolge de dwangbevelen van de UST (OFAC).
Commissie voor de Bescherming van de Persoonlijke Levenssfeer, "Aanbeveling nr. 02/2007 uit eigen beweging inzake de verspreiding van beeldmateriaal", 28 November 2007.
Commissie voor de Persoonlijke Levenssfeer, "Decision of 9 December 2008 regarding the Control and recommendation procedure initiated with respect to the company SWIFT", 9 December 2008.
Commissie voor de Bescherming van de Persoonlijke Levenssfeer, "Aanbeveling nr 09/2012 uit eigen beweging in verband met authentieke gegevensbronnen in de overheidssector (CO-AR-2010-005)", 23 May 2012.
Commissie voor de Bescherming van de Persoonlijke Levenssfeer, Sectoraal Comité van de Sociale Zekerheid en van de Gezondheid, Afdeling «Gezondheid», Beraadslaging nr. 11/088 van 18 oktober 2011, gewijzigd op 9 juni 2015, met betrekking tot de nota betreffende de elektronische bewijsmiddelen van een therapeutische relatie en van een zorgrelatie, SCSZG/15/088.
Commission National Informatique et Libertés (CNIL), "Les transferts de données à caractère personnel hors Union européenne", not dated.
Commission National Informatique et Libertés (CNIL), "Les questions posées pour la protection des données personnelles par l'externalisation hors de l'Union européenne des traitements informatiques", September 2010.
Commission Nationale de l'Informatique et Libertés (CNIL), Recommendations for companies planning to use Cloud computing services, not dated.
College Bescherming Persoonsgegevens, "Publicatie van Persoonsgegevens op het Internet", *CBP Richtsnoeren*, December 2007.
Data Protection Commissioner, "Report of Audit – Facebook Ireland Ltd.", 21 December 2011.
Agencia Española de Protección de Datos, "Statement on Internet Search Engines", December 2007.
E. Denham (Assistant Privacy Commissioner of Canada), "Report of Findings into the complaint filed by the Canadian Internet Policy and Public Interest Clinic (CIPPIC) against Facebook Inc. under the Personal Information Protection and Electronic Documents Act", 22 July 2009.
Office of the Privacy Commissioner of Canada, "PIPEDA – Processing Personal Data Across Borders Guidelines", 27 January 2009.
United States Federal Trade Commission (FTC), *In the matter of Facebook Inc. – Decision and Order*, Docket No. C-4365, 27 July 2012.
Garante per la protezione dei dati personali, Provvedimento dell'11 febbraio 2016 [doc. web n. 4833448], 11 Feburary 2016.

5. RECOMMENDATIONS AND DECLARATIONS

COUNCIL OF EUROPE

Parliamentary Assembly of the Council of Europe, Recommendation 509 (1968) concerning Human rights and modern scientific and technological developments, 31st January 1968 (16th Sitting).

Committee of Ministers of Council of Europe, Resolution (73)22 on the protection of privacy of individuals vis-à-vis electronic data banks in the private sector, 26 September 1973 (224th meeting of the Ministers' Deputies).

Committee of Ministers of the Council of Europe, Resolution (74)29 on the protection of the privacy of individuals vis-à-vis electronic data banks in the public sector, 20 September 1974 (236th meeting of the Ministers' Deputies).

Committee of Ministers of the Council of Europe, Recommendation R(86)1 on the protection of personal data for social security purposes, 23 January 1986 (392nd meeting of the Ministers' Deputies).

Committee of Ministers of the Council of Europe, Recommendation R(99)5 for the protection of privacy on the internet, 23 February 1999 (660th meeting of the Ministers' Deputies).

Committee of Ministers of the Council of Europe, Declaration on freedom of communications on the Internet, 28 May 2003 (840th meeting of the Ministers' Deputies).

Project Group on Data Protection (CJ-PD) of the Council of Europe, Guiding principles for the protection of personal data with regard to smart cards, 12 May 2004 (adopted at the 79th Plenary the European Committee on Legal Co-operation (CDCJ).

Consultative Committee of the Convention for the protection of individuals with regard to automatic processing of personal data of the Council of Europe, Opinion of the T-PD in the interpretation of the concepts of automatic processing and controller of the file in context of worldwide telecommunications networks, T-PD-BUR (2006) 08 E fin, Strasbourg, 15 March 2007.

Council of Europe, Recommendation of the Committee of Ministers to member States on the protection of human rights with regard to search engines, CM/Rec(2012)3, 4 April 2012 (adopted at the 1139th meeting of the Ministers' Deputies).

OECD

Organisation for Economic Co-operation and Development (OECD), Guidelines on the Protection of Privacy and Transborder Flows of Personal Data, 23 September 1980.

Organisation for Economic Co-operation and Development (OECD), Declaration on Transborder Data Flows, 11 April 1985.

Organisation for Economic Co-operation and Development (OECD), Declaration on the Protection of Privacy in Global Networks, adopted at the Ottawa Ministerial Conference 7–9 October 1998, adopted as OECD Council Resolution on 19 October 1998.

Organisation for Economic Co-operation and Development (OECD), Recommendation on Cross-border Co-operation in the Enforcement of Laws Protecting Privacy, 12 June 2007.

Organisation for Economic Co-operation and Development (OECD), Recommendation of the Council concerning Guidelines governing the Protection of Privacy and Transborder Flows of Personal Data, C(80)58/FINAL, as amended on 11 July 2013 by C(2013)79.

Organisation for Economic Co-operation and Development (OECD), Recommendation of the Council on Digital Security Risk Management for Economic and Social Prosperity, C(2015)115, 17 September 2015.

OTHER

International Working Group on Data Protection in Telecommunications, Report and Guidance on Privacy in Social Network Services – "Rome Memorandum", adopted 3-4 March 2008.

International Data Protection and Privacy Commissioners' Conference: Resolution on Privacy Protection and Search Engines, 28th edition, London, 2–3 November 2006.

International Working Group on Data Protection in Telecommunications, Working Paper on Cloud Computing – Privacy and data protection issues – "Sopot Memorandum", adopted 23–24 April 2012.

6. DOCTRINE

MONOGRAPHS

Ausloos, J., *The Right to Erasure: Safeguard for informational self-determination in a digtial society?*, Dissertation presented in partial fulfilment of the requirements for the degree of Doctor in Laws, KU Leuven, 2018, 481 p.

Bainbridge, D., *EC Data Protection Directive*, London, Butterworths, 1996, 328 p.

Baldwin, R. and Cave, M., *Understanding regulation – Theory Strategy and Practice*, Oxford, Oxford university press, 1999, 363 p.

Bennett, C.J., *Regulating Privacy*, Ithaca, Cornell University Press, 1992, 263 p.

Boonk, M.L., *Zeker over zoeken? Naar een juridisch kader voor verichtingen van zoeksystemen met betrekking tot via internet beschikbare open content*, Zutphen, Uitgeverij Paris, 2013, 466 p.

Bygrave, L.A., *Data protection law: approaching its rationale, logic and limits*, The Hague, Kluwer Law International, 2002, 426 p.

Cannataci, J.A., *Privacy and Data Protection Law: International Development and Maltese Perspectives*, Oslo, Norwegian University Press, 1986, 239 p.

Coene, B. *De wenselijkheid van de investeringsbescherming geboden door de sui generis intellectuele rechten rond chips, computerprogramma's en databanken*, Proefschrift aangeboden tot het behalen van de titel van Doctor in de Rechten aan de KU Leuven en de UGent, Academiejaar 2015–2016, 3 February 2016, 935 p.

Dammann, U., Mallmann, O. and Simitis, S., (eds.), *Data Protection Legislation. An International Documentation. English – German*, 1977, Frankfurt am Main, Alfred Metzner Verlag GmbH, 203 p.

Dammann, U. and Simitis, S., *EG-Datenschutzrichtlinie*, 1997, Baden-Baden, Nomos Verlagsgesellschaft, 346 p.

De Bot, D., *Verwerking van Persoonsgegevens*, Antwerpen, Kluwer, 2001, 403 p.

De Bot, D., *Privacybescherming bij e-government in België. Een kritische analyse van het Rijksregister, de Kruispuntbank van Ondernemingen en de elektronische identiteitskaart*, Brugge, Vandenbroele, 2005, 469 p.

De Cock, D., *Contributions to the Analysis and Design of Large-Scale Identity Management Systems*, Dissertation presented in partial fulfillment of the requirements for the degree of Doctor in Engineering, June 2011, 234 p.

De Hert, P., Gutwirth S. and Debeuckelaere, W., *Anthologie privacy: referentietekst*, published by Commissie voor de Bescherming van de Persoonlijke Levenssfeer, 2013, 93 p.

Demeyere, S., Samoy, I. and Stijns, S., *Aansprakelijkheid van een contractant jegens derden – De rechtspositie van de nauw betrokken derde*, Brugge, die Keure, 2015, 167 p.

Dierickx, L., "Recht op afbeelding" in X., Reeks *Instituut voor Familierecht en Jeugdrecht KU Leuven*, no. 89, Antwerpen, Intersentia, 2005, 345 p.

Flaherty, D.H., *Protecting Privacy in Surveillance Societies. The Federal Republic of Germany, Sweden, France, Canada, & the United States*, 1989, Chapel Hill, The University of North Carolina Press, 483 p.

George, A.L. and Bennet, A., *Case Studies and Theory Development in the Social Sciences*, 2005, London, MIT Press, 331 p.

González Fuster, G., *The Emergence of Personal Data Protection as a Fundamental Right of the EU*, Dordrecht, Springer, 2014, 284 p.

Gutwirth, S., *Privacy and the information age*, Lanham, Rowman & Littlefield Publ., 2002, 152 p.

Hensler, D.R., *Designing Empirical Legal Research: A Primer for Lawyers*, 2011, second revision, 145 p.

Hijmans, H., *The European Union as a constitutional guardian of internet privacy and data protection*, Academisch proefschrift ter verkrijging van de graad van doctor aan de Universiteit van Amsterdam en de Vrije Universiteit Brussel, 2016, 543 p.

Hondius, F. W., *Emerging data protection in Europe*, Amsterdam, North-Holland Publishing Company, 1975, 282 p.

Hutter, B.M., *Regulation and Risk. Occupational Health and Safety on the Railways*, Oxford, Oxford University Press, 2001, 356 p.

Jones, A. and Sufrin, B., *EU Competition Law – Texts, Cases and Materials*, Oxford, Oxford University Press, Fourth Edition, 2011, 1287 p.

Kayser, P., *La protection de la vie privée. Protection du secret de la vie privée*, Paris, Economica, 1984, 605 p.

Kosta, E., *Unravelling consent in European data protection legislation: a prospective study on consent in electronic communications*, Doctoral Thesis, Submitted 1 June 2011, 364 p.

Kuczerawy, A., *Intermediary Liability and Freedom of Expression in the EU: from Concepts to Safeguards*, KU Leuven Centre for IT & IP Law Series, Intersentia, 2018, 425 p.

Kuner, C., *European data protection law: corporate compliance and regulation*, 2nd edition, Oxford, Oxford University Press, 2007, 552 p.

Lievens E., *Protecting Children in the Digital Era – the Use of Alternative Regulatory Instruments*, Leiden, Martinus Nijhoff Publishers, International Studies in Human Rights, 2010, 584 p.

Marchini, R., *Cloud computing: A Practical Introduction to the Legal Issues*, London, BSI Standards Institution, 2010, 166 p.

Menezes, A.J., Van Oorschot, P.C. and Vanstone, S.A., *Handbook of Applied Cryptography*, Boca Raton, CRC Press, 1997, 780 p.

Moerel, L., *Binding Corporate Rules: Corporate Self-Regulation of Global Data Transfers*, Oxford, Oxford University Press, 2012, 354 p.

Newman, A., *Protectors of Privacy: Regulating personal data in a global economy*, 2008, New York, Cornell University, 221 p.

Niblett, G.B.F., "Digital information and the privacy problem", *OECD Informatics Studies*, no. 2, 1971, Paris, OECD, 58 p.

Nugter, A.C.M., *Transborder Flow of Personal Data within the EC. A comparative analysis of the privacy statutes of the Federal Republic of Germany, France, the United Kingdom and The Netherlands and their impact on the private sector*, Deventer, Kluwer, Computer/Law Series no. 6, 1990, 430 p.

Oderkerk, A.E., *De preliminaire fase van het rechtsvergelijkend onderzoek*, Ph. D. Thesis, 1999, msterdam Center for International Law (ACIL), 484 p.

Overkleeft-Verburg, M., *De Wet persoonsregistraties – norm, toepassing en evaluatie*, Proefschrift ter verkrijging van de graad van doctor aan de Katholieke Universiteit Brabant, Hilvarenbeek, 1995, 607 p.

Solove, D.J., *The Future of Reputation: Gossip, Rumor and Privacy on the Internet*, 2007, New Haven, Yale University Press, 247 p.

Stijns, S., *Verbintenissenrecht*, Boek 1*bis*, Brugge, die Keure, 2013, 152 p.

Thijssen, M.B.J., *De Wbp en de vennootschap*, Deventer, Kluwer, 2009, 342 p.

Tridimas, T., *The General Principles of EU Law*, 2nd edition, Oxford, Oxford University Press, 2006, 591 p.

Van Hoboken, J., *Search engine freedom. On the implications of the right to freedom of expression for the legal governance of Web search engines*, Academisch Proefschrift ter verkrijging van de graad van doctor aan de Universiteit van Amsterdam, defended on 23 March 2012, 357 p.

Vansweevelt, T. en Weyts, B., *Handboek Buitencontractueel Aansprakelijkheidsrecht*, Antwerpen, Intersentia, 2009, 935 p.

Vinge, P.G., *Swedish Data Act*, Federation of Swedish Industries, No. 43, Stockholm, Svanbäck & Nymans Boktr., 1974 (original release: 1973), 22 p.

Yin, R.K., *Case Study Research – Design and Methods*, 2009, London, Sage Publications, Fourth Edition, 219 p.

Yin, R.K. Applications of Case Study Research, 2012, London, Sage Publications, Third Edition, 231 p.

Zhang, L., *Knowledge Graph Theory and Structural Parsing*, PhD Thesis, University of Twente, Twente University Press, 2002, 232 p.
Zittrain, J., *The Future of the Internet- And How to Stop It*, New Haven, Yale University Press, 2008, 342 p.

ARTICLES, BOOK CHAPTERS AND EDITED WORKS

Agre, P.E. and Rotenberg M. (eds.), *Technology and Privacy: The New Landscape*, 1998, London, MIT Press, 325 p.
Alhadeff, J., Van Alsenoy, B. and Dumortier, J., "The accountability principle in data protection regulation: origin, development and future directions", in D. Guagnin, L. Hempel, C. Ilten a.o. (eds.), *Managing Privacy through Accountability*, Houndmills (UK), Palgrave Macmillan, 2012, p. 49–82.
Aronstein, C., "Défense de la vie privée. Essai pour contribuer à la survie de notre civilisation", *Journal des Tribunaux* 1971, p. 453–463.
Ausloos, J. and Kuczerawy, A., "From Notice-and-Takedown to Notice-and-Delist: Implementing the Google Spain ruling", *CiTiP Working Paper Series* 2015, 38 p.
Balboni, P. "Data Protection and Data Security Issues Related to Cloud Computing in the EU", in N. Pohlmann, H. Reimer and W. Schneider (eds.), *ISSE 2010 Securing Electronic Business Processes*, Springer, 2010, p. 163–172.
Bagherjeiran, A., Bhatt, R.P., Parekh, R. and Chaoji, V., "Online Advertising in Social Networks", in B. Furht (ed.), *Handbook of Social Network Technologies and Applications*, 2010, New York, Springer, p. 651–689.
Beer, D., "Social network(ing) sites ... revisiting the story so far: A response to danah boyd & Nicole Ellison", *Journal of Computer-Mediated Communication* 2008, Vol. 13, p. 516–529.
Bender, J., "eIDAS regulation: eID – Opportunities and Risks", 25th SmartCard Workshop, 4–5 February 2015, p. 157–166.
Bing, J., "A Comparative Outline of Privacy Legislation", *Comparative Law Yearbook* 1978, Vol. 2, p. 149–181.
Bing, J., Forsberg, P. and Nygaard, E., "Legal problems related to transborder data flows", in OECD, *An Exploration of Legal Issues in Information and Communication Technologies*, Information Computer Communication Policy no. 8, Paris, OECD, 1983, 135 p.
Bing, J., "The Council of Europe Convention and the OECD Guidelines on Data Protection", *Michigan Yearbook of International Legal Studies* 1984, Vol. 5, p. 271–303.
Bing, J., "Data Protection in a Time of Changes", in W.F. Korthals Altes a.o. (eds.), *Information law towards the 21st Century*, Information law series 2, Deventer, Kluwer Law and Taxation Publishers, 1992, p. 247–259.
Birnhack, M., "Reverse Engineering Information Privacy Law", *Yale Journal of Law and Technology* 2012, Vol. 24, p. 24–91.
Black, J., "The Rise, Fall and Fate of Principles Based Regulation", *LSE Law Society and Economy Working Papers* 17/2010, 2010, 26 p.

Blume, P., "Controller and processor: is there a risk of confusion?", *International Data Privacy Law* 2013, Vol. 3, No. 2, p. 140–145.

Blume, P., "An alternative model for data protection law: changing the roles of controller and processor", *International Data Privacy Law* 2015, Vol. 5, No. 4, p. 292–297.

Bocken, H., "Samenloop contractuele en buitencontractuele aansprakelijkheid", *NjW* 2007, no. 169, p. 722–731.

Börjesson, M., "The Swedish Data Act in Transition", in P. Blume (ed.), *Nordic Studies in Information Technology and Law*, Computer/Law Series, Kluwer, 1991, p. 151–162.

Boulanger, M.-H., De Terwangne, C., Léonard, T., Louveaux, S., Moreau, D. and Poullet, Y., "La Protection des Données à caractère personnel en droit communautaire", *Journal de Tribunaux Droit Européen* 1997, p. 121–155.

Bovens, M., "Analysing and Assessing Accountability: A conceptual Framework", *European Law Journal* 2007, vol. 13, p. 946–967.

boyd, d. "Friendster and Publicly Articulated Social Networks", in *Conference on Human Factors and Computing Systems* (CHI 2004), Vienna, ACM, April 24–29, 2004, p. 1279–1282.

boyd, d.m. and Ellison, N.B., "Social Networking Sites: Definition, History and Scholarship", *Journal of Computer-Mediated Communication* 2008, vol. 13, p. 210–230.

Boyd, J. and Ingberman, D.E., "The 'Polluter pays principle': Should Liability be Extended When the Polluter Cannot Pay?", *The Geneva Papers on Risk and Insurance* 1996, Vol. 21, No. 79, p. 182–203.

Brugger, W., "Legal Interpretation, Schools of Jurisprudence, and Anthropology: Some Remarks from a German Point of View", *American Journal of Comparative Law* 1994, Vol. 42, No. 2, p. 395–421.

Buquicchio, G., "The work of the Council of Europe in the field of data protection", in Council of Europe, *Legislation and Data Protection. Proceedings of the Rome Conference on problems relating to the development and application of legislation on data protection*, 1983, Rome, Camera dei Deputati, Annex I, p. 229–233.

Burkert, H. "Privacy – Data Protection A German/European Perspective", in C. Engel K.H. Keller (eds.), *Governance of Global Networks in the Light of Differing Local Values*, 2000, Baden-Baden, Nomos, p. 43–69.

Bygrave, L.A., "Core principles of data protection", *Privacy Law and Policy Reporter* 2001, vol. 7, issue 9, p. 169.

Callens, S., a.o. (ed.), *Chapters on pharmaceutical law*, Antwerpen, Intersentia, 2000, 194 p.

Campbell, D. and Fisher, J. (eds.), *Data transmission and privacy*, Center for International Legal Studies, Dordrecht, Martinus Nijhoff Publishers, 1994, 509 p.

Casteluccia, C., "Behavioural Tracking on the Internet: A Technical perspective", S. Gutwirth et al. (eds.), *European Data Protection: In Good Health?*, 2013, Dordrecht, Springer Science+Business Media, p. 21–33.

Cate, F.H., "The EU Data Protection Directive, Information Privacy, and the Public Interest", *Iowa Law Review* 1995, 431–443.

Centrum voor Internationaal Strafrecht, "De Belgische privacy-wetgeving, een eerste analyse", *Rechtskundig Weekblad* 1992–1993, no. 34, p. 1145–1154.

Chadwick, D., "Federated Identity Management", in Alessandro Aldini, Gilles Barthe and Roberto Gorrieri (eds.), *Foundations of Security Analysis and Design V*, FOSAD 2007/2008/2009 Tutorial Lectures, Springer, 2009, p. 96–120.

Claeys, I., "Buitencontractuele aansprakelijkheid van contractanten en hulppersonen? Als het contractuele evenwicht maar niet wordt verstoord", in S. Stijns (ed.), *Verbintenissenrecht*, Brugge, die Keure, 2004, Reeks 'Themis', no. 23, p. 27–42.

Cook, T., "The law relating to computer bureaux", in C. Edwards and N. Savage (eds), *Information Technology & The Law*, 1986, MacMillan Publishers, p. 159–167.

Cousy, H. and Droshout, D., "Fault under Belgian Law", in P. Widmer (ed.), Unification of Tort Law: Fault, 2005, The Hague, Kluwer Law International, p. 27–51.

Cousy, H. and Droshout, D., "Belgium", in B.A. Koch and H. Koziol (ed.), *Unification of Tort Law: Strict Liability*, 2002, The Hague, Kluwer International, p. 43–74.

Cousy, H. and Droshout, D., "Liability for Damage Caused by Others under Belgian Law", in J. Spier (ed.), *Unification of Tort Law: Liability for Damage Caused by Others*, The Hague, Kluwer law International, p. 37–54.

Cousy, H. and Droshout, D., "Multiple Tortfeasors under Belgian Law", in. W.V.H. Rogers (Ed.), *Unification of Tort Law: Multiple Tortfeasors*, The Hague, Kluwer Law International, 2004, p. 29–52.

Crook, A., "Data Protection in the United Kingdom, Part 2", *Journal of Information Science* 1983, Vol. 7, p. 47–57.

Cruquenaire, A. and Henrotte, J.F., "Le devoir de Conseil dans le Règlement général sur la protection des données: bis repetita placent?", in C. De Terwangne a.o. (eds.), *Law, Norms and Freedoms in cyberworld / Droit, Normes et Libertés dans le cybermonde – Liber amicorum Yves Poullet*, p. 599–617.

Cuijpers, C. and Schroers, J., "eIDAS as guideline for the development of a pan European eID framework in FutureID", *Open Identity Summit* 2014 vol. 237, p. 23–38.

de Andrade, N.N.G., "'Electronic Identity for Europe': Moving from Problems to Solutions", *Journal of International Commercial Law and Technology* 2013, Vol. 8, No.2, p. 104–109.

de Azevedo Cunha, M.V., Marin, L. and Sartor, G., "Peer-to-peer privacy violations and ISP liability: data protection in the user-generated web", *International Data Privacy Law* 2012, Vol. 2, No. 2, p. 50–67.

De Boeck, A., "Aansprakelijkheid voor gebrekkige dienstverlening", in X., *Bestendig Handboek Vennootschap & Aansprakelijkheid*, Mechelen, Kluwer, 2008, looseleaf.

De Bot, D., "Art. 15*bis* Wet Persoonsgegevens", in X., *Personen- en familierecht. Artikelsgewijze commentaar met overzicht van rechtspraak en rechtsleer*, Mechelen, Kluwer, 2001, looseleaf.

De Cock, D., Van Alsenoy, B., Preneel, B. and Dumortier, J. "The Belgian eID Approach", in W. Fumy and M. Paeschke, *Handbook of eID Security. Concepts, Practical Experiences, Technologies*, 2011, Erlangen, Publicis, p. 117–139.

Defreyne, E. and Romain, R., "L'arrêt «Google Spain» : commentaire et mise en perspective", *Revue du Droit des Technologies de l'Information* 2014, no. 56, p. 73–114.

De Groef, W., Devries, D., Reynaert, T. and Piessens, F., "Security and Privacy of Online Social Network Applications", in L. Caviglione, M. Coccoli and A. Merlo (eds.), *Social Network Engineering for Secure Web Data and Services*, IGI Global, 2013, p. 206–221.

De Hert, P., "Een betere bescherming van de privacy door de nieuwe wet verwerking persoonsgegevens? Analyse van nieuwigheden en tekortkomingen", in X., *CBR Jaarboek 2000-2001*, Antwerpen, Maklu, 2001, 365–409.

De Hert, P. and Gutwirth, S. "Privacy, data protection and law enforcement. Opacity of the individual and transparency of power", in E. Claes, A. Duff and S. Gutwirth (eds.), *Privacy and the Criminal Law*, Antwerpen/Oxford, Intersentia, 2006, p. 61–104.

De Hert, P. and Gutwirth, S. "Data Protection and the Case Law of Strasbourg and Luxemburg: Constitutionalism in Action", in S. Gutwirth, Y. Poullet, P. De Hert, J. Nouwt and C. De Terwangne (eds.), *Reinventing data protection?*, Dordrecht, Springer Science, 2009, p. 3–44.

De Hert, P., Papakonstantinou, V. and Kamara, I., "The new cloud computing ISO/IEC 27018 standard through the lens of the EU legislation on data protection", *Brussels Privacy Hub Working Paper*, Vol. 1, No. 2, November 2014, 26 p.

De Hert, P. and Papakonstantinou, V., "The proposed data protection Regulation replacing Directive 95/46/EC: A sound system for the protection of individuals", *Computer Law & Security Review* 2012, vol. 28, p. 130–142.

De Hert, P. and Papakonstantinou, V., "Comment – Google Spain -Addressing Critiques and Misunderstandings One Year Later", *Maastricht Journal of European and Comparative Law* 2015, Vol. 22, No. 4, p. 624–638.

De Hert P. and Saelens, R., "Recht op afbeelding", *TPR* 2009, afl. 2, p. 867–917.

Delforge, A., "Les obligations générales du responsable du traitement et la place du sous-traitant", in C. De Terwangne and K. Rosier (eds.), *Le Règlement Général sur la Protection des Données (RGPD/GDPR) – Analyse approfondie*, CRIDS, Brussels, Larcier, 2018, p. 371–406.

Determann, L., "Data Privacy in the Cloud–Myths and Facts", *Institute for IT Law*, 10 April 2012, online publication at http://www.iitr.us/publications/40-data-privacy-in-the-cloud-a-dozen-myths-and-facts.html.

De Terwangne, C., "Les principes relatifs au traitement des données à caractère personnel et sa licéité", in C. De Terwangne and K. Rosier (eds.), *Le Règlement Général sur la Protection des Données (RGPD/GDPR) – Analyse approfondie*, CRIDS, Brussels, Larcier, 2018, p. 87–142.

Dirix, E., "Aansprakelijkheid van en voor hulppersonen", in. M. Storme (ed.), *Recht Halen uit Aansprakelijkheid*, Gent, Mys & Breesch, 1993, p. 342.

Docquir, B., "Le 'cloud computing' ou l'informatique dématérialisée: la protection des données au coeur de la relation contractuelle", *Revue de Droit Commercial* 2011, Vol. 10, p. 1000–1015.

Dumortier, J., "Privacybescherming en gegevensverwerking. Aantekeningen bij de Wet tot bescherming van de persoonlijke levenssfeer t.o.v. de verwerking van persoonsgegevens", *Vlaamse Jurist* 1993, p. 4–14.

Dumortier, J. and Vandezande, N., "Trust in the proposed EU regulation on trust services?", *Computer Law and Security Review* 2012, Vol. 28, p. 568–576.

Dworkin, G., "The Younger Committee Report on Privacy", *The Modern Law Review* 1973, Vol. 36, No. 4, p. 399–406.

Edwards, C. and Savage, N., "Data Privacy: the UK Experience", in C. Edwards and N. Savage (eds), *Information Technology & The Law*, Basingstoke, MacMillan Publishers, 1986, p. 75–142.

Ehrleich, I. and Posner, R. A., "An Economic Analysis of Legal Rulemaking", *The Journal of Legal Studies* 1974, Vol. 3, No. 1, p. 257–286.

Enders, A., Hungenberg, H., 'The long tail of social networking. Revenue models of social networking sites", *European Management Journal* 2008, Vol. 26, p. 199–211.

Erdos, D., "Filling Defamation's Gaps: Data Protection and the Right to Reputation", *Oxford Legal Studies Research Paper* 2013, No. 69, 41 p.

Esayas, S.Y., "A walk in to the cloud and cloudy it remains: The challenges and prospects of 'processing' and 'transferring' personal data", *Computer, Law & Security Review* 2012, Vol. 28, p. 662–678.

Evans, A.C., "Data Protection Law", *The American Journal of Comparative Law* 1981, vol. 29, no. 4, p. 571–582.

Fang, Z., "E-Government in Digital Era: Concept, Practice, and Development", *International Journal of The Computer, The Internet and Management* 2002, Vol. 10, No.2, p. 1–22.

Fon, V. and Parisi, F., "Codifications and the optimal specificity of legal rules", Law and Economics Working Paper Series 04–32, *George Mason University School of Law*, 2007, 22 p.

Freese, J., "The Swedish Data Act", *Current Sweden* 1977, No. 178, p. 1–8.

Fuster, G.G., De Hert, P. and Gutwirth, S., "SWIFT and the vulnerability of transatlantic data transfers", *International Review of Law Computers & Technology* 2008, Vol. 22, p. 191–202.

Garcia, F.J., "Bodil Lindqvist: A Swedish Churchgoer's Violation of the European Union's Data Protection Directive Should Be a Warning to U.S. Legislators", *Fordham Intell. Prop. Media & Ent. L.J.* 2005, Vol. 15, p. 1204–1243.

Garcia, S.S., Oliva, A.G., Belleboni, E.P. and De La Cruz, I.P., "Current Trends in Pan-European Identity Management Systems", *IEEE Technology and Society Magazine* 2012, Vol. 31, Issue 3, p. 1204–1243.

Garrie, D.B., Duffy-Lewis, M., Wong, R. and Gillespie, R.L., "Data Protection: the Challenges Facing Social Networking", *International Law & Management Review* 2010, Vol. 6, p. 127–152.

Gellert, R., "Understanding data protection as risk regulation", *Journal of Internet Law* 2015, p. 3–16.

Gelman, L., "Privacy, Free Speech, and "Blurry-Edged" Social Networks", *Boston College Law Review* 2009, vol. 50, p. 1315–1344.

Gilbert, F., "Cloud service providers as joint-data controllers", *Journal of Internet Law* 2011, p. 3–13.

Godin, B., "The information economy: the history of a concept through its measurement, 1949–2005", *History and Technology: An International Journal* 2008, Vol. 24, n. 3, p. 255–287.

Goettke, R. and Christiana, J., "Privacy and Online Social Networking Websites", Computer Science 199r: Special Topics in Computer Science Computation and Society: Privacy and Technology, May 14, 2007. http://www.eecs.harvard.edu/cs199r/fp/RichJoe.pdf.

Grimmelmann, J., "Speech engines", *Minnesota Law Review* 2014, Vol. 98, p. 868–952.

Grönlund, A. and Horan, T.A., "Introducing e-Gov: history, definitions and issues", *Communications of the Association for Information Systems* 2004, Vol. 15, p. 713–729.

Gross, R. and Acquisti, A., "Information Revelation and Privacy in Online Social Networks", in *Proceedings of the 2005 ACM Workshop on Privacy in the Electronic Society* (WPES'05), Virginia, 2005, p. 71–80.

Guiliams, S., "Eenzelfde schade of andere schade bij pluraliteit van aansprakelijken", *Nieuw Juridisch Weekblad* (NJW) 2010, afl. 230, p. 699–700.

Guiliams, S., "De verdeling van de schadelast bij samenloop van een opzettelijke en een onopzettelijke fout", *Rechtskundig Weekblad* (R.W.) 2010–2011, no. 12, p. 474–485.

Gürses, S. and van Hoboken, J. "Privacy After the Agile Turn", in J. Polonetsky, O. Tene and E. Selinger (eds.), *Cambridge Handbook of Consumer Privacy*, Cambridge Univeristy Press, 2017, 31 p.

Gutwirth, S., "De toepassing van het finaliteitsbeginsel van de Privacywet van 8 december 1992 tot bescherming van de persoonlijke levenssfeer ten opzichte van de verwerking van persoonsgegevens", *Tijdschrift voor Privaatrecht* 1993, vol. 4, p. 1409–1477.

Harris, E.C., "Personal Data Privacy Tradeoffs and How a Swedish Church Lady, Austrian Public Radio Employees, and Transatlantic Air Carriers Show That Europe Does Not Have All the Answers", *Am. U. Int'l L. Rev.* 2007, Vol. 22, p. 745–799.

Hartzog, W. and Stutzman, F., "The Case for Online Obscurity", *California Law Review* 2013, Vol. 101, No. 1, p. 1–49.

Heidemann, J., Klier, M. and Probst, F., "Online social networks: A survey of a global phenomenon", *Computer Networks* 2012, vol. 56, p. 3866–3878.

Helberger, N. and Van Hoboken, J., "Little Brother Is Tagging You – Legal and Policy Implications of Amateur Data Controllers", *Computer Law Review International* (Cri) 2010, Vol. 4, p. 101–109.

Heyman, R. and Pierson, J., "An Explorative Mapping of the Belgian Social Media Value Network and its Usage of Personal Identifiable Information", in M. Hansen a.o. (eds.), *Privacy and Identity*, IFIP, AICT, 2013, p. 203–213.

Hijmans, H., "Right to Have Links Removed – Evidence of Effective Data Protection", *Maastricht Journal of European and Comparative Law* 2014, Vol. 21, No. 3, p. 555–563.

Hildebrandt, M. and Koops, B.J., "The Challenges of Ambient Law and Legal Protection in the Profiling Era", *The Modern Law Review* 2010, p. 428–460.

Hintze, M. "Data Controllers, Data Processors, and the Growing Use of Connected Products in the Enterprise: Managing Risks, Understanding Benefits, and Complying with the GDPR", *Journal of Internet Law* 2018, 21 p.

Holleaux, A., "La loi du 6 Janvier 1978 sur l'informatique et les libertés (I) ", *La Revue Administrative* 1978, Vol. 31, no. 181, p. 31–40.

Holleaux, A., "La loi du 6 Janvier 1978 sur l'informatique et les libertés (II) ", *La Revue Administrative* 1978, Vol. 32, no. 182, p. 160–165.

Hornung, G., "A General Data Protection Regulation for Europa? Light and Shade in the Commission's Draft of 25 January 2012", *Scripted* 2012, Volume 9, Issue 1, p. 64–81.

Huber, M., Mulazzani, M., Schrittwieser, S., Weippl, E.R., "AppInspect – Large-scale Evaluation of Social Apps", *Proceedings of ACM Conference on Online Social Networks* (CSON) 2013, p. 143 – 154.

Hustinx, H., "Data Protection in the Light of the Lisbon Treaty and the Consequences for Present Regulations", speech delivered at the 11th Conference on Data Protection and Data Security, Berlin, 8 June 2009.

Hustinx, P., European Data Protection Supervisor, Data protection and Cloud Computing under EU law, speech delivered at the Third European Cyber Security Awareness Day, European Parliament, 13 April 2010.

Ilshammar, L., "When Computers Became Dangerous: The Swedish Computer Discourse of the 1960s", *HUMAN IT* 2007, Vol. 9, No. 1, p. 6–37.

Itzcovich, G. "The Interpretation of Community Law by the European Court of Justice", *German Law Journal* 2009, Vol. 10, No. 5, p. 537–560.

Jacobs, F.G., "Recent Development in the Principle of Proportionality in European Community Law", in E. Ellis (ed.), *The Principle of Proportionality in the Laws of Europe*, 1999, Hart Publishing, Oxford, p. 1–22.

Joint, A. and Baker, E. "Knowing the past to understand the present – issues in the contracting for cloud based services", *Computer Law & Security Review* 2011, Vol. 27, p. 407–415.

Källner, C.G., "Personal Data: The Open Access Approach", in OECD, *Policy issues in data protection and privacy. Concepts and perspectives*, Proceedings of the OECD Seminar 24th–26th June 1974, Paris, OECD Informatics Studies, no. 10, 1976, p. 59–65.

Kaplow, L., "Rules versus Standards: An Economic Analysis", *Duke Law Journal* 1992, Vol. 42, p. 557–629.

Karner, E., "The Function of the Burden of Proof in Tort Law", in Koziol and Steininger (eds.), *European Tort Law 2008*, Springer, 2009, p. 68–78.

Karst, K.L., "'The Files': Legal Controls over the Accuracy and Accessibility of Stored Personal Data', *Law and Contemporary Problems* 1966, vol. 31, no. 2, 342–376.

Kestemont, L., "Methods for traditional legal research, Reader Research Master in Law: Methods of Legal Research", KU Leuven – University of Tilburg (Leuven/Tilburg), 2015, 36 p.

Kestemont, L., "A typology of research objectives in legal scholarship", *Electronic Supplement to the Russian Juridical Journal* 2015, Vol. 5, p. 5–21.

Keuleers, E. and Dinant, J.M., "Multi application smart card schemes – Data protection: multi-application smart cards: the use of global unique identifiers for crossprofiling purposes – Part I", *Computer Law and Security Report* 2003, vol. 19, no. 6, p. 480–486.

Kindt, E.J., "Why research may no longer be the same: About the territorial scope of the New Data Protection Regulation", *Computer Law & Security Review 2016*, vol. 32, p. 729–748.

Kirby, M.D., "Transborder Data Flows and the 'Basic Rules' of Data Privacy", *Stanford Journal of International Law* 1980, Vol. 16, no. 42, p. 27–66.

Kirby, M. "The history, achievement and future of the 1980 OECD guidelines on privacy", *International Data Privacy Law* 2011, Vol. 1, No. 1, 6–14.

Ko, M.N., Cheek, G.P. and Shebab, M., "Social-Networks Connect Services", *Computer* 2010, Issue no. 8, IEEE Computer Society, p. 37–43.

Kohl, U. "Google: the rise and rise of online intermediaries in the governance of the Internet and beyond (Part 2)", *International Journal of Law and Information Technology* 2013, p. 1–48.

Koops, B.J., "Forgetting Footprints, Shunning Shadows. A Critical Analysis of the "Right to be Forgotten" in Big Data Practice", *Scripted* 2011, Vol. 8, Issue 3, p. 229–256.

Kontaxis, G., Polychronakis, M., Keromytis, A.D. and Markatos, E.P., "Privacy-Preserving Social Plugins", *Proceedings of the 21st USENIX conference on Security symposium*, 2012, 16 p.

Koppell, J., "Pathologies of Accountability: ICANN and the Challenge of "Multiple accountabilities Disorder"", *Public Administration Review* 2005, Vol. 65, Issue 1, p. 94–108.

Korobkin, R.B., "Behavioural analysis and legal form: Rules vs. Standards Revisited", *Oregon Law Review* 2000, Vol. 79, No. 1, p. 23–58.

Kosta, E. and Dumortier, J., "The Data Retention Directive and the principles of European Data protection legislation", *Medien und Recht International* 2007, Issue 3, p. 130–136.

Kosta, E. Zibuschka, J., Scherner, T. and Dumortier, J., "Legal considerations on privacy-enhancing Location Based Services using PRIME technology", *Computer, Law & Security Review* 2008, Vol. 24, p. 139–146.

Kosta, E., Kalloniatis, C., Mitrou, L. and Kavakli, E., "Search Engines: Gateway to a New "Panopticon"?", in S. Fischer-Hübner a.o. (eds.), *Trust, Privacy and Security in Digital Business*, Lecture Notes in Computer Science Volume 5695, 2009, p. 11–21.

Kosta, E., Kalloniatis, C., Mitrou, L. and Gritzalis, S., "Data protection issues pertaining to social networking under EU law", *Transforming Government: People, Process and Policy* 2010, Vol. 4, No. 2, p. 193–201.

Krishnamurthy, B., and Wills, C.E., "Characterizing Privacy in Online Social Networks", WOSN 2008, *Proceedings of the 1st ACM workshop on Online social networks*, 2008, p. 37–42.

Krishnamurthy, B. and Wills, C.E., "On the Leakage of Personally Identifiable Information Via Online Social Networks", WOSN 2009, *Proceedings of the 2nd ACM workshop on Online social networks*, 2009, p. 7–12.

Kuan Hon, W., Millard, C. and Walden, I., "Who is Responsible for 'Personal Data' in Cloud Computing? The Cloud of Unknowing, Part 2", Queen Mary University of London, School of Law, Legal Studies Research Paper No. 77/2011, 31 p.

Kuczerawy, A. and Coudert, F., "Privacy Settings in Social Networking Sites: Is It Fair?", in S. Fischer-Hübner et al. (eds.): *Privacy and Identity Management for Life*, 2011, p. 231–243.

Kuner, C., "Proportionality in European Data Protection Law And Its Importance for Data Processing by Companies", *Privacy & Security Law Report* 2008, vol. 07, no. 44, p. 1–5.

Kuner, C., "Regulation of Transborder Data Flows under Data Protection and Privacy Law: Past, Present, and Future", *TILT Law & Technology Working Paper Series*, 2010, 90 p.

Kuner, C. "The European Commission's Proposed Data Protection Regulation: A Copernican Revolution in European Data Protection Law", Bloomberg BNA, *Privacy and Security Law Report*, 2 June 2012, p. 1–15.

Lando, O. and Beale, H. (eds.), *Principles of European Contract Law – Parts I and II*, prepared by the Commission on European Contract Law, The Hague, Kluwer Law International, 2000, 610 p.

Lauvaux, M., "De burgerlijke aansprakelijkheid van werknemers", *Oriëntatie* (Or.) 2005, afl. 3, p. 65–75.

Layton, C. "Protection of Privacy – Future Prospects at the European Communities Level", in OECD, "Transborder Data Flows and the Protection of Privacy", Information Computer Communications Policy, no. 1, 1979, Paris, OECD, p. 213–216.

Leenes, R., "Who Controls the Cloud?", *Revista D'Internet, Dret I Política* (IDP) 2010, no. 11, p. 1–10.

Leitold, H. and Zwattendorfer, B., ""STORK: Architecture, Implementation and Pilots", in N. Pohlmann a.o. (eds.), *ISSE 2010 Securing Electronic Business Processes*, Springer, 2010, p. 131–142.

Lenoir, N., "La loi 78-17 du 6 janvier 1978 et la Commission national de l'informatique et des liberté: Éléments pour un premier bilan de cinq années d'activité", *La Revue administrative* 1983, Vol. 36, no. 215, p. 451–466.

Léonard, T., and Poullet, Y., "La protection des données à caractère personnel en pleine (r)évolution", *J.T.* 1999, p. 377–396.

Léonard, T., "La protection des données à caractère personnel et l'entreprise", in X., *Guide juridique de l'entreprise*, Brussels, Kluwer, 2004, livre 112.1, pp. 9–64.

Léonard, T. and Mention, A., "Transferts transfrontaliers de données: quelques considérations théorique et pratiques", in B. Docquir and A. Puttemans (eds.), *Actualités du droit de la vie privée*, Bruxelles, Bruylant, 2008, p. 98–137.

Lynskey, O., "Control over Personal Data in a Digital Age: Google Spain v AEPD and Mario Costeja Gonzalez", *The Modern Law Review* 2015, Vol. 78, no. 3, p. 522–548.

Mahieu, R., van Hoboken, J., Asghari, H., "Responsibility for Data Protection in a Networked World. On the question of the controller, "effective and complete protection" and its application to data access rights in Europe", *JIPITEC* 2019, Vol. 10(1), forthcoming.

Mahler, T., "Defining legal risk", paper presented at the conference "Commercial Contracting for Strategic Advantage – Potentials and Prospects", Turku University of Applied Sciences, 2007, 31 p.

Mantelero, A., "Cloud computing, trans-border data flows and the European Directive 95/46/EC: applicable law and task distribution", *European Journal for Law and Technology* 2012, Vol. 3, No. 2, 6 p.

Mayer-Schönberger, V., "Generational Development of Data Protection in Europe", in P.E. Agre and M. Rotenberg (eds.), *Technology and Privacy: The New Landscape*, 1998, London, MIT Press, p. 219–241.

MacCormick, N., "Argumentation and Interpretation in Law", *Ratio Juris* 1993, Vol. 6, No. 1, p. 16–29.

Marston, S. a.o., "Cloud computing – The business perspective", Decision Support Systems 2011, Vol. 51, p. 176–189.

McBride, J., "Citizen's Privacy and Data Banks: Enforcement of the Standards in the Data Protection Act 1984 (U.K.)", *Les Cahiers de Droit* 1984, vol. 25, no. 3, p. 533–552.

Merchant, K.A. and Otley, D.T., "A Review of the Literature on Control and Accountability", in C. S. Chapman, A. G. Hopwood and M. D. Shields (eds.), *Handbook of Management Accounting Research*, Vol. 2, 2007, Amsterdam, Elsevier, p. 785–802.

Miller, A.R., "Personal Privacy in the Computer Age: The Challenge of a New Technology in an Information-Oriented Society", *Michigan Law Review* 1969, vol. 67, p. 1089–1246.

Moerel, L.,"The long arm of EU data protection law: Does the Data Protection Directive apply to processing of personal data of EU citizens by websites worldwide?", *International Data Privacy Law* 2011, Vol. 1, No. 1, p. 28–46.

Moerel, L., "Back to basics: when does EU data protection law apply?", *International Data Privacy Law* 2011, Vol. 1, No. 2, p. 92–110.

Montéro, E. "Les responsabilités liées au web 2.0", *Revue du Droit des Technologies de l'Information* 2008, no. 32, p. 363–388.

Mulgan, R., "'Accountability': an ever-expanding concept?", *Public Administration* 2000, vol. 78, No. 3, p. 55–573.

Mustonen, J. (ed.), The World's First Freedom of Information Act. Anders Chydenius' Legacy Today, Anders Chydenius Foundation's Publications 2, 2006, 103 p.

Odudu, O. and Bailey, D., "The single economic entity doctrine in EU competition law", *Common Market Law Review* 2014, Vol. 51, p. 1721–1758.

Olsen, T. and Mahler, T., "Identity management and data protection law: Risk, responsibility and compliance in 'Circles of Trust' – Part II", *Computer, Law & Security Review* 2007, Vol. 23, no. 5, p. 415–426.

Onstad, P.C., "Data Processing Services and Transborder Data Flows, in OECD, *Transborder Data Flows and the Protection of Privacy*, Proceedings of a Symposium held in Vienna, Austria, 20th–23rd September 1977, Paris, OECD, 1979,p. 178–182.

Pagano, R., "Panorama of Personal Data Protection Laws", in Council of Europe, Legislation and Data Protection. Proceedings of the Rome Conference on problems relating to the development and application of legislation on data protection, 1983, Rome, Camera dei Deputati, Annex II, p. 236–348.

Pallis, G., Zeinalipour-Yazti, D. and Dikaiakos, M.D. in Vakali, A. and Jain, L.C., (eds.), "Online Social Networks: Status and Trends", *New Directions in Web Data Management, Studies in Computational Intelligence* 2011, Vol. 331, Berlin, Springer-Verlag, p. 213–234.

Papakonstantinou, V., "A data protection approach to data matching operations among public bodies", *International Journal of Law and Information Technology* 2001, vol. 9, issue 1, 2001, 39–64.

Patrick, P.H., "Privacy Restrictions on Transnational Data Flows: A Comparison of the Council of Europe Draft Convention and OECD Guidelines", *Jurimetrics Journal* 1980–1981, Vol. 21, p. 405–420.

Peguera, M. "The Shaky Ground of the Right to Be Delisted", (Draft, August 2015, forthcoming in Vanderbilt Journal of Entertainment & Technology Law), 52 p., available at http://ssrn.com/abstract=2641876.

Peterson, H.E. and Turn, R., "System implications of information privacy", in *Proceeding AFIPS '67*, (Spring) Proceedings of the April 18–20, 1967, spring joint computer conference, ACM, New York, p. 291–300.

Raitio, J., "The Expectation of Legal Certainty and Horizontal Effect of EU Law", in U. Bernitz, X. Groussot and F. Schulyok (eds.), *General Principles of EU Law and European Private Law*, 2013, Croyden, Kluwer Law International, p 199–212.

Reed, C., "The Law of Unintended Consequences – Embedded Business Models in IT Regulation", *Journal of Information Law and Technology* 2007, vol. 2, p. 1–34.

Reich, N., "The Principle of Effectiveness and EU Private Law", in U. Bernitz, X. Groussot and F. Schulyok (eds.), *General Principles of EU Law and European Private Law*, 2013, Croyden, Kluwer Law International, p. 301–326.

Reid, E., "Liability for Dangerous Activities: A Comparative Analysis", *The International and Comparative Law Quarterly* 1999, Vol. 48, No. 4, p. 731–756.
Robben, F., "Toepassingsgebied en begripsdefinities", in J. Dumortier en F. Robben, Persoonsgegevens en privacybescherming. Commentaar op de wet tot bescherming van de persoonlijke levenssfeer, Brugge, die Keure, 1995, p. 20–61.
Rodotà, S., "Data Protection – Some problems for Newcomers", in Council of Europe, Legislation and Data Protection. Proceedings of the Rome Conference on problems relating to the development and application of legislation on data protection, 1983, Rome, Camera dei Deputati, p. 186–193.
Roosendaal, A., "Facebook tracks and traces everyone: Like this!", *Tilburg Law School Legal Studies Research Paper Series*, No. 03/2011, 10 p.
Roosendaal, A.P.C., "We Are All Connected to Facebook … by Facebook!", in S. Gutwirth et al. (eds), *European Data Protection: In Good Health?*, Dordrecht, Springer, 2012, p. 3–19.
Rosier K. and Delforge, A., "Le régime de responsabilité civile du responsable du traitement et du sous-traitant dans le RGPD", in C. De Terwangne and K. Rosier (eds.), *Le Règlement Général sur la Protection des Données (RGPD/GDPR) – Analyse approfondie*, CRIDS, Brussels, Larcier, 2018, p. 665–702.
Roth, P. "Data Protection Meets Web 2.0 – Two Ships Passing in the Night", *UNSW Law Journal* 2010, Vol. 33, p. 532–561.
Salom, J.A., "'A third party to whom data are disclosed': A third group among those processing data", *International Data Privacy Law* 2014, Vol. 4, No. 3, p. 177–188.
Samyn, B., "Raad van Bestuur", in X., *Bestendig Handboek Vennootschap & Aansprakelijkheid*, Mechelen, Wolters Kluwer, 2000-, looseleaf.
Sancho-Villa, D., "Developing Search Engine Law: It Is Not Just about the Right to Be Forgotten", *Legal Issues of Economic Integration* 2015, Vol. 42, no. 4, p. 357–381.
Sartor, G., "Providers' liabilities in the new EU Data Protection Regulation: A threat to Internet freedoms?", *International Data Privacy Law* 2013, Vol. 3, No. 1, p. 3–12.
Sartor, G. "Search Engines as Controllers – Inconvenient implications of a Questionable Classification", *Maastricht Journal of European and Comparative Law* 2014, Vol. 21, No. 3, p. 564–575.
Sayaf, R. and Clarke, D., "Access control models for online social networks", in L. Caviglione, Coccoli, M. and Merlo, A. (eds.) *Social Network Engineering for Secure Web Data and Services*, Hershey, IGI, 2013, p. 32–56.
Schmidtchen, D. a.o., "The Internalisation of External Costs in Transport: From the Polluter Pays to the Cheapest Cost Avoider Principle", *CSLE discussion paper series*, No. 2007-03, 2007, 157 p.
Schmidl, M., "The Challenges of Subprocessing and Suggested Solutions under German and EU Privacy Law", *Bloomberg BNA World Data Protection Report* 2013, Vol. 13, No. 2, p. 1–5.
Schneier, B., "A Taxonomy of Social Networking Data", *Security & Privacy* 2009, IEEE, Vol. 8, Issue 4, p. 88.
Schwartz, P. "Information Privacy in the Cloud", *University of Pennsylvania Law Review* 2013, Vol. 161, p. 1623–1662.
Seawright, J. and Gerring, J. "Case Selection Techniques in Case Study Research – A Menu of Qualitative and Quantitative Options", *Political Research Quarterly* 2008, Vol. 61, No. 2, p. 294–308.

Seipel, P., "The Right to Know – Computers and Information Power", in P. Blume (ed.), *Nordic Studies in Information Technology and Law*, Computer/Law series no. 7, Deventer, Kluwer, 1991, p. 7–43.

Sethi, N., "Reimagining Regulatory Approaches: on the Essential Role of Principles in Health Research Regulation", *Scripted 2015*, Vol. 12, Issue 2, p. 91–116.

Simitis, S., "Establishing Institutional Structures to Monitor and Enforce Data Protection", in OECD, "Policy issues in data protection and privacy. Concepts and perspectives", *OECD Informatics Studies*, no. 10, Paris, OECD, 1976, p. 83–94.

Simitis, S., "Zwanzig Jahre Datenschutz in Hessen – eine kritische Bilanz", *Hessischer Landtag*, Neunzehnter Tätighkeitsbericht des hessischen Datenshutzbeauftragten, 1990, Drucksache 12/7651, p. 68–75.

Simitis, S., "Datenschutz", in H. Meyer and M. Stolleis (eds.), *Staats- und Verwaltungsrecht für Hessen*, 1996, fourth edition, Baden-Baden, Nomos Verlagsgesellschaft, p. 109–146.

Simitis, S., (ed.), *Kommentar zum Bundesdatenschutzgesetz*, 5th edition, Baden-Baden, Nomos Verlagsgesellschaft, 2003, 1623 p.

Simitis, S. "Privacy – An Endless Debate?", *California Law Review* 2010, Vol. 98, Issue 6, p. 1989–2005.

Sinclair, A., "The Chameleon of Accountability: Forms and Discourses", *Accounting, Organisations and Society* 1995, Vol. 20, p. 219–237.

Sjöblom, G., "Control in the History of Computing: Making an Ambiguous concept Useful", *IEEE Annals of the History of Computing* 2011, p. 86–870.

Solove, D., "A taxonomy of privacy", *University of Pennsylvania Law Review* 2006, Vol. 154, No. 3, p. 477–560.

Stadler, G., and Herzog, T., "Data Protection: International Trends and the Austrian Example", Guest Seminar at the International Institute for Applied Systems analysis, Laxenburg, Austria, 1981, 28 p.

Svantesson, D. and Clarke, R., "Privacy and consumer risks in cloud computing", *Computer Law & Security Review* 2010, Vol. 26, p. 391–397.

Svenonius, P., "Address", OECD, *Policy issues in data protection and privacy. Concepts and perspectives*, OECD Informatics Studies, no. 10, 1976, OECD, Paris, p. 48

Tene, O., "What Google Knows: Privacy and Internet Search Engines", *Utah Law Review* 2008, no. 4, p. 1433–1492.

Tene, O., "Privacy: The new generations", *International Data Privacy Law* 2011, Vol. 1, No. 1, p.15–27.

Thijssen, M.B.J., "Data Protection and group companies", 17th BILETA Annual Conference April 5th – 6th, 2002, 12 p.

Thompson, M. "Beyond Gatekeeping: The Normative Responsibility of Internet Intermediaries", *University of Hong Kong Faculty of Law Research Paper* No. 2015/45, 55 p.

Treacy, B. C. "Lessons from SWIFT: the 'controller' v 'processor' dilemma", *Complinet* 2008, 3 p.

Treacy, B., "Working Party confirms 'controller' and 'processor' distinction", *Privacy & Data Protection Journal* 2010, Vol. 10, Issue 5, p. 3–5.

Treacy, B., "Challenging times ahead for data processors", *Privacy & Data Protection Journal* 2012 Vol. 12, Issue 7, p. 3–6.

Tsormpatzoudi, P. and Coudert, F., "Technology providers' responsibility in protecting privacy... dropped from the sky?", *Paper presented at the Amsterdam Privacy Conference (APC)*, 23–26 October 2015, 13 p.

Turn, R. and Ware, W.H., "Privacy and Security Issues in Information Systems", *IEEE Transactions on Computers* 1976, Vol. C-25, No. 12, 1353–1361.

Turn, R., "Data security: costs and constraints" in OECD, *Policy issues in data protection and privacy. Concepts and perspectives, OECD Informatics Studies*, 1976, no. 10, OECD, Paris, p. 243–265.

Van Alsenoy, B., Ballet, J., Kuczerawy, A. and Dumortier, J., "Social networks and web 2.0: are users also bound by data protection regulations?", *Identity in the information society* 2009, Vol. 2, no.1, p. 65–79.

Van Alsenoy, B., De Cock, D., Simoens, K., Dumortier, J. and Preneel, B., "Delegation and digital mandates: Legal requirements and security objectives", *Computer, Law and Security Review* 2009, Vol. 25, no 5, p. 415–431.

Van Alsenoy, B., "Allocating responsibility among controllers, processors, and "everything in between": the definition of actors and roles in Directive 95/46/EC", *Computer Law & Security Review* 2012, Vol. 28, p. 25–43.

Van Alsenoy, B., Kindt, E. and Dumortier, J., "Privacy and data protection aspects of e-government identity management", in S. Van der Hof, M.M. Groothuis (eds.), *Innovating Government – Normative, Policy and Technological Dimensions of Modern Government*, Information Technology and Law Series (IT & Law), Vol. 20, T.M.C. Asser Press, Springer, 2011, p. 251–282.

Van Alsenoy, B., Kosta, E. and Dumortier, J., "Privacy notices versus informational self-determination: Minding the gap", *International Review of Law, Computers & Technology* 2013, p. 185–203.

Van Alsenoy, B., Kuczerawy A., and Ausloos, J., "Search Engines after *Google Spain*: Internet@Liberty or Privacy@Peril?", *ICRI Working Paper Series*, Working paper 15/2013, September 2013, 74 p.

Van Alsenoy, B., "The evolving role of the individual under EU data protection law", *ICRI Working Paper Series*, Working paper 23/2015, Augustus 2015, 35 p.

Van Alsenoy, B., and Koekkoek, M., "Internet and jurisdiction after Google Spain: the extraterritorial reach of the 'right to be delisted'", *International Data Privacy Law* 2015, Vol. 5, No. 2, p. 105–120.

Van Alsenoy, B., "Reconciling the (extra)territorial reach of the GDPR with public international law", in G. Vermeulen and E. Lievens (eds.), *Data Protection and Privacy under Pressure Transatlantic tensions, EU surveillance, and big data*, Antwerp, Maklu, 2017, p. 77–100.

Van Alsenoy, B., "Liability under EU Data Protection Law: From Directive 95/46 to the General Data Protection Regulation", JIPITEC 2016, Vol. 7, 271–288.

Vandenberghe, H., "Aansprakelijkheid van de aansteller", *Tijdschrift voor Privaatrecht* (TPR) 2011, afl. 2, p. 575–612.

van der Sloot, B., "Welcome to the Jungle: the Liability of Internet Intermediaries for Privacy Violations in Europe", *JIPITEC* 2015, Vol. 6, p. 211–228.

van der Wees, J.G.L., "De verantwoordelijke en de bewerker in de cloud", *Computerrecht* 2011, Afl. 3, p. 108–114.

Van Eecke, P., "Online service providers and liability: a plea for a balanced approach", *Common Market Law Review* 2011, Vol. 48, p. 1455–1502.

Van Eecke P. and Truyens, M., "Privacy and social networks", *Computer, Law & Security Review* 2010, Vol. 26, no. 5, p. 535–546.

Van Gyseghem, J.M., "Cloud computing et protection des données à caractère personnel: mise en ménage possible?", *Revue du Droit des Technologies de l'Information* 2011, vol. 42, p. 35–50.

Vegleris, P., "Preadvies" in X., *Privacy en de rechten van de mens. Handelingen van het Derde Internationaal Colloquium over het Europees Verdrag tot Bescherming van de Rechten van de Mens,* Leuven, Acco, 1974, p. 337–342.

Waters, R.D., Burnett, E., Lamm, A. and Lucas, J., "Engaging stakeholders through social networking: How nonprofit organisations are using Facebook", *Public Relations Review* 2009, Vol. 35, Issue 2, p. 102–106.

Witting, C., "Breach of the non-delegable duty: defending limited strict liability in tort", *University of New South Wales Law Journal* 2006, Vol. 29, No. 3, p. 33–60.

Wojtan, B., "The new EU Model Clauses: One step forward, two steps back?", *International Data Privacy Law* 2011, Vol. 1, No. 1, p. 76–80.

Wong, K, "Data Protection Law", *Data Processing* 1984, Vol. 26, no. 1, p. 34–37.

Wong, R., "The Shape of Things to Come: Swedish Developments on the Protection of Privacy", *SCRIPT-ed* 2005, Vol. 2, Issue 1, p. 107–124.

Wong, R. and Savirimuthu, J., "All or Nothing: This is the Question? The Application of Article 3(2) Data Protection Directive 95/46/EC to the Internet", *The John Marshall Journal of Information Technology and Privacy Law* 2008, Vol. 25, Issue 2. p. 241–266.

R. Wong, "Social Networking: Anybody is a Data Controller!", (last revised) 2008, 16 p. published online at http://papers.ssrn.com/sol3/papers.cfm?abstract_id=1271668

R. Wong, "Social networking: a conceptual analysis of a data controller", *Communications Law* 2009, Vol. 14, No. 5, p. 142–149.

Wynant, L., "Aansprakelijkheid voor en van derden die voor de vennootschap werken: Personeel ter beschikking stellen van werknemers, onderaannemers", in X., *Bestendig Handboek Vennootschap & Aansprakelijkheid,* Mechelen, Wolters Kluwer, 2000-, looseleaf.

Xanthoulis, N., "Negotiating the EU Data Protection Reform: Reflections on the Household Exemption", in A. B. Sideridis a.o. (eds.*), E-Democracy, Security, Privacy and Trust in a Digital World,* 5th International Conference, E-Democracy 2013, Springer, Communications in Computer and Information Science, 2014, p. 135–152.

J. Zittrain, "Privacy 2.0", *University of Chicago Legal Forum* 2008, No. 1, article 3, p. 65–119.

REPORTS BY (INTER)GOVERNMENTAL BODIES

- *Council of Europe*

Council of Europe, Explanatory Report accompanying the Convention for the Protection of Individuals with regard to Automatic Processing of Personal Data, ETS. 108, paragraph 13, available at http://conventions.coe.int/treaty/en/Reports/Html/108.htm.

Council of Europe, Legislation and Data Protection. Proceedings of the Rome Conference on problems relating to the development and application of legislation on data protection, 1983, Rome, Camera dei Deputati, 356 p.

- *European Union*

Commission des Communautés Européens, "Systèmes à grande puissance de traitement automatique de l'information. Besoins et applications dans la Communauté européenne et au Royaume-Uni vers les années soixante-dix", *Études, Série Industrie* 1971, no. 6, 64 p.

European Commission, First Report on the Application of Directive 2000/31 of the European Parliament and of the Council of 8 June 2000 on the Directive on Electronic Commerce, COM(2003) 702 final, Brussels, 21 November 2003, 25 p., available at http://eur-lex.europa.eu/legal-content/EN/TXT/PDF/?uri=CELEX:52003DC0702&from=EN.

European Commission, Summary of the results of the Public Consultation on the future of electronic commerce in the Internal Market and the implementation of the Directive on electronic commerce (2000/31/EC), 2010, 17 p. available at: http://ec.europa.eu/internal_market/consultations/docs/2010/e-commerce/summary_report_en.pdf.

European Commission, Commission Staff Working Document Online services, including e-commerce, in the Single Market, Brussels, 11 January 2012 SEC(2011) 1641 final, 141 p., available at http://ec.europa.eu/internal_market/e-commerce/docs/communication2012/SEC2011_1641_en.pdf.

European Commission, The Internal Market Information (IMI) System User Handbook, Update 2012, Publications Office of the European Union, Luxembourg, 2012, 64 p., available at http://ec.europa.eu/internal_market/imi-net/_docs/library/user_handbook_en.pdf.

European Commission, Directorate-General Informatics, "EU activities in the field of eID interoperability", December 2013, 3 p., available at http://ec.europa.eu/isa/documents/eu-activities-in-the-field-of-eid-interoperability.pdf.

European Commission, "Data protection guidelines for IMI users", not dated, 6 p., available at http://ec.europa.eu/internal_market/imi-net/docs/data_protection/data_protection_guidelines_en.pdf.

European Commission, "IMI roles and responsibilities", not dated, 6 p., accessible at http://ec.europa.eu/internal_market/imi-net/_docs/training/roles_responsibilities_en.pdf.

European Commission, Managing my authority and users, not dated, accessible at http://ec.europa.eu/internal_market/imi-net/_docs/training/managing_authority_users_en.pdf

European Union Agency for Fundamental Rights (FRA) and Council of Europe, Handbook on European Data Protection Law, 2014, 203 p., available at http://www.echr.coe.int/Documents/Handbook_data_protection_ENG.pdf.

European Commission, Introduction to the Connecting Europe Facility eID building block, Version 1.01, 2015, 34 p., accessible at https://joinup.ec.europa.eu/sites/default/files/introduction_to_the_connecting_europe_facility_eid_building_block_v1_01_0.pdf.

European Parliamentary Research Service (EPRS), "eGovernment – Using technology to improve public services and democratic participation", July 2015, 28 p., available at http://www.europarl.europa.eu/RegData/etudes/IDAN/2015/565890/EPRS_IDA%282015%29565890_EN.pdf.

- *OECD*

Organisation for economic co-operation and development (OECD), "Policy issues in data protection and privacy. Concepts and perspectives", *OECD Informatics Studies*, 1976, no. 10, OECD, Paris, 324 p.

Organisation for economic co-operation and development (OECD), "Transborder Data Flows and the Protection of Privacy", *Information Computer Communications Policy*, 1979, no. 1, OECD, Paris, 335 p.

Organisation for economic co-operation and development (OECD), Explanatory Memorandum to the OECD Guidelines on the Protection of Privacy and Transborder Flows of Personal Data, 1980, Paris, 32 p.

Organisation for economic co-operation and development (OECD), *Privacy and data protection: issues and challenges*, OECD, Paris, 1994, 71 p.

Organisation for economic co-operation and development (OECD), *The Economic and Social Role of Internet Intermediaries*, 2010, Paris, OECD Publishing, 49 p., available at http://www.oecd.org/internet/ieconomy/44949023.pdf.

Organisation for economic co-operation and development (OECD), *Digital Identity Management: Enabling Innovation and Trust in the Internet Economy*, 2011, Paris, OECD Publishing, 183 p., available at http://www.oecd.org/sti/ieconomy/49338380.pdf.

Organisation for economic co-operation and development (OECD), "The Evolving Privacy Landscape: 30 Years After the OECD Privacy Guidelines", *OECD Digital Economy Papers* 2011, No. 176, Paris, OECD Publishing, 176 p. available at http://dx.doi.org/10.1787/5kgf09z90c31-en.

Organisation for economic co-operation and development (OECD), "The App Economy", *OECD Digital Economy Papers* 2013, No. 230, Paris, OECD Publishing, 57 p., available at http://dx.doi.org/10.1787/5k3ttftlv95k-en.

Organisation for economic co-operation and development (OECD), *Supplementary explanatory memorandum to the revised recommendation of the Council concerning guidelines governing the protection of privacy and transborder flows of personal data*, 2013, Paris, p. 19–27, available at http://www.oecd.org/sti/ieconomy/2013-oecd-privacy-guidelines.pdf.

Organisation for economic co-operation and development (OECD), "Exploring data-driven innovation as a new source of growth: Mapping the policy issues raised by "big data"", in OECD, *Supporting Investment in Knowledge Capital, Growth and Innovation*, 2013, Paris, OECD Publishing, 306 p.

- *Hesse*

Hessischer Landtag, *Plenarprotokolle der 77. Sitzung*, 8 Juli 1970, 6. Wahlperiode, Stenographischer Bericht no. 77, 74 p.

Hessischer Landtag, *Plenarprotokolle der 80. Sitzung*, 30 September 1970, 6. Wahlperiode, Stenographischer Bericht no. 80, 115 p.
Hessischer Landtag, *Vorlage des Datenshutzbeauftragten betreffend den Ersten Tätighkeitsbericht*, 29 March 1972, 7. Wahlperiode, Drucksache 7/1495, 40 p.
Hessischer Landtag, *Vorlage des Datenshutzbeauftragten betreffend den Vierten Tätighkeitsbericht*, 26 March 1975, 8. Wahlperiode, Drucksache 8/438, 44 p.

- *Belgium*

Deprest, J. and Robben, F., *eGovernment: the approach of the Belgian federal administration*, 2003, 57 p.

- *France*

Commission Nationale de l'Informatique et des Libertés (CNIL), *Premier rapport au Président de la République et au Parlement 1978-1980*, La Documentation Française, Paris, 1980, 219 p.

- *United Kingdom*

Home Office (Great Brittain), *Report of the Committee on Privacy*, Cmnd. 5012, HMSO, London, 1972, 349 p. (the "Younger report")
Home Office (Great Brittain), *Computers and Privacy*, Cmnd. 653, Her Majesty's Stationary Office (HMSO), London, 1975, 13 p.; reproduced by Home Office (Great Brittain), *Report of the Committee on Data Protection*, Cmnd. 7341, HMSO, London, 1978, 460 p.
Home Office (Great Brittain), *Report of the Committee on Data Protection*, Cmnd. 7341, HMSO, London, 1978, 460 p. (the "Lindop report")
Home Office (Great Brittain), Data Protection: the Government's proposal for Legislation, Cmnd. 8539, HMSO, London, 1982, 23 p.
House of Lords, European Union Committee, "EU Data Protection Law: A 'right to be forgotten'?", *HL Paper* 40, London, The Stationary Office Limited, 30 July 2014, 24 p.

- *United States*

Federal Trade Commission, *Protecting Consumer Privacy in an Era of Rapid Change*, FTC Report, March 2012, 112 p.
U.S. Senate Committee on Commerce, Science and Transportation, "A Review of the Data Broker Industry: Collection, Use, and Sale of Consumer Data for Marketing Purposes", Office of Oversight and Investigations – Majority Staff, Staff Report for Chairman Rockefeller, 2013, 42 p.

OTHER REPORTS

Alhadeff, J. and Van Alsenoy, B. (eds.), "Requirements: Privacy, governance and contractual options", *Trusted Architecture for Securely Shared Services* (TAS^3),

Deliverable 6.1, v2.0, 2009, 80 p., available at http://vds1628.sivit.org/tas3/content/deliverables/TAS3_D6p1_v2_TRequirements:_Privacy,_governance_and_contractual_options.pdf.

Alhadeff, J. and Van Alsenoy, B. (eds.), "D6.2 Contractual framework", *Trusted Architecture for Securely Shared Services* (TAS³), v2.0, 2009, 123 p., available at http://vds1628.sivit.org/tas3/content/deliverables/TAS3_D6p2_v2_TContractual_Framework.pdf.

Alhadeff, J. and Van Alsenoy, B. (eds.), "Legal and Policy handbook for TAS³ implementations", *Trusted Architecture for Securely Shared Services* (TAS³), Deliverable 6.1–6.2, v1.0, 2012, 331 p., available at http://homes.esat.kuleuven.ac.be/~decockd/tas3/final.deliverables/pm48/TAS3-D06p1-2_Legal_and_Policy_Handbook_final_versionforthereviewers.pdf.

Ausloos, J., Lievens, E., Kindt, E. and Dumortier, J., "Guidelines for privacy-friendly default settings", *SPION*, Deliverable D6.4, 2012, 37 p., available at www.spion.me.

Badger, L. Grance, T., Patt-Corner, R. and Voas, J., *Cloud Computing Synopsis and Recommendations*, NIST Special Publication 800–146, National Institute of Standards and Technology (NIST), May 2012, 81 p.

Bigo, D., a.o., "Fighting cyber crime and protecting privacy in the cloud", Study for the European Parliament, Committee on Civil Liberties, Justice and Home Affairs, PE 462.509, 2012, 63 p.

Bruegger, B., "Reference Architecture", FutureID deliverable D21.4, v1.1. 2014, 108 p., available at http://futureid.eu/data/deliverables/year1/Public/FutureID_D21.04_WP21_v1.1_Reference%20Architecture.pdf.

Buitelaar, J.C., Meints, M. and Van Alsenoy, B. (eds.), "Conceptual Framework for Identity Management in eGovernment", *FIDIS*, Deliverable D16.1, 2008, 143 p, available at http://www.fidis.net/fileadmin/fidis/deliverables/new_deliverables3/2009_04_16_D16.1_Framework_IDM_in_eGov_Final_2__1_.pdf.

Buitelaar, J.C., Meints, M. and Kindt, E., "Towards requirements for privacy-friendly identity management in eGovernment", *FIDIS*, Deliverable D16.3, 2009, 88 p, available at http://fidis.net/fileadmin/fidis/deliverables/new_deliverables3/2009_06_14_Fidis_D16.3_Reqs_PF_eGov_v1.2_final.pdf.

Capgemini, IDC, Sogeti, and Politecnico di Milano, "Future-proofing eGovernment for a Digital Single Market", Final Insight Report, June 2015, Study prepared for the European Commission DG Communications Networks, Content and Technology, 2015,37 p.

Catteddu, D. and Hogben G., (eds.), *Cloud computing – Benefits, risks and recommendations for information security*, ENISA, 2009, 125 p.

Deadman S., (ed.), "Circles of Trust: The Implications of EU Data Protection and Privacy Law for Establishing a Legal Framework for Identity Federation", *Liberty Alliance Project*, February 23, 2005, 34 p.

Decker, M. and Hogben, G., *Appstore security: 5 lines of defence against malware*, ENISA, 2011, 20 p.,

European Network and Information Security Agency (ENISA), "Online as soon as it happens", *ENISA*, February 2010, 49 p.

Farkas, L. and O'Farrell, L., "Reversing the burden of proof: Practical dilemma's at the European and national level", European Commission, Directorate-General for Justice and Consumers, 2015, 100 p.

Graux, H. and Majava, J., "eID Interoperability for PEGS. Analysis and Assessment of similarities and differences – Impact on eID interoperability", *IDABC*, 2007, 210 p.

Graux, H., "Initial Data Protection Report", *STORK 2.0*, Deliverable D3.7, 20 November 2012, 20 p., available at https://www.eid-stork2.eu/index.php?option=com_phocadownload&view=file&id=9:d37-initial-data-protection-report&Itemid=175.

Graux, H., "Consolidated Data Protection Report", *STORK 2.0*, Deliverable D3.8, 9 October 2015, 39 p., available at https://www.eid-stork2.eu/index.php?option=com_phocadownload&view=file&id=74:d38-consolidated-data-protection-report&Itemid=175

Hon, K, Kosta, E., Millard, C. and Stefanatou, D., "White paper on the proposed data protection regulation", *Cloud Accountability Project*, 28 February 2014, 49 p., available at http://www.a4cloud.eu/sites/default/files/D25.1%20White%20paper%20on%20new%20Data%20Protection%20Framework.pdf

Huysmans, X. and Van Alsenoy, B. (eds.), D1.3 Conceptual Framework – Annex I. Glossary of Terms, IDEM, v1.07, 2007, 36 p.

International Chamber of Commerce (ICC), ICC Task Force on Privacy and the Protection of Personal Data, "Summary of the Workshop on the Distinction between Data Controllers and Data Processors", Paris, Thursday, 25 October, 2007, 6 p.

Irion, K and Luchetta, G., "Online Personal Data Processing and EU Data Protection Reform – Report of the CEPS Digital Forum, Centre for European Policy Studies (CEPS), April 2013, 97 p.

ISO/IEC Information technology -- Security techniques -- Entity authentication assurance framework, ISO/IEC 29115:2013(E), 1 April 2013, 36 p.

International Telecommunication Union (ITU), Telecommunication Standardization Sector Focus Group on Identity Management, Report on Identity Management Framework for Global Interoperability, 30 p., published online https://www.itu.int/ITU-T/studygroups/com17/fgidm.

International Telecommunication Union (ITU), Entity authentication assurance framework, Recommendation ITU-T X.1254, September 2012, 44 p., available at https://www.itu.int/ITU-T/recommendations/rec.aspx?rec=11608.

International Telecommunication Union (ITU), "Security Compendium. Part 2 – Approved ITU-T Security Definitions", ITU-T SG 17, 13 May 2005, 52 p., available at http://www.itu.int/ITU-T/studygroups/com17/def005.doc.

Konarski, X., Karwala, D., Schulte-Nölke, H. and Charlton, C., "Reforming the Data Protection Package", Study commissioned by the European Parliament, Directorate-General for Internal Policies, Policy Department A: Economic and Scientific Policy, IP/A/IMCO/ST/2012-02, PE 492.431, September 2012, 92 p., accessible at http://www.europarl.europa.eu/RegData/etudes/etudes/join/2012/492431/IPOL-IMCO_ET%282012%29492431_EN.pdf.

Korff, D., "EC Study on Implementation of Data Protection Directive 95/46/EC", Study Contract ETD/2001/B5-3001/A/49, 2002, 253 p., accessible at http://papers.ssrn.com/sol3/papers.cfm?abstract_id=1287667

Kuczerawy, A., "Legal and ethical analysis", *Exploiting Social Networks for Building the Future Internet of Services* (SocIoS), Deliverable D3.5, v0.3, 2012, 45 p.

Larouche, P., Peitz, M. and Purtova, N., "Consumer privacy in network industries – A CERRE Policy Report", *Centre on Regulation in Europe*, 25 January 2016, 74 p., available at http://cerre.eu/sites/cerre/files/160125_CERRE_Privacy_Final.pdf

Le Borgne-Bachschmidt, F. et al., "User-Created-Content: Supporting a participative Information Society", Study for the European Commission, SMART 2007/2008, 2008, 302 p., available at http://www.ivir.nl/publicaties/download/233.

Modinis project, Common Terminological Framework for Interoperable Electronic Identity Management, Consultation Paper, prepared for the eGovernment Unit of DG Information Society and Media of the European Commission, v2.01, 23 November 2005, 18 p., accessible at: https://www.cosic.esat.kuleuven.be/modinis-idm/twiki/pub/Main/GlossaryDoc/modinis.terminology.paper.v2.01.2005-11-23.pdf

Olsen, T. and Mahler, T., "Privacy – Identity Management Data Protection Issues in Relation to Networked Organisations Utilizing Identity Management Systems", *Legal IST* project, Deliverable D11, 4 November 2005, 144 p.

Robinson, N., Graux, H., Botterman, M. and Valeri, L., "Review of the European Data Protection Directive", *RAND Europe*, 2009, 100 p.

Ruggie, J., "Protect, Respect and Remedy – A Framework for Business and Human Rights", Report of the Special Representative of the United Nations Secretary-General on the issue of human rights and transnational corporations and other business enterprises, *innovations* (a United Nations publication), 2008, p. 189–212.

Ruggie, J., "Clarifying the Concepts of "Sphere of influence" and "Complicity"", Report of the Special Representative of the Secretary-General on the Issue of Human Rights and Transnational Corporations and other Business Enterprises, A/HRC/8/16, 15 May 2008, 22 p., available at http://198.170.85.29/Ruggie-companion-report-15-May-2008.pdf.

von Bar, C. a.o. (eds.) "Principles, Definitions and Model Rules of European Private Law – Draft Common Frame of Reference (DCFR)", Study Group on a European Civil Code and the Research Group on EC Private Law, 2009, 4795 p., accessible at http://ec.europa.eu/justice/contract/files/european-private-law_en.pdf.

Van Alsenoy, B. "E-government Solutions: Trends and Developments in Belgian e-Government", in M. Meints and H. Zwingelberg (eds.), *Identity Management Systems – recent developments, FIDIS*, Deliverable D3.17, 2009, p. 39–49, accessible at http://www.fidis.net/fileadmin/fidis/deliverables/new_deliverables/fidis-wp3-del3.17_Identity_Management_Systems-recent_developments-final.pdf.

Van Alsenoy, B., Vandezande, N., Janssen, K, a.o., "Legal Provisions for Deploying INDI services", Global Identity Networking for Individuals (GINI), Deliverable D3.1, 2011, 83 p.

Van Alsenoy, B., Lievens, E., Janssen, K., a.o., "A Regulatory Framework for INDI Operators", Global Identity Networking for Individuals (GINI), Deliverable D3.2, 2012, 63 p.

Van Alsenoy, B., Verdoodt, V., Heyman, R., Ausloos, J., Wauters; E. and Acar, G. "From social media service to advertising network – A critical analysis of Facebook's Revised Policies and Terms", v1.3, 25 August 2015, 109 p.

Van Eecke, P., Truyens, M., et al. (eds.), "The future of online privacy and data protection, EU study on the Legal analysis of a Single Market for the Information Society – New rules for a new age?", *DLA Piper*, November 2009, 69 p.

Zwenne, G.-J., Duthler, A-W., Groothuis, M., a.o., "Eerste fase evaluatie Wet bescherming persoonsgegevens – Literatuuronderzoek en knelpuntenanalyse", Ministerie van Justitie (NL), 2007, 211 p.

X., "The Advisory Council to Google on the Right to be Forgotten", 6 February 2015, 44 p., available at https://drive.google.com/file/d/0B1UgZshetMd4cEI3SjlvV0hNbDA/view.

7. POLICY DOCUMENTS

EUROPEAN COMMISSION

Commission of the European Communities, "Community Policy on Data Processing", Communication of the Commission to the Council, SEC(73) 4300 final, 21 November 1973, 34 p.

European Commission, "Report from the Commission – First Report on the implementation of the Data Protection Directive (95/46/EC)", COM(2003) 265 final, 15 May 2003, 27p.

European Commission, First Report on the Application of Directive 2000/31 of the European Parliament and of the Council of 8 June 2000 on the Directive on Electronic Commerce, COM(2003) 702 final, Brussels, 21 November 2003, 25 p.

European Commission, i2010 eGovernment Action Plan: Accelerating eGovernment in Europe for the Benefit of All, SEC(2006) 511, 24 April 2006, 12 p., available at http://eur-lex.europa.eu/legal-content/EN/TXT/PDF/?uri=CELEX:52006DC0173&from=EN

European Commission, A Roadmap for a pan-European eIDM Framework by 2010, 2006, v1.0, 20 p., available at http://ec.europa.eu/information_society/activities/ict_psp/documents/eidm_roadmap_paper.pdf

European Commission, Summary of the results of the Public Consultation on the future of electronic commerce in the Internal Market and the implementation of the Directive on electronic commerce (2000/31/EC), 2010, 17 p., available at: http://ec.europa.eu/internal_market/consultations/docs/2010/e-commerce/summary_report_en.pdf

European Commission, Commission Staff Working Document Online services, including e-commerce, in the Single Market, Brussels, 11 January 2012, SEC(2011) 1641 final, 141 p.

European Commission, Communication on the follow-up of the Work programme for a better implementation of the Data Protection Directive, 7 March 2007, COM(2007)87 final, 11 p., accessible at http://eur-lex.europa.eu/legal-content/EN/TXT/PDF/?uri=CELEX:52007DC0087&from=EN

European Commission, "Summary of Replies to the Public Consultation on the Commission's Communication on comprehensive approach on personal data protection in the European Union", 4 November 2010, Annex 4, 22 p.

European Commission, "Communication from the Commission to the European Parliament, the Council, the European Economic and Social Committee and the

Committee of the Regions, Better governance of the Single Market through greater administrative cooperation: A strategy for expanding and developing the Internal Market Information System ('IMI')", 21 February 2011, COM(2011) 75 final, 18 p.
European Commission, "Safeguarding Privacy in a Connected World – A European Data Protection Framework for the 21st Century", Communication from the Commission to the European Parliament, the Council, the European Economic and Social Affairs Committee and the Committee of the Regions, COM(2012) 9 final, 25 January 2012, 13 p.
European Commission, "Unleashing the Potential of Cloud Computing in Europe", Communication of the Commission to the European Parliament, the Council, the European Economic and Social Committee and the Committee of the Regions, COM(2012) 529 final, 27 September 2012, 16 p.

STAKEHOLDER RESPONSES

Association of Consumer Credit Information Suppliers (ACCIS), Position paper on proposed Data Protection Regulation, April 2012, 21 p., available at http://ec.europa.eu/justice/news/consulting_public/0006/contributions/organisations/accis_en.pdf.
Bird & Bird, "Response to European Commission Consultation on the Legal Framework for the Fundamental Right to Protection of Personal Data", 2009, 4 p., available at http://ec.europa.eu/justice/news/consulting_public/0003/contributions/organisations_not_registered/bird_bird_en.pdf.
BEUC, "A Comprehensive Approach on Personal Data Protection in the European Union – European Commission's Communication", 24 January 2011, 18 p., available at http://ec.europa.eu/justice/news/consulting_public/0006/contributions/organisations/beuc_en.pdf.
Business Europe, "Commission Proposal on a General Data Protection Regulation", Position Paper, 17 October 2012, 18 p., available at https://www.businesseurope.eu/sites/buseur/files/media/imported/2012-01161-E.pdf
European Banking Federation, "EBF Position on the European Commission's Proposal for a Regulation on the protection of individual with regard to the processing of personal data and on the free movement of such data (General Data Protection Regulation), 22 May 2015, 5 p., available at http://ec.europa.eu/justice/news/consulting_public/0006/contributions/organisations/ebf_en.pdf
European Privacy Officers Forum (EPOF), "Comments on the Review of European Data Protection Framework", 2009, 12 p., available at http://ec.europa.eu/justice/news/consulting_public/0003/contributions/organisations_not_registered/european_privacy_officers_forum_en.pdf
Information Commissioner's Office (ICO), "The Information Commissioner's response to the European Commission's consultation on the legal framework for the fundamental right to protection of personal data", 7 p., available at http://ec.europa.eu/justice/news/consulting_public/0003/contributions/public_authorities/ico_uk_en.pdf.

Information Commissioner's Office (ICO), "The Information Commissioner's (United Kingdom) response to A comprehensive approach on personal data protection in the European Union", 14 January 2011, 15 p., accessible at http://ec.europa.eu/justice/news/consulting_public/0006/contributions/public_authorities/ico_infocommoffice_en.pdf

International Pharmaceutical Privacy Consortium, "Comments in Response to the Consultation on the Legal Framework for the Fundamental Right to Protection of Personal Data", 2009, 10 p., available at http://ec.europa.eu/justice/news/consulting_public/0003/contributions/organisations_not_registered/international_pharmaceutical_privacy_consortium_en.pdf

International Chamber of Commerce (ICC), ICC Commission on E-business, IT and Telecoms, "ICC Response to the European Commission Consultation on the Legal Framework for the Fundamental Right to Protection of Personal Data", December 2009, 10 p., available at http://ec.europa.eu/justice/news/consulting_public/0003/contributions/organisations_not_registered/international_chamber_of_commerce_icc_en.pdf.

INDUSTRY WHITE PAPERS

Microsoft, "Protecting Data and Privacy in the Cloud", *Reactive Security Communications*, 2014, 16 p., available at http://download.microsoft.com/download/2/0/A/20A1529E-65CB-4266-8651-1B57B0E42DAA/Protecting-Data-and-Privacy-in-the-Cloud.pdf

Microsoft, "Trusted Cloud: Microsoft Azure Security, Privacy, and Compliance", April 2015, p. 14, available at https://www.microsoft.com/en-us/Openness/TrustedCloud.

Amazon Web Services, "Whitepaper on EU Data Protection", October 2015, 16 p., available at http://d0.awsstatic.com/whitepapers/compliance/AWS_EU_Data_Protection_Whitepaper.pdf.

KU Leuven Centre for IT & IP Law

The KU Leuven Centre for IT & IP Law Series brings together the results of research activities of the Centre for IT & IP Law. The central research themes of the series concern the legal and ethical aspects of information technology, innovation and intellectual property.

Each book in the series focuses on the essential developments in the current legal framework, necessitated by the rapid evolution of technology in various fields, such as government, media, health care, informatics, digital economy, banking, transport and culture. The research is characterised by an interdisciplinary approach, constantly cross-fertilising legal, technical, economic, ethical and socio-cultural perspectives.

Books are published in English, Dutch and/or French.

Recently published in this series:

1. Rán Trygvadóttir, *European Libraries and the Internet: Copyright and Extended Collective Licences*, 2018.
2. Niels Vandezande, *Virtual Currencies*, 2018.
3. Aleksandra Kuczerawy, *Intermediary Liability and Freedom of Expression in the EU: From Concepts to Safeguards*, 2018.
4. Letizia Paoli, Jonas Visschers Cedric Verstraete, Elke van Hellemont, *The Impact of Cybercrime on Belgian Businesses*, 2019
5. Niels Vandezande, *When An Original Is Not Original. The Originality Requirement in Belgian Law*, 2019

www.ingramcontent.com/pod-product-compliance
Ingram Content Group UK Ltd.
Pitfield, Milton Keynes, MK11 3LW, UK
UKHW051846100926
8556IPUK00005B/469